The SAGE Handbook of
Communication and Instruction

The SAGE Handbook of
Communication and Instruction

Edited by

Deanna L. Fassett
San José State University

John T. Warren
Southern Illinois University Carbondale

Los Angeles | London | New Delhi
Singapore | Washington DC

For information:

SAGE Publications, Inc.
2455 Teller Road
Thousand Oaks, California 91320
E-mail: order@sagepub.com

SAGE Publications Ltd.
1 Oliver's Yard
55 City Road
London EC1Y 1SP
United Kingdom

SAGE Publications India Pvt. Ltd.
B 1/I 1 Mohan Cooperative Industrial Area
Mathura Road, New Delhi 110 044
India

SAGE Publications Asia-Pacific Pte. Ltd.
33 Pekin Street #02-01
Far East Square
Singapore 048763

Printed in the United States of America

Library of Congress Cataloging-in-Publication Data

The SAGE handbook of communication and instruction/editors: Deanna L. Fassett, John T. Warren.
 p. cm.
Includes bibliographical references and index.
ISBN 978-1-4129-7087-7 (cloth)

 1. Communication—Study and teaching—Handbooks, manuals, etc. I. Fassett, Deanna L. II. Warren, John T., 1974. III. Title: Handbook of communication and instruction.

P91.3.S24 2010
302.2071—dc22   2009038557

This book is printed on acid-free paper.

10 11 12 13 14 10 9 8 7 6 5 4 3 2 1

Acquisitions Editor:	Todd R. Armstrong
Editorial Assistant:	Nathan Davidson
Production Editor:	Astrid Virding
Copy Editor:	QuADS Prepress (P) Ltd.
Typesetter:	C&M Digitals (P) Ltd.
Proofreader:	Scott Oney
Indexer:	William Ragsdale
Cover Designer:	Candice Harman
Marketing Manager:	Helen Salmon

Contents

Acknowledgments

Because edited collections involve so many different people in so many different capacities, the task of identifying individuals to whom we feel grateful is daunting. Even though it seems impossible to acknowledge everyone who has been so kind and helpful and patient during the preparation of this *Handbook*, we would still like to try to offer a few heartfelt words of appreciation.

First, it is important to note that this *Handbook* is possible in large measure because, almost a century ago, a group of committed teacher-scholars of public speaking left the Modern Language Association and formed their own organization dedicated to the scholarly study of teaching and learning communication. While, as the contributors herein recognize, the discipline goes back much further than 100 years, it is this association of radicals to whom we are grateful.

Second, we would like to thank our colleagues in communication studies, in general, and those who study pedagogy in particular. For every person we were able to include here, there are many others, quietly yet passionately engaged in the research and the community building that makes this work possible. Each References page in this *Handbook* pays tribute to a community that holds meaningful teaching as fundamental to our lives, in and apart from the academy.

Third, we are particularly indebted to the people whose voices have shaped this volume directly. Ann Darling and Scott Myers were invaluable and irreplaceable in the construction of this *Handbook*. As section editors ourselves, we understand the kind and volume of work such responsibility entails, and we were relieved to know that these sections—as well as their contributing authors—were in capable hands. Their willing spirit made possible our commitment to the integrity and relevance of each section. The SAGE team was supportive from start to finish, from idea to advertising. Particularly, this project would not be the same were it not for the effort and encouragement of Todd Armstrong and Aja Baker, along with Nathan Davidson and Astrid Virding. We would also like to thank the reviewers of the project's initial prospectus: Joyce Ferguson (University of North Carolina—Greensboro), Mark Gring (Texas Tech University), Kristen Treinen (Minnesota State University—Mankato), and David Williams

(Texas Tech University); and our copyeditor, Rajasree Ghosh, and her team at QuADS Prepress (P) Ltd. And, most important of all, we are deeply appreciative of each of the authors who contributed to this volume; their generosity shapes not only this collection but also our field of study, and we hope you find their thoughts as inspiring as we have.

Finally, over the past 2 years, as both general editors and section editors, we have been busy inviting and cajoling, writing and revising, reading and editing, formatting and e-mailing. Our students and colleagues at San José State University and Southern Illinois University, Carbondale, have been gracious and patient with us. But we are most grateful to our families, who made time and space for us to bring this project to fruition: Thanks to Ed, Gina, Elias, and Isaac—as always, we owe you.

Introduction

Deanna L. Fassett and John T. Warren

Handbooks, as a general rule, tend to have functional, seemingly unambiguous titles. For example, recent entries in the SAGE Handbook Series include volumes on conflict communication, performance studies, organizational communication, interpersonal communication, and so forth. This *Handbook* is no exception. Still, we found it initially difficult to name this collection. Largely this is because, as our discipline teaches us (from the Sophists to more contemporary scholars such as Lakoff & Johnson, 1980; Stewart, 1995), even the most seemingly neutral, transparent description has a history, an imprint of past and present beliefs, values, and actions. As communication scholars, we know that language is more than representational—does more than mirror or reflect reality—it is also constitutive; our language choices, because they illuminate some aspects of an experience and obfuscate others, both make possible and delimit our understandings and actions with respect to communication phenomena.

Where we are concerned, as a discipline, with the intersections of communication and instruction, our language has been shaped by values, assumptions, misunderstandings, and multiple meanings. Teacher-scholars already at work in this area of study have their own, often shared, understandings of "communication education" and "instructional communication." While a small number of colleagues outside this area still use these terms interchangeably, most of us rely on Staton's (1989) definition of these two areas:

> Communication education (formerly speech education), one of the oldest fields of our discipline, is the study of teaching of speech communication. The emphasis historically has been on teaching speech communication in traditional college classrooms ranging from kindergarten to the college/ university level. . . . Instructional communication [however] is defined typically as the study of human communication process as it occurs in instructional contexts—across subject matter, grade levels and types of settings. The focus

[handwritten margin note: strategies — teacher/student interaction]

is on communication variables that can or do affect all instructional environments (e.g., teacher power, nonverbal immediacy, teacher communicator style). (p. 365)

Furthermore, Sprague's (1992, 1993) agenda setting for these two areas of study remains useful and relevant today, as evidenced by how frequently her scholarship has served as impetus or support for work both in and beyond this collection. In effect, "communication education" and "instructional communication" are distinct and meaningful descriptors; though many of our colleagues, ourselves included, engage in scholarship in both areas, they are not interchangeable, nor are they the same. Different ontological and epistemological commitments, histories and trajectories, influential scholars, and foundational texts inform each. Hence, this is not a handbook of communication education, nor is it a handbook of instructional communication, though both areas are represented in this collection.

Further complicating the question of the title is the role of critical, cultural studies, and social justice–oriented work at the intersections of communication and instruction. Finding traction in communication studies in the past 20 years, this growing body of scholarship is not a subdiscipline, on a par with communication education or instructional communication, but rather an extension or respecification (in Garfinkel's, 1967, sense) of both. To refer to this collection as a handbook of "communication pedagogy" would similarly call forward one approach to the study of the intersections of communication and instruction, one that might speak to this current strand of work in our field; but this would not connote the openness, the opportunities for multiple perspectives, theories, values, methods, investments, and so forth, present in our collective efforts.

Hence, the *SAGE Handbook of Communication and Instruction* is a title that represents this spirit of community. That we say community here is not to suggest that all perspectives are harmonious and equally embraced but that all are present in our discipline and, taken together, constitute a more complex and nuanced understanding of not only how we teach and learn communication but also how communication is an essential component of all teaching and learning.

Furthermore, this *Handbook* is a collaborative effort. We have divided it into three sections: Communication Education, Instructional Communication, and Critical Communication Pedagogy. In doing so, we do not mean to suggest that these are isolable and discrete areas of study—in reading across the entire collection of chapters, there is considerable overlap in areas of concern; however, the sections of this *Handbook* provide an architecture for inviting colleagues, in the form of section editors, to help us create an accurate representation of the field as it has been, as it is, and as how it might be. We are indebted to Scott Myers, West Virginia University, and Ann Darling, University of Utah, for their work as section editors; section editors helped identify prospective contributors to this *Handbook*, working with those authors to create what is, at the time of this writing, the most comprehensive collection to date on scholarship in communication and instruction. In particular, we were fortunate to work closely with colleagues who were intimately familiar with the work in their respective niches of the field—both the foundational and the cutting edge.

It was important to us that this *Handbook* take shape through the guidance of different colleagues with different disciplinary backgrounds and research programs. Each of the sections in this *Handbook*, as is apparent from their section editors' introductions and chapters regarding theoretical and methodological assumptions, is characterized fundamentally by different paradigms. In effect, the authors in each of these sections is motivated to ask different questions about communication, engage in different means and methods to answer those questions, and put her or his findings to work in the world in different ways. We felt that it was essential that the people most connected to and appreciative of the different paradigms of study identify these research foundations, questions, and functions. Together, all section editors worked to select chapters that would illuminate key themes, topics, and issues with respect to each body of scholarship. We are, as a result of seeing the collection in its entirety, grateful to the authors who contributed to this *Handbook*. Without their expertise, this *Handbook* could not have been possible and would certainly not be the rich chorus of voices that it became. The diversity of works this *Handbook* represents is unprecedented in our field to date and is thus the most comprehensive text complied for communication and instruction.

It is our hope that, above all else, this *Handbook* will be useful for all who encounter it. Researchers engaged in work at the intersections of communication and instruction will not only find support for their efforts but also find inspiration for future investigation. They will find their research methods validated, but they will also find other, possible ways of studying particular communication phenomena, whether this is the question of how best to craft and use textbooks, of how to trace the effects of power, or of how to understand students', teachers', and researchers' identities as constituted in daily discourse. Students learning the field will find direction, a comprehensive guide, and a platform on which to build their own investigations; to this end, instructors of graduate and advanced undergraduate seminars in communication and instruction will find this a helpful addition to their reading lists.

We find ourselves at a historical juncture when careful and systematic attention to communication and instruction is, by people and institutions outside our discipline, grossly undervalued and desperately needed. At the time of this writing, we find ourselves in an unprecedented global economic crisis; this crisis has affected teaching and learning at all levels, from communication between parents and children, to diminished state support for public primary, secondary, and postsecondary education, to the training and development of industry professionals, to the question of whether and how to educate a migrant and migratory population. We also find ourselves struggling, in fits and starts, toward greater connection and community, in the face of challenges to our efforts at sustainability (of our fragile global and local ecosystems, of our mental and physical health and wellness) and humanity (e.g., in the face of assaults on human rights, free speech, and self-determination in Iran or south-central China, growing hunger and poverty, and inconsistently checked abuses of political and industry power). Further complicating these challenges, though certainly enriching our experiences as educators, researchers, and students, is the profound and heretofore unprecedented cultural diversity (racial, ethnic, economic, gendered, sexual, spiritual, and physical—i.e., dis/abled) of the people we teach and who will enter teaching. We are, in many ways, as educators and researchers, expected by the communities we serve to do the same or more with less (sometimes quite literally so in the face of furloughs and layoffs). Perhaps we might also think of our community, our diversity—in persons and paradigms—as a strength? As a way to do more with more?

While it is not our intention here to suggest that we might simply redefine all these problems, threats, and challenges away, languaging them into opportunities for success, it is important to bear in mind that how we respond, as a discipline, the directions we take as individuals and as connected communities of teacher-scholars, will reveal our work as relevant, timely, and meaningful to others, in and beyond the academy.

References

Garfinkel, H. (1967). *Studies in ethnomethodology.* Cambridge, UK: Polity Press.

Lakoff, G., & Johnson, M. (1980). *Metaphors we live by.* Chicago: University of Chicago Press.

Sprague, J. (1992). Expanding the research agenda for instructional communication: Raising some unasked questions. *Communication Education, 41,* 1–25.

Sprague, J. (1993). Retrieving the research agenda for communication education: Asking the pedagogical questions that are "embarrassments to theory." *Communication Education, 42,* 106–122.

Staton, A. Q. (1989). The interface of communication and instruction: Conceptual considerations and programmatic manifestations. *Communication Education, 38,* 364–391.

Stewart, J. (1995). *Language as articulate contact: Toward a post-semiotic philosophy of communication.* Albany: State University of New York Press.

Part I

Communication Education

Communication Education 1

An Association of Radicals

Ann L. Darling

As is true of many communities, we share a lore about who we are and what we do. This lore is carried in stories that virtually all the community members know because the stories are told and retold at moments calling for ritualistic declarations of community identity. For the community of communication education scholars, the story commonly begins with the often related moment when the 17 then members of the National Council of Teachers of English finally became sufficiently dismayed at the lack of scholarly attention to teaching public speaking that they convened a special meeting of the Public Speaking Section to debate a motion on establishing the first National Association of Academic Teachers of Public Speaking, today's National Communication Association (Jeffrey, 1964). This story has been told countless times at meetings of the National Communication Association, in books about the history of our discipline (e.g., Benson, 1985), in essays contextualizing the history or charge of our field (e.g., Craig, 1989), in special issues of our national journal *Communication Education*, and even in this volume (see Nainby, Chapter 2; McGarrity, Chapter 6).

Given the constant telling of this story with emphasis on the end result (i.e., the establishment of the National Association of Academic Teachers of Public Speaking), curiosity about the sentiments and events that led to this outcome has been limited. There were actually 34 people at the meeting when the motion was originally debated; the debate was anything but one-sided, and it actually took two meetings to get the job done. At the end of the initial meeting, the vote was 18 to 16 to table the motion, hardly a resounding statement of intent. It wasn't until the next morning that the group of 17 people resumed the debate and voted to break away from the National Council of Teachers of English. So what motivated the initial motion, and why was the debate protracted? Answers to this question are difficult to pin down, but rich accounts provided by Jeffrey (1964),

Wallace (1954), Weaver (1959), Gray (1964), and Reid (2002) lead us to believe that the motion was the result of the extensive frustration felt by teachers of public speaking, who believed that they were being held to elocutionist principles for teaching public speaking and not given the support or resources to pursue a research agenda related to teaching public speaking (Jeffrey, 1964). The debate was likely about resources. Given the paucity of resources for public higher education, these 17 scholar-teachers probably had concerns about the wisdom of establishing a new professional organization and about the academic viability of a new field of study. In the end, evidently, their frustrations about being unable to approach the teaching of public speaking from a base of research were more compelling than fears about fiscal or political vulnerability. Told this way, the story suggests that our founding fathers were brave radicals determined to make a difference; they intended to change the way we teach and study speech in American public universities and were willing to make sacrifices to accomplish their goal.

Given our radical beginnings and the efforts of those brave founders, we might rightly ask ourselves, what have we done lately to acknowledge and celebrate their accomplishment? What have we done lately to ensure that the study and teaching of communication as a discipline remains vibrant and vital and whole? In what ways do we remain radical in our work? Those founding members were determined to and did establish an association with each other; the seeds of our community were built in their talk and in their commitment to support and guide each other in the pursuit of scholarly and pedagogical excellence in communication education research and teaching. As someone who began her career in communication education almost 30 years ago, it has been my experience that, while the discipline of communication has blossomed (some might argue exploded), the field of communication education—the field charged with ensuring a vibrant, vital, radical, and scholarly conversation about the pedagogy of the discipline—has fractured into a million little pieces of devoted, exciting, passionate but disparate and separated communities of scholars and teachers. Until now.

With this, the first comprehensive handbook of research in communication and instruction, Deanna Fassett and John Warren have done us the great service of creating a context to begin our collective commitments anew. They have invited us, in each section of this *Handbook*, to highlight and celebrate the best and the freshest essays on topics that are germane to three general fields of inquiry: (1) communication education, (2) instructional communication, and (3) critical communication pedagogy. Remembering the community lore, that we are all academic descendants of teachers of public speaking, they rightfully placed the communication education section first.

Those 17 colleagues of long ago were interested in advancing scholarship in the teaching of public speaking.[1] Since this auspicious beginning, we have been passionately engaged in developing pedagogy for and a pedagogical scholarship about communication. As several of my teachers, mentors, and friends have reported elsewhere (Book, 1989; Friedrich, 1987; Sprague, 1993; Staton, 1989), since the very beginning of our association, we have been asking questions not only about teaching public speaking but also about how to employ a variety of instructional methods in the service of teaching communication. This section of the *Handbook* provides evidence that we are still fulfilling the promise of our founders; we are radically committed to advancing scholarship on teaching communication.

But our founders were interested in two things: enhancing research on teaching speech *and* establishing a community of individuals who could support each other in producing and promoting that research. In fact, as Jeffrey (1964) notes, concerns about protecting the strength of the community as a group of scholars supporting each other was evident in discussions on the first constitution of the fledgling organization and decades later as various regional associations began to form. This *Handbook*, because of its commitment to present a comprehensive account of scholarship at the intersection of communication and instruction, creates an opportunity to renew a sense of community in our association with one another.

In working with the authors who have contributed to this section, I invited them to approach their chapters with special attention to the "new" and "fresh" and "important" scholarship that they were doing and in which they wanted others to engage. Each of these essays is devoted to acknowledging the charge of our fore-creators in demanding a rigorous scholarship about teaching communication. Each essay also reflects the radical commitment of those 17 fore-creators by pushing us to ask questions that expand contemporary understandings of communication and that address the vexing problems teachers and students face each time they enter a classroom.

Keith Nainby provides a historical account of the philosophical and methodological underpinnings of communication education scholarship. In Chapter 2, he reminds us of our rhetorical roots and demonstrates how ancient debates continue to foster growth in our contemporary scholarship. Nainby provides a particularly careful account of our evolution from a field strongly influenced by social scientific research agendas into one embracing interpretive and critical scholarship. His invitation to widen our investment in critical and interpretive scholarship is striking in the context of his historical analysis; it seems that cycles do indeed repeat themselves.

Deanna Sellnow and Jason Martin (Chapter 3) report on research about the introductory course in communication. Reading their account, we are reminded that the introductory, or basic, course serves important functions for the department because it often brings in a steady stream of revenue, for the discipline because it provides a wide base of exposure to individuals (students, faculty, and administrators) who might not otherwise come into contact with communication as a discipline of study, and for students because it is commonly the only arena in which they can develop communication skills that will be vital to their personal and professional success beyond college. Sellnow and Martin discuss the fresh and important research being conducted on the basic course, particularly with regard to problem-based learning, online delivery systems, and questions about how best to incorporate research from critical whiteness studies into the curriculum. These authors invite, with some urgency, communication education scholars to conduct experimental or quasi-experimental studies that document the efficacy of our basic course teacher training programs and the success of basic course instruction in relation to specific and communally ratified outcome measures.

Deanna Dannels (Chapter 4) reports on a close neighbor to research on the introductory course: communication across the curriculum (CXC) research. This research also explores questions about teaching communication to noncommunication majors, but in this case, the instruction occurs within other disciplinary curricula. Dannels describes the rich body of work that has emerged over the past 30 years and then uses that foundational work to invite us to take on important challenges. Her invitation is one that would have us engage in communication education that even more broadly connects us with publics not directly involved with university instruction, with spaces beyond the brick-and-mortar classroom, and with media other than textbooks and scholarly articles.

Katherine Hendrix's chapter (Chapter 5) draws our attention to research about communication education and the preparation of future faculty. Placing her review in the context of contemporary conditions in which faculty should be prepared to teach, she asks, How can we help junior faculty approach and manage the many incoherencies they face? These incoherencies include having to work with an undergraduate population that is increasingly overcommitted to a multitude of activities and obligations other than education and that may have developed a healthy (or unhealthy) cynicism about authority in general and educational authority in particular. At the same time, resources for faculty are dwindling, and expectations for incorporating a wide range of technological approaches are increasing. This creates a dynamic context in which new faculty must work and thrive. Hendrix's chapter invites us to explore research about how to bring these complex incoherencies into some kind of balance.

Matt McGarrity (Chapter 6) begins his chapter with an observation that scholarly discussions of the textbook are as old as the discipline itself. In fact, McGarrity asserts that textbooks could be viewed as "the trilobites of the disciplinary fossil record." His chapter presents a model for organizing and conducting research on communication textbooks; that model, a life-cycle approach, begins with questions about the production of textbooks and moves through research about the content, the use, and, finally, the history of communication textbooks. McGarrity points out the relative paucity of methodological pluralism in communication textbook research and laments that several rich questions remain unasked as a result.

Jami Warren and Timothy Sellnow (Chapter 7) report on the status of research about service learning in communication pedagogy. Service learning has expanded on college and university campuses in the past 20 years, and the discipline of communication has played an important role in its growth. As these authors report, research about how and to what end to incorporate service learning in communication courses is both rich and diverse. Courses in communication research methods, in organizational communication, and, especially relevant for this section of the *Handbook*, in communication education have integrated service learning, explored the effects of that integration, and published studies for others to review and share. Warren and Sellnow end their chapter with an invitation to communication education scholars to ask how communication pedagogy is essential to any application of service learning, regardless of disciplinary affiliation. Research exploring this question would make an important contribution to theorizing about communication pedagogy.

My *Oxford American Dictionary* (Ehrlich, Flexner, Carruth, & Hawkins, 1980) provides some interesting fodder for thinking about the term *radical*. The first definition listed is as follows: "going to the root or foundation of something fundamental." The second offers a contrasting interpretation: "drastic, thorough, changes or reforms" (p. 739). Looking at these descriptions together, I understand that *radical* means a change of or at the core of something. Reflecting on common usage of the term, I understand that radicals are often given that name or assume that name because they are unsettled with the way things are. They are restless and seem to be driven by a need to change the status quo. Like our 17 fore-creators, the work of these eight authors can also be seen as restless and unsettled. We can read these as inciting change to the ways we conceptualize, enact, and research communication pedagogy.

As a whole, the essays in this section address common themes/issues about disciplinary pedagogy, and they call for a radical commitment to fundamental growth and change. Both Book (1989) and Sprague (1993) have asked that we invest scholarly interest in the development of a discipline-specific pedagogy. Such a pedagogy would answer questions about how best to teach communication and would acknowledge the unique and defining features of communication; namely, it is social, complex/ongoing, embodied, unconscious/automatic, tied to personal/cultural identity, and embedded with/connected to power (Sprague, 1993). Developing a robust and comprehensive disciplinary pedagogy requires the concerted, devoted, and radical efforts of a wide range of communication education scholars like the original 17 and these eight here.

Focusing attention on the problems with a decontextualized, ahistorical, self-reported, and singularly cognitive assessment of learning outcomes (as Dannels, Chapter 4; Hendrix, Chapter 5; Sellnow & Martin, Chapter 3; and Warren & Sellnow, Chapter 7, do here) is a perfectly radical move. This is especially true at a time when state and national funding sources are increasingly tied to high-stakes testing, and administrative calls for accountability are associated with "objective" standards of assessment. The tendency to surrender to these pressures will be great, but we must resist. Instead, as the authors in this *Handbook* demonstrate, we can and should continue to develop assessment measures that are sensitive to the complex/ongoing, unconscious/automatic, and social dimensions of communication skill development. Sellnow and Martin (Chapter 3), Dannels (Chapter 4), Warren and Sellnow (Chapter 7), and Hendrix (Chapter 5) provide important insights into how the discipline can develop meaningful forms of assessment and how their use can further understanding of discipline-specific pedagogical practices. As Dannels and Housley-Gaffney (2009) report elsewhere, much of the CXC work is built on the development of localized outcome measures, and while there are some issues associated with this inclination, it is still an inclination in keeping with the accepted theoretical tenets and empirical findings of our disciplinary knowledge. These authors are quite astute, insistent, and radical in articulating the problems with current approaches to assessing learning outcomes in communication.

Placing embodied relationships in the center rather than on the periphery of our vision is also a perfectly radical position that these authors take. Exploring communication instruction that is deeply embedded in community settings encourages theorizing beyond individual-level outcomes to those that are essentially embodied, relational, and communal. Such explorations allow us to imagine discipline-specific pedagogical practices that seek the development of relationship and community communicative competence, and they rob us of the limiting focus on the individual so prevalent in our theorizing. Teaching situated within community contexts, and research on that teaching, necessarily reveals how particular bodies come into contact, develop understanding (or not), accomplish goals (or not), and commit to ongoing relationships (or not). So when Sellnow and Martin (Chapter 3), Warren and Sellnow (Chapter 7), and Hendrix (Chapter 5) insist that we expand our commitment to service learning and civically engaged curricula and when Dannels (Chapter 4) imagines using university extension services as a model for communication pedagogy, they are being radical in helping build discipline-specific pedagogical practices that are embodied, contextual, and relational.

Hendrix (Chapter 5) is especially radical in her contribution to the understanding of embodied practice in communication pedagogy. She reminds us that physical and spiritual well-being are also appropriate foci for our work. Too often, scholarship about preparing future faculty is silent on issues of how to care for our teaching bodies and our teaching souls, yet we can't teach without them. Her essay, then, is a unique gift to an otherwise antiseptic literature. Within this frame of embodiment, her reminder of the particular challenges to identity faced by faculty and graduate teaching assistants of color is, above all, radical.

Examining the ways in which communication education structures power and how pedagogy constitutes culture and identity is radical. In fact, questions about how communication in classrooms produces and reproduces social inequity are foundational to radical research about pedagogy (Freire, 1990; Giroux, 1988; Sprague, 1992). As Nainby (Chapter 2) notes, there are many important questions to ask about communication pedagogy and power, and several of those are advanced in this *Handbook*.

McGarrity (Chapter 6), for instance, observes the relatively unchallenged power that textbook publishers and publishing organizations have over the content and design of many textbooks. He invites communication education scholars to use critical organizational communication theories and methods to help explore how the discourses of the publisher and publishing company assert influence over the content and design of textbooks. Sellnow and Martin (Chapter 3) invite reflection on how the results of critical whiteness studies can be integrated into the basic course. They note that one obvious place in which to explore the integration of critical whiteness into the basic course is the typically unchallenged assumption that Westernized conceptions of communication skills are used to structure the curriculum of the basic course. Given the disciplinary commitment to critical scholarship, to exploring the many and insidious ways in which communication is complicit with the power that structures inequity, it is disappointing that more communication education scholarship has not incorporated a critical perspective. Given the initial investments articulated by these eight authors, we can certainly hope for more.

Maybe the next edition of this *Handbook* will, like the last section of this edition of the *Handbook*, have more to say about how communication pedagogy intersects with the communicative creation and sustenance of power and identity. I can imagine, for example, explorations of communicative practices that allow the enactment of critical communication pedagogy, just as I can imagine philosophical discussions of the hoped-for outcomes of communication education that have emancipatory goals. I can also imagine studies that reveal the ways in which constructions of race, gender, class, heteronormativity, and ableism are communicatively not only accomplished but encouraged *inside of* communication pedagogy. In other words, while this is painful to assert, we may have the opportunity to explore the ways in which our very curriculum is structured on the foundations of whiteness. Radical work indeed!

I am proud to have had the opportunity to add another line to the story of how communication education scholarship came to be. With these eight authors, we continue the tradition of being restless and unsettled with the way things are and hopeful that we can make a difference. Questions about how best to teach and learn communication may be foundational to the whole enterprise of being an educated person. They are certainly radical elements of an academic conversation about communication.

Note

1. Attention quickly turned to the broader concept of "speech" rather than "public speaking." In fact, by the time of the first actual convention, in 1915, the name of the association had changed to the "National Association of Teachers of Speech" (Jeffrey, 1964; Philipsen, 2007).

References

Benson, T. W. (1985). *Speech communication in the twentieth century.* Carbondale: Southern Illinois University Press.

Book, C. L. (1989). Communication education: Pedagogical content knowledge needed. *Communication Education, 38,* 315–321.

Craig, R. T. (1989). Communication as a practical discipline. In B. Dervin, L. Grossberg, B. J. O'Keefe, & E. Wartella (Eds.), *Rethinking communication: Vol. 1. Paradigm issues* (pp. 97–122). Newbury Park, CA: Sage.

Dannels, D. P., & Housley-Gaffney, A. L. (2009). Communication across the curriculum and in the disciplines: A call for cross-curricular scholarly advocacy. *Communication Education, 58,* 124–153.

Ehrlich, E., Flexner, S. B., Carruth, G., & Hawkins, J. (Eds.). (1980). *Oxford American dictionary* (Heald Colleges Edition). New York: Avon Books.

Freire, P. (1990). *Pedagogy of the oppressed.* New York: Continuum.

Friedrich, G. W. (1987). Instructional communication research. *Journal of Thought, 22,* 4–10.

Giroux, H. A. (1988). *Teachers as intellectuals: Toward a critical pedagogy of learning.* Boston: Bergin & Garvey.

Gray, G. W. (1964). The founding of the Speech Association of America: Happy birthday. *Quarterly Journal of Speech, 50,* 342–444.

Jeffrey, R. C. (1964). A history of the Speech Association of America, 1914–1964. *Quarterly Journal of Speech, 50,* 432–444.

Philipsen, G. (2007). The early career rise of "Speech" in some disciplinary discourses, 1914–1946. *Quarterly Journal of Speech, 93*(3), 352–354.

Reid, L. (2002). The speech teacher: Early years. *Communication Education, 51,* 333–336.

Sprague, J. (1992). Expanding the research agenda for instructional communication: Raising some unasked questions. *Communication Education, 41,* 181–203.

Sprague, J. (1993). Retrieving the research agenda from communication education: Asking the pedagogical questions that are "embarrassments to theory." *Communication Education, 42,* 106–122.

Staton, A. Q. (1989). The interface of communication and instruction: Conceptual considerations and programmatic manifestations. *Communication Education, 38,* 364–371.

Wallace, K. R. (1954). *History of speech education in America: Background studies.* New York: Appleton-Century-Crofts.

Weaver, A. T. (1959). Seventeen who made history. *Quarterly Journal of Speech, 45,* 195.

The Philosophical and Methodological Foundations of Communication Education

2

Keith Nainby

I n unearthing the traces of how our sense of ourselves, as teachers and scholars of communication, has evolved within the ecological niche of a specific academic discipline, we might start, as Phillips and Wood (1990) start, with the establishment of our leading scholarly association:

> In 1914, seventeen speech teachers formed The National Association of Academic Teachers of Public Speaking to provide academic identity and to promote professional development of members and the discipline. . . . Notably, the organization is currently called the Speech Communication Association. (p. vii)

Equally notably, the National Communication Association dropped the designation "Speech" from its name completely in 1997, a mere 7 years after the above preface was published, reflecting broadening conceptions of research and teaching in communication that have evolved beyond the connotations of the term *speech*. Two conclusions may be drawn from this history: First, organized scholarly inquiry into communication has, from the beginning, been deeply intertwined with teachers and with questions surrounding the teaching of communication. Second, attempts to define subject matter, scope, and method within communication research are just as long-standing and continue, necessarily, to evolve.

This chapter tells the story of one branch of this evolving disciplinary family tree: the story of communication education scholarship, or scholarship exploring teaching and learning communication. This vital branch might even be called one of the two branches of communication (along with rhetoric) that is closest to the "trunk" of our discipline, as it can be directly traced to the oldest roots of the communication discipline, roots that were thriving—long before the formation of educational associations in the United States—in classical studies of the art of speaking, of how and to whom this art should be taught, and of the social implications of its teaching and learning. These roots continue to flourish today, supporting researchers who consider power, culture, and identity development and how these dimensions shape the contemporary teaching and learning of communication.

In the present chapter, I narrate several of the twists and turns of this epic story of scholarly branching, depicting the dynamic process of collective intellectual commitments that have been shaped by the interactions of particular historical contexts and long-term disciplinary developments. I offer this analysis in an effort to identify the primary philosophical and methodological foundations of communication education, foundations that grew from historically specific pathways and that still nourish this vital area of communication inquiry as it continues to grow.

I take the "roots" metaphor from Friedrich (1989), who describes our recent academic foundations in this way:

> Tracing their roots to the study of rhetoric (an established part of the curriculum since medieval times), departments of English originally claimed responsibility for both oral and written communication instruction. . . . Drawing on two sources (the rhetorical tradition, a tradition as classical as that of literature, and modern science, a tradition foreign to the interests of English departments), early communication instructors developed theories of practical discourse that guided them as they provided instruction in the diverse arts of oral communication. Thus, from the beginning, the communication discipline has been . . . a practical discipline whose essential purpose is to cultivate communication as a practical art through critical study. (p. 297)

Here, Friedrich marks the fundamental importance of communication education as a bridge between practice and critique by invoking a story familiar to advanced students in our field: the emergence of communication as a sphere of academic inquiry. This story involves three movements, from (1) the ancient study of speaking as an "art" in the highest classical sense of a thorough integration of theory and practice, through (2) efforts in the 19th and 20th centuries to reconcile theory and practice in speech communication pedagogy after centuries-long denigration of the teaching of the mere craft of "delivery," to (3) the incorporation of theories and methods from disciplines such as psychology and sociology that steered us toward the project of accumulating scientifically ratified knowledge about human communication phenomena. I track the ebb and flow of these three movements as an organizing principle in this analysis.

These three wide-spanning historical streams of communication-education-related development are currently joined by a fourth that has coalesced since Friedrich's discussion: Fed by disciplines such as critical theory, cultural studies, and postmodern philosophy, this stream of studies addresses power, identity, and social justice as they pertain to teaching and learning communication. The present chapter is, like all such analyses and like all forces shaping the foundations of communication education, strongly influenced by both the light and the heat of the most pressing contemporary discussions in the field; I believe that future scholars will recognize critical, postmodern research in communication education as a significant shift, but only time will tell.

Philosophical and Methodological Foundations

Although the following sections provide a more detailed view of the struggles that have shaped communication education (CE), the present section offers a cursory enumeration of the philosophical and methodological foundations to help orient readers to the major elements of the terrain. Sprague explored the view of communication inherent in CE research in several essays, initially describing these in 1993 (Sprague, 1993) and summarizing them succinctly in 2002:

> A discipline specific pedagogy recognizes that communication is inherently complex, processual, and frequently unconscious or automatic. It treats human speech communication as a performative, embodied, usually oral, social enactment. It honors the ties of communication to cultural and social identity and acknowledges its implication in the structures of power. (p. 347)

The view of communication articulated by Sprague reflects unfolding historical developments in the field as a whole. Throughout this chapter, I track several of these historical developments, exploring how they have, through ongoing debate, shaped the constitution of the core issues surrounding discipline-specific pedagogy. Here, I identify several philosophical and methodological assumptions that are, again debatably, entailments of this view—entailments that not all CE scholars would necessarily affirm. I contend, however, that these entailments reflect the most salient issues in contemporary CE and that their emergence as core issues is grounded in the disciplinary history Sprague invokes. They include the following:

Philosophical Assumptions of CE

(P1) Communication acts are principally responsive, through oral/aural interaction or otherwise—meaning that they are direct engagements with other communicators (some physically present, some imagined) and are performed in social contexts.

(P2) Communicative acts shape both people and the human world.

(P3) Communication is a process in which participants actively make meanings within dynamic contexts.

(P4) Communication practices are learned and become habituated over time.

Methodological Assumptions of CE

(M1) Communicative acts can best be understood in relation to context.

(M2) Communicative acts are affected by the (communicative) act of conducting research.

(M3) Communicative acts are often complex and require multileveled analysis.

The Ancient Study of Speaking: Why Teach Communication?

Given that the primary concern of communication education scholars is with the teaching and learning of communication, the foundational philosophical question would be, why? Why place so much emphasis on the teaching and learning of oral/aural communication? This question can be answered, historically, by locating the source of this emphasis in liberal arts and humanistic education.

The emergence of the city-state in Greece was frequently linked, in formative CE scholarship (roughly the first half of the 20th century), to the focus on public speechmaking as the most significant vehicle for the democratic process. Brigance (1952), for example, argues for the centrality of what we would now call communication education in observing that "systematic speechmaking grew out of the attempt of free people to govern themselves. . . . That is why every citizen in every free society needs to be trained in its discipline" (p. 158). Brigance stresses that the significant development in the Greek rhetorical tradition, from a teaching and learning standpoint, is the "systematization" of speechmaking and of instruction in this art, most obviously in the work of Aristotle, and that the systematization of training in the art of speech is at one with the establishment of political liberty in Greece (pp. 157–159). Shorey (1922) similarly yokes effective speaking with efficacious public deliberation throughout the classical tradition:

> True political eloquence . . . can flourish only where the votes of parliaments and people determine the destinies of states. After the death of Cicero, Greek and Roman critics both recognized this truth. . . . Many besides Quintilian wrote treatises on the causes of the decline and corruption of eloquence and found the dominant cause in the loss of the old political freedom. (p. 122)

For early CE scholars, success in oral communication, at least in the form of oral communication that contemporary texts would now label "public speaking," occupies a keystone position in the education of a democratic citizenry—and so, too, then, does instruction in the means to achieve this success (e.g., in mastering artistic and inartistic proofs, in adhering to the five canons). Here, we see traces of the development of two philosophical assumptions:

> (P1) Communication acts are principally responsive (through oral/aural interaction or otherwise) and are performed in social contexts in collaboration with other communicators.

> (P2) Communicative acts shape both people and the human world.

It is the fundamentally social, responsive character of the spoken word, and its capacity to shape public belief and sentiment, that made the teaching and learning of oratory paramount in classical education and ensured its place in the liberal arts educational tradition that continues to undergird contemporary universities (Miller, 2007; Neiman, 1997). Furthermore, the emphasis in the classical tradition was never on the mere analytical dimension of rhetorical study but always included attention to the practice of oratory, an early example of the precept of speech as a performed act at its core.

In light of this strong relationship between speaking and public deliberation on social concerns, the founding CE scholars, who approached classical rhetoric for insights about speech instruction, consistently highlighted the moral and ethical dimensions of pedagogy—such as Flynn (1957) synthesizing Aristotle's position: "At best, society is a manifestive, not a constitutive, norm of morality" (p. 184). In line with the mainstream scholarly discussions of instruction in public speaking at that time, Flynn follows Aristotle in arguing,

> Since the teacher should contribute to a speaker's effectiveness the former ought to be concerned with his student's choice of objectives and the appropriate steps he takes to reach them. As teachers we need sound basic principles for determining when a speaker's attitudes and methods are ethical. (p. 179)

This call for "basic principles," however, while reflective of the foundational disciplinary approaches to speaking instruction, was tempered with respect for the complexity of the speaking act; again following Aristotle, Flynn (1957) qualifies the pedagogical process through which students—and the university educators who philosophize speaking instruction—can come to rely on Aristotelian moral determinants:

> Even after we understand these basic elements and their application to ethical problems we must carefully analyze the agent's intent, the object, and the circumstances. Besides, we should seek to broaden our understanding of human nature and human society, both key factors in the study of ethics. (p. 187)

Flynn's (1957) perspective on a classically grounded pedagogy of speaking indicates the relevance of two methodological assumptions for CE:

(M1) Communicative acts can best be understood in relation to context—what Aristotle would label "intent, object and circumstances."

(M3) Communicative acts are often complex and require multilevel analysis—a position illustrated by Aristotle's elaborated taxonomy of rhetorical methods, poetical forms, and moral determinants as necessary components of speaking instruction.

The Aristotelian foundation of CE topics at the formation of our discipline is significant, as McGee (1985) maintains, because Isocrates offers an alternative view of morality and of pedagogy, in which a successful person can achieve greater moral wisdom through the careful development of the art of speaking in particular deliberative settings, what McGee describes as an "applied political aesthetic" (p. 2). McGee explains the stakes, for a discipline-specific pedagogy, in the struggle of early-20th-century communication scholars to establish their place within the university community by appealing to this classical topic—the proper situation of truth in relation to rhetorical practice. McGee notes that "speech teachers had to justify their practice within a traditional conception (which we get from Plato) that scholarship should soar high 'above' political interest" (p. 4). The effort to carve out a disciplinary territory that fellow university scholars would recognize not only as a valid area of study but also as the domain of neither philosophy departments (aesthetics) nor political science departments (politics) led, according to McGee, to our disciplinary emphasis on argumentation; but this area of inquiry, because of the expectations of colleagues in the university elite, was first oriented to the Platonic and Aristotelian conceptions described above, in which rhetoric per se, in research and in teaching, must involve the search for universalizable principles applicable across particular contexts.

The historical forces that led to the "renaissance" of rhetoric McGee (1985) identifies in late-19th-century and early-20th-century universities contrast with the Platonic views of truth and of rhetoric, however: "Argumentation was taken up, not by *scholars* committed to ivory-tower research into the writings of dead Greeks, but by *teachers* interested in . . . our political system in crisis [in postindustrial society]" (p. 3). Again we see that questions about the teaching and learning of communication are at the forefront of our coming together as a distinct "speech" discipline, and again we see that historical forces shape the debate over pedagogical theory and practice. As McGee observes,

We have a contradiction, then, between a pedagogical practice justified by a need to develop a polity competent to manage the affairs of a democracy, and a scholarly practice justified by the need to understand the mechanics and tactics of text formation. (p. 4)

McGee concludes with an explicit call for communication scholars to acknowledge the minimization of an Isocratic rhetoric, a call that has been answered in much contemporary CE research (as I show below) and that contrasts with earlier trends in the development of discipline-specific pedagogies. These historical forces that shape the debate over discipline-specific pedagogy, however, affirm the importance of a second methodological assumption in CE: (M2), Communicative acts are affected by the (communicative) act of conducting research.

As McGee suggests, the early speech communication scholars' advocacy of a general communication practice that could stand "above" the particularities of any given community (whether on moral, logical, or aesthetic grounds), and proposing of guidelines for instruction that could lead to such a general practice, can be seen frequently in teaching and learning–centered articles in Speech Communication Association (SCA)/National Communication Association (NCA) journals (e.g., *Quarterly Journal of Speech* and *Speech Teacher*) from their inception until the 1960s. However, it is not exclusive; early CE scholarship also reveals extensive attention to CE questions that continue to foster philosophical and methodological debate today—for instance, the significance of student-teacher identification (Osmer, 1923), the teaching of communication for specific communities of disabled students (Bruhn, 1923), and the embodied nature of communication (Pardoe, 1923), all of which appear in the same volume of *Quarterly Journal of Speech*. Moreover, the struggle between a pedagogy of general communication competencies (Platonic) and a pedagogy of particular communication competencies (Isocratic) persists today in the communication in the disciplines (CID)/communication across the curriculum (CXC) dialogue (discussed later in this chapter). The seeds of this pedagogical debate were, indeed, sown even earlier than in the time of Aristotle; for example, Johnstone (2001) finds significant evidence that the Older Sophists approached instruction in public speaking by thoroughly integrating theory, critique, and oral performance practice—an Isocratean pedagogy more complex, and more like contemporary communication instruction, than that with which the Sophists have typically been credited.

The tension between Platonic/Aristotelian and Isocratic perspectives on pedagogy can be said to turn on two more philosophical assumptions within CE:

(P3) Communication is a process in which participants actively make meanings within dynamic contexts—an assumption that would be anathematic to the Platonic view of meaning but that is at the heart of the Isocratic view.

(P4) Communication practices are learned and become habituated over time—which, for the Platonic school, requires vigilant uncovering of the calcifying, truth-obscuring elements of everyday interaction and which, for Isocrates, requires vigilant attention to the lessons embedded in these same elements of interaction.

Scholars who grapple with the fundamental rift between the Platonic and the Isocratic views are not only helping define the nature and importance of communication; they are also helping define the character of the professional-community communication of communication teachers, as I explore in the following section.

Speech as More Than Mere Style: Who Teaches Communication?

A major challenge facing those who appealed to the classical rhetorical tradition in defending "speech" as valuable disciplinary territory in the academy is that rhetoric had not fared well within the academy in the previous 2,000 years. Despite the occasional modern theoretical clarifications and extensions of the rhetorical tradition offered by Campbell or Blair (Golden & Corbett, 1990), for instance, academically ratified, systematic study of oral communication was not in place in Western universities when the "speech teachers" McGee (1985) references emerged to reclaim the classical rhetorical tradition. In 1947, Parrish reviewed the treatment of rhetoric in predominant college-level English and speech textbooks, concluding that the classical rhetorical tradition has been "abandoned" by English departments and "left in our hands" (p. 467).

This "abandonment" of the classical tradition necessitated some treatment of the perspectives on rhetoric that had prevailed in the past several centuries, principally the Ramian and elocutionist schools. Parrish (1947) acknowledges the importance of recovering a more substantive role for rhetoric than that allowed by Ramus, appealing like so many of his contemporaries to Aristotle and characterizing "sophistic" as an "exclusive preoccupation with style" (p. 466). In a similar effort to provide a firm footing for speech instruction, Baldwin (1928) crystallizes this distinction: "Rhetoric is conceived by Aristotle as the art of giving effectiveness to the truth; it is conceived alike by the earlier and the later sophists and by their successors as the art of giving effectiveness to the speaker" (p. 3).

The battles to recover a role for teaching and learning speech are unified by their sustained attention to the complexities of speaking in a variety of settings—from the political arena to the interpretive stage to other institutional and professional settings. Gray (1960), for example, shows that the much maligned elocutionist movement, though later narrowed to mean only the most myopic study of particular oral/aural habits and routines, was initially an effort to attend seriously to the intensive learning process at the heart of effective speaking in given social conditions. The mid-20th-century scholarly movement to integrate speech teaching into a widening range of academic and professional settings was an implicit recognition of the intensely polymath

character of speech teachers themselves and of everyday speech instruction. Reid (2002) recalls that in the formative years of the SCA community of teacher/scholars, "most speech teachers were beginners" (p. 333).
He maintains that instructors with a separate disciplinary identity were
uncommon: "Speech or theatre majors, or even minors, were rare on
university campuses; almost impossible to find in high schools. Basically
we were trained in English; we had debated, we had acted, but mostly on
an extracurricular basis" (p. 333). This question remained a cogent one
even in 1961, when Tarver and Peterson analyzed the demands of
college-level teaching positions to consider the question of whether it
was professionally reasonable for graduate students to specialize in "speech"
teaching alone—quite an interesting fluidity of identity for the future
professorate of a discipline that had been holding formal meetings and
publishing peer-reviewed scholarship for half a century by that point!

This amorphous pedagogical identity, though one consequence of the
unpleasant (for communication teaching and scholarship) historical
period of academic debate that stretches approximately from Quintillian
to Dewey, came to be respected, perhaps paradoxically, as a strength for
communication educators. Haberman (1961), studying the characteristics
of the "ideal teacher of speech" at several educational levels through a
combination of survey results and philosophical argument, finds that
speech teachers play a unique role in the intellectual development of students because our curricula involve students with the processes of discovering, shaping, and communicating ideas, across a breadth of areas, within
the especially demanding performative context of the public speech. He
holds that "there is scarcely any teacher in the entire curriculum of the
public school who is so close at crucial moments to the intellectual creativity that goes on inside the pupil" (p. 3). Like several writers in our discipline before and after him, Haberman enumerates the impressive range
of scholarly knowledge required of the "ideal" speech teacher, which
includes knowledge of physiology and audiology, psychology, linguistics,
aesthetics, history of communication, and the specializations we would
now call media studies and performance studies (p. 4).

While this list may seem daunting, it does circumscribe a group of people committed to several of the core philosophical and methodological
assumptions discussed above, assumptions that begin to take firmer shape
in this period of defining speech communication as a discipline: (P1),
Communication acts are principally responsive (through oral/aural interaction or otherwise) and are performed in social contexts in collaboration
with other communicators. This assumption, because it centers on the
spoken word as well as the collaboration necessary between audience and
rhetor, grounds the very territorial viability of the discipline itself, helping
differentiate the orientation to rhetorical arts in speech communication
from the orientations to related topics in the departments of English,
drama/theater, philosophy, and political science.

Three related assumptions played the productive role of tethering the discipline, in its early years, to emerging scholarship in other new areas of the academy that had first flourished in the mid-to-late 19th century: (P2), Communicative acts shape both people and the human world. This assumption not only followed from the original impetus for the reclamation of speech instruction in the concern for democratic process and public deliberation following the social upheavals of the industrial revolution but also opened up avenues for communication research that paralleled those in psychology, sociology, and, especially, social psychology and social interactionism (Mead, 1934). This assumption would lead communication scholars into the sphere of social science research (discussed more fully in the next section) and, in this way, would help strongly reinforce two methodological entailments of Communication Education: (M1), Communicative acts can best be understood in relation to context, and (M3), Communicative acts are often complex and require multilevel analysis. Both of these assumptions flow from psychological and social psychological models of communication, in which communicators' engagement with one another is mediated by the contingent particularities of personal development and of the robust social world rather than merely structured by universal principles and apposite circumstance.

The philosophical assumption that communication practices are learned and become habituated over time (P4) became singularly important within the then nascent area of specialized research on communication in all instructional settings because it was a point of connection with the developing empirical research on the psychology of learning as well as with philosophical arguments about the goals of public schooling related to citizenry and the deep relationship of communication to those goals (Dewey, 1921). This root would later flower into much of contemporary CE research on topics such as instructional communication and teaching and learning communication in particular educational settings (discussed in the next section) and power, culture, and identity (discussed in its own section) and—in an often overlooked symbiosis—would later help ground, regrettably primarily through philosophy rather than through communication scholarship, core texts in critical pedagogy.

The philosophical assumption that communication is a process in which participants actively make meanings within dynamic contexts (P3) linked the young discipline—sometimes by way of contrast—to the new explorations of meaning taking place in anthropology, structural linguistics, and semiotics. The study of meaning making has been linked in communication with the performative dimensions of the first assumption identified in this chapter (P1) and in research areas such as speech act theory (Austin, 1962) and performance studies (Pelias & VanOosting, 1987), and has helped ground constitutive philosophies of communication (Stewart, 1995). Moreover, philosophical debates across these disciplines and our own centered on the balance between universality and particularity with respect to meaning making and communicative practices; when these took on a political character, they helped lead CE scholars and their like-minded colleagues to question the methodological assumptions of objectivist research in communication, leading to the reinforcement of one final methodological assumption of CE: (M2), Communicative acts are affected by the (communicative) act of conducting research. This story is the story of a key struggle at the core of communication scholarship related to teaching and learning and is told in the following section.

The Social Science of Communication Education: How Should We Study the Teaching and Learning of Communication?

An important, and likely necessary, marker of the maturation of the speech communication discipline in general, and CE in particular, is the concomitant generation of a technical vocabulary for identifying communication phenomena and a set of procedures for studying these phenomena in systematic ways. In CE scholarship, this was first evident in two related efforts prior to the mid-1960s: (1) analyses of the causes of and potential "remedies" for students' experience of fear in public speaking settings, which was alternately labeled "stage fright" and "speech anxiety," and (2) application of the tools of psychology and speech therapy to "correct" speech "disorders" such as stuttering and various other oral practices among students (Greenleaf, 1952; Hegarty, 1967; Lomas, 1937; Robinson, 1959). The titles of two articles that form an arc from 1942 (Hayworth, "A Search for Facts on the Teaching of Public Speaking, IV") to 1959 (Clevenger, "A Synthesis of Experimental Research in Stage Fright") indicate how significant it was to foreground the introduction of empirical studies incorporating social science methods in CE scholarship in the middle of the 20th century.

The process of generating social scientific knowledge about teaching and learning through journals and conferences on communication ramped up quickly beginning around 1965, with increasing attention to both definitional work and methodological orthodoxy. For example, topics that were previously known as "stage fright" or "speech anxiety" became codified as "communication apprehension." Daly (1974) provides a 241-item bibliography of scholarship on communication apprehension, approximately two thirds of which had been in print for less than a decade.

The proliferation of scholarship on communication apprehension is especially significant with respect to the clarification of philosophical and methodological assumptions within CE, for one paramount reason: Communication apprehension scholarship was extended beyond the public speaking setting into communication areas such as small-group decision making (Lustig & Grove, 1975) and, critically, across a range of educational environments (McCroskey, Ralph, & Barrick, 1970; Wheeless, 1971). This final turn to communication apprehension in educational settings more generally helped foster a major shift within CE research, from a concern with teaching and learning communication (a discipline-specific pedagogy) to a concern with the role of communication in a variety of instructional settings. This latter focus has come to be known as instructional communication, or IC, and is distinct from CE not merely in topical focus but in several philosophical and methodological senses as well. Rich debates between CE and IC scholars in the past few decades over definitional questions, research goals and methods, social relevance, and—especially—philosophical perspectives on communication have led to further reinforcement of the philosophical and methodological assumptions that are the subject of this chapter. This debate is what I turn to now, in an effort to explicate these assumptions in their contemporary form. In this explication, I do not attempt to mask my own stance in this debate nor my commitment to the CE assumptions themselves; these will be evident throughout.

A spark igniting the extended debate over the assumptions embedded in both IC and CE is the valorization of a particular model of programmatic accumulation of scholarly knowledge, a model Sprague (1994) characterizes as an objectivist epistemology, in which the researcher "assumes that there is a separation between knower and known—or at least that it is possible and desirable to act as if that were the case by following certain rules of observation and using language in certain technical ways" (p. 275). Clearly, not all researchers working within the IC paradigm embrace this exact objectivist stance. Just as clearly, many of those who embrace it in some form have worked in tandem with a large group of scholars across the entire communication discipline to develop a substantial foundational literature undergirding the academic merit of these approaches to the study of communication phenomena. However, Friedrich's (2002) consideration of the relative merits of recently published scholarship in IC and CE is one powerful indicator of how much the objectivist stance determines what counts as quality research:

> A very large percentage of the essays in *Communication Education* that help us with our tasks as communication instructors can be characterized as either non–research based opinion pieces or as isolated, non-programmatic research projects. . . . A notable exception to this generalization is the research conducted in the domain of instructional communication. (pp. 372–373)

Friedrich's goal in making these claims is a laudable one: to call, as Sprague (2002) does in the same anniversary issue of *Communication Education*, for a more comprehensive, sustained focus on the theoretical and practical issues associated with CE. Yet this contrast of CE with IC misconstrues CE in two related ways.

First, CE research is generating sophisticated theoretical and practical knowledge but doing so in a variety of areas. This may result in a less robust understanding of the impact of CE, especially when it is compared with IC research in "communication and instruction"–centered contexts such as *Communication Education*, because only some of these areas of study (the scholarship of teaching and learning, graduate teaching assistant [GTA] training, articles in *Communication Teacher*) are directly aligned with the traditional "effective speech teacher" line of research described above. Other CE branches are flourishing today—CXC/CID, communication through service learning, subdiscipline-specific pedagogies such as teaching and learning argumentation and debate, intercultural communication, and so on—but may be somewhat harder to recognize as "programmatic" given the wide range of their topical focus. In terms of historical developments in CE literature, Sprague (2002) analyzes 50 years of historical trends in the journal now titled *Communication Education* (formerly *Speech Teacher*), finding that several of the questions currently at the forefront of communication education scholarship have been subjects of scholarly articles for at least five decades (p. 338). These include teaching communication in business, health care, correctional settings, and other nonclassroom settings; service learning; and CXC. As Sprague (1992, 1993) notes, in this case what should be a strength of CE, its potential to inform all teachers and researchers of communication, instead becomes a weakness when CE is contrasted with a more narrowly defined topical area of communication inquiry such as IC.

Second, and much more substantive, is a misunderstanding of (or refusal to acknowledge) what makes for "programmatic knowledge" according to CE scholars. The most direct way, in any area of study, to amass research findings that are systematically related to one another, that build on one another, and that therefore can be said to constitute programmatic knowledge is to adopt the objectivist epistemology discussed above. In the post-Galileo period of quantification of natural phenomena, technization of subject terminology and methodology, and advancement of the scientific method—not only in the natural sciences but in the social sciences as well—it is little exaggeration to say that this has been the only way we have recognized programmatic knowledge of any kind; this is especially true in the demarcation of disciplinary and subdisciplinary territory, which is almost always accomplished through the development of technical terminology in a given range of study (Husserl, 1970).

The most obvious manifestation of this objectivist epistemology in our own discipline is adherence to particular methodological procedures, an adherence that, as I have suggested above, has a historical cause in resistance to the long-term devaluation of oral/aural communication knowledge and the resultant embrace of the research methods of disciplines such as psychology and sociology. These procedures include forming initial hypotheses based on prior findings, some accepted and others controversial; operationalizing variables, scales, or coding categories; testing the reliability of survey instruments or observational coding procedures; and clarifying testing or observational conditions to help account for the influence of untested factors on the outcomes used to evaluate the hypothesis.

When researchers (both the authors of a study and those who subsequently build on the study in question) respect the limitations of the knowledge generated by the use of such procedures and allow this respect to inform the situation of knowledge within the larger sphere of communication scholarship generated by a range of other methodologies, these procedures are extremely fruitful, as they often have been in IC research and other social scientific inquiry in communication. Yet what has been to this point too common in our field, indicated by Friedrich's framing of CE and IC research, is to take the highly systematic form of objectivist-oriented studies, from their design to their incorporation of previous findings, as normative of programmatic research as such. Given the philosophical and methodological assumptions I trace in this chapter—assumptions, such as (P1): Communication acts are principally responsive (through oral/aural interaction or otherwise) and are performed in social contexts in collaboration with other communicators, that continue to serve as a foundation for CE—such a perspective is untenable.

The notion of a "speech act" in contemporary research is perhaps the least controversial of the assumptions across the CE/IC debate, though it is worth noting that the performative element in this assumption troubles the extensive reliance in IC definitional work on personality types, trait-versus-state distinctions, and other stable characterizations of individual personality. This troubling has helped clarify the foundations of CE, in which all experiences of apprehension and indeed all communication, instructional or otherwise, would be viewed as a "state" of human life in the most robust sense. For this reason, CE scholars also emphasize the correlative methodological assumption (M1), Communicative acts can best be understood in relation to context; it is this assumption that accounts, for instance, for the more extensive use of participation-observation and interviewing in scholarly CE projects compared with IC and accounts as well for its (typically) longer period of gestation in the research process. While this may have been a "weakness" of sorts in the relative youth of the discipline, it should be much less problematic in the contemporary landscape of multiple scholarly associations and multiple publication venues.

Several philosophical and methodological assumptions intersected one another at this point in the development of CE—for example, (P2), Communicative acts shape both people and the human world, which leads in CE scholarship to (M2), Communicative acts are affected by the (communicative) act of conducting research. Importantly, while Sprague (1992) cites scholars in disciplines such as sociology (Habermas, 1971) and education (Shulman, 1986) when developing a critique of approaches to research that overemphasize technical knowledge, the serious limitations of the goal of precision in communication inquiry have been explored in depth in our own literature as well (Shotter, 1993; Stewart, 1995). These scholars argue for an expansion of our approaches to the study of communication on philosophical as well as methodological grounds. A central implication of the communication philosophy shared by these authors is that there is no set of systematically ordered, preexisting traits, capacities, or orientations that might be identified through careful testing of the scientific questions that are supremely relevant for communication theorizing. Instead, any traits, capacities, or orientations that researchers find will have been, according to this philosophy of communication paradigm, constituted in and through the research process itself, and no further evidence of priority for such categories is retrievable—because we can only undertake such retrieval efforts as communicators sharing a world that we have already co-constituted, in the act of research, with our research participants.

(P4), Communication practices are learned and become habituated over time, and (P3), Communication is a process in which participants actively make meanings within dynamic contexts, are perhaps the most strident areas of departure for CE scholars with respect to IC and similar objectivist research. CE scholars, in committing to a process-based understanding in which communication practices are dynamic, transactional, nonsummative, and often more deeply embedded in cultural and social micropractices than researchers or participants can recognize, maintain skepticism about how effectively we might operationalize variables, scales, or coding categories when these pertain to communication. These procedures enable us to generate, at best, a synchronic view or "snapshot" of fluid, multichanneled communication practices at a single moment of observation or testing; at worst, they encapsulate a range of cognitive and affective reflections on one's own life in the reductive form of a scaled self-report question. This assumption does not entail abandoning the scholar's responsibility to clarify research questions or procedures; rather, a process-centered perspective heightens the demand for reflexivity on the part of the researcher at all stages of research, from design to observation to writing, which entails the methodological assumption (M3), Communicative acts are often complex and require multilevel analysis. One consequence of these two related assumptions—(P3) and (M3)—is the turn toward interpretive and critical scholarship in CE; this turn is the subject of the next section.

This debate, or point of departure, between core philosophies and methodologies in CE and IC continues today. It marks important points of distinction in the scholarly work taken up in these two subfields. In CE, the story has yet another turn to make, the turn to critical inquiry.

Contemporary Communication Education: How Does Communication Constitute Us and Our World?

To return, at the end of our story, to the overarching purpose of communication education, Sprague (1993), following Shulman (1986), clarifies the highest goals of communication educators and scholars: subject matter knowledge, pedagogical content knowledge, and curricular knowledge. These three forms of knowledge depend on one another to develop most fully, given the importance of clarity and heuristic value for both the classroom and the journal: The more thoroughly we understand how we learn and teach communication, the more thoroughly we can identify, explore, debate, and respecify communication questions, even those questions considered by the most highly specialized scholars in our field. Research may often be initiated and guided by quite specific concerns associated with narrow forms of knowledge in communication; yet even the most specific concerns will be subsumed within a developing body of academic knowledge that is more general, ratified through the coherence of connections with other specific areas of research, and communicated to curious people across a range of levels of expertise and disciplinary training. Sprague (1993) articulates the significance of this deep commitment to pedagogical and curricular knowledge: "Teachers with discipline-specific pedagogical or curricular knowledge have achieved that elegant form of simplicity; they can make their content starkly clear without trivializing it" (p. 110).

Such "elegant simplicity" is certainly worth striving for in the presentation of scholarship and therefore might usefully inform the design and conduct of research as well. In this rests the potential importance of a focus on discipline-specific pedagogy for all communication scholars. Angus and Langsdorf (1993) link the ability to meaningfully communicate with the broader community, inside and outside the discipline, to a critical, reflexive focus on epistemological assumptions, in a passage that reaches conclusions much like Sprague's (1993) in the above call for elegant simplicity:

> The lesson . . . is that we make the most of the plurality of roads of inquiry, and that we are most faithful to the pluralities of the human condition, if we declare openly the persuasions that each of us practices and do not pretend to engage in them in the service of esoteric knowledge. The beginner and the generalist do not have to wait; they can be assured of prompt, piecemeal gratification of their epistemic and ethical needs to know. (Angus & Langsdorf, 1993, p. 7)

This raising of the profile of the situated, contextualized knowledge of everyday practices held in different forms by formal scholars and non-scholars alike, and the simultaneous lowering of the profile of "esoteric knowledge," is one way to understand what is at stake in the interpretive and critical "turns" in the academy.

The first of these, the interpretive turn, was associated, as noted previously, with the opening of humanistic inquiry into the plenitude of human practices in disciplines such as history, anthropology, and sociology. The goal of interpretive scholarship in CE is to understand, in rich detail, the meaning-making processes that shape the teaching and learning of communication for particular students and teachers in specific contexts. Representative interpretive scholarship in contemporary CE includes the study of teacher socialization (Smith, 2005; Staton & Huntington, 1992; Staton-Spicer & Darling, 1986) and explorations of communication instruction through programs in particular disciplines (Dannels, 2002; Darling, 2005). Indeed, 2005 saw a lively debate within interpretive CE circles on whether traditional CXC programs in universities might be fruitfully extended through the implementation of CID programs that foster the development of discipline-specific, and potentially richer and more meaningful, communication skills in a variety of subject areas (Dannels, 2001). The primary concern with this, expressed by Fleury (2005), is that such CID programs may lose sight of the more universal goals of liberal education associated with communication instruction, which include "core styles" that "transcend" particular disciplines (pp. 74–75). What is interesting about this debate is that it re-creates, in many ways, the Platonic/Isocratic debate marked by McGee (1985) at the founding of our discipline, suggesting that core issues such as the relationship of the general to the particular remain the subject of lively dialogue within interpretive scholarship.

Another, equally lively, debate has emerged in response to authors whose "turn" extends interpretive work into critical work. The goal of critical scholarship in CE is to uncover structures of power and privilege that are communicatively constituted among contingent social and cultural systems, with consideration of how these structures shape the teaching and learning of communication. Representative critical scholarship in contemporary CE includes studies of race (Cooks, 2003; Miller & Harris, 2005; Warren & Hytten, 2004), gender (Godley, 2003), race and gender (Johnson & Bhatt, 2003), culture (Jones & Bodtker, 1998), and identity (Fassett & Warren, 2004; Fitch & Morgan, 2003; Hendrix, Jackson, & Warren, 2003; Orbe, 2004).

The focus on identity links interpretive and critical contemporary CE scholarship; both of these bodies of work are rooted in a postmodern view of the self as constituted, at least in part, in and through contingent social and cultural practices—chief among these being, from our disciplinary perspective, communication. Interpretive CE scholars may, as a group, be less likely than critical CE scholars to wholly accept the most "radical" version of the social constitution of reality, in which all phenomena experienced by human beings derive their ontological force solely from communication

(Stewart, 1995). Nevertheless, what unifies this "fourth stream" of historical movement in CE, as of this writing, can be encapsulated by the following extended philosophical and methodological assumptions:

Constitutive Philosophical Assumptions

(P1a) Communication acts are principally responsive (through oral/aural interaction or otherwise) and are performed in social contexts in collaboration with other communicators.

(P2a) Communicative acts constitute social reality, including identities and cultures, within contingent social systems.

(P3a) Communication is a process in which participants actively make meanings within dynamic contexts.

(P4a) Communication practices are complex, learned, and (frequently) habituated at many different levels of cognitive and social experience, some distinct from the fully conscious or intentional.

(P5a) Communication is characterized by enduring, yet shifting, power relationships along a variety of axes of communicative experience.

Constitutive Methodological Assumptions

(M1a) Communicative acts can only be understood in context, and these contexts are often opaque to researchers in various ways.

(M2a) Communicative acts and those who engage in them are affected by the (communicative) act of conducting research (the Schrödinger's Cat problem at its most acute level).

(M3a) Goals, motives, perceptions, and expectations are partial, irreducibly interconnected, and frequently obfuscated—intentionally or not—by communicators; therefore, they are open to question in all research conditions, regardless of the reliability of research methods.

Taken together, this group of eight augmented and clarified assumptions helps define CE scholarship as a distinctive approach to communication, one that seeks to provide the discipline with a foundation for teaching and learning that attends carefully to the active negotiation of identity and meaning, in and through communication, in a variety of social contexts. In so doing, contemporary CE work fulfills the promise of a scholarly tradition that began with questions about the effects of speech in the public sphere and that gained tremendous momentum in recent decades as a core pedagogical linchpin for the burgeoning scientific and interpretive body of literature in communication. Indeed, this fertile group of eight assumptions might be understood as fulfilling another promise as well, that of Sprague's (1993) vision of a disciplinewide and discipline-specific bedrock of curricular and pedagogical knowledge that can nourish all teaching and all research in our academic subject.

Conclusion

Sprague (1993) identifies a historically compelling parallel among advancements in communication theory and pedagogy, noting,

> For many decades communication education was a valued professional concentration in a discipline that, after all, sprang from such master pedagogues as Isocrates, Aristotle, and Quintillian. . . . Gladys Borchers, Loren Reid, and Karl Wallace were revered along with their contemporaries in rhetorical theory and public address. (p. 107)

These enduring pedagogical and scholarly veins connect us, through the middle and the early 20th century, to classical scholars as far back as ancient Greece—when education in the art of public speaking involved disciplined practice meant to develop the whole student, intellectually and spiritually, through a sustained spiral of reflection and action, thereby producing a speaker who could shape social reality (in the case of Isocrates) or become an excellent leader of self and others (in the cases of Aristotle and Quintillian). As communication theorists—during the 20th-century move toward social scientific research—shifted from presenting a linear model involving message transmission between fixed participants to postulating complex, multilayered systems enmeshing participants, messages, and contexts, we can see historical evidence of the emergence of the contemporary foundational assumptions described here within our entire disciplinary tradition.

Communication education research, even in its contemporary formulations, has an unbroken connection to our disciplinary history that is firmly rooted in evolving trends in the study of communication—a symbiosis even richer than our broad interest, as communication pedagogues, in the practical issues in teaching communication. Considering these strong linkages, it is no exaggeration to say that the history of communication education is at one with the history of communication.

We began as a domain interested in teaching the "good man" [*sic*] how to speak well. Today, our questions focus on how the person is constituted in and through social contexts that define "good," "speaking well," and "man." We are also, for the record, recognizing eloquence in all kinds of voices these days. The postmodern era allows us the comfort of knowing that our worlds are constituted and reconstituted in our talk, and yes, that means we were right all along in focusing on the art of speaking.

References

Angus, I., & Langsdorf, L. (1993). Unsettled borders: Envisioning critique at the postmodern site. In I. Angus & L. Langsdorf (Eds.), *The critical turn: Rhetoric and philosophy in postmodern discourse* (pp. 1–19). Carbondale: Southern Illinois University Press.

Austin, J. L. (1962). *How to do things with words.* Cambridge, MA: Harvard University Press.

Baldwin, C. S. (1928). *Medieval rhetoric and poetic (to 1400).* New York: Macmillan.

Brigance, W. N. (1952). Demagogues, "good" people, and teachers of speech. *Speech Teacher, 1*(3), 157–162.

Bruhn, M. E. (1923). Teaching speech reading to the deaf. *Quarterly Journal of Speech Education, 9*(4), 334–339.

Clevenger, T. J. (1959). A synthesis of experimental research in stage fright. *Quarterly Journal of Speech, 45,* 134–145.

Cooks, L. (2003). Pedagogy, performance, and positionality: Teaching about whiteness in interracial communication. *Communication Education, 52,* 245–257.

Daly, J. A. (1974). *Communication apprehension: A preliminary bibliography of research.* Retrieved July 3, 2009, from Educational Resources Information Center (ED101406), http://eric.ed.gov/ERICDocs/data/ericdocs2sql/content_storage_01/0000019b/80/39/ac/2e.pdf

Dannels, D. P. (2001). Time to speak up: A theoretical framework of situated pedagogy and practice for communication. *Communication Education, 50,* 144–158.

Dannels, D. P. (2002). Communication across the curriculum and in the disciplines: Speaking in engineering. *Communication Education, 51,* 254–268.

Darling, A. L. (2005). Public presentations in mechanical engineering and the discourse of technology. *Communication Education, 54,* 20–33.

Dewey, J. (1921). *Democracy and education: An introduction to the philosophy of education.* New York: Macmillan.

Fassett, D. L., & Warren, J. T. (2004). "You get pushed back": The strategic rhetoric of educational success and failure in higher education. *Communication Education, 53,* 21–39.

Fitch, F., & Morgan, S. E. (2003). "Not a lick of English": Constructing the ITA identity through student narratives. *Communication Education, 52,* 297–310.

Fleury, A. (2005). Liberal education and communication against the disciplines. *Communication Education, 54,* 72–79.

Flynn, L. J. (1957). The Aristotelian basis for the ethics of speaking. *Speech Teacher, 6*(3), 179–187.

Friedrich, G. W. (1989). A view from the office of the SCA president. *Communication Education, 38,* 297–302.

Friedrich, G. W. (2002). The communication education research agenda. *Communication Education, 51,* 372–375.

Godley, A. J. (2003). Literacy learning as gendered identity work. *Communication Education, 52,* 273–285.

Golden, J. L., & Corbett, E. P. J. (1990). *The rhetoric of Blair, Campbell, and Whately* (Rev. ed.; Landmarks in Public Address). Carbondale: Southern Illinois University Press.

Gray, G. W. (1960). What was elocution? *Quarterly Journal of Speech, 46*(1), 1–7.

Greenleaf, F. I. (1952). An exploratory study of speech fright. *Quarterly Journal of Speech, 38*(3), 326–330.

Haberman, F. W. (1961). Toward the ideal teacher of speech. *Speech Teacher, 10*(1), 1–9.

Habermas, J. (1971). *Knowledge and human interests* (J. J. Shapiro, Trans.). Boston: Beacon.

Hayworth, D. (1942). A search for facts on the teaching of public speaking, IV. *Quarterly Journal of Speech, 28*(3), 347–354.

Hegarty, I. E. (1967). Group therapy for adolescent stutterers. *Speech Teacher, 16*(3), 195–199.

Hendrix, K. G., Jackson, R. L., II, & Warren, J. R. (2003). Shifting academic landscapes: Exploring co-identities, identity negotiation, and critical progressive pedagogy. *Communication Education, 52,* 177–190.

Husserl, E. (1970). *The crisis of the European sciences and transcendental phenomenology: An introduction to phenomenological philosophy* (D. Carr, Trans.). Evanston, IL: Northwestern.

Johnson, J. R., & Bhatt, A. J. (2003). Gendered and racialized identities and alliances in the classroom: Formations in/of resistive space. *Communication Education, 52,* 230–244.

Johnstone, C. L. (2001). Communicating in classical contexts: The centrality of delivery. *Quarterly Journal of Speech, 87*(2), 121–143.

Jones, T. S., & Bodtker, A. (1998). A dialectical analysis of a social justice process: International collaboration in South Africa. *Journal of Applied Communication Research, 26*(4), 357–373.

Ledbetter, A. M., & Schrodt, P. (2008). Family communication patterns and cognitive processing: Conversation and conformity orientations as predictors of informational reception apprehension. *Communication Studies, 59*(4), 388–401.

Lomas, C. W. (1937). The psychology of stage fright. *Quarterly Journal of Speech, 23*(1), 35–44.

Lustig, M. W., & Grove, T. G. (1975). Interaction analysis of small problem-solving groups containing reticent and non-reticent members. *Western Speech Communication, 39*(3), 155–165.

McCroskey, J. C., Ralph, D. C., & Barrick, J. E. (1970). The effect of systematic desensitization on speech anxiety. *Speech Teacher, 19*(1), 32–36.

McGee, M. C. (1985). The moral problem of *argumentum per argumentum*. In J. R. Cox, M. O. Sillars, & G. B. Walker (Eds.), *Argument and social practice: Proceedings of the fourth SCA/AFA Conference on argumentation* (pp. 1–12). Annandale, VA: Speech Communication Association.

Mead, G. H. (1934). *Mind, self and society* (C. W. Morris, Ed.). Chicago: University of Chicago Press.

Miller, A. (2007). Rhetoric, *paideia* and the old idea of a liberal education. *Journal of Philosophy of Education, 41*(2), 183–206.

Miller, A. N., & Harris, T. M. (2005). Communicating to develop white racial identity in an interracial communication class. *Communication Education, 54,* 223–242.

Neiman, A. M. (1997). Pragmatism, Thomism, and the metaphysics of desire: Two rival versions of liberal education. *Educational Theory, 47*(1), 91–117.

Orbe, M. P. (2004). Negotiating multiple identities within multiple frames: An analysis of first-generation college students. *Communication Education, 53,* 131–149.

Osmer, L. C. (1923). The function of the teacher's taste in oral English. *Quarterly Journal of Speech Education, 9*(4), 340–346.

Pardoe, T. E. (1923). Language of the body. *Quarterly Journal of Speech Education, 9*(3), 252–258.

Parrish, W. (1947). The tradition of rhetoric. *Quarterly Journal of Speech, 33*(4), 464–467.

Pelias, R. J., & VanOosting, J. (1987). A paradigm for performance studies. *Quarterly Journal of Speech, 73*(2), 219–231.

Phillips, G. M., & Wood, J. T. (1990). Preface. In G. M. Phillips & J. T. Wood (Eds.), *Speech communication: Essays to commemorate the 75th anniversary of the Speech Communication Association* (pp. vii–xiii). Carbondale: Southern Illinois University Press.

Reid, L. (2002). *The Speech Teacher:* Early years. *Communication Education, 51,* 333–336.

Robinson, E. R. (1959). What can the speech teacher do about students' stage-fright? *Speech Teacher, 8*(1), 8–14.

Rodriguez, J. I., & Cai, D. A. (1994). When your epistemology gets in the way: A response to Sprague. *Communication Education, 43,* 263–272.

Shorey, P. (1922). What teachers of speech may learn from the theory and practice of the Greeks. *Quarterly Journal of Speech Education, 8*(2), 105–131.

Shotter, J. (1993). *Conversational realities: Constructing life through language.* Thousand Oaks, CA: Sage.

Shulman, L. S. (1986). *The wisdom of practice: Essays on teaching, learning, and learning to teach.* San Francisco: Jossey-Bass.

Smith, E. R. (2005). Learning to talk like a teacher: Participation and negotiation in co-planning discourse. *Communication Education, 54,* 52–71.

Sprague, J. (1992). Expanding the research agenda for instructional communication: Raising some unasked questions. *Communication Education, 41,* 1–25.

Sprague, J. (1993). Retrieving the research agenda for communication education: Asking the pedagogical questions that are "embarrassments to theory." *Communication Education, 42,* 106–122.

Sprague, J. (1994). Ontology, politics, and instructional communication research: Why we can't just "agree to disagree" about power. *Communication Education, 43,* 273–290.

Sprague, J. (2002). Communication education: The spiral continues. *Communication Education, 51,* 337–354.

Staton, A., & Huntington, S. (1992). Teacher socialization: Review and conceptualization. *Communication Education, 41,* 109–137.

Staton-Spicer, A. Q., & Darling, A. L. (1986). Communication in the socialization of preservice teachers. *Communication Education, 35,* 215–230.

Stewart, J. (1995). *Language as articulate contact: Toward a post-semiotic philosophy of communication.* Albany: State University of New York Press.

Tarver, J. L., & Peterson, O. (1961). Specialization in college speech teaching. *Speech Teacher, 10*(4), 304–308.

Warren, J. T., & Hytten, K. (2004). The faces of whiteness: Pitfalls and the critical democrat. *Communication Education, 53,* 321–339.

Wheeless, L. R. (1971). Communication apprehension in the elementary school. *Speech Teacher, 20*(4), 297–299.

The Basic Course in Communication 3

Where Do We Go From Here?

Deanna D. Sellnow and Jason M. Martin

A question that continually perplexes basic communication course teacher-scholars is simultaneously simple and complex: Just what is the basic course in communication? As a point of departure, the basic course is essentially considered a general education course "either required or recommended for . . . all or most undergraduates" (Morreale, Hanna, Berko, & Gibson, 1999, p. 3). Beyond this broad definition, however, opinions vary as to what should be taught in it and how. Regarding content, should the basic course be a purely public speaking fundamentals course; or a hybrid course that teaches some combination of public speaking, interpersonal, and teamwork skills; or something else? Regarding pedagogy, can the basic course be taught effectively online, in large lecture halls, and by graduate teaching assistants (GTAs) and adjunct instructors? Moreover, how might problem-based and service learning influence student achievement in the basic course?

To understand what research tells us in response to these questions and then to suggest lines of research for the future, we begin by describing the issues confronting the basic communication course as a general education requirement. Then, we focus on more specific issues regarding content and pedagogy in the basic course. Finally, we propose some important strategies to promote and draw attention to rigorous empirical research on the basic course in communication journals.

The Basic Course and General Education

The concept of a general education curriculum was first introduced in the United States in the 1930s, and training in oral communication was a major component (Miller, 1988) of it. John Dewey's (1937) democratic philosophy of education guided the development of required general education curricula through the 1940s; but these curricula gradually faded away in the 1950s when the concept of a compulsory program of courses "came under . . . suspicion as being un-American" (Rudolph, 1977, p. 263), and the launching of Sputnik incited a systemic curricular reform movement from liberal arts to science education (Dow, 1991). By the early 1970s, however, the reform efforts began to wane. Thus, the resurgence of general education that guides our programs today can be traced to the late 1970s and early 1980s (Gaff, 1983). At that time "instruction in speaking and listening [became] one of the essential features of a minimum required curriculum for a coherent undergraduate education" (Ford & Wolvin, 1993, p. 215).

By the late 1980s, most American colleges and universities had developed general education programs that included a course in oral communication as an answer to Boyer's (1987) charge that "to succeed in college, undergraduates should be able to write and speak with clarity, and to read and listen with comprehension" (p. 73). Because communication skills continue to top the lists of what employers want in college graduates (National Association of Colleges and Employers, 2008), a basic communication course remains part of the general education curriculum at most colleges and universities today. Hence, the basic course is a "first opportunity to introduce students to communication skills and theories" (Morreale, Hugenberg, & Worley, 2006, p. 416).

Although it is certainly gratifying to know that business and industry professionals value communication skills, servicing all undergraduates in the form of a required general education course can be a daunting, if not impossible, task. The charge becomes increasingly difficult as the size of the undergraduate student population grows.

Many of the issues we grapple with in offering the basic course as a general education requirement are rooted in economic constraints. For example, communication departments are sometimes forced to use salary dollars to hire instructors to teach the basic course at the expense of offering a breadth and depth of courses for majors. Moreover, because we need to offer multiple sections when servicing an entire undergraduate population, we often rely on adjunct instructors and GTAs. Certainly, adjuncts and GTAs can be outstanding teachers (Harper, 1991). However, issues must be addressed regarding how to maintain consistency, curriculum integrity, and instructional quality across sections when taught by multiple and novice instructors. Much research dealing with these general education issues to date focuses on (a) mentoring and teacher training and (b) communication labs and centers of excellence.

MENTORING AND TEACHER TRAINING

When the basic communication course became a general education requirement, scholars in the field faced serious issues in terms of managing multiple sections taught by a range of experienced and inexperienced instructors. The earliest solutions to be published focused on mentoring and teacher training programs (e.g., Buerkel-Rothfuss & Gray, 1991; Gibson, Hanna, & Leichty, 1990; Monroe & Denman, 1991; Trank, 1989). Hill, Bahniuk, and Dobos (1989), for example, argued that "scholars in instructional communication should direct increased attention to the nature and impact of instruction through mentoring and collegial relationships" (p. 31). Similarly, Trank (1989) and Buerkel-Rothfuss and Gray (1991) described model teacher training programs to help new teachers succeed, and Goulden (1990) proposed a rater-training program for teaching new teachers to evaluate public speeches consistently.

Somewhat troubling, however, is the fact that publications 5, 10, and 15 years later continue to consist primarily of either rationales for or descriptions of mentoring and teacher training programs (e.g., Buerkel-Rothfuss, 1999; Buerkel-Rothfuss, Fink, & Amaro, 1994; Dixson, 1996; Gray & Murray, 1994; Hendrix, 2000; Hugenberg, Morreale, Worley, Hugenberg, & Worley, 2007; Quigley, Hendrix, & Freisem, 1998; Sellnow & Tyma, 2007; Strom-Gottfried & Dunlap, 2004; Williams, 1995; Ziegler & Reiff, 2006). In 1996, for instance, Dixson wrote, "Training sessions or workshops may be used to orient new instructors . . . including how to grade student speeches, choosing assignments and practicing lecturing" (p. 189). And, as recently as 2006, Ziegler and Reiff argued for the integration of "a comprehensive adjunct mentoring program . . . to operationalize a quality educational experience for every student" (p. 263). Of course, there is an important role for describing model approaches to train and mentor teachers. What tends to be noticeably absent, however, are a similarly substantial array of articles empirically examining and assessing what works and what does not work in terms of teacher training and mentoring workshops, programs, and curricula. In other words, we can locate a good number of publications that offer descriptions of programs that provide suggestions as to what programmatic features to include, but we have too little data attaching those programmatic features to outcomes such as student learning, teacher effectiveness, or student retention.

Although far too few published articles assessing the utility of mentoring and training approaches exist to date, some have begun to appear in the journals. One study by Meyer et al. (2007), for example, examines a classroom management teacher training approach (CMT) and what its results suggest for future teacher training programs. Another article, published in the new "educational assessment" section of *Communication Teacher*, examines the effects of information literacy instruction in the basic course and its implications for teacher training programs (Meyer et al., 2008). And an article published in the *Journal of General Education* assesses the degree to which the basic course fosters critical thinking and suggests implications for teacher training (Mazer, Hunt, & Kuznekoff, 2008). Perhaps these recent publications signal a trend for publishing this type of assessment research regarding training and mentoring programs in the basic course. From this point forward, it is imperative to conduct and publish more research that assesses the efficacy of the programs in place now. Doing so will essentially legitimize innovative revision decisions regarding teacher training and mentoring programs for the basic course (Preston & Holloway, 2006). Doing so will also engage basic course directors in enriched academic exchange toward improving the approaches we take to train and mentor basic course instructors.

Along with a call for additional empirical research assessing teacher training and mentoring programs is a need for systematic approaches for teacher assessment. That is, how do we know that basic course instructors are doing a good job? Similarly, how do we know that the instructional strategies they employ and the assignments they require are effective? Relying solely on end-of-semester course evaluations from students is clearly not adequate (e.g., Ellington & Ross, 1994; Harper, 1991; Hay, 1992; Rice, Stewart, & Hujber, 2000; Stankeviciene, 2007). Nor is relying too heavily on studies that correlate student perceptions of, for instance, teacher immediacy with teacher assessment (e.g., Mottet, Parker-Raley, Beebe, & Cunningham, 2007; Smythe & Hess, 2005; Titsworth, 2004). Although the relationship between student perceptions of teacher immediacy and affective and cognitive learning has utility, such studies only suggest one dimension of teacher effectiveness.

A few studies do describe different methods of teacher assessment in the basic course (e.g., reflective teaching portfolios, peer coaching, reflective self-assessment papers, and alumni teaching effectiveness surveys). Buerkel-Rothfuss, Gray, and Yerby (1993), for example, examined the structured model of competency-based instruction (SMCI) and its impact on student achievement of basic course learning outcomes. More recently, Hunt, Simonds, and Hinchcliffe (2000) demonstrated the utility of student portfolios as a form of authentic assessment, and Jones, Simonds, and Hunt (2005) examined written application essays as an effective tool for assessing instruction in the basic communication course. Also, Smith and King (2004) examined how different amounts and types of teacher feedback affect public speaking performance. These approaches to teacher assessment move beyond mere analyses of end-of-semester teacher evaluations completed by students to examinations of actual teaching practices and their impact on student learning. Hence, what is needed from this point forward is continued academic dialogue in the journals highlighting a variety of rigorous approaches (with conclusions and implications) to systematic teacher assessment and its relationship to improving the quality of instruction in the basic course.

COMMUNICATION LABS AND CENTERS OF EXCELLENCE

By the late 1980s, some colleges and universities were creating communication labs and centers of excellence to help students achieve the *communication competence* outcome of their general education programs. Some departments designed communication labs "to assist students enrolled in basic public speaking and communication courses" (Jones, Hunt, Simonds, Comadena, & Baldwin, 2004, pp. 105–106). Communication labs augment basic course instruction by providing students with additional opportunities to practice and record speeches, as well as get feedback for improvement from lab assistants (e.g., Brownell & Watson, 1984; Hunt & Simonds, 2002; Morreale, 2001; Teitelbaum, 2000). Essentially, communication labs assist instructors who are expected to teach the basic course to and refine the speaking skills of all students as a general education requirement.

Communication centers transformed the concept of labs in ways that addressed the communication across the curriculum (CXC) component of general education (e.g., Cronin & Glenn, 1991; Dannels & Housley-Gaffney, 2009; Weiss, 1998). The goal of such centers is to maintain the integrity of the communication discipline within CXC programs, in addition to training teachers, assessing instruction, and tutoring speakers. A primary rationale for creating CXC programs was based on business and industry professionals' complaints that "college graduates do not possess adequate written and oral communication skills" (Cronin & Glenn, 1991, p. 356). Most college graduates typically take only one basic oral communication course, and this level of instruction is not sufficient to refine these skills to the degree desired by future employers. Like labs, most centers assist basic course instructors via training, assessment, and tutoring services; but they also (a) assist faculty across the university in developing oral communication assignments and evaluation tools for their courses, as well as (b) provide training for implementing oral communication in their courses (e.g., Cronin & Grice, 1993; Dannels, 2001; Darling, 2005; Huang, Normandia, & Greer, 2005; Morton & O'Brien, 2005). Interestingly, a follow-up study of the programs implemented before 1990 revealed that half of the communication centers established in the 1980s had been discontinued a decade later (Weiss, 1998). Reasons stemmed from financial exigencies, to leader dependence, to insufficient institutionalization.

Perhaps because the idea of communication centers as a means by which to execute CXC has merit, the implementation of communication centers gained renewed momentum in 2001 with the establishment of the National Association of Communication Centers. Preston (2006) write, for example, that communication centers "have become integral to the working of their campuses and have been legitimized with expanded staff, assigned space, and a budget" (p. 57). They argue further that communication centers will gain additional credibility "when we can develop strategic plans, conduct research on our work, and disseminate that research broadly" (pp. 58–59). It appears that communication center directors have learned from the failures of the early pioneers and are making strategic choices to ensure sustaining such centers on college and university campuses.

Since both the basic communication course and CXC programs function similarly to meet a fundamental general education outcome at most institutions, and because labs and centers exist to assist faculty in fulfilling that outcome, the assessment of work accomplished in labs and centers should continue to be the focus of basic course research. Moreover, if Dannels and Housley-Gaffney (2009) are correct in claiming that CXC and WAC (writing across the curriculum) programs are now beginning to work together, then additional research regarding the utility of shared curricular content, instructors, training, and assessment strategies should also be a focus of future studies. For instance, at the University of Kentucky, the director of the writing center and director of the basic course in communication have been charged with developing a two-course, six-credit-hour sequence of "integrated communication general education skills," which will each focus on oral, written, visual, and digital communication.

Basic Course Curricular Content

According to the results of a series of seven surveys spanning over 40 years, opinions vary regarding what content should be included in the basic course. The earliest surveys indicated the existence of several different basic course orientations (Gibson, Gruner, Brooks, & Petrie, 1970). The most recent survey suggests, however, that the focus has narrowed to two predominant orientations: *public speaking* and *hybrid* (which encompasses a combination of public speaking, interpersonal communication, and teamwork skills) (Morreale et al., 2006). Moreover, ideas about what should constitute the focus of the basic course is continually being debated in our journals and at our professional conferences (e.g., Fassett & Warren, 2008; Goulden, 1996; Hugenberg, 1996; Morreale et al., 1999; Trank & Lewis, 1991; Treinen & Warren, 2001). In fact, Volume 3 of the *Basic Communication Course Annual* devoted several articles to this debate by publishing articles promoting, for example, a public speaking focus (Verderber, 1991), a hybrid focus (Pearson & West, 1991), a small group focus (Brilhart, 1991), a communication theory focus (Donaghy, 1991), an interpersonal focus (DeVito, 1991), and a diversity/multicultural focus (e.g., Braithwaite & Braithwaite, 1991). Since then, scholars also have contended that we should make ethics (Hess, 2001), social change (Leeman & Singhal, 2006), creating community (King, 2006), political engagement (Hunt, Simonds, & Simonds, 2009), or civic engagement (Gullicks, 2006) a primary foundation. Healthy debate about what ought to be taught in the basic course can be an excellent tool to foster innovative change. One potential problem, though, is the perception it might create with potential stakeholders outside the discipline that our own field does not even know of—or at least cannot agree on—the fundamental communication concepts/skills/competencies that are or should be addressed in the basic course.

Interestingly, examinations of "public speaking" and "hybrid" basic course textbooks reveal that there is, in fact, a set of consistent concepts and skills covered among them (e.g., Hess & Pearson, 1992; Worley, Worley, & McMahan, 1999). Moreover, surveys of departments offering a basic course, as well as of leaders in business and industry, yield similar results (e.g., Morreale et al., 2006; National Association of Colleges and Employers, 2008). Although additional concepts and skills might be included in some textbooks and in some versions of the basic course (e.g., public speaking, hybrid, and interpersonal), several key concepts and skills seem to cut across all of them. These are verbal and nonverbal communication, public speaking, listening, interpersonal (one-on-one) and small group (team-based) communication, diversity, critical thinking, and communication apprehension. These preliminary analyses suggest that today, some 40 years after the first surveys were conducted, we are beginning to agree more about the fundamental concepts of the basic course than the different course titles (orientations) imply.

A good deal of research has been published regarding many of these concepts, though not necessarily focused specifically on how they pertain to the basic course. Acknowledging that, we focus this section more narrowly on publications about these concepts that directly relate to the basic course.

One concept that has received a good deal of research study specific to the basic course is communication apprehension (e.g., Beatty & Friedland, 1990; Duff, Levine, Beatty, Woolbright, & Sun Park, 2007; Dwyer, 2000; Dwyer, Carlson, & Dalbey, 2003; Dwyer, Carlson, & Kahre, 2002; Dwyer & Fus, 1999; Dwyer & Fus, 2002; Finn, Sawyer, & Schrodt, 2009; Lubbers & Gorcyca, 1992; McKinney & Pullum, 1994; Neer & Kirchner, 1991; Newberger & Hemphill, 1992; Rubin, Rubin, & Jordan, 1997; Whitworth & Cochran, 1996; Witt & Behnke, 2006). These studies have examined, for example, the degree to which systematic desensitization (e.g., Friedrich, Goss, Cunconan, & Lane, 1997), visualization (e.g., Ayres & Hopf, 1985), and skills training (Robinson, 1997) reduces speech anxiety, as well as the relationship between specific teaching strategies (e.g., Bourhis & Berquist, 1990) or assignments (e.g., Sellnow & Golish, 2000) and communication apprehension. Managing communication apprehension continues to be an important outcome for students in the basic course. As such, continued empirical research on how best to teach apprehension management skills ought to be included in our research agenda.

Two additional concepts that have received a good deal of research attention specific to the basic course are public speaking and diversity. Most of the public speaking research focuses on evaluating speeches (e.g., Foster, Smilowitz, Foster, & Phelps, 1990; Goulden, 1990; Jensen & Lamoureux, 1997; Semlak, 2008; Sims, 2003; Turman & Barton, 2004; Whitecap, 1992; Williams & Stewart, 1994). Anderson and Jensen (2002), for example, examined the degree to which previous speech grading experience, formal training, and the actual forms used affect ratings. Sellnow and Treinen (2004) focused on gender differences in student peer critiques by males and females when evaluating a male and a female speaker of similar ability giving the same speech. Similarly, Turman and Barton (2004) studied potential evaluation bias by student critics related to speaker order, speaker quality, and gender. And Sims (2003) focused on student perceptions about evaluating peers on streaming video rather than in a face-to-face environment. Obviously, assessment of public speaking evaluation methods and potential biases will continue to be an important area of research as long as public speaking skills training remains a fundamental learning outcome of the basic course.

A fair amount of research has also been published that focuses on addressing diversity in the basic course (e.g., Braithwaite & Braithwaite, 1991; Cooper, 1994; Goulden, 1996; LaWare, 2004; Modaff, 2004). How do we address diversity in ways that honor differences while still teaching best practices? Is it sufficient to require assignments that force students to think beyond the boundaries of their own worldview (Sellnow & Littlefield, 1996), to insert mention of diverse perspectives as additional standpoints in the textbooks, or to provide sample speeches from speakers of different races, sexes, and ethnicities (Powell, 1996)? In response to these questions, some interesting research being conducted in recent years focuses on approaching diversity through a lens rooted in antiracist pedagogy and whiteness studies (e.g., Fassett & Warren, 2008; Nakayama & Krizek, 1995; Prividera, 2006; Treinen & Warren, 2001).

To clarify, "whiteness" is the "everyday, invisible, subtle, cultural, and social practices, ideas, and codes that discursively secure the power and privilege of White people" (Shome, 1996, p. 503). Among others, Warren (1999) suggests that we acknowledge and examine "whiteness" as the center of power in "the hope that the center will fall apart" (p. 197). To do so in the basic course involves "more than figuring out where to include materials about diversity in the curriculum" (Treinen, 2004, p. 156), or "simply adding the voices and perspectives of cultures other than white culture" (p. 157), or "treating students as though they are all the 'same'" (p. 157). Rather, to do so means critically examining what it means to be white and to have and exercise white privilege. The rationale for addressing diversity in the basic course through a lens rooted in antiracist pedagogy and whiteness studies is compelling. Since public speaking as it is traditionally taught in the basic course tends to reflect an inherently Western bias, approaching the basic course from this critical/cultural perspective acknowledges that fact fundamentally. In other words, doing so admits that the linear approach we typically use to frame speeches is not the only way nor is it necessarily the best way to do so. It is, however, one effective approach that is generally successful in the dominant American culture. What is now needed is a series of models for approaching diversity in the basic courses, along with cognitive, affective, and performance-based assessments of student learning related to diversity approached in these various ways.

The other concepts and skills that appear central to the basic course have received far less attention in terms of empirical research (i.e., communication contexts and models, verbal and nonverbal communication, presentational aids, listening, small groups, and ethics). Although a number of innovative teaching strategies focused on them have been published in *Communication Teacher* over the years, very few articles have been published in any of the other communication journals that offer insight into the degree to which students can understand and apply these concepts and skills or the effects of these innovative teaching approaches on student learning.

Moreover, although many research-based instructional communication articles published primarily in *Communication Education* and the various regional journals do, in fact, focus on students enrolled and instructional strategies employed in the basic course, rarely are implications for the basic course spelled out in the conclusions. Moreover, "basic course" is almost never offered as a key word. As such, the potential value of their conclusions for the basic course is, unfortunately, often overlooked except perhaps by those readers who make the inferences themselves.

With these limitations in mind, there still exists a need for more research focused on assessing teaching strategies employed and communication concepts addressed in the basic course as they affect student learning. To clarify, a few articles focus on how to create and integrate computer-generated slideshows for presentational aids in the basic course, but nothing exists to date assessing how effective they are in terms of audience perception, comprehension, or retention. How do we know that the approaches touted as *best practices* are really effective? Moreover, are these computer-generated slideshows any better than well-done posterboards, handouts, or flipcharts? Are there instances when handouts or posterboards might be a better choice for public speakers? If so, when and why? Similarly, listening is deemed central by potential employers, is given attention in textbooks and syllabi, and is claimed to be important via instructor surveys. Consequently, innovative pedagogical strategies for teaching listening skills have been published in *Communication Teacher*. But little attention has been given to assessing pedagogical approaches to listening in the basic course. How do we know whether any of these innovative strategies actually improve basic course students' listening skills? Do some strategies yield better results in terms of students' listening skills than others? Essentially, a good number of articles suggest how we ought to teach various concepts and skills in the basic course. What we now need are articles that focus on their utility in general and that compare the utility of them to current methods.

Finally, if these concepts and skills are central to the basic course—whether we label the course as hybrid, public speaking, or something else—and are, in fact, the skills future employers want to see in job candidates, then we ought to be conducting studies that measure the degree to which students can understand and apply them on completing the course and track their ability to do so in courses across the curriculum at various points along their degree completion journey.

In sum, what we know now about curricular content in the basic course suggests two important lines of future research. First, additional research ought to be conducted that compares the similarities among the different basic course orientations as well as explores empirically what the foundational course concepts and learning objectives ought to be. In doing so, we ought to make public the cross-cutting foundational concepts and skills of the basic course. Certainly, the amount of attention given to each concept and skill might vary in different versions of the basic course, but it seems the time has come to share a unified answer to the question that we have grappled with for over 40 years: Just what is fundamental in the basic communication course? This is not to suggest that we stifle academic freedom. Rather, doing so will ensure that, as a discipline, we do know and agree on a set of foundational concepts and skills to be learned in our basic course regardless of its particular orientation. The ability to present a unified answer when talking with colleagues in our own field, across our campuses, and in our communities when they ask, "What do you teach in the basic course in communication?" will enhance our image as members of a coherent and legitimate field of study (and not just as in possession of a skill set void of "content").

A second important line of research would assess student learning regarding each of these basic communication course competencies. National surveys of employers report that public presentation skills, interpersonal skills, and teamwork skills are both what they seek and what is lacking in college graduates (National Association of Colleges and Employers, 2008). We must conduct more performance-based assessment research focused on the degree to which students demonstrate improvement in these very communication skills as a result of what and how we teach them in the basic course.

Basic Course Pedagogy

Some fascinating basic-course-related research that has developed over the past decade focuses on pedagogical issues—that is: How should we teach the basic course to best meet the needs of students in the 21st century? More specifically, this research focuses on various delivery systems and instructional designs as they influence student achievement of basic course learning outcomes.

DELIVERY SYSTEMS

With regard to delivery systems, the debate continues as to whether it is better to offer the basic course in a lecture/lab format or in autonomous sections. Todd, Tilson, Cox, and Malinauskas (2000) discovered, for example, essentially no differences regarding perceptions of teacher immediacy from students enrolled in lecture/lab and self-contained sections of the basic course. In contrast, Cox and Todd (2001) found verbal immediacy, student motivation, and instructor credibility to be statistically higher in self-contained sections of the basic course. Still, Morreale et al. (2006) explain, "only 10.3% of institutions use the mass lecture/small performance laboratory system in the basic course" compared with 89.7% who reported using self-contained sections (p. 424).

Even more interesting, however, is the debate about whether or not the basic course can be taught effectively online, whether in part or in its entirety (e.g., Allen, 2006; Carrell & Menzel, 2001; Goodnight & Wallace, 2005; Morreale et al., 2006; Schwartzman, 2006; Sellnow, Child, & Ahlfeldt, 2005; Sellnow, Child, Brown, & Liu, 2005; Shedletsky & Aitkin, 2001; Sims, 2003). Research to date is somewhat contradictory and suggests a need for further examination before determining its viability as an effective delivery system. Interestingly, some research suggests that the worth of online delivery systems may be more related to instructor competence regarding the use of technology than about anything inherently related to the software or the Internet per se (Sims, 2003). Finally, most of the research about the utility of online instruction is focused on student perceptions. What is needed from this point forward is empirical performance-based assessment data regarding student learning outcomes comparing online and face-to-face basic course classrooms.

INSTRUCTIONAL DESIGNS

A growing concern among basic course instructors has to do with what instructional design will best help students achieve the learning outcomes we have set out for the course. To clarify, students who demonstrate effective communication skills by the time they complete the basic course often fail to transfer them successfully to other courses or the workplace (National Association of Colleges and Employers, 2008). Several innovative instructional strategies have emerged recently to address this transferability issue. Each of them actually stems from the experiential learning theory as first conceived by John Dewey (1937). Essentially, these approaches reframe our approach to teaching and learning in ways that address a four-stage cycle of learning via (1) concrete experience, (2) reflective observation, (3) abstract conceptualization, and (4) active experimentation (Kolb, 1984).

Problem-based learning, for example, has been shown to promote student learning in business, education, medicine, law, and physics (Duch, Groh, & Allen, 2001). Research determining the utility of this approach in the basic communication course, however, has only just begun. To that end, a problem-based learning approach does appear to foster interactive engagement (Ahlfeldt & Sellnow, 2009) and improve student speech quality (Ahlfeldt, 2003) in the basic communication course. To clarify, educational research using the National Survey of Student Engagement (NSSE) illustrates that student learning is enhanced when students are actively engaged in the material. Ahlfeldt and Sellnow (2009) demonstrated how approaching public speech assignments via problem-based learning (i.e., student teams that each focus on a different real-world issue and develop a series of individual and group speeches about that issue over the course of the semester) fosters significantly more engagement than a basic course classroom employing a more traditional approach to speech assignments (i.e., students prepare and present speeches on a variety of topics over the course of the term). Although these results are encouraging, more research to assess cognitive, affective, and behavioral learning is needed to confirm the value of this approach in the basic course.

As reviewed in this volume by Warren and Sellnow (see Chapter 7), another instructional strategy being adopted and assessed, as it may improve student achievement and basic course skill transferability, is service learning. Although much has been published in other disciplines regarding the value of service learning, relatively few published studies focus specifically on communication curricula (e.g., Frymier & Houser, 2000; Frymier & Shulman, 1995; Frymier, Shulman, & Houser, 1996; Isaacson, Dorries, & Brown, 2001; Novak, Markey, & Allen, 2007; Oster-Aaland, Sellnow, Nelson, & Pearson, 2004; Quintanilla & Wahl, 2005; Sellnow & Oster, 1997), and fewer still focus specifically on the basic course (e.g., Ahlfeldt, 2009; Gullicks, 2006; Harter, Kirby, Hatfield, & Kuhlman, 2004). Essentially, the research suggests that employing a service learning approach helps students see the relevance of coursework to the "real world" and, in doing so, increases motivation and produces better speeches. As with problem-based learning, however, more research must be conducted, particularly in the form of performance-based assessments to confirm the utility of a service learning pedagogy in the basic course. For instance, how does concept comprehension compare between students taught in service learning and traditional sections of the basic course? What impact, if any, does service learning have on speech quality (content, structure, and delivery)? And does a service learning approach influence student perceptions of the relevance of the basic course?

Promoting Basic Course Research

Obviously, since the primary goal of the *basic course* is to foster *communication competence*, we ought to be actively engaged in an ongoing assessment regarding the degree to which communication competence is being achieved. Moreover, basic course teacher-scholars need to share results with one another as a means to promote positive change. We offer two suggestions for promoting basic course research.

First, research that offers implications for basic course instruction should be more easily accessed. By that we mean that it is often difficult to locate articles that pertain specifically to the basic course even though they are being published in communication journals. Certainly, the *Basic Communication Course Annual* is an important and valuable outlet dedicated to basic course issues. What is unfortunate, however, is how often articles that are relevant to the basic course and published in other communication journals fail to make a transparent link from conclusions to implications for the basic course. Moreover, these same articles fail to include "basic course" as a key term. When appropriate, articles already being published in the communication journals would actually enhance intellectual exchange among basic course scholars simply by making their utility to improving the basic course more apparent.

Second, basic course directors and instructors engage in ongoing research about the basic course on a daily basis. Moreover, many basic course scholars use the results of such research to prepare assessment reports for internal audiences at their institutions. What is being shared internally ought to be used simultaneously to foster dialogue with colleagues across the country by making a conscious effort to also submit these manuscripts to our conferences and our journals. The research is being done. We just need to make the effort to share our results not only with campus administrators but also with our colleagues who deal with similar issues related to the basic course.

Conclusions and Implications

The *basic course* in communication serves as both a gateway course for students choosing to major in communication and a core component in the education of all college students. For these reasons, it is imperative to engage in an ongoing investigation of how it may best achieve its goals. Research ought to continue regarding how we might best balance course integrity and economic feasibility in the basic course that functions as a core component in the general education of all college students. Similarly, we must continue to grapple with finding suitable answers to the question, "What communication concepts and skills ought to be taught in the basic course?" Moreover, we must continue to examine pedagogical strategies, assess the degree to which we are addressing learning outcomes, and improve teaching and learning processes. Finally, whenever possible, we must make transparent the potential implications of instructional communication research projects for the basic course. Failing to do so sends an important message to basic course scholars about the discipline's perception regarding the value and centrality of the basic course in the discipline. We must embrace our "bread-and-butter course" by publishing and drawing attention to rigorous research focused on it. Doing so is the only way the basic course will stay where it belongs—that is, rooted in the communication discipline.

References

Ahlfeldt, S. (2003). *Problem-based learning in the public speaking classroom.* Unpublished doctoral dissertation, North Dakota State University, Fargo.

Ahlfeldt, S. (2009). Thoughtful and informed citizens: An approach to service-learning for the communication classroom. *Communication Teacher, 23,* 1–6.

Ahlfeldt, S., & Sellnow, D. (2009). Problem-based learning and student engagement in the public speaking classroom. *Basic Communication Course Annual, 21,* 134–150.

Allen, T. H. (2006). Is the rush to provide on-line instruction setting our students up for failure? *Communication Education, 55,* 122–126.

Anderson, K., & Jensen, K. K. (2002). An examination of the speech evaluation process: Does the evaluation instrument and/or evaluator's experience matter? *Basic Communication Course Annual, 14,* 113–163.

Ayres, J., & Hopf, T. S. (1985). Visualization: A means of reducing speech anxiety. *Communication Education, 34,* 318–323.

Beatty, M. J., & Friedland, M. H. (1990). Public speaking state anxiety as a function of selected situational and predispositional variables. *Communication Education, 39,* 142–147.

Bourhis, J., & Berquist, C. (1990). Communication apprehension in the basic course: Learning styles and preferred instructional strategies of high and low apprehensive students. *Basic Communication Course Annual, 2,* 27–46.

Boyer, E. L. (1987). *College: The undergraduate experience.* New York: Harper & Row.

Braithwaite, C. A., & Braithwaite, D. O. (1991). Instructional communication strategies for adapting to a multicultural introductory course. *Basic Communication Course Annual, 3,* 145–160.

Brilhart, J. L. (1991). Small group communication as an introductory course. *Basic Communication Course Annual, 3,* 35–50.

Brownell, W. W., & Watson, A. K. (1984, November). *Creating a speech communication laboratory in a university retention program.* Paper presented at the annual conference of the Speech Communication Association, Chicago.

Buerkel-Rothfuss, N. L. (1999). How basic course directors evaluate teaching assistants: Social constructionism in basic course land. *Basic Communication Course Annual, 11,* 37–54.

Buerkel-Rothfuss, N. L., Fink, E. S., & Amaro, C. A. (1994). The incorporation of mentors and assistant basic course directors into the basic course program: Creating a safety net for new teaching assistants. *Basic Communication Course Annual, 6,* 105–128.

Buerkel-Rothfuss, N. L., & Gray, P. L. (1991). Models for graduate teaching assistant training: The real, the necessary, and the ideal. *Basic Communication Course Annual, 3,* 247–268.

Buerkel-Rothfuss, N. L., Gray, P. L., & Yerby, J. (1993). The structured model of competency-based instruction. *Communication Education, 42,* 22–36.

Carrell, L. J., & Menzel, K. E. (2001). Variations in learning, motivation, and perceived immediacy between live and distance education classrooms. *Communication Education, 50,* 230–240.

Cooper, P. (1994). Stories as instructional strategy: Teaching in another culture. *Basic Communication Course Annual, 6,* 207–216.

Cox, S. A., & Todd, T. S. (2001). Contrasting the relationships between teacher immediacy, teacher credibility, and student motivation in self-contained and mass-lecture courses. *Basic Communication Course Annual, 13,* 23–45.

Cronin, M., & Glenn, P. (1991). Oral communication across the curriculum in higher education: The state of the art. *Communication Education, 40,* 356–367.

Cronin, M. W., & Grice, G. L. (1993). A comparative analysis of training models versus consulting/training models for implementing oral communication across the curriculum. *Communication Education, 42,* 1–9.

Dannels, D. P. (2001). Time to speak up: A theoretical framework of situated pedagogy and practice for communication across the curriculum. *Communication Education, 50,* 144–158.

Dannels, D. P., & Housley-Gaffney, A. L. (2009). Communication across the curriculum and in the disciplines: A call for scholarly cross-curricular advocacy. *Communication Education, 58,* 124–153.

Darling, A. L. (2005). Public presentations in mechanical engineering and the discourse of technology. *Communication Education, 54,* 20–33.

DeVito, J. A. (1991). The interpersonal communication course. *Basic Communication Course Annual, 3,* 73–87.

Dewey, J. (1937). *Democracy and education: An introduction to the philosophy of education.* New York: Macmillan.

Dixson, M. D. (1996). Associate faculty: Directing a rich resource of the basic course. *Journal of the Association for Communication Administration, 3,* 187–204.

Donaghy, W. C. (1991). Introductory communication theory: Not another skills course. *Basic Communication Course Annual, 3,* 51–72.

Dow, P. (1991). *Schoolhouse politics: Lessons from the Sputnik era.* Cambridge, MA: Harvard University Press.

Duch, B. J., Groh, S. E., & Allen, D. E. (Eds.). (2001). *The power of problem-based learning.* Sterling, VA: Stylus.

Duff, D. C., Levine, T. R., Beatty, M. J., Woolbright, J., & Sun Park, H. (2007). Testing public speaking anxiety treatments against a credible placebo control. *Communication Education, 56,* 72–88.

Dwyer, K. K. (2000). The multidimensional model: Teaching students to self-manage high communication apprehension by self-selecting treatments. *Communication Education, 49,* 72–81.

Dwyer, K. K., Carlson, R. E., & Dalbey, J. (2003). Oral communication apprehension. *Basic Communication Course Annual, 15,* 117–143.

Dwyer, K. K., Carlson, R. E., & Kahre, S. A. (2002). Communication apprehension and basic course success: The lab-supported public speaking course intervention. *Basic Communication Course Annual, 14,* 87–112.

Dwyer, K. K., & Fus, D. A. (1999). Communication apprehension, self-efficacy, and grades in the basic course: Correlations and implications. *Basic Communication Course Annual, 11,* 108–132.

Dwyer, K. K., & Fus, D. A. (2002). Perceptions of communication, competence self-efficacy, and trait communication apprehension: Is there an impact on basic course success? *Communication Research Reports, 19,* 29–37.

Ellington, H., & Ross, G. (1994). Evaluating teaching quality throughout a university: A practical scheme based on self-assessment. *Quality Assurance in Education, 2*(2), 4–9.

Fassett, D. L., & Warren, J. T. (2008). Pedagogy of relevance: A critical communication pedagogy agenda for the "basic" course. *Basic Communication Course Annual, 20,* 1–24.

Finn, A. N., Sawyer, C. R., & Schrodt, P. (2009). Examining the effect of exposure therapy on public speaking state anxiety. *Communication Education, 58,* 92–109.

Ford, W. S. Z., & Wolvin, A. D. (1993). The differential impact of a basic communication course on perceived communication competencies in class, work, and social contexts. *Communication Education, 42,* 215–223.

Foster, T. J., Smilowitz, M., Foster, M. S., & Phelps, L. A. (1990). Some student perceptions of grades received on speeches. *Basic Communication Course Annual, 2,* 121–142.

Friedrich, G., Goss, B., Cunconan, T., & Lane, D. (1997). Systematic desensitization. In J. A. Daly, J. C. McCroskey, J. Ayres, T. Hopf, & D. M. Ayres (Eds.), *Avoiding communication: Shyness, reticence, and communication apprehension* (2nd ed., pp. 305–330). Cresskill, NJ: Hampton Press.

Frymier, A. B., & Houser, M. L. (2000). The teacher-student relationship as an interpersonal relationship. *Communication Education, 49,* 207–219.

Frymier, A. B., & Shulman, G. M. (1995). What's in it for me? Increasing content relevance to enhance students' motivation. *Communication Education, 44,* 40–50.

Frymier, A. B., Shulman, G. M., & Houser, M. (1996). The development of a learner empowerment measure. *Communication Education, 45,* 181–199.

Gaff, J. G. (1983). *General education today.* San Francisco: Jossey-Bass.

Gibson, J., Gruner, C., Brooks, W., & Petrie, C. (1970). The first course in speech: A survey of U.S. colleges and universities. *The Speech Teacher, 19,* 13–20.

Gibson, J. W., Hanna, M. S., & Leichty, G. (1990). The basic speech course at United States colleges and universities: V. *Basic Communication Course Annual, 2,* 233–257.

Goodnight, L. J., & Wallace, S. P. (Eds.). (2005). *The basic communication course online: Scholarship and application.* Dubuque, IA: Kendall/Hunt.

Goulden, N. R. (1990). A program of rater training for evaluating public speeches combining accuracy and error approaches. *Basic Communication Course Annual, 2,* 143–165.

Goulden, N. R. (1996). Teaching communication behaviors/skills related to cultural diversity in the basic course classroom. *Basic Communication Course Annual, 8,* 145–161.

Gray, P. L., & Murray, M. G. (1994). TA mentoring: Issues and questions. *Basic Communication Course Annual, 6,* 129–159.

Gullicks, K. A. (2006). *What's service got to do with it? Investigating student sensemaking of required service in the basic communication course.* Unpublished doctoral dissertation, North Dakota State University, Fargo.

Harper, B. (1991). Who does the better job teaching the basic course: Teaching assistants or faculty? *Association for Communication Administration Bulletin, 77,* 68–70.

Harter, L. M., Kirby, E. L., Hatfield, K. L., & Kuhlman, K. N. (2004). From spectators of public affairs to agents of social change: Engaging students in the basic course through service-learning. *Basic Communication Course Annual, 16,* 165–194.

Hay, E. A. (1992). A national survey of assessment trends in communication departments. *Communication Education, 41,* 247–257.

Hendrix, K. G. (2000). Peer mentoring for graduate teaching assistants: Training and utilizing a valuable resource. *Basic Communication Course Annual, 12,* 161–192.

Hess, J. A. (2001). Rethinking our approach to the basic course: Making ethics the foundation of introduction to public speaking. *Basic Communication Course Annual, 13,* 76–115.

Hess, J. A., & Pearson, J. C. (1992). Basic public speaking principles: An examination of twelve popular texts. *Basic Communication Course Annual, 4,* 16–34.

Hill, S. E. K., Bahniuk, M. H., & Dobos, J. (1989). The impact of mentoring and collegial support on faculty success: An analysis of support behavior, information adequacy, and communication apprehension. *Communication Education, 38,* 15–33.

Huang, J., Normandia, B., & Greer, S. (2005). Communicating mathematically: Comparison of knowledge structures in teacher and student discourse in a secondary math classroom. *Communication Education, 54,* 34–51.

Hugenberg, L. W. (1996). Introduction to cultural diversity in the basic course: Differing points of view. *Basic Communication Course Annual, 8,* 136–144.

Hugenberg, L. W., Morreale, S., Worley, D. W., Hugenberg, B., & Worley, D. A. (Eds.). (2007). *Basic communication course best practices: A training manual for instructors.* Dubuque, IA: Kendall/Hunt.

Hunt, S. K., & Simonds, C. J. (2002). Extending learning opportunities in the basic communication course: Exploring the pedagogical benefits of speech laboratories. *Basic Communication Course Annual, 14,* 61–86.

Hunt, S. K., Simonds, C. J., & Hinchcliffe, L. J. (2000). Using student portfolios as authentic assessment of the basic communication course. *Journal on Excellence in College Teaching, 11,* 57–77.

Hunt, S. K., Simonds, C. J., & Simonds, B. K. (2009). Uniquely qualified, distinctively competent: Delivering 21st century skills in the basic course. *Basic Communication Course Annual, 21,* 1–29.

Isaacson, R., Dorries, B., & Brown, K. (2001). *Service learning in communication studies: A handbook.* Belmont, CA: Thomson Wadsworth.

Jensen, K. K., & Lamoureux, E. R. (1997). Written feedback in the basic course: What instructors provide and what students deem helpful. *Basic Communication Course Annual, 9,* 37–58.

Jones, A. C., Hunt, S. K., Simonds, C. J., Comadena, M. E., & Baldwin, J. R. (2004). Speech laboratories: An exploratory examination of potential pedagogical effects on students. *Basic Communication Course Annual, 16,* 105–137.

Jones, A. C., Simonds, C. J., & Hunt, S. K. (2005). The use of application essays as an effective tool for assessing instruction in the basic communication course. *Communication Education, 54,* 161–169.

King, J. L. (2006). Re-focusing the basic public speaking course: Changing to an epideictic framework to create community. *Basic Communication Course Annual, 18,* 210–229.

Kolb, D. A. (1984). *Experiential learning: Experience as the source of learning and development.* Englewood Cliffs, NJ: Prentice Hall.

LaWare, M. R. (2004). The public speaking classroom as public space: Taking risks and embracing difference. *Basic Communication Course Annual, 16,* 279–291.

Leeman, M., & Singhal, A. (2006). The basic course as social change. *Basic Communication Course Annual, 18,* 230–243.

Lubbers, C. A., & Gorcyca, D. A. (1992). Academic success in the basic course: The influence of apprehension and demographics. *Basic Communication Course Annual, 4,* 1–15.

Mazer, J. P., Hunt, S. K., & Kuznekoff, J. H. (2008). Revising general education: Assessing a critical thinking instructional model in the basic communication course. *Journal of General Education, 56,* 173–199.

McKinney, B. C., & Pullum, S. J. (1994). Obstacles to overcome in the implementation of a program to reduce communication apprehension in the basic public speaking course. *Basic Communication Course Annual, 6,* 70–86.

Meyer, K. R., Hunt, S. K., Hopper, K. M., Thakkar, K. V., Tsoubakopoulos, V., & Van Hoose, K. J. (2008). Assessing information literacy in the basic communication course. *Communication Teacher, 22*(1), 22–34.

Meyer, K. R., Simonds, C. J., Simonds, B. K., Baldwin, J. R., Hunt, S. K., & Comadena, M. E. (2007). Designing classroom management training for basic course instructors. *Basic Communication Course Annual, 19,* 1–36.

Miller, G. E. (1988). *The meaning of general education: The emergence of a curriculum paradigm.* New York: Teachers College Press.

Modaff, D. P. (2004). Native virtues: Traditional Sioux philosophy and the contemporary basic communication course. *Basic Communication Course Annual, 16,* 261–278.

Monroe, C., & Denman, S. (1991). Assimilating adjunct faculty: Problems and opportunities. *Association for Communication Administration Bulletin, 77,* 56–62.

Morreale, S. (2001). *Communication labs enhance student learning and promote awareness of the discipline.* Retrieved September 2, 2009, from www.natcom.org

Morreale, S. P., Hanna, M. S., Berko, R. M., & Gibson, J. W. (1999). The basic communication course at U.S. colleges and universities: VI. *Basic Communication Course Annual, 11,* 1–36.

Morreale, S., Hugenberg, L., & Worley, D. (2006). The basic communication course at U.S. colleges and universities in the 21st century: Study VII. *Communication Education, 55*(4), 415–437.

Morton, J., & O'Brien, D. (2005). Selling your design: Oral communication pedagogy in design education. *Communication Education, 54,* 6–19.

Mottet, T. P., Parker-Raley, J., Beebe, S. A., & Cunningham, C. (2007). Instructors who resist college-lite: The neutralizing effect of instructor immediacy on students' course-workload violations and perceptions of instructor credibility and affective learning. *Communication Education, 56,* 145–167.

Nakayama, T., & Krizek, R. (1995). Whiteness: A strategic rhetoric. *Quarterly Journal of Speech, 81,* 291–309.

National Association of Colleges and Employers. (2008). *Class of 2008 steps into good job market* [Electronic version]. Retrieved April 17, 2008, from www.jobweb.com/studentarticles.aspx?is=1219

Neer, M. R., & Kirchner, W. F. (1991). Classroom interventions for reducing public speaking anxiety. *Basic Communication Course Annual, 3,* 202–223.

Newberger, C., & Hemphill, M. (1992). Video-modeling and pre-performance apprehension: Is ignorance bliss? *Basic Communication Course Annual, 4,* 72–79.

Novak, J. M., Markey, V., & Allen, M. (2007). Evaluating cognitive outcomes of service learning in higher education: A meta-analysis. *Communication Research Reports, 24,* 149–157.

Oster-Aaland, L. K., Sellnow, T. L., Nelson, P. E., & Pearson, J. C. (2004). The status of service learning in departments of communication: A follow-up study. *Communication Education, 53,* 348–356.

Pearson, J. C., & West, R. (1991). The introductory communication course: The hybrid approach. *Basic Communication Course Annual, 3,* 16–34.

Powell, K. A. (1996). Meeting the challenges of cultural diversity: Ideas and issues for the public speaking course. *Basic Communication Course Annual, 8,* 197–201.

Preston, M. M. (2006). Communication centers and scholarship possibilities. *International Journal of Listening, 20,* 56–59.

Preston, M. M., & Holloway, R. (2006). Case study of a basic course: Using assessment to legitimize innovation. *Basic Communication Course Annual, 18,* 283–302.

Prividera, L. C. (2006). Suppressing cultural sensitivity: The role of Whiteness in instructors' course content and pedagogical practices. *Basic Communication Course Annual, 18,* 28–62.

Quigley, B. L., Hendrix, K. G., & Freisem, K. (1998). Graduate teaching assistant training: Preparing instructors to assist ESL students in the introductory public speaking course. *Basic Communication Course Annual, 10,* 58–89.

Quintanilla, K. M., & Wahl, S. T. (2005). Incorporating service learning into communication courses: Benefits, guidelines, and challenges. *Texas Speech Communication Journal, 30,* 67–96.

Rice, R., Stewart, L., & Hujber, M. (2000). Extending the domain of instructional effectiveness assessment in student evaluations of communication courses. *Communication Education, 49,* 253–266.

Robinson, T. E. (1997). Communication apprehension and the basic public speaking course: A national survey of in-class treatment techniques. *Communication Education, 46,* 188–197.

Rubin, R. B., Rubin, A. M., & Jordan, F. F. (1997). Effects of instruction on communication apprehension and communication competence. *Communication Education, 46,* 104–114.

Rudolph, R. (1977). *Curriculum: A history of the American undergraduate course of study since 1636.* San Francisco: Jossey-Bass.

Schwartzman, R. (2006). Virtual group problem solving in the basic communication course: Lessons for online learning. *Journal of Instructional Psychology, 33,* 3–14.

Sellnow, D. D., Child, J. T., & Ahlfeldt, S. A. (2005). Textbook technology supplements: What are they good for? *Communication Education, 54,* 243–253.

Sellnow, D. D., Child, J. T., Brown, A., & Liu, M. (2005, April). *Can public speaking be taught online? A comparative examination of student speech quality in traditional and online courses.* Paper presented at the annual conference of the Central States Communication Association, Kansas City, MO.

Sellnow, D. D., & Golish, T. (2000). The relationship between a required self-disclosure speech and public speaking anxiety: Considering gender equity. *Basic Communication Course Annual, 12,* 28–59.

Sellnow, D. D., & Littlefield, R. S. (1996). The speech on diversity: A tool to integrate cultural diversity into the basic course. *Basic Communication Course Annual, 8,* 185–196.

Sellnow, D. D., & Treinen, K. P. (2004). The role of gender in perceived speaker competence: An analysis of student peer critiques. *Communication Education, 53,* 286–296.

Sellnow, D., & Tyma, A. (2007). Teaching new teachers to reflect: Training and assessment strategies. In L. W. Hugenberg, S. Morreale, D. W. Worley, B. Hugenberg, & D. A. Worley (Eds.), *Basic communication course best practices: A training manual for instructors* (pp. 217–224). Dubuque, IA: Kendall/Hunt.

Sellnow, T. L., & Oster, L. K. (1997). The frequency, form, and perceived benefits of service learning in speech communication departments. *Journal of the Association for Communication Administration, 26,* 190–198.

Semlak, J. (2008). Traditional pedagogical tools: Examining peer feedback in the basic communication course. *Basic Communication Course Annual, 20,* 72–100.

Shedletsky, L. J., & Aitken, J. E. (2001). The paradoxes of online academic work. *Communication Education, 50,* 206–217.

Shome, R. (1996). Race and popular cinema: The rhetorical strategies of whiteness in City of Joy. *Communication Quarterly, 44,* 502–518.

Sims, J. R. (2003). Streaming student speeches on the Internet: Convenient and connected feedback in the basic course. *Basic Communication Course Annual, 15,* 1–40.

Smith, C. D., & King, P. E. (2004). Student feedback sensitivity and the efficacy of feedback interventions in public speaking performance improvement. *Communication Education, 53,* 203–216.

Smythe, M.-J., & Hess, J. A. (2005). Are student self-reports a valid method for measuring teacher nonverbal immediacy? *Communication Education, 54,* 170–179.

Stankeviciene, J. (2007, September). *Assessment of teaching quality: Survey of university graduates.* Paper presented at the European Conference on Educational Research, University of Ghent, Belgium.

Strom-Gottfried, K., & Dunlap, K. (2004). Assimilating adjuncts: Strategies for orienting contract faculty. *Journal of Social Work Education, 40,* 445–452.

Teitelbaum, J. (2000, November). *Use of a communication lab to enhance teaching communication courses.* Paper presented at the National Communication Association, Seattle, WA.

Titsworth, B. S. (2004). Students' notetaking: The effects of teacher immediacy and clarity. *Communication Education, 53,* 305–320.

Todd, T. S., Tilson, L. D., Cox, S. A., & Malinauskas, B. (2000). Assessing the perceived effectiveness of the basic communication course: An examination of the mass-lecture format versus the self-contained format. *Journal of the Association for Communication Administration, 29,* 185–195.

Trank, D. M. (1989). Training or teaching: A professional development program for graduate teaching assistants. *Basic Communication Course Annual, 1,* 169–196.

Trank, D. M., & Lewis, P. (1991). The introductory communication course: Results of a national survey. *Basic Communication Course Annual, 3,* 106–122.

Treinen, K. (2004). Creating a dialogue for change: Educating graduate teaching assistants in whiteness studies. *Basic Communication Course Annual, 16,* 139–164.

Treinen, K., & Warren, J. T. (2001). Antiracist pedagogy in the basic course: Teaching cultural communication as if whiteness matters. *Basic Communication Course Annual, 13,* 46–75.

Turman, P. D., & Barton, M. H. (2004). Bias in the evaluation process: Influences of speaker order, speaker quality, and gender on rater error in the performance based course. *Basic Communication Course Annual, 16,* 1–35.

Verderber, R. F. (1991). The introductory communication course: The public speaking approach. *Basic Communication Course Annual, 3,* 3–15.

Warren, J. T. (1999). Whiteness and cultural theory: Perspectives on research and education. *Urban Review, 31,* 185–203.

Weiss, R. O. (1998, November). *Sustaining speaking across the curriculum programs.* Paper presented at the annual conference of the National Communication Association, New York.

Whitecap, V. A. (1992). The introduction of a speech: Do good introductions predict a good speech? *Basic Communication Course Annual, 4,* 141–153.

Whitworth, R. H., & Cochran, C. (1996). Evaluation of integrated versus unitary treatments for reducing public speaking anxiety. *Communication Education, 45,* 306–314.

Williams, D. E., & Stewart, R. A. (1994). An assessment of panel vs. individual instructor ratings of student speeches. *Basic Communication Course Annual, 6,* 87–104.

Williams, G. (1995). TA training beyond the first week: A leadership perspective. *Basic Communication Course Annual, 7,* 59–82.

Witt, P. L., & Behnke, R. R. (2006). Anticipatory speech anxiety as a function of public speaking assignment type. *Communication Education, 55,* 167–177.

Worley, D. W., Worley, D. A., & McMahan, D. (1999). *A descriptive analysis of best-selling basic course texts.* (ERIC Document Reproduction Service No. ED437687)

Ziegler, C. A., & Reiff, M. (2006). Adjunct mentoring, a vital responsibility in a changing educational climate: The Lesley University adjunct mentoring program. *Mentoring & Tutoring, 14,* 247–269.

Communication Across the Curriculum Problematics and Possibilities

Standing at the Forefront of Educational Reform

Deanna P. Dannels

4

"U R on FB Dr. D.?"

"Yes. Of course."

"LOL."

"What?"

"Laugh out loud."

"OK . . . why are you laughing?"

"U on FB?"

"Yes. Me on facebook. Facebook is the place to be, yes?"

"GMTA, Dr. D. ☺"

"GMTA—explain?"

"Great minds think alike!"

✳ ✳ ✳

Within a couple of weeks of setting up my Facebook account (on encouragement and nagging of several old friends), a small window popped up on my screen with the picture of one of my graduate students with whom I have worked fairly closely. After the above "chat," I decided to declare to the Facebook world my willingness to be open to the ways of the next generation. I immediately wrote on my own "wall" (a general posting area that I soon found out was intended for others to write on)— "Deanna is having fun learning about Facebook." Within moments, my stepson (who was on Facebook in the other room) yelled, "You aren't supposed to write on your own wall . . . newwwwwbie!" Moments later, I received a request on Facebook to "have drinks" with a different graduate student. I immediately e-mailed her to ask whether she was having difficulties with her committee or her GTA work—trying to electronically communicate my willingness to meet with her and provide mentoring on any pending crises. Imagine my surprise (and embarrassment) when she kindly responded (I'm sure shaking her head the whole time): "it isn't a real drink Dr. D., its virtual, just a facebook thing."

Such were my first, failed attempts to engage in the new landscape of social technologies. Yet today's students are engaged in countless social interactions and communicative endeavors within these technological environments. They have complex languages that help them make decisions, multiple means for "chatting" with others, and countless tiers of "friends" with whom they communicate. They have different acronyms that communicate—with few letters—emotion, desire, and intent. In short, they have a communicative culture in which there are norms, rules, and expectations for behavior. In my attempts to enter this culture, I had to take some risks—engaging in communicative activities that were unfamiliar, making mistakes that were somewhat embarrassing and uncomfortable, and participating in rituals that were seemingly disconnected from my expertise.

As a communication across the curriculum (CXC) scholar and practitioner, I essentially ask students and faculty in other disciplines to engage in similar risks—to step into a culture of more formalized communication education that is probably somewhat uncomfortable, unfamiliar, and disconnected from their areas of expertise. I essentially ask them to walk into a landscape that at times feels as foreign as Facebook did to me—knowing they will make mistakes, break rules, and probably struggle in learning the norms. Even though they have engaged in informal communicative activities in numerous settings—within and outside the classroom—in terms of the formal teaching and learning of communication, they are (in my stepson's language) "newbies." The task for CXC scholars and practitioners, then, is to help them (faculty and students) navigate this somewhat foreign landscape.

The CXC initiative focuses on providing and supporting communication instruction in noncommunication courses. Responding to consistent refrains from business leaders, accreditation agencies, and the popular press, CXC programs focus on helping non-communication-focused faculty and students understand the power of communication and become competent in using communication to achieve multiple goals in various settings (Cronin & Grice, 1992; Mehren, 1999; Zernike, 1999). In this way, CXC programs share similar foundational goals as many communication departments. Yet CXC programs implement these goals within disciplines that do not focus entirely, or sometimes even partially, on communication as a content area. Rather, CXC programs are working within disciplines such as engineering, business, design, agriculture, and math (to name a few) to explore ways in which communication can be woven within and around the content to supplement students' learning and professional development. Given this structure, CXC programs often work with discipline-specific faculty who are untrained and often unaware and students who are fearful and often unhappy about the prospect of adding more to their plate (Cronin, 1996; Cronin & Glenn, 1991). In other words, CXC programs are often in a position of having to persuade faculty and students to take uncomfortable risks with activities that could seem foreign and irrelevant to them.

In some cases, these risks involve learning new kinds of communication genres. In other cases, these risks involve learning how to give and receive feedback on oral work. In yet other cases, these risks involve providing evaluations to students on their professional communicative development. In the best of scenarios, these risks are undertaken with one-on-one support of the communication specialist, ongoing faculty development, a well-funded student lab, and incentives for students and faculty to take communication seriously when it officially sits outside the realm of their chosen area of expertise. Yet in reality, many faculty and students are in the unfortunate position of having to take these risks within budgetary, administrative, and pedagogical landscapes that are fragile and consistently shifting underfoot. Monetary support for new curricular initiatives now is the exception (rather than the rule) in times in which fiscal trimming of nonprofitable programs is becoming habitual practice. Administrative freedom to explore interdisciplinary innovations has been constricted by the consistent demand for accountability and assessment. Pedagogical initiatives that once engaged learners in active participation with content have become mundane for learners who spend much of their life in technological matrices of social interaction. As a cross-curricular initiative fiscally and programmatically connected with such changes, CXC faces the threat of budget cuts, administrative bureaucracy, and pedagogical antiquity. Yet as a cross-curricular initiative relationally connected with students and faculty across countless programs, disciplines, and courses, CXC has an opportunity to engage in bold, innovative strategies to extend its reach, affirm its relevance as an initiative, and stand at the cornerstone of educational reform. This opportunity is risky, but vital.

Before discussing the opportunities and risks facing the CXC initiative, I first provide some background information on the history of CXC. I describe general types of CXC program structures and goals that have typified the initiative over the past 30 years. I then provide an overview of trends in CXC research and scholarship. Drawing on those trends, I then discuss the problematics that face the CXC initiative, and finally, I entertain several possibilities for the future of CXC that address the emergent problematics. Ultimately, I pose a challenge for CXC program staff, directors, and invested participants to consider new and innovative ideas in order to take advantage of the central position and unique expertise CXC has within educational settings.

CXC Goals and Program Structures

Over the past 30 years, CXC programs have had a number of different foci.[1] The earliest speaking across the curriculum (SAC) program began at Center College, Iowa, in 1974 (Hay, 1987; Tomlinson, 1999). Many other programs followed suit—some of the most sustained early programs emerging at institutions such as Radford University, University of Colorado at Colorado Springs, DePauw University, and Hamline University (Cronin & Grice, 1991b; Morreale, Shockley-Zalabak, & Whitney, 1993; Palmerton, 1990; Weiss, 1988). In the earliest stage of CXC programs, CXC (or SAC) was often used as an overall term for multiple activities—individual course development with faculty or lectures in other departments on communication skills, the development of a speaking lab, the training of tutors or faculty to support students' communication activities, or full development of a cross-curricular program (Grice & Cronin, 1992; Hay, 1987). Although a number of these consultative activities emerged in the early decades of the CXC movement, it was not until the early 1990s that institutions started to have established, funded, university-wide programs (Hay, 1987; Olsen, 1996). Currently, CXC has become distinct from (although complementary to) many of those early activities (e.g., speaking labs, tutoring centers, or larger communication centers)—carving out its niche as an initiative working campuswide or within particular disciplines (typically with faculty and students) on communication activities and competencies (Cronin, Grice, & Palmerton, 2000; Tomlinson, 1999).

Also, over the past 30 years, CXC programs have been hailed by a number of different names that provide some insight into changes in the CXC mission over time. Whereas programs emergent in early CXC history seemed to focus on generalized communication instruction for noncommunication disciplines, as evidenced by more generic program names such as communication across the curriculum, speaking across the curriculum, and oral communication across the curriculum (Cronin & Grice, 1990), current programs seem to reflect more clearly defined emphases—communication in the disciplines; writing and SAC; speaking, arguing, and writing in the disciplines; written, oral, visual, and electronic communication; communication and ethics; and leadership development (Dannels, 2001a).[2] Regardless of the various structures and goals, though, in the past 30 years, the CXC initiative has established itself as an important and relevant activity on many campuses (Cronin et al., 2000; Dannels, 2001a; Steinfatt, 1986).

CXC PROGRAMMATIC STRUCTURES

Although there are no standardized CXC program structures, national discussions on CXC have resulted in principles that typify good CXC programs (Dannels, Jackson, Robertson, Sheckels, & Tomlinson, 2001). These principles suggest that CXC programs are best constructed as a supplement to general education courses (such as an introductory course); are ideally driven by the specific needs of the institution; and are created with commitments to scholarship, disciplinarity, breadth of goals and assignments, trained and compensated leadership, assessment, and ongoing faculty development. In practice, each CXC program manages these principles in distinct ways—making multiple decisions about issues of focus, administrative structure, audience, and program activities. The various decision-making clusters reflected in any CXC program provide a heuristic for understanding and distinguishing program structures and goals. Although this heuristic might not necessarily reflect the depth of many CXC programs, it does afford the opportunity to sketch out distinctions and similarities (and it can stand as a guide for future planning, as well).

1. *Institutional context:* What was the impetus of this program? What need does the program fill? Where is the program fiscally located? What is the funding source for the program? What are key partnerships for the CXC program (e.g., writing across the curriculum [WAC])? What is the overall institutional culture on matters of teaching and learning initiatives?

2. *Program goals:* What are the goals of the CXC program? How does the CXC program fit within the larger mission and curricular structure of the institution? How do these goals connect with other institutional initiatives focused on teaching and learning?

3. *Program activities:* What kinds of administrative and pedagogical activities are at the core of the program? What curricular models typify the program? Does this program use an "intensive" model where particular courses are designed and implemented with speaking requirements? Or is the program set up for more of a full saturation model, in which faculty teaching all courses are encouraged and supported for incorporating oral communication in alignment with course goals? Does the program target general education courses? Or is the program situated

within one particular discipline, targeting a specific disciplinary audience? Is the program connected with a speaking or writing center or other campus initiatives (e.g., teaching and learning centers, etc.)?[3]

4. *Program audiences:* Who is the target audience of the program? Is the program more focused on faculty development or is the program more focused on assisting students? Who are audiences that are relevant but peripheral? Is the program accountable—formally or informally—to any external audiences (e.g., alumni, business leaders, accreditation agencies)?

5. *Role of the CXC practitioner:* Is the CXC practitioner a trainer who focuses on helping faculty to become self-sufficient in their communication instruction? If so, how and when does this training happen (e.g., ongoing faculty development workshops, learning communities, orientation sessions, etc.)? Or is the CXC practitioner more of a consultant, bearing the full responsibility for the communication instruction with students? If this is the case, how and when does the CXC practitioner implement instruction (e.g., workshops in classes, tutoring on communication assignments in lab periods, meeting with students outside of class time, etc.)?[4]

6. *Expertise and training of CXC practitioners:* Who are the CXC practitioners? Is the program staffed with faculty who implement its activities? To what extent does the program make use of graduate or undergraduate students or adjunct faculty to assist in its mission? How are the CXC practitioners identified and chosen? Do CXC practitioners come from a communication department or are there students from different disciplines trained in communication instruction? How are the practitioners trained (if training is necessary)? What topics of training require the most attention and need continuous support?

7. *Assessment:* What counts as a successful CXC program? What data are accepted as measures of success in the program (e.g., student performance, perceptual data, faculty attendance data)? What are the expectations for assessment of the CXC program? Who has the responsibility for assessment of the CXC program? What assessment mechanisms are already in place at the institution or with external constituencies (e.g., accreditation)? What kinds of assessment are valued at the institutional and programmatic level?

8. *Inquiry:* To what extent does the CXC program produce and engage in scholarly inquiry? What scholarly principles or methodologies typify the work in the program? How is scholarly inquiry integrated in the programmatic work of CXC practitioners?

Answers to these clusters have resulted in a number of different programmatic combinations. Any CXC program can be mapped along this heuristic—and probably provides additional layers of activities or institution-specific parameters that make it unique and distinct from other programs. Although each cluster merits further discussion (specifically for new program leaders or administrators considering CXC programs), one that provides helpful insight into understanding the CXC initiative as a whole is that of CXC program goals—because these goals often become the foundation on which other decisions are made.

CXC GOALS

A number of different goals have been and continue to be relevant to CXC programs. Three that have been explored in recent discussions are professionalization, learning, and civic engagement (Dannels, 2005a; Fleury, 2005; Palmerton, 2005). Although programs typically have multiple and overlapping goals (that are often reflective of institutional missions), they can generally be identified according to the extent to which they value, emphasize, and further one or more of these goals in their program activities and materials. It is important to note, though, that although programs can be distinguished by their primary goal or focus, it is possible and typical for them to achieve multiple goals without necessarily intending to do so (e.g., civic engagement programs could also be reinforcing professional training for business leaders; programs primarily using communication to learn could also be reinforcing increased engagement with communities outside academia).

Professionalization. Many disciplines, such as business, accounting, engineering, medicine, and mathematics (to name a few), are hearing calls from industry to prepare students for the specific kinds of communication tasks they will face in the workplace. In business management, for example, calls from management companies suggest a need for more competent communicators in managerial positions. In the medical field, many experts are requesting increased attention to the communication competencies specific to doctors' and nurses' interaction with patients. In engineering, industry representatives are recognizing the importance and relevance of communication on the job and wanting students to be able to handle that reality. In design disciplines (architecture, landscape architecture, graphic design), practitioners recognize that students need to be proficient in the "critique" (the name for the genre in which students present their design and receive feedback) in order to be prepared for the client/designer meetings in the workplace (for a sample of such research illustrating the importance of communication within preprofessional contexts of business, design, engineering, and medicine, see Baren, 1993; Bennett & Olney, 1986; Brennan, 1997; Burke, 1991; Darling & Dannels, 2003; Dowd & Liedtka, 1994; Krapels & Arnold, 1996; Kreps & Kunimoto, 1994; Oak, 2000; Pabbati & Rathod, 1995; Paradis, Dobrin, & Miller, 1985; Vest, Long, & Anderson, 1996).

There are various ways in which CXC programs can and do respond to these calls to provide support for professional communication development. In an engineering course, for example, students might give "request for funding" presentations to simulate those they would give to external sponsors of a design. Students in food science courses could be asked to engage in a mock phone interview with a customer concerned about food safety issues. Students in a business management course might participate in mock "cocktail hours" in which they need to respond to targeted questions about their own abilities and professional preparation. Finally, students in a parks, recreation, and tourism course could practice responding to questions from the public about particular local parks and tourist sites. Underlying these activities, though, is helping students become more competent communicators within the expectations and norms of their chosen professional arena. In some cases, the communication activities can be very formal—even bringing in external audiences to provide feedback or to make the activity more reflective of the workplace. In other cases, the communication activities can be more classroom based—simply providing students with exposure to the kinds of communication events they will face in the workplace and giving them an opportunity to experience such events.

Learning. Another goal of many CXC programs is to use oral communication activities to help students learn course material in more sophisticated and thoughtful ways. This emphasis on learning has been captured by the phrase "speaking to learn" and closely parallels the "writing to learn" initiative (Miller, 2003; Palmerton, 1989, 1992; Russell, 2002; Smith, 1997)—with a focus on using communication activities to help students think critically, engage course material, and learn content in deeper ways (rather than the focus being placed on students becoming competent professional communicators in their chosen discipline). In higher education, there are a number of different initiatives that complement this learning-based CXC goal. These initiatives all work on the premise that getting students involved as active and engaged participants in the classroom is beneficial to learning the course material. Such initiatives include (but are not limited to) active learning, problem-based learning, inquiry-guided instruction, service learning, and e-learning (see Helman & Horswill, 2002; Silvan, Wong Leung, Woon, & Kember, 2000; Springer, Stanne, & Donovan, 1997, for a sample of studies illustrating the activities and benefits of active learning initiatives).

In congruence with these movements in higher education, there are a number of activities within CXC programs that promote oral communication as a way to engage students in learning course material. In a soil science class, for example, students could engage in a mock debate format in class to explore the benefits and drawbacks of different pesticides. In a psychology class, students might play patient "roles" to better understand, from an insider perspective, different psychological diagnoses. In history, students could respond to problematic historical analyses in short 1-minute presentations that require them to identify the biases in the historical argument. In an English course, students might engage in a fishbowl discussion (where half the class discusses a particular topic while the others observe, take notes, and then join the discussion at a predetermined time) on the recent novel assigned to them.

These communication activities necessarily have varied structures and levels of formality, but most are less formal in terms of needed preparation time and level of assessment, although not necessarily less formal in terms of the intellectual processes necessary to complete the learning activity. Some might also simulate professional contexts (e.g., take the psychology activity described above), but the intent is not to have students focus on their development as professional communicators but rather to have them focus on the process of communication as it helps them wrestle with the material.

Civic Engagement. The third goal that often characterizes CXC programs and activities is civic engagement. Building on many discussions in higher education that have lamented the loss of an educational focus on citizenship and character—citing challenges such as vocationalism and consumerism (ironically, these are potential outcomes of programs with professionalism as a key goal)—some CXC programs have focused communication instruction on creating more informed citizens. These programs typically have, as a foundation, the goal of helping students understand the importance of civic responsibility and preparing them to take an active and engaged role in the public forum (e.g., Ehrlich, 2000; Fleury, 2005; *Liberal Arts College Presidents Speak Out,* n.d.).

Activities within CXC programs that promote citizenship can be varied. In a chemistry course, for example, students could engage in small group discussions about particular societal issues related to nanotechnology and the production of sunscreen. In an education course, K–12 in-service teachers might create 3-minute arguments for a number of different audiences (parents, school board, and legislature) on the role of teachers in moral education. In a statistics course, students could debate solutions to different ethical dilemmas statisticians face in the completion and publication of their work for consumption by the general public. In an engineering course, students might participate in a net forum discussion about engineering failures—with a focus on the community issues that influence these particular failures. In a landscape architecture course, students might be asked to wrestle with tensions that emerge when their community partners suggest landscape needs in direct conflict with the mapping information they have garnered in the computer-based site assessment. In all these cases, the focus of CXC becomes about helping students understand the ethical, moral, and societal implications of their role as citizens.

In summary, there are a number of ways to distinguish CXC programs in terms of their overall programmatic structures, goals, and placement in particular institutions. These program goals not only shed light on different program structures but also have necessary implications for those programs that engage in scholarship and research. Similar to many other educational initiatives, there has been a strand of research emerging from some CXC program activities. As suggested in the earlier decision-making heuristic for CXC programs, the engagement in research is a decision CXC leaders have to address—and not all programs are involved in or engaged in CXC research (some because of the mission of the institution, others because of the explicit structure of the program and its leaders). Yet over the 30 years of the CXC initiative, the emergent lines of inquiry have addressed a number of different scholarly and programmatic questions.

CXC Research and Scholarship

The scholarship emerging from the CXC initiative has provided important theoretical, empirical, and programmatic insights.[5] CXC research and scholarship over the past 30 years can be broken down into three general eras: (1) establishment and justification, (2) expansion and critical reflection, and (3) reinvention and empiricism (Dannels & Gaffney, 2009). In the establishment and justification era (1983–1995), research focused on providing detailed descriptions of new CXC programs, explanations of CXC activities, and reports of assessment data to support the success of CXC as a university initiative. This research worked, as a whole, to create a solid foundation for CXC by detailing its growth, success, and specific programmatic structures at numerous universities (e.g., Bowers, 1997; Cronin, 1993; Cronin & Grice, 1991a, 1993; Glenn, Dobkins, Kennan, & Cronin, 1989; Grice, 1992; Weiss, 1993). In the expansion and critical reflection era (1996–2000), CXC research surfaced a number of important internal questions about the initiative and its potential harm or benefit within and outside the communication discipline (e.g., Braithwaite, 1988; "Colloquy: Responses," 1999; Morreale, 1997; Schneider, 1999). Critics questioned whether CXC initiatives were supporting a watered-down, atheoretical view of communication, and whether noncommunication faculty could do justice to the complexity of communication instruction. Supporters answered with a commitment to continuous training and development of noncommunication faculty on the complexities of communication and an argument for the important role CXC could play in institutions without established communication departments. The debate that ensued brought a new level of publicity to the CXC initiative that, in tandem with other educational calls for attention to communication, expanded its reach beyond the initial early-adopter institutions (Boyer Commission, 1998). In the reinvention and empiricism era (2001–2008), CXC research reflected a shift in focus from program development and assessment to more theoretical and empirical curiosity about specific disciplinary contexts such as engineering and design—focused on questions about teaching, learning, and engaging in situated, disciplinary communication activities (e.g., Cyphert, 2002; Dannels, 1999, 2000c, 2001b; Dannels, Housley Gaffney, & Norris Martin, 2008; Dannels & Norris Martin, 2008).

Beyond the three eras that characterize the history of CXC research, four central trends typify the current state of CXC scholarship. First, there has been a move from a generalized framework of CXC to a more discipline-specific framework of CXC. This research emerged in congruence with a similarly focused "communication in the disciplines" theoretical framework (Dannels, 2001b) that claims—from a situated learning perspective—that oral genres are sites for disciplinary learning, oral argument is situated practice, communication competence is locally negotiated, and learning to communicate is a context-driven activity. Research that best represents this move to a communication in the disciplines (CID) framework has occurred within engineering disciplines, in which oral communication is explored as a situated and distinct event. For example, studies suggest that successful communication in engineering involves numerical evidence, simplicity, a focus on the object/visual, and a results-oriented structure (Dannels, 2002, 2003; Darling, 2005)—characteristics distinct from expectations in other disciplines such as design (Dannels, 2005b). This move toward discipline specificity has also called into question generalized methods of assessing oral communication (Dannels, 2000c), suggesting that disciplinary norms and expectations for success necessitate disciplinary assessment.

The second trend in CXC research is a move from program-based inquiry toward interpretive empirical research. In the early CXC eras, research focused in large part on describing and showcasing newly developed CXC programs and providing assessment data to illustrate the successes and challenges of such programs. Recent research has shown a commitment to interpretive and empirical methodologies—exploring oral communication in its naturalistic setting from more ethnographic frameworks (e.g., Dannels, 2000b; Dannels, Anson, Bullard, & Peretti, 2003). For example, research in the discipline of design has used multiple empirical methodologies (interpretive, ethnographic, linguistic, discursive) to explore ways of achieving success in design critiques. Specifically, this empirical research has suggested that students who are successful in design critiques comprehensively explain visuals, demonstrate the design evolution in a systematic manner, advocate transparently for their design intent, credibly stage their presentation, manage interactions appropriately, and use rhetorical strategies to convey a narrative style and a close relationship between themselves and the design (Dannels, 2005b; Dannels et al., 2008; Morton, 2006; Morton & O'Brien, 2005). Research in design is emblematic of the shift from program description to interpretive exploration—showcasing the ways in which designers value and frame communication rather than describing the ways in which designers teach communication (or the ways in which CXC practitioners teach communication within design).

The third trend in CXC scholarship reflects a focus on outcomes-based assessment data instead of the self-report, perceptual data that characterized early eras. Scholars in CXC arenas have called for and recognized the importance of outcomes-based assessment (Dannels, 2000a, 2000c)—yet only recently has there been some research exploring the extent to which students involved in CXC endeavors have achieved particular discipline-specific outcomes. For example, one study of design presentations in chemical engineering explored the rhetorical strategies, organizational structures, and oral styles that differentiated successful and unsuccessful student teams as they completed their final design presentations (Dannels, 2009). Additionally, research in the discipline of design (architecture, landscape architecture, graphic design, industrial design, and art/design) has suggested that critics' feedback provides insight into the extent to which design students have achieved disciplinary communicative outcomes and competencies necessary for professional arenas (Dannels & Norris Martin, 2008). This research illustrates a focus on looking at actual communication behavior (presentations, feedback, etc.) instead of relying solely on students' or teachers' perceptions of communication behavior.

The final trend in CXC scholarship is that of a renewed reliance on and contribution to theoretical sophistication. Drawing on rhetorical theory, feminist theory, activity theory, situated learning, learning development, and genre theory, recent CXC research has explored a number of lines of inquiry previously unexplored (e.g., Anson & Dannels, 1999; Dannels, 2001b; Garside, 2002). For example, there is a large body of CXC research that interrogates the challenges involved with teaching and learning of communication in preprofessional disciplinary classrooms such as engineering and design. Drawing on activity theory and situated learning theory, researchers engaged in this line of inquiry suggest that students in these situations are caught between two social systems of practice—work and school—and tend to (regardless of the suggestions to act as professionals) revert to the academic expectations when enacting communication performances (Dannels, 2003). Additionally, recent research builds on genre theory, rhetorical theory, and activity theory by suggesting a new theoretical construct that can better capture the relational aspects that complicate oral genre learning—"relational genre knowledge" (Dannels, 2009). In each of these examples, there is more of a reliance on theoretical foundations and an attempt to expand those foundations in ways that are distinct to the teaching and learning of oral communication.

In sum, CXC scholarship has reflected some clear trends over the past 30 years—moving from the important foundational work that included program descriptions, self-report assessment data, generalized tools for implementation, and CXC justifications to more recent work characterized by empiricism, theoretical inquiry, outcomes-oriented data, and disciplinarity. Such research, as mentioned, has provided salient information to practitioners and scholars about the teaching and learning of communication in other disciplines. Yet although this work has generated a clear and important body of scholarship, it also brings to the fore certain problematics for CXC scholars and practitioners to explore. Such problematics are important to discuss, address, and explore when considering the future role of CXC in pedagogical, curricular, and scholarly conversations.

CXC Problematics

Looking forward, CXC scholars and practitioners are at a critical crossroads. As suggested, increasingly there are more and more pressures from administrative structures to produce concrete evidence of success, calls from industries to attend more thoroughly to communication competence, changes in communicative mediums and technologies, and challenges for competitive funding among various initiatives. At the same time, there are few institutions training new faculty for administration in and scholarship about CXC. Therefore, although CXC is theoretically (and sometimes programmatically) a central and relevant initiative for many institutions, it faces a number of challenges that could determine the extent to which the future is one of growth or one of stagnancy. Preventing the latter necessitates exploring and addressing several CXC problematics—four of which are paramount in considering the future of CXC: (1) interdisciplinarity, (2) relevance, (3) agency, and (4) self-limiting propagation.

Ask any CXC administrator for one of the best and worst stories of his or her administrative experience, and you will find that they typically involve moments in which interdisciplinarity is front and center—either rearing its ugly head or showing its benevolence. Interdisciplinarity can either provide huge benefits for CXC programs and scholarship or set up monumental roadblocks to success. For example, disciplines typically have distinct values and norms that might be in conflict with those that communication scholars and practitioners know as good pedagogical practice. I once worked with an engineering department in which I was given 2 minutes once a week for communication instruction—and I was expected to transform the engineering students into competent, confident professional speakers! The engineers placed a huge value on time—being succinct, keeping it short and sweet, and not adding any "fluff" (a direct quotation from a faculty member in that department). Yet I knew that good pedagogical practice necessitated practice, rehearsal, reflection, and continuous engagement with oral activities—something that I simply could not accomplish in 2 minutes every week.

Therefore, the question remains—how can CXC practitioners engage in pedagogical work and scholarly inquiry with disciplinary faculty who might hold different assumptions about communication? More specifically (and even more difficult), what if disciplinary faculty value different methodologies, forms of evidence, and kinds of data? How can CXC practitioners gain trust from faculty who value different measures of success to establish a productive research and instructional climate? These are foundational questions that do not even touch on the more practical interdisciplinary challenges with scheduling meetings, coteaching or cofacilitating workshops, managing fiscal responsibilities, and negotiating administrative turnover. The ways in which CXC scholars and practitioners handle these questions of interdisciplinarity, though, have important implications for CXC growth.

Not only does interdisciplinarity pose a significant issue for CXC, but it also brings to the fore a second problematic—relevance. The recent trend toward more theoretical inquiry is significant, and it is often accompanied with a wealth of empirical thick description about communication activities in various courses. But what is missing from this new trend of research are clear and concrete answers to the question "What evidence do we have that CXC works?" Regardless the methodological commitments of CXC scholars and practitioners, many disciplinary members we work with will (rightfully so) ask that very question. In fact, many of them will want statistical evidence garnered from controlled experimental studies. For example, I was once involved in a meeting with a dean and associate dean in a college of design. The purpose of the meeting was for me and my research team to update them on the curricular progress we had made. Within a minute of starting my opening remarks, the dean interrupted and said, "Prove to me my money was well spent. Show me the evidence that your work is helping this college."

Questions such as this will and should be at the doors of CXC scholars and practitioners. CXC practitioners and administrators need to be able to answer them. So how can CXC practitioners and scholars ask good, scholarly questions about CXC that not only will build on the strong theoretical traditions already forming but will be relevant and timely for our target audiences? And if CXC scholars and practitioners are able to balance the need for theoretical exploration with practical contributions, the challenge of translation still remains. How can CXC scholars translate data into language that target audiences can understand (again, necessitating an interdisciplinary process)? And practically—when consulting about communication to other disciplines—how do CXC practitioners translate our discipline in ways that not only preserve its complexity but also are persuasive to other disciplines? Bottom line, it seems as if CXC is consistently called on to make research and practice relevant for audiences who may not necessarily find thick description and theoretical sophistication important to fiscal and pedagogical decisions.

Another problematic for CXC scholars and practitioners to consider when looking ahead is that of agency. To what extent should CXC scholars be agents of change? Recent CXC research recommends a stance of curiosity for CXC practitioners and scholars (Dannels, 2005a). Such a stance begs for listening, asking questions, and empathic neutrality—without a central focus on change. Yet is this the best stance for the future? In a recent interaction with faculty in a food science department, for example, I was explaining to them the importance of a new CXC initiative focused on understanding their curriculum, their communication assignments, and their current instructional practices with regard to communication activities. In this initiative, the goal was to understand and provide information back to the department for them to enact change as they wanted. Although I firmly believe in this ground-up approach of supporting disciplines in making their own changes, I had to pause in an interview with one of those food science faculty (with whom I had worked on a number of university-wide committees), when he jokingly said to me, "You mean you aren't going to tell us what we're doing wrong? You're the experts. We don't need information. We need help! Make us better; don't rely on us to figure it out."

Therein lies the tension: Should CXC focus solely on understanding, describing, hearing, and interpreting what is within the target disciplines? Or should CXC practitioners go in more blatantly and unapologetically as agents of change? What if faculty in the disciplines present CXC practitioners and scholars with firmly held and beloved communication activities and genres that seem, at best, instructionally weak; at worst, unethical? What if there are opportunities to teach students new ways of being in their disciplinary and preprofessional skins? Should CXC practitioners help students follow the norms of their future professional worlds? Or should the CXC role be to encourage students to disrupt those norms in the name of communicative innovation and social change? If CXC practitioners encourage disruption of the norms, what interdisciplinary challenges might we create? Bottom line, the question is simple: To what extent should CXC scholars and practitioners adopt a stance committed to conversion and change rather than to empathy and neutrality?

Finally, although showing evidence of growth, rather than dormancy, the nature of CXC scholarship has contributed to a fourth problematic—that of self-limiting propagation of research and practice. In terms of research, scholarly inquiry is emerging most systematically from the kinds of academic contexts that value, support, and reward empirical scholarship. It is also these kinds of contexts that are necessarily disciplinary focused (e.g., large institutions with multiple colleges, departments, and other campus units). Therefore, the research relies and builds on this notion of disciplinarity as does much of the curricular and programmatic practice. This has been a significant and important move for CXC initiatives, as it has challenged notions of generalized instruction and assessment. Structurally, though, the research and practice becomes self-limiting—drawing from those disciplinary contexts that are available to program curricular activities and to engage in scholarly work, then taking those program activities and scholarly conclusions and using them to attract and speak to those same kinds of disciplinary contexts. Yet there are numerous contexts in which disciplinarity is not the relevant construct for pedagogical structures—community colleges, primary and secondary settings, international institutions, and perhaps even liberal arts institutions. For example, in a recent consultation with a rural community college, I received blank stares when talking with them about creating discipline-specific communication outcomes for their majors. One faculty member said to me, "We really don't want discipline-specific outcomes—our students are coming to learn a trade, not a discipline. They have to know certain skills and they get those skills in all our classes, regardless the course name or focus."

In this case, the faculty member was suggesting a different unit of analysis for this community college—one not grounded in disciplines or departments. Yet these places are typically not ones in which CXC scholarly inquiry is being done—and therefore we do not have research exploring teaching and learning communication in noncommunication contexts within institutions in which disciplinarity is perhaps irrelevant (and perhaps not; we simply do not have the research). Disciplinarity is simply one example of self-limiting propagation—there are most likely others that can be called into question given the current trends in CXC scholarship and practice. Given this, how can CXC scholars and practitioners gain breadth in institutional presence and scholarly inquiry in a way that is collaborative and respectful of various communicative needs?

The problematics facing CXC scholarship and practice—interdisciplinarity, relevance, agency, and self-limiting propagation—emerge (ironically) as by-products of a strong and growing area of research and practice. The body of scholarship has many strengths, yet its strengths also present challenges. These problematics could be viewed as a potential threat to CXC, but they could also be seen as an opportunity for CXC practitioners and scholars to think creatively and act innovatively in the future.

From Problematics to Possibilities

The problematics facing CXC scholarship and practice are the tip of the iceberg within a system in which administrative, budgetary, and pedagogical changes have shifted the very foundation of many educational initiatives. Although the status quo has generated strong programmatic and scholarly trends, the educational landscape provides opportunities for future growth. Three potential ways of addressing these problematics and seriously considering future growth include establishing an extension strand of CXC work, engaging socially based technologies for CXC educational use, and exploring more accessible and broad methodologies and products of research.

First, one way to expand the relevance of CXC and to stand at the cornerstone of educational reform would be to establish an extension strand of CXC research and practice. In many institutions that have agriculture disciplines, extension is a standard part of what they do—with the mission to connect their work with the public. In my state, for example, extension agents from soil science will come and test our garden soil to check its acidity. Extension agents will also provide assistance to budding beekeepers who are interested in keeping bees as a hobby. In plant biology, extension agents provide disease diagnoses and identification of insects to help grow healthy crops. In fact, in my state, there are extension agents in all 100 counties. The mission of extension agents is to provide needed service to the public in a variety of agricultural arenas. This might be a grand task for CXC, but imagine for a moment starting an extension strand of CXC that works, for example, to assist children in rural high schools to polish their skills at speaking at church, school, or community meetings. Or perhaps CXC extension agents can assist new managers to learn how to run business meetings. CXC extension agents could also work with community college students and provide them assistance in becoming more proficient in job interviews.

Regardless of the communicative content, there seems to be a wide opportunity to expand the reach of CXC by supplementing our academic audience with a wider, community audience—using extension as a model for doing so (as opposed to a consulting model that connotes activities separate from the academic context for external pay). Doing this would necessitate asking and answering several questions. What kinds of extension activities might CXC scholars pursue in different institutions? What extension audiences are most in need of communication assistance? What is a manageable starting point in terms of an extension service? What funds are available to assist such kinds of extension work? How can CXC partner with or adopt current extension models to gain access to a wider community?

Second, another way for CXC scholars and practitioners to innovate beyond the realm of current practice is to explore the uses and adaptations of socially based technologies in CXC education. As suggested in the opening vignette, being hailed as "digital natives" (Palfrey & Gasser, 2008), our students come to our classrooms with competencies in many social technologies—Facebook, text messaging, YouTube, online gaming, and Twitter, to name a few. It is only recently, though, that there has been some exploration of educational adaptations and uses of such technologies (e.g., Dannels & de Souza e Silva, 2009). CXC could place itself as a leader of this charge. With a central focus on communication, disciplinary cultures, and instructional effectiveness, CXC scholars and practitioners are in a unique position to contribute greatly to conversations about technology in a variety of classrooms. This would require moving beyond discussions of PowerPoint, though. It might even require a leap of faith—working against the assumption that entertaining these social technologies academically would be making a deal with the devil.

In doing this, CXC practitioners would have to sincerely, aggressively, and responsibly entertain the claim that social technologies could be used productively in CXC instructional activities—in a programmatic and scholarly way. Why not, for example, use YouTube to expand the CXC audience to the K–12 context? Why not create YouTube videos that showcase communication competencies, complexities, and dilemmas that might face our students? How can CXC practitioners help students adopt disciplinary communicative identities in social technologies such as Facebook? How could CXC help teach about disciplinary communicative decision-making processes within online gaming activities? How can virtual gaming open new avenues for collaboration and teamwork in CXC endeavors? A number of questions emerge, and to the extent that these social technologies invoke communicative elements, CXC is well positioned to ask and answer them.

Finally, CXC scholars and practitioners might extend their reach by considering a broader methodological foundation and more publicly accessible products (or genres). As mentioned, there is very little experimental research that provides statistically significant claims about the success or failure of particular CXC activities. Granted there are extremely difficult issues to manage when doing this research (especially in educational settings)—confounding variables, the ethics of controlling instructional research, informed consent—but CXC scholars could at least entertain the challenge rather than claim this kind of research impossible. If we are being asked to prove CXC instruction matters, we might need to consider traditional experimental designs to explore focused hypotheses. On the other end of the continuum, it might be insightful for CXC scholars and practitioners to explore narrative avenues of research and writing, constructing stories that bring to the fore those challenges that are difficult to discuss: interdisciplinarity, power, and resistance (to name a few). Such stories could bring insight not only to practitioners but also to disciplinary members for whom a narrative structure is persuasive and salient.

If CXC practitioners and scholars are able to create a broader methodological foundation, why not explore more publicly accessible genres to get the message out? What about writing an editorial about communication competencies for the local newspaper? How about developing a white paper on the importance of CXC? Publishing a children's book on communication anxiety? Constructing a video on YouTube about the importance of communication in different disciplines? Creating a podcast with conflict management strategies for struggling managers? Why not get some time in front of local legislators or boards of trustees about communication initiatives in the state or institutional system? Methodological and genre breadth and accessibility can only help CXC practitioners, as it provides a number of different tools for administrators to use in order to speak to varied audiences. The challenge becomes embracing methodological and genre breadth in ways that do justice to the complexities of communication teaching and learning and that provide succinct information for time-pressed audiences. Yet in doing so, methodological and genre breadth might actually teach CXC scholars and practitioners something new.

I recognize these are bold suggestions that probably seem unmanageable and difficult within the bureaucracies that often characterize cross-curricular work. Yet the potential for CXC to be left behind within the turmoil of administrative, budgetary, and pedagogical changes is real. The problematics facing CXC scholarship and practice can grow and lead to stagnation, but the possibilities (given the important and central space CXC occupies at various institutions) for innovation and leadership are great. Taking on this leadership, admittedly, might require walking into landscapes in which CXC is unfamiliar, uncomfortable, and somewhat disconnected. It might require making some mistakes in order to learn the norms and expectations of new innovations. It might require some humility and careful walking into spaces that are foreign and some advocacy in speaking about what is crucial in new communicative settings. The opportunity is risky, but vital.

Conclusion

In the spirit of my own recommendations, I end with a different genre—a story. Recently, I was teaching my daughter how to snow ski. She had been in ski school for a couple of days, but I figured that it was now my turn to take the instructional reins. She was doing quite well, and we decided to do a few runs down the bunny slope. We would ride the short lift up the mountain, and I would ski down the easy slope and wait for her to ski down to me. She was having great success. After about 30 minutes, I even stopped yelling "Pizza! Pizza!" as she flew by me, which was the word she learned for snow plowing—the way you stop on skis.

After doing this for a couple of days, my daughter finally said to me:

"Mommy, I want to go down the big hill."

"What do you mean?" I asked.

"I want to go down THAT one," she said, pointing to the long run that headed straight down the mountain. "Can I do that one?"

"Well, that is actually the next one you will try—it is a green run and that means it is harder than the bunny slope. Maybe we can do that one next year. For now, let's stay here and keep working on this hill, okay? We are doing just fine."

"But mommy, I want to go on the big hill. This is boring. Just the same thing over and over. Let's do something new, Mommy."

The CXC initiative can easily stay on its current path. CXC has established important roots in a number of different universities; produced good, solid research that has influenced many new scholars and practitioners; and generated a number of curricular and pedagogical activities that have influenced faculty and students across countless disciplines. Yet with the educational landscape changing, CXC is facing a number of administrative, budgetary, and pedagogical challenges. CXC initiatives could continue down the easy path (over and over), but there is a danger that may tire, and then look ahead and outward for other possibilities. But there is also the opportunity for CXC to stand on the edge of educational reform, with its keen insight into interdisciplinary relationships, its practitioners' structural positioning as quasi-insiders in numerous disciplines, its unique positioning to speak within relevant and frequently used technological contexts, and its vital expertise in something that is at the core of pedagogical and educational success: communication.

"Let's do something new, Mommy."

"Yes, let's do something new."

GMTA.

Notes

1. For a thorough history on early and recent CXC programs and scholarship, see Cronin and Glenn (1991), Cronin et al. (2000), and Dannels and Gaffney (2009).

2. Although there are a number of different acronyms used to refer to CXC initiatives, for the remainder of this chapter, I use CXC as a generic acronym to refer to the initiative.

3. CXC program structures/activities have historically aligned with three different models—communication-intensive, full saturation, and discipline-specific models. These general types of programs are not inclusive of all adaptations of CXC program structures and should only be used loosely to distinguish different programs. To better understand any CXC initiative, it is important to have a full understanding of the university structure and program placement within that structure.

4. The training and consulting models (and the hybrid CONTRA [combined consulting and training] model) were empirically explored early in the history of the CXC initiative and have been adapted in a number of different forms over time. For a full discussion of definitions of the consulting, training, and combined (CONTRA) models, see Cronin and Grice (1993).

5. For a comprehensive review of CXC scholarship and a full explanation of the three eras summarized here, see Dannels and Gaffney (2009).

References

Anson, C. M., & Dannels, D. P. (1999, November). *Becoming disciplined in talk and text: Genre as social action across the curriculum.* Paper presented at the meeting of the National Communication Association, Chicago.

Baren, R. (1993). Teaching writing in required undergraduate engineering courses: A materials course example. *Journal of Engineering Education, 82,* 59–61.

Bennett, J. C., & Olney, R. J. (1986). Executive priorities for effective communication in an information society. *Journal of Business Communication, 23*(2), 13–22.

Bowers, A. A., Jr. (1997). *A descriptive study of speaking across the curriculum programs in four-year public higher education institutions in the United States.* Unpublished doctoral dissertation, University of Toledo, Toledo, OH.

Boyer Commission on Educating Undergraduates in the Research University. (1998). *Reinventing undergraduate education: A blueprint for America's research universities.* Stony Brook: State University of New York.

Braithwaite, D. (1988, November). *Anyone can teach speech, right? The impact of speaking across the curriculum on the discipline.* Paper presented at the meeting of the Speech Communication Association, New Orleans, LA.

Brennan, M. (1997). Job market healthy for new chemistry graduates. *Chemical and Engineering News, 75,* 10.

Burke, J. D. (1991). The emergence of career wellness programs. *Chemical and Engineering News, 76,* 77–78.

Colloquy: Responses. (1999). *The Chronicle.* Retrieved June 27, 2008, from http://chronicle.com/article/Taking-Aim-at-Student-Incoh/11515/

Cronin, M. W. (1993, November). *Empirical measures of learning outcomes from oral communication across the curriculum.* Paper presented at the meeting of the Speech Communication Association, Miami Beach, FL.

Cronin, M. W. (1996, November). *Lessons we've learned: What does it take to maintain and implement oral communication across the curriculum proposals.* Panel presentation at the meeting of the Speech Communication Association, San Diego, CA.

Cronin, M. W., & Glenn, P. (1991). Oral communication across the curriculum in higher education: The state of the art. *Communication Education, 40,* 356–367.

Cronin, M. W., & Grice, G. L. (1990, November). *Oral communication across the curriculum: Designing, implementing and assessing a university-wide program.* Program presented at the meeting of the Speech Communication Association, Chicago.

Cronin, M. W., & Grice, G. L. (1991a, April). *Implementing oral communication across the curriculum.* Paper presented at the meeting of the Central States Communication Association, Chicago.

Cronin, M. W., & Grice, G. L. (1991b, April). *Speech communication across the curriculum: Development of the Radford University Oral Communication Program.* Paper presented at the annual meeting of the Southern States Communication Association, Tampa, FL.

Cronin, M. W., & Grice, G. L. (1992, April). *Meeting the SACS guidelines in oral communication.* Panel presented at the meeting of the Southern States Communication Association, San Antonio, TX.

Cronin, M. W., & Grice, G. L. (1993). A comparative analysis of training models versus consulting/training models for implementing oral communication across the curriculum. *Communication Education, 42,* 1–9.

Cronin, M. W., Grice, G. L., & Palmerton, P. (2000). Oral communication across the curriculum: The state of the art after twenty-five years of experience. *Journal of the Association for Communication Administration, 29,* 66–87.

Cyphert, D. (2002). Integrating communication across the MBA curriculum. *Business Communication Quarterly, 65,* 81–86.

Dannels, D. P. (1999, November). *Disciplinary assessment of oral presentations: Initial steps and strategies.* Paper presented at the meeting of the National Communication Association, Chicago.

Dannels, D. P. (2000a, November). *Evidence of communication competence: Student video portfolios as outcome-based assessment tools for CXC.* A paper presented at the meeting of the National Communication Association Convention, Seattle, WA.

Dannels, D. P. (2000b). Learning to be professional: Technical classroom discourse, practice, and professional identity construction. *Journal of Business and Technical Communication, 14,* 5–37.

Dannels, D. P. (2000c, June). *A model for discipline-specific outcome-based assessment of writing and speaking.* Paper presented at the meeting of the American Association of Higher Education Assessment Conference, Charlotte, NC.

Dannels, D. P. (2001a). Taking the pulse of communication across the curriculum: A view from the trenches. *Journal of the Association of Communication Administration, 30,* 50–71.

Dannels, D. P. (2001b). Time to speak up: A theoretical framework of situated pedagogy and practice for communication across the curriculum. *Communication Education, 50,* 144–158.

Dannels, D. P. (2002). Communication across the curriculum and in the disciplines: Speaking in engineering. *Communication Education, 51,* 254–268.

Dannels, D. P. (2003). Teaching and learning design presentations in engineering: Contradictions between academic and workplace activity systems. *Journal of Business & Technical Communication, 17,* 139–169.

Dannels, D. P. (2005a). Leaning in and letting go. *Communication Education, 54,* 1–5.

Dannels, D. P. (2005b). Performing tribal rituals: A genre analysis of "crits" in design studios. *Communication Education, 54,* 136–160.

Dannels, D. P. (2009). Features of success in engineering design presentations: A call for relational genre knowledge. *Journal of Business and Technical Communication, 23*(4), 399–427.

Dannels, D. P., Anson, C. M., Bullard, L., & Peretti, S. (2003). Challenges in learning communication skills in chemical engineering. *Communication Education, 52*, 50–56.

Dannels, D. P., & de Souza e Silva, A. (2009). OnSite and engaged: Hybrid-reality gaming in communication across the curriculum initiatives. In A. de Souza e Silva & D. Sutko (Eds.), *Digital cityscapes: Merging digital and urban playspaces* (pp. 321–338). New York: Peter Lang.

Dannels, D., & Gaffney, A. (2009). Communication across the curriculum and in the disciplines: A call for scholarly cross-curricular advocacy. *Communication Education, 58*(1), 124–153.

Dannels, D. P., Housley Gaffney, A. L., & Norris Martin, K. (2008). Beyond content, deeper than delivery: What critique feedback reflects about communication expectations in design education. *International Journal for the Scholarship of Teaching and Learning, 2*(2). Retrieved January 15, 2009, from http://academics.georgiasouthern.edu/ijsotl

Dannels, D. P., Jackson, N., Robertson, T., Sheckels, T., & Tomlinson, S. (2001). *Proceedings from the communication across the curriculum strand.* Program presented at the NCA Summer Conference, Washington, DC.

Dannels, D. P., & Norris Martin, K. (2008). Critiquing critiques: A genre analysis of feedback across novice to expert design studios. *Journal of Business & Technical Communication, 22*, 135–159.

Darling, A. L. (2005). Public presentations in mechanical engineering and the discourse of technology. *Communication Education, 54*, 20–33.

Darling, A. L., & Dannels, D. P. (2003). Practicing engineers talk about the importance of talk: A report on the role of oral communication in the workplace. *Communication Education, 52*, 1–16.

Dowd, K. O., & Liedtka, J. (1994). What corporations seek in MBA hires: A survey. *Selections, 10*(2), 34–39.

Ehrlich, T. (2000). *Civic engagement.* Retrieved January 2, 2009, from http://measuringup.highereducation.org/2000/articles/ThomasEhrlich.cfm

Fleury, A. (2005). Liberal education and communication against the disciplines. *Communication Education, 54*, 72–79.

Garside, C. (2002). Seeing the forest through the trees: A challenge facing communication across the curriculum programs. *Communication Education, 51*, 51–64.

Glenn, P., Dobkins, D., Kennan, W., & Cronin, M. (1989, June). *An oral communication program: Goals and implementation.* Paper presented at the meeting of the Speech Writing Conference of the Canadian Speech Communication Association, Ontario, Canada.

Grice, G. (1992, November). *Implementing required oral communication intensive courses as part of the GE curriculum.* Paper presented at the meeting of the Speech Communication Association, Chicago.

Grice, G. L., & Cronin, M. (1992, April). *The comprehensive speech communication laboratory: We have ways of making you talk.* Paper presented at the meeting of the Southern States Communication Association, San Antonio, TX.

Hay, E. (1987, November). *Communication across the curriculum.* Paper presented at the meeting of the Speech Communication Association, Boston.

Helman, S., & Horswill, M. S. (2002). Does the introduction of non-traditional teaching techniques improve psychology undergraduates' performance in statistics? *Psychology Learning and Teaching, 2*(1), 12–16.

Krapels, R. H., & Arnold, V. D. (1996). The legitimacy of business communication. *Journal of Business Communication, 33,* 331–351.

Kreps, F., & Kunimoto, E. N. (1994). *Effective communication in multicultural health care settings.* Thousand Oaks, CA: Sage.

Liberal arts college presidents speak out on liberal arts colleges' role in shaping moral values. (n.d.). Retrieved January 2, 2008, from www.collegenews.org/x3716.xml

Mehren, E. (1999, February 22). Colleges, like focus on speech. *Los Angeles Times,* p. A1.

Miller, P. C. (2003). *Speaking across the curriculum: An annotated bibliography of resources by topics.* Retrieved June 20, 2008, from http://eric.ed.gov:80/ERICDocs/data/ericdocs2sql/content_storage_01/0000019b/80/1b/1f/87.pdf

Morreale, S. (1997, April). Communication across the curriculum and in undergraduate education debated and clarified. *Spectra, 33,* 5–14.

Morreale, S., Shockley-Zalabak, P., & Whitney, P. (1993). The Center for Excellence in Oral Communication: Integrating communication across the curriculum. *Communication Education, 42,* 10–21.

Morton, J. (2006). The integration of images into architecture presentations: A semiotic analysis. *Art, Design & Communication in Higher Education, 5*(1), 21–37.

Morton, J., & O'Brien, D. (2005). Selling your design: Oral communication pedagogy in design education. *Communication Education, 54,* 6–19.

Oak, A. (2000). It's a nice idea, but it's not actually real: Assessing the objects and activities of design. *International Journal of Art and Design Education, 19*(1), 86–95.

Olsen, R. (1996, November). *The future of OCAC: An argument for the conceptual framing of the oral communication across the curriculum movement.* Paper presented at the meeting of the Speech Communication Association, San Diego, CA.

Pabbati, P. V., & Rathod, M. S. (1995). Study of curriculum models that integrate mathematics, physical sciences, computers, and communication in technical courses. In *Proceedings of the 1995 Annual ASEE Conference* (pp. 215–220). Washington, DC: American Society for Engineering Education.

Palfrey, J., & Gasser, U. (2008). *Born digital.* New York: Basic Books.

Palmerton, P. R. (1989, November). *Talking, writing, learning.* Paper presented at the meeting of the Speech Communication Association, San Francisco.

Palmerton, P. R. (1990, March). *Speaking across the curriculum: The Hamline experience.* Paper presented at the meeting of the Conference of College Composition and Communication, Chicago.

Palmerton, P. R. (1992). Teaching skills or teaching thinking? *Journal of Applied Communication Research, 20,* 334–341.

Palmerton, P. R. (2005). Liberal education and communication across the curriculum: A response to Anthony Fleury. *Communication Education, 54,* 80–85.

Paradis, J., Dobrin, D., & Miller, R. (1985). Writing at Exxon ITD: Notes on the writing environment of an R & D organization. In L. Odell & D. Guswami (Eds.), *Writing in non-academic settings* (pp. 281–307). New York: Guilford Press.

Russell, D. (2002). *Writing in the academic disciplines: A curricular history* (2nd ed.). Carbondale: Southern Illinois University Press.

Schneider, A. (1999, March 26). Taking aim at student incoherence: Spread of speech programs across the curriculum irks some communications professors. *Chronicle of Higher Education,* p. A16.

Silvan, A., Wong Leung, R., Woon, C., & Kember, D. (2000). An implementation of active learning and its effect on the quality of student learning. *Innovations in Education and Teaching International, 37,* 381–389.

Smith, G. (1997). Learning to speak and speaking to learn. *College Teaching, 45,* 49–51.

Springer, L., Stanne, M. E., & Donovan, S. S. (1997*). Effects of small-group learning on undergraduates in science, mathematics, engineering, and technology: A meta-analysis* (Research Monograph No. 11). Madison: University of Wisconsin, National Institute for Science Education.

Steinfatt, T. (1986). Communication across the curriculum. *Communication Quarterly, 34,* 460–470.

Tomlinson, S. D. (1999). *Communication across the curriculum: Status of the movement and recommendations.* Unpublished master's project, University of Washington, Seattle.

Vest, D., Long, M., & Anderson, T. (1996). Electrical engineers' perceptions of communication training and their recommendation for curricular change: Results of a national survey. *IEEE Transactions of Professional Communication, 39,* 38–42.

Weiss, R. O. (1988, November). *Start-up strategies for speaking and listening across disciplines.* Paper presented at the meeting of the Speech Communication Association, New Orleans, LA.

Weiss, R. O. (1993, November). *Speaking across the curriculum as an alternative assessment process.* Paper presented at the meeting of the Speech Communication Association, Miami Beach, FL.

Zernike, K. (1999, January 31). Talk is, like, you know, cheapened. *The Boston Globe,* p. A1.

Communication and the Preparation of Future Faculty 5

Learning to Manage Incoherencies

Katherine Grace Hendrix

> *Given the importance of the ability to communicate competently, the communication discipline should be viewed as central on college campuses. Humans are born with the ability to vocalize; but not with the knowledge, attitudes, and skills that define communication competence. The ability to communicate effectively and appropriately is learned and, therefore, must be taught . . . by specialists in departments that are devoted to the study of communication.*
>
> —Morreale, Osborn, and Pearson (2000, p. 2)

Managing Incoherencies

Light and Cox (2008) posit that we live in an age of "super complexity," and they argue that a major challenge for higher education professionals is the management of ever-increasing incoherencies that appear not only in the form of alternate ways of knowing but in the demands of our professional associations, external agencies, institutions, and campus departments. We must update our teaching, find time for professional development, and somehow balance career and family. In conjunction with macrolevel professional demands, today we face the ever-mounting challenge of teaching to older, commuter students as well as the "Millennials" who, characteristically, (a) are the children of the late Baby Boomers (1954–1964) or Generation Xers (1965–1981), (b) constitute

36% of the U.S. population, (c) spend more than 6.5 hours daily on various media, and (d) are more diverse than any previous group of students (Halpern, 2009). This time of "super complexity" places new and uncommon challenges before the new teacher, and these challenges can seem unmanageably incoherent.[1]

Clearly, we are called to move toward an updated way of thinking about what constitutes effective teaching that promotes learning while meeting the social and personal needs of the individuals enrolled in our courses. Kuh, Kinzie, Schuh, Whitt, and Associates (2005) note our charge to convert these incoherencies into opportunities, shifting from a passive, instructor-dominated pedagogy to more engaged activities that, for instance, allow us to interact with older, nontraditional students in the workforce as paraprofessionals whose experiences can be of benefit to all enrolled in our classes.

However, the challenge is much greater than determining the correct mix of content, approach, and assessment. According to Light and Cox (2008), we are caught up in the demands linked to a call *for* professionalism (i.e., accountability) and a call *to* professionalism (i.e., defending academic values and practices while simultaneously working to transform the institution) at a time when our student bodies are more diverse than at any other time in the history of U.S. education—a demographic fact that brings with it increased pressures apart from learning subject matter content. From a curriculum development standpoint, Kuh et al. (2005) acknowledge the tension associated with continuously improving our offerings, thereby adding to an expected professional pace and workloads that are spiraling out of control.

From an alternate standpoint, one can ascertain the stresses and strains experienced by our students that cannot help but detract from their focus on the subject matter. In *Campus Confidential: The Complete Guide to the College Experience by Students for Students*, Miller (2006) addresses predictable topics such as what courses to take, choosing a major, and managing Greek Life, but he also discusses areas that we, as professors, may not consider—keeping peace with a roommate, functioning on campus as an athlete, "coming out" on campus, campus safety, stress and health, and so on. Others add to Miller's overview of student concerns: wrestling with culture shock endured by domestic (Orbe, 2004) and international students (Rubin & Turk, 1997; Wadsworth, Hecht, & Jung, 2008); working and studying (Pike, Kuh, & Massa-McKinley, 2008); balancing working, studying, and family (Gorsline, Holl, Pearson, & Child, 2006; Rizer, 2005); achieving success as a student of color on a predominantly white campus (Davidson & Foster-Johnson, 2001; Feagin, Vera, & Imani, 1996); and even oral communication performance anxiety (Witt & Behnke, 2006).

In short, our students have far more on their minds than internalizing our course material, and all of these worries are exacerbated by the mindset of some students, such as our Millennials:

It is imperative that someone studying this generation realize that we have the world at our fingertips—and the world has been at our fingertips for our entire lives. I think this access to information seriously undermines this generation's view of authority, especially traditional scholastic authority. (Clysdale, 2009, p. B8)

Thus, adding to the process of managing the incoherencies previously noted is the additional task of keeping up with technology ourselves while increasing the competency of our students who are not techno-savvy.

In regard to managing incoherencies, Liston and Zeichner (1996) observe that, while of critical importance, instructional methodology and learner psychology are often emphasized in teacher education without acknowledging that classrooms and schools are neither separate nor immune from influences of their larger environment. Specifically, these educators indicate that

> what goes on inside schools is greatly influenced by what occurs outside of schools. The students who attend and the teachers and administrators who work within those walls bring into the school building all sorts of cultural assumptions, social influences, and contextual dynamics. (p. x)

They go on to state that "unless some concerted attention is given to those assumptions, influences, and dynamics, to the reality of school life and to the social conditions of schooling, our future teachers will be ill prepared" (p. x).

There is hope in all this apparent complexity and incoherence. Despite the challenges ahead, after requesting narratives, lessons, and questions about teaching from the National Communication Association (NCA) membership, West (2008) concluded that the responses reflected passion; more specifically, they showed "communication teachers [who] are engaged, resourceful, innovative, and witty" (p. 1). Three communication professors from institutions of varying size and type exemplified that passion as they reported, "We want to be in the classroom because it is where we can have a positive and lasting impact on individual students" (Chisholm, 2008, p. 8); "What you gain [in a small school environment] is, first, an in-depth understanding of the entire educational endeavor and, second, a greater understanding of the students you teach . . . in a wider range of contexts" (Sheckels, 2008, p. 9); and "I teach because it allows me to live in these places we call classrooms. Because I believe that classrooms must necessarily challenge, stretch, and even frighten all members of the community, even teachers . . ." (Darling, 2008, p. 10).

In view of the incoherencies facing all teachers and students, the remainder of this chapter first offers an overview of recent research pertaining to teaching and uses that research to offer suggestions about preparing to teach in these complicated contexts. The chapter will then address several specific topics that offer particularly important opportunities to learn about managing incoherence: incivility, diversity, and online teaching/learning (see Note 1). Finally, professional development is explored along the dimensions of the scholarship of teaching as well as active conference participation.

Teaching

When asked to envision a masterful college teacher, Lowman (1984) presents three images: (1) an awe-inspiring lecturer whose students lean forward to catch every word, (2) a warm, approachable person seated at a seminar table "gently guiding" his or her students to think critically, and (3) a "freewheeling" session between an instructor and several students in the instructor's office or laboratory or over beer at a local bar. In all three instances, Lowman notes that the teacher is "pictured not while studying alone or presenting a paper to learned colleagues but while interacting with students"; consequently, all three scenarios convey the ability of the professor to have a profound effect on his or her students (pp. 1–2).

In this section, literature addressing the process of transferring and/or co-constructing knowledge with our students will be viewed from a macrolevel, in the form of reflective teaching, holistic teaching, and mentoring. However, it is best to begin from a point of introspection.

INTROSPECTION

Sometimes teachers and educators are not honored enough for their role as unsung heroes in mentoring and molding young people. . . . It is the obligation of the mentor or teacher to redefine the impossible, to bolster the child's uniqueness by helping them to become a whole person, a mature adult. Someone who knows how to make good choices. A mentor is someone whose presence stays with you, someone who makes you understand the straight and narrow and that [it] is not a restricted place to be. (Jamieson, 2009)

Implicit within Jamieson's definition of an effective teacher is a person capable of making wise decisions on his or her own behalf, for how can one counsel another in the midst of chaos within his or her own life? Hence, we begin from the self outward, and such a process inevitably involves revisiting our impression of self-concept, self-esteem, and the corresponding belief system (i.e., attitudes, beliefs, and morals) safeguarding our image.

Although we frequently discuss the foundations of self-concept and self-esteem with our students, I am suggesting that it is imperative that we not only present the material to our students but also actively participate in that same contemplative process. What are our major characteristics? Which are our strengths? Weaknesses? Do we possess an accurate sense of self?

What are we perfectly satisfied with about ourselves in contrast to areas where we know we can stand to improve? Do we need to make any modifications to our thoughts, actions, or beliefs and, if so, are we willing to put forth the necessary effort (on our own or with the assistance of others) to make the changes?

In complete honesty, Parker Palmer (1998) admits,

> Good teaching cannot be reduced to technique; good teaching comes from the identity and integrity of the teacher . . . by identity and integrity, I do not mean only our noble features, or the good deeds we do, or the brave faces we wear to conceal our confusions and complexities. Identity and integrity have as much to do with our shadows and limits, our wounds and fears, as with our strengths and potentials. (pp. 12–13)

We are quite familiar with Rosenberg's (1979) constructs of the desired, perceived, and public selves and Goffman's (1959) notion of center stage versus backstage face. We teach but fail to apply the material. To manage the incoherencies of our professional life, we must first pull together the disparate strands of our personal relationships and can then connect who we are as an individual, outside of academia, to our classroom persona.

REFLECTIVE TEACHING

Traditionally, communication education and instructional communication scholars have called for reflective teaching—a time to review one's knowledge and ability to effectively communicate subject matter content to students. Liston and Zeichner (1996) define such reflection as "an examination of our own theories and beliefs . . . [that are] formed and arise from our past experiences, our received knowledge, and our basic values" (p. xviii). Reflective student teachers share several characteristics: (a) They consider it important for their students to learn by investigating and structuring things themselves; (b) they have previously been encouraged to structure their own experiences and problems; (c) they have strong feelings of personal security and self-efficacy; and (d) they appear to talk or write relatively easily about their experiences (Korthagen & Wubbels, 1991). As Schon (1983) notes,

> A practitioner's reflection can serve as a corrective to overlearning. Through reflection, he can surface and criticize the tacit understandings that have grown up around the repetitive experiences of a specialized practice, and can make new sense of the situations of uncertainty or uniqueness which he may allow himself to practice. (p. 61)

Using Schon as a foundation, Killion and Todnem (1991) created the three-part explanation of reflection-on-action, reflection-in-action, and reflection-for-action, with the first two types distinguished by *when* reflection occurs and the latter representing a desired outcome.

Noting that the relative importance of the type of reflection changes depending on the stage of our teaching career, reflection-in-action is most closely associated with the advanced/master teacher. An alternative conception is offered by Sparks-Langer and Colton's (1991) three elements of reflective practice, including the cognitive, critical, and narrative. Cognition is concerned with the knowledge teachers must have to make sound decisions (also see Shulman, 1987); a critical approach engenders social justice and ethical issues, including not only the desired education product but also the process goals relative to acceptable achievement of the end product; and narrative allows the instructor to account for his or her own experience in the classroom. The narrative element is explained as "serv[ing] to contextualize the classroom experience for the teacher and for others and thereby provid[ing] a much richer understanding of what takes place in the classroom and in the teacher's construction of reality than would otherwise be possible" (Norlander-Case, Reagan, & Case, 1999, p. 35).

More recently, reflective teaching has been reconceptualized to include contemplation about not only one's persona in relation to students but also the presentation of one's soul in the classroom. In contrast to the traditional forms of education that accentuate the "rational," a holistic pedagogy suggests that acknowledging spirituality in one's classroom and professional life is a mandatory aspect of human development and achievement. Many scholars now promote the value of holistic teaching, which encompasses not only the mind but also the soul. The basic foundational premise of this line of scholarship is that failing to understand and nurture human wholeness leads to fractured, unhappy, unhealthy, and unproductive lives (Palmer, 1998, 2004).

Consequently, a holistic pedagogy offers an opportunity to manage the complexities of our professional lives by enhancing our ability to cope with stressors, tolerate ambiguities and increased demands, and embrace innovation. In essence, a holistic approach possesses the potential to bring some semblance of order into the midst of chaos. As we learn to teach for the first time, learn new material, learn new technologies, and/or learn about a wider range of diverse student/colleague characteristics, we must seek pedagogical approaches allowing us, and our students, to successfully manage incoherency.

HOLISTIC TEACHING: THE SPIRITUAL CONNECTION

Holistic teaching is a related construct based on the premise that each person finds identity, meaning, and purpose in life through connections

to spiritual values. Holistic education includes four processes: (1) cultivating the whole person; (2) sensing one's connection to the universe;
(3) attending to our students' minds, bodies, and spirits; and (4) inviting
emotion and soul into our classrooms (Baesler, 2009; Dillard, 2006;
Miller, 2000; Moore, 2005; Orr, 2005). Arduini (2004) offers three orientations toward spirituality: the existence of individual spirit, an entity
providing context for a larger reality (e.g., God, life force), and the invo-
cation of specific religious traditions. Hence, three songbirds potentially
sing in our classrooms—the self, the world, and/or "the Way." While
positing that each of the spiritual orientations provides a venue for presenting more of ourselves in our educational practice, the scholar
reminds us to take caution not to oppress the beliefs of others but instead
to ensure that "there must always be room for affirmation of spirit, but
also students in particular must be given space for their own, possibly
contradictory, orientations" (p. 13).

Scholars are beginning to articulate their own spiritual practices as educators. In her essay titled "Engaging Spirituality and an Authentic Self in
the Intercultural Communication Class," Hamlet (2009) describes the
daily spiritual ritual she enacts to place herself in the right frame of mind
to enter the class:

> My spiritual practices include the daily ritual of prayer. . . . Other activities
> reinforce and/or complement my connection to the spirit, such as my daily
> drive to campus which is enhanced with musical renditions from my
> favorite gospel artists blasting from the car's CD player. The music puts me
> in a good mood for the day (or at least the morning). My morning ritual is
> complete after I arrive in my office, water the plants, make coffee (this is not
> a spiritual practice but a necessary one), then read a scripture card from the
> elegant porcelain box that sits on my desk. I'm now ready to begin my work
> day with the belief that I will have *divine guidance and intervention* with
> whatever I have to confront that day, especially in the classroom.

Once in the classroom, Parker Palmer (1998) desires a creative tension
that maintains the attention of his students as well as his own. He has
discovered six paradoxical tensions evoking a teaching and learning
space that allow him to manage the complexities of physical room
arrangement, environmental feeling, conceptual framework pertinent to
the subject matter, interaction ground rules, and emotional ethos.
Palmer manages the incoherencies by creating the following spacial tensions: (a) bounded/open, (b) hospitable/charged, (c) individual voice/group
voice, (d) solitude/community, and (e) silence/speech. In addition, he
advises that our classroom space "should honor the 'little' stories of the
students and the 'big' stories of the disciplines and tradition" (p. 74). In
my view, the latter paradox—little and big stories—radically twists
our typical approaches to determining what counts as knowledge

(epistemology), what is real (ontology), and what knowledge is deemed valuable (axiology). In this last paradox, we respect both our personal upbringing and the life histories of our students by holding both individual experience and disciplinary doctrine up for inspection.

Whether one takes a spiritually guided or secularly oriented path when teaching, the commonality involves being reflexive in one's practice and providing similar opportunities for one's students. Mentoring and service learning are two common approaches to promoting increased awareness of self and others.

MENTORING

"Out-of-class communication" is an alternate phrase reminding us that our teaching is not confined to the subject matter at hand or within the walls of a classroom or lecture hall. The editors of *Beyond Teaching to Mentoring* (2001) suggest that given the "shifting educational, social, and technical environment[s]" that affect institutions of higher learning, educators must consider our changing roles and how to mentor our students under evolving circumstances (Reinarz & White, 2001, p. 1). These scholars further maintain that if mentoring is accepted as a metaphor for teaching,

> We are provided with the opportunity to reflect on what we do both in the classroom and outside of it . . . [which] can lead then to a renewal of spirit and a chance to see just how far the student can outperform the teacher. (p. 2)

Reinarz and White (2001) offer several alternative forms of mentoring linked to one's disciplinary center (e.g., science, business, mass communication). In contrast, Buell's (2004) three-phase research highlighted the mentoring practices of communication and journalism faculty and included focus group data collected from graduate students. Buell's analysis led her to posit that there are four models of mentoring among communication professors: cloning, nurturing, friendship, and apprenticeship.

Even though cloning had been part of the experience of some participants (i.e., controlling more than directing a mentee's path), Buell (2004) found that approach "in disfavor" and "falling into relative disuse" (p. 56). The nurturing model was described as akin to parental guidance—empathic, encouraging, involving mutual decision making—sometimes hampered by dependency and difficulty in letting the relationship end. The friendship model was described as more collaborative and co-constructed, consistent with the development phases of female mentoring relationships (see Kalbfleisch & Keyton, 1995), with a focus on personal bonds, reciprocity, and honesty. Finally, the apprentice model evolved as an alternative to the cloning model. The apprenticeship model centers on learning from one's mentor without any personal commitment; it is a "hands off" approach, where the sole purpose is the short-term professional relationship. Such alliances, for instance, might be viewed as a means to further one's career through association with a particular scholar in the communication field.

Mentoring in the Community: Service Learning. Mentoring can occur in the traditional professor-student relationship, but the belief (see Warren & Sellnow, Chapter 7 in this volume) in the need for civic education (McDevitt, 2006; Murphy, 2004) is capable of moving teaching/mentoring from the deliberative college or high school classroom into wider arenas such as political discussion with one's friends, family, and coworkers and to community volunteerism (e.g., service learning). Service learning entails learning by doing and interacting with members of one's community within particular, supervised contexts. Barnett (1996) defines service learning as "integrating community service with academic instruction, emphasizing critical reflection and civic responsibility" (p. 15), as she discerns that such service corroborates the community college mission of teaching and serving the local community.

An important (and often overlooked) dimension of mentoring others one-on-one and via service learning projects is the effect of the exchange of ideas on our growth as professors, family members, and individuals. Researcher-practitioners say that, as faculty, being involved in service learning aided their personal and professional development by (a) promoting more cohesive classroom interactions, (b) referring to students' past experiences to enhance the learning of current enrollees, (c) sharing the responsibility for creating knowledge with students and community partners, (d) promoting invigorated teaching generated by experimentation, (e) sparking new research opportunities, (f) increasing self-learning prompted by involvement with their community, and (g) making a difference where they live (Pinzon-Perez & Rodriguez, 2006; University of Nebraska, Omaha, Service-Learning Academy, 2008).

Unfortunately, in their overview of service learning and communication departments, Oster-Aaland, Sellnow, Nelson, and Pearson (2004) discovered that despite increases in the number of communication majors participating in service learning projects, only a few departments provide meaningful community projects with structured reflection as a component. As a result, it appears that we communication scholars are not allowing ourselves to reflect on or reflect for action along this dimension of out-of-class communication.

In this section, we have viewed teaching from the inside (introspection) outward (reflection, wholeness, mentoring). Before discussing specific incoherencies that present themselves in our teaching, it is essential to recognize that, in contrast to the more individually oriented perspectives regarding reflective teaching, as Ross, Cornett, and McCutcheon (1992) remind us, teacher education (and, I would add, self-development and graduate teaching assistant [GTA] training) "should be concerned with more than just the transformation of individuals into reflective practitioners, but also with the development of self-critical communities of teachers in the schools" (p. 179). Ross et al. argue that

> the failure to acknowledge the truly interactive nature of reflection has led to conceptions of reflective teacher education that fail to sufficiently address the impact that social and institutional contexts have on the teacher's practice. . . . Working from a Deweyan perspective, the aim of teacher education is not limited to the development of reflective individuals that work within schools as they presently exist, but *the reconstruction of experience that will lead to new understandings of self-as-teacher and the discovery (restoration) of community among teachers and others working in schools* [italics added]. (pp. 181, 186)

Hence, managing academic incoherencies requires the help that comes from interfacing, dialoguing, debating, lamenting, listening, and collaborating with others—including our students. Enlightenment emanating from a clearer awareness of self, laboring in conjunction with colleagues, and conceding the value of our students' life experiences and intelligence better equips us to promote engaging exchanges in the midst of attempts at incivility, diversity, and even physical distance (i.e., online teaching).

Specific Incoherencies

Up to this point, my approach to the chapter has been somewhat global in nature. My goal has been to provide an aerial view of the field of teaching expansive enough to reflect the depth of complexity and breadth of contradictions. We now move in for a closer vantage point of three areas where we as faculty, experienced as well as novice, may find ourselves entangled in a net of confusion. Teacher/student, student/student, student/class, and teacher/class communication can be incoherent due to two primary factors: (1) lack of clarity and/or (2) lack of cohesion. Verbal and nonverbal messages may be incoherent to us because they are not delivered clearly, the information is new to us, or the information is *complex and new to us*. Furthermore, we may wrestle with incoherence because the information shared does not fit within our personal or professional belief system. Along this same vein, what we convey as individuals and/or as disciplinary dogma may not mesh well with what our students perceive as truth. As a result, in our role as teachers, we must not only manage the teaching encounter by making sense of its sometimes disparate components but also bring some sense of order and reason to our students—that may entail partnering with our students to make the myriad ideas, experiences, and evolving technologies more intelligible.

INCIVILITY

Partnering with our students can sometimes in itself present us with incoherencies in the form of incomprehensible behavior. Research on disruptive behavior (also referred to as incivility, resistance, and reactive behavior) at the postsecondary level is gradually appearing in our scholarly journals (see Braxton & Bayer, 2005a; Richardson, 1999) and professional discussion boards (Bochner, 2008). Orlich, Harder, Callahan, Trevisan, and Brown (2004) examined the critical value of meeting teacher and student needs by establishing goals, routines, and classroom management systems, asserting that these should incorporate moral reasoning (citing Kohlberg), behavior modification (citing Skinner), desist strategies (citing Kounin & Wallen), reality therapy (citing Glasser), and needs (citing Maslow).

Before addressing incivility in the classroom, let us begin with a macro perspective addressing the behavior of the U.S. citizenry. Sypher (2004) vows that we are engaged in conflict on a "battleground of colliding value systems and contentious discourse" (p. 257) in our workplaces, which, as a result, contribute to what Forni (2002) depicts as the coarsening of America, including uncivil behavior such as bullying, sly remarks, rude e-mails, and emotional tirades. Civility moves beyond politeness to entail appropriately handling encounters with others, some degree of self-sacrifice (i.e., restraint), and considering the needs of the collective. Conversely, incivility encompasses rude or disrespectful behavior without regard for the needs and/or feelings of others. Of course, many of the individuals exposed to the stresses of family disputes, desk rage, and road rage enter our classrooms in the role of "student," exhibiting some of the identical behavior carried out at home, at work, and in their cars.

Classroom Incivility (CI). According to Boice (1996), we often discuss the intimidation and, in some cases, violence inflicted on high school teachers, but college professors rarely discuss incivility in higher education and, should the topic arise, we normally assign blame to some student we describe as not suitable for college work. The limited focus on postsecondary incivility may connect with our desire to, at least, pretend that we have control. Ironically, Palmer (1998) characterizes pretense as "another name for dividedness, a state that keeps us from cultivating the capacity of connectedness on which good teaching depends" (p. 86).

Twenty years ago, Long (1989) identified four traits that coincide with the personality types aggressive independents, aggressive dependents, passive independents, and passive dependents. Each trait/personality type has its own serious implications for higher education, as each style manifests different reactions to class material and teaching styles. Particularly noteworthy is the aggressive-independent personality often displayed as phobic, impulsive, obsessive-compulsive, and hysterical, because students manifesting these traits are most likely to spin out of control. Consistent with Long's findings, Dziuban (1996) discovered that 63% of the pupils identified as discipline problems were aggressive independents, and Cioffi (1995) indicated that 81% of the high school students placed in gifted/advanced courses were aggressive dependent.

About the same time that Long was investigating reactive behavior types and personality traits, Sandler (1991) chronicled the experiences of women in the classroom indicating, as part of addressing the chilly classroom climate for women and minorities, that it was time to address "how students (male and female) treat women and men faculty differently" (p. 6). Sandler discussed the dissonance created by the presence of a woman in a traditionally male position and attributed the differential (i.e., less respectful, more aggressive) treatment of female faculty to (a) society's devaluation of what women do in general, and (b) students' comfort factor—being uncomfortable in asserting oneself as a female or comfortable in challenging females.

When discussing authority and challenge as relational elements in the classrooms of Black male teachers and students, Alexander (2004) conceptualized resistance as challenging an un-inclusive educational system and/or constituting a test of teacher caring whereas Hendrix (2007b) set forth several viable explanations for disrespectful student of color behavior, when teacher and student are of the same racial heritage, "ranging from the innocuous, understandable behavior experienced as they grow into adulthood to a complex range of expected professor behavior [dependent] on how the student views his or her racial identity at [their] current stage of psychological, social, and racial development" (p. 92).

Of course, students are not the only potential source of inappropriate behavior. In some cases, it is the teacher who enacts negative behavior in the classroom.

Professor Classroom Incivility. The results of Boice's (1996) longitudinal study of 16 professors over 3 years indicated that students perceived CI in professors who were more than 5 minutes late to class, proffered surprise test items, belittled students, and were cold, distant teachers. Chory-Assad and Paulsel (2004) used the term *antisocial classroom behavior* in their research investigating student responses to perceived classroom injustice. They found that student behaviors could be placed in one of three categories: (a) indirect interpersonal aggressiveness, (b) hostility, or (c) student resistance. Indirect interpersonal aggressiveness constituted the act of harming a professor without engaging in face-to-face interaction (e.g., withholding information the instructor values, spreading rumors, facilitating the instructor's failure). Hostility involved verbal, face-to-face behavior aimed directly at a professor, whereas student resistance disrupted on-task teaching and learning behaviors with the primary intent of resisting an instructor's persuasive attempts to moderate their behavior. All three types of uncivil behavior were *in response to perceived injustices* carried out by a professor.

Also, related to the notion of professor CI, Kelsey, Kearney, Plax, and Allen (2001) found that teacher misbehaviors were interpreted as internal in origin, which they inferred to be more salient than the positive teacher behaviors that convey immediacy (e.g., smiling, direct eye contact, close proximity). In essence, they found that "prior claims that implied that immediate teachers can escape assignments of negative attributions are not supported in this investigation . . . teacher immediacy cannot undo students' perceptions and attributions of negative teacher behavior" (p. 23). Therefore, acting appropriately and effectively in response to student CI and self-monitoring our own behavior in the classroom are vital to maintaining our credibility and a classroom environment conducive to learning.

No matter how hostile and egregious the student's behavior, one must remain professional, which means in-kind verbally aggressive (and physically aggressive) behavior is not allowed. With this cornerstone in place, several scholars proffer instructor codes of conduct. Holton's model of conflict management (Holton, 1999) calls for a three-stage process for conflict resolution: (a) problem identification, (b) solution identification, and (c) solution implementation. Braxton and Bayer (2005b) indicate that our undergraduate classes should be carefully planned, important course details should be conveyed, materials should reflect the latest advancements in our field, students should be treated with respect, faculty members should avoid sexual relationships with students enrolled in their courses, and they should not arrive in class intoxicated from drugs and/or alcohol. Hendrix (2007b) offers 13 strategies,[2] including being careful not to overreact, determining what you consider disrespectful behavior at the onset of the term, and reminding your students of those expectations if you witness several incidents of concern, among others (for recommendations from K–12 teachers, see National Education Association, 2000).

DIVERSITY

Let us begin with a topic often reduced to an afterthought in our own teaching as well as in the training of the future professoriate. Faculty quite commonly overlook diversity as part of course design until presented with an obvious contrast to our expected classroom demographic makeup. We may become conscious of diversity when (a) one or several female students enroll in a typically male-dominated class, (b) one or several students of color enroll in a typically white-dominated class, (c) one or several obviously international students enroll in a typically U.S.—English as first language—course, (d) a non-Christian student or students enroll in a course where one would normally only discuss Christianity, if religion were discussed at all, (e) a visibly disabled (e.g., paraplegic) student enrolls in a course where we normally assume students are able-bodied and healthy, (f) we enter the classroom as young GTAs of similar age or younger than our students, (g) we enter a U.S. American classroom as international GTAs or professors with English as a second language, (h) we enter a predominantly white classroom as a GTAs or professors of color,[3] or (i) for the first time, we enter the classroom as white GTAs or professors at a predominantly minority college or university (historically black college or university [HBCU], Hispanic-serving institutions [HSI], tribal colleges and universities, etc.).

It is imperative to reinforce that efforts to attend to diversity are crucial to the education of all undergraduate and graduate students (in conjunction with our own professional/personal development) because, as stated earlier, per Nakayama (2008), we live in "an increasingly international and intercultural world" (p. 28). Consequently, we can no longer (erroneously) assume that being well versed in issues of diversity is only necessary in the presence of noteworthy degrees of observable "difference" within our respective classrooms and campuses. In fact, as Kuh et al. (2005) appropriately declare, in the absence of racial/ethnic campus diversity, some Documenting Effective Educational Practice (DEEP) institutions have recognized that it is critical to

> redoubl[e] efforts to incorporate diverse perspectives into the curriculum. Class discussions and assignments featured socioeconomic class, internationalism, global consciousness, and how various perspectives could result in theoretical and practical differences in how the world is viewed and problems are solved. (p. 292)

Culturally Relevant Teaching. When investigating successful teaching of African American children, Ladson-Billings (1994) defined culturally relevant teaching as that which "empowers students intellectually, socially, emotionally, and politically by using cultural referents to impart knowledge, skills, and attitudes," with those referents not merely being "vehicles for bridging or explaining the dominant culture" but also being "aspects of the curriculum in their own right" (p. 18). At least three levels of analysis contribute toward developing a philosophical orientation to diversity: (a) intrapersonal discovery; (b) insight guiding our interactions with others—neighbors, community members, staff, students, and academic colleagues; and (c) knowledge and understanding that lays a foundation for the selection of course content. In other words, it is not enough to incorporate an occasional lesson unit or discussion in our classrooms. An appreciation of the impact of diverse cultural experiences and world-views begins with situating oneself—a self-assessment of our mind-set (i.e., attitudes, values, and beliefs), co-cultural membership (gender, race, nationality, religion, sexual orientation, able-bodiedness, profession, etc.), and external perceptions of our dominant cultural identity within our native country and the world.

Once an understanding of how an individual's own situated "self" has been developed, it is appropriate to consider how our identity and status in the world affect communication with those we deem as similar to and others we perceive as different from us (see Hecht, 1998). At this juncture of analysis, issues of power will undoubtedly surface as a factor influencing our behavior toward others, and we must be cautious not to move into fallacious thinking—for instance, perceiving that we have a good relationship with the Hmong custodian in our building does not allow us to infer that we have an amicable bond with the Hmong faculty member in our department. Instead of creating such assumptions, we might be well-advised to ask ourselves questions such as the following: Am I comfortable with one person because of the status and socioeconomic differential (placing me on a higher plane) and subconsciously uncomfortable with the second individual as I experience difficulties correlating that particular individual as an equal or more advanced academic colleague? (See McPhail, in press, for a more thorough explication of such issues.)

Finally, as is the case of any new course preparation, we must become familiar with literature that expands the perspectives/experiences pertaining to the knowledge base of our class(es). Just as we prepare by learning the most recent relevant scholarship and placing the new information within a historical context, the same process applies to incorporating culturally relevant material into our coursework. A 2008 article by Johnson, Rich, and Cargile is of particular significance, as it offers three specific pedagogical interventions designed to mitigate white students' denial of the existence of racism and resistance to classroom discussion. In "Why Are You Shoving This Stuff Down Our Throats? Preparing Educators to Challenge Performances of White Racism," these three scholars outline interventions (i.e., anticipating student responses, understanding how students reify resistance, and critical self-inquiry) designed to move one's students past the "ceasefire" status of politically correct conversation that often quickly quells in-depth analysis and tends to disguise the undercurrent of tension just below the surface of our in-class exchanges.

We must learn, analyze, confer with others, internalize, and synthesize the material, keeping in mind the goals and objectives of our course, the makeup of the student enrollees, the impact of our mind-set and experience on the presentation of the subject matter, and the influence of our physical "body" in the classroom.[4] Teaching as the detached, objective individual is a facade that we must acknowledge and move out of; if we expect honesty from our students, as teachers, we must initiate an atmosphere of authenticity. Ironically, a new challenge is conveying this same authenticity online (see Wood & Fassett, 2003).

TECHNOLOGY AND ONLINE TEACHING

Thirteen years ago, Sandell, Stewart, and Stewart (1996) researched the introduction of computer-mediated communication (CMC) into the postsecondary classroom by investigating the use of electronic mail (e-mail), class listservs, and internet assignments in 13 classes enrolling more than 700 students across several disciplines. They found that students with a positive attitude toward CMC ended up with a more positive attitude toward their class and, conversely, students with negative attitudes toward computerized assignments and correspondence disliked their course. On a cautionary note, Sandell et al. warned that students may resist communication technologies but, since they are "vitally important in the business world," faculty should "incorpo[rate] into classes interactivity that forces students to get on-line" (p. 72). They then briefly mentioned several problems faculty encountered (e.g., student reluctance, low use of e-mail in courses meeting on a frequent basis) but did not outline difficulties experienced by faculty in learning and/or incorporating such technology. After discovering online distance learning faculty in ambiguous, ill-defined roles, Easton (2003) portrayed the use of technology as involving a paradigm shift regarding management of our time, classes, and student engagement.

A decade after Sandell et al.'s (1996) study, Allen (2006) identified the competing agendas of academic institutions—in particular, those large in size—as (a) the rush to provide technology such as general education and skills courses using distance and online learning, and (b) the goal of retaining and graduating students. Concomitant with these competing agendas, a debate rages over the value of online coursework in particular and online degrees in general (Adams & DeFleur, 2006). Considering the presence of technology in preschool (Wei & Hendrix, 2009) and kindergarten classes (Hyun & Davis, 2005), the need to make sense of and become competent in the use of technology in a postsecondary environment is inevitable. The move from hard-copy instructional materials to computerized ancillary textbook resources is further proof of the unavoidable, despite findings such as Sellnow, Child, and Ahlfeldt's (2005) conclusion that students perceived technology supplements as less helpful than they initially anticipated.

In *Engaging the Online Learner*, Conrad and Donaldson (2004) present a detailed set of icebreakers, activities, and simulations that can be incorporated into online teaching. After discussing how to construct activities for online learners, these authors introduce a chapter on building students' skills in using technology. Interestingly, this and other texts, assume that faculty possess a technological knowledge base. If teachers do possess some knowledge, a logical question is, "How effectively are we incorporating technology into our classrooms?" After studying the use of presentation technology in the public speaking classroom, Cyphert (2007) called for a stronger integration of "visual, verbal, and haptic forms of communication" instead of presenting technology to public speaking students as a "subset of visual aids" (p. 168). So, when familiar with technological resources, teachers must decide how to incorporate them into traditional and online classrooms alike, including *what* CMC resources to use; *how* to employ online assignments to distinguish lower, upper, and graduate coursework; *whether* to set up the class for one-to-one, one-to-many, or both types of social networking; and, of course, *what* venues to employ in our efforts to express immediacy. In the 21st century, most teachers and/or our students face a series of incoherencies relative to technology ranging from having limited knowledge of various technologies to possessing advanced skills with limited convenient access to online resources.

Professional Development

Menges's (1996) research revealed that new and junior faculty are anxious about surviving their jobs, normally sacrifice their personal life and professional activities to focus on teaching,[5] feel dissonance regarding the time spent on teaching in contrast to their advancement heavily depending on research, undergo professional stress spilling over into their personal lives, and experience a sense of isolation. In the midst of all the aforementioned demands[6] outlined in this chapter and Menges's studies from a decade ago, it is clear that teachers often suffer from debilitating stress and burnout (also see Froyen, 1993). This was true prior to the dominant presence of technology on our campuses and is now exacerbated by a new set of expectations and assumptions that we are proficient in even the most recent software programs. As a result, leading a "balanced" life allowing professional and personal development is essential to our total well-being.

DEVELOPING THE TEACHING PROFESSION

Borrowing from Ross et al.'s (1992) notion of the usefulness of communal experiences, it is essential to consider not only how to improve our individual teaching but also the quality of teaching within our profession. In their overview of the scholarship of teaching (SoT), Kreber and Cranton (2000) lay out three perspectives—(1) SoT as discovery research leading to visible products such as publications, conference presentations, and text-books on teaching; (2) excellence in teaching as evidenced by outstanding teaching awards and student evaluations; and (3) the application of educational theory to teaching practice. These scholars then contend that an accurate view of SoT "includes both ongoing learning about teaching and the demonstration of teaching knowledge" grounded in the perception of teachers as adult learners (p. 478). McCroskey, Richmond, and McCroskey (2002) argue that the scholarship of teaching and learning (SoTL) is now being accepted as "on par with the Scholarship of Research" in "response to the recognition that many college professors are less than fully competent teachers" (p. 383). The scholarship of teaching and learning (SoTL), as defined by Shulman (1999), is research on teaching that becomes public and subject to critical assessment by other teachers and that can be used as a foundation on which one's colleagues can build (also see McKinney, 2007). Hutchings (2003) adds to these definitions the importance of meta-analysis, deep engagement, listening to students, and detailed contextualization of the teaching environment. Darling (2003) further clarifies the SoTL by explaining that it is

> work that encourages an empirical examination of teaching in relation to student learning. It is distinct from scholarly teaching in that it goes beyond teaching well, even superbly, to participating in a focused inquiry process and reflective practice about one's own teaching. (p. 47)

More specific to our discipline, Darling (2003) then introduces the scholarship of teaching and learning in communication (SoTL/C) as akin to traditional communication education work in its focus on "how to best teach/learn communication" and as reminiscent of instructional communication scholars' ability to "examine the ways in which communication functions in a variety of pedagogical contexts." But ultimately, SoTL/C is unlike either, because it "merges the inquiry process with the teacher/scholar's *own* teaching," thereby "examin[ing] that teaching in light of the student learning that happens as a result" (pp. 47–48).

We are capable of advancing our profession by enhancing the quality of our teaching. Such enhancement requires a respect for the teaching profession, which facilitates an appreciation and understanding of pedagogical principles. Learning pedagogical principles (rather than, e.g., assuming anyone who earns good grades can teach); investigating teaching—ours and that of others; and helping provide useful, empirically grounded findings (incorporating a variety of methodological approaches) capable of benefitting the teaching of our colleagues are steps we can take not only to improve the caliber of our instruction but to grow our research skills and disciplinary content knowledge.

DEVELOPING OURSELVES

Somewhere and somehow in between learning and preparing to teach, reconceptualizing our teaching (for the more experienced faculty members), grading assignments, mentoring, keeping abreast of the newest developments in our field, and so on, there must be time devoted to self-development. One means of accomplishing such development is sharing our scholarship at professional conferences.[7] Our conference participation can occur on many levels. Directly related to the conference, we may participate by attending panels, probing panelists during question/answer periods, supporting business meetings, serving as an officer or in some other official capacity for regional or national associations, being a panelist (paper or roundtable), offering reviewer critique, and so forth.

Hickson (2006) extends our understanding of the value of conference attendance by submitting that

> professionalism requires that we become and remain active in our field of study. We do that by maintaining membership in our professional national and regional associations . . . [which give] opportunities for us to listen to the work of others, present our own research, access the most current information in the discipline, organize programs and interest groups, and become part of a network of lifelong professional and personal friends. (p. 465)

His observations set forth two levels of participation: (1) actual conference participation in the sharing/debating/co-construction of scholarship and (2) the communal aspect grounded in the collective experience of one's profession that brings about a consciousness allowing for mentoring, networking, and even commiserating.

Professional development cannot be fully realized by sequestering ourselves in a campus office, locked library carrel, or home study to review the latest journal issues and recently published texts. Individual study only partially represents the process of remaining current in our disciplinary knowledge; operating as an active, valuable member of our profession; and successfully contributing to the communities in which we live. Research findings and pedagogical principles must be tested, critiqued, and amended based on application and subsequent discussion with our peers, students, and even family. Sharing how we process information and being aware of alternate interpretations is central to gaining a broad, rather than myopic perspective that we can, in turn, hold up for our students' inspection to enhance their critical thinking as well as promote their intellectual maturity and holistic growth.

Conclusion

> We are akin to caterpillars, all of us. At some critical moment through our own will power or through the assistance of others we enter a chrysalis, evolve through an amorphous state, and emerge changed. (McEntee, 2003, p. 102)

We live and must teach in a super complex world with steadily increasing demands on our time and mounting expectations relative to what we should know and be able to impart to our students. Reflective and holistic teaching are discussed as approaches to maintaining an outlook that will reduce stress, promote and maintain high caliber instruction, and impart some degree of balance across our personal and professional lives. Three specific incoherencies (i.e., classroom incivility, diversity, and technology and online teaching) are explored along with two dimensions of professional development (i.e., the scholarship of teaching and learning and conference participation).

In this chapter, I have responded to one implicit question that inherently reflects the complex milieu of teaching: How do we manage the incoherencies of our life—professional and personal—well enough to sustain mental and physical well-being and a healthy personal life and to contribute effectively to the teaching profession? The answer appears to lie somewhere in the communal experience—be that communing spiritually with a greater power (Baesler, 2009), ensuring time for family and friends, joining circles of trust (see Palmer, 2004), actively participating at professional conferences, sharing knowledge in the capacity of consultant (Beebe, 2007; Plax, 2006), and/or becoming part of a research team. Removing ourselves from isolation and presenting an authentic self—frailties and all—in the presence of others who reciprocate is central to decreasing doubts and stress while increasing our ability to perform at our very best in the midst of frequently incoherent circumstances.

Notes

1. I know that my directive is to discuss what one must do to be an effective *communication* professor but, of course, I can't discuss teaching communication well without discussing issues associated with teaching in general. So I find myself in the intersection where communication education and instructional communication overlap.

2. These strategies are designed to assist professors of color confronted with uncivil behavior from students with whom they share the same racial heritage; however, many of these guidelines can be applied to untoward behavior in general.

3. I would argue that GTAs, instructors, and professors of color would possess a sense of the challenges associated with establishing their credibility in a

predominantly white classroom/institution given the history of strained race relations in the United States. The extent of the challenges and how to address them, however, might not be clear to these individuals.

4. Recommended readings include Banks and McGee Banks (2006), Beauboeuf-Lafontant and Augustine (1996), Boyer (1990), Braithwaite and Thompson (1999), Gonzalez, Houston, and Chen (2003), Hendrix (2007a), Jackson and Hendrix (2003), McKeachie and Svinicki (2006), Rosenblum and Travis (2008), Svinicki (2004), Tokarczyk and Fay (1993), TuSmith and Reddy (2002), Valverde (2008), and Wu (2002).

5. Research I institutions may give priority and expect more time to be devoted to empirical investigations rather than teaching.

6. Although not addressed within this chapter, yet another responsibility is to serve as a model of ethical behavior and decision making as well as to encourage such in our students.

7. Teaching portfolios, peer assessment, scholarly publications, community and professional service, earning tenure (Defleur, 2007), and posttenure professional engagement are all potential areas related to professional development. However, due to space limitations, the discussion in this chapter revolves around the SoTL and conference participation.

References

Adams, J., & DeFleur, M. H. (2006). The acceptability of online degrees earned as a credential for obtaining employment. *Communication Education, 55,* 32–45.

Alexander, B. K. (2004). Negotiating cultural identity in the classroom. In M. Fong & R. Chuang (Eds.), *Communicating ethnic and cultural identity* (pp. 329–343). Lanham, MD: Rowman & Littlefield.

Allen, T. H. (2006). Is the rush to provide on-line instruction setting our students up for failure? *Communication Education, 55,* 122–156.

Arduini, T. (2004). The songbird in the superstore: How the spirit enters the classroom. In D. Denton & W. Ashton (Eds.), *Spirituality, action, and pedagogy: Teaching from the heart* (pp. 9–20). New York: Peter Lang.

Baesler, E. J. (2009). Prayer life of a professor. *New Directions for Teaching and Learning, 120,* 9–16.

Banks, J. A., & McGee Banks, C. (2006). *Multicultural education: Issues and perspectives* (6th ed.). Hoboken, NJ: Wiley.

Barnett, L. (1996). Service learning: Why community colleges? *New Directions for Community Colleges, 93,* 7–15.

Beauboeuf-Lafontant, T., & Augustine, D. S. (Eds.). (1996). *Facing racism in education* (2nd ed.). Cambridge, MA: Harvard Educational Review.

Beebe, S. A. (2007). What do communication trainers do? *Communication Education, 56,* 249–254.

Bochner, A. (2008, August 7). *Things that boggle my mind.* Message posted to Communication Research and Theory Network (CRTNET) at CRTNET@Lists .psu.edu

Boice, B. (1996). Classroom incivilities. *Research in Higher Education, 37,* 453–486.

Boyer, E. L. (1990). *Scholarship reconsidered: Priorities of the professoriate.* San Francisco: Jossey-Bass.

Braithwaite, D. O., & Thompson, T. L. (Eds.). (1999). *Handbook of communication and people with disabilities: Research and application.* Mahwah, NJ: Lawrence Erlbaum.

Braxton, J. M., & Bayer, A. E. (Eds.). (2005a). *Addressing faculty and student classroom improprieties* (New Directions for Teaching and Learning, Vol. 99). San Francisco: Jossey-Bass.

Braxton, J. M., & Bayer, A. E. (2005b). Toward a code of conduct for undergraduate teaching. In J. M. Braxton & A. E. Bayer (Eds.), *Addressing faculty and student classroom improprieties* (New Directions for Teaching and Learning, Vol. 99, pp. 47–55). San Francisco: Jossey-Bass.

Buell, C. (2004). Models of mentoring in communication. *Communication Education, 53,* 56–73.

Chisholm, M. (2008, September). Why I became a teacher: The community college perspective [Special issue]. *Spectra, 44*(8), 8.

Chory-Assad, R. M., & Paulsel, M. L. (2004). Classroom justice: Student aggression and resistance as reactions to perceived unfairness. *Communication Education, 53,* 253–273.

Cioffi, D. H. (1995). *A description of reactive behavior patterns in gifted adolescents.* Unpublished doctoral dissertation, University of Central Florida, Orlando.

Clysdale, T. (2009, January 23). Wake up and smell the new epistemology. *Chronicle of Higher Education,* pp. B7–B9.

Conrad, R., & Donaldson, J. A. (2004). *Engaging the online learner: Activities and resources for creative instruction.* San Francisco: Jossey-Bass.

Cyphert, D. (2007). Presentation technology in the age of electronic eloquence: From visual aid to visual rhetoric. *Communication Education, 56,* 168–192.

Darling, A. (2003). Scholarship of teaching and learning in communication: New connections, new directions, new possibilities. *Communication Education, 52,* 47–49.

Darling, A. (2008, September). Why I became a teacher: The large school perspective [Special issue]. *Spectra, 44*(8), 10, 12.

Davidson, M. N., & Foster-Johnson, L. (2001). Mentoring in the preparation of graduate researchers of color. *Review of Educational Research, 71,* 549–574.

Defleur, M. L. (2007). Raising the question #5: What is tenure and how do I get it? *Communication Education, 56,* 106–112.

Dillard, C. (2006). *On spiritual striving: Transforming an African American woman's academic life.* Albany: State University of New York Press.

Dziuban, J. I. (1996). *A study of the distribution of reactive behavior patterns in elementary age children and their relationship to selected demographics.* Unpublished doctoral dissertation, University of Central Florida, Orlando.

Easton, S. S. (2003). Clarifying the instructor's role in online distance learning. *Communication Education, 52,* 87–106.

Feagin, J. R., Vera, H., & Imani, N. (1996). *The agony of education: Black students at White colleges and universities.* New York: Routledge.

Forni, P. M. (2002). *Choosing civility.* New York: St. Martin's Press.

Froyen, L. A. (1993). *Classroom management: The reflective teacher-leader* (2nd ed.). New York: Macmillan.

Goffman, E. (1959). *The presentation of self in everyday life.* Chicago: Anchor Books.

Gonzalez, A., Houston, M., & Chen, V. (Eds.). (2003). *Our voices: Essays in culture, ethnicity, and communication* (4th ed.). New York: Oxford University Press.

Gorsline, D., Holl, A., Pearson, J. C., & Child, J. T. (2006, December). It's more than drinking, drugs, and sex: College student perceptions of family problems. *College Student Journal, 40*(4), 802–806. Retrieved September 3, 2009, from www.higheredcenter.org/research/its-more-drinking-drugs-and-sex-college-student-perceptions-family-problems

Halpern, D. F. (2009). *Thinking and assessing critical thinking: Better thinking skills really can be a college outcome* (Society for the Teaching of Psychology Web Conference). Retrieved January 23, 2009, from http://mediasite.bsu.edu/BSU40/Catalog/default.aspx?cid=77e49b84–4c5a-4e76-b68e-1c81615f007e

Hamlet, J. (2009). Engaging spirituality and an authentic self in the intercultural communication class. *New Directions for Teaching and Learning, 120,* 25–33.

Hecht, M. L. (Ed.). (1998). *Communicating prejudice.* Thousand Oaks, CA: Sage.

Hendrix, K. G. (Ed.). (2007a). *Neither white nor male: Female faculty of color* (New Directions for Teaching and Learning, Vol. 110). San Francisco: Jossey-Bass.

Hendrix, K. G. (2007b). She must be trippin': The secret of disrespect from students of color toward faculty of color. In K. G. Hendrix (Ed.), *Neither white nor male: Female faculty of color* (New Directions for Teaching and Learning, Vol. 110, pp. 85–96). San Francisco: Jossey-Bass.

Hickson, M., III. (2006). Raising the question #4: Why bother attending conferences? *Communication Education, 55,* 464–468.

Holton, S. A. (1999). After the eruption: Managing conflict in the classroom. In S. M. Richardson (Ed.), *Promoting civility: A teaching challenge* (New Directions for Teaching and Learning, Vol. 77, pp. 59–68). San Francisco: Jossey-Bass.

Hutchings, P. (2003). The scholarship of teaching and learning in communication: A few words from the Carnegie Academy. *Communication Education, 52,* 57–59.

Hyun, E., & Davis, G. (2005). Kindergartners' conversations in a computer-based technology classroom. *Communication Education, 54,* 118–135.

Jackson, R., II, & Hendrix, K. G. (Eds.). (2003). Racial, cultural, and gendered identities in educational contexts: Communication perspectives on identity negotiation [Special issue]. *Communication Education, 52.*

Jamieson, J. (2009). *The BET Honors.* Retrieved March 28, 2009, from www.bet.com/Specials/bethonors09/bethonors09_videos/bethonors09_video_FullSpeeches.htm?episodeid=2666&playerid=betawards08&videoindex=3

Johnson, J. R., Rich, M., & Cargile, A. C. (2008). Why are you shoving this stuff down our throats? Preparing educators to challenge performances of White racism. *Journal of International and Intercultural Communication, 1,* 113–135.

Kalbfleisch, P. J., & Keyton, J. (1995). Power and equality in mentoring relationships. In P. J. Kalbfleisch & M. J. Cody (Eds.), *Gender, power, and communication in human relationships* (pp. 189–222). Hillsdale, NJ: Lawrence Erlbaum.

Kelsey, D., Kearney, P., Plax, T. G., & Allen, T. H. (2001, November). *A test-retest of teacher misbehaviors.* Paper presented at the annual meeting of the National Communication Association, Atlanta, GA.

Killion, J. P., & Todnem, G. R. (1991). A process for personal theory building. *Educational Leadership, 48,* 14–16.

Korthagen, F., & Wubbels, T. (1991, April). *Characteristics of reflective practitioners: Towards an operationalization of the concept of reflection.* Paper presented at the annual meeting of the AERA, Chicago.

Kreber, C., & Cranton, P. A. (2000). Exploring the scholarship of teaching. *Journal of Higher Education, 71,* 476–495.

Kuh, G. D., Kinzie, J., Schuh, J. H., Whitt, E. J., & Associates. (2005). *Student success in college: Creating conditions that matter.* San Francisco: Jossey-Bass.

Ladson-Billings, G. (1994). *The dreamkeepers: Successful teachers of African American children.* San Francisco: Jossey-Bass.

Light, G., & Cox, R. (2008). *Learning and teaching in higher education: The reflexive professional.* Thousand Oaks, CA: Sage.

Liston, D. P., & Zeichner, K. M. (1996). *Culture and teaching.* Mahwah, NJ: Lawrence Erlbaum.

Long, W. A., Jr. (1989). Personality and learning: 1988 John Wilson memorial address. *Focus on Learning Problems in Math, 11,* 1–16.

Lowman, J. (1984). *Mastering the techniques of teaching.* San Francisco: Jossey-Bass.

McCroskey, L. L., Richmond, V. P., & McCroskey, J. C. (2002). The scholarship of teaching and learning: Contributions from the discipline of communication. *Communication Education, 51,* 383–391.

McDevitt, M. (2006). Deliberative learning: An evaluative approach to interactive civic education. *Communication Education, 55,* 247–264.

McEntee, G. H. (2003). Growing reflective practitioners. In G. H. McEntee, J. Appleby, J. D. Grant, S. Hole, P. Silva, & J. W. Check (Eds.), *At the heart of teaching: A guide to reflective practice* (pp. 102–119). New York: Teachers College Press.

McKeachie, W. J., & Svinicki, M. (2006). *McKeachie's teaching tips: Strategies, research, and theory for college and university teachers* (12th ed.). Boston: Houghton-Mifflin.

McKinney, K. (2007). *Enhancing learning through the scholarship of teaching and learning: The challenges and joys of juggling.* San Francisco: Anker.

McPhail, M. L. (in press). Dark menexenus: Black opportunism in an age of white anxiety. *Southern Communication Journal.*

Menges, R. J. (1996). Experiences of newly hired faculty. In L. Richlin (Ed.), *To improve the academy* (Vol. 15, pp. 169–182). Stillwater, OK: New Forums Press and the Professional and Organizational Development Network in Higher Education.

Miller, R. (2000). *Caring for a new life: Essays on holistic education.* Brandon, VT: Foundation for Educational Renewal.

Miller, R. (2006). *Campus confidential: The complete guide to the college experience by students for students.* San Francisco: Jossey-Bass.

Moore, T. (2005). Educating for the soul. In J. P. Miller, S. Karsten, D. Denton, D. Orr, & I. C. Kates (Eds.), *Holistic learning and spirituality in education: Breaking new ground* (pp. 9–15). Albany: State University of New York Press.

Morreale, S. P., Osborn, M. M., & Pearson, J. C. (2000). Why communication is important: A rationale for the centrality of the study of communication. *Journal of the Association for Communication Administration, 29,* 1–25.

Murphy, T. A. (2004). Deliberative civic education and civil society: A consideration of ideals and actualities in democracy and communication education. *Communication Education, 53,* 74–91.

Nakayama, T. (2008, March). New Journal of International and Intercultural Communication launches. *Spectra, 44*(3), 1, 28.

National Education Association. (2000). *Dilemma: How do you handle disruptive students?* Retrieved March 29, 2009, from http://findarticles.com/p/articles/mi_qa3617/is_200011/ai_n8916327

Norlander-Case, K. A., Reagan, T. G., & Case, C. W. (1999). *The professional teacher: The preparation and nurturance of the reflective practitioner.* San Francisco: Jossey-Bass.

Orbe, M. P. (2004). Negotiating multiple identities within multiple frames: An analysis of first-generation college students. *Communication Education, 53,* 131–149.

Orlich, D. C., Harder, R. J., Callahan, R. C., Trevisan, M. S., & Brown, A. H. (2004). *Teaching strategies: A guide to effective instruction* (7th ed.). Boston: Houghton-Mifflin.

Orr, D. (2005). Minding the soul in education: Conceptualizing and teaching the whole person. In J. P. Miller, S. Karsten, D. Denton, D. Orr, & I. C. Kates (Eds.), *Holistic learning and spirituality in education: Breaking new ground* (pp. 87–99). Albany: State University of New York Press.

Oster-Aaland, L. K., Sellnow, T. L., Nelson, P. E., & Pearson, J. C. (2004). The status of service learning in departments of communication: A follow-up study. *Communication Education, 53,* 348–356.

Palmer, P. J. (1998). *The courage to teach: Exploring the inner landscape of a teacher's life.* San Francisco: Jossey-Bass.

Palmer, P. J. (2004). *A hidden wholeness: The journey toward an undivided life.* San Francisco: Jossey-Bass.

Pike, G. R., Kuh, G. D., & Massa-McKinley, R. C. (2008). First-year students' employment, engagement, and academic achievement: Untangling the relationship between work and grades (Report). *NASPA Journal, 5*(4). Retrieved June 1, 2009, from http://publications.naspa.org/cgi/viewcontent.cgi?article=2011&context=naspajournal

Pinzon-Perez, H., & Rodriguez, M. (2006). Service learning in the classroom: Faculty and student viewpoints. *Exchanges: The Online Journal of Teaching and Learning in the CSU.* Retrieved April 19, 2009, from www.calstate.edu/ITL/exchanges/print/print_1247.html

Plax, T. G. (2006). Raising the question #2: How much are we worth? Estimating fee for services. *Communication Education, 55,* 242–246.

Reinarz, A. G., & White, E. R. (Eds.). (2001). *Beyond teaching to mentoring* (New Directions for Teaching and Learning, Vol. 85). San Francisco: Jossey-Bass.

Richardson, S. M. (Ed.). (1999). *Promoting civility: A teaching challenge* (New Directions for Teaching and Learning, Vol. 77). San Francisco: Jossey-Bass.

Rizer, M. (December 16, 2005). When students are parents. *Chronicle of Higher Education, 52,* 17. Retrieved June 1, 2009, from Educator's Reference Complete via Gale Web site: http://find.galegroup.com.ezproxy.memphis.edu/itx/start.do?prodId=PROF

Rosenberg, M. (1979). *Conceiving the self.* New York: Basic Books.

Rosenblum, K., & Travis, T.-M. (2008). *The meaning of difference: American constructions of race, sex and gender, social class, sexual orientation, and disability.* Boston: McGraw-Hill.

Ross, E. W., Cornett, J. W., & McCutcheon, G. (1992). *Teacher personal theorizing: Connecting curriculum practice, theory, and research.* Albany: State University of New York Press.

Rubin, D. L., & Turk, D. (1997). The basic communication course: Options for accommodating non-native speakers of mainstream North American English. *Journal of the Association for Communication Administrators, 2,* 140–148.

Sandell, K. L., Stewart, R. K., & Stewart, C. K. (1996). Computer-mediated communication in the classroom: Models for enhancing student learning. In L. Richlin (Ed.), *To improve the academy* (Vol. 15, pp. 59–74). Stillwater, OK: New Forums Press and the Professional and Organizational Development Network in Higher Education.

Sandler, B. R. (1991). Women faculty at work in the classroom, or, why it still hurts to be a woman in labor. *Communication Education, 40,* 6–15.

Schon, D. A. (1983). *The reflective practitioner: How professionals think in action.* New York: Basic Books.

Sellnow, D. D., Child, J. T., & Ahlfeldt, S. L. (2005). Textbook technology supplements: What are they good for? *Communication Education, 54,* 243–253.

Sheckels, T. F. (2008, September). Why I became a teacher: The small school perspective [Special issue]. *Spectra, 44*(8), 9, 11.

Shulman, L. S. (1987). Knowledge and teaching: Foundations of the new reform. *Harvard Educational Review, 57,* 8.

Shulman, L. S. (1999). Taking learning seriously. *Change, 31,* 10–17.

Sparks-Langer, G. M., & Colton, A. B. (1991). Synthesis of research on teachers' reflective thinking. *Educational Leadership, 48,* 37–44.

Svinicki, M. D. (2004). *Learning and motivation in the postsecondary classroom.* San Francisco: Anker Press.

Sypher, B. D. (2004). Reclaiming civil discourse in the workplace. *Southern Communication Journal, 69,* 257–269.

Tokarczyk, M. M., & Fay, E. A. (Eds.). (1993). *Working-class women in the academy: Laborers in the knowledge factory.* Boston: University of Massachusetts Press.

TuSmith, B., & Reddy, M. T. (Eds.). (2002). *Race in the classroom: Pedagogy and politics.* Piscataway, NJ: Rutgers University Press.

University of Nebraska, Omaha, Service-Learning Academy. (2008). Faculty faq. Retrieved May 26, 2009, from www.unomaha.edu/servicelearning/faq_faculty.php

Valverde, L. A. (2008). *Latino change agents in higher education: Shaping a system that works for all.* San Francisco: Jossey-Bass.

Wadsworth, B. C., Hecht, M., & Jung, E. (2008). The role of identity gaps, discrimination, and acculturation in international students' educational satisfaction in American classrooms. *Communication Education, 57,* 64–87.

Wei, F. F., & Hendrix, K. G. (2009). Gender differences in preschool children's recall of competitive and noncompetitive computer mathematics games. *Learning, Media and Technology, 34,* 27–43.

West, R. (2008, September). In the classroom [Special issue]. *Spectra, 44*(8), 1.

Witt, P. L., & Behnke, R. R. (2006). Anticipatory speech anxiety as a function of public speaking assignment type. *Communication Education, 55,* 167–177.

Wood, A. F., & Fassett, D. L. (2003). Remote control: Identity, power, and technology in the communication classroom. *Communication Education, 52,* 286–296.

Wu, F. H. (2002). *Yellow: Race in America beyond Black and White.* New York: Basic Books.

Communication Textbooks 6

From the Publisher to the Desk

Matt McGarrity

G iven a broad enough definition, one can trace the topic of this chapter, communication textbooks, back to the rhetorical handbooks of antiquity. While some Greek rhetorics are lost to time, successful Roman rhetorics such as the *Rhetorica ad Herennium* and *De Inventione* continued to be used in classrooms hundreds of years after their creation. The history of communication textbook analysis is only slightly shorter. Isocrates railed against the inflexibility of the handbook tradition in his *Against the Sophists;* we can also look to our own disciplinary roots to see similar critiques. Shortly after breaking away from the National Council of Teachers of English (NCTE) in 1914 to establish the National Association of Academic Teachers of Public Speaking (NAATPS), our National Communication Association (NCA) predecessors found themselves discussing teaching and textbooks. Such sustained attention makes sense when considering that textbooks serve as a discipline's public face. In communication, they introduce undergraduates to new concepts, provide guidance to first-time teaching assistants (TAs), and serve as reference books for those within and outside the discipline. As such, textbooks highlight how we see ourselves as a discipline and how we project that self-conception to others.

Of course, a number of disciplines investigate their textbooks' roles and content. Most notably, the field of education has a deep research literature on a wide range of issues. Some recent examples include studies into histories of textbooks (Hughes, 2007; Moreau, 2004; Sanchez, 2007; Von Heyking, 2006), student-textbook interactions (Clariana & Koul, 2008; Hiebert & Sailors, 2009; Johnston & Huczynski, 2006), and textbooks and political identity (De la Caba Collado & Lopez Atxurra, 2006; Rodden, 2006; Torsti, 2007), as well as gender (Macgillivray & Jennings, 2008; Temple, 2005). Additionally, the sciences contribute to our knowledge about textbooks. For example, Roth, Pozzer-Ardenghi, and Han (2005) examined how students learn from visual representations of data. English composition seems to bear the closest similarity to communication in its efforts to understand how students interact with textbooks. Gale and Gale's (1999) edited volume on the introductory English composition textbook, *(Re)visioning Composition Textbooks: Conflicts of Culture, Ideology, and Pedagogy,* provides a number of models for research into the introductory public speaking textbook. In this chapter, I draw on these related fields to map the scholarship on communication textbooks. After presenting a model for researching communication textbooks, I summarize the research and opportunities for new study in the areas of textbook production, content, usage, and history. I conclude with a discussion of the nature of research on communication textbooks.

A Model for Researching Communication Textbooks

The communication textbook is a multifaceted artifact embedded within a number of overlapping contexts. I have classified the existing disparate research into four broad categories: (1) the production of communication textbooks, (2) communication textbook content, (3) communication textbook usage, and (4) the histories of communication textbooks. Such an approach opts for a "life cycle" metaphor to preserve the complexity of how textbooks emerge and function. Any one element of a textbook is affected by the others. A design decision at the production level affects the content of the book and thus, possibly, its use. For example, there are a number of content analyses that track gender equity in textbooks at the level of the photograph. The inclusion of these photos was not a random decision; it was made within the context of a publishing company. That decision thus has the potential to reinforce negative assumptions about gender roles. Other reviews of scholarship on textbooks have adopted similar life-cycle approaches (Gale & Gale, 1999; Johnsen, 1993). Let us overview each category.

Textbooks are developed within disciplinary and publishing contexts. The author, industry, and subject matter operate within a relational matrix. As a for-profit industry, publishers respond to perceived demands from their market—the communication discipline—and tap insiders to produce instructional texts. These authors generate drafts, which undergo editing to render them more marketable, before turning to industry representatives who sell the texts office door to office door. Teachers and students thus come to a text that already bears the marks of many hands. Communication research in this area seeks to illuminate the often unseen processes of production.

Understanding textbooks' industrial origins allows for a richer study of their content. The textbook is an act of communication; it explains theories and recommends communication skills to readers in particular ways.

Studies of textbook content examine and critique these representations. Additionally, work in this area examines how textbooks reflect larger ideological structures, such as gender and race. The underlying concern is that negative textbook portrayals can encourage negative reader perceptions. Content analyses are the most common type of study in the research literature on communication textbooks.

Production and content certainly affect usage. Yet student readers engage the text in ways unforeseen, in some instances undermining the author's careful planning. As publishers have reached out to students, they have created an entire secondary level of ancillary materials aimed at further shaping the reader's usage through video clips, exercises, and practice exams. Of course, students are not the sole users of textbooks. Both textbooks and instructors teach the students. The instructor and the textbook may maintain a friendly relationship, a coolly cordial one, or an overtly hostile one; regardless, that relationship is performed regularly in class. Research in this area traces all manner of usage, from a textbook's readability to teachers' adoption decisions.

Finally, textbooks evolve over time. We could even say that textbooks serve as the trilobites of the disciplinary fossil record. While they probably do not trigger the extraordinary events of the age in the same way a revolutionary book or theorist might, they do record daily pedagogical activities. Looking back at the development of these ideas can tell us much about our discipline's present condition and the current cohort of textbooks. Some studies in this area have explored the changing narratives textbooks tell about the communication discipline.

The Production of Communication Textbooks

Clearly, textbook authors shape the nature and direction of their texts; yet there are also the many workers who contract, design, and market communication textbooks to communication teachers. The U.S. Government Accountability Office (2005) reported that the cost of textbooks increased 186% between 1986 and 2004 due largely to the added cost of textbook supplements. Yet such pricing strategies have not saved the industry from the tumult of financial troubles and mergers. Workers in the industry, who may or may not have a background in communication, make design and marketing decisions that fundamentally shape the final product. Once produced, the textbook is then placed in the hands of advertisers and textbooks representatives who influence the perception and implementation of the text.

There is surprisingly little research on the industry and its impact on the resulting communication textbooks. We do know that authors and publishers maintain complicated relationships. In a short opinion piece,

Mencher (1996) described his own experiences as an author of a journalism textbook, noting a problematic editorial influence. McGarrity (2005) interviewed public speaking textbook authors about their industry experiences. In these interviews, authors articulated a market pressure that influenced the design of their textbooks. Based on his experiences as a textbook writer and consultant, Winterowd (1989) discussed some of the unwritten practices that occur prior to entering into an agreement with a publisher, as well as some items to keep in mind when signing the contract. Newburger, Smith, and Pledger (1993) provided recommendations for working with publishing houses to produce custom-designed introductory textbooks. Unfortunately, all these accounts are anecdotal and/or opinion based. In preparing this review, I was unable to uncover any research that studied industrial influence on communication textbooks in a deeper, more systematic manner. Clearly, such research is needed.

OPPORTUNITIES FOR PRODUCTION RESEARCH

New research into communication textbook publishing might begin with questions about the organizational structures, language, and persons that affect content and design decisions. For example, one might investigate the organizational discourses of managers, editors, and marketing representatives to reveal some of the decision-making processes that shape textbooks. Since communication textbooks are written by disciplinary insiders but filtered through the publishing industry, it seems important to determine where and how these interests and priorities overlap and where they stand in divergence. Textbook authors themselves should also be studied more comprehensively. One could easily envision an excellent study that interviews textbooks authors and probes their rationales for the choices they made. Such knowledge would seem to be an almost essential counterpart to the many content analyses that critique the presence or absence of particular concepts (described below). Finally, authors and editors may have an ongoing relationship with each other but not with the teachers who make adoption decisions; this is the realm of the textbook representative. These representatives may or may not exert significant influence in terms of what books enjoy widespread use. But they certainly serve as intermediaries gauging the interest level of teachers and trying to respond with appropriate curricular materials.

The industrial side of textbooks can reveal intriguing aspects of the intellectual foundations of the discipline. Zebroski (1999) performed a fascinating study of composition textbook advertisements from the 1970s to the 1990s. Specifically, he turned to advertisements as a way of challenging the notion that expressivism became a dominant model for the teaching of composition in the late 1960s and early 1970s. For instance, in his review of expressivist pedagogy, Burnham (2001) wrote,

> Expressivism places the writer in the center, articulates its theory, and develops its pedagogical system by assigning highest value to the writer and her imaginative, psychological, social, and spiritual development and how that development influences individual consciousness and social behavior. (p. 19)

The established narrative posited that the expressivist movement reached its nadir in the late 1960s and early 1970s; conversely, Zebroski (1999) noted that the number of expressivist textbook advertisements did not reach their peak until 1985. His historical analysis of industrial documents upended a prevailing assumption about the discipline's intellectual trajectory.

Research into these publishing cultures might best be achieved through interviews with textbook authors, editors, and sales representatives or surveys of these populations. While her focus was not on understanding textbook production, Laura Prividera (2004) performed an exemplary analysis of teacher interview transcripts. After interviewing teachers about their teaching of diversity issues, she sorted the data to identify recurring themes. This type of ethnographic study of pedagogical decision makers would no doubt reveal a number of assumptions that remain hidden when simply examining the finished textbook.

It is a shame that little work has been done on the publishing industry's role in shaping textbooks. As we will see next, content analysis is the most prevalent type of research in communication textbooks. The starting point for many content analyses is the published text; yet these studies would be greatly enriched with a deeper understanding of the cultures and decision-making processes that gave rise to the texts. It is to textbook content that we now turn.

Communication Textbook Content

Textbooks are defined by their content; thus it is an obvious point of entry into the text. Perhaps because of this clear connection, investigations into content represent the largest body of published research on communication textbooks reviewed in this chapter. Questions here generally center on presence and/or absence; researchers track the different elements that are included or excluded from a text. Given the amount of research in this area, I have divided the section into the three most commonly studied topics: (1) communication theory and research, (2) gender, and (3) intercultural issues.

COMMUNICATION THEORY AND RESEARCH

Persistently, researchers report that textbooks lag behind or misrepresent communication theory and research. Such concerns have a long history. In

1977, Doolittle argued that communication textbooks failed to represent the current thinking about conflict. After identifying common theoretical themes in five popular interpersonal textbooks, Webb and Thompson-Hayes (2002) more recently concluded, "When theory was discussed in the textbooks, often it was presented in a simplistic manner, perhaps in an effort to present the material in a way students could readily understand" (p. 220). In their analysis of introductory course textbooks, Janusik and Wolvin (2002) argued, "The amount of space allotted for listening instruction is insufficient, and the quality of the content does not reflect current listening scholarship" (p. 188). Public relations textbooks also demonstrate a lack of contemporary research (Duffy, 2000).

Public speaking textbooks, in particular, are often accused of failing to reflect accurately contemporary communication research and theory. Hugenberg and Moyer (1998) rejected public speaking textbooks' advice because they found much of it to be "opinion-based, based on personal preference or personal experience" (p. 169). Allen and Preiss (1990) also claimed that public speaking textbooks, on average, failed to represent contemporary social science findings on effective persuasion. Turning from social scientific research to rhetorical theory, Frobish (2000) critiqued Stephen Lucas's textbook, *The Art of Public Speaking*, for not reflecting Kathleen Hall Jamieson's insights into modern eloquence. Jamieson's (1988) understanding of a new eloquence for the media age was premised on intimacy and disclosure rather than on formal logic and argument. Frobish (2000) argued that adopting Jamieson's (1988) theory would require emphasizing narrative as a structuring device, foregrounding the influence of television on audience expectations, and incorporating modern rhetorical theory.

Critics also argue that public speaking textbooks fail to adequately reflect all aspects of communication apprehension (CA) research. Before CA developed as the larger research frame, earlier scholars often studied aspects of speech anxiety as "stage fright." As far back as 1959, Clevenger and Phifer asserted that textbook coverage of stage fright was "fragmentary and incomplete" (p. 7). Thirty years later, Pelias (1989) similarly concluded, "A few textbooks devote considerable attention to CA; several make only brief reference to the phenomenon" (p. 51). More recently, Pearson, DeWitt, Child, Kahl, and Dandamudi (2007) tracked textbooks' coverage of CA. They found significant variation in the amount of space different textbooks devoted to aspects of CA. Nonetheless, overall coverage appeared to have increased from earlier studies.

As with theory and research, communication textbooks are often critiqued for insufficiently addressing ethical communication. Hess (1993) and Schwartzman (2004) both critiqued public speaking textbooks for spending far too little time discussing speakers' ethical obligations. Pearson, Child, Mattern, and Kahl (2006) identified common ethical topics and their coverage in different public speaking textbooks. They noted that textbook authors tended to offer ethical directives instead of examining ethics within contexts. This lack of nuance was also noted in Hartung's (1998) analysis of ethical discussions in technical communication textbooks.

GENDER

Communication textbooks' representations of gender continue to be problematic; while there may be numerical parity, significant power differences remain. Campbell (1991) argued that women are underrepresented in public speaking anthologies and as models in public speaking textbooks. Cawyer et al. (1994) concluded that while men and women are given equal coverage in introductory communication textbooks, men were often depicted in positions of power, thus reinforcing conventional gender roles. This finding is consistent with Hanson's (1999) study that surmised that the coverage of gender issues had improved, but texts continued to suggest a white male standard for effective delivery. Business communication textbooks might in fact do a better job of equally representing men and women, as was found by Pomerenke, Varner, and Mallar (1996). This cannot be said for public speaking textbooks. Gullicks, Pearson, Child, and Schwab (2005) conducted a content analysis of photographs in public speaking textbooks and discovered that men were pictured in positions of power more often than women.

INTERCULTURAL ISSUES

Communication research has canvassed textbooks to identify the complex manifestations of intercultural issues. Intercultural representations may be increasing numerically, but with mixed results. Webb et al. (2004) noted that the family communication textbooks they examined all addressed gender issues in similar ways, but texts varied significantly in how they attended to diversity issues; some texts devoted sizable portions of the texts to diversity examples, whereas others made little to no mention of diversity issues. Gullicks et al. (2005) found that multiple ethnicities were more likely to be shown in positions of power than Caucasians in public speaking textbooks. This appears to be an improvement over Kern-Foxworth's (1990) earlier study that identified few depictions of minorities in public relations textbooks.

Other analyses of intercultural coverage tend to be more overtly critical. Starck and Wyffels (1990), for example, concluded, "Journalism education, as reflected in this sampling of reporting textbooks, is ignoring or skimming the subject of intercultural reportage" (p. 44). Hardin and Preston (2001) reached a similar conclusion when looking at textbooks' coverage of disability reporting. Turning to technical writing, Miles (1997) pointed out that although technical communication textbooks were increasing their coverage of international issues, they exoticized the international "other" and framed foreigners as consumers of English discourse rather than as producers. Building on Miles (1997), Matveeva (2007) noted that while intercultural concepts had become a recognized part of technical communication, textbooks treated such issues superficially.

While we can examine how textbooks address intercultural themes, so too can we study the intercultural work textbooks are actually doing. For example, Chang, Holt, and Luo (2006) used two popular intercultural communication textbooks as a lens for examining the broader challenges of intercultural pedagogy. Miller (2002) looked at how traditional public speaking textbooks are used in other cultures. She noted that some elements of traditional U.S. textbooks did not work well in Kenyan culture. For example, ceremonial speaking was more common in Kenyan culture and demanded more attention than was given in most American textbooks. Kubota and Shi (2005) examined Chinese and Japanese junior high school language arts textbooks to identify the types of reading instruction provided. They argued that these texts encouraged a linear pattern of opinion writing but did not emphasize the importance of preview statements.

OPPORTUNITIES FOR CONTENT RESEARCH

Given the depth of the literature on textbook content, it is perhaps surprising that so much work remains to be done. Clearly, researchers have proven willing to perform content analyses on passages or pictures to determine a text's emphasis; however, there are relatively few interpretive and critical works that read textbook content as representative of larger discourses. Exceptionally, Clasen and Lee (2006) argued that public speaking textbooks operate with a suburban notion of politics. Such a focus makes public speaking textbooks blind to matters of political access and influence. In a similar interpretive vein, Rowan (1995) discussed the Belletristic influences on contemporary public speaking pedagogy.[1] By tracing the development of informative speaking pedagogy from the 18th century forward, Rowan argued that rather than focusing on the possible obstacles to audience understanding, public speaking textbooks continue to teach informative speaking using "ready-made 'solutions' or arrangement forms" (p. 237). Clasen and Lee (2006) and Rowan (1995) point to some of the interesting avenues for deep interpretative analysis of textbook content.[2]

As Clasen and Lee (2006) demonstrated, communication textbooks can be viewed through the lenses of class. In *Democratic Eloquence*, Cmiel (1990) studied the debates surrounding proper linguistic use in the 19th century. He touched on the role of communication skills training as a vehicle for class crossing. One wonders how much this border-crossing ethos remains, given the current emphasis on effectiveness in various communication contexts. Bloom (1996) explored how the English composition class was largely a middle-class enterprise. One could easily pose some troubling questions about how class operates in public speaking, interpersonal, or small group communication textbooks. Keshishian's (2005) study of class in communication textbooks serves as an excellent model to follow. She examined the priority given to competition and consumerism in intercultural textbooks and concluded that textbooks do not pay enough attention to the relationship between economies and cultures.

In addition to class, communication textbooks often weigh in on basic cultural issues. This takes on particular importance when culturally specific textbooks argue for normative communication practices. Public speaking textbooks are perhaps the most obvious example of this type of normative instruction (e.g., public speaking textbooks privilege certain ways of speaking over others). Hugenberg (1996) claimed that public speaking instruction expects students to become "Westernized." This critique was reinforced by Treinen and Warren (2001), who argued that the basic course desperately needs an antiracist pedagogy to overcome its current tendencies to ignore or exoticize difference. Neither Hugenberg (1996) nor Treinen and Warren (2001) actually proved or studied the power of such a normative framework; rather, they assumed that it exerted influence on students. Such an assumption is reasonable, but it demands much closer scrutiny. One study could easily chart out where and how students are encouraged to adopt specific Western practices. Even more telling would be a study that sought to understand how (if at all) this instruction influenced student behaviors in multicultural classrooms.

The communication discipline is made up of a number of subfields, and our textbooks follow suit. So it is entirely reasonable to study our textbook genres: the introductory text, public speaking text, interpersonal text, and so on. Doing so should lead to a set of content-specific questions. For example, Welch (1987) argued that writing textbooks rely on the rhetorical canon but ignore delivery, resulting in a lack of emphasis on the situatedness of writing. Welch serves as simply one example of how a good case study into a specific genre of textbook can move from the basic questions of presence and absence into an interpretive account that provides sound pedagogical advice. Returning to public speaking textbooks, we might ask how such textbooks address matters of argument invention, the most written about aspect of rhetoric in the classical tradition.

Studies of textbook content work with the tacit assumption that how a textbook discusses issues can shape how readers understand them. Yet to delve more deeply into this relationship, we need to examine how textbooks are actually being used in and out of the classroom. Production and content are vitally important contexts of the textbook's life cycle, but unless the book is used, its impact cannot be felt. Let us now turn to the complex event of using a communication textbook.

Communication Textbook Usage

Textbooks are designed to be used. Yet how exactly do students use our textbooks? How do teachers and TAs interact with these texts? The answers to these questions seem to be of tremendous importance to the study of communication textbooks. Unfortunately, such research requires some fairly extensive surveying, interviewing, and/or fieldwork. Perhaps as a result of these barriers, little has been done to trace how students and teachers use textbooks.

Readability studies have tried to understand textbooks from the students' perspective. Studies have used the Flesch, Fry, or Dunning scales (or a combination of all three) to assess readability based on sentence length and word or syllable complexity. Razek and Cone (1981) found that 10 of 12 popular business communication textbooks rated a college-level readability score. Schneider (1991) found that the 24 hybrid textbooks he examined ranged from an average 10th grade reading level up to a 14th grade level. Schneider (1992) found similar variability in the reading levels of public speaking and interpersonal textbooks, which he suggested allowed teachers to better select books appropriate to their students' reading level.

Apart from readability, there are few studies on student interactions with textbooks. Besser, Stone, and Nan (1999) surveyed 1,170 students to discover what they identified as helping them read textbooks effectively. They found that students were interested in the clarity of the writing and the presence of cues to help them interpret the writing. Interestingly, mass communication students were more likely to identify bad writing as an interference to learning and were more likely to rank highly clarifying structural elements (chapter summaries, charts and illustrations, etc.). Sellnow, Child, and Ahlfeldt (2005) reported that students found textbook technology supplements (e.g., self-guided quizzes, exercises, CD-ROM speech clips) to be less useful than expected. Technology supplements were perceived as more useful when they were an assigned part of the course rather than simply optional.

While we have no analyses of how teachers choose particular textbooks, we do have a number of guides for aiding that decision. Seidman (2003), for example, developed an organized overview of the different genres of presentation media textbooks as a guide for instructors of media courses. Tindell (1999) wrote a similar guide for selecting argumentation textbooks. Barker and Matveeva (2006) went beyond this book review approach and developed and tested a Burkean model for making adoption decisions. Combining course goals with Burke's (1945) pentad, they provided a system for charting and choosing textbooks based on pentadic ratios.

The rise of departmental publishing and in-house textbooks allows researchers to closely observe teacher-textbook interactions on a small scale. Ross (2003) examined how a particular program, the composition sequence at University of California at Irvine, developed an in-house textbook. Through an examination of multiple editions of the student writing guide, she traced a gradual retreat from the process-orientated pedagogy that the original edition was designed to support. Over the years, various community revisions to the common textbook reflected the teachers' commitment to a product orientation in writing pedagogy. That is, University of California–Irvine (UCI) had attempted to reform their program but failed to make sure that all the participants were deeply committed to the new vision. Consequently, small trade-offs here and there transformed the departmental textbook into a hybrid that reflected the conflicting pedagogical assumptions of the actual department instead of the more narrowly conceived reform agenda.

Questions of usage also raise questions of context. Our discipline supports a number of different learning contexts that can change how one interacts with a text. Erickson (2004), for example, reviewed four business communication textbooks for use with accounting students. She found most of the textbooks useful but noted a need for more writing instruction and less small group instruction. A special review forum in the Fall 1999 edition of *Communication Education* questioned the appropriate uses of a textbook in a class on performance. All the essays affirmed that the textbook does, indeed, have a place in the performance classroom. Yet they all seemed to indicate that the textbook by itself is insufficient, lacking ethical (Hess, 1999) and philosophical depth (Russ & McClish, 1999), or failing to attend closely enough to diversity (Yook, 1999) and mass mediated issues (Cole, 1999). Regrettably, I find the need to repeat here the argument that K–12 contexts are underrepresented in the academic literature. There have been few recent reviews and discussions of high school communication textbooks and/or the use of textbooks in high school settings (Allen, 1986; O'Keefe, 1992).

OPPORTUNITIES FOR USAGE RESEARCH

The field of education has produced some excellent book-length studies into textbook usage that point to some interesting avenues for communication research. LaSpina (1998) explored matters of design in a hotly debated social sciences textbook. Through eight chapters, he probed how text and image worked with and against each other in aiding student learning. Levin and Mayer (1993) detailed ways in which illustrations help students learn from a text. Woodward (1993) examined how illustrations function within texts. Future study into pictures and illustrations in communication textbooks might follow these leads and probe the educational work being done by such images. Such work seems especially important because of obvious connections to the robust fields of visual rhetoric and visual communication.

There are a few studies that report on student uses of textbooks through survey data but nothing with a significant qualitative dimension. Communication textbooks attempt to shape students' knowledge and, often, their communication choices; as such, we should work more diligently to peek into students' interactions with the text. While Janet Emig's (1971) seminal work, *The Composing Processes of Twelfth Graders*, does have its fair share of critics, her case study method sought to uncover how actual writers made decisions during their writing process. Emig recorded students as they were composing and had them voice out loud their entire thought process. Flower (1994) also borrowed this general protocol as a way of illuminating the composing process. Communication textbooks are overflowing with models for writing and speaking, yet we could be doing more to track how these models influence students' message construction.

Emig's (1971) method was similar to the wealth of educational methods already in place to better understand literacy and the process by which a beginning reader becomes literate. A key text here is Mallette and Duke's (2004) excellent summary of all the different methodologies for researching literacy. While such literacy studies tend to aim more at beginning readers, they approach the reading process from the student's perspective. For example, Hiebert and Sailors (2009) collected a significant amount of research on how to select texts for beginning readers. Such a frame would be tremendously helpful in decoding communication textbooks. While readability studies attempt to reveal the reader's experience, they only touch the surface. Armed with some learning theory, researchers might be surprised to find what actually helps students learn from communication textbooks.

We now finally turn to the area of history. Production, content, and usage all direct us to the present moment: making changes to better educate a particular class. Yet my own bookshelf is filled with old textbooks, now in disuse. These textbooks continue to say much about the development of the discipline and the rise and fall of ideas.

Histories of Communication Textbooks

Many of the early founders of the discipline were also textbook authors. James Winans (1917), for example, penned a public speaking textbook. As Benson (2003) pointed out, Winans's textbook set out a basic rationale for an independent study of public speaking (apart from English or elocution) that formed the core of the Cornell School of Rhetoric. Not surprisingly, textbooks served an important role in a discipline that started as the National Association of Academic Teachers of Public Speaking. At the first meeting of the association in 1915, the first topic for discussion (following the president's address) was "The Freshman Course in Public Speaking" (Jeffrey, 1964, p. 434).

While not told from the perspective of the textbook, many speech communication histories make special note of the textbooks used by teachers or departments since they served as important markers of disciplinary identity. Cohen's (1994) history of the field often references some of the key textbook authors of the day (most notably, Adams Sherman Hill). Wallace's (1954) excellent edited volume, *History of Speech Education in America*, makes multiple references to the importance of the textbook in shaping a curriculum. In particular, Guthrie's (1954) history of rhetorical theory in the American colonies chronicles the major rhetoric programs through their textbooks. Even departmental histories merge with textbook history as one stretches further back. My own department at the University of Washington produced a slim volume tracing the history of the communication department (Nilsen, 1991). Nilsen's story begins, as do most, with the classes and textbooks that gave rise to the modern department. Such histories operate within each department. Sometimes, they are written down; all too often, they merely live within the yellowing files of the underused departmental library.

When using textbooks to examine history, the authors themselves provide one of the richest areas to mine. Mortensen (2008) detailed Cicero's varied use of *loci* and argues that Cicero uses *locus* as a metaphor rather than as a specific unified concept or theory. While modern textbook authors may not aspire to the mantle of Cicero, a sorting through their various inventional concepts could well reveal a similar metaphoric grounding. The textbooks of William Norwood Brigance registered the changes in speech communication's understanding of the speaker-audience relationship. J. Jeffrey Auer (1989) made a passing reference to this in a speech before the Central States Communication Association. He noted that Brigance's four major public speaking texts (published in 1927, 1938, 1947, and 1952) moved from an exclusive focus on the speaker to a focus on the immediate audience and then to the larger society in which communication occurs. Brigance's books (as well as his role as Speech Communication Association [SCA] president in 1946 and editor of the *Quarterly Journal of Speech* from 1942 to 1944) helped influence how teachers understood and taught public speaking. Brigance's history is not communication's history, but his changes reveal much about the discipline's development.

Such historical work often must situate the textbook within the background culture that gave rise to it. One only need turn to the pages of the journal *Rhetorica* to find a wealth of excellent historical scholarship devoted to exploring the richness of ancient rhetorical texts and textbooks. For example, Richardson (2001) and Camargo (2001) provided two solid investigations of medieval *Ars Dictaminis;* these instructional texts serve as windows into the practical business and writing concerns of the day. Adopting a more contemporary approach, Connors (1986) presented a careful study of the development of the genre of English handbooks. He traced how handbooks emphasizing mechanical correctness emerged, beginning in the mid-1800s, in response to the demand on teachers to grade many student essays. Keith (2007) drew heavily on discussion and debate textbooks (as well as their authors) to better understand the important role speech education played in the American forums movement of the 1930s. American forums, such as the Chautauquas before them, sought to bring citizens together in an educational setting to discuss political issues. Clearly then, textbooks have the potential to reflect and affect the social conditions of the origins of the discipline.

Such historical investigation proves worthwhile since textbooks present disciplinary narratives about the field, introducing students to the originating myth. Norris (1980) presented another model for historical research of textbooks. He investigated the historical narrative of advertising offered in advertising textbooks and found that such stories were generally naive and inaccurate. Rather than discussing advertising as an economic institution that affects the pricing of services, textbooks framed advertising as merely a conduit of information linking products with interested purchasers. Hoy, Raaz, and Wehmeier (2007) adopted a similar approach in looking at the historical narratives about the field of public relations in public relations textbooks. They too found that textbooks tended to present an anecdote-based history of the discipline instead of a more theory-driven approach to understanding public relations' history. Speech-oriented communication textbooks often include a similar legitimizing historical narrative; one wonders how well our own stories stand up to the historical record.

OPPORTUNITIES FOR HISTORICAL RESEARCH

We now have a long enough continuous history as a discipline to map developments over the years. A good example here would be Gibson and Glenn (1982), who looked at the changes in business communication textbooks over a 24-year period. They found that business communication students were being taught basically the same information as speech communication students; there was only a slightly heavier emphasis on oral communication in business communication—an attempt to better accommodate the needs of business and professional students. One can easily envision studies that track the changes in how communication textbooks discuss certain topics. For example, a number of introductory communication textbooks include chapters on library research, yet research technology is significantly different from what it was even 20 years ago. As research technology evolves, one wonders if our textbooks have changed in their understanding of plagiarism. Additionally, some potential historical studies already have a baseline in place. In 1980, Bryant, Gula, and

Zillmann reported that communication textbooks included a great deal of humor. There has yet to be a follow-up study that evaluates how, if at all, communication textbooks have changed over the past 30 years.

While a historical study of textbooks can be done with an eye to better understanding the present pedagogy, deep research of primary texts is needed to ensure that we operate with an accurate view of the past. Spoel (2001) returned to the textbooks that made up the heart of the elocutionist movement and attempted some recovery. He argued that elocutionist textbooks operated with a complex theory of performance that worked in tandem with the concerns of late 18th-century British culture. Such research requires a close investigation of primary texts. Composition and English textbooks have produced collections of documentary materials (Brereton, 1995; Graff & Warner, 1989). Students of composition can easily pick up Brereton's (1995) volume and scan through some of the excerpted readings, and develop a set of historical questions that then can be pursued with greater archival research. Communication would be well served by such a documentary history with selections from our textbooks.

Conclusion

Kuhn (1962/1996) famously saw science textbooks as flawed vehicles for legitimizing scientific paradigms, stitching the past scientific revolutions together with the current paradigm. He argued that science textbooks report on past events and problems from within the vocabulary of the present. All textbooks thus operate within frames that shape how they discuss ideas. As such, our textbooks potentially reveal more about the discipline than we would wish. They display our knowledge, values, teaching models, and normative visions for communicative practice. Perhaps uncomfortably, they also demonstrate how our scholarly knowledge is influenced by outside factors (production) and bends when in the hands of others (usage). All these issues continue to evolve over time. In this way, textbooks reveal our discipline's situatedness. Textbooks are remarkably complex documents. They emerge from a production process that tries to balance a broad marketability with disciplinary expertise. The resulting text reflects choices about what content to include and exclude. All these decisions fade into the background as teachers and students use the text. This entire life cycle repeats, marking off distinct eras in our pedagogical and intellectual history.

Since textbooks are such deceptively complex works, they call for investigation from all corners of the discipline: social scientific surveys of how content affects students, ethnographic analyses of authors' decision-making processes, studies of organizational discourse, rhetorical critiques of content, and so forth. Unfortunately, such methodological pluralism is not currently the norm. In the scholarship surveyed here, content analyses are the most common studies by far. It is perhaps understandable that communication scholars opt to study the text as it stands. Yet to focus our critical gaze simply on the presence or absence of particular elements in textbooks misses much of the complexity of textbooks' life cycles.

Recently, I was discussing public speaking pedagogy with a colleague from another university. She was nonplussed that I did not require students to deliver a speech using technology, despite the fact that our rooms come equipped with all manner of presentational media. I responded that while I think such technology is important, I am more concerned with other concepts in the introductory public speaking course. This brief exchange highlights one of the most interesting aspects of the study of pedagogy and pedagogical texts; they require decisions. While both this teacher and I would quickly fall into agreement about the general importance of presentational technology, she assigns a technology speech and I do not. The constraints of a quarter or semester system drive us to reach different conclusions about the priority of certain skills and ideas. Academic discussions can easily become additive. For example, teaching research skills in the public speaking course is important, but so are ethical frameworks, as are models of reasoning. While the world of ideas may be boundless, I have only so much room on my 10-week syllabus. The same holds true for textbooks; they cannot include everything, but it is this factor that reveals the choices of companies and authors and shades the content for students and teachers.

Notes

1. Scholars often point to the literary qualities of the Belletristic rhetoric movement of the late 1700s. Warnick (1993) noted that studies of the belles lettres "were particularly concerned with examining the specific qualities of discourse and their effects" (p. 4).

2. If one wishes to retain some of the empiricism of a content analysis, critical discourse studies offers some methodological routes. Oteiza (2003), for example, studied how grammatical and lexical choices in Chilean history textbooks maintained an objective tone while interlacing judgments about previous governments.

References

Allen, M., & Preiss, R. (1990). Using meta-analyses to evaluate curriculum: An examination of selected college textbooks. *Communication Education, 39,* 103–116.

Allen, R. R. (1986). Selected secondary school textbooks in speech communication. *Communication Education, 35,* 102–109.

Auer, J. J. (1989). Pride in our past: Faith in our future. In W. Work & R. C. Jeffrey (Eds.), *Past is prologue: A 75th anniversary history of the SCA* (pp. 59–64). Annandale, VA: Speech Communication Association.

Barker, T., & Matveeva, N. (2006). Teaching intercultural communication in a technical writing service course: Real instructors' practices and suggestions for textbook selection. *Technical Communication Quarterly, 15,* 191–214.

Benson, T. W. (2003). The Cornell School of Rhetoric: Idiom and institution. *Communication Quarterly, 51,* 1–56.

Besser, D., Stone, G., & Nan, L. (1999). Textbooks and teaching: A lesson from students. *Journalism & Mass Communication Educator, 53*(4), 4–17.

Bloom, L. Z. (1996). Freshman composition as a middle-class enterprise. *College English, 58,* 654–675.

Brereton, J. C. (1995). *The origins of composition studies in the American college, 1875–1925: A documentary history.* Pittsburgh, PA: University of Pittsburgh Press.

Brigance, W. N. (1927). *The spoken word: A textbook of speech composition.* New York: Crofts.

Brigance, W. N. (1938). *Speechmaking: Principles and practice.* New York: Crofts.

Brigance, W. N. (1947). *Speech Communication: A brief textbook.* New York: Crofts.

Brigance, W. N. (1952). *Speech: Its techniques and disciplines in a free society.* New York: Appleton-Century-Crofts.

Bryant, J., Gula, J., & Zillmann, D. (1980). Humor in communication textbooks. *Communication Education, 29,* 125–134.

Burke, K. (1945). *A grammar of motives.* New York: Prentice Hall.

Burnham, C. (2001). Expressive pedagogy: Practice/theory. In G. Tate, A. Rupiper, & K. Shick (Eds.), *A guide to composition pedagogies* (pp. 19–35). New York: Oxford University Press.

Camargo, M. (2001). The waning of medieval Ars Dictaminis. *Rhetorica, 19,* 135–140.

Campbell, K. K. (1991). Hearing women's voices. *Communication Education, 40,* 33–48.

Cawyer, C. S., Bystrom, D., Miller, J., Simonds, C., O'Brien, M., & Storey-Martin, J. (1994). Communicating gender equity: Representation and portrayal of women and men in introductory communication textbooks. *Communication Studies, 45,* 325–331.

Chang, H., Holt, R., & Luo, L. (2006). Representing East Asians in intercultural communication textbooks: A select review. *Review of Communication, 6,* 312–328.

Clariana, R. B., & Koul, R. (2008). The effects of learner prior knowledge when creating concept maps from a text passage. *International Journal of Instructional Media, 35,* 229–236.

Clasen, P. R. W., & Lee, R. (2006). Teaching in a sanitized world: An exploration of the suburban scene in public communication pedagogy. *Communication Education, 55,* 463–483.

Clevenger, T., & Phifer, G. (1959). What do beginning college speech texts say about stage fright? *The Speech Teacher, 8,* 1–7.

Cmiel, K. (1990). *Democratic eloquence: The fight over popular speech in nine-teenth-century America*. New York: William Morrow.

Cohen, H. (1994). *The history of speech communication: The emergence of a discipline, 1914–1945*. Annandale, VA: Speech Communication Association.

Cole, R. A. (1999). Beyond the textbook: Teaching communication concepts through computers and music videos. *Communication Education, 48,* 327–328.

Connors, R. J. (1986). Textbooks and the evolution of the discipline. *College Composition and Communication, 37,* 178–194.

De la Caba Collado, M., & Lopez Atxurra, R. (2006). Democratic citizenship in textbooks in Spanish primary curriculum. *Journal of Curriculum Studies, 38,* 205–228.

Doolittle, R. (1977). Conflicting views of conflict: An analysis of basic speech communication textbooks. *Communication Education, 26,* 121–127.

Duffy, M. (2000). There's no two-way symmetric about it: A postmodern examination of public relations textbooks. *Critical Studies in Media Communication, 17,* 294–315.

Emig, J. A. (1971). *The composing processes of twelfth graders*. Urbana, IL: National Council of Teachers of English.

Erickson, S. (2004). Adapting to the communication needs of business and accounting students in introductory communication textbooks: Meeting the objectives of the accounting education change commission and the profession. *Review of Communication, 4,* 248–255.

Flower, L. (1994). *The construction of negotiated meaning: A social cognitive theory of writing*. Carbondale: Southern Illinois University Press.

Frobish, T. S. (2000). Jamison meets Lucas: Eloquence and pedagogical model(s) in the art of public speaking. *Communication Education, 49,* 239–252.

Gale, X. L., & Gale, F. G. (Eds.). (1999). *(Re)visioning composition textbooks: Conflicts of culture, ideology, and pedagogy*. Albany: State University of New York Press.

Gibson, G. M., & Glenn, E. C. (1982). Oral communication in business textbooks: A twenty-four year survey. *Journal of Business Communication, 19*(4), 39–49.

Graff, G., & Warner, M. (1989). *The origins of literary studies in America: A documentary anthology*. New York: Routledge.

Gullicks, K. A., Pearson, J. C., Child, J. T., & Schwab, C. R. (2005). Diversity and power in public speaking textbooks. *Communication Quarterly, 53,* 19–26.

Guthrie, W. (1954). Rhetorical theory in colonial America. In K. R. Wallace (Ed.), *History of speech education in America: Background studies* (pp. 48–59). New York: Appleton-Century-Crofts.

Hanson, T. L. (1999). Gender sensitivity and diversity issues in selected basic public speaking texts. *Women and Language, 22*(2), 13–19.

Hardin, M., & Preston, A. (2001). Inclusion of disability issues in news reporting textbooks. *Journalism & Mass Communication Educator, 56*(2), 43–54.

Hartung, K. K. (1998). What are students being taught about the ethics of technical communication? An analysis of the ethical discussions presented in four textbooks. *Journal of Technical Writing & Communication, 28,* 363–364.

Hess, J. (1999). Integrating the textbook into a philosophical foundation for the course. *Communication Education, 48,* 319–320.

Hess, J. A. (1993). Teaching ethics in introductory public speaking: Review and proposal. *Basic Communication Course Annual, 5,* 101–126.

Hiebert, E. H., & Sailors, M. (2009). *Finding the right texts: What works for beginning and struggling readers*. New York: Guilford Press.

Hoy, P., Raaz, O., & Wehmeier, S. (2007). From facts to stories or from stories to facts? Analyzing public relations history in public relations textbooks. *Public Relations Review, 33,* 191–200.

Hugenberg, L. W. (1996). Introduction to cultural diversity in the basic course: Differing points of view. *Basic Communication Course Annual, 8,* 136–144.

Hugenberg, L. W., & Moyer, B. S. (1998). The research foundation for instruction in the beginning public speaking course. *Basic Communication Course Annual, 10,* 157–170.

Hughes, R. L. (2007). A hint of whiteness: History textbooks and social construction of race in the wake of the sixties. *The Social Studies, 98,* 201–207.

Jamieson, K. H. (1988). *Eloquence in an electronic age: The transformation of political speechmaking*. New York: Oxford University Press.

Janusik, L., & Wolvin, A. D. (2002). Listening treatment in the basic communication course text. *Basic Communication Course Annual, 14,* 164–210.

Jeffrey, R. C. (1964). A history of the Speech Association of America, 1914–1964. *Quarterly Journal of Speech, 50,* 432–444.

Johnsen, E. B. (1993). *Textbooks in the kaleidoscope: A critical survey of literature and research on educational texts*. New York: Oxford University Press.

Johnston, S. P., & Huczynski, A. (2006). Textbook publishers' website objective question banks: Does their use improve students' examination performance? *Active Learning in Higher Education, 7,* 257–271.

Keith, W. M. (2007). *Democracy as discussion: Civic education and the American forum movement*. Lanham, MD: Lexington Books.

Kern-Foxworth, M. (1990). Ethnic inclusiveness in public relations textbooks and reference books. *Howard Journal of Communications, 2,* 226–237.

Keshishian, F. (2005). A historical-materialist critique of intercultural communication instruction. *Communication Education, 54,* 205–222.

Kubota, R., & Shi, L. (2005). Instruction and reading samples for opinion writing in L1 junior high school textbooks in China and Japan. *Journal of Asian Pacific Communication, 15,* 97–127.

Kuhn, T. S. (1996). *The structure of scientific revolutions* (3rd ed.). Chicago: University of Chicago Press. (Original work published 1962)

LaSpina, J. A. (1998). *The visual turn and the transformation of the textbook*. Mahwah, NJ: Lawrence Erlbaum.

Levin, J. R., & Mayer, R. E. (1993). Understanding illustrations in text. In B. K. Britton, A. Woodward, & M. Binkley (Eds.), *Learning from textbooks: Theory and practice* (pp. 95–113). Hillsdale, NJ: Lawrence Erlbaum.

Macgillivray, I. K., & Jennings, T. (2008). A content analysis exploring lesbian, gay, bisexual, and transgender topics in foundations of education textbooks. *Journal of Teacher Education, 59,* 170–188.

Mallette, M. H., & Duke, N. K. (2004). *Literacy research methodologies*. New York: Guilford Press.

Matveeva, N. (2007). The intercultural component in textbooks for teaching a service technical writing course. *Journal of Technical Writing & Communication, 37,* 151–166.

McGarrity, M. (2005). The public speaking public: An analysis of a rhetoric of public speaking pedagogy (Doctoral dissertation, Indiana University, 2005). *Dissertation Abstracts International, 66*(06), 2200.

Mencher, M. (1996). Travails of a textbook author. *Nieman Reports, 50*(3), 43–47.

Miles, L. (1997). Globalizing professional writing curricula: Positioning students and re-positioning textbooks. *Technical Communication Quarterly, 6*, 179–200.

Miller, A. N. (2002). An exploration of Kenyan public speaking patterns with implications for the American introductory public speaking course. *Communication Education, 51*, 168–182.

Moreau, J. (2004). *Schoolbook nation: Conflicts over American history textbooks from the Civil War to the present.* Ann Arbor: University of Michigan Press.

Mortensen, D. E. (2008). The loci of Cicero. *Rhetorica, 26*, 31–56.

Newburger, C., Smith, R., & Pledger, L. (1993). Departmental textbook publishing for the introductory communication course: Pedagogical boon or exploitation? *Journal of the Association for Communication Administration, 3*, 31–36.

Nilsen, T. R. (1991). *Speech communication at the University of Washington: An informal history.* Seattle: University of Washington Publication Services.

Norris, V. P. (1980). Advertising history: According to the textbooks. *Journal of Advertising, 9*(3), 3–11.

O'Keefe, V. (1992). Review essay: Intermediate and secondary level textbooks in speech communication. *Communication Education, 41*, 440–451.

Oteiza, T. (2003). How contemporary history is presented in Chilean middle school textbooks. *Discourse & Society, 14*, 639–660.

Pearson, J., Child, J., Mattern, J., & Kahl, D. (2006). What are students being taught about ethics in public speaking textbooks? *Communication Quarterly, 54*, 507–521.

Pearson, J., DeWitt, L., Child, J., Kahl, D., & Dandamudi, V. (2007). Facing the fear: An analysis of speech-anxiety content in public-speaking textbooks. *Communication Research Reports, 24*, 159–168.

Pelias, M. (1989). Communication apprehension in basic public speaking texts: An examination of contemporary textbooks. *Communication Education, 38*, 41–53.

Pomerenke, P., Varner, I. I., & Mallar, S. (1996). The depiction of female and male professionals in business communication textbooks. *Business Communication Quarterly, 59*(4), 36–46.

Prividera, L. C. (2004). Assessing sensitivity: A critical analysis of gender in teaching basic communication courses. *Basic Communication Course Annual, 16*, 195–229.

Razek, J., & Cone, R. (1981). Readability of business communication textbooks: An empirical study. *Journal of Business Communication, 18*(2), 33–40.

Richardson, M. (2001). The fading influence of the medieval Ars Dictaminis in England after 1400. *Rhetorica, 19*, 225–247.

Rodden, J. (2006). *Schoolbooks, ideology, and East German identity: Textbook reds.* University Park: Pennsylvanian State University Press.

Ross, C. (2003). Education reform and the limits of discourse: Rereading collaborative revision of a composition program's textbook. *College Composition and Communication, 55*, 302–329.

Roth, W. M., Pozzer-Ardenghi, L., & Han, J. Y. (2005). *Critical graphicacy: Understanding visual representation practices in school science*. Dordrecht, The Netherlands: Springer.

Rowan, K. E. (1995). A new pedagogy for explanatory speaking: Why arrangement should not substitute for invention. *Communication Education, 44*, 236–250.

Russ, S., & McClish, G. (1999). Foundational text as textbook. *Communication Education, 48*, 320–321.

Sanchez, T. R. (2007). The depiction of Native Americans in recent (1991–2004) secondary American history textbooks: How far have we come? *Equity & Excellence in Education, 40*, 311–320.

Schneider, D. (1992). A comparison of readability levels of textbooks in public speaking and interpersonal communication. *Communication Education, 41*, 400–404.

Schneider, D. E. (1991). An analysis of readability levels of contemporary textbooks that employ a hybrid approach to the basic communication course. *Communication Education, 40*, 165–171.

Schwartzman, R. (2004). What's basic about the basic course? Enriching the ethosystem as a corrective for consumerism. *Basic Communication Course Annual, 13*, 116–150.

Seidman, S. (2003). In quest of a textbook for a presentation-media course. *International Journal of Instructional Media, 30*, 419–427.

Sellnow, D., Child, J., & Ahlfeldt, S. (2005). Textbook technology supplements: What are they good for? *Communication Education, 54*, 243–253.

Spoel, P. M. (2001). Rereading the elocutionists: The rhetoric of Thomas Sheridan's *A Course of Lectures on Elocution* and John Walker's *Elements of Elocution*. *Rhetorica, 19*, 49–91.

Starck, K., & Wyffels, R. (1990). Seeking intercultural dimensions in textbooks. *Journalism Educator, 45*(3), 39–45.

Temple, J. R. (2005). People who are different from you: Heterosexism in Quebec high school textbooks. *Canadian Journal of Education, 28*, 271–294.

Tindell, J. (1999). Argumentation and debate textbooks: An overview of content and focus. *Argumentation & Advocacy, 35*, 185–191.

Torsti, P. (2007). How to deal with a difficult past? History textbooks supporting enemy images in post-war Bosnia and Herzegovina. *Journal of Curriculum Studies, 39*, 77–96.

Treinen, K. P., & Warren, J. T. (2001). Antiracist pedagogy in the basic course: Teaching cultural communication as if whiteness matters. *Basic Communication Course Annual, 13*, 46–76.

U.S. Government Accountability Office. (2005, July). *College textbooks: Enhanced offerings appear to drive recent price increases* (Publication No. GAO-05-806). Retrieved September 4, 2009, from Government Accountability Office Reports Online via GPO Access Web site: http://www.gao.gov/new.items/d05806.pdf

Von Heyking, A. (2006). Talking about Americans: The image of the United States in English-Canadian schools, 1900–1965. *History of Education Quarterly, 46*, 382–408.

Wallace, K. R. (Ed.). (1954). *History of speech education in America: Background studies*. New York: Appleton-Century-Crofts.

Warnick, B. (1993). *The sixth canon: Belletristic rhetorical theory and its French antecedents*. Columbia: University of South Carolina Press.

Webb, L. M., Bourgerie, A. J., Schaper, M. W., Johnson, K. B., Dubbs, K. L., Mountain, K. N., et al. (2004). Gender and diversity in family communication: A content analysis of the four undergraduate textbooks. *Journal of Family Communication, 4,* 35–52.

Webb, L., & Thompson-Hayes, M. (2002). Do popular collegiate textbooks in interpersonal communication reflect a common theory base? A telling content analysis. *Communication Education, 51,* 210–224.

Welch, K. E. (1987). A critique of classical rhetoric: The contemporary appropriation of ancient discourse. *Rhetoric Review, 6,* 79–86.

Winans, J. A. (1917). *Public speaking.* New York: Century.

Winterowd, W. R. (1989). Composition textbooks: Publisher-author relationships. *College Composition and Communication, 40,* 139–151.

Woodward, A. (1993). Do illustrations serve an instructional purpose in U.S. textbooks? In B. K. Britton, A. Woodward, & M. Binkley (Eds.), *Learning from textbooks: Theory and practice* (pp. 115–134). Hillsdale, NJ: Lawrence Erlbaum.

Yook, E. L. (1999). Giving more than lip service to cultural diversity in the basic text. *Communication Education, 48,* 321–323.

Zebroski, J. T. (1999). Textbook advertisements in the formation of composition: 1969–1990. In X. L. Gale & F. G. Gale (Eds.), *(Re)visioning composition textbooks: Conflicts of culture, ideology, and pedagogy* (pp. 231–248). Albany: State University of New York Press.

Learning Through Service 7

The Contributions of Service Learning to the Communication Discipline

Jami L. Warren and Timothy L. Sellnow

O ver the past two decades, interest in service learning has continued to expand in nearly all disciplines. Many universities in the United States encourage and monitor service learning campuswide in an effort to demonstrate community involvement and innovative education opportunities. The communication discipline shares in this enthusiasm with an increasing number of programs adopting service learning (Oster-Aaland, Sellnow, Nelson, & Pearson, 2004; Sellnow & Oster, 1997). By definition, service learning is a pedagogical strategy in which students engage in volunteer work that enhances their understanding of course concepts and enables them to make contributions to their communities (Rhodes & Davis, 2001). More specifically, Eyler and Giles (1999) suggest that the service learning experience should meet four criteria in order for it to be considered successful. These criteria include (1) personal and interpersonal development, (2) understanding and applying knowledge learned in class, (3) perspective transformation, and (4) a developed sense of citizenship. Communication educators observe that these criteria can be met in all major areas of study, ranging from interpersonal communication to public speaking (Oster-Aaland et al., 2004).

The rising popularity of service learning is matched by a growing body of research addressing the benefits and constraints of this approach to instruction. A wide variety of disciplines, including communication (e.g., see recent edited collections by Tannenbaum, 2008; see also Droge & Murphy, 1999), have contributed to the literature addressing service learning. In this chapter, we provide an overview of the existing research on service learning with specific attention to the work done in communication. In doing so, we first establish the foundation and theoretical underpinnings of service learning. Next, we summarize what is currently known about the potential benefits of service learning. This summary is followed by a discussion of the research associated with implementing and evaluating service learning programs. Throughout this process of reviewing the service learning literature, we identify current gaps in research and application within the communication discipline. We conclude with an overall assessment of the contributions service learning makes to our discipline as well as opportunities for further contributions.

Theoretical Perspectives on Service Learning

Although there is no dominant service learning theory, sufficient research has been conducted to draw some consistent theoretical conclusions. Service learning is situated in the greater context of experiential learning. Dewey (1938) is often credited as being the first to discuss experiential education. He argued that traditional education does not provide students with skill development to deal with potential present and future issues. Instead, he suggested that students need hands-on experience or engagement in real-life problem solving to facilitate understanding of course concepts.

Kolb (1984) further clarified the expectations of experiential learning by suggesting that students comprehend best when experiencing four stages of learning. Specifically, he argued that students should engage in each of the following stages: (1) concrete experience abilities, (2) reflective observation, (3) abstract conceptualization, and (4) active experimentation. In other words, students learn better when they focus on factual material regarding a concept, contemplate stories and specific real-life examples that exemplify that concept, examine visual representations of that concept, and engage in activities that assist them with applying that specific concept. Although students are typically able to engage in the first three of the aforementioned stages within a traditional classroom, they are often unable to engage in "active experimentation," or in activities that assist them with applying a specific concept, in those traditional classrooms. Service learning approaches provide students with this missing opportunity for active experimentation. Particularly, service learning asks students to participate in real-life, hands-on experiences that engage them in their course material and encourages them to apply specific concepts that they are learning in class.

Active experimentation is a form of engagement. Specifically, Rockquemore and Schaffer (2000) developed a stage theory of engagement regarding service learning experiences. They suggest that, although researchers know a great deal about students' attitudes and perceptions of learning before and after completing a service learning course, little is known about how or why this process occurs. After conducting surveys and qualitative analysis of journal entries from students participating in a service learning course, Rockquemore and Schaffer proposed a theory of engagement that includes three stages students encounter while involved in a course that includes service learning: (1) shock, (2) normalization, and (3) engagement. The first stage, "shock," suggests that when students first begin their service experience, they are truly in shock because they are surprised by the conditions in which they are expected to work and also at the conditions in which others exist. The second stage, "normalization," suggests that the shock of the new experience eventually wears off and students adapt to the experience. During this stage, students begin to feel more comfortable with their service location and see it as a "normal" experience. Finally, the third and most important stage for the purposes of this discussion is the "engagement" stage. During the engagement stage, students begin to ask questions about their service experiences. They begin to apply what they are learning in class to the real-life examples from their service location. Therefore, students become truly engaged in their course material and start to make connections between their service and what they have learned in class.

Students realize several benefits as a result of their engagement in course material. Because students are participating in real-life problem solving and applying their course material to these experiences, the relevance of the course content should increase for them. Frymier and Shulman (1995) found that when content relevance increased, students' state motivation to study also increased. This idea is further supported by Flournoy's (2007) observation that students' motivation to study increased as a result of their involvement in a service learning journalism course. Furthermore, Frymier, Shulman, and Houser (1996) found that increasing content relevance also increased students' affect toward the course material and the instructor. Additionally, as state motivation to study increases, one would also expect that cognitive learning would increase as well. This is to say that as students study more, one would anticipate that student learning of course concepts would increase as well. Both of these ideas are also supported in the service learning literature. For instance, Moely, McFarland, Miron, Mercer, and Ilustre (2002) found that students involved in a service learning course rated the value of that course significantly higher at the end of the semester when compared with their non–service learning counterparts. Furthermore, both Strage (2000) and Lundy (2007) found that examination scores were higher among students involved in service learning courses when compared with students involved in non–service learning courses. Therefore, students who participate in a service learning course should perceive the content in that course as more relevant, which should consequently increase their motivation to study. Content relevance should also increase affective and cognitive learning. The model in Figure 7.1 summarizes this process.

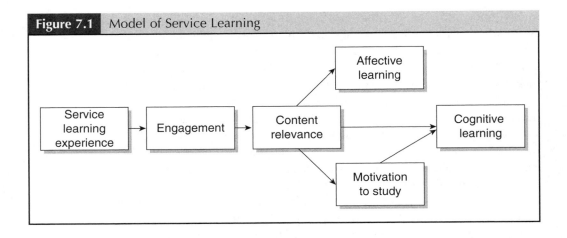

Figure 7.1 Model of Service Learning

Benefits of Service Learning

A significant amount of research exists regarding the effect that service learning has on higher-order thinking (Eyler & Giles, 1999), empathy (Lundy, 2007), cultural awareness (Bloom, 2008; Borden, 2007; Gutheil, Chernesky, & Sherratt, 2006), personal and interpersonal development (Gullicks, 2006), motivation to engage in social issues (Lee, Olszewski-Kubilius, Donahue, & Weimholt, 2008), motivation to study (Flournoy, 2007), life skills (Astin & Sax, 1998), self-efficacy (Simons & Cleary, 2006; Stewart, 2008), and civic engagement/responsibility (Astin & Sax, 1998; Einfeld & Collins, 2008; Gullicks, 2006; Lee et al., 2008; Prentice, 2007; Simons & Cleary, 2006). In this section, we review a variety of studies that identify the potential benefits of service learning. Although much of this research was conducted outside the communication discipline, the findings have relevance across disciplines. Specifically, we address potential benefits of enhanced civic engagement, student learning, and knowledge application, as well as the associated dilemma of measuring cognitive learning.

CIVIC ENGAGEMENT

Previous research consistently indicates that service learning has the potential to enhance the level of student civic engagement. Prentice (2007) conducted research on the impact of service learning on civic engagement among students at several different community colleges over a number of semesters. Both pre- and posttest surveys were given to students involved in service and non–service learning courses at several community colleges. Two surveys created by the researcher were used to measure student civic engagement. The study was based on a data set of 166 pre- and posttest surveys. As a result, Prentice found that service learners, when compared with non–service learners, significantly differed on the civic engagement measures at posttest.

Simons and Cleary (2006) conducted a study of service learning's effect on students' community self-efficacy and civic engagement. Specifically, they employed a pre-post test design with 142 psychology students. Students participated in a 16-hour service requirement as part of their course requirements. Several measures were administered in this study, including the Civic Attitudes and Skills Questionnaire, the Community Service Self-Efficacy Scale, and the Texas Social Behavior Inventory–Short Form. Results of this study indicated that students involved in service learning had an increased level of civic engagement and community self-efficacy as well as an increased level of political awareness and improved diversity attitudes.

Several studies reveal that civic engagement was further improved by the students' development of a greater appreciation for dissimilar popula-tions. For instance, Borden (2007) studied the impact of service learning on ethnocentrism in an intercultural communication course. Specifically, students were required to complete a minimum of 15 service hours over a 12-week period at one of two service locations. Students completed the Generalized Ethnocentrism (GENE) scale both before participating in their service requirements and after finishing the requirement. Borden found that students' ethnocentrism significantly decreased after partici-pating in the service learning course.

Similarly, Gutheil et al. (2006) conducted a study on the effect service learning had on student attitudes toward aging in Bermuda. Bermuda needed its citizens to perform a needs assessment of their elderly popula-tion, creating a unique collaboration between a research center in Bermuda and the community college. The researchers chose to work with students who were involved in a course on aging as interviewers of elderly citizens. A total of 300 elderly individuals were interviewed by 11 students. A qualitative analysis of students' final papers indicated that students' atti-tudes changed and stereotypes regarding the elderly population decreased as a result of their service experience.

STUDENT LEARNING AND APPLICATION OF KNOWLEDGE

A considerable amount of research exists on the impact of service learn-ing on several attitudinal measures. However, little experimental research has been conducted on whether service learning experiences enhance stu-dent learning or ability to apply course concepts. Novak, Markey, and Allen (2007) conducted a meta-analysis to evaluate cognitive outcomes of service learning in higher education. Only nine studies that examined service learning and cognitive outcomes emerged as a result of their analysis. While these studies did measure students' understanding of the subject matter and their ability to apply the knowledge or skills learned, many of these studies did so using student self-report or faculty testimonials. Therefore, instead of measuring actual learning, many of these studies examined student and faculty *perceptions* of learning.

For example, Litke (2002) examined final reflection papers of 60 students involved in a service learning course. Student papers were coded in six different categories, including (1) personal development, (2) sense of belonging, (3) active citizenship, (4) enhanced academic understanding of subject matter, (5) ability to apply knowledge and skills learned, and (6) ability to reframe complex social issues. As a result of her analysis, Litke found that students involved in the course reported personal development as the most significant benefit of the service learning course, followed by the ability to apply knowledge and skills learned, an increased sense of belonging, enhanced academic understanding of subject matter, active citizenship, and the ability to reframe complex social issues. While these knowledge gains are significant, this study depended on students' reports of their ability to apply knowledge and skills learned and understanding of the subject matter rather than more concrete measures of cognitive learning.

Similarly, Moely et al. (2002) examined data from a total of 541 students, 271 of whom were involved in 26 different service learning courses compared with 324 students involved in four non–service learning courses. Scales measuring student attitudes, course value, learning about the academic field, and learning about the community were completed by students in this study. Results of the data analysis showed an increase among service learning students' attitudes, perceptions of course value, and perception of learning about the community over the course of the semester when compared with non–service learners. However, results also suggested a slight decrease in learning about the academic field among service learners over the course of the semester. While these results are informative, this study still depended on student self-reports to measure learning. The tendency of scholars to rely on self-reports from students is likely due to the difficulty of measuring cognitive learning.

THE DILEMMA OF MEASURING COGNITIVE LEARNING

The dilemma regarding measurement of cognitive learning is very common within instructional communication and communication education research (Richmond, Lane, & McCroskey, 2006). While these disciplines are similar, instructional communication research focuses on the role of communication within instruction whereas communication education examines the teaching of communication concepts. Although these disciplines are slightly different, learning outcomes should be the "bottom line" of research within both of these fields (Sprague, 2002). However, measuring learning has become a dilemma within these fields. Researchers have relied on instruments that measure student and/or faculty perceptions of student cognitive learning instead of measuring true cognitive learning. Measures such as the Learning Loss Measure (Richmond, Gorham, & McCroskey, 1987) and Learning Indicators Scale (Frymier & Houser, 2000) that measure students' perceptions of their own learning have become the norm. The cognitive learning dilemma still remains a problem for instructional communication and communication education researchers today. There is still no widely accepted measure for cognitive learning and, therefore, researchers continue to rely on measuring student perceptions of learning. This is problematic because student perceptions of their own learning may not be accurate and may be affected by other variables such as affect for the course and/or the instructor, teacher immediacy, and so on.

Although some of the studies included in the previously mentioned meta-analysis depended on self-report data to measure learning outcomes, several did not. For example, Strage (2000) studied the impact of service learning on learning outcomes, specifically examination scores, among students enrolled in an introductory child development course. Students involved in the service learning course were compared with students who had previously taken the same course and were not involved in service learning. The service learning students were required to complete a minimum of 20 hours of service at a school site. Students involved in the service learning course scored significantly higher on all three exams when compared with non–service learning students.

Additionally, although not included in the previously mentioned meta-analysis, Lundy (2007) conducted research on the impact of service learning on exam scores within a life-span development course. Students were required to choose one of three course projects, one of which was a service learning project. Other project possibilities included an interview project and a research paper. Service learning students were required to complete 2 hours of service a week for 12 weeks, totaling 24 hours of service. Lundy found that students who completed the service learning project scored significantly higher on exams than their non–service learning counterparts.

While the previously mentioned studies did measure learning through examination scores, neither did so within the communication discipline. At present, little or no research published in refereed communication journals has been conducted on cognitive learning outcomes, using examination scores, as a learning outcome among service learning courses within the communication discipline.

Providing evidence that demonstrates learning outcomes derived from service learning is imperative for educators. First, administrations often desire proof that a concept "works" or provides significant improvement in student learning over traditional methods before they will support and/or fund such an initiation at an institution. Of equal importance, educators need to be sure that adding a service learning component to a course does not detract from student learning. Therefore, more experimental or quasi-experimental research needs to address the effect that service learning has on student learning outcomes, especially among communication courses.

Assessment and Implementation of Service Learning

Although a significant amount of research exists in the service learning literature regarding effective implementation of service learning programs, assessment and evaluation of those programs, and building meaningful community partnerships, less research has been conducted within the communication discipline. In the future, it will be important for those within the communication discipline to continue to conduct research on the implementation and evaluation of service learning programs to determine whether there are unique challenges and opportunities for faculty and students within communication. Additionally, and wherever possible, we should be conducting research that provides community partners with an outlet to voice their perspective on the process. Although some aspects of implementation, evaluation, and community partnerships span disciplines, understanding how these objectives relate to all levels of communication would assist instructors in the communication discipline, specifically, as they plan their service learning courses. Such information would also aid in justifying the use of service learning to students, other faculty members, and administrators.

Research within the service learning literature provides educators with important information on characteristics of faculty who implement service learning in their courses as well as the processes that accompany the implementation of service learning programs. For instance, empirical studies have shown that faculty who implement service learning in their courses tend to prioritize teaching and are motivated by student learning outcomes and receive greater personal satisfaction from teaching these types of courses (Abes, Jackson, & Jones, 2002; Hammond, 1994). Conversely, faculty members who do not incorporate service learning in their courses often prioritize research before teaching. Additionally, math and science faculty tend to value service learning less than other faculty members.

While understanding what characterizes and motivates faculty members to include service learning in their courses is important, understanding how to implement a service learning program is equally relevant. Bringle and Hatcher (1995) described a curriculum designed for a series of faculty workshops, including workshops on introducing service learning and building effective community partnerships. Furthermore, Coyle, Jamieson, and Sommers (1997) described a model for implementing service learning specifically in an engineering curriculum. In their research, they described not only the phases and structure of projects used in their program but also their goals and preliminary evaluation of their program. Research studies such as those mentioned above have the potential to provide educators with a guide for implementing their own service learning programs.

The communication discipline addressed this need through a special issue of the *Southern Communication Journal* that was devoted to service learning research. Several of the articles included in this special issue discussed the implementation of service learning in communication courses. For instance, Gibson, Kostecki, and Lucas (2001) discussed how they implemented service learning in a communication training and development course. More specifically, they used 11 principles of best practice adapted from the National Society for Experiential Education to implement service learning in the course. These principles included practices such as making sure that students were provided with an authentic service experience, that they had an opportunity to reflect on their experiences, and that the program was evaluated in terms of student outcomes. Gibson and colleagues determined that the principles of best practice provided a useful framework for developing a quality service learning course. Similarly, Keyton (2001) made the argument that service learning can be implemented in communication research methods courses as well. She described three case studies in which service learning was used in a research methods course. For example, in one such case study, students in a communication research methods course at the University of Memphis were assigned to determine the effectiveness of the Crimestoppers' radio public service announcements (PSAs) that were broadcasted on University of Memphis's noncommercial radio station. Overall, students in the course discovered that the majority of participants in their study could not recall the Crimestoppers' phone number announced during the PSA. This provided Crimestoppers with valuable information about their PSAs and also provided students with real-world research experience. Additional articles within the special issue of the *Southern Communication Journal* examined how service learning can be implemented in communication education (Staton & Tomlinson, 2001), organizational communication (Braun, 2001), critical ethnography in communication (Artz, 2001), and communication capstone courses (O'Hara, 2001).

Additionally, there is some research on implementation within communication that has been presented at conferences or in books. For instance, Bachen (1999) described how faculty in the communication department at Santa Clara University became involved with the Eastside Project, a university-wide program that matches students with service agencies. Specifically, this program has been used in the introductory communication course among others at Santa Clara. Bachen explained how students used a structured-journal approach to help make connections between their course material and their service learning experiences. For instance, while students in these classes were learning about interpersonal communication concepts in their class readings and discussions, they were also using journal entries to reflect on how their preconceptions about the people in their service placement affected their interpersonal interactions. This journaling activity allowed the students to see how the concepts they were studying in class occurred in the real world. Similarly, Bergstrom and Bullis (1999) implemented service learning in the communication research course at the University of Utah. One group within this course conducted research for a large nonprofit organization that delivers food to 212 distribution sites in the state. The students involved in this project assessed the organizational communication by designing on-site surveys. For example, students working on this project examined the relationships between the amount of food provided by each of the distribution sites and the amount of food provided by each site to its customers. In both of these examples, the experiential activity enabled students to better understand their audiences and, through applied research, provide practical solutions to communication-relevant problems.

Research such as that mentioned above is particularly accessible when scholars publish in mainstream journals. The fact that the *Southern Communication Journal* devoted an entire issue to service learning is encouraging. Continued efforts to publish such research in mainstream journals will help identify those unique motivations, opportunities, and challenges facing faculty who teach service learning courses within the communication discipline. Moreover, this type of research will provide a broader understanding of how service learning programs are best implemented within communication courses.

Conducting research on implementation of service learning programs is necessary to facilitate understanding of this process among communication educators. Similarly, understanding how to effectively evaluate service learning programs is essential. Driscoll, Holland, Gelmon, and Kerrigan (1996) discussed a comprehensive case study model they created as a response to the lack of instruments or models available for measuring the impact that service learning courses have on students, faculty, the community, and the institution itself. In this particular study, Driscoll and colleagues piloted their model in four service learning courses. While data analysis was still in progress at the time their study was published, studies such as this one are essential because they provide a tool for educators to consistently and systematically evaluate the effectiveness of service learning programs. Furthermore, Gilchrist, Mundy, Felton, and Shields (2003) detailed the transition of a non–service learning course to a service learning course. They discussed the transition of a course titled "Values and Community Service" that eventually became required of all freshmen majoring in human and organization development at their institution. The course is now titled "Principles of Community Engagement." Gilchrist and colleagues provided a thorough description of the process of this transition, including the evolution of the course over time. They also commented on the importance of assessment and reflection to this process.

Several studies offer advice on assessing service learning in communication classes. For example, Gibson et al. (2001) described how they evaluated their service learning course. Throughout the semester, students reflected on their service experiences in journal form, which provided the researchers with several pages of narrative for each student. Additionally, they conducted focus groups at the end of the course. Gibson et al. reported that students felt that their service experience prepared them for employment; improved their public speaking, teambuilding, and leadership skills; increased their learning of course content; and increased their understanding of community issues. Similarly, Staton and Tomlinson (2001) collected student reflection articles throughout their communication education course. Overall, they found that students in the course felt positive about their service experiences. Additionally, high final performance ratings suggested that students learned course concepts as well.

Research on evaluation has also been presented at conferences or published in books. For example, Bachen (1999) discusses preliminary evaluation of the use of the Eastside Project. Bachen discovered that the service experiences seem to increase students' awareness of social issues, which allows them to reflect on their course material in a meaningful way. Conversely, other students also reported the difficulty of adding another component, such as completing their service requirements, to their already busy schedules. Although this information is important, most of this discussion was based purely on informal student feedback and not on more concrete measures of program assessment. Bergstrom and Bullis (1999) described a similar strategy for evaluating their service learning programs. They examined student reflections of their service experiences and found that students seem to be making meaningful connections between their service experiences and their course material in addition to understanding perspectives of those less fortunate. Again, while the existing research is valuable, continuing to publish research of this kind within communication journals would provide accessible recommendations designed to ensure that service learning programs within communication courses are effective for the students, the faculty, the community, and the institution. Such work will also help build a more comprehensive understanding of communication education pedagogy, perhaps even making theorizing arguments about how best to teach and learn communication knowledge.

Finally, there is a significant amount of research within the service learning literature that focuses on the community partners' perspectives. Because service learning should focus on both learning course concepts and giving back to the community, the perspective of the community partner is extremely important. Most research on this issue has found that community agency personnel have positive perspectives on both the campuses and the students with whom they work (Bushouse, 2005; Ferrari & Worrall, 2000; Sandy & Holland, 2006; Vernon & Ward, 1999). However, most of these agency personnel also report a greater need for communication and coordination with the campus and faculty involved in the service learning program (Sandy & Holland, 2006; Vernon & Ward, 1999). While research of this kind has been conducted among health profession departments (Gelmon, Holland, Seifer, Shinnamon, & Connors, 1998), management courses (Bushouse, 2005), and Spanish courses (Jorge, 2003), despite diligent efforts on our part, we were unable to find research of this kind that has been conducted within communication departments. Research of this kind from communication scholars is needed because the community partners' support is so vital to the success of a service learning program.

As mentioned previously, little substantive research exists within the communication discipline regarding the implementation and evaluation of service learning programs. However, there are several studies that are noteworthy. First, Panici and Lasky (2002) conducted an empirical study to determine how service learning is both implemented and evaluated within journalism and mass communication courses. They surveyed journalism and mass communication faculty members and found that most members integrated service learning by incorporating a service learning component into an existing course. Furthermore, faculty in this study suggested that students' activity reports and/or site or supervisor evaluation served to assess the service learning experience. Additionally, Corbett and Kendall (1999) sought to determine the success of service learning communication courses from the students' perspectives. After surveying 153 students enrolled in service learning communication courses, they found that, overall, students felt that the service learning experience helped them understand the course concepts they learned in class. Students also suggested that the service learning course increased their sense of citizenship.

While these studies are an important step forward for communication scholars, most communication research that is focused on service learning is anecdotal and/or simply provides an argument for including certain pedagogical strategies such as reflection and critical approaches in service learning communication courses (McEachern, 2006; Turnley, 2007). How service learning courses are implemented and evaluated within the communication discipline has received relatively little attention. Furthermore, there is a lack of research within the communication discipline that focuses on the community perspective.

Overall Assessment and Potential Contributions

This analysis reveals that service learning has considerable momentum, appearing with notable frequency in myriad disciplines. The communication discipline is no exception. The number of communication programs advocating service learning continues to rise (Oster-Aaland et al., 2004). Despite the rising frequency of service learning in communication programs, limited research on the subject appears in refereed communication journals. Dedication to service learning research by communication scholars could further discern the unique opportunities and constraints of service learning in the context of communication pedagogy.

A clear theoretical basis for service learning has been established. The long-standing work of Dewey (1938) as well as learning styles and stage theory have established a solid foundation for exploring the impact of service learning strategies on student learning. The general benefits of service learning, such as civic engagement, knowledge acquisition, and knowledge application, are known. Likewise, constraints, such as difficulties in measuring cognitive learning, have been identified on an interdisciplinary level. The degree to which those benefits are bolstered or limited in the context of communication instruction, however, has received only limited attention in refereed communication journals. As communication educators contemplate continuing, implementing, or revising service learning assignments in the classes they teach, they could also provide a needed service to their peers by establishing research questions and procedures for collecting evidence regarding student performance and perception.

An immediate area of interest involves the implementation of service learning programs in the communication discipline. Other disciplines offer detailed guides for how, when, and where service learning has been and can be implemented in various courses. Many communication departments have long-standing service learning projects in a variety of courses. Reflecting on the strengths and weaknesses of how these programs were implemented could serve as inspiration for others to follow suit. Moreover, more research focusing on examples of successful implementation in communication programs or consistent themes of successful implementation among programs would allow other programs to introduce or revise service learning projects more efficiently and effectively.

Formal assessment of learning, based on service learning opportunities, is another promising and essential area of research. Nearly every program is required to engage in the formal process of assessing student learning. Service learning is no less amenable to the assessment process than other forms of learning. Data collection may introduce some complications regarding access; yet, the richness of such data provides a level of authenticity that may exceed more traditional forms of assessment data. Service learning requires students to apply their knowledge in a real-world setting, thereby testing their preparation to meet such demands. By publishing experimental research focusing on assessment findings and strategies in refereed communication journals, scholars could make a helpful contribution to many programs as they undertake the assessment process.

Another area of interest involves the formation of community partners. Many communication programs establish advisory boards and engage in outreach activities to establish a productive link with their surrounding communities. In fact, such community connections are a vital part of the mission embraced by many universities. Compelling evidence suggests that service learning provides ample opportunities for communication departments to establish such connections. Despite this assumed opportunity, only limited data-based research has been published in communication journals. Future research assessing the community connections or failures based on service learning is needed in our discipline.

While we emphasize various opportunities for filling gaps in communication education research focusing on service learning, we realize that calling for such refereed scholarship cannot occur without publishing access to existing communication journals. Our hope is that research that is well designed, enacted, and summarized will find a place in our journals. We have reason for optimism. In addition to the special issue of the *Southern Communication Journal*, *Communication Teacher* now invites scholarship based on assessment of student learning. Access to other national and regional journals in the form of special issues, traditional articles, research notes, and commentaries will enable the communication discipline to match the research productivity of other disciplines in the study of service learning.

Conclusion

Service learning remains a viable option for communication educators in a multiplicity of content areas. Students who embark on service learning projects have the potential to experience benefits such as civic engagement and enhanced opportunities for knowledge application. Evidence suggests that a growing number of communication faculty are recognizing the potential benefits of service learning and creating such opportunities for their students. If service learning is to reach its full potential in our discipline, however, this enthusiasm for application must be matched by an enthusiasm for research and publication of that research. The best practices for service learning in the communication discipline cannot likely be perfected based on anecdote and word of mouth alone. Rather, an extensive body of refereed research dedicated to discerning the best means of implementation and assessment is essential.

References

Abes, E. S., Jackson, G., & Jones, S. R. (2002). Factors that motivate and deter faculty use of service learning. *Michigan Journal of Community Service Learning, 1*, 5–17.

Artz, L. (2001). Critical ethnography for communication studies: Dialogue and social justice in service-learning. *Southern Communication Journal, 66,* 239–250.

Astin, A. W., & Sax, L. J. (1998). How undergraduates are affected by service participation. *Journal of College Student Development, 39,* 251–263.

Bachen, C. M. (1999). Integrating communication theory and practice in community settings: Approaches, opportunities, and ongoing challenges. In D. Droge & B. O. Murphy (Eds.), *Voices of a strong democracy: Concepts and models for service-learning in communication studies* (pp. 13–23). Sterling, VA: Stylus.

Bergstrom, M. J., & Bullis, C. (1999). Integrating service-learning into the communication curriculum at a research university: From institutionalization to assessment of effectiveness. In D. Droge & B. O. Murphy (Eds.), *Voices of a strong democracy: Concepts and models for service-learning in communication studies* (pp. 25–33). Sterling, VA: Stylus.

Bloom, M. (2008). From the classroom to the community: Building cultural awareness in first semester Spanish. *Language, Culture, and Curriculum, 21,* 103–119.

Borden, A. W. (2007). The impact of service-learning on ethnocentrism in an intercultural communication course. *Journal of Experiential Education, 30,* 171–183.

Braun, M. J. (2001). Using self-directed teams to integrate service-learning into an organizational communication course. *Southern Communication Journal, 66,* 226–238.

Bringle, R. G., & Hatcher, J. A. (1995). A service learning curriculum for faculty. *Michigan Journal of Community Service Learning, 2,* 112–122.

Bushouse, B. (2005). Community non-profit organizations and service-learning: Resource constraints to developing partnerships with universities. *Michigan Journal of Community Service Learning, 12,* 35–40.

Corbett, J. B., & Kendall, A. R. (1999). Evaluating service learning in the communication discipline. *Journalism and Mass Communication Educator, 53,* 66–76.

Coyle, E. J., Jamieson, L. H., & Sommers, L. S. (1997). EPICS: A model for integrating service learning into the engineering curriculum. *Michigan Journal of Community Service Learning, 4,* 81–90.

Dewey, J. (1938). *Experience and education.* New York: Macmillan.

Driscoll, A., Holland, B., Gelmon, S., & Kerrigan, S. (1996). An assessment model for service learning: Comprehensive case studies of impact on faculty, students, community, and institution. *Michigan Journal of Community Service Learning, 3,* 66–71.

Droge, D., & Murphy, B. O. (Eds.). (1999). *Voices of a strong democracy: Concepts and models for service learning in communication studies.* Sterling, VA: Stylus.

Einfeld, A., & Collins, D. (2008). The relationships between service learning, social justice, multicultural competence, and civic engagement. *Journal of College Student Development, 49,* 95–109.

Eyler, J. S., & Giles, D. E. (1999). *Where's the learning in service learning?* San Francisco: Jossey-Bass.

Ferrari, J. R., & Worrall, L. (2000). Assessments by community agencies: How "the other side" sees service learning. *Michigan Journal of Community Service Learning, 7,* 35–40.

Flournoy, C. (2007). Investigative reporting and service learning. *Journalism and Mass Communication Educator, 62,* 47–61.

Frymier, A. B., & Houser, M. L. (2000). The teacher-student relationship as an interpersonal relationship. *Communication Education, 49,* 207–219.

Frymier, A. B., & Shulman, G. M. (1995). "What's in it for me?" Increasing content relevance to enhance students' motivation. *Communication Education, 44,* 40–50.

Frymier, A. B., Shulman, G. M., & Houser, M. (1996). The development of a learner empowerment measure. *Communication Education, 45,* 181–199.

Gelmon, S. B., Holland, B. A., Seifer, S. D., Shinnamon, A., & Connors, K. (1998). Community-university partnerships for mutual learning. *Michigan Journal of Community Service Learning, 5,* 97–107.

Gibson, M. K., Kostecki, E. M., & Lucas, M. K. (2001). Instituting principles of best practice for service-learning in the communication curriculum. *Southern Communication Journal, 66,* 187–200.

Gilchrist, L. Z., Mundy, M. E., Felton, P., & Shields, S. L. (2003). Course transitions, midsemester assessment, and program design characteristics: A case study. *Michigan Journal of Community Service Learning, 10,* 51–58.

Gullicks, K. A. (2006). *What's service got to do with it? Investigating student sensemaking of required service in the basic communication course.* Unpublished doctoral dissertation, North Dakota State University, Fargo.

Gutheil, I. A., Chernesky, R. H., & Sherratt, M. L. (2006). Influencing student attitudes toward older adults: Results of a service-learning collaboration. *Educational Gerontology, 32,* 771–784.

Hammond, C. (1994). Integrating service and academic study. *Michigan Journal of Community Service Learning, 1,* 21–28.

Jorge, E. (2003). Outcomes for service learning in an unmediated service-learning program. *Michigan Journal of Community Service Learning, 10,* 28–38.

Keyton, J. (2001). Integrating service-learning in the research methods course. *Southern Communication Journal, 66,* 201–210.

Kolb, D. A. (1984). *Experiential learning: Experience as the source of learning and development.* Englewood Cliffs, NJ: Prentice Hall.

Lee, S. Y., Olszewski-Kubilius, P., Donahue, R., & Weimholt, K. (2008). The civic leadership institute: A service-learning program for academically gifted youth. *Journal of Advanced Academics, 19,* 272–308.

Litke, R. A. (2002). Do all students "get it"? Comparing students' reflections to course performance. *Michigan Journal of Community Service Learning, 8,* 27–34.

Lundy, B. L. (2007). Service learning in life-span developmental psychology: Higher exam scores and increased empathy. *Teaching of Psychology, 34,* 23–27.

McEachern, R. W. (2006). Incorporating reflection into business communication service-learning courses. *Business Communication Quarterly, 69,* 312–316.

Moely, B. E., McFarland, M., Miron, D., Mercer, S., & Ilustre, V. (2002). Changes in college students' attitudes and intentions for civic involvement as a function of service learning experiences. *Michigan Journal of Community Service Learning, 9,* 18–26.

Novak, J. M., Markey, V., & Allen, M. (2007). Evaluating cognitive outcomes of service learning in higher education: A meta-analysis. *Communication Research Reports, 24,* 149–157.

O'Hara, L. S. (2001). Service-learning: Students' transformative journey from communication student to civic-minded professional. *Southern Communication Journal, 66,* 251–266.

Oster-Aaland, L. K., Sellnow, T. L., Nelson, P. E., & Pearson, J. C. (2004). The status of service learning in departments of communication: A follow-up study. *Communication Education, 53,* 348–356.

Panici, D., & Lasky, K. (2002). Service learning's foothold in communication scholarship. *Journalism and Mass Communication Educator, 57,* 113–125.

Prentice, M. (2007). Service learning and civic engagement. *Academic Questions, 20,* 135–145.

Rhodes, N. J., & Davis, J. M. (2001). Using service learning to get positive reactions in the library. *Computers in Libraries, 21,* 32–35.

Richmond, V. P., Gorham, J. S., & McCroskey, J. C. (1987). The relationship between selected immediacy behaviors and cognitive learning. In M. L. McLaughlin (Ed.), *Communication Yearbook 10* (pp. 574–590). Newbury Park, CA: Sage.

Richmond, V. P., Lane, D. R., & McCroskey, J. C. (2006). Teacher immediacy and the teacher-student relationship. In T. P. Mottet, V. P. Richmond, & J. C. McCroskey (Eds.), *Handbook of instructional communication: Rhetorical and relational perspectives* (pp. 167–193). Boston: Pearson.

Rockquemore, K. A., & Schaffer, R. H. (2000). Toward a theory of engagement: A cognitive mapping of service-learning experiences. *Michigan Journal of Community Service Learning, 7,* 14–25.

Sandy, M., & Holland, B. A. (2006). Different worlds and common ground: Community partner perspectives on campus-community partnerships. *Michigan Journal of Community Service Learning, 13,* 30–43.

Sellnow, T. L., & Oster, L. (1997). The frequency, form and perceived benefits of service learning in communication departments. *Journal of the Association for Communication Administration, 3,* 190–197.

Simons, L., & Cleary, B. (2006). The influence of service learning on students' personal and social development. *College Teaching, 54,* 304–319.

Sprague, J. (2002). Communication education: The spiral continues. *Communication Education, 51,* 337–354.

Staton, A. Q., & Tomlinson, S. D. (2001). Communication education outreach in elementary school classrooms. *Southern Communication Journal, 66,* 211–224.

Stewart, T. (2008). Community service, self-efficacy and first-year undergraduate honors service learning. In M. A. Bowdon, S. H. Billig, & B. A. Holland (Eds.), *Scholarship for sustaining service-learning and civic engagement* (pp. 29–53). Charlotte, NC: Information Age.

Strage, A. A. (2000). Service-learning: Enhancing student learning outcomes in a college-level lecture course. *Michigan Journal of Community Service Learning, 7,* 5–13.

Tannenbaum, S. C. (2008). *Researching advocacy and political engagement: Multidisciplinary perspectives through service learning.* Sterling, VA: Stylus.

Turnley, M. (2007). Integrating critical approaches to technology and service-learning projects. *Technical Communication Quarterly, 16,* 103–123.

Vernon, A., & Ward, K. (1999). Campus and community partnerships. *Michigan Journal of Community Service Learning, 6,* 30–37.

Part II

Instructional Communication

Instructional Communication 8

The Emergence of a Field

Scott A. Myers

Since its inception, the field of instructional communication has enjoyed a healthy existence. Unlike its related subareas of communication education and developmental communication (Friedrich, 1989), instructional communication is considered to be a unique area of study rooted in the tripartite field of research conducted among educational psychology, pedagogy, and communication studies scholars (Mottet & Beebe, 2006). This tripartite field focuses on the learner (i.e., how students learn affectively, behaviorally, and cognitively), the instructor (i.e., the skills and strategies necessary for effective instruction), and the meaning exchanged in the verbal, nonverbal, and mediated messages between and among instructors and students. As such, the study of instructional communication centers on the study of the communicative factors in the teaching-learning process that occur across grade levels (e.g., K–12, postsecondary), instructional settings (e.g., the classroom, the organization), and subject matter (Friedrich, 1989; Staton, 1989).

Although some debate exists as to the events that precipitated the emergence of instructional communication as a field of study (Rubin & Feezel, 1986; Sprague, 1992), McCroskey and McCroskey (2006) posited that the establishment of instructional communication as a legitimate area of scholarship originated in 1972, when the governing board of the International Communication Association created the Instructional Communication Division. The purpose of the Division was to "focus attention on the role of communication in all teaching and training contexts, not just the teaching of communication" (p. 35), and provided instructional communication researchers with the opportunity to showcase their scholarship at the Association's annual convention and to publish their research in *Communication Yearbook*, a yearly periodical sponsored by the Association. In 1977, *Communication Yearbook* started the practice of publishing the top convention papers submitted to the Division as well as an overview chapter devoted to some component of instructional communication (McCroskey & McCroskey, 2006). These overview chapters were literature reviews (rather than empirical studies) intended to provide readers with an extensive synthesis of topics such as instructional theory and research (Scott & Wheeless, 1977), learning theory (Lashbrook & Wheeless, 1978), instructional strategies and systems (Wheeless & Hurt, 1979), classroom interaction (Daly & Korinek, 1980), and developmental communication (Van Kleeck & Daly, 1982).

Although this practice was discontinued in 1986 (McCroskey & McCroskey, 2006), by this time, instructional communication scholars had obtained another distribution outlet for their scholarship. In 1975, the journal *Speech Teacher* (sponsored by the Speech Communication Association) was renamed *Communication Education* and shifted its solicitation of manuscripts from those aiding instructors of speech communication courses to manuscripts that could "assist teachers of all disciplines and academic levels to apply communication theory and research to classroom teaching and learning" (Sprague, 1993, p. 107). Despite its name, the journal centered largely on the dissemination of instructional communication scholarship and has continued to be the primary research outlet for instructional communication research, a fact that prompted Waldeck, Kearney, and Plax (2001) to suggest that the journal be renamed to embrace its focus on instructional communication research. Supplementing this initial foray into scholarship was the publication in 1978 of the first instructional communication textbook, written by Hurt, Scott, and McCroskey. This textbook not only helped establish the field of instructional communication as a legitimate arena of both teaching and scholarship but also introduced readers (i.e., students, researchers) to several instructional communication variables (e.g., instructor credibility, homophily, and power; student motivation; student communication apprehension) that later morphed into viable lines of instructional communication research, many of which are still studied.

The late 1970s to early 1980s witnessed the birth of the variable-analytic approach to the study of instructional communication—an approach still associated heavily with instructional communication research—which was guided by a heavy reliance on logical empiricism as its philosophical frame (Nussbaum & Friedrich, 2005). This approach centers largely on the identification of particular communicative behaviors, traits, or attributes used by instructors with their students; these behaviors were believed to be linked with students' reports of their affective, behavioral, or cognitive learning; students' assessments of their instructors' positive teaching practices; and students' perceptions of effective classroom communication management practices (Nussbaum, 1992; Waldeck, Plax, & Kearney, 2009). Exemplars of the research conducted during this time period include the origins of the study of instructor nonverbal immediacy (Andersen, 1979), instructor communicator style (Norton, 1977), instructor humor (Bryant,

Comisky, & Zillmann, 1979), instructor communication concerns (Staton-Spicer & Marty-White, 1981), student communication apprehension (McCroskey, 1977), and the "Power in the Classroom" series (McCroskey & Richmond, 1983; Richmond & McCroskey, 1984). Furthermore, it was during this time period that instructional communication researchers began their quest to measure quantitatively the variables they were studying (e.g., nonverbal immediacy, communicator style, and power) as well as to measure student affective, behavioral, and cognitive learning (see Waldeck, Plax, & Kearney, Chapter 9, this volume, for a description of the development of learning measures).

These lines of research continued to develop further in the mid-1980s. For example, the study of instructor nonverbal immediacy bore its companion study of instructor verbal immediacy (Gorham, 1988), the study of instructor power gave rise to the emergence of instructor behavior alteration techniques and student resistance (see Chory & Goodboy, Chapter 10, this volume, for a review of these three research lines), the study of instructor communicator style was extended to explore further instructors' use of dramatic verbal communication behaviors (i.e., humor, self-disclosure, and narratives) (e.g., Downs, Javidi, & Nussbaum, 1988; Javidi, Downs, & Nussbaum, 1988), and the study of communication apprehension continued its exploration of its causes, correlates, and treatments across elementary, secondary, and postsecondary classrooms. During this time, the exploration of student communication competence commenced, and appropriate measures were developed for assessing this construct (Backlund, Brown, Gurry, & Jandt, 1982; Rubin, 1982; Rubin & Graham, 1988).

By the 1990s, several lines of research introduced in the late 1970s to early 1980s (i.e., power, immediacy, and humor) flourished, and newer lines of research emerged. Similar to the research conducted in the 1980s, instructional communication research continued to center primarily on instructor communicative behaviors, traits, or attributes, although a growing interest emerged in the examination of student communication variables (Staton-Spicer & Wulff, 1984; Waldeck et al., 2001). Some of these newer lines of research included instructor aggressive communication (e.g., Myers, 1998), instructor socio-communicative style (e.g., Thomas, McCroskey, & Richmond, 1994; see Martin & Myers, Chapter 4, this volume, for a review of this line), instructor use of affinity-seeking (e.g., McCroskey & McCroskey, 1986) and relevance strategies (e.g., Frymier & Shulman, 1995), instructor misbehaviors (e.g., Kearney, Plax, Hays, & Ivey, 1991), student clarifying techniques (e.g., Kendrick & Darling, 1990), student motivation (e.g., Christophel, 1990; Gorham & Millette, 1997), student learner empowerment (e.g., Frymier, Shulman, & Houser, 1996), and student motives to communicate with their instructors (e.g., Martin, Myers, & Mottet, 1999). Instructor clarity, which originally was studied among educational psychologists, also gained the attention of communication studies scholars during this time (see Titsworth & Mazer, Chapter 13, this volume, for a review of the development of this construct).

As instructional communication research moved into the first decade of 2000, much of the variable analytic research continued. Continued lines of research include the study of instructor power, immediacy, humor, clarity, aggressive communication, self-disclosure, socio-communicative style, and misbehaviors; new lines of research, such as instructor confirmation (e.g., Ellis, 2000) and instructor temperament (e.g., McCroskey, Valencic, & Richmond, 2004), also were introduced. Researchers also began to show an increased interest in the role technology plays in the instructional environment (Lane & Shelton, 2001) by focusing on issues such as distance education, classroom digital technology, e-mail, and social networking sites (Waldeck et al., 2009). From the student perspective, the research conducted on student motives to communicate with their instructors thrived, and a host of new research studies examined the reasons, functions, and correlates of students' out-of-class communication with their instructors (e.g., Bippus, Kearney, Plax, & Brooks, 2003; Jaasma & Koper, 2001). Instructional communication researchers continued to refine their measurement instruments, and the communibiological perspective was introduced as an additional research paradigm through which instructional communication could be studied (see Ayres, 2000, for a special issue on the communibiological perspective).

Across the decades, however, three lines of research retained a high level of visibility. The first line was instructor nonverbal immediacy (see Witt, Schrodt, and Turman, Chapter 11, this volume, for a review of the literature), the second line was communication apprehension (see McCroskey & Beatty, 1998), and the third line was instructor credibility. Instructor credibility, which is defined as the "attitude of a receiver which references the degree to which a source is seen to be believable" (McCroskey, 1998, p. 80), exists across three dimensions: (1) competence, which is the extent to which an instructor is considered to be an expert on the subject matter; (2) character, which is the extent to which an instructor is viewed as honest and trustworthy; and (3) caring, which is the extent to which an instructor is perceived to be concerned about the welfare of students (McCroskey, 1998). Since its initial introduction to the instructional communication setting (McCroskey, Holdridge, & Toomb, 1974), both the conceptualization and the measurement of the instructor credibility construct have evolved extensively (McCroskey & Teven, 1999; McCroskey & Young, 1981; Teven & McCroskey, 1997). A meta-analysis conducted by Finn and her colleagues (2009) revealed that perceived instructor credibility is moderately associated with a host of instructor attributes (e.g., sex, sexual orientation, and race), instructor communicative behaviors and traits (e.g., argumentativeness and verbal aggressiveness, confirmation, and nonverbal immediacy), and student outcomes (e.g., state motivation, affective learning, and cognitive learning). Most recently, Zhang and Sapp (2009) found that instructor burnout has a negative impact on instructor credibility. Based on these collective findings, it is not surprising that Myers (2001) claimed that instructor credibility is one of the most important variables affecting the instructor-student relationship.

The Chapters

This section of the *Handbook* focuses on some of the most widely studied constructs in the instructional communication domain, many of which date back to the initial research conducted among instructional communication scholars. In Chapter 9, Jennifer Waldeck, Timothy Plax, and Patricia Kearney examine the philosophical and methodological foundations of instructional communication. Building on their earlier work (Waldeck et al., 2001), they begin their chapter by reviewing several prominent lines of research and theoretical frameworks associated with instructional communication research across the content areas of student communication, instructor communication, and instructor-student interaction. These lines of research include communication apprehension and student motivation (i.e., student communication), instructor confirmation and misbehaviors (i.e., instructor communication), and mentoring (i.e., instructor-student interaction). They then identify recent developments that have occurred in the study of instructional communication, which include an increase in researchers' interest in instructor-student interaction, the transfer of traditional instructional communication research to the training and development context, and the proliferation of technology in the learning process. Central to the learning process is the conceptualization and measurement of student affective, behavioral, and cognitive learning, which Waldeck and her colleagues summarize concisely. This summary is followed by two suggestions they recommend instructional communication researchers should heed. The first suggestion centers on the development of theoretical models that succinctly capture the essence and tone of instructional communication; the second suggestion focuses on the exploration of the interfaces between technology use, communication, and learning. By doing so, Waldeck et al. are confident that the contributions made by instructional communication researchers to the field of communication studies will remain heuristic.

In Chapter 10, Rebecca Chory and Alan Goodboy provide a comprehensive chronology of the "Power in the Classroom" series. They begin their chapter with a thorough review of the first two "Power in the Classroom" articles, which introduced French and Raven's (1959, 1968) concept of power bases (i.e., coercive, reward, legitimate, expert, and referent) to the instructional communication setting by identifying the correlates and outcomes associated with each power base. Chory and Goodboy then review the findings of the next five "Power in the Classroom" articles.

In this review, they provide a history and synthesis of the research conducted on the compliance-gaining strategies, which are referred to as behavioral alteration techniques (BATs), used by college instructors, graduate teaching assistants, and K–12 teachers. From this review, they then explore the research conducted on student resistance, which arguably is an attendant of the power research, and how student resistance is linked to students' perceptions of instructor use of BATs, immediacy behaviors, and classroom justice. To aid researchers in their study of power, compliance gaining, and resistance, Chory and Goodboy identify the measures used to assess these constructs. However, as they note, the power and compliance-gaining research has been mired in mild controversy over issues surrounding its measurement. These issues are addressed briefly, as are the strengths, limitations, and future research directions of this body of research. Chory and Goodboy conclude their chapter by challenging instructional communication researchers to continue the theoretical and pragmatically important work conducted to date on the power, compliance-gaining, and resistance classroom communication constructs.

In Chapter 11, Paul Witt, Paul Schrodt, and Paul Turman examine the extensive body of work conducted on instructor immediacy. After reviewing the development of the nonverbal and the verbal immediacy constructs, they identify the research conducted to date on nonverbal and verbal immediacy with the traditional areas of instructional communication research—namely, the influence of student communication variables (e.g., motivation, empowerment), instructor communication variables (e.g., power, clarity), and student learning (e.g., affective learning, cognitive learning). They also examine whether students' perceptions of instructor immediacy vary across cultures (e.g., China, Germany, Puerto Rico, and Japan, as well as the United States) and classroom settings (e.g., distributed learning environments, use of technology) as well as summarize the designs and measures used in immediacy research. They then synthesize the theoretical explanations that underlie the immediacy construct, pay particular attention to the four theoretical models (i.e., the learning model, the motivation model, the affect model, and the integrated model) that have evolved from immediacy research, and identify the critiques and challenges associated with immediacy research. They conclude their chapter by proposing that researchers examine further the viability of the measurement of verbal immediacy, continue to explore the relationship between immediacy and cognitive learning, and engage in additional testing of theoretical models of immediacy and learning. By doing so, Witt and colleagues contend that instructional communication researchers will be able to uncover *why* and *how* instructor immediacy works, which instructional communication researchers have not yet done.

In Chapter 12, Melanie Booth-Butterfield and Melissa Wanzer review the role that humor plays in the instructional setting. They begin their chapter by providing an overview and theoretical background of the study of humor, addressing the three seminal theories (i.e., arousal relief or relief theory, incongruity theory, and disparagement or superiority theory) that have guided humor research and introducing a new theory (i.e., instructional humor processing theory) to explain further the purported link between instructor use of humorous messages and student learning. They then explore the benefits instructors and students associate with humor use in the classroom before reviewing the various typologies of humor used by instructors. From this review, they shift their focus to highlighting the Humor Orientation Scale (Booth-Butterfield & Booth-Butterfield, 1991)—one measurement tool used extensively to assess both instructor and student perceptions of humor in the classroom—by assessing the reliability and validity of the scale, summarizing the characteristics of individuals who possess a humor orientation, and identifying the ways in which humor orientation operates in the classroom. They conclude their chapter by offering directions for future research and encouraging instructional communication researchers to continue the study of humor across instructional contexts.

In Chapter 13, Scott Titsworth and Joseph Mazer trace the evolution of the instructor clarity construct from its roots in educational psychology to its current state in communication studies. Their chapter commences with a provision of the theoretical foundations of clarity research, which is followed by a cumulative review of the research efforts undertaken by educational psychologists (i.e., the Ohio State studies) and researchers in communication studies (i.e., the perception studies) to conceptualize and operationalize the instructor clarity construct. They then examine the classroom effects of instructor clarity by identifying the links between instructor clarity and student affective and cognitive learning; highlighting the linguistic dimensions of instructor clarity; recognizing the interaction effects between instructor clarity, instructor immediacy, and student test anxiety; reporting the results gleaned from instituting training on instructor clarity; and exploring the role culture plays in student perceptions of instructor clarity. They offer recommendations for the future study of instructor clarity by offering three observations: (1) instructor clarity is multidimensional, (2) future studies should emphasize the process of instructor clarity (rather than its product), and (3) instructor clarity research is foreshadowed by a positive bias. They conclude their chapter by reminding instructional communication researchers who are interested in studying instructor clarity to do so in a manner that avoids conflating the study of clarity with the study of effective instructional communicative behaviors.

In Chapter 14, Matthew Martin and Scott Myers explore the relational side of instructional communication by focusing on the relational approach to teaching via the influence of instructor presentational communication traits in the college classroom. They begin their chapter by providing an overview of the trait approach to the study of instructor communication. They then narrow their focus to the explication of three instructor presentational traits, which are instructor self-disclosure, instructor communicator style, and instructor socio-communicative style. For each trait, they review its operationalization (i.e., definition, components) and summarize the research conducted on its outcomes (e.g., links with other instructor communication traits, behaviors, or attributes) and effects (e.g., student perceptions of instructors, student learning). Positing that the continued study of instructor communication traits is warranted, Martin and Myers recommend that instructional communication researchers consider analyzing the situations in which student behavior occurs, focusing on students' reports of their communication traits, and relying less on student self-reports as the primary mode of data gathering. They conclude their chapter by suggesting that instructional communication researchers who embrace the trait approach to instructional communication should be able to enhance the study of the relational approach to teaching.

Conclusion

Based on this collective body of research, it appears that the field of instructional communication has continued (and will continue) to enjoy a healthy existence. As instructional communication research moves into the next decade, it stands to reason that not only will researchers continue to study the communicative factors in the teaching-learning process that occur across grade levels, instructional settings, and subject matter; they will also identify, investigate, and expatiate the factors that make the study of instructional communication unique.

References

Andersen, J. F. (1979). Teacher immediacy as a predictor of teaching effectiveness. In D. Nimmo (Ed.), *Communication yearbook 3* (pp. 543–559). New Brunswick, NJ: Transaction Books.

Ayres, J. (Ed.). (2000). The nature/nurture balance [Special issue]. *Communication Education, 49*(1).

Backlund, P. M., Brown, K. L., Gurry, J., & Jandt, F. (1982). Recommendations for assessing speaking and listening skills. *Communication Education, 31,* 9–17.

Bippus, A. M., Kearney, P., Plax, T. G., & Brooks, C. F. (2003). Teacher access and mentoring abilities: Predicting the outcome value of extra class communication. *Journal of Applied Communication Research, 31,* 260–275.

Booth-Butterfield, S., & Booth-Butterfield, M. (1991). The communication of humor in everyday life. *Southern Communication Journal, 56,* 205–218.

Bryant, L., Comisky, P., & Zillmann, D. (1979). Teachers' humor in the college classroom. *Communication Education, 28,* 110–118.

Christophel, D. M. (1990). The relationships among teacher immediacy behaviors, student motivation, and learning. *Communication Education, 39,* 323–340.

Daly, J. A., & Korinek, J. T. (1980). Instructional communication theory and research: An overview of classroom interaction. In D. Nimmo (Ed.), *Communication yearbook 4* (pp. 515–532). New Brunswick, NJ: Transaction Books.

Downs, V. C., Javidi, M., & Nussbaum, J. F. (1988). An analysis of teachers' verbal communication within the college classroom: Use of humor, self-disclosure, and narratives. *Communication Education, 37,* 127–141.

Ellis, K. (2000). Perceived teacher confirmation: The development and validation of an instrument and two studies of the relationship to cognitive and affective learning. *Human Communication Research, 26,* 264–291.

Finn, A.N., Schrodt, P., Witt, P. L., Elledge, N., Jernberg, K.A., & Larson, L.M. (2009, November). A meta-analytical review of teacher credibility and its associations with teacher behaviors and student outcomes. *Communication Education, 58,* 516–537.

French, J. R. P., & Raven, B. (1959). The bases for social power. In D. Cartwright (Ed.), *Studies in social power* (pp. 150–167). Ann Arbor: University of Michigan Press.

French, J. R. P., & Raven, B. H. (1968). The bases of social power. In D. Cartwright & A. Zander (Eds.), *Group dynamics: Research and theory* (pp. 259–270). New York: Harper & Row.

Friedrich, G. W. (1989). A view from the office of the SCA president. *Communication Education, 38,* 297–302.

Frymier, A. B., & Shulman, G. M. (1995). "What's in it for me?" Increasing content relevance to enhance students' motivation. *Communication Education, 44,* 40–50.

Frymier, A. B., Shulman, G. M., & Houser, M. (1996). The development of a learner empowerment measure. *Communication Education, 45,* 181–199.

Gorham, J. (1988). The relationship between verbal immediacy behaviors and student learning. *Communication Education, 37,* 40–53.

Gorham, J., & Millette, D. M. (1997). A comparative analysis of teacher and student perceptions of sources of motivation and demotivation in college classes. *Communication Education, 46,* 245–261.

Hurt, H. T., Scott, M. D., & McCroskey, J. C. (1978). *Communication in the classroom.* Reading, MA: Addison-Wesley.

Jaasma, M. A., & Koper, R. J. (2001, May). *Talk to me: An examination of the content of out-of-class interaction between students and faculty.* Paper presented at the annual meeting of the International Communication Association, Washington, DC.

Javidi, M., Downs, V. C., & Nussbaum, J. F. (1988). A comparative analysis of teachers' use of dramatic style behaviors at higher and secondary educational levels. *Communication Education, 37,* 278–288.

Kearney, P., Plax, T. G., Hays, E. R., & Ivey, M. J. (1991). College teacher misbehaviors: What students don't like about what teachers say or do. *Communication Quarterly, 39,* 309–324.

Kendrick, W. L., & Darling, A. L. (1990). Problems of understanding in classrooms: Students' use of clarifying tactics. *Communication Education, 39,* 15–29.

Lane, D. R., & Shelton, M. W. (2001). The centrality of communication education in classroom computer-mediated communication: Toward a practical and evaluation pedagogy. *Communication Education, 50,* 241–255.

Lashbrook, V. J., & Wheeless, L. R. (1978). Instructional communication theory and research: An overview of the relationship between learning theory and instructional communication. In B. D. Ruben (Ed.), *Communication yearbook 2* (pp. 439–456). New Brunswick, NJ: Transaction Books.

Martin, M. M., Myers, S. A., & Mottet, T. P. (1999). Students' motives for communicating with their instructors. *Communication Education, 48,* 155–164.

McCroskey, J. C. (1977). Oral communication apprehension: A summary of recent theory and research. *Human Communication Research, 4,* 78–96.

McCroskey, J. C. (1998). *An introduction to communication in the classroom* (2nd ed.). Acton, MA: Tapestry Press.

McCroskey, J. C., & Beatty, M. J. (1998). Communication apprehension. In J. C. McCroskey, J. A. Daly, M. M. Martin, & M. J. Beatty (Eds.), *Communication and personality: Trait perspectives* (pp. 215–231). Cresskill, NJ: Hampton Press.

McCroskey, J. C., Holdridge, W., & Toomb, J. K. (1974). An instrument for measuring the source credibility of basic speech communication instructors. *Speech Teacher, 23,* 26–33.

McCroskey, J. C., & McCroskey, L. L. (1986). The affinity-seeking of classroom teachers. *Communication Research Reports, 3,* 158–167.

McCroskey, J. C., & McCroskey, L. L. (2006). Instructional communication: The historical perspective. In T. P. Mottet, V. P. Richmond, & J. C. McCroskey (Eds.), *Handbook of instructional communication: Rhetorical and relational perspectives* (pp. 33–47). Boston: Allyn & Bacon.

McCroskey, J. C., & Richmond, V. P. (1983). Power in the classroom I: Teacher and student perceptions. *Communication Education, 32,* 175–184.

McCroskey, J. C., & Teven, J. J. (1999). Goodwill: A reexamination of the construct and its measurement. *Communication Monographs, 66,* 90–103.

McCroskey, J. C., Valencic, K. M., & Richmond, V. P. (2004). Toward a general model of instructional communication. *Communication Quarterly, 52,* 197–210.

McCroskey, J. C., & Young, T. J. (1981). Ethos and credibility: The construct and its measurement after three decades. *Central States Speech Journal, 32,* 24–34.

Mottet, T. P., & Beebe, S. A. (2006). Foundations of instructional communication. In T. P. Mottet, V. P. Richmond, & J. C. McCroskey (Eds.), *Handbook of instructional communication: Rhetorical and relational perspectives* (pp. 3–32). Boston: Allyn & Bacon.

Myers, S. A. (1998). Instructor socio-communicative style, argumentativeness, and verbal aggressiveness in the college classroom. *Communication Research Reports, 15,* 141–150.

Myers, S. A. (2001). Perceived instructor credibility and verbal aggressiveness in the college classroom. *Communication Research Reports, 18,* 354–364.

Norton, R. W. (1977). Teacher effectiveness as a function of communicator style. In B. D. Ruben (Ed.), *Communication yearbook 1* (pp. 525–542). New Brunswick, NJ: Transaction Books.

Nussbaum, J. F. (1992). Effective teacher behaviors. *Communication Education, 41,* 167–180.

Nussbaum, J. F., & Friedrich, G. (2005). Instructional/developmental communication: Current theory, research, and future trends. *Journal of Communication, 55,* 578–593.

Richmond, V. P., & McCroskey, J. C. (1984). Power in the classroom II: Power and learning. *Communication Education, 33,* 125–136.

Rubin, R. B. (1982). Assessing speaking and listening competence at the college level: The communication competency assessment instrument. *Communication Education, 31,* 19–32.

Rubin, R. B., & Feezel, J. D. (1986). A needs assessment of research in communication education. *Central States Speech Journal, 37,* 113–118.

Rubin, R. B., & Graham, E. E. (1988). Communication correlates of college success: An exploratory investigation. *Communication Education, 37,* 14–27.

Scott, M. D., & Wheeless, L. R. (1977). Instructional communication theory and research: An overview. In B. D. Ruben (Ed.), *Communication yearbook 1* (pp. 495–511). New Brunswick, NJ: Transaction Books.

Sprague, J. (1992). Expanding the research agenda for instructional communication: Raising some unasked questions. *Communication Education, 41,* 1–25.

Sprague, J. (1993). Retrieving the research agenda for communication education: Asking the pedagogical questions that are "embarrassments to theory." *Communication Education, 42,* 106–122.

Staton, A. Q. (1989). The interface of communication and instruction: Conceptual considerations and programmatic manifestations. *Communication Education, 38,* 364–371.

Staton-Spicer, A. Q., & Marty-White, C. R. (1981). A framework for instructional communication theory: The relationship between teacher communication concerns and classroom behavior. *Communication Education, 30,* 354–366.

Staton-Spicer, A. Q., & Wulff, D. H. (1984). Research in communication and instruction: Categorization and synthesis. *Communication Education, 33,* 377–391.

Teven, J. J., & McCroskey, J. C. (1997). The relationship of perceived teacher caring with student learning and teacher evaluation. *Communication Education, 46,* 1–9.

Thomas, C. E., McCroskey, J. C., & Richmond, V. P. (1994). The association between immediacy and socio-communicative style. *Communication Research Reports, 11,* 107–115.

Van Kleeck, A., & Daly, J. A. (1982). Instructional communication research and theory: Communication development and instructional communication—an overview. In M. Burgoon (Ed.), *Communication yearbook 5* (pp. 685–715). New Brunswick, NJ: Transaction Books.

Waldeck, J. H., Kearney, P., & Plax, T. G. (2001). Instructional and developmental communication theory and research in the 1990s: Extending the agenda for the 21st century. In W. B. Gudykunst (Ed.), *Communication yearbook 24* (pp. 207–229). Thousand Oaks, CA: Sage.

Waldeck, J. H., Plax, T. G., & Kearney, P. (2009, November). *Philosophical and methodological foundations of instructional communication.* Paper presented at the annual meeting of the National Communication Association, Chicago.

Wheeless, L. R., & Hurt, H. T. (1979). Instructional communication theory and research: An overview of instructional strategies as instructional communication systems. In D. Nimmo (Ed.), *Communication yearbook 3* (pp. 525–541). New Brunswick, NJ: Transaction Books.

Zhang, Q., & Sapp, D. A. (2009). The effect of perceived teacher burnout on credibility. *Communication Research Reports, 26,* 87–90.

Philosophical and Methodological Foundations of Instructional Communication

9

Jennifer H. Waldeck,
Timothy G. Plax, and Patricia Kearney

Instructional communication enjoys a rich history within the discipline, dating to the 1972 International Communication Association conference and subsequent *Communication Yearbook* reviews designed to introduce the area and provide a conceptual scope for the study of communication in instruction. Since then, international, national, and regional communication professional associations have created divisions related to the study of instructional communication; a number of communication departments have developed graduate programs in the area; and research in instructional communication has flourished across regional, national, and international journals. Instructional communication scholars have developed a number of psychometrically sound measures and generated knowledge on student and instructor variables, as well as the nature of relationships that form among students and instructors.

This chapter provides an overview of the assumptions, theories, and methods that characterize the history of instructional communication research. It begins with the identification and explication of prominent lines of research and theoretical frameworks, followed by a review of developments in instructional communication. This chapter concludes by defining the research agenda in a way that addresses the contemporary challenges and opportunities of both learning and conducting research on the instructional communication process.

Prominent Lines of Research and Theoretical Frameworks

To identify the most prominent lines of instructional communication research, we conducted a systematic analysis of the literature published from 1970 to the present in communication journals. This task yielded an extensive list of constructs studied, measures developed, and theories employed. We applied several criteria in identifying the most important areas of research to cover in this chapter: (a) heuristic value (i.e., programs of research were chosen over isolated studies), (b) frequency with which the construct appeared in the literature, (c) evidence of a theoretical framework in at least some studies within the research program (i.e., the theory may have driven or resulted from the study), and (d) value to instructional practitioners across disciplines (in general, lines of research pertaining exclusively to communication education were excluded). Importantly, we excluded lines of research that, critical to an understanding of instructional communication, are covered elsewhere in this handbook (i.e., instructor power, immediacy, humor, and clarity).

We then classified the areas that met our criteria according to the general foci of instructional communication research identified by Waldeck, Kearney, and Plax (2001b): student communication, instructor communication, and instructor-student interaction. Student-focused research variables covered in the following section include communication apprehension and motivation; instructor-focused scholarship includes studies on confirmation and misbehaviors, and instructor-student interaction research focuses on mentoring.

STUDENT-FOCUSED RESEARCH

Communication Apprehension (CA). During the 1970s and 1980s, no other construct received such systematic attention in the instructional communication literature as communication apprehension and its corollaries of willingness to communicate, reticence, and shyness. (For an extensive review of research findings on CA, see Richmond & McCroskey, 1998.) Communication apprehension is defined by Richmond and McCroskey as "an individual's level of fear or anxiety associated with either real or anticipated communication with another person or persons" (p. 41). Research efforts in this area, launched by McCroskey (1970), examined the broad effects of CA on human communication outcomes, with the instructional communication literature isolating the correlates and consequences of CA on student learning and performance of communication skills such as public speaking and presentation preparation (e.g., high CAs avoid classes with participation requirements, interactive formats, and heavy discussion load).

Additionally, CA often interferes with learning and achievement. High CA students may take longer than low CA students to finish their degrees or may not complete them at all (Ericson & Gardner, 1992). Anxiety related to communicating about course material appears to interfere with cognitive learning and recall; conversely, students with low CA appear to behave in ways that increase their chances of positive learning outcomes (Richmond & McCroskey, 1998). Although no meaningful correlation exits between apprehension and intelligence, instructors and classmates tend to misperceive quiet students as incompetent or unintelligent. Similarly, peers perceive quiet others as less approachable and less friendly than those peers who are talkative; thus, high CA students may miss collaborative learning and study opportunities. Although these negative attributions about quiet students may be faulty, they often lead to self-fulfilling prophecies that diminish students' self-esteem and eventual learning. Similarly, research indicates that quiet or apprehensive instructors are not as well liked by students as extroverted instructors, leading to diminished affective learning and skill transfer.

Numerous CA studies have been grounded in theoretical frames that propose predictors, correlates, and treatments of CA. Beatty, Plax, and Kearney (1985) tested reinforcement theory and modeling as explanations for childhood development of CA and found that CA is not acquired through the modeling of parents' communication behaviors but that reinforcement—regardless of parental CA level—was the better predictor of a child's apprehension. Witt and Behnke (2006) successfully used uncertainty-reduction theory to explain why students experience more anticipatory anxiety related to certain speaking assignments. Beatty, McCroskey, and Heisel (1998) proffered a neurological explanation for the etiology of CA in their theory of communibiology. Elsewhere, Duff, Levine, Beatty, Woolbright, and Park (2007) tested various treatment theories (e.g., systematic desensitization, visualization therapy) and found no evidence that treatment results in more or longer-lasting improvement in CA levels than placebo control and enrollment in a public speaking skills class.

Student Motivation. Instructional communication research clearly demonstrates that student success is a result of participation and engagement (Frymier & Shulman, 1995) and that motivation is a necessary and critical, but usually insufficient, condition for engagement that increases students' desire to learn (Christophel, 1990; Dweck, 1986). Richmond (1990) succinctly argued that motivation exists when learners do something because they prefer to do so, rather than doing something because someone else wants them to even though they prefer not to. Furthermore, motivation has been described as a process, rather than a singular activity, which includes directive and stimulating activities designed to instigate particular behaviors among students, make those behaviors persistent, and equip students to direct their own behavior with regard to the subject matter (Ames, 1986). Notably, although instructors play an important role in student motivation, no one individual can be responsible for either motivating or demotivating a learner (Christophel, 1990).

Motivation is conceptualized further as either a trait or a state orientation (Brophy, 1987). Trait motivation is a learner's enduring predisposition toward learning and accomplishment; state motivation occurs with regard to specific classes or subject matters. Surprisingly, Christophel (1990) demonstrated that although students may be trait motivated to learn, a predisposition toward motivation in general contributes little to learning in specific courses. Instead, student state motivation, modifiable within a specific course environment, "unequivocally" (p. 337) explains the unique variance in learning. Instructor behaviors, course material, tests, projects, and technologies used within a course may all affect students' state motivation to learn in a particular course. For example, student state motivation is related positively to student perceptions of instructor fairness (Chory-Assad, 2002), trustworthiness (Jaasma & Koper, 1999), self-disclosure (Mazer, Murphy, & Simonds, 2007), argumentativeness (Myers & Knox, 2000), and immediacy (Allen, Witt, & Wheeless, 2006). State motivation may contribute to student receiver apprehension (Ayres, Wilcox, & Ayres, 1995), and collaborative learning situations may enhance state motivation (Dobos, 1996). Although student state motivation is affected negatively when instructors are verbally aggressive (Myers, 2002) or engage in other misbehaviors (Wanzer & McCroskey, 1998), out-of-class interaction between instructors and students appears to enhance student state motivation (Jaasma & Koper, 1999; Jones, 2008). Moreover, positively valenced computer-mediated word-of-mouth communication about instructors (e.g., RateMyProfessor.com) may heighten student state motivation (Edwards, Edwards, Qingmei, & Wahl, 2007).

Gorham and Millette (1997) found that instructors and students assign credit or blame for motivation (or the lack thereof) differently. Whereas instructors tend to credit themselves for their students' motivation (e.g., how they organize the class, the quality of assignments), students assume credit for their own motivation (e.g., interest in the subject matter, desire to succeed). Consistent with this pattern of attributions, instructors tend to blame students for being demotivated (e.g., students' lack of preparation), while students tend to blame their instructors (e.g., poor presentational skills, lack of clarity). Without question, instructor behaviors affect the motivational climate of the classroom, but this relationship may not be as straightforward as imagined.

Instructional communication researchers have employed Keller's (1983) ARCS theoretical framework to explain the role of motivation in various instructional contexts. The ARCS model of motivational design indicates that instructors who make material relevant to students' lives or goals increase motivation to learn. The model delineates four concepts that, in sum, define learners' motivation: attention focused on the subject matter, relevance of the content or instructional medium to students' personal goals or interests, confidence or self-efficacy in mastering the material, and satisfaction with the outcome of the learning experience. Frymier and Shulman (1995) found that the more effectively instructors communicated relevance in their instruction, the more motivated students were to learn. Waldeck and Dougherty (2008) demonstrated that when students attend to the reasons for using course-related technology, perceive the relevance of the technology to the course, have confidence using the medium, and are satisfied with the outcome, their motivation to learn ensues.

INSTRUCTOR-FOCUSED RESEARCH

Instructor Confirmation. Instructor confirmation refers to a series of communication behaviors through which instructors signal to students that they are valuable and significant (Ellis, 2000, 2004). This line of research emanates from confirmation theory (Buber, 1957), which argues that confirmation may be the most important facet of human interaction. Although instructor confirmation can be communicated in interactions with the class as a whole, the most confirming behaviors are those behaviors that occur in personalized communication with students. Ellis (2000, 2004) identified four dimensions of confirming communication. First, instructors confirm students by responding to questions in ways that students perceive as showing instructor interest and availability. Second, instructors confirm students when they demonstrate interest in, and communicate concern for, their students as individuals. Third, teaching strategies can communicate confirmation to students. For instance, when students perceive that an instructor has provided a meaningful exercise or activity to help them understand a concept, they report feeling confirmed. Fourth, confirming instructors avoid antisocial communication behaviors, such as making rude remarks or embarrassing students. Ellis (2000) reported a small but significant and positive relationship between students' perceptions of instructor confirmation behaviors and their affective and cognitive learning. Later, Ellis (2004) found that students' perceptions of how confirmingly or disconfirmingly their instructors behave influence their overall feelings of confirmation. Furthermore, Ellis found that the absence of instructor confirmation results in student receiver apprehension and that confirmation indirectly affects student state motivation, cognitive learning, and affective learning, although this relationship is mediated by student receiver apprehension.

Schrodt, Turman, and Soliz (2006) found evidence that instructor confirmation both directly and indirectly affects students' perceptions of instructor credibility and instructor evaluations. Confirming messages directly influence how students perceive their instructors; at the same time, confirming messages influence positively students' perceived understanding, which, in turn, further affects how they evaluate their instructors. Goodboy and Myers (2008) examined how instructor confirmation behaviors influence student communication and learning. They concluded, overall, that students are motivated to communicate with instructors who are confirming and that students participate more and challenge less in courses with instructors who engage in confirming communication. Moreover, instructor confirmation was related positively to student affective and cognitive learning, satisfaction, and motivation. In sum, instructors who confirm students are likely to be perceived as caring and understanding, prompting positive student engagement and learning outcomes.

Instructor Misbehaviors. Not so unlike student misbehaviors that interfere with instruction, instructor misbehaviors irritate, demotivate, or substantially distract students from learning. Departing from the traditional perspective of students as the source of learning interference, Kearney, Plax, Hays, and Ivey (1991) argued that not only do instructors misbehave, but those behaviors can influence how students think about, feel, and act toward the instructor, school, and themselves. Inductively deriving types of instructor misbehaviors from student reports, they identified 28 categories of instructor misbehaviors that could be reduced to three underlying dimensions, profiled as incompetence, offensiveness, and indolence. Incompetent instructors engage in a cluster of misbehaviors that reflect a lack of caring for either the course or the students by failing to learn students' names and/or being unable or unwilling to help students succeed. Offensive instructors are characterized as mean and cruel; they humiliate, embarrass, and intimidate students. Indolent instructors engage in misbehaviors that are seemingly irresponsible, such as showing up to class late or neglecting to grade homework.

This early research on instructor misbehaviors has proven to be highly heuristic. Relying on attribution theory, Kelsey, Kearney, Plax, Allen, and Ritter (2004) found that when their instructors misbehave, students more readily assign causal attributions of internality than of externality. Surprisingly, instructor nonverbal immediacy failed to neutralize these attributions; students continued to ascribe dispositional, not situational, causes to instructors who engage in offensive, indolent, or incompetent misbehaviors. In short, students hold instructors responsible for their behaviors and appear to be unconcerned or unaware that instructors may have mitigating or plausible reasons for what they do or fail to do. McPherson and Young (2004) focused on a specific type of offensive instructor misbehavior—anger—and found that students assign greater internal attributions to instructors who display anger aggressively and fewer internal attributions to instructors who display anger assertively.

Conceptualizing instructor misbehaviors as a form of classroom norm violation, Berkos, Allen, Kearney, and Plax (2001) reported that students preferred imagining what they might say or could have said with norm-violating instructors as a substitute for directly interacting with or confronting these instructors. McPherson, Kearney, and Plax (2003) found that how instructors expressed anger influenced whether or not students perceived the misbehavior as a norm violation to the extent that intense and aggressive anger displays were perceived as inappropriate and associated with lower student affect. Related research on instructor aggressiveness illustrates how this misbehavior type negatively influences perceptions of instructor credibility (Myers, 2001; Schrodt, 2003; Teven, 2001) as well as students' inclination to ask questions in class and seek further interaction with their instructors, both in and out of class (Myers, Edwards, Wahl, & Martin, 2007).

INSTRUCTOR-STUDENT INTERACTION

In the instructional context, mentoring is a communication process involving a seasoned instructor who counsels, guides, and tutors a student protégé in academic, career, and social matters (Waldeck, Orrego, Plax, & Kearney, 1997). Research indicates that faculty mentors function in capacities beyond academic advising and provide important personal and social support to their student protégés. Instructional communication researchers have documented numerous benefits of mentoring (Kogler-Hill, Bahniuk, & Dobos, 1989). For instance, student-faculty mentorships allow students increased face time with their instructors, an important correlate with student retention, academic progress, and graduation. Mentored students secure higher postgraduation incomes than their nonmentored counterparts, and they tend to be more self-confident, empowered, and well connected in important communication networks (Waldeck et al., 1997).

In a study of graduate student–faculty mentoring across the disciplines, Waldeck et al. (1997) identified 10 diverse communication strategies that students rely on to initiate mentoring relationships with faculty. The strategies ranged from very passive (e.g., "Assume it will just happen") to a variety of more direct approaches (e.g., "Seek counsel from target mentor" and "Appeal to target directly"). Graduate students successful in initiating a mentoring relationship characterized these relationships as "extremely pleasurable, meaningful, and productive" (p. 105). Moreover, students reported that in graduate student–faculty mentoring relationships, the psychosocial function predominates in both frequency and importance over the career function. That is, students who form close, personal relationships with their mentors also reported more satisfying learning and professional benefits than protégés who did not form a close, personal relationship with their mentors.

Mentoring is related to a number of important learning variables in the undergraduate context as well (Bippus, Kearney, Plax, & Brooks, 2003; Waldeck, 2007). Undergraduates who perceive their instructors to have strong course- and career-related mentoring abilities are more likely to predict a positive outcome from engaging in out-of-class communication with those instructors (Bippus et al., 2003). Out-of-class (or "extra-class") communication (see Myers, 2008, for a review) is an important predictor of student learning (Terenzini, Pascarella, & Blimling, 1996). Moreover, participation in a mentoring relationship is associated with undergraduate students' perceptions of personalized education, which is a correlate of both cognitive and affective learning (Waldeck, 2007).

Notably, despite the many benefits of academic mentoring, Waldeck et al. (1997) reported that finding mentored graduate students is difficult. In particular, minority students appear to be underrepresented in mentoring relationships. Even students who successfully initiate a mentoring relationship report their efforts to elicit mentoring from a faculty member as difficult and often ineffective, requiring multiple attempts.

Developments in Instructional Communication

Instructional communication research has advanced in recent years as researchers have investigated a range of contemporary, relevant constructs. Additionally, instructional communication researchers have employed increasingly sophisticated thinking, research designs, and data analyses in interpreting findings.

Although the earliest instructional communication researchers investigated instructor communication behaviors and their relationship to student learning almost exclusively, interest in the kinds of communication that occur between instructor and student and among students has grown steadily. Waldeck et al. (2001b) completed a systematic analysis of research published in international (i.e., International Communication Association), national (i.e., National Communication Association or NCA), and regional journals between 1990 and 2000 and concluded that "although we know about 'instructor' behaviors and 'student' behaviors independent of one another, we know very little about how instructor-student *interactions* influence learning" (p. 224). They argued for an increased focus on instructor-student relational constructs as well as the dynamics of groups and collaborative learning. Subsequently, researchers have examined the relationship between student predispositions to communication and instructor reciprocity (Allen, Long, & Judd, 2008) and the impact of extraclass communication on a number of student readiness-to-learn variables and learning (Bippus et al., 2003; Jones, 2008; Waldeck, 2007).

Recent years have further shown a growing interest among instructional scholars in research on training and development. In her editorial statement, 2006–2008, *Communication Education* editor Patricia Kearney explicitly solicited "research that extends beyond the more traditional context to include training and development in small and large organizations" and worked to encourage collaboration between the Training and Development division of the NCA and Instructional/Developmental division (IDD) researchers. This important initiative resulted in a special issue of the journal (Kearney, 2008) devoted to the practices of training and consulting by instructional communication researchers. Moreover, Beebe (2007) addressed the training activities of communication scholars in an essay designed to stimulate interest in the study and practice of training. Specific to instructor training, Hunt, Simonds, and Cooper (2002) advocated instruction in communication for all preservice instructors, and McCroskey and Richmond (1992) articulated the development and execution of the successful MA in Instructional Communication program offered at extension sites throughout the state of West Virginia by the West Virginia University (WVU) Department of Communication Studies (also see McCroskey & McCroskey, 2006, for a discussion of the WVU program). Whether through training instructors to be more effective communicators or training employees in business settings to apply the skills and knowledge of instructional communication research, instructional communication scholars appear to be in demand as trainers and consultants.

Within the past decade, instructional communication researchers have become increasingly focused on the role of technology in learning (see Waldeck & Dougherty, 2008, for a review). Early instructional communication investigations of the role of technology in learning focused on distance learning. Working from expectancy theory, Witt and Wheeless (1999) found that students enrolled in distance learning courses tend to have lower expectations for instructor immediacy than students in face-to-face courses; however, they argued that immediacy may play an important role in distance education. They learned, for instance, that students with previous distance learning experiences have significantly higher expectations for instructor immediacy than students with no experience. Given the wide range of sophisticated media available to instructors for making their distance courses engaging, interactive, and immediate, these findings are even more relevant now than they were 10 years ago. As e-mail began to proliferate on college campuses, Waldeck, Kearney, and Plax (2001a) investigated reasons why students use e-mail to communicate with instructors and examined the specific message strategies instructors employ intended to encourage students to e-mail them. Kelly, Duran, and Zolten (2001) reported that reticent students prefer using e-mail over oral communication channels to contact instructors and that nonreticent students experience less comfort with e-mail as a medium for communicating with instructors than reticent students. These findings merit reexamination now and in the future; it might be expected that due to the near-universal acceptance of electronic communication channels, including e-mail, text messaging, and social networking sites, even nonreticent students might enjoy and even prefer these channels for communication related to instruction.

As society has become more immersed in a variety of advanced communication and information technologies, instructional communication scholars have kept pace with how such innovations as e-mail (Waldeck et al., 2001a), cell phones (Campbell, 2006), social networking (Mazer et al., 2007), and streaming video (Boster, Meyer, Roberto, Inge, & Strom, 2006) facilitate or inhibit learning. Traditional technologies, such as presentational software (Cyphert, 2007), computer-assisted classroom instruction (Timmerman & Kruepke, 2006), and distance learning (Allen, 2006; Carrell & Menzel, 2001; Shedletsky & Aitken, 2001) have been examined and reconceptualized as means to enhance learning. Importantly, instructional communication researchers have demonstrated that moderate technology use in the classroom results in heightened student affective learning (Turman & Schrodt, 2005) and that this positive effect of technology use increases when the instructor is nonverbally immediate (Witt & Schrodt, 2006).

Research Design and Measurement Issues

One pressing research-design issue that instructional communication researchers faced as the field emerged was that of data collection. Because instructional communication researchers are interested in how communication functions in learning experiences across disciplines, using intact classes as research participants was limiting. Furthermore, researchers often experienced difficulty finding enough instructors willing to let them collect data, and institutional review boards sometimes frowned on instructional communication data collection in intact classes, as they view it as an unofficial form of faculty evaluation by a party other than the institution itself. Plax, Kearney, McCroskey, and Richmond (1986) reasoned that asking students enrolled in classes taught by cooperative instructors to report on the instructor they had in the "class before this one" (i.e., prior to completing any research instrument or participation in the research project) would obviate these problems. Not only did this technique address the issue of finding enough instructors willing to allow data collection in their classes, but the practice also allowed researchers to obtain data on instructors across the university, thus enhancing the generalizability of findings, and was acceptable to institutional review boards. This "prior class" data collection model continues to be widely used.

In addition to developing a data collection model, instructional communication researchers have developed unique measures of student affective, behavioral, and cognitive learning. Affective learning refers to students' internalization of positive liking toward instructional content or subject matter. Instructional communication scholars have long argued that student affect may be a more powerful and relevant outcome of instructional effectiveness than cognitive learning, and numerous studies have provided support for that claim. Affect is an important predictor of students' willingness to learn, use, and generalize course concepts beyond the instructional environment. More important, affective learning mediates the relationship between instructor communicative behavior and student cognitive learning (Rodriguez, Plax, & Kearney, 1996).

Andersen (1979) developed the first measure of affective learning (ALM) used by instructional communication researchers. Her scale measured both lower-order affect, including student attitudes toward (a) course, (b) subject matter, and (c) instructor, and also higher-order affect, including student intentions of (a) engaging in behaviors taught in the class and (b) taking additional classes in the subject matter. Although the original ALM was highly reliable, McCroskey (1994) argued that two sets of its items suffered from validity problems that possibly may have overinflated researchers' conclusions about affective learning. Specifically, McCroskey contended that students' attitudes toward the instructor as well as their probability of taking another course with the same instructor do not represent an adequate conceptual fit with Bloom's original definition of affective learning. The Revised ALM (McCroskey, 1994; Mottet & Richmond, 1998) eliminated these two measures of affect toward instructor, offering a more parsimonious operationalization of affective learning. (These eliminated measures can be used instead to assess students' evaluation of the instructor.) Notably, the Revised ALM continues to include items that measure students' affect toward "behaviors recommended in the course" and the "likelihood of actually attempting to engage in behaviors recommended in the course." While both of these scales assess higher-order affect, they should not be confused with behavioral or psychomotor learning.

Behavioral, or psychomotor, learning refers to students' ability to perform physical action and skills as a result of instruction. Perhaps no field has amassed such a large and sound collection of measures that assess discipline-specific skills as communication studies. Designed to measure individuals' actual speaking and/or listening skills, behavioral learning measures are typically the domain of communication education researchers who focus on the diagnosis of communication strengths and weaknesses. However, the size and quality of this collection of measures makes it worth mentioning in this chapter. The NCA has been concerned with the assessment of public speaking behaviors since the organization's inception; since 1970, it has sponsored a Committee on Assessment and Testing (CAT), which has produced a number of oral-communication behavioral assessments, including the Large Scale Assessment in Oral Communication (assessment of college student competency in speech communication), the K–12 and Higher Education Program Assessment in Speech Communication, the Conversational Skills Rating Scale, the Competent Speaker Speech

Evaluation Form, and the Motivation to Communicate Assessment. (These instruments are available through the NCA's national office or at www.nat com.org.) Other important behavioral learning measures used by instructional communication researchers include the Watson-Barker Listening Test (Watson & Barker, 1984), the Student Nonverbal Behaviors Inventory (Andersen, Andersen, & Mayton, 1985), and the Communication Competency Assessment Instrument (Rubin, 1982). These assessments are valuable to researchers as well as practitioners because they measure observable communication skills, which then allow instructors and trainers to determine learning objectives, instructional strategies, and learning activities.

Cognitive learning involves acquiring, understanding, synthesizing, evaluating, and using information or knowledge (Bloom, 1956). The problem faced by instructional communication researchers has been the development of meaningful measures of cognitive learning that can be used across disciplines and classes. In the 1970s, standardized test scores, recall measures, and course grades were used as measures of cognitive learning; however, the use of such scores presented reliability and validity problems. For instance, not all instructors are adequately trained in test-construction techniques and teaching strategies, and classroom variables that predict scores in an intact classroom may not be valid indicators of instructional effectiveness across instructors, subject matter, or students. Kearney and Beatty (1994) noted that "students themselves complain that examination scores, course grades, and grade point averages only partially reflect what they have learned" (p. 8).

To address these problems, Richmond, McCroskey, Kearney, and Plax (1987) devised a two-item student self-report measure that has been used widely across disciplines, classrooms, and content. The first item asks students, "On a scale of 0 to 9, how much did you learn in the class you had with this instructor, with 0 meaning you learned nothing, and 9 meaning you learned more than in any other class you've had?" The second item asks, "How much do you think you could have learned in this class if you had had the ideal instructor?" By subtracting the score on the first item from the score on the second item, a "learning loss" score is derived. Unlike test scores and recall measures, the learning loss assessment allows researchers to examine more sophisticated perceptions of student learning than mere recall, takes into account students' own perceptions of learning (which arguably are potentially more valid than instructors' perceptions), and facilitates systematic data collection across classes and instructors.

Examining the validity of this instrument, Chesebro and McCroskey (2000) demonstrated only a modest association (−.50) between learning loss and students' answers to a simple recall quiz under experimental conditions that should have optimized this correlation. Moreover, Witt, Wheeless, and Allen (2004) found evidence that questions whether students' self-perceived learning is a valid indicator of cognitive learning. The single-item nature of the instrument also precludes estimation of reliability.

Recently, King and Witt (2009) drew from the fields of psychology and education an alternative measure of cognitive learning known as confidence testing. Confidence testing requires students to respond to a test question and then estimate their confidence in their answer. They found a modest positive association between confidence testing, learning loss ($r = .37$), and course grade ($r = .33$) and concluded that confidence testing should be "regarded with a degree of skepticism" (p. 118) and does not provide a solution to problems associated with the measurement of cognitive learning. Still, though better models for the measurement of cognitive learning are needed, the development of the learning loss measure represents an important initial contribution to the assessment of instructional communication and remains the primary measure of cognitive learning used by instructional communication researchers to date.

Defining the Research Agenda

In 2001, Waldeck et al. (2001b) argued that although instructional communication researchers were productive and energetic, this area of scholarship suffered from some fundamental problems that would inhibit its growth until addressed. They pointed to a lack of programmatic research and a number of variable analytic studies that, while interesting, did little to advance theory. Since publication of that critique, the field has continued to mature. As illustrated in this chapter, research programs focused on several instructional communication constructs have been characterized by heuristic value and increasingly reliable conclusions about communication and learning. Many of these studies are grounded in theoretical frameworks, and the field is showing growing interest in theoretical models (McCroskey, Valencic, & Richmond, 2004; Mottet, Frymier, & Beebe, 2006). However, more work needs to be done in order to further legitimize instructional communication as central to, and influential outside of, the communication studies discipline. Accordingly, researchers should consider two primary paths of scholarship.

First, although researchers have recently made efforts to build a theory of instructional communication, their work is better characterized as proposed models that can be used for depicting overall processes. The predominant explanations offered for instructional communication—rhetorical and relational perspectives (Mottet & Beebe, 2006)—are interesting and informative but do not meet the criteria of middle-range theories (see Merton, 1957). In general, efforts to construct and test a theory of instructional communication have identified some empirical generalizations but lack the organizational and heuristic qualities of a true theory (see Heath & Bryant, 1992) that explains, predicts, and controls a range of phenomena. As instructional communication scholars continue to search for a paradigm appropriate to instructional communication, scholars must consider the importance of parsimony, pragmatism, and testability and avoid the tendency to develop models that are so comprehensive that they ultimately fail to yield any empirically and pedagogically useful information.

Second, instructional communication researchers are positioned uniquely to study the power and influence of communication technology on learning in contemporary society. Although instructional communication researchers have studied technology, the field should assume a greater leadership role in exploring the interconnections among technology use, human interaction, and learning. Technology will play an increasing role in how instructors teach and how students learn and process information. As such, instructional communication researchers should attend to a wider array of advanced communication technologies as they relate to learning, such as digital textbooks, social networking media, assessment using visual media (e.g., PowerPoint-based quizzes and tests, classroom "clicker" response technologies), and educational gaming technologies. Additionally, although instructor and student technology use may positively influence student learning outcomes, instructional communication researchers should pursue Boster et al.'s (2006) directive that researchers explain *why* this relationship exists.

Conclusion

Chapters such as this one often end with a long list of suggested directions for researchers. However, we argue that instructional communication scholars might profitably focus on just two primary areas: true theory development and focused, programmatic research on communication technology and learning. As a maturing area of the field, instructional communication will benefit from focused attention to the most relevant and timely constructs affecting the learning process. Such activity will help the area continue to rise to greater prominence both in and out of the communication studies discipline.

References

Allen, J. L., Long, K. M., & Judd, B. B. (2008). Students' predispositions and orientations toward communication and perceptions of instructor reciprocity and learning. *Communication Education, 57,* 20–40.

Allen, M., Witt, P. L., & Wheeless, L. R. (2006). The role of instructor immediacy as a motivational factor in student learning: Using meta-analysis to test a causal model. *Communication Education, 55,* 21–31.

Allen, T. A. (2006). Is the rush to provide online instruction setting our students up for failure? *Communication Education, 55,* 122–126.

Ames, R. (1986). Effective motivation: The contribution of the learning environment. In R. S. Feldman (Ed.), *The social psychology of education: Current research and theory* (pp. 235–256). Cambridge, UK: Cambridge University Press.

Andersen, J. F. (1979). Instructor immediacy as a predictor of teaching effectiveness. In D. Nimmo (Ed.), *Communication yearbook 3* (pp. 543–559). New Brunswick, NJ: Transaction Books.

Andersen, P. A., Andersen, J. F., & Mayton, S. M. (1985). The development of nonverbal communication in the classroom: Instructors' perceptions of students in grades K–12. *Western Journal of Speech Communication, 49,* 188–203.

Ayres, J., Wilcox, A. K., & Ayres, D. M. (1995). Receiver apprehension: An explanatory model and accompanying research. *Communication Education, 44,* 223–235.

Beatty, M. J., McCroskey, J. C., & Heisel, A. M. (1998). Communication apprehension as temperamental expression: A communibiological paradigm. *Communication Monographs, 65,* 197–220.

Beatty, M. J., Plax, T. G., & Kearney, P. (1985). Reinforcement vs. modeling theory in the development of communication apprehension: A retrospective analysis. *Communication Research Reports, 2,* 80–85.

Beebe, S. A. (2007). What do communication trainers do? *Communication Education, 56,* 249–254.

Berkos, K. M., Allen, T. H., Kearney, P., & Plax, T. G. (2001). When norms are violated: Imagined interactions as processing and coping mechanisms. *Communication Monographs, 68,* 289–300.

Bippus, A. M., Kearney, P., Plax, T. G., & Brooks, C. F. (2003). Instructor access and mentoring abilities: Predicting the value of extra-class communication. *Journal of Applied Communication Research, 31,* 260–276.

Bloom, B. S. (1956). *Taxonomy of educational objectives: Handbook I: Cognitive domain.* New York: McKay.

Boster, F. J., Meyer, G. S., Roberto, A. J., Inge, C., & Strom, R. (2006). Some effects of video streaming on educational achievement. *Communication Education, 55,* 46–62.

Brophy, J. (1987). Synthesis of research on strategies for motivating students to learn. *Educational Leadership, 18,* 40–48.

Buber, M. (1957). Distance and relation. *Psychiatry, 20,* 97–104.

Campbell, S. (2006). Perceptions of mobile phones in college classrooms: Ringing, cheating, and classroom policies. *Communication Education, 55,* 280–294.

Carrell, L. J., & Menzel, K. E. (2001). Variations in learning, motivation, and perceived immediacy between live and distance education classrooms. *Communication Education, 50,* 230–240.

Chesebro, J. L., & McCroskey, J. C. (2000). The relationship between students' reports of learning and their actual recall of lecture material: A validity test. *Communication Education, 49,* 297–301.

Chory-Assad, R. M. (2002). Classroom justice: Perceptions of fairness as a predictor of student motivation, learning, and aggression. *Communication Quarterly, 50,* 58–77.

Christophel, D. M. (1990). The relationships among instructor immediacy behaviors, student motivation, and learning. *Communication Education, 39,* 323–340.

Cyphert, D. (2007). Presentation technology in the age of electronic eloquence: From visual aid to visual rhetoric. *Communication Education, 56,* 168–192.

Dobos, J. A. (1996). Collaborative learning: Effects of student expectations and communication apprehension on student motivation. *Communication Education, 45,* 119–134.

Duff, D., Levine, T. R., Beatty, M. J., Woolbright, J., & Park, H. S. (2007). Testing public anxiety treatments against a placebo control. *Communication Education, 56,* 72–88.

Dweck, C. C. (1986). Motivational processes and affective learning. *American Psychologist, 41,* 1040–1048.

Edwards, C., Edwards, A., Qingmei, Q., & Wahl, S. T. (2007). The influence of computer-mediated word-of-mouth communication on student perceptions of instructors and attitudes toward learning course content. *Communication Education, 56,* 255–277.

Ellis, K. (2000). Perceived instructor confirmation: The development and validation of an instrument and two studies of the relationship to cognitive and affective learning. *Human Communication Research, 26,* 264–291.

Ellis, K. (2004). The impact of perceived instructor confirmation on receiver apprehension, motivation, and learning. *Communication Education, 53,* 1–20.

Ericson, P. M., & Gardner, J. W. (1992). Two longitudinal studies of communication apprehension and its effects on college students' success. *Communication Quarterly, 40,* 127–137.

Frymier, A. B., & Shulman, G. M. (1995). "What's in it for me?" Increasing content relevance to enhance students' motivation. *Communication Education, 44,* 40–51.

Goodboy, A. K., & Myers, S. A. (2008). The effect of instructor confirmation on student communication and learning outcomes. *Communication Education, 57,* 153–179.

Gorham, J., & Millette, D. M. (1997). A comparative analysis of instructor and student perceptions of motivation and demotivation in college classes. *Communication Education, 46,* 245–261.

Heath, R. L., & Bryant, J. (1992). Why study communication theories and conduct research? In R. L. Heath & J. Bryant (Eds.), *Human communication theory and research* (pp. 1–27). Hillsdale, NJ: Lawrence Erlbaum.

Hunt, S. K., Simonds, C. J., & Cooper, P. J. (2002). Communication and instructor education: Exploring a communication course for all instructors. *Communication Education, 51,* 81–94.

Jaasma, M. A., & Koper, R. J. (1999). The relationships of student/faculty out-of-class communication to instructor immediacy and trust and to student motivation. *Communication Education, 48,* 41–47.

Jones, A. C. (2008). The effects of out-of-class support on student satisfaction and motivation to learn. *Communication Education, 57,* 373–388.

Kearney, P. (Ed.). (2008). Instructional communication in organizational contexts: Innovations in training and consulting [Special issue]. *Communication Education, 57*(4).

Kearney, P., & Beatty, M. J. (1994). Measures of instructional communication. In R. B. Rubin, P. Palmgreen, & H. E. Sypher (Eds.), *Communication research measures: A sourcebook* (pp. 7–20). New York: Guilford Press.

Kearney, P., Plax, T. G., Hays, E. R., & Ivey, M. (1991). College instructor misbehaviors: What students don't like about what instructors say and do. *Communication Quarterly, 39,* 309–324.

Keller, J. M. (1983). Motivational design of instruction. In C. M. Reigeluth (Ed.), *Instructional design theories and models: An overview of their current status* (pp. 383–429). Hillsdale, NJ: Lawrence Erlbaum.

Kelly, L., Duran, R. L., & Zolten, J. J. (2001). The effect of reticence on college students' use of electronic mail to communicate with faculty. *Communication Education, 50,* 170–176.

Kelsey, D. M., Kearney, P., Plax, T. G., Allen, T. H., & Ritter, K. J. (2004). College students' attributions of instructor misbehaviors. *Communication Education, 53,* 40–55.

Kogler-Hill, S. E., Bahniuk, M. H., & Dobos, J. (1989). The impact of mentoring and collegial support on faculty success: An analysis of support behavior, information adequacy, and communication apprehension. *Communication Education, 38,* 15–31.

King, P., & Witt, P. (2009). Teacher immediacy, confidence testing, and the measurement of cognitive learning. *Communication Education, 58,* 110–123.

Mazer, J. P., Murphy, R. E., & Simonds, C. J. (2007). I'll see you on "Facebook": The effects of computer-mediated instructor self-disclosure on student motivation, affective learning, and classroom climate. *Communication Education, 56,* 1–17.

McCroskey, J. C. (1970). Measures of communication-bound anxiety. *Speech Monographs, 37,* 269–277.

McCroskey, J. C. (1994). Assessment of affect toward communication and affect toward instruction in communication. In S. Morreale & M. Brooks (Eds.), *1994 SCA summer conference proceedings and prepared remarks* (pp. 55–71). Annandale, VA: Speech Communication Association.

McCroskey, J. C., & McCroskey, L. L. (2006). Instructional communication: The historical perspective. In T. P. Mottet, V. P. Richmond, & J. C. McCroskey (Eds.), *Handbook of instructional communication: Relational and rhetorical perspectives* (pp. 33–47). Boston: Allyn & Bacon.

McCroskey, J. C., & Richmond, V. P. (1992). An instructional communication program for in-service instructors. *Communication Education, 41,* 215–223.

McCroskey, J. C., Valencic, K. M., & Richmond, V. P. (2004). Toward a model of instructional communication. *Communication Quarterly, 52,* 197–210.

McPherson, M. B., Kearney, P., & Plax, T. G. (2003). The dark side of instruction: Instructor anger as classroom norm violations. *Journal of Applied Communication Research, 31,* 76–90.

McPherson, M. B., & Young, S. L. (2004). What students think when instructors get upset: Fundamental attribution error and student-generated reasons for instructor anger. *Communication Quarterly, 52,* 357–369.

Merton, R. K. (1957). *Social theory and social structure* (Rev. ed.). Glencoe, IL: Free Press.

Mottet, T. P., & Beebe, S. A. (2006). Foundations of instructional communication. In T. P. Mottet, V. P. Richmond, & J. C. McCroskey (Eds.), *Handbook of instructional communication: Rhetorical and relational perspectives* (pp. 3–32). Boston: Allyn & Bacon.

Mottet, T. P., Frymier, A. B., & Beebe, S. A. (2006). Theorizing about instructional communication. In T. P. Mottet, V. P. Richmond, & J. C. McCroskey (Eds.), *Handbook of instructional communication: Rhetorical and relational perspectives* (pp. 255–282). Boston: Allyn & Bacon.

Mottet, T. P., & Richmond, V. P. (1998). Newer is not necessarily better: A reexamination of affective learning measurement. *Communication Research Reports, 15,* 370–378.

Myers, S. A. (2001). Perceived instructor credibility and verbal aggressiveness in the college classroom. *Communication Research Reports, 18,* 354–364.

Myers, S. A. (2002). Perceived aggressive instructor communication and student state motivation, learning, and satisfaction. *Communication Reports, 15,* 113–121.

Myers, S. A. (2008). Classroom student-instructor interaction. In W. Donsbach (Ed.), *The international encyclopedia of communication* (Vol. 2, pp. 514–520). Malden, MA: Blackwell.

Myers, S. A., Edwards, C., Wahl, S. T., & Martin, M. M. (2007). The relationship between perceived instructor aggressive communication and college student involvement. *Communication Education, 56,* 495–508.

Myers, S. A., & Knox, R. L. (2000). Verbal aggression in the college classroom: Perceived instructor use and student affective learning. *Communication Quarterly, 47,* 33–45.

Plax, T. G., Kearney, P., McCroskey, J. C., & Richmond, V. P. (1986). Power in the classroom VI: Verbal control strategies, nonverbal immediacy, and affective learning. *Communication Education, 35,* 43–55.

Richmond, V. P. (1990). Communication in the classroom: Power and motivation. *Communication Education, 39,* 181–195.

Richmond, V. P., & McCroskey, J. C. (1998). *Communication apprehension, avoidance, and effectiveness* (5th ed.). Boston: Allyn & Bacon.

Richmond, V. P., McCroskey, J. C., Kearney, P., & Plax, T. G. (1987). Power in the classroom VII: Linking behavior alteration techniques to cognitive learning. *Communication Education, 36,* 1–12.

Rodriguez, J. I., Plax, T. G., & Kearney, P. (1996). Clarifying the relationship between instructor nonverbal immediacy and student cognitive learning: Affective learning as the central causal mediator. *Communication Education, 45,* 293–306.

Rubin, R. B. (1982). Assessing speaking and listening competence at the college level: The Communication Competency Assessment Instrument. *Communication Education, 31,* 19–32.

Schrodt, P. (2003). Students' appraisals of instructors as a function of students' perceptions of instructors' aggressive communication. *Communication Education, 52,* 106–121.

Schrodt, P., Turman, P. D., & Soliz, J. (2006). Perceived understanding as a mediator of perceived instructor confirmation and students' ratings of instruction. *Communication Education, 55,* 370–388.

Shedletsky, L. J., & Aitken, J. E. (2001). The paradoxes of online academic work. *Communication Education, 50,* 206–218.

Terenzini, P. T., Pascarella, E. T., & Blimling, G. S. (1996). Students' out-of-class experiences and their influence in learning and cognitive development: A literature review. *Journal of College Student Development, 37,* 149–162.

Teven, J. J. (2001). The relationships among instructor characteristics and perceived caring. *Communication Education, 50,* 159–169.

Timmerman, C. E., & Kruepke, K. A. (2006). Computer-aided instruction, media richness, and college student performance. *Communication Education, 55,* 73–104.

Turman, P. D., & Schrodt, P. (2005). The influence of instructional technology use on students' affect: Do course designs and biological sex make a difference? *Communication Studies, 56,* 109–129.

Waldeck, J. H. (2007). Answering the question: Student perceptions of personalized education and the construct's relationship to learning outcomes. *Communication Education, 56,* 409–432.

Waldeck, J. H., & Dougherty, K. (2008, May). *Collaborative communication technologies and learning in college courses: Which are used, for what purposes, and to what ends?* Paper presented at the annual meeting of the Eastern Communication Association, Pittsburgh, PA.

Waldeck, J. H., Kearney, P., & Plax, T. G. (2001a). Instructor email message strategies and student willingness to communicate online. *Journal of Applied Communication Research, 29,* 54–70.

Waldeck, J. H., Kearney, P., & Plax, T. G. (2001b). The state of the art in instructional communication research. In W. R. Gudykunst (Ed.), *Communication yearbook 24* (pp. 207–230). Thousand Oaks, CA: Sage.

Waldeck, J. H., Orrego, V. O., Plax, T. G., & Kearney, P. (1997). Graduate student/faculty mentoring relationships: Who gets mentored, how it happens, and to what end. *Communication Quarterly, 45,* 93–109.

Wanzer, M. B., & McCroskey, J. C. (1998). Instructor socio-communicative style as a correlate of student affect toward instructor and course material. *Communication Education, 47,* 43–52.

Watson, K. W., & Barker, L. L. (1984). *Watson-Barker Listening Test.* New Orleans, LA: Speech Communication Association.

Witt, P. L., & Behnke, R. R. (2006). Anticipatory speech anxiety as a function of public speaking assignment type. *Communication Education, 55,* 166–177.

Witt, P. L., & Schrodt, P. (2006). The influence of instructional technology use and instructor immediacy on student affect for instructor and course. *Communication Reports, 19,* 1–15.

Witt, P. L., & Wheeless, L. R. (1999). Nonverbal communication expectancies about instructors and enrollment behavior in distance learning. *Communication Education, 48,* 149–154.

Witt, P. L., Wheeless, L. R., & Allen, M. (2004). A meta-analytical review of the relationship between instructor immediacy and student learning. *Communication Monographs, 71,* 184–207.

Power, Compliance, and Resistance in the Classroom

10

Rebecca M. Chory
and Alan K. Goodboy

I n the first of their seminal "Power in the Classroom" studies, McCroskey and Richmond (1983) stated that the ultimate purpose of the research program was "to determine how teacher power affects student learning and how teachers may modify their communication behavior and use of power to enhance learning in the classroom" (p. 178). In the subsequent studies, power use also has been considered as a means of classroom management (Kearney, Plax, Richmond, & McCroskey, 1985; Plax, Kearney, McCroskey, & Richmond, 1986). As such, the "Power in the Classroom" research program has produced a typology of instructor compliance-gaining strategies (i.e., behavior alteration techniques and messages) that has continued to spark lines of research currently studied (e.g., student resistance, student compliance gaining).

To examine the evolution of this program of research, this chapter is organized into 6 sections. The first section focuses on the "Power in the Classroom" theory and research, the second section reviews the compliance-gaining research, and the third section centers on the student resistance research. The fourth section reviews the measurement of power, compliance gaining, and resistance. The fifth section describes the controversies concerning the "Power in the Classroom" series. The sixth section identifies the strengths, limitations, and future research directions associated with this research program.

"Power in the Classroom" Theory and Research

In "Power in the Classroom I," McCroskey and Richmond (1983) found that although instructors and students perceived instructors as using reward, expert, and referent power most frequently, the degree of their shared perceptions was not particularly strong. They reasoned that future research should focus on students' versus instructors' perceptions because students respond (e.g., learn) based on their interpretations of instructors' behavior. As a result, virtually all the subsequent instructional communication research on power has defined power from the perspective of the receiver; that is, the targets of the influence attempt (i.e., students) must perceive that the source (i.e., the instructor) "has" power. Beginning with "Power in the Classroom II" (Richmond & McCroskey, 1984), scholars have investigated the relationships between perceptions of instructor power and instructional outcomes. The following section reviews this research.

BASES OF POWER IN THE CLASSROOM

Coercive Power. Coercive power is grounded in students' expectations that instructors will punish them (i.e., introduce a negative element into the environment or remove a positive element from the environment) if they do not conform to their requests (French & Raven, 1959, 1968; McCroskey & Richmond, 1983). Generally, students' perceptions of their instructors' use of coercive power and cognitive learning are related negatively in the United States (Richmond, 1990; Richmond & McCroskey, 1984; Roach, 1999) but are related positively in France (Roach, Cornett-DeVito, & DeVito, 2005). Among students in the United States, perceptions of instructors' coercive power use are related negatively to affective learning (Richmond, 1990; Richmond & McCroskey, 1984; Roach, 1999), affect toward the instructor (Roach et al., 2005; Schrodt, Witt, & Turman, 2007), evaluations of instruction (Schrodt et al., 2007; Schrodt et al., 2008), and ratings of instruction (Roach, 1999; Roach et al., 2005). Among students in Germany, perceptions of instructors' coercive power are related negatively to student ratings of instruction (Roach & Byrne, 2001). In addition, student perceptions of instructor coercive power use are associated negatively with student state motivation (Richmond, 1990), instructor confirmation (Turman & Schrodt, 2006), and perceptions of procedural and interactional classroom justice (Paulsel, Chory-Assad, & Dunleavy, 2005).

In terms of students' communicative responses to instructor coercive power, students who perceived their instructors as employing coercive power frequently report using all five power bases more frequently themselves (Golish & Olson, 2000). When seeking accommodations for their learning disabilities, students respond to instructors' use of coercive power by censoring themselves and avoiding the instructors (Worley & Cornett-DeVito, 2007).

Reward Power. Reward power is based on students' perceptions that their instructors will give them rewards (i.e., introduce a positive element into the environment or remove a negative element from the environment) for complying with their requests (French & Raven, 1959, 1968; McCroskey & Richmond, 1983). Students' perceptions of their instructors' use of reward power are related positively to cognitive learning (Richmond & McCroskey, 1984; Roach, 1999), affective learning (Roach, 1999), student ratings of instruction (Roach, 1999), instructor confirmation (Turman & Schrodt, 2006), learner empowerment (Schrodt et al., 2008), perceptions of distributive and interactional classroom justice (Paulsel et al., 2005), and perceptions of instructor character and caring (Teven & Herring, 2005). Students also report that teaching assistants (TAs) who are moderate in trait argumentativeness are perceived to use reward power (Roach, 1995a) and TAs who are anxious about communicating in the classroom exercise less reward power (Roach, 1999). Students who perceive that their instructors use reward power more frequently report that they use reward, legitimate, expert, and referent power more frequently with their instructors (Golish & Olson, 2000).

Legitimate Power. Legitimate, or assigned, *power* refers to students' perceptions that their instructors have the right, by virtue of their position as the instructor, to make certain demands or requests of students (French & Raven, 1959, 1968; McCroskey & Richmond, 1983). Legitimate power use generally is associated with routine classroom issues and usually does not extend beyond the classroom (McCroskey & Richmond, 1983). Students' perceptions of instructor legitimate power use are related negatively to student cognitive and affective learning (Richmond & McCroskey, 1984; Roach, 1999), students' ratings of instruction (Roach, 1999), and their learner empowerment (Schrodt et al., 2008). In contrast, perceived instructor legitimate power is related positively to perceptions of instructor competence (Teven & Herring, 2005) and perceptions of distributive, procedural, and interactional classroom justice (Paulsel et al., 2005). Students also perceive that TAs who are low in trait argumentativeness use more legitimate power than moderately or highly argumentative TAs (Roach, 1995a). Students with learning disabilities perceive instructors' use of legitimate power in responding to students' accommodation requests as incompetent communication (Worley & Cornett-DeVito, 2007).

Expert Power. Expert power refers to students' beliefs that their instructors are competent, qualified, and knowledgeable in the area in which they try to exert influence (French & Raven, 1959, 1968; McCroskey &

Richmond, 1983). According to French and Raven (1968), expert power has its primary effect on changing targets' cognitions, which may lead to changes in behavior. Students' perceptions of instructor expert power use are related positively to student state motivation (Richmond, 1990), cognitive learning (Richmond, 1990; Roach, 1999; Roach et al., 2005), affective learning (Richmond, 1990; Richmond & McCroskey, 1984; Roach et al., 2005), affect toward the instructor (Roach et al., 2005; Schrodt et al., 2007), ratings of instruction (Roach, 1999; Roach et al., 2005), evaluations of the instructor (Schrodt et al., 2007), and instructor confirmation (Turman & Schrodt, 2006). Instructors' expert power use also is related positively to students' perceptions of instructor competence, character, and caring (Teven & Herring, 2005) and to perceptions of distributive, procedural, and interactional classroom justice (Paulsel et al., 2005). In addition, students perceive TAs who are low in trait argumentativeness (Roach, 1995a) and anxious about communicating in the classroom (Roach, 1999) as using expert power, although TAs perceive their own levels of argumentativeness to be related positively to their use of expert power (Roach, 1995b). Golish and Olson (2000) found that students were more likely to use expert power in attempting to influence nonverbally immediate (vs. nonimmediate) instructors.

Referent Power. Referent power is based on students' desire to please their instructors and to identify with them (French & Raven, 1959, 1968; Kearney et al., 1985; McCroskey & Richmond, 1983). Referent power stems from students' interpersonal attraction to and affinity for their instructors, perceptions of similarity with their instructors, and/or their desire to be like their instructors (Kearney et al., 1985; McCroskey & Richmond, 1983; Schrodt et al., 2007). In the United States, students' perceptions of their instructors' use of referent power are related positively to their cognitive learning (Richmond, 1990), though in Germany, students' perceptions of instructors' use of referent power are related negatively to their cognitive learning (Roach & Byrne, 2001). Students' perceptions of their instructors' use of referent power in the classroom are related positively to their state motivation (Richmond, 1990), affective learning (Richmond, 1990; Richmond & McCroskey, 1984; Schrodt et al., 2007), instructor confirmation (Turman & Schrodt, 2006), learner empowerment (Schrodt et al., 2008), and evaluations of the instructor (Schrodt et al., 2007). Students also report positive associations between instructor referent power use and perceptions of instructor competence, character, and caring (Teven & Herring, 2005) and of procedural and interactional classroom justice (Paulsel et al., 2005). Students perceive TAs who are low in argumentativeness (Roach, 1995a) and anxious about communicating in the classroom (Roach, 1999) as using referent power; however, TAs perceive their own argumentativeness and referent power to be related positively (Roach, 1995b). Students with learning disabilities perceive instructors' use of referent power in responding to accommodation requests as competent communication (Worley & Cornett-DeVito, 2007).

Compliance Gaining

Although instructors' bases of power were examined in the first two "Power in the Classroom" studies (McCroskey & Richmond, 1983; Richmond & McCroskey, 1984), subsequent studies in the research program have investigated how instructors communicate power through compliance-gaining strategies known as behavioral alteration techniques (BATs) and examples of such techniques known as behavioral alteration messages (BAMs). The majority of this research has focused on K–12 and college instructor use of BATs/BAMs, which have been conceptualized and analyzed as prosocial (reward-oriented) or antisocial (punishment-oriented) compliance-gaining techniques.

In "Power in the Classroom III" ("Power III"), Kearney et al. (1985) developed a typology of instructor compliance-gaining strategies. They asked college students to generate messages they would use to get other people to do things they may not want to do. These same students then categorized and grouped responses into approximately 150 categories, which the authors reduced to 18 BATs. Kearney et al. then created accompanying BAMs for each technique. They discovered that K–12 teachers use six BATs most frequently: (1) reward from behavior and source, (2) personal responsibility, (3) expert, (4) self-esteem, (5) altruism, and (6) duty. Teachers perceived that the BATs they used were effective. Teacher variables (i.e., sex, experience, satisfaction, and grade) generally did not predict BAT use.

In "Power in the Classroom IV" (Kearney, Plax, Richmond, & McCroskey, 1984), the BAT/BAM typology was revised, validated, and expanded by having K–12 teachers provide examples of how they routinely attempted to get students to do things they may not want to. In groups, they then categorized their messages into the 18 BATs/BAMs identified in "Power III" by Kearney et al. (1985). Messages that were unable to be classified into the existing categories were placed into new ones, which yielded four additional BATs. Using these 22 BATs, Kearney et al. (1984) found that (a) teachers used reward-related BATs, self-esteem, and teacher feedback more frequently than other BATs and believed this use was effective; (b) teachers infrequently used punishment-related BATs, guilt, teacher-student relationship: negative, legitimate teacher authority, debt, altruism, peer modeling, and teacher modeling; (c) BAT use varied by teacher sex such that women used immediate reward from behavior, self-esteem, and teacher feedback more frequently than did men, whereas men used expert teacher more frequently than did women; and (d) the grade level taught yielded differences in BAT use (i.e., teachers in upper grade levels used more deferred reward from behavior, punishment from teacher, debt, and expert teacher, whereas lower grade teachers used more reward from teacher and reward from others), perceptions of BAT effectiveness (i.e., upper grade level teachers perceived deferred reward from behavior as more effective, whereas lower grade level teachers perceived reward from teacher as more effective), and perceptions of colleagues' BAT use (i.e., upper grade level teachers perceived their colleagues as using more deferred reward from behavior, punishment from teacher, legitimate higher authority, debt, and teacher modeling, whereas lower grade level teachers perceived their colleagues as using more immediate reward from behavior, reward from others, and self-esteem).

Shortly after these two studies, Kearney, Plax, Sorensen, and Smith (1988) factor analyzed the BATs typology and confirmed a two-factor structure: prosocial BATs and antisocial BATs. Of the 22 BATs identified by Kearney et al. (1984), 10 BATs are considered to be prosocial, 8 BATs are considered to be antisocial, and 4 BATs are neither prosocial nor antisocial. The prosocial BATs are immediate reward from behavior and deferred reward from behavior, reward from others, self-esteem, responsibility to class, normative rules, altruism, peer modeling, teacher modeling, expert teacher, and teacher responsiveness. The antisocial BATs are guilt, punishment from behavior and punishment from others, teacher-student relationship: negative, legitimate higher authority and legitimate teacher authority, and debt. The BATs that did not load on either factor are reward from teacher, punishment from teacher, teacher-student relationship: positive, and personal (student) responsibility. (For a definition of each BAT, see Plax & Kearney, 1992.)

In "Power V," McCroskey, Richmond, Plax, and Kearney (1985) found that prosocial BATs were associated positively with student affective learning, whereas antisocial BATs were associated negatively with affective learning. In a comparison between teachers and students (Grades 7 to 12), teachers perceived themselves as using more self-esteem, teacher-student relationship: positive, expert teacher, teacher feedback, guilt, responsibility to class, normative rules, and peer modeling. Students, however, perceived teachers as using more legitimate teacher authority. Additionally, student and teacher perceptions of BAT use were largely uncorrelated, suggesting that student perceptions of teacher BAT use should be examined when assessing student outcomes. Also, perceptions of BAT use varied as a function of student quality. Finally, teachers with training in instructional communication were perceived by students as using fewer antisocial BATs.

In "Power VI," Plax, Kearney, McCroskey, et al. (1986) found that junior and senior high school and university students' perceptions of instructor prosocial BAT use were correlated positively with their affective learning, and perceptions of antisocial BAT use were correlated negatively with affective learning. Similar correlations between instructor BAT use and student affective learning were discovered in both the junior and senior high school and university student samples. In addition, instructor immediacy mediated the relationship between perceptions of instructor prosocial BAT use and affective learning, suggesting that perceptions of prosocial BAT use increase student affect by increasing student perceptions of instructor immediacy.

In "Power VII," Richmond, McCroskey, Kearney, and Plax (1987) studied BATs by having college students report on their best or worst instructor or a former instructor who taught a course in or outside their major. They discovered that "good" and "bad" instructor BAT use differed. For instance, students perceived that their best instructors used more responsibility-related BATs, whereas their worst instructors used more punishment-related BATs. Most important, prosocial BATs were related positively to cognitive learning, whereas antisocial BATs were related negatively.

Other researchers have investigated the role that BATs play in the college classroom. Both Plax, Kearney, and Tucker (1986) and Kearney and Plax (1987) examined the extent to which instructor experience affects the use of BATs. They found that prospective and experienced instructors reported using the self-esteem and teacher feedback BATs most frequently, although experienced instructors used a wider range of BATs than did prospective instructors. They also observed that prospective and experienced instructors implemented prosocial BATs when dealing with passive student misbehaviors (e.g., inattention, apathy) and antisocial BATs when dealing with active misbehaviors (e.g., talking out of turn, overactivity). Moreover, instructors were more likely to use both prosocial and antisocial BATs in response to frequent versus occasional student misbehavior. However, Roach (1994) discovered that, in addition to varying as a function of instructor experience, the frequency of instructor BAT use depended on the point in the semester in which students were sampled. Students perceived that instructors used more prosocial BATs in the middle of the semester than at the beginning of the semester, and instructors used more antisocial BATs at the end of the semester than at the beginning of the semester.

Instructor satisfaction is another variable that affects teacher BAT use. Plax, Kearney, and Downs (1986) observed that among elementary and secondary school teachers, the frequency of using antisocial BATs was related negatively to satisfaction with teaching and students. However, among college instructors, the frequency of using prosocial BATs was associated positively with satisfaction with teaching and students.

Culture has been shown to influence instructors' use of BATs. With the exception of the self-esteem BAT, Lu (1997) found that Chinese instructors use the same BATs as American instructors in addition to a BAT Lu referred to as "self-consciousness." Chinese instructors also were more likely to use some BATs (e.g., punishment from behavior, deferred reward from behavior) and less likely to use others (e.g., immediate reward from behavior, punishment from others). Subsequent research has uncovered no differences in the use of prosocial or antisocial BATs between Chinese and American instructors (Liu, Sellnow, & Venette, 2006; Sellnow, Liu, & Venette, 2006).

Similar to instructors, graduate teaching assistants (GTAs) use BATs in the college classroom. Roach (1991) found that GTAs used teacher feedback, expert teacher, legitimate higher authority, immediate reward from behavior, and teacher modeling most frequently and used punishment from others, guilt, debt, peer modeling, and reward from others least frequently. Student affective learning was correlated positively with GTAs' use of immediate reward from behavior and deferred reward from behavior. Furthermore, students reported higher affective learning from professors than from GTAs, the latter of whom were perceived as using significantly more BATs.

In terms of student outcomes, instructor BAT use has been linked to motivation, fairness, and aggression. Richmond (1990) established that student state motivation was associated positively with instructors' use of the immediate reward and teacher feedback BATs and associated negatively with the punishment and legitimate authority BAT types, teacher-student relationship: negative, and teacher-modeling BATs. Chory-Assad and Paulsel (2004a) observed that instructors' use of antisocial BATs was correlated negatively with students' perceptions of interactional justice and predicted a higher likelihood of students indirectly aggressing against instructors.

Additionally, students use BATs with their GTAs and instructors. Golish (1999) found that students use a set of 19 unique compliance-gaining techniques to make requests of their instructors. These student BATs are honesty-sincerity, blame, complaining, begging, guilt, flattery, play on GTA's ability to relate, group persuasion, public persuasion, private persuasion, evidence of preparation/logic, earned credibility/past performance, stress/overload, utilitarian justice, emotional displays, general excuses, punish teacher, reference to higher authority, and verbal force/demand. Although these strategies are generally prosocial in nature, students reported using antisocial strategies if their prosocial attempts failed. In a follow-up study, Golish and Olson (2000) found that students used most frequently the strategies of honesty-sincerity, flattery, group persuasion, private persuasion, and evidence of preparation/logic; the least frequently used strategies were begging, emotional displays, punish teacher, reference to higher authority, and verbal force/demand. Most recently, Kennedy-Lightsey and Myers (2009) discovered that verbally aggressive students perceived the strategies of complaining, guilt, playing on teachers' ability to relate, public persuasion, general excuses, and verbal force/demand as appropriate. They perceived complaining, pleading, guilt, playing on teachers' ability to relate, and public persuasion as effective. Furthermore, argumentative students perceived pleading as effective, whereas verbally aggressive students were more likely to use antisocial student BATs.

Student Resistance

Student resistance refers to students' constructive or destructive oppositional behaviors used in the classroom to resist instructor attempts at compliance gaining (Burroughs, Kearney, & Plax, 1989). Constructive resistance enhances students' on-task behavior and learning (e.g., asking for clarification, expressing classroom concerns), whereas destructive resistance disrupts student on-task behavior and learning (e.g., distracting other students, failing to complete assignments).

In their initial attempt to explore student resistance, Burroughs et al. (1989) discovered that college students use 19 resistance strategies. Through factor analysis, Kearney, Plax, and Burroughs (1991) revealed that five of these strategies were *teacher owned* (i.e., the student perceives the instructor as the cause of the problem), five strategies were *student owned* (i.e., the student accepts the blame for the problem), and nine strategies involved no attribution. The teacher-owned strategies are teacher advice, teacher blame, appeal to powerful others, modeling teacher behavior, and modeling teacher affect; the student-owned resistance strategies are deception, ignoring the teacher, priorities, hostile defensive, and student rebuttal; the remaining strategies are avoidance, reluctant compliance, active resistance, disruption, direct communication, excuses, challenge the teacher's basis of power, rallying student support, and revenge. Although students use all 19 strategies, they are most likely to use reluctant compliance, direct communication, and priorities and least likely to use active resistance, disruption, and challenge the teacher's basis of power (Kearney, Plax, & Burroughs, 1991). More recently, Burroughs (2007) examined students' self-reported use of resistance strategies in their actual classes (as opposed to using hypothetical scenarios as stimulus material) through open-ended questions and found that only 45% of her sample reported resisting in an actual class, with students most frequently engaging in complete compliance, passive rejection, and partial compliance.

Interestingly, research suggests that student resistance varies as a function of the type of BAT used. For instance, students are very likely to resist antisocial BATs that involve significant punishment, they are moderately likely to resist the other six antisocial BATs, and they are least likely to resist prosocial BATs (Plax, Kearney, Downs, & Stewart, 1986). When studied in tandem with instructor immediacy, however, instructor use of both prosocial and antisocial BATs produced no differences in student resistance (Kearney, Plax, & Burroughs, 1991). Other research has indicated that students are more likely to resist antisocial than prosocial BATs (Lee,

Levine, & Cambra, 1997), and resistance and individual antisocial BAT use are related positively (Paulsel & Chory-Assad, 2004).

Along with instructor BAT use, a great deal of student resistance research has focused on instructor immediacy. Overwhelmingly, research suggests that immediate instructors face less student resistance. Burroughs et al. (1989) found that the students generated more potential resistance messages to a hypothetical nonimmediate instructor than to a hypothetical immediate instructor. Likewise, Kearney, Plax, Smith, and Sorensen (1988) discovered that students are less likely to resist an immediate instructor who uses prosocial BATs than an immediate instructor who uses antisocial BATs or a nonimmediate instructor who uses either prosocial or antisocial BATs. Moreover, Kearney, Plax, and Burroughs (1991) reported that students are more likely to use teacher-owned resistance strategies with nonimmediate instructors and student-owned resistance strategies with immediate instructors, regardless of the type of instructor BATs employed. Burroughs (2007) found that students are more likely to use passive-rejection resistance and less willing to comply with an instructor's request when the instructor was perceived as nonimmediate. Moreover, students who used passive-rejection resistance reported lower levels of cognitive and affective learning. Thus, it appears that immediacy may diminish resistance, or perhaps, less student resistance allows instructors to relax and engage in immediate communication with their students.

Perceptions of classroom justice also seem to dictate student resistance. Chory-Assad and Paulsel (2004b) found that student perceptions of procedural injustice predicted a stronger likelihood to resist through revenge (e.g., giving negative course evaluations, not recommending an instructor to others) and deception (e.g., lying to an instructor, pretending to have complied). Paulsel and Chory-Assad (2005) observed that students' perceptions of interactional injustice predicted a stronger probability of resisting with all the teacher-owned strategies except modeling teacher behavior. In a related vein, Goodboy and Bolkan (2009) observed that teacher misbehaviors directly and indirectly (through their relationship with affective learning) increased teacher- and student-owned resistance.

Measurement of Power, Compliance Gaining, and Resistance

POWER

Four means of assessing student perceptions of instructor power exist; all are self-report measures. The first measure is the Perceived Power Measure (PPM; McCroskey & Richmond, 1983), which is based on Student's

(1968) and Richmond, McCroskey, Davis, and Koontz's (1980) measures of French and Raven's (1968) power bases. This measure features descriptions of each power base followed by the phrase "My teacher uses _____ power." Respondents indicate their agreement with the phrase on five 7-point bipolar scales (i.e., *agree-disagree, false-true, incorrect-correct, wrong-right, yes-no*). The second measure is the Relative Power Measure (RPM; McCroskey & Richmond, 1983), also based on Student's (1968) and Richmond et al.'s (1980) measure of French and Raven's power bases. The RPM includes descriptions of each power base. Respondents then estimate the proportion of their instructors' total power use that comes from each power base.

The third measure is the Power Base Measure (PBM) developed by Roach (1995a) that contains four statements reflecting each of French and Raven's (1959) five power bases for a total of 20 items. The PBM's items contain reasons for compliance (e.g., "because it is required by the instructor") and outcomes for compliance or noncompliance (e.g., "the student will receive some kind of tangible or intangible reward") that invoke the bases of power. Respondents are instructed to indicate the frequency with which their instructor uses each strategy on a 5-point Likert-type scale ranging from *never* to *very often*. The fourth measure is the Teacher Power Use Scale (TPUS) developed by Schrodt et al. (2007), which focuses on observed instructor communication behaviors that communicate power to students in the college classroom and contains 30 items (6 per power base). Respondents indicate the frequency with which their instructors engage in the given behavior on a 7-point Likert-type scale ranging from *never* to *always*.

COMPLIANCE GAINING

Although the means of assessing compliance gaining in the classroom are usually based on the Kearney et al. (1984) BATs typology, there is no standard measure of BAT use. Initially, instructor BAT use was assessed by providing participants with a categorized list containing four to five BAMs representing each of the BATs in the typology (the BAT labels were not included). Participants then were instructed to indicate the frequency with which the instructor used each of the 22 BATs by providing one overall rating for each BAT (Kearney et al., 1985; McCroskey et al., 1985; Plax, Kearney, McCroskey, et al., 1986; Richmond et al., 1987). In later examinations of the 22-item BAT typology, Kearney, Plax, Sorensen, et al. (1988) discovered a dual factor structure consisting of prosocial and antisocial BATs. Based on this two-factor solution, composite measures of prosocial and antisocial BAT use were developed and used to assess compliance gaining in the classroom (e.g., Roach, 1994). Most recently, researchers have created composite indices of individual BATs to assess the use of specific BATs (e.g., Chory-Assad & Paulsel, 2004a; Paulsel &

Chory-Assad, 2004; Roach, 1990, 1991). In these studies, participants rate two to five BAMs representing each of the BATs.

Responses to the BATs measures have been solicited using varying formats, including a dichotomous format of *yes* or *no* (Richmond et al., 1987), 5-point Likert-type scales (Chory-Assad & Paulsel, 2004a; McCroskey et al., 1985; Paulsel & Chory-Assad, 2004; Plax, Kearney, & Downs, 1986; Plax, Kearney, Downs, et al., 1986; Roach, 1990, 1991, 1994; Sellnow et al., 2006), 7-point Likert-type scales (Kearney, Plax, Sorensen, et al., 1988), and a combination of the dichotomous and 5-point Likert-type formats (Richmond, 1990). Response options for the Likert-type scales have ranged from *never* to *very often* (Kearney et al., 1985; Richmond, 1990; Roach, 1990, 1991, 1994) and *extremely unlikely* to *extremely likely* (Chory-Assad & Paulsel, 2004a; Paulsel & Chory-Assad, 2004).

To date, the use of Golish's (1999) student BATs typology has only been studied by Kennedy-Lightsey and Myers (2009). They assessed college students' perceptions of the appropriateness and effectiveness of each student BAT and their likelihood of using each BAT via 5-point Likert-type scales. Response options ranged from *appropriate* to *inappropriate, effective* to *ineffective,* and *very likely (to use)* to *not very likely (to use).* They discovered two factors resulting from a principal components analysis and labeled these factors "likelihood to use prosocial BATs" and "likelihood to use antisocial BATs."

STUDENT RESISTANCE

Similar to BATs, there is no standard measure of student resistance, though most assessments are based on the Burroughs et al. (1989) student resistance typology. Student resistance initially was measured by providing participants with a categorized list containing multiple examples of each of the 19 resistance strategies in the Burroughs et al. typology (the resistance labels were not included). Participants were asked to report their likelihood of using each strategy with an instructor on a 7-point Likert-type scale ranging from *extremely unlikely* to *extremely likely.* Participants provided one overall rating for each resistance strategy. Kearney, Plax, Hays, and Ivey (1991) later revealed a dual-factor structure in the typology consisting of five teacher-owned and five student-owned strategies.

Recently, Chory and her colleagues have treated the individual resistance strategies as separate variables. In these studies, participants respond to multiple items representing each of the resistance strategies, and composite indices for the individual resistance strategies are created. For example, the teacher-owned resistance strategies have been examined as five individual variables (Chory-Assad & Paulsel, 2004b; Paulsel & Chory-Assad, 2004, 2005); Chory-Assad and Paulsel (2004b) examined five destructive student resistance strategies (disruption, challenging the teacher's basis of power, rallying student support, revenge, and deception) as five separate variables.

Controversies of the "Power in the Classroom" Series

Despite the widespread study of power in the classroom, Sprague (1992) offered several critiques of this line of research. Sprague objected to conceptualizing power as the rational behavioral intentions of instructors, claiming it ignored more indirect means of exerting power and the societal forces that drive compliance. According to Sprague, power does not involve instructors simply selecting strategies to keep students on task nor students simply deciding to resist such attempts, but involves more complex relationships within classrooms and between the interpersonal dynamics of classrooms and factors in the external envirnoment.

Sprague (1992) also noted that classroom power has more important implications for education and society than the "Power in the Classroom" research program suggests. For example, Sprague stated that the "Power in the Classroom" vocabulary positioned students as workers and schools as institutions preparing laborers who passively comply. She suggested that student misbehaviors may be considered acts of resistance against attempts to devalue and dehumanize their work. Furthermore, she argued that the "Power in the Classroom" research implicitly involves domination of students by instructors. In short, Sprague criticized instructional power research for failing to consider whether its approach liberates or dehumanizes instructors and students.

Sprague (1992) encouraged researchers to consider who deserves to have power over students, who decides how that power is used, and how students and teachers can be sensitized to alternatives to power. To answer these and related questions, Sprague directed researchers to consider the social, cultural, economic, and political context in which classroom power is exercised. Similarly, she urged scholars to include the impact of race, gender, sexual orientation, and other individual characteristics important in interpersonal interactions in their studies. She suggested that researchers examine how these microlevel and macrolevel characteristics interact with each other in defining, negotiating, and constraining classroom power relations. Sprague stated that only research that considers all the complexities of power in the classroom offers real potential for emancipatory transformation.

CONTROVERSIES REGARDING BATS

Although scholars attest to the reliability and validity of BATs measurement (e.g., Kearney & Plax, 1997; Roach, 1990; Sorensen, Plax, Kearney, & Burroughs, 1988), criticisms of the checklist procedure used in the measure have arisen. Burleson et al. (1988) argued that studies using selectionist methodologies produced an item-desirability bias that did not occur with constructionist methodologies. In response, Sorensen, Plax, and Kearney (1989) and Plax, Kearney, and Sorensen (1990) used a constructionist approach to examine BATs. Their results were in line with previous research that had used the selectionist approach. They argued that the methods were functionally equivalent.

Waltman (1994, 1995) claimed that the BAT checklist suffered from an item-desirability bias because prospective and experienced teachers' likelihood of using particular BATs was correlated positively with social appropriateness scores for those BATs. Consequently, Waltman argued that teachers report using more prosocial than antisocial BATs because it is socially appropriate to do so, not because they actually use them more frequently. Moreover, Waltman and Burleson (1997a) questioned the validity of the BATs measure because the results it produced (respondents frequently report using prosocial BATs and infrequently report using antisocial BATs) were inconsistent with half a century of observational research, indicating that "teachers typically employ *negative and antisocial* strategies to correct the misbehavior of students" (p. 77). Again, they purported that the BATs measure suffered from an item-desirability bias due to respondents using a politeness heuristic in processing the items and found that when prospective teachers completed the BATs checklist under conditions in which heuristic processing was inhibited, they endorsed fewer polite BATs and more impolite ones than prospective teachers who completed the BATs measure under normal conditions.

Kearney and Plax (1997) concluded that Waltman and Burleson's (1997a) claims were unwarranted and that there was "*no single study* that demonstrates that teachers are mostly or even typically negative or antisocial in their compliance-gaining attempts" (p. 96). Kearney and Plax pointed out that Waltman and Burleson incorrectly equated BATs with desist and reinforcement techniques, as opposed to compliance-gaining strategies geared toward student on-task behavior, and stated that results showing teachers rely more on prosocial than antisocial BATs have been found using a variety of data collection methods. Kearney and Plax also faulted the experimental manipulation, the use of undergraduate education majors as participants, and the way in which the data that were used to test their hypotheses were selected and aggregated. Indeed, Waltman and Burleson (1997b) asserted that Kearney and Plax (1997) did not dispute the data showing an item-desirability bias in the BATs checklist and that the data they did invoke did not support their claims that teachers use more prosocial than antisocial strategies.

Strengths, Limitations, and Future Research Directions

There are three main strengths of the power, compliance, and resistance research programs. First, research in these areas has involved focused, programmatic investigations with attainment of replicable results. Second, researchers have revised and refined measures in all three areas of inquiry, reflecting their concern with producing accurate, reliable results. Third, this line of research has been quite heuristic, generating programs of inquiry that intersect with contemporary instructional communication topics such as classroom justice (e.g., Chory-Assad & Paulsel, 2004a, 2004b; Paulsel & Chory-Assad, 2004, 2005; Paulsel et al., 2005), learner empowerment (e.g., Schrodt et al., 2008), instructor confirmation (e.g., Turman & Schrodt, 2006), instructor misbehaviors (e.g., Goodboy & Bolkan, 2009), and classroom diversity (Lee et al., 1997; Liu et al., 2006; Worley & Cornett-DeVito, 2007).

Two weaknesses of this research program are (1) its reliance on self-report data and correlational analyses, and (2) its examination of power, compliance, and resistance from a primarily social science and quantitative perspective. Accordingly, other research methods and theoretical points of view are needed to triangulate the extant research findings. These recommendations include using (a) observations and coding of actual teacher power use and compliance as well as student resistance in both K–12 and college classrooms; (b) behavioral manipulations of instructor power, compliance gaining, and resistance as stimuli; (c) focus groups and in-depth interviews examining instructors' and students' insights and experiences with these topics; and (d) longitudinal and experimental designs to delineate patterns of causality. Future research should employ more conservative statistical techniques (e.g., hierarchical multiple regression) to more accurately determine the relative importance of various power-based strategies in the classroom. In addition, moderating and mediating variables that draw theoretical boundaries and offer explanations, respectively, should be investigated via analyses of variance, linear equation modeling, path analysis, and other appropriate statistical means.

Future research also should be guided by a broader range of theoretical perspectives, such as that advocated by Sprague (1992) and executed by Worley and Cornett-DeVito (2007). Examination of power, compliance, and resistance from these, as well as other, perspectives would only extend and advance findings in an already pragmatic and pedagogically relevant area of instructional communication research. Through theoretical and methodological triangulation, the most comprehensive and representative picture of power, compliance, and resistance in the classroom is likely to be drawn.

Conclusion

The bodies of work reviewed in this chapter demonstrate that power, compliance, and resistance in the classroom are theoretically and pragmatically important instructional communication constructs. As the educational environment and the student-instructor relationship continue to evolve and change over time, the approach taken by instructional communication researchers to examine and theorize power, compliance, and resistance must also continue to evolve. We believe the instructional communication field is well poised for such a challenge.

References

Burleson, B. R., Wilson, S. R., Waltman, M. S., Goering, E. M., Ely, T. K., & Whaley, B. B. (1988). Item desirability effects in compliance-gaining research: Seven studies documenting artifacts in the strategy selection procedure. *Human Communication Research, 14,* 429–486.

Burroughs, N. F. (2007). A reinvestigation of the relationship of teacher non-verbal immediacy and student compliance-resistance with learning. *Communication Education, 56,* 453–475.

Burroughs, N. F., Kearney, P., & Plax, T. G. (1989). Compliance-resistance in the college classroom. *Communication Education, 38,* 214–229.

Chory-Assad, R. M., & Paulsel, M. L. (2004a). Antisocial classroom communication: Instructor influence and interactional justice as predictors of student aggression. *Communication Quarterly, 50,* 58–77.

Chory-Assad, R. M., & Paulsel, M. L. (2004b). Classroom justice: Student aggression and resistance as reactions to perceived unfairness. *Communication Education, 53,* 255–275.

French, J. R. P., & Raven, B. (1959). The bases for social power. In D. Cartwright (Ed.), *Studies in social power* (pp. 150–167). Ann Arbor: University of Michigan Press.

French, J. R. P., & Raven, B. H. (1968). The bases of social power. In D. Cartwright & A. Zander (Eds.), *Group dynamics: Research and theory* (pp. 259–270). New York: Harper & Row.

Golish, T. D. (1999). Students' use of compliance gaining strategies with graduate teaching assistants: Examining the other end of the power spectrum. *Communication Quarterly, 47,* 12–32.

Golish, T. D., & Olson, L. N. (2000). Students' use of power in the classroom: An investigation of student power, teacher power, and teacher immediacy. *Communication Quarterly, 48,* 293–310.

Goodboy, A. K., & Bolkan, S. (2009). College teacher misbehaviors: Direct and indirect effects on student communication behavior and traditional learning outcomes. *Western Journal of Communication, 73,* 204–219.

Kearney, P., & Plax, T. G. (1987). Situational and individual determinants of teachers' reported use of behavior alteration techniques. *Human Communication Research, 14,* 145–166.

Kearney, P., & Plax, T. G. (1997). Item desirability bias and the BAT checklist: A reply to Waltman and Burleson. *Communication Education, 46,* 95–99.

Kearney, P., Plax, T. G., & Burroughs, N. F. (1991). An attributional analysis of college students' resistance decisions. *Communication Education, 40,* 325–342.

Kearney, P., Plax, T. G., Hays, E. R., & Ivey, M. J. (1991). College teacher misbehaviors: What students don't like about what teachers say and do. *Communication Quarterly, 39,* 309–324.

Kearney, P., Plax, T. G., Richmond, V. P., & McCroskey, J. C. (1984). Power in the classroom IV: Alternatives to discipline. In R. N. Bostrom (Ed.), *Communication yearbook 8* (pp. 724–746). Beverly Hills, CA: Sage.

Kearney, P., Plax, T. G., Richmond, V. P., & McCroskey, J. C. (1985). Power in the classroom III: Teacher communication techniques and messages. *Communication Education, 34,* 19–28.

Kearney, P., Plax, T. G., Smith, V. R., & Sorensen, G. (1988). Effects of teacher immediacy and strategy type on college student resistance to on-task demands. *Communication Education, 37,* 54–67.

Kearney, P., Plax, T. G., Sorensen, G., & Smith, V. R. (1988). Experienced and prospective teachers' selections of compliance-gaining messages for "common" student misbehaviors. *Communication Education, 37,* 150–164.

Kennedy-Lightsey, C., & Myers, S. A. (2009). College students' use of behavioral alteration techniques as a function of aggressive communication. *Communication Education, 58,* 54–73.

Lee, C. R., Levine, T. R., & Cambra, R. (1997). Resisting compliance in the multicultural classroom. *Communication Education, 46,* 29–43.

Liu, M., Sellnow, D. D., & Venette, S. (2006). Integrating nonnatives as teachers: Patterns and perceptions of compliance-gaining strategies. *Communication Education, 55,* 208–217.

Lu, S. (1997). Culture and compliance gaining in the classroom: A preliminary investigation of Chinese college teachers' use of behavior alteration techniques. *Communication Education, 46,* 10–28.

McCroskey, J. C., & Richmond, V. P. (1983). Power in the classroom I: Teacher and student perceptions. *Communication Education, 32,* 175–184.

McCroskey, J. C., Richmond, V. P., Plax, T. G., & Kearney, P. (1985). Power in the classroom V: Behavior alteration techniques, communication training and learning. *Communication Education, 34,* 214–226.

Paulsel, M. L., & Chory-Assad, R. M. (2004). The relationships among instructors' antisocial behavior alteration techniques and student resistance. *Communication Reports, 17,* 103–112.

Paulsel, M. L., & Chory-Assad, R. M. (2005). Perceptions of instructor interactional justice as a predictor of student resistance. *Communication Research Reports, 22,* 283–291.

Paulsel, M. L., Chory-Assad, R. M., & Dunleavy, K. D. (2005). The relationship between student perceptions of instructor power and classroom justice. *Communication Research Reports, 22,* 207–215.

Plax, T. G., & Kearney, P. (1992). Teacher power in the classroom: Defining and advancing a program of research. In V. P. Richmond & J. C. McCroskey (Eds.), *Power in the classroom: Communication, control, and concern* (pp. 67–84). Hillsdale, NJ: Lawrence Erlbaum.

Plax, T. G., Kearney, P., & Downs, T. M. (1986). Communicating control in the classroom and satisfaction with teaching and students. *Communication Education, 35*, 379–388.

Plax, T. G., Kearney, P., Downs, T. M., & Stewart, R. A. (1986). College student resistance toward teachers' use of selective control strategies. *Communication Research Reports, 3*, 20–27.

Plax, T. G., Kearney, P., McCroskey, J. C., & Richmond, V. P. (1986). Power in the classroom VI: Verbal control strategies, nonverbal immediacy and affective learning. *Communication Education, 35*, 43–55.

Plax, T. G., Kearney, P., & Sorensen, G. (1990). The strategy selection-construction controversy II: Comparing pre- and experienced teachers' compliance-gaining message constructions. *Communication Education, 38*, 128–141.

Plax, T. G., Kearney, P., & Tucker, L. K. (1986). Prospective teachers' use of behavior alteration techniques on common student misbehaviors. *Communication Education, 35*, 32–42.

Richmond, V. P. (1990). Communication in the classroom: Power and motivation. *Communication Education, 39*, 181–195.

Richmond, V. P., & McCroskey, J. C. (1984). Power in the classroom II: Power and learning. *Communication Education, 33*, 125–136.

Richmond, V. P., McCroskey, J. C., Davis, L. M., & Koontz, K. A. (1980). Perceived power as a mediator of management communication style and employee satisfaction: A preliminary investigation. *Communication Quarterly, 28*, 37–46.

Richmond, V. P., McCroskey, J. C., Kearney, P., & Plax, T. G. (1987). Power in the classroom VII: Linking behavior alteration techniques to cognitive learning. *Communication Education, 36*, 1–12.

Roach, K. D. (1990). A reliability assessment of the Kearney, Plax, Richmond, and McCroskey (1984) BATs and BAMs model. *Communication Research Reports, 7*, 67–74.

Roach, K. D. (1991). Graduate teaching assistants' use of behavior alteration techniques in the university classroom. *Communication Quarterly, 39*, 178–188.

Roach, K. D. (1994). Temporal patterns and effects of perceived instructor compliance-gaining use. *Communication Education, 43*, 236–245.

Roach, K. D. (1995a). Teaching assistant argumentativeness: Effects on affective learning and student perceptions of power use. *Communication Education, 44*, 15–29.

Roach, K. D. (1995b). Teaching assistant argumentativeness and perceptions of power use in the classroom. *Communication Research Reports, 12*, 94–103.

Roach, K. D. (1999). The influence of teaching assistant willingness to communicate and communication anxiety in the classroom. *Communication Quarterly, 47*, 166–182.

Roach, K. D., & Byrne, P. R. (2001). A cross-cultural comparison of instructor communication in American and German classrooms. *Communication Education, 50*, 1–14.

Roach, K. D., Cornett-DeVito, M. M., & DeVito, R. (2005). A cross-cultural comparison of instructor communication in American and French classrooms. *Communication Quarterly, 53*, 87–107.

Schrodt, P., Witt, P. L., Myers, S. A., Turman, P. D., Barton, M. H., & Jernberg, K. A. (2008). Learner empowerment and teacher evaluations as a function of teacher power use in the college classroom. *Communication Education, 57*, 180–200.

Schrodt, P., Witt, P. L., & Turman, P. D. (2007). Reconsidering the measurement of teacher power use in the college classroom. *Communication Education, 56,* 308–332.

Sellnow, D., Liu, M., & Venette, S. (2006). When in Rome, do as the Romans do: A comparative analysis of Chinese and American new teachers' compliance-gaining strategies. *Communication Research Reports, 23,* 259–264.

Sorensen, G., Plax, T. G., & Kearney, P. (1989). The strategy selection-construction controversy: A coding scheme for analyzing teacher compliance-gaining message construction. *Communication Education, 38,* 102–118.

Sorensen, G., Plax, T. G., Kearney, P., & Burroughs, N. F. (1988). Developing coding systems for explicating teacher compliance-gaining messages. *World Communication, 17,* 241–251.

Sprague, J. (1992). Expanding the research agenda for instructional communication: Raising some unasked questions. *Communication Education, 41,* 1–25.

Student, K. R. (1968). Supervisory influence and work-group performance. *Journal of Applied Psychology, 52,* 188–194.

Teven, J. J., & Herring, J. E. (2005). Teacher influence in the classroom: A preliminary investigation of perceived instructor power, credibility, and student satisfaction. *Communication Research Reports, 22,* 235–246.

Turman, P. D., & Schrodt, P. (2006). Student perceptions of teacher power as a function of perceived teacher confirmation. *Communication Education, 55,* 265–279.

Waltman, M. S. (1994). An assessment of the convergent validity of the checklist of behavior alteration techniques: The association between teachers' likelihood-of-use ratings and informants' frequency-of-use ratings. *Journal of Applied Communication Research, 22,* 295–308.

Waltman, M. (1995). An assessment of the discriminant validity of the checklist of behavior alteration techniques: A test of the item desirability bias in prospective and experienced teachers' likelihood-of-use ratings. *Journal of Applied Communication Research, 23,* 201–211.

Waltman, M. S., & Burleson, B. R. (1997a). Explaining bias in teacher ratings of behavior alteration techniques: An experimental test of the heuristic processing account. *Communication Education, 46,* 75–94.

Waltman, M. S., & Burleson, B. R. (1997b). The reality of item desirability and heuristic processing in BAT ratings: Respecting the data. *Communication Education, 46,* 100–103.

Worley, D. W., & Cornett-DeVito, M. M. (2007). College students with learning disabilities (SWLD) and their response to teacher power. *Communication Studies, 58,* 17–33.

Instructor Immediacy $\mathbf{11}$

Creating Connections Conducive to Classroom Learning

Paul L. Witt, Paul Schrodt, and Paul D. Turman

Instructor immediacy is arguably the most widely researched variable in classroom communication research. For more than three decades, instructional communication scholars have delved into the effects of instructor immediacy on various classroom outcomes, leading some scholars to conclude that instructor immediacy has nearly universal classroom appeal and that it elicits consistently positive responses from students around the world. The psychologist Albert Mehrabian (1969) conceptualized immediacy as a cluster of communication behaviors that "enhance closeness to and nonverbal interaction with another" (p. 203). Grounding the construct in approach-avoidance theory, Mehrabian (1981) identified sets of verbal and nonverbal communication behaviors that contribute to reducing the perceived physical or psychological distance between communicators (Mehrabian, 1969, 1971; Wiener & Mehrabian, 1968). In the classroom, students perceive immediacy cues as expressions of interpersonal approach and liking by their instructor, thereby enhancing the instructor-student connection as an interpersonal relationship (Frymier & Houser, 2000). Perhaps as many as 200 immediacy studies have reported positive associations between instructor immediacy and various classroom outcomes such as student motivation, student satisfaction, instructor evaluations, and student learning.

Despite the breadth and depth of the literature, however, considerable controversy exists concerning the measures, findings, and theoretical underpinnings of immediacy research. Consequently, in this chapter, we proffer a compilation and synthesis of the instructor immediacy literature across four sections. First, we review general findings from nonverbal and verbal immediacy research. Second, we discuss current theoretical explanations for classroom immediacy. Third, we provide a brief overview of the critiques and challenges associated with immediacy research before concluding our chapter with a proposed agenda for future research.

Findings From Nonverbal and Verbal Immediacy Research

NONVERBAL IMMEDIACY AND LEARNING

As an interpersonal communication construct, teacher immediacy consists of a cluster of behavioral cues that implicitly communicate interpersonal approach or liking (Mehrabian, 1981). In the classroom, nonverbal immediacy may be expressed by both instructors and students through eye gaze, smiles, nods, relaxed body posture, forward leans, movement, gestures, and appropriate touch (Andersen, 1978). Nonverbal immediacy also may include paralinguistic variables such as tone, pace, intensity, variety, pause, and articulation, but not the verbal content of spoken messages. Most nonverbal immediacy researchers have focused on the use of these cues by instructors and subsequent effects on student learning outcomes. In her seminal study of immediacy in the classroom, for example, Andersen (1979) detected a significant relationship between teacher nonverbal immediacy behaviors and students' affective learning but no measurable relationship with cognitive learning as measured by test grades. A few early studies did link nonverbal immediacy to cognitive learning performance (Jordan, 1989; Kelley & Gorham, 1988), but the first decade of immediacy research produced more consistent findings related to affective learning, including both student attitudes and behavioral predispositions (Andersen & Withrow, 1981; Kearney, Plax, & Wendt-Wasco, 1985; Plax, Kearney, McCroskey, & Richmond, 1986; Sorenson, 1989). Overall, these studies reported a low to moderate association between teacher nonverbal immediacy and greater liking for the instructor and course, greater likelihood of engaging in the behaviors learned, and greater likelihood of enrolling in another course of the same type.

Increased attention was given to the association between nonverbal immediacy and cognitive learning after Richmond, McCroskey, Kearney, and Plax (1987) introduced the *learning loss* procedure to measure students' perceptions of their own learning. These researchers found an inverse relationship between nonverbal immediacy and learning loss, which represents the difference between students' perceived learning in the course and the predicted learning they believe would have occurred had they been taught by the ideal instructor. Researchers who employed learning loss (or the single item, "How much did you learn in this course?") treated the proce-dure as a cognitive learning measure, thus generating claims about the effects of instructor immediacy on cognitive learning (Chesebro & McCroskey, 2001; Gorham & Christophel, 1990; Zhang, Oetzel, Gao, Wilcox, & Takai, 2007). However, many communication scholars disagree with this interpretation, instead considering learning loss as a measure of affective or perceived learning (Hess & Smythe, 2001; King & Witt, 2009; Witt, Wheeless, & Allen, 2004). Despite the controversy, this procedure has been used widely in immediacy research, sometimes as the only learning instrument (Christensen & Menzel, 1998; Menzel & Carrell, 1999) but, more often, in conjunction with measures of affective learning (Baker & Woods, 2004; Frymier, 1994; Neuliep, 1995, 1997; Zhang et al., 2007).

Like other nonverbal behaviors, nonverbal immediacy cues are highly inferential and vary by culture and context (Gudykunst & Ting-Toomey, 1988). Researchers have detected positive relationships between nonverbal immediacy and classroom outcomes in several countries, including China (Myers, Zhong, & Guan, 1998; Zhang et al., 2007), Germany (Roach & Byrne, 2001), Kenya (Johnson & Miller, 2002), and Japan (Neuliep, 1997), as well as Australia, Finland, and Puerto Rico (McCroskey, Fayer, Richmond, Sallinen, & Barraclough, 1996; McCroskey, Sallinen, Fayer, Richmond, & Barraclough, 1996). Other researchers have examined immediacy in multi-ethnic classrooms in the United States (Neuliep, 1995; Sanders & Wiseman, 1990). Although differences in the magnitude of effects have been observed across cultural groups within and outside of the United States, collectively, researchers have found a generally positive association between teacher nonverbal immediacy and students' affective and perceived learning.

Instructor immediacy also is present in distributed learning environ-ments (Walker & Hackman, 1991; Witt & Wheeless, 1999), where reducing the distance between teacher and students is a primary communication goal. Research findings have indicated that the medium of instructional video does support the transmission of teacher nonverbal immediacy cues, with similar effects on student outcomes as in the traditional, face-to-face classroom (Peterson, 1994). Even in computer-mediated contexts, where nonverbal immediacy cues are filtered by a text-only medium, instructors may be able to substitute for the loss of nonverbal immediacy through exaggerated or more frequent use of verbally immediate cues (Baker & Woods, 2004; Hackman & Walker, 1990).

To empirically assess the effects of teacher immediacy on student learn-ing outcomes across decades, cultures, and contexts, Witt and colleagues (2004) conducted a meta-analysis of 81 studies conducted since 1978. They reported overall effects for teacher nonverbal immediacy in relation to affective learning ($r = .49$), perceived learning/learning loss ($r = .51$), and cognitive learning ($r = .17$). Their results demonstrated the predomi-nantly relational nature of nonverbal immediacy in the classroom, where immediate behaviors establish and maintain a communicative connection that enhances the instructor-student relationship. In such a supportive learning environment, students' perceptions, attitudes, and feelings are influenced positively by the instructor's expressions of liking and approach. Thus, students report greater liking for the instructor and course, as well as greater perceptions of having learned from the course experience. In contrast, meta-analytical results indicated that teacher non-verbal immediacy accounts for less than 3% of the variance in cognitive learning as measured by test grades, course grades, or recall of specific course content. Collectively, then, researchers have failed thus far to demonstrate substantial cognitive learning effects for teacher nonverbal immediacy, leading to the conclusion that "even though students like more highly immediate instructors and think they learn more from their courses, actual cognitive learning is not affected as much as they think it is" (Witt et al., 2004, p. 201).

NONVERBAL IMMEDIACY
AND OTHER CLASSROOM VARIABLES

Instructors' nonverbal immediacy cues not only affect student learning outcomes but also influence a host of classroom variables. Research has shown that teacher nonverbal immediacy is associated positively with students' state motivation (Christophel & Gorham, 1995; Frymier, 1994) and motivation to study (Frymier, 1993), as well as students' evaluations of the course and instructor (Moore, Masterson, Christophel, & Shea, 1996). Thus, immediate instructors are viewed positively by most students who apparently enter the classroom with expectations that their instructors will, in fact, demonstrate a degree of personal warmth and approach. Schrodt and Witt (2006) examined those expectations in connection with instructors' use of classroom technology and con-cluded that regardless of the level of technology use, students perceived immediate instructors as being "more competent, trustworthy, and caring than instructors described as being non-immediate" (p. 17). Researchers have detected positive associations between teacher non-verbal immediacy and students' perceptions of instructor credibility (Chamberlin, 2000; Thweatt & McCroskey, 1998), clarity (Chesebro & McCroskey, 1998, 2001), effectiveness (Andersen, 1979), and power (Plax et al., 1986). Furthermore, instructor immediacy has been shown to influence positively student behaviors such as extraclass communi-cation (Fusani, 1994) while contributing to decreased levels of commu-nication apprehension (Ellis, 1995; Frymier, 1993) and student resistance to compliance-gaining messages (Kearney & Plax, 1991). To date, no other instructional communication variable has demonstrated more widespread impact on classroom processes and outcomes than teacher nonverbal immediacy.

VERBAL IMMEDIACY AND LEARNING

Current understandings of instructor immediacy were broadened by Gorham's (1988) pivotal study that expanded the focus of immediacy research to include explicit verbal cues. As part of the original immediacy construct, Mehrabian (1969, 1971; Wiener & Mehrabian, 1968) had constructed a taxonomy of word choices and syntactic structures that could result in perceptions of immediacy or nonimmediacy. Examples included, among others, expressions of proximity (this vs. that), duration (of attention), probability (will vs. might), object participation (use of names), activity (active vs. passive voice), and inclusivity (we, our goal vs. you, your goal). Gorham (1988) introduced the construct of *teacher verbal immediacy* by expanding Mehrabian's taxonomy to include items such as concern (about students), self-disclosure (openness), detail (of explanations), appropriate use of humor, and conversations with students before and after class. Positing a comprehensive model of immediacy that included both nonverbal and verbal cues, Gorham introduced the 20-item Verbal Immediacy Behaviors (VIB) instrument to be used in combination with Richmond, Gorham, and McCroskey's (1987) 14-item Nonverbal Immediacy Behaviors (NIB) scale. Despite serious criticism about the validity of the VIB (Robinson & Richmond, 1995), some researchers have followed Gorham's lead and combined the two types of immediacy into a single construct (Neuliep, 1995, 1997; Sanders & Wiseman, 1990; Titsworth, 2001), though most researchers conduct separate tests for the two types of instructor immediacy (Christensen & Menzel, 1998; Christophel, 1990; Frymier, 1994; Menzel & Carrell, 1999).

Obviously, most classroom messages involve the simultaneous use of both nonverbal and verbal cues. Scholars have investigated the comparative effects of both types of instructor immediacy and found generally similar effects, though outcomes related to verbal immediacy may be mediated or overridden by instructors' nonverbal behaviors. For example, in studies of instructors' compliance-gaining message strategies, the potentially negative effects of nonimmediate, antisocial compliance messages were mitigated by the overriding positive effects of teacher nonverbal immediacy cues (Kearney, Plax, Smith, & Sorenson, 1988; Plax et al., 1986). In other words, instructors' use of nonverbal cues such as smiling, eye contact, and physical proximity can potentially suppress the negative effects of nonimmediate verbal content. Furthermore, Witt and Wheeless (2001) conducted an experiment manipulating both types of immediacy (i.e., in high and low combinations) and found that students recalled the least amount of message content when the instructor used verbally immediate language but nonimmediate nonverbal cues. As they reasoned, this combination of immediacy cues created cognitive dissonance as the students became distracted by the instructor's inconsistent communication style. Thus, in classroom messages combining verbal and nonverbal cues, it appears that the more robust effect emanates from instructors' nonverbal behaviors, even if the content of the message is potentially negative.

In their meta-analysis of immediacy and learning, Witt and colleagues (2004) reported overall effects for teacher verbal immediacy in relation to affective learning ($r = .49$), perceived learning/learning loss ($r = .49$), and cognitive learning ($r = .06$) that were similar to the results for teacher nonverbal immediacy. Again, their findings demonstrated the relational nature of verbal immediacy in the classroom, where instructors' syntax and specific word choice can lead to perceptions of liking and closeness, thus enhancing the teacher-student relationship. It is important to note, however, that instructor verbal immediacy had little to no effect on the cognitive learning outcomes of test grades, course grades, or recall of specific course content (Witt et al., 2004).

VERBAL IMMEDIACY AND OTHER CLASSROOM VARIABLES

Given the challenges associated with valid measurement of verbal immediacy, this construct has not been as widely researched as has nonverbal immediacy. Some scholars have combined verbal and nonverbal cues into a single teacher immediacy construct (Booth-Butterfield, Mosher, & Mollish, 1992; Neuliep, 1995), but other researchers have examined specific verbal immediacy cues in relation to various classroom variables. For example, positive associations have been reported between verbal immediacy and teacher clarity (Powell & Harville, 1990), effectiveness (Christophel, 1990; Powell & Harville, 1990), social style (Frymier & Thompson, 1995), and end-of-course evaluations (Moore et al., 1996). Student variables such as motivation (Frymier, 1993), out-of-class communication (Jaasma & Koper, 1999), and information-seeking strategies (Myers & Knox, 2001) have been found positively correlated with instructors' verbal immediacy cues. In addition, Frymier and Thompson (1995) observed a negative association between teacher verbal immediacy and students' communication apprehension. Collectively, these studies suggest that when instructors engage in distance-reducing language in the classroom, a number of positive instructional outcomes may be enhanced.

IMMEDIACY AS A MODERATOR OF OTHER INSTRUCTOR COMMUNICATION BEHAVIORS

As investigators have examined teacher immediacy in relation to other classroom variables, they have detected various moderating effects. For example, nonverbal immediacy cues are so intertwined with other instructor behaviors that they often moderate the effects of instructional technology use (Schrodt & Witt, 2006; Witt & Schrodt, 2006), instructor misbehaviors (Thweatt & McCroskey, 1998), and behavior alteration techniques (Plax et al., 1986). Immediacy also moderates the influence of teacher clarity (Chesebro & McCroskey, 1998), credibility (Pogue & AhYun, 2006), and caring (Comadena, Hunt, & Simonds, 2007) as these variables affect student motivation and learning outcomes. Collectively, these studies have demonstrated that immediacy cues typically occur in conjunction with other instructor behaviors and that the use of appropriate immediacy cues can either enhance the positive effects of prosocial communication behaviors or help mitigate the negative consequences of antisocial communication behaviors (Kearney et al., 1988). Of course, how immediacy operates within a given investigation varies as a function of research design and methodology.

RESEARCH DESIGNS AND MEASURES

Most studies of instructor immediacy have employed survey research designs in which students complete perceptual measures related to their instructor's immediacy and their own learning. Following the innovative methodology introduced by Plax and colleagues (1986), students are typically asked at a point in the semester to complete a survey questionnaire while referencing "the instructor you have in the course which meets prior to this class." This procedure has been used successfully in previous research and assures that instructors from a wide variety of disciplines are referenced by the students. In contrast, other researchers have designed experimental and quasi-experimental investigations to compare learning effects in the presence of various controlled manipulations of instructor immediacy (Comadena et al., 2007; Pogue & AhYun, 2006; Titsworth, 2001; Witt & Wheeless, 2001; Zhang & Sapp, 2007). Witt and colleagues (2004) observed that, on average, experimental designs have produced smaller effect sizes for instructor immediacy on learning outcomes than have survey research designs.

In addition to research designs, the *measurement* of nonverbal immediacy has evolved over time as well. Considered the first immediacy scale used in instructional communication research, the high-inference Generalized Immediacy (GI) scale (Andersen, 1979) consists of nine semantic differential items that measure gestalt responses to the overall level of instructor nonverbal immediacy. Although the GI scale sometimes is used as the only measure of immediacy given its relatively high internal reliability (ranging from .84 to .97; see Comstock, Rowell, & Bowers, 1995; Rubin, Palmgreen, & Sypher, 1994), it is used more often in conjunction with behavioral measures, such as the Behavioral Indicants of Immediacy (BII) scale (Andersen, 1979). The low-inference BII consists of 15 instructor behaviors (e.g., gestures, eye contact, smiles) that are assessed in terms of frequency using a 7-point Likert-type response format. The BII was modified by Richmond et al. (1987) and renamed the Nonverbal Immediacy Behaviors (NIB) scale, further modified and renamed the Nonverbal Immediacy Measure (NIM; Gorham & Zakahi, 1990), and finally abbreviated and renamed the Revised Nonverbal Immediacy Measure (RNIM; McCroskey, Sallinen, et al., 1996). The most current measure of nonverbal immediacy is the Nonverbal Immediacy Scale (NIS), which exists in both self-report (NIS-S) and other-report (NIS-O) formats (Richmond, McCroskey, & Johnson, 2003). Using a 5-point Likert-type response format, the NIS includes 26 items worded in such a way that they are not specific to the classroom only, as previous measures have been.

Although these measures are widely used and highly reliable, some researchers have questioned the validity of these perceptual instruments in measuring instructor nonverbal immediacy as originally conceived by Mehrabian (Hess & Smythe, 2001; Moore et al., 1996). In particular, their use in cross-cultural contexts has been challenged by Zhang and Oetzel (2006), who developed the Chinese Teacher Immediacy Scale (CTIS) to overcome various culture-bound artifacts in the underlying conceptual framework of earlier measures. Likewise, measurement of verbal immediacy has been so problematic as to generate calls for the cessation of verbal immediacy research until a valid measure can be developed (Hess & Smythe, 2001; Robinson & Richmond, 1995). Each critique is reviewed in further detail later in this chapter, but first, the theoretical explanations for the effects of immediacy in the classroom should be considered.

Current Theoretical Explanations for Classroom Immediacy

Although instructor immediacy may be the most widely researched variable in classroom communication research, it may be the least theoretically developed of all the classroom variables. Although scholars know *that* immediacy works, they do not yet know *why* or *how*. To date, researchers have not developed a specific theory that explains why immediacy cues such as smiles, eye contact, gestures, and inclusive language bring about positive outcomes such as student affect, motivation, and learning. Furthermore, no universally accepted theoretical model exists that demonstrates how instructor immediacy cues function to influence other variables. This is not to say that every immediacy study is variable-analytic in nature (although this criticism is heard frequently) or disconnected from the body of communication theory that may come to bear on the phenomenon. On the contrary, scholars have drawn on a number of theories to support their immediacy research, and they have tested and replicated several different models in their search for a theoretical framework to explain immediacy in the classroom. The results, however, are not conclusive.

Following the lead of Mehrabian (1969, 1981), for example, some scholars have studied nonverbal immediacy in terms of approach-avoidance theory. People move closer to individuals they like and farther away from those individuals they dislike. Thus, instructors are posited to draw near to their students psychologically and/or physically when they engage in behaviors such as eye contact, forward body leans, proximity, smiles, and gestures. On the other hand, verbal immediacy may be partially explained in terms of communication accommodation theory (Giles, Mulac, Bradac, & Johnson, 1987; Jordan & Wheeless, 1990) in that people adapt the manner and content of their verbal communication to the perceived preference or style of the receiver and context. Thus, instructors may engage in classroom immediacy cues because students expect instructors to be personable and engaging. By adapting their linguistic code to normative classroom expectations, instructors may be perceived as more similar to and, therefore, more liked by their students.

Several other explanatory viewpoints have been put forward as well, including the idea that (a) immediacy attracts or arouses students' attention, which in turn enhances learning outcomes (Comstock et al., 1995; Kelley & Gorham, 1988); (b) immediacy elicits certain positive emotional responses from students, which in turn increase learning (Butland & Beebe, 1992; Mottet & Beebe, 2002; Mottet, Frymier, & Beebe, 2006); and (c) immediacy cues establish and maintain a meaningful interpersonal connection that supports the exchange of messages, including course-related information (Witt, 2008). Although each of these perspectives has some validity, to date no single theory satisfactorily explains the functions and effects of immediacy in the classroom.

Similarly, several theoretical models have been developed and tested, particularly in relation to immediacy and learning. Although each model has been shown to be the best fit in at least one investigation, none has proven to be consistently better than the others. This theoretical ambiguity may be justified if the functions of immediacy vary according to external influences such as classroom environment, class size, course content, culture, time of the semester, time of day, or age and sex of the students and instructor. Nevertheless, researchers have either directly or indirectly tested four conceptual models explaining the link between immediacy cues and student learning. The *learning model* posits that instructor immediacy behaviors function directly to increase students' learning. Frymier (1994) attributed this model to Andersen (1979), who, like other early immediacy researchers, assumed that instructor immediacy had a direct effect on student outcomes. The assumption simply is that students learn more when instructors engage in immediacy cues (Kearney et al., 1985; Plax et al., 1986). In the *motivation model*, however, immediacy serves to increase students' state motivation to study, which in turn increases their learning (Frymier, 1994). Although Frymier provided preliminary results in support of this model, researchers have yet to test the motivation model in relation to performed cognitive learning, as indicated by course grades, test grades, or recall of instructional content.

The *affect model* posits that immediacy enhances affect for the instructor and course content, thereby increasing cognitive learning (Allen, Witt, & Wheeless, 2006; Rodriguez, Plax, & Kearney, 1996). To explain the association between teacher immediacy and various types of student learning, this model posits that affect precedes cognitive learning (see Krathwohl, Bloom, & Masia, 1964). Proponents of this model have acknowledged the conceptual overlap between affect and motivation, such that greater liking for the instructor and course understandably serves to motivate students to apply themselves in a more diligent and focused manner. In a recent test of this model, Allen et al. (2006) provided initial support for this approach for both verbal and nonverbal immediacy in relation to both perceived and performed cognitive learning outcomes.

In the *integrated model*, Zhang et al. (2007) compared the three preceding models using structural equation modeling and student samples from four countries. Using a revised measure of immediacy (i.e., the CTIS; Zhang & Oetzel, 2006), they found that all three models explain part of the variance in motivation, affective learning, and perceived learning. The results of their study prompted Zhang and her colleagues (2007) to posit an integrated model that combines the learning, motivation, and affect perspectives into one theoretical model. According to this model, in particular learning contexts and cultures, instructor immediacy has direct effects on affective and perceived learning. Simultaneously or separately, the effects of immediacy also may be mediated by affect and/or motivation. Instead of resolving the ambiguities associated with the three contrasting theoretical models, the integrated model confirms each model and acknowledges that the models are all partially valid. It should be noted, however, that the integrated model has not yet been assessed in relation to students' actual academic performance (e.g., grades or recall of instructional content) or other outcomes such as students' ratings of instruction.

Critiques and Challenges Associated With Immediacy Research

Two primary criticisms have been levied against instructor immediacy research. First, survey research designs have been the most common methodology employed to assess students' perceptions of instructor immediacy behaviors. Although employing Plax et al.'s (1986) procedure assures that instructors from a wide variety of disciplines are referenced by the students, a number of scholars have cautioned against an overreliance on measurement techniques that rely solely on student recall. As Hess and Smythe (2001) argued, there is little evidence to suggest that perceptions of immediacy would not be confounded by other judgments students have of their instructor (e.g., out-of-class communication, grading practices, prior relationships). As a result, instructor behaviors deemed to produce a sense of liking by students may indirectly increase perceived immediacy scores. In support of their earlier claim, Smythe and Hess (2005) video recorded instructors in the classroom environment and then sought student perceptions of their instructors' nonverbal immediacy behaviors. After the recorded content was coded for actual immediacy cues and compared with student ratings, results indicated limited correspondence between the two measures. Accordingly, Smythe and Hess concluded that "researchers may not be justified in making claims about instructor immediacy behaviors based on student perceptions" (p. 177). As Rubin (2002) observed, "This research literature is not so much about observed teacher immediacy behavior as it is about students' perceptions of teacher immediacy" (p. 415), an issue often overlooked in the interpretation of immediacy research.

The second, but perhaps more important line of critique involves the validity of both the verbal and nonverbal immediacy instruments (Hess & Smythe, 2001; Rubin, 2002). Gorham (1988) argued that an instructor's verbal communicative behaviors would operationally influence students' perceptions of immediacy, thus necessitating the development of the VIB to measure verbal immediacy cues. Robinson and Richmond (1995) called into question the validity of the VIB, however, raising concerns about the directionality employed in the wording of immediate and nonimmediate behaviors and suggesting that the VIB was in reality a measure of instructor effectiveness rather than instructor immediacy. They argued that "this distinction is very important, since the constructs of effectiveness and immediacy are far from isomorphic" (p. 81). Specifically, Robinson and Richmond raised concerns about the face, construct, and predictive validity of the VIB, concluding that "the scale is not recommended for continued use in communication research prior to its reformulation and additional testing for validity" (p. 80).

Hess and Smythe (2001) extended these concerns about the VIB by criticizing the survey development procedures employed by Gorham (1988). Specifically, asking students to report on the behaviors of their *best teacher* positioned immediacy as interchangeable with effective teaching (Hess & Smythe, 2001). However, neither Mehrabian's (1966, 1969) original articulation of immediacy nor Andersen's (1979) conceptualization of teacher immediacy render such an interchange tenable. As Mottet and Richmond (1998) noted, efforts at developing a measure of verbal immediacy stemmed from Mehrabian's (1967) early work, which was designed to help therapists provide better interpretations of the linguistic features of their clients' messages. Attempting to reposition immediacy into an instructional context, then, may have unintentionally resulted in the development of a *relational maintenance* typology similar to those found within everyday talk in interpersonal relationships (Mottet & Richmond, 1998). For example, Mottet and Richmond found that respondents were more likely to employ a nonverbal linguistic code of silence when they wanted to avoid relationship formation in instructor and peer-friend interactions. Consequently, "if verbal immediacy exists linguistically, it does not appear to be consciously employed" (p. 39), raising further concerns about the possibility of developing a measure of verbal immediacy that coincides with Mehrabian's original conceptualization of the immediacy construct. Although the research of Mottet and Richmond was not restricted to the classroom communication context, it was conducted among college student participants, and some of the survey items related to the communication cues of their instructors.

Although verbal immediacy and the VIB have received the majority of scholarly criticism within this body of research, the measurement of teacher nonverbal immediacy also has been called into question. Moore and colleagues (1996) observed that factors such as class size, academic discipline (e.g., task-oriented vs. people-oriented courses), and expected grade may influence students' perceptions of instructor immediacy. The fact that students who expected to receive an "A" in the course perceived higher levels of nonverbal immediacy when compared with those who expected a "C" adds further support to the criticism that students' perceptions of nonverbal immediacy are subject to halo effects and confounded with other instructor behaviors. Furthermore, when developing the most recent version of the NIS, Richmond and colleagues (2003) found unanticipated sex differences in their results. They observed that female students were more likely than male students to rate their instructors as highly immediate, which led the researchers to posit that females are better able to interpret nonverbal cues. Nonetheless, when coupled with Moore et al.'s (1996) findings, Richmond et al.'s (2003) research only further supports current concerns about the validity of relying solely on survey-based research when measuring nonverbal immediacy.

Collectively, then, instructional communication scholars have voiced a number of concerns and cautions about extant research on instructor immediacy, the most notable of which include an overreliance on cross-sectional, survey-based research of students' *perceptions* of instructors' immediacy in the classroom, as well as construct validity concerns about the VIB. With these criticisms in mind, the final section of this chapter highlights the three most pressing, and potentially promising, directions for future research.

Proposed Agenda for Future Research

In their recent review of instructor immediacy, Richmond, Lane, and McCroskey (2006) outlined a number of future directions scholars can take as they continue to investigate the use of immediacy behaviors in classroom settings. For instance, they called for continued intercultural investigations of instructor immediacy (see Zhang et al., 2007); comparisons of immediate behaviors across different levels of education, class sizes, technological media, and subject matters; and further research on the consequences that immediacy use may have for instructors themselves, to name a few. These future directions certainly merit continued research, but we contend that three issues in particular need immediate attention given their theoretical and methodological implications for this body of work.

First, instructional communication scholars should reconsider extant measures of verbal immediacy and determine whether the construct itself merits further research in classroom settings. Our knowledge claims about instructor immediacy are only as valid as the measures and research designs used to advance the claims in the first place. Although Gorham's (1988) VIB has received considerable scrutiny and some researchers have questioned whether verbal immediacy can be measured using self-reports in the instructor-student relationship (e.g., Mottet & Richmond, 1998), other scholars have demonstrated through the use of experimental manipulations that verbal immediacy cues do influence classroom learning (e.g., Witt & Wheeless, 1999). Ironically, measures of nonverbal immediacy have undergone continued revisions over the past several years, yet the verbal communicative behaviors that reduce the perceived psychological distance between two communicators have received far less attention. Thus, future research is needed to reexamine Mehrabian's (1969) taxonomy, to query students themselves on the salience of verbal immediacy cues in the classroom, and to reconstruct a more valid set of indicators measuring verbal immediacy cues.

Second, we echo Richmond et al.'s (2006) call for continued research on the relationship between immediacy and cognitive learning. Some scholars have argued that the relationship is curvilinear, where optimal cognitive learning is most likely to occur when instructors use moderate levels of immediacy (Comstock et al., 1995). Other scholars have reported a linear relationship between the two constructs (Andersen, 1979; Jordan, 1989; Kelley & Gorham, 1988). Before researchers can fully examine the precise nature of this relationship, however, more valid measures of cognitive learning are needed. In general, most instructional communication researchers have relied primarily on measures of *perceived learning* using the learning loss procedure (Richmond, McCroskey, et al., 1987) or other indirect indicators of cognitive learning, such as exam scores, course grades, and other learning performance instruments (Witt et al., 2004). The validity of using exam scores and course grades or relying solely on students' perceptions of learning loss has been questioned (McCroskey & Richmond, 1992; Witt et al., 2004), and the continued search for highly valid measures of cognitive learning remains elusive at best. Thus, future research is needed not only to strengthen the construct validity of the verbal and nonverbal immediacy measures but also to identify and construct valid measures of cognitive learning as well. Bloom (1956) originally described cognitive learning as the recall, comprehension, application, and synthesis of newly acquired information. Perhaps a more valid approach to measuring cognitive learning, then, would necessitate triangulating multiple indicators of learning that span across the levels of Bloom's taxonomy (King & Witt, 2009).

Third, and perhaps most important, future research is needed to more carefully test competing theoretical models of immediacy and learning that, in essence, identify the theoretical mechanisms primarily responsible for this relationship. Such efforts would move researchers one step closer to developing a specific theory of instructor immediacy useful for integrating this body of research. Initial efforts at testing competing models, though heuristic in nature, have yielded inconsistent results, primarily as a function of not establishing measurement and structural invariance for measures of nonverbal immediacy across cultures (Zhang et al., 2007). Nevertheless, structural equation modeling provides a statistical tool useful for comparing the direct effects model with the affect, motivation, and integrated models. Furthermore, researchers have generally neglected the role that student characteristics play in moderating the effects of an instructor's immediacy cues. Building from the assumptions of emotional response theory (Mottet et al., 2006), for instance, emotional intelligence (Mayer, Salovey, & Caruso, 2004) and emotional contagion (Hatfield, Cacioppo, & Rapson, 1994) are two student characteristics that may moderate the association between instructor immediacy and student affect. Ultimately, it is through continued investigations of competing and complementary theoretical explanations for instructor immediacy that scholars may further the understanding of the complex nature of the teacher-student relationship.

Conclusion

There is little doubt that instructor immediacy plays a meaningful role in building and sustaining the kinds of relationships that ultimately enhance student learning. Now, researchers simply need to know *why* and *how* immediacy works.

References

Allen, M., Witt, P. L., & Wheeless, L. R. (2006). The role of teacher immediacy as a motivational factor in student learning: A meta-analysis and causal model. *Communication Education, 55*, 21–31.

Andersen, J. F. (1978). *The relationship between teacher immediacy and teaching effectiveness.* Unpublished doctoral dissertation, West Virginia University, Morgantown.

Andersen, J. F. (1979). Teacher immediacy as a predictor of teaching effectiveness. In D. Nimmo (Ed.), *Communication yearbook 3* (pp. 543–559). New Brunswick, NJ: Transaction Books.

Andersen, J. F., & Withrow, J. G. (1981). The impact of lecturers' nonverbal expressiveness on improving mediated instruction. *Communication Education, 30,* 342–353.

Baker, J. D., & Woods, R. (2004). Immediacy, cohesiveness, and the online classroom. *Journal of Computing in Higher Education, 15,* 133–151.

Bloom, B. S. (1956). *A taxonomy of educational objectives.* New York: Longmans, Green.

Booth-Butterfield, S., Mosher, N., & Mollish, D. (1992). Teacher immediacy and student involvement: A dual process analysis. *Communication Research Reports, 9,* 13–21.

Butland, M. J., & Beebe, S. A. (1992, May). *A study of the application of implicit communication theory to teacher immediacy and student learning.* Paper presented at the annual meeting of the International Communication Association, Miami, FL.

Chamberlin, C. R. (2000). Nonverbal behaviors and initial impressions of trustworthiness in instructor-supervisor relationships. *Communication Education, 49,* 352–364.

Chesebro, J. L., & McCroskey, J. C. (1998). The relationship of teacher clarity and teacher immediacy with students' experiences of state receiver apprehension. *Communication Quarterly, 46,* 446–456.

Chesebro, J. L., & McCroskey, J. C. (2001). The relationship of teacher clarity and immediacy with student state receiver apprehension, affect, and cognitive learning. *Communication Education, 50,* 59–68.

Christensen, L. J., & Menzel, K. E. (1998). The linear relationship between student reports of teacher immediacy behaviors and perceptions of state motivation, and of cognitive, affective, and behavioral learning. *Communication Education, 47,* 82–90.

Christophel, D. M. (1990). The relationships among teacher immediacy behaviors, student motivation and learning. *Communication Education, 39,* 323–340.

Christophel, D. M., & Gorham, J. (1995). A test-retest analysis of student motivation, teacher immediacy, and perceived sources of motivation and demotivation in college classes. *Communication Education, 44,* 292–306.

Comadena, M. E., Hunt, S. K., & Simonds, C. J. (2007). The effects of teacher clarity, nonverbal immediacy, and caring on student motivation, affective and cognitive learning. *Communication Research Reports, 24,* 241–248.

Comstock, J., Rowell, E., & Bowers, J. W. (1995). Food for thought: Teacher nonverbal immediacy, student learning, and curvilinearity. *Communication Education, 44,* 251–266.

Ellis, K. (1995). Apprehension, self-perceived competency, and teacher immediacy in the laboratory-supported public speaking course: Trends and relationships. *Communication Education, 44,* 64–78.

Frymier, A. B. (1993). The relationships among communication apprehension, immediacy, and motivation to study. *Communication Reports, 6,* 8–17.

Frymier, A. B. (1994). A model of immediacy in the classroom. *Communication Quarterly, 42,* 133–144.

Frymier, A. B., & Houser, M. L. (2000). The teacher-student relationship as an interpersonal relationship. *Communication Education, 49,* 207–219.

Frymier, A. B., & Thompson, C. A. (1995). Using student reports to measure immediacy: Is it a valid methodology? *Communication Research Reports, 12,* 85–93.

Fusani, D. S. (1994). "Extra-class" communication: Frequency, immediacy, self-disclosure, and satisfaction in student-faculty interaction outside the classroom. *Journal of Applied Communication Research, 22,* 232–257.

Giles, H., Mulac, A., Bradac, J. J., & Johnson, P. (1987). Speech accommodation theory: The first decade and beyond. In M. L. McLaughlin (Ed.), *Communication yearbook 10* (pp. 13–48). Newbury Park, CA: Sage.

Gorham, J. (1988). The relationship between verbal teacher immediacy and student learning. *Communication Education, 37,* 40–53.

Gorham, J., & Christophel, D. M. (1990). The relationship of teachers' use of humor in the classroom to immediacy and student learning. *Communication Education, 30,* 46–62.

Gorham, J., & Zakahi, W. R. (1990). A comparison of teacher and student perceptions of immediacy and learning: Monitoring process and product. *Communication Education, 39,* 354–368.

Gudykunst, W. G., & Ting-Toomey, S. (1988). *Culture and interpersonal communication.* Newbury Park, CA: Sage.

Hackman, M. Z., & Walker, K. B. (1990). Instructional communication in the televised classroom: The effects of system design and teacher immediacy on student learning and satisfaction. *Communication Education, 39,* 196–206.

Hatfield, E., Cacioppo, J. T., & Rapson, R. L. (1994). *Emotional contagion.* New York: Cambridge University Press.

Hess, J. A., & Smythe, M. J. (2001). Is teacher immediacy actually related to student cognitive learning? *Communication Studies, 52,* 197–219.

Jaasma, M. A., & Koper, R. J. (1999). The relationship of student-faculty out-of-class communication to instructor immediacy and trust and to student motivation. *Communication Education, 48,* 41–47.

Johnson, S. D., & Miller, A. N. (2002). A cross-cultural study of immediacy, credibility, and learning in the U.S. and Kenya. *Communication Education, 51,* 280–292.

Jordan, F. F. (1989). *An examination of the relationship between perceived verbal and paralinguistic immediacy and accommodation to perceived cognitive learning.* Unpublished doctoral dissertation, West Virginia University, Morgantown.

Jordan, F. F., & Wheeless, L. R. (1990, November). *An investigation of the relationships among teachers' verbal immediacy, paralinguistic immediacy, and speech accommodation in diverse classrooms.* Paper presented at the annual meeting of the Speech Communication Association, Chicago.

Kearney, P., & Plax, T. G. (1991). An attributional analysis of college students' resistance decisions. *Communication Education, 40,* 325–342.

Kearney, P., Plax, T. G., Smith, V. R., & Sorenson, G. (1988). Effects of teacher immediacy and strategy type on college student resistance to on-task demands. *Communication Education, 37,* 54–67.

Kearney, P., Plax, T. G., & Wendt-Wasco, N. J. (1985). Teacher immediacy for affective learning in divergent college classes. *Communication Quarterly, 33,* 61–71.

Kelley, D. H., & Gorham, J. (1988). Effects of immediacy on recall of information. *Communication Education, 37,* 198–207.

King, P. E., & Witt, P. L. (2009). Teacher immediacy, confidence testing, and the measurement of cognitive learning. *Communication Education, 58,* 110–123.

Krathwohl, D. R., Bloom, B. S., & Masia, B. B. (1964). *Taxonomy of education objectives: Handbook II. Affective domain.* New York: David McKay.

Mayer, J. D., Salovey, P., & Caruso, D. R. (2004). Emotional intelligence: Theory, findings, and implications. *Psychological Inquiry, 15,* 197–215.

McCroskey, J. C., Fayer, J. M., Richmond, V. P., Sallinen, A., & Barraclough, R. A. (1996). A multi-cultural examination of the relationship between nonverbal immediacy and affective learning. *Communication Quarterly, 44,* 297–307.

McCroskey, J. C., & Richmond, V. P. (1992). Increasing teacher influence through immediacy. In V. P. Richmond & J. C. McCroskey (Eds.), *Power in the classroom: Communication, control, and concern* (pp. 101–119). Hillsdale, NJ: Lawrence Erlbaum.

McCroskey, J. C., Sallinen, A., Fayer, J. M., Richmond, V. P., & Barraclough, R. A. (1996). Nonverbal immediacy and cognitive learning: A cross-cultural investigation. *Communication Education, 45,* 200–211.

Mehrabian, A. (1966). Immediacy: An indicator of attitudes in linguistic communication. *Journal of Personality, 34,* 26–34.

Mehrabian, A. (1967). Attitudes inferred from neutral verbal communication. *Journal of Consulting Psychology, 31,* 414–417.

Mehrabian, A. (1969). Some referents and measures of nonverbal behavior. *Behavioral Research Methods and Instrumentation, 1,* 203–207.

Mehrabian, A. (1971). *Silent messages.* Belmont, CA: Wadsworth.

Mehrabian, A. (1981). *Silent messages* (2nd ed.). Belmont, CA: Wadsworth.

Menzel, K. E., & Carrell, L. J. (1999). The impact of gender and immediacy on willingness to talk and perceived learning. *Communication Education, 48,* 31–40.

Moore, A., Masterson, J. T., Christophel, D. M., & Shea, K. A. (1996). College teacher immediacy and student ratings of instruction. *Communication Education, 45,* 29–39.

Mottet, T. P., & Beebe, S. A. (2002). Relationships between teacher immediacy, student emotional response, and perceived student learning. *Communication Research Reports, 19,* 77–88.

Mottet, T. P., Frymier, A. B., & Beebe, S. A. (2006). Theorizing about instructional communication. In T. P. Mottet, V. P. Richmond, & J. C. McCroskey (Eds.), *Handbook of instructional communication: Rhetorical and relational perspectives* (pp. 255–282). Boston: Allyn & Bacon.

Mottet, P. T., & Richmond, V. P. (1998). An inductive analysis of verbal immediacy: Alternative conceptualization of relational verbal approach/avoidance strategies. *Communication Quarterly, 46,* 25–40.

Myers, S. A., & Knox, R. L. (2001). The relationship between college student information-seeking behaviors and perceived instructor verbal behaviors. *Communication Education, 50,* 343–357.

Myers, S. A., Zhong, M., & Guan, S. (1998). Instructor immediacy in the Chinese college classroom. *Communication Studies, 49,* 240–254.

Neuliep, J. W. (1995). A comparison of teacher immediacy in African-American and Euro-American classrooms. *Communication Education, 44,* 267–277.

Neuliep, J. W. (1997). A cross-cultural comparison of teacher immediacy in American and Japanese college classrooms. *Communication Research, 24,* 431–452.

Peterson, S. J. (1994). *Interactive television: Continuing education participant satisfaction.* Unpublished doctoral dissertation, University of Missouri, Columbia.

Plax, T. G., Kearney, P., McCroskey, J. C., & Richmond, V. P. (1986). Power in the classroom VI: Verbal control strategies, nonverbal immediacy and affective learning. *Communication Education, 35,* 43–55.

Pogue, L. L., & AhYun, K. (2006). The effect of teacher nonverbal immediacy and credibility on student motivation and affective learning. *Communication Education, 55,* 331–344.

Powell, R., & Harville, B. (1990). The effects of teacher immediacy and clarity on instructional outcomes: An intercultural assessment. *Communication Education, 39,* 369–379.

Richmond, V. P., Gorham, J. S., & McCroskey, J. C. (1987). The relationship between selected immediacy behaviors and cognitive learning. In M. L. McLaughlin (Ed.), *Communication yearbook 10* (pp. 574–590). Newbury Park, CA: Sage.

Richmond, V. P., Lane, D. R., & McCroskey, J. C. (2006). Teacher immediacy and the teacher-student relationship. In T. P. Mottet, V. P. Richmond, & J. C. McCroskey (Eds.), *Handbook of instructional communication: Rhetorical and relational perspectives* (pp. 167–193). Boston: Allyn & Bacon.

Richmond, V. P., McCroskey, J. C., & Johnson, A. E. (2003). Development of the Nonverbal Immediacy Scale (NIS): Measures of self- and other-perceived nonverbal immediacy. *Communication Quarterly, 51,* 502–515.

Richmond, V. P., McCroskey, J. C., Kearney, P., & Plax, T. G. (1987). Power in the classroom VII: Linking behavior alteration techniques to cognitive learning. *Communication Education, 36,* 1–12.

Roach, K. D., & Byrne, P. R. (2001). A cross-cultural comparison of instructor communication in American and German classrooms. *Communication Education, 50,* 1–14.

Robinson, R. Y., & Richmond, V. P. (1995). Validity of the verbal immediacy scale. *Communication Research Reports, 12,* 80–84.

Rodriguez, J. I., Plax, T. G., & Kearney, P. (1996). Clarifying the relationship between teacher nonverbal immediacy and student cognitive learning: Affective learning as the central causal mediator. *Communication Education, 45,* 293–305.

Rubin, D. L. (2002). Binocular vision for communication education. *Communication Education, 51,* 412–419.

Rubin, R. B., Palmgreen, P., & Sypher, H. E. (1994). *Communication research measures: A sourcebook.* New York: Guilford Press.

Sanders, J. A., & Wiseman, R. L. (1990). The effects of verbal and nonverbal teacher immediacy on perceived cognitive, affective, and behavioral learning in the multicultural classroom. *Communication Education, 39,* 341–353.

Schrodt, P., & Witt, P. L. (2006). Students' attributions of instructor credibility as a function of students' expectations of instructional technology use and non-verbal immediacy. *Communication Education, 55,* 1–20.

Smythe, M. J., & Hess, J. A. (2005). Are student self-reports a valid method for measuring teacher nonverbal immediacy? *Communication Education, 54,* 170–179.

Sorenson, G. A. (1989). The relationships among teachers' self-disclosive statements, students' perceptions, and affective learning. *Communication Education, 38,* 259–276.

Thweatt, K. S., & McCroskey, J. C. (1998). The impact of teacher immediacy and misbehaviors on instructor credibility. *Communication Education, 47,* 348–358.

Titsworth, S. B. (2001). The effects of teacher immediacy, use of organizational lecture cues, and students' notetaking on cognitive learning. *Communication Education, 50,* 283–297.

Walker, K. B., & Hackman, M. Z. (1991, November). *Information transfer and nonverbal immediacy as primary predictors of learning and satisfaction in the televised course.* Paper presented at the annual meeting of the Speech Communication Association, Atlanta, GA.

Wiener, M., & Mehrabian, A. (1968). *Language within language: Immediacy, a channel in verbal communication.* New York: Appleton-Century-Crofts.

Witt, P. L. (2008, May). *Communicative connection: A theoretical clarification of the role of teacher immediacy in classroom communication.* Paper presented at the annual meeting of the International Communication Association, Montreal, Quebec, Canada.

Witt, P. L., & Schrodt, P. (2006). The influence of instructional technology use and teacher immediacy on student affect for teacher and course. *Communication Reports, 19,* 1–15.

Witt, P. L., & Wheeless, L. R. (1999). Nonverbal communication expectancies about teachers and enrollment behavior in distance learning. *Communication Education, 48,* 149–154.

Witt, P. L., & Wheeless, L. R. (2001). An experimental study of teachers' verbal and nonverbal immediacy and students' affective and cognitive learning. *Communication Education, 50,* 327–342.

Witt, P. L., Wheeless, L. R., & Allen, M. (2004). A meta-analytical review of the relationship between teacher immediacy and student learning. *Communication Monographs, 71,* 184–207.

Zhang, Q., & Oetzel, J. G. (2006). Constructing and validating a teacher immediacy scale: A Chinese perspective. *Communication Education, 55,* 218–241.

Zhang, Q., Oetzel, J. G., Gao, Z., Wilcox, R. G., & Takai, J. (2007). A further test of immediacy-learning models: A cross-cultural investigation. *Journal of Intercultural Communication Research, 36,* 1–13.

Zhang, Q., & Sapp, D. (2007, November). *A burning issue in teaching: The impact of teacher burnout and nonverbal immediacy on student motivation and affective learning.* Paper presented at the annual convention of the National Communication Association, Chicago.

Humor and Communication in Instructional Contexts

12

Goal-Oriented Communication

*Melanie Booth-Butterfield
and Melissa Bekelja Wanzer*

"We're not laughing *at* you, we're laughing *with* you." Anyone who has ever heard this conversational assurance can probably be assured of only one thing—that the person who was the source of the behavior leading to laughter did not *intend* to be funny. In that situation, humor was not a goal-oriented communication strategy. Communicators who intentionally enact humor may give the illusion that they are surprised, embarrassed, or unaffected by other communicators' responses, but in actuality their communication plan is to send humorous messages to achieve a variety of objectives. Humorous communication, like other forms of communication, often is strategic and goal oriented.

This chapter examines how humor is intentionally used in instructional contexts, with special attention paid to the mechanisms, benefits, and skills involved in humor production across five sections. The first section provides a general overview and theoretical background on the communication of humor. The second section discusses the benefits of humorous communication in instructional settings. The third section describes several typologies of humor enactment. The fourth section describes the measurement of humorous communication. The fifth section explores directions for future humorous communication research.

Overview and Theoretical
Background on the Communication of Humor

Over the years, humor has been described in various ways (Martin, 2001). It has sometimes been studied as receivers' trait response to humor (i.e., sense of humor). Humor also has been described as a message stimulus (i.e., seeing the humor in a situation), and humor also has received attention as the cognitive processing and selection of potentially humorous enactments (i.e., how an individual encodes humorous messages). Generally, a humor response involves a positive affect state that is different from other positive emotions such as tenderness, love, or hope, partly due to higher levels of arousal associated with humor.

In this chapter, humorous communication is defined broadly as "intentional verbal and nonverbal messages which elicit laughter, chuckling, and other forms of spontaneous behavior taken to mean pleasure, delight, and/or surprise in the targeted receiver" (Booth-Butterfield & Booth-Butterfield, 1991, p. 206). Thus, humorous communication (a) is intentional or goal directed; (b) integrates both verbal and nonverbal elements, although these elements are not necessarily balanced in every enactment; and (c) represents a clear sequential progression of humorous communication enactment leading to a targeted response, which ideally is positive.

It is useful to view the process of humor enactment from a communication competence perspective, which includes the components of knowledge, skill, and motivation (Spitzberg, 1983). Competent humor-oriented individuals appear to have a memory for humor: schematic knowledge of what will be funny, how it will be funny, and who will be amused. Humor-oriented people also possess the behavioral skill to enact amusing communication. They do not just recognize humor but can also behave in entertaining ways, whether in the form of verbal witticism, physical gestures and nonverbal expressions, timing, inflections and intonations, or other actions. Humor-oriented people are motivated to be funny and often do so for a variety of reasons, such as easing or creating tension, seeking affinity, or demonstrating their own expertise. They want to insert humor into diverse situations and are willing to be the focus of attention when they enact these behaviors.

Whenever researchers examine humorous communication, there is an imperative distinction to be made: Is the research predicated on and developed from the source or the receiver perspective? Both perspectives are valuable areas of study, but they do not address the same construct. When studying the benefits of humor in instruction, laughter in medicine, a sense of humor, or levels of perceived appropriateness, scholars are examining *receiver* responses. In other words, how do receivers process and interpret humorous messages? That is a different research perspective from the study of humor enactment.

When examining how communicators create humorous messages, the types of behaviors they formulate, or the objectives they hope to achieve, then humor is studied from the *source* perspective. What is it that the source does to achieve a humorous outcome? How is the humor attempt encoded? Confusion results when researchers are not clear about which perspective is their focus. In this chapter, humor research that has adopted both source and receiver perspectives is the focus, because research from both these perspectives has contributed to the knowledge and understanding of humor in the classroom.

While there are over 100 identified humor theories (Foot & McCreaddie, 2006), three theories are considered seminal and often are delineated in humor studies: (1) arousal relief or relief theory (Berlyne, 1969), (2) incongruity theory (Berlyne, 1960), and (3) disparagement or superiority theory (Wolff, Smith, & Murray, 1934). These theories and their by-products offer viable explanations for why students might find classroom humor funny. Proponents of arousal relief or relief theory argue that individuals experience humor and laughter in response to some stressful or difficult event or situation (Berlyne, 1972; Morreall, 1983). Working from this theory, humorous reactions result primarily from the cathartic release of pent-up emotions or tensions. Thus, when an instructor tells a humorous joke or a story at the beginning of a lecture, students may laugh and subsequently release pent-up anxiety or stress.

According to incongruity theory, humorous reactions result from exposure to stimuli that are unexpected, shocking, or surprising (Berger, 1976; Berlyne, 1960; McGhee, 1979). A basic premise behind this theory is that people enter communication situations with a set of specific expectations, and when something happens unexpectedly, it often is perceived as funny. Interestingly, Frymier and Weser (2001) found that students do not necessarily expect their instructors to use classroom humor; therefore, any instructor attempts at classroom humor, even unintentional or weak attempts, often may be recognized by students as humorous. For example, when an instructor trips, this event may be perceived by students as funny. Similarly, if an instructor does a rendition of the moonwalk, this may also be perceived as humorous because it is unexpected by students.

The third theory is disparagement or superiority theory (Feinberg, 1978; Gruner, 1978, 1997). This theory is based on the premise that people laugh at others' shortcomings, failings, or inadequacies (Wolff et al., 1934). Gruner (1997), a proponent of this theory, argued that all attempts at humor are synonymous with games, where there are often clear winners and losers in the process. By poking fun at either the self or others and eliciting laughter from receivers, the humorist "wins" the communication event. Similarly, when instructors tease students about their inability to answer questions in class, they may also do so to make themselves feel better about their own inadequacies.

Despite the body of knowledge generated on such theories of humor, researchers have not developed a theory that addresses humor in the classroom/learning context. Recently, Wanzer, Frymier, and Irwin (2010) advanced an integrative theory to explain the humorous message/learning link. Instructional humor processing theory (IHPT) draws from incongruity resolution theory, disposition theory, and the elaboration likelihood model (ELM). The first step in IHPT is that students must recognize and resolve any incongruity in an instructor's humorous message. If incongruity is not resolved, students will be distracted or confused by the message, rather than perceiving its humor. Because humor is arousing, students' attention will be increased. However, for the humor message to have a positive impact on learning, it must increase motivation and ability to process the instructional message.

The ELM explains how individuals process persuasive messages (Cacioppo & Petty, 1984); it also can describe how individuals process instructor humor. For example, one factor that influences motivation to process is whether a message is personally relevant (Claypool, Mackie, Garcia-Marques, McIntosh, & Udall, 2004; Johnson & Eagly, 1989). Applying IHPT, students who perceive relevance should be more motivated to process the information, resulting in greater content understanding and retention. Consistent with this thinking, several studies have reported positive correlations among students' perceptions of content relevance, motivation to study, empowerment, and perceived learning (Frymier & Shulman, 1995; Frymier, Shulman, & Houser, 1996; Keller, 1983).

Therefore, humorous instructional messages that are perceived as relevant heighten students' motivation to process course material, which in turn enhances their learning. IHPT predicts that instructor use of humorous messages should result in increasing students' motivation to process course content to the extent that the humorous message gained their attention, created positive affect, made content relevant, and increased the clarity of the content. Preliminary research conducted using IHPT indicated that instructors' use of related humor increased student learning while offensive and other disparaging types of humor did not (Wanzer et al., 2010).

Benefits of Humorous Communication in Instructional Settings

There are two major beneficiaries of humor use in classroom contexts: instructors and students. Instructors note positive classroom atmosphere, higher student ratings, and possibly advantages in student learning when humor is incorporated. Instructors' use of humor has been linked repeatedly to important outcomes in the educational setting, such as improved perceptions of teacher competence (Scott, 1976), higher teacher evaluations (Bryant, Crane, Comisky, & Zillmann, 1980), enhanced quality of the student-teacher relationship (Welker, 1977), and recognition of teaching excellence (Javidi, Downs, & Nussbaum, 1988). When comparing the behaviors of award-winning instructors with the behaviors of non-award-winning instructors, researchers noted that award-winning secondary- and higher-education instructors consistently enacted more humor, self-disclosure, and narratives in the classroom than those instructors who did not win awards (Javidi et al., 1988). Humor is an effective way to create a low-stress working environment from the first day of class. It helps instructors learn more about their students and foster relationships. Instructors can use humor as a classroom management tool to create conducive work environments for everyone and maintain control (Proctor, 1994). Kher, Molstad, and Donahue (1999) suggested that instructors display a humorous "Top Ten Peeves" to clearly state classroom rules in order to avoid sounding preachy to students. Humor can benefit the instructor by eliciting positive student behaviors; students who are encouraged to laugh and use humor in the classroom often are less likely to cause disturbances (Walter, 1990).

Most instructional humor research has focused on how students benefit from instructors' humor and, in particular, how instructor humor affects student learning, quality of relationships, and classroom environment (Aylor & Oppliger, 2003; Bryant, Comisky, & Zillmann, 1979; Bryant et al., 1980; Bryant & Zillmann, 1988; Conkell, Imwold, & Ratliffe, 1999; Davies & Apter, 1980; Downs, Javidi, & Nussbaum, 1988; Dunleavy, 2006; Frymier & Weser, 2001; Gorham & Christophel, 1990; Kaplan & Pascoe, 1977; Sadowski, Gulgoz, & LoBello, 1994; Wanzer & Frymier, 1999; White, 2001). For example, instructor humor can improve the classroom climate (Stuart & Rosenfeld, 1994) as well as the formal and informal conversations that occur between instructors and students outside the classroom (Aylor & Oppliger, 2003).

Studies that have provided support for the relationship between instructor humor and student learning (Davies & Apter, 1980; Downs et al., 1988; Gorham & Christophel, 1990; Hauck & Thomas, 1972; Wanzer & Frymier, 1999) often assert that instructor humor is a means of gaining and keeping students' attention (Ziv, 1979). This same explanation was advanced to describe the relationship between instructor immediacy and student learning (Kelley & Gorham, 1988). Instructor humor often is cited as a type of immediacy behavior that can increase student learning (Gorham & Christophel, 1990). Thus, similar to instructor immediacy behaviors that also affect student learning, instructors' use of classroom humor may reduce student anxiety and help create a more enjoyable classroom environment (Neuliep, 1991) where students can more easily assimilate course content. Instructors' use of humor, particularly relevant humor, helps clarify course material and facilitate learning (Downs et al., 1988; Wanzer et al., 2010).

While a number of studies have provided support for the relationship between instructor humor and student learning, results for other similar investigations have been equivocal. For example, Ziv (1988) examined 18 studies that tested the humor-learning relationship, identifying 11 studies that found either a direct or an indirect relationship between humor and learning and 7 studies that failed to identify any significant relationship. One explanation for the failed relationship between humor and learning was the short length of the manipulation used in some of the studies. In several studies, the length of time students were exposed to humorous content may have been too short (e.g., 10 minutes) to adequately affect their ability to retain information. Another important methodological concern was the extent to which humorous stimuli were actually perceived as funny by the study participants (Gorham & Christophel, 1990; Ziv, 1988). If the humorous material is not perceived as funny, participants may not be sufficiently aroused to attend to and process material in the humor condition. Ziv (1988) also established that many of the original studies investigating the relationship between humor and learning were conducted in settings that did not resemble real classrooms. Gorham and Christophel (1990) argued that it is nearly impossible to compare early study results because of the variability in the types of humorous stimuli researchers used (e.g., cartoons, jokes), as well as the inconsistency in the placement of the humor. Differences in earlier instructor humor results may be best explained by examining how these studies were conducted, as well as how humor was operationalized.

Typologies of Humor Enactment

Several humor communication typologies have been developed that operate at different levels (e.g., more abstract vs. specific enactments) or for different functions depending on the context (e.g., instructional vs. social goals). Although communicators may use multiple simultaneous strategies to be funny, nine distinct categories of humor types have been identified (Booth-Butterfield & Booth-Butterfield, 1991; Wanzer, Booth-Butterfield, & Booth-Butterfield, 2005). These categories form the basis for behaviors and can be applied across various contexts, including classroom enactments. Research also has found that higher-humor-oriented individuals use more diverse categories than lower-humor-oriented individuals; that is, they are less likely to rely on one form of humor enactment. Table 12.1 includes categories of humor enactments that can be enacted in instructional as well as other contexts (Wanzer et al., 2005).

Table 12.1	Categories of Humor Enactments

Low humor entails communication that is stupid, silly, absurd, or simplistic. For example, low humor could be a dumb joke, acting like a fool, showing low IQ, and any humor that is active, specific, and concrete. Think of *Animal House*, most Adam Sandler movies, and the shenanigans of the *Jackass* crew.

Nonverbal humor incorporates specific communicative behaviors such as gestures, facial and body displays, vocal tones, and inflection variety. Examples might include grinning, making funny faces, eye contact, whistling, rolled eyes, singing, and dancing.

Impersonation is interaction that portrays a specific character, action, or situation. Examples include assuming the character, talking in different voices, imitating someone, or wearing certain apparel to look like someone. Note here that for the impersonation to be funny, the audience must recognize the character; for example, the enactment of the school principal is only amusing if you know him or her.

Language or verbal communication is widely used, both alone and in conjunction with nonverbal elements. Language that is witty, clever, ironic, innuendo, or specific qualifies. Examples include word play, teasing or making fun of someone, and using sarcasm, slang, verbal mistakes, and regional language.

Other orientation is somewhat less directly observable than some other forms. It involves communication that shows awareness and adaptation to the audience members and their response to humor. Examples include noticing and pointing out people reacting, ignoring outside distractions, taking control, including everyone, waiting for listeners, and so on.

Expressiveness/general humor encompasses communication emphasizing intensity, dynamism, and emotionality and includes general references to being friendly, enthusiastic, positive, and happy. Examples include making light of situations, joking, and even laughing at oneself.

Laughter is also a category of humor. As odd as it may sound, since we tend to think of laughter solely as a response, laughter can be used as a communication mechanism to elicit laughter in others. Laughter tends to be contagious. Examples include snickering, bursting out guffawing, snorting, and getting the giggles.

Funny props are widely used as a humor mechanism, often enacted with other types of humor such as impersonation. Situation-related "tools" that communicators use might include humorous calendars, cartoons, hats, water pistols, whistles, and funny faces on beverage cups or food.

Seeking others is likely to be used more often by lower-humor-oriented people who are challenged to be humorous by themselves. It is a proactive strategy in which they intentionally find a funny coworker or other person close by who is recognized as funny. They communicate with this person, who offers a humorous comment, a light perspective, and/or the sought-after humor.

Research focusing specifically on the various types of humor used by instructors has provided classroom-oriented information. Bryant and colleagues (1979) developed one of the first lists of different types of humor used by college instructors. Based on audio-taped data, it was found that college instructors used humorous messages 3.34 times during a 50-minute class period, with male instructors using humor more often than female instructors. Using a deductive method, they identified six types of teacher humor: jokes, riddles, puns, funny stories, funny comments, and other/ miscellaneous. They further clarified the type of humor instructors used by coding it as sexual or nonsexual, hostile or nonhostile, and related or unrelated to course material and determined whether it disparaged the student, teacher, or a third person or group. The primary way instructors communicated humor in the classroom was through the use of funny stories, with 39% of their sample indicating that they used this type.

Subsequent research by Downs and colleagues (1988) and Javidi and Long (1989) examined different types of instructional humor using a category system developed by Nussbaum, Comadena, and Holladay (1985). The category system involved different types of classroom "play-offs" or quick, intentional humor attempts directed toward a particular target (i.e., self, students, others in class, course material, or object). Downs and colleagues examined the target of the instructors' humor attempts and whether the humor was related to course content. Not surprisingly, they found that award-winning instructors employed more humor in the classroom than non-award-winning instructors, and humor attempts often were related to course material (Downs et al., 1988; Javidi & Long, 1989).

While research conducted by Bryant et al. (1979) and Nussbaum et al. (1985) used deductive methods, Gorham and Christophel (1990) adopted an inductive method to develop a typology of typical instructor humor. In their study, students were asked to keep a log of the actual humor behaviors their instructors exhibited over five consecutive class meetings. Specifically, students were instructed to record "things this teacher did or said today which shows he/she has a sense of humor" (Gorham & Christophel, 1990, p. 51). To develop their classification system of teacher humor, Gorham and Christophel used grounded theory constant comparison procedures. Once the data were transcribed and unitized, the data were placed into categories and cross-coded by the researchers. This coding resulted in the identification of the following categories of humorous behavior: (1) brief tendentious comments directed at individual students, the class as a whole, the university, department, or state, national or world events, world events or personalities, the topic or subject matter, and the self (self-deprecating); (2) personal anecdotes or stories related to the subject; (3) general anecdotes or stories related to the subject; (4) general anecdotes or stories not related to the subject; (5) jokes; (6) physical or vocal comedy; or (7) other. Neuliep (1991) studied the humorous behaviors used by high school teachers, their perceived appropriateness, and the reasons for using humor. He found that high school teachers typically used the same types of humorous messages as college professors, but at a less frequent rate.

Torok, McMorris, and Lin (2004) examined college students' and instructors' perceptions of the Bryant et al. (1979) types of classroom humor. Three instructors and 124 college students reported their perceptions of Bryant's types of classroom humor. Torok and his colleagues assumed that seven types of humor (i.e., funny stories, funny comments, jokes, professional humor, puns, cartoons, and riddles) would be considered generally positive in the college classroom, for which they found preliminary support. They predicted that four types of instructor humor (i.e., sarcasm, sexual humor, ethnic humor, and aggressive/hostile humor) would be rated negatively by students. All types, with the exception of sarcastic humor, were found to be used infrequently by college professors and were not recommended for the classroom by respondents. However, sarcasm, initially thought to be a negative behavior, was rated as appropriate for instructional humor. Although the Torok et al. (2004) study has some limitations, it is important to note that it is the first recent study that has attempted to distinguish between appropriate and inappropriate forms of classroom humor.

More recently, researchers have attempted to identify a comprehensive list of appropriate and inappropriate uses of instructional humor to study the relationship between instructor humor and student learning with greater precision (e.g., Wanzer, 2002). Wanzer, Frymier, Wojtaszczyk, and Smith (2006) asked students to recall and construct examples of both appropriate and inappropriate uses of humor by their instructors. Constant comparative methods were employed to place the student-generated humor examples into categories of appropriate and inappropriate humor. This inductive methodology produced four broad categories of appropriate humor (i.e., related humor, unrelated humor, self-disparaging humor, and unplanned humor) that were similar to those categories identified in prior research (Bryant et al., 1979; Downs et al., 1988; Gorham & Christophel, 1990). Four broad categories of inappropriate teacher humor also were identified (i.e., offensive humor, disparaging student humor, disparaging other humor, and self-disparaging humor). For both appropriate and inappropriate humor, the categories were further divided into numerous subcategories of specific types of humor enactments. Table 12.2 provides a comprehensive list of the categories and subcategories identified by Wanzer et al. (2006).

In a follow-up investigation, Frymier, Wanzer, and Wojtaszczyk (2008) used the Wanzer et al. (2006) typology of appropriate and inappropriate instructor humor to create a humor appropriateness measure and test three explanations for differences in interpretations of teacher humor. The first explanation for student perceptions of instructor humor was predicated on incongruity resolution and disposition theories. They argued

| Table 12.2 Categories of Appropriate and Inappropriate Teacher Humor ||
Appropriate Classroom Humor	Inappropriate Classroom Humor
Related to class material • Humor related to material (nonspecific) • Using media or external objects • Jokes • Examples • Stories • Critical/cynical • College life stereotypes • Directed toward students/teasing • Teacher performance • Role-playing/activities • Creative language use	Offensive humor • Sexual jokes/comments • Vulgar verbal and nonverbal expressions • Drinking • Inappropriate jokes • Personal life • Drugs/illegal activities • Morbid humor • Sarcasm

Humor unrelated to class material
 	
• Stories
• Jokes
• Critical/cynical
• Directed toward students/teasing
• College life stereotypes
• Teacher performance
• Creative language use
• Current events/political
• Using media/external objects
	Disparaging humor: student target
	
	• Students (as a group)
	  – Nonspecific response
	  – Based on intelligence
	  – Based on gender
	  – Based on appearance
	
	• One student (singled out)
	  – Nonspecific response
	  – Based on intelligence
	  – Based on student's personal life/opinions/interests
	  – Based on appearance
	  – Based on gender
	  – Based on religion

Self-disparaging humor
 	
• Make fun of himself/herself (nonspecific)
• Make fun of personal characteristics
• Tell embarrassing stories
• Make fun of mistakes made in class
• Make fun of abilities
	Disparaging humor: "other" target
	
	• Using stereotypes in general
	• Using specific targets
	  – Gender
	  – Racial/ethnic
	  – University related
	  – Religious groups
	  – Sexual orientation
	  – Appearance
	  – Political motivation

Unplanned humor • Unplanned/unintentional	Self-disparaging humor

that students generally would perceive certain types of humor as more inappropriate when they did not recognize and resolve it (i.e., incongruity resolution) and when it made fun of liked or similar others (i.e., disposition theory). Not surprisingly, students viewed teacher humor as inappropriate when it was perceived as offensive and when it demeaned students as a group or individually. The second explanation for student variability in perceptions of humor appropriateness is based on the premise that student personality traits or receiver characteristics influence perceptions of instructor humor. As expected, students' humor orientation, verbal aggressiveness, and communication competence were related directly to how they viewed instructors' use of appropriate or inappropriate humor. The third explanation was that instructor traits or characteristics influence student perceptions of instructor behavior; that is, students expect instructors possessing certain traits to exhibit behaviors congruent with those traits. Instructors' perceived humor orientation, verbal aggressiveness, and nonverbal immediacy also were related to how students viewed instructors' use of humor. For example, students expected verbally aggressive instructors to use humor that targeted other students or student groups. These results suggest that a combination of both student and instructor factors, as well as message content, can help explain differences in ratings of classroom humor appropriateness.

Measurement of Humorous Communication

Although there are a few observational studies (e.g., McIlheran, 2006; Wanzer, Booth-Butterfield, & Booth-Butterfield, 1995), humorous communication largely has been measured via self-report methods. Perhaps the most widely used assessment of humorous communication enactments is the Humor Orientation (HO) scale developed by Booth-Butterfield and Booth-Butterfield (1991). The HO scale is a 17-item, Likert-type scale that measures an individual's predisposition to enact humor successfully across a wide variety of contexts. Considered to be a reliable and valid measure (Graham, 2009), the HO scale has been reliably adapted as an other-report as well as a self-report measure (Campbell, Martin, & Wanzer, 2001; Rizzo, Wanzer, & Booth-Butterfield, 1999). People who score higher on the HO scale tend to be less lonely, be more popular as supervisors, be perceived as more socially attractive, enjoy humor more, be more communicatively adaptive and other-oriented, and be recognized as being "funnier" in presentations than those individuals who score low on the HO scale (Wanzer et al., 1995; Wanzer, Booth-Butterfield, & Booth-Butterfield, 1996; Wrench & Booth-Butterfield, 2003). Higher-humor-oriented individuals also tend to cope better with work-related stress (Booth-Butterfield, Booth-Butterfield, & Wanzer, 2007). Although some people may use humor in negative ways to attack others, humor orientation is not correlated with verbal aggressiveness (Wanzer et al., 1996), which implies that the fact that someone is funny does not indicate that they use humor in a mean-spirited manner. (See also Martin, Puhlik-Doris, Larsen, Gray, & Weir, 2003, for an explanation of humor styles that include the negative strategies of aggressiveness.)

Classroom studies have noted that instructors perceived as higher in humor orientation are viewed as more immediate and more effective at facilitating student learning (Wanzer & Frymier, 1999). Not surprisingly, Wanzer and Frymier (1999) identified an interaction effect between student and instructor levels of humor orientation, with higher-humor-oriented students indicating that they learned the most from higher-humor-oriented instructors and the least from lower-humor-oriented instructors. Importantly, when instructor humor orientation, nonverbal immediacy, assertiveness, and responsiveness were evaluated as predictors of students' affective learning and learning behaviors, instructor humor orientation emerged as a significant positive predictor that explained the unique variance in student affective learning and learning behaviors. Instructor humor orientation also is linked positively with students' perceptions of their instructors' competence, character, and caring (Dunleavy, 2006).

A question that has arisen is whether the HO scale is simply measuring verbal joke telling (Wrench & McCroskey, 2001). Widely published research indicates that the humor orientation concept encompasses both verbal and nonverbal mechanisms for making people laugh and is implicated in decoding ability as well (Merolla, 2006). The HO scale correlates at .51 with the Richmond Humor Assessment Instrument, suggesting substantial overlap (Wrench & McCroskey, 2001). In addition, brief versions of the HO scale have recently shown promise and are in the developmental stages (M. Booth-Butterfield, personal communication, February 27, 2009).

Again, there is a need to ensure that the operationalization matches the conceptualization in humor research. If sense of humor (e.g., trait orientation in receivers) or humor and amusement as a specific reaction is being studied, commonly used scales include general ratings of message "funniness," coping with stress, or contextual measures such as the Situational Humor Response Questionnaire (Martin, 1996, 2001; Martin & Lefcourt, 1984). In sum, the communication of humor has proven to have valid and reliable measures, whether from the source or the receiver perspective.

Directions for Future Humorous Communication Research

The study of humorous communication as a goal-oriented strategy has expanded in recent decades, but being funny needs to be taken "seriously" from a scholarly perspective. At present, stringent theoretical frameworks are preliminary, and empirical testing of humor concepts is underdeveloped. The active communication of humor also can benefit from adherence to rigorous programmatic and theory-based research efforts. These efforts to conduct high-quality research and to understand the mechanisms, benefits, and pitfalls of communicating humor in instruction have the potential to produce great benefits.

The current scholarly focus indicates a need for more experimental testing of the effects of humor in the classroom. Given that most of the studies on the benefits of humor use a correlational design, it is not clear whether instructors' enactments of communication objectively increase student comprehension, learning, and motivation. It is known that when instructors enact humor that is perceived as appropriate, students like them more and report that they learn more. A potential mechanism for these effects is that humor increases liking or positive affect for the content and the instructor. Humor often is described as an indirect form of persuasion (Weinberger & Gulas, 1992); that is, humor facilitates liking, which then leads to persuasion, hence serving as an elaboration moderator.

Alternatively, it could be that well-liked instructors are perceived as more immediate and well-intentioned and that their communication is tolerated more even if they enact potentially inappropriate humorous messages. Clearly, one required area for research is to manipulate instructor humor (e.g., using both appropriate and inappropriate types of humor) to determine how learning outcomes occur and may be mediated by liking. Additional research should embrace an experimental approach and examine both qualitative and quantitative differences in humorous enactments and how such enactments potentially affect relevant outcomes such as learning and coping with both instructional challenges and classroom interactions.

Another area of study entails the strategic use of humor by children. Simply put, are some children funnier than others? Do children use humorous messages to achieve goals? Socha and Kelly (1994) studied children's use of humor and impression management, gender differences, and target differences, and noted changes over time from prosocial to antisocial humor use. As children aged, they were more likely to enact antisocial humorous messages with their peer groups. Other researchers, such as Kotthoff (2006), describe playfulness and teasing communication among even very young children. Many perspectives on children's use of humor have emerged from a clinical perspective. For example, Peller (1956) noted that children seem to use humor when they feel guilty and want to avoid consequences. McGhee (2002) indicated that even parents often observe predispositional differences in humorous communication among their children. Much more stringent empirical work is needed in this area to explore how and why children enact humor in their interactions.

Another area of study includes building the skill of humor communication. Transforming low-humor-oriented individuals into high-humor-oriented individuals may be unlikely because humor orientation is a communication trait that builds over a lifetime. However, as with many other communication skills, the behaviors involved with enacting humor can be improved with training, practice, and positive reinforcement (Clark et al., 1998; McIlheran, 2006; Rancer, Whitecap, Kosberg, & Avtgis, 1997; Wigley, 2008). People can become more competent in communicating humor by increasing their knowledge base of what contributes to good humorous messages and improving their behavioral skill in enacting humor correctly through repetition. Currently, little empirical research exists that addresses humor skill development over time.

There also is a need to study humorous communication at a more micro level to understand precisely what makes something funny, or how it is communicated on a very meticulous level. Such study might entail experiments comparing appropriate use of humor (e.g., related, self-disparaging) with inappropriate (e.g., offensive, disparaging others) use of humor, and additional closely coded studies of specific behaviors that differentiate funny from nonfunny enactments. Such research would involve detailed examination of pausing effects, intonations, duration, and potentially physiological measures such as electromyographic readings (e.g., Cacioppo, Petty, Losch, & Kim, 2008) to determine which facial muscles are activated in humor enactments. New research also is beginning to examine the debilitating effects brain damage has specifically on humor enactments and the processing of humor (Heath & Blonder, 2005).

Finally, what elicits humor and amuses people certainly differs from culture to culture. However, it seems reasonable that within any culture, individuals can be funny (or not). That is, regardless of the ethnic background or nationality under consideration, it is likely that some citizens are better at creating humor than others. Therefore, cross-cultural comparisons of the skill and propensity to enact humorous communication are needed.

Conclusion

What do we know about the communication of humor in instructional contexts? Based on numerous published studies by a variety of scholars, we know that (a) enacted humor in the classroom is positive if used competently, especially for enhancing student affect toward course material; (b) the predisposition to enact humor is measurable, relates to a wide variety of positive perceptions in others, and enhances positive coping; (c) multiple effective ways exist to measure humorous communication, although the choice of measurement will depend on the specific variables under study; and (d) it is imperative to distinguish between source orientations and receiver orientations in humor research. As such, it becomes clear that there are continually emerging aspects of humorous communication yet to study!

References

Aylor, B., & Oppliger, P. (2003). Out-of-class communication and student perceptions of instructor humor orientation and socio-communicative style. *Communication Education, 52,* 122–134.

Berger, A. A. (1976). Anatomy of the joke. *Journal of Communication, 26,* 113–115.

Berlyne, D. E. (1960). *Conflict, arousal, and curiosity.* New York: McGraw-Hill.

Berlyne, D. E. (1969). Arousal, reward, and learning. *Annals of the New York Academy of Science, 159,* 1059–1070.

Berlyne, D. E. (1972). Affective aspects of aesthetic communication. In T. Alloway, L. Krames, & P. Pliner (Eds.), *Communication and affect: A comparative approach* (pp. 97–118). New York: Academic Press.

Booth-Butterfield, M., Booth-Butterfield, S., & Wanzer, M. (2007). Funny students cope better: Patterns of humor enactment and coping effectiveness. *Communication Quarterly, 55,* 299–315.

Booth-Butterfield, S., & Booth-Butterfield, M. (1991). The communication of humor in everyday life. *Southern Communication Journal, 56,* 205–218.

Bryant, J., Comisky, P., & Zillmann, D. (1979). Teachers' humor in the college classroom. *Communication Education, 28,* 110–118.

Bryant, J., Crane, J. S., Comisky, P. W., & Zillmann, D. (1980). Relationship between college teachers' use of humor in the classroom and students' evaluations of their teachers. *Journal of Educational Psychology, 72,* 511–519.

Bryant, J., & Zillmann, D. (1988). Using humor to promote learning in the classroom. *Journal of Children in Contemporary Society, 20,* 49–78.

Cacioppo, J. T., & Petty, R. E. (1984). Elaboration likelihood model of persuasion. *Advances in Consumer Research, 11,* 673–675.

Cacioppo, J., Petty, R., Losch, M., & Kim, H. (2008). Electromyographic activity over facial muscle regions can differentiate the valence and intensity of affective reactions. In R. Fazio & R. Petty (Eds.), *Attitudes: Their structure, function, and consequences* (pp. 69–83). New York: Psychology Press.

Campbell, K. L., Martin, M. M., & Wanzer, M. B. (2001). Employee perceptions of manager humor orientation, assertiveness, responsiveness, approach/avoidance strategies, and satisfaction. *Communication Research Reports, 18,* 67–74.

Clark, N., Gong, M., Schork, A., Evans, D., Roloff, D., Hurwitz, M., et al. (1998). Impact of education for physicians on patient outcomes. *Pediatrics, 5,* 831–836.

Claypool, H. M., Mackie, D. M., Garcia-Marques, T., McIntosh, A., & Udall, A. (2004). The effects of personal relevance and repetition on persuasive processing. *Social Cognition, 22,* 310–335.

Conkell, C. S., Imwold, C., & Ratliffe, T. (1999). The effects of humor on communicating fitness concepts to high school students. *Physical Educator, 56,* 8–18.

Davies, A. P., & Apter, M. J. (1980). Humor and its effect on learning in children. In P. E. McGhee & A. J. Chapman (Eds.), *Children's humor* (pp. 237–254). New York: Wiley.

Downs, V. C., Javidi, M. M., & Nussbaum, J. F. (1988). An analysis of teachers' verbal communication within the college classroom: Use of humor, self-disclosure, and narratives. *Communication Education, 37,* 127–141.

Dunleavy, K. N. (2006). The effect of instructor humor on perceived instructor credibility, student state motivation, and student motives to communicate in the classroom. *Kentucky Journal of Communication, 25,* 39–56.

Feinberg, L. (1978). *The secret of humor.* Amsterdam: Rodopi.

Foot, H., & McCreaddie, M. (2006). Humour and laughter. In O. Hargie (Ed.), *The handbook of communications skills* (pp. 293–322). New York: Routledge.

Frymier, A. B., & Shulman, G. M. (1995). "What's in it for me?" Increasing content relevance to enhance students' motivation. *Communication Education, 44,* 40–50.

Frymier, A. B., Shulman, G. M., & Houser, M. (1996). The development of a learner empowerment measure. *Communication Education, 45,* 181–199.

Frymier, A. B., Wanzer, M. B., & Wojtaszczyk, A. (2008). Assessing students' perceptions of inappropriate and appropriate teacher humor. *Communication Education, 57,* 266–288.

Frymier, A. B., & Weser, B. (2001). The role of student predispositions on student expectations for instructor communication behavior. *Communication Education, 50,* 314–326.

Gorham, J., & Christophel, D. M. (1990). The relationship of teachers' use of humor in the classroom to immediacy and student learning. *Communication Education, 39,* 46–62.

Graham, E. E. (2009). Humor Orientation Scale. In R. Rubin, A. Rubin, E. Graham, E. Perse, & D. Seibold (Eds.), *Communication research measures: A sourcebook* (Vol. 2, pp. 158–163). New York: Routledge/Taylor & Francis.

Gruner, C. R. (1978). *Understanding laughter: The working of wit and humor.* Chicago: Nelson-Hall.

Gruner, C. R. (1997). *The game of humor.* New Brunswick, NJ: Transaction Books.

Hauck, W. E., & Thomas, J. W. (1972). The relationship of humor to intelligence, creativity, and intentional and incidental learning. *Journal of Experimental Education, 40,* 52–55.

Heath, R., & Blonder, L. (2005). Spontaneous humor among right hemisphere stroke survivors. *Brain and Language, 93,* 267–276.

Javidi, M. M., Downs, V. C., & Nussbaum, J. F. (1988). A comparative analysis of teachers' use of dramatic style behaviors at higher and secondary educational levels. *Communication Education, 37,* 278–288.

Javidi, M. M., & Long, L. W. (1989). Teachers' use of humor, self-disclosure, and narrative activity as a function of experience. *Communication Research Reports, 6,* 47–52.

Johnson, B. T., & Eagly, A. H. (1989). Effects of involvement on persuasion: A meta-analysis. *Psychological Bulletin, 106,* 290–314.

Kaplan, R. M., & Pascoe, G. C. (1977). Humorous lectures and humorous examples: Some effects upon comprehension and retention. *Journal of Educational Psychology, 69,* 61–65.

Keller, J. M. (1983). Motivational design of instruction. In C. M. Reigeluth (Ed.), *Instructional design theories: An overview of their current status* (pp. 383–434). Hillsdale, NJ: Lawrence Erlbaum.

Kelley, D. H., & Gorham, J. (1988). Effects of immediacy on recall of information. *Communication Education, 37,* 198–207.

Kher, N., Molstad, S., & Donahue, R. (1999). Using humor in the college class-room to enhance teaching effectiveness in "dread courses." *College Student Journal, 33,* 400–407.

Kotthoff, H. (2006). Let's have a joke! Children's joking and humor; some age and intercultural differences. *Television, 19,* 10–14.

Martin, R. (1996). The Situational Humor Response Questionnaire (SHRQ) and Coping Humor Scale (CHS): A decade of research findings. *Humor: International Journal of Humor Research, 9,* 251–272.

Martin, R. (2001). Humor, laughter, and physical health: Methodological issues and research findings. *Psychological Bulletin, 127,* 504–519.

Martin, R., & Lefcourt, H. (1984). Situational Humor Response Questionnaire: Quantitative measure of the sense of humor. *Journal of Personality and Social Psychology, 45,* 145–155.

Martin, R. A., Puhlik-Doris, P., Larsen, G., Gray, J., & Weir, K. (2003). Individual differences in uses of humor and their relation to psychological well-being: Development of the humor styles questionnaire. *Journal of Research in Personality, 37,* 48–75.

McGhee, P. E. (1979). *Humor: Its origin and development.* San Francisco: W. H. Freeman.

McGhee, P. E. (2002). *Understanding and promoting the development of children's humor.* New York: Kendall/Hunt.

McIlheran, J. (2006). The use of humor in corporate communication. *Corporate Communications, 11,* 267–274.

Merolla, A. (2006). Decoding ability and humor production. *Communication Quarterly, 54,* 175–189.

Morreall, J. (1983). *Taking laughter seriously.* Albany: State University of New York Press.

Neuliep, J. W. (1991). An examination of the content of high school teachers' humor in the classroom and the development of an inductively derived tax-onomy of classroom humor. *Communication Education, 40,* 343–355.

Nussbaum, J. F., Comadena, M. E., & Holladay, S. J. (1985, May). *Verbal commu-nication within the college classroom.* Paper presented at the meeting of the International Communication Association, Chicago.

Peller, L. E. (1956). Review of the book *Children's humor: A psychological analysis. Psychoanalysis Quarterly, 25,* 106–108.

Petty, R. E., & Cacioppo, J. T. (1981). *Attitudes and persuasion: Classic and con-temporary approaches.* Dubuque, IA: W. C. Brown.

Petty, R., & Cacioppo, J. (1986). *Communication and persuasion: The central and peripheral routes to attitude change.* New York: Springer-Verlag.

Proctor, R. F. (1994, April). *Communicating rules with a grin.* Paper presented at the annual meeting of the Central States Communication Association, Oklahoma City, OK.

Rancer, A., Whitecap, V., Kosberg, R., & Avtgis, T. (1997). Testing the efficacy of a communication training program to increase argumentativeness and argu-mentative behavior in adolescents. *Communication Education, 46,* 273–286.

Rizzo, B., Wanzer, M., & Booth-Butterfield, M. (1999). Individual differences in managers' use of humor: Subordinate perceptions of managers' humor. *Communication Research Reports, 16,* 360–369.

Sadowski, C. J., Gulgoz, S., & LoBello, S. G. (1994). An evaluation of the use of content-relevant cartoons as a teaching device. *Journal of Instructional Psychology, 21,* 368–371.

Scott, T. M. (1976). Humor in teaching. *Journal of Physical Education & Recreation, 47*(8), 18.

Socha, T. J., & Kelly, B. (1994). Children making "fun": Humorous communication, impression management, and moral development. *Child Study Journal, 24,* 1–11.

Spitzberg, B. (1983). Communication competence as knowledge, skill, and impression. *Communication Education, 32,* 323–329.

Stuart, W. D., & Rosenfeld, L. B. (1994). Student perceptions of teacher humor and classroom climate. *Communication Research Reports, 11,* 87–97.

Torok, S. E., McMorris, R. F., & Lin, W. (2004). Is humor an appropriate teaching tool? Perceptions of professors' teaching styles and use of humor. *College Teaching, 52,* 14–20.

Walter, G. (1990). Laugh, teacher, laugh! *Educational Digest, 55*(9), 43–44.

Wanzer, M. B. (2002). Use of humor in the classroom: The good, the bad, and the not-so-funny things that teachers say and do. In J. L. Chesebro & J. C. McCroskey (Eds.), *Communication for teachers* (pp. 116–125). Boston: Allyn & Bacon.

Wanzer, M., Booth-Butterfield, M., & Booth-Butterfield, S. (1995). The funny people: A source-orientation to the communication of humor. *Communication Quarterly, 43,* 142–154.

Wanzer, M., Booth-Butterfield, M., & Booth-Butterfield, S. (1996). Are funny people more popular: The relationship of humor orientation, loneliness, and social attraction. *Communication Quarterly, 44,* 42–52.

Wanzer, M., Booth-Butterfield, M., & Booth-Butterfield, S. (2005). "If we didn't use humor we'd cry": Use of humor as coping in healthcare. *Journal of Health Communication, 10,* 105–125.

Wanzer, M. B., & Frymier, A. B. (1999). The relationship between student perceptions of instructor humor and student's reports of learning. *Communication Education, 48,* 48–62.

Wanzer, M. B., Frymier, A. B., & Irwin, J. (2010). An explanation of the relationship between instructor humor and student learning: Instructional humor processing theory. *Communication Education, 59,* 1–18.

Wanzer, M. B., Frymier, A. B., Wojtaszczyk, A., & Smith, T. (2006). Appropriate and inappropriate uses of humor by teachers. *Communication Education, 55,* 178–196.

Weinberger, M. G., & Gulas, C. S. (1992). The impact of humor in advertising: A review. *Journal of Advertising, 18*(4), 35–59.

Welker, W. A. (1977). Humor in education: A foundation for wholesome living. *College Student Journal, 11,* 252–254.

White, G. W. (2001). Teachers' report of how they used humor with students' perceived use of such humor. *Education, 122,* 337–348.

Wigley, C. (2008). Verbal aggression interventions: What should be done? *Communication Monographs, 75,* 339–350.

Wolff, H. A., Smith, C. E., & Murray, H. A. (1934). The psychology of humor. *Journal of Abnormal and Social Psychology, 28,* 341–365.

Wrench, J., & Booth-Butterfield, M. (2003). Increasing patient satisfaction and compliance: An examination of physician humor orientation, compliance-gaining strategies, and perceived credibility. *Communication Quarterly, 51,* 482–503.

Wrench, J., & McCroskey, J. C. (2001). A temperamental understanding of humor communication and exhilaratability. *Communication Quarterly, 49,* 142–159.

Ziv, A. (1979). *L'humor en education: Approche psychologique.* Paris: Editions Social Francaises.

Ziv, A. (1988). Teaching and learning with humor: Experiment and replication. *Journal of Experimental Education, 57,* 5–15.

Clarity in Teaching and Learning 13

Conundrums, Consequences, and Opportunities

Scott Titsworth and Joseph P. Mazer

Contemporary interest in instructor clarity generally is traced to the initial research efforts of Rosenshine and Furst (Rosenshine, 1971; Rosenshine & Furst, 1971), who summarized the results of more than 50 teacher-effects studies and concluded that, among the 11 categories of teacher behaviors related to student learning, teacher clarity had the strongest connection. Stemming from their conclusion, scholars in educational psychology and communication studies have explored a diverse array of questions surrounding the relationships between clarity, student affect, and student learning. Yet despite continued interest in the topic, research on clarity has become seemingly mired in issues of how to define and operationalize clarity. These that have dominated entire programs of research on the topic and, as noted by Civikly (1992), this research has done little to increase precision. While a single definition of clarity might be elusive, much research has been conducted to precisely indicate behaviors and dimensions associated with the construct. Moreover, many fruitful areas for research remain for those researchers interested in exploring the process of clarity in instructional settings.

This chapter begins with an analysis of the theoretical foundations of clarity research. The focus then shifts to an examination of the research efforts sustained to define and operationalize clarity in both educational psychology and communication studies, which is followed by a summary of the classroom effects of instructor clarity. The chapter concludes with recommendations for future research.

Theoretical Foundations of Clarity Research

Instructor clarity emerged from a series of early teacher-effects studies in educational psychology. Following a conventional variable-analytic tradition, these studies attempted to establish relationships between observed teacher behaviors and student achievement (see Brophy, 1988) and, in many cases, did not explicitly attribute observed relationships to broad theoretical positions. That said, scholars in both educational psychology and communication studies implicitly draw on two sorts of theoretical foundations: information processing and what loosely could be called adaptive instruction.

Information processing theory dominated educational psychology research conducted in the 1960s and 1970s (Mayer, 1996a). Succinctly, this theory views teachers as dispensers of information and learners as information processors. Learners take information that is input into short-term memory by teachers and apply mental operations to the information. Through this process, information is added to long-term memory. As teachers enact clarity behaviors, students are better able to attend to, process, store, and retrieve information.

Complementary to the information processing perspective, some clarity researchers assumed that instructors must adapt (i.e., adaptive instruction) their clarity behaviors to students through communication. For example, both Civikly (1992) and Simonds (1997) argued that clarity occurs as instructors and students negotiate meaning within the instructional setting. Through ongoing classroom communication, instructors plan and present information; students react through questions, comments, and performance on formal and informal assessment opportunities, and instructors respond as necessary to enhance understanding. This perspective is complementary to information processing because it expands the programming metaphor to be iterative rather than linear. That is, clarity does not happen in one message, but rather, clarity is a process of communication where meanings are negotiated.

These broad theoretical foundations have led to more specific, theory-driven explanations of how clarity influences learning. Mayer (1977), for instance, developed assimilation-to-schema theory to draw distinctions between rote and meaningful learning. Meaningful learning occurs when students receive information, integrate new information to existing schema, and then activate appropriate schema to accomplish tasks. Conversely, rote learning simply involves the reception of information. Mayer theorized that advance organizers, or statements explaining what students will learn from a lesson (see Kibler, Cegala, Barker, & Miles, 1974), assist in creating schema, or knowledge structures, to which new information can be assimilated. Thus, as instructors present information and students expand their structures of understanding, their ability to both remember and accurately use information is enhanced.

Research Efforts to Define and Operationalize Clarity

After Rosenshine and Furst's observation that clarity was a promising process-product variable, various researchers undertook the task of conceptually and operationally defining the construct. Two groups of scholars, one from educational psychology and one from communication studies, attempted to devise measurement scales that could be used to assess clarity within classroom situations.

THE OHIO STATE LOW-INFERENCE STUDIES

Through the mid-1970s, research exploring teacher clarity suffered from a common problem: the conceptual and operational definition of teacher clarity lacked precision. As explained by Bush, Kennedy, and Cruickshank (1977), "Considering the most commonly used definition of teacher clarity, 'being clear and easy to understand,' the difficulties can be readily appreciated. Not only is the common definition circular but, as stated, clarity cannot be directly observed or easily measured" (p. 53). In response to such imprecision, a team of researchers from Ohio State University undertook a large-scale effort to empirically derive a precise operational definition of teacher clarity. This effort was primarily centered on the three broad classifications of clarity behaviors. *High-inference* clarity behaviors (e.g., being clear) often are defined vaguely and open to subjectivity. *Intermediate-inference* behaviors are less vague and can include clarity dimensions such as "organization" and "explanation." The intermediate-inference dimension of "organization" can be readily observed and understood through a *low-inference* teacher behavior (e.g., clearly previewing the main points of a lecture), which can be clearly observed and objectively quantified.

Initial work by the Ohio State researchers involved asking more than 1,000 students in the Columbus Public School system to list five behaviors performed by their clearest teacher (see Bush et al., 1977). Responses to their open-ended survey were used to create items and measurement scales, which were administered to more than 1,500 junior high school students in Cleveland to determine whether factor structures were present. Examining separate factor analyses for various versions of the scales, two factors were found to be consistent. The first factor was a relatively general dimension involving the explanation of concepts and directions in an "understandable manner and appropriate pace" (p. 57). Examples of low-inference items associated with the first factor were "Takes time when explaining" and "Gives explanations that the student understands." The second factor dealt specifically with how teachers use examples and illustrations when presenting information. Examples of low-inference items for the second factor included "Gives an example on the board of how to do something" and "Gives students an example and then lets them try to do it."

Given the highly specific sample used in the 1977 study, Kennedy, Cruickshank, Bush, and Myers (1978) attempted to cross-validate the previous findings using a more diverse sample of junior high school students from Ohio ($n = 425$), Tennessee ($n = 307$), and Australia ($n = 531$). Results of their study revealed 29 prime discriminators (i.e., items) classified into 4 dimensions: (1) assesses student learning (e.g., "tries to find out if we don't understand and then repeats things"), (2) provides time to think (e.g., "gives us a chance to think about what's being taught"), (3) uses examples (e.g., "works examples and explains them"), and (4) reviews and organizes (e.g., "prepares us for what we will be doing next").

Although the Ohio State instruments did not result in a legacy of use by other scholars, this program of research undertook important steps in operationalizing and defining a previously opaque construct through identifying low- and intermediate-inference dimensions of clarity. The Ohio State studies also provided initial evidence of a broad relationship between teacher clarity, student achievement, and student satisfaction. For instance, in a 1985 study, Hines, Cruickshank, and Kennedy studied preservice teachers ($n = 202$) in the Ohio State University College of Education who were engaging in reflexive teaching activities. Results of that study, coupled with the results reported in the 1977 study, indicated that teacher clarity was related positively to both students' achievement and satisfaction. These findings served as a rationale for continued exploration of the construct.

PERCEPTION STUDIES IN COMMUNICATION STUDIES

Similar to the Ohio State team, various communication researchers attempted to devise scales tapping students' perceptions of instructor clarity. For instance, Powell and Harville (1990) developed a 15-item Teacher Clarity Scale (TCS) based on categories of clarity behaviors found in an unpublished manuscript by Book and McCaleb; no example items were provided in their manuscript. Their 15-item scale was factor analyzed and it was concluded that a 1-factor solution was most appropriate.

Using the TCS as a foundation, Sidelinger and McCroskey (1997) created an expanded 22-item scale that included 10 items from the TCS and 12 new items, with the intent to assess students' perceptions of oral and written instructor clarity. Chesebro and McCroskey (1998a) later revised the TCS into a shortened version to be more commensurate in length with other measures. The Teacher Clarity Short Inventory (TCSI) contained 10 items that were found to load on a single factor. Example items include "My teacher is straightforward in her or his lecture" and "In general, I understand my teacher."

The TCSI became the *de facto* option for much of the correlational research on clarity conducted in the communication discipline. For instance, in using the TCSI, Avtgis (2001) found clarity to be correlated positively with students' attributional confidence, and Chesebro and McCroskey (2001) observed that clarity had significant positive relationships with instructor nonverbal immediacy, student motivation, student affect for the instructor, and affect for the course but had significant negative relationships with student state receiver apprehension and perceived learning loss. Faylor, Beebe, Houser, and Mottet (2008) surveyed adult learners and found that trainer clarity was the only significant predictor of affective learning in a training environment. In an examination of ninth-grade classrooms, Mottet and colleagues (2008) found that teacher clarity was related positively to perceived teacher nonverbal immediacy, perceived relevance of information, use of study strategies, and students' affect toward learning but was related negatively to perceived instructor disconfirmation.

Guided by Civikly's (1992) treatment of clarity, Simonds (1997) argued for an additional expansion of the clarity construct. Her work resulted in a 20-item, two-dimensional instrument assessing content clarity (e.g., "My instructor is clear when presenting content") and process clarity (e.g., "Asks if we know what to do and how to do it"); however, a factor analysis of the scale revealed only a single dimension of clarity. While communication researchers provided conceptually distinct alternatives to the Ohio State instruments, those alternatives have resulted in a less precise analysis of clarity behaviors because they essentially tap a broad, one-dimensional view of the construct.

Classroom Effects of Instructor Clarity

Although questions of how to define clarity have been and remain dominant in the literature, an impressive program of research examining the effects of clarity on classroom outcomes and processes has emerged. This section begins with a broad overview of research findings before addressing more specific issues in the literature, including interaction effects, the negotiation of clarity though communication, cultural dimensions of clarity, and teacher training.

THE EFFECTS OF CLARITY: AN OVERVIEW

Although multiple outcome variables are important in classroom contexts, most studies attempt to determine relationships between clarity behaviors and students' affective and cognitive learning. Nine studies using either correlational or experimental designs explored the main effect of clarity on students' affect or motivation toward a class. As shown by the summary of findings in Table 13.1, the direction of effects was consistently positive: Higher levels of instructor clarity were associated with

Table 13.1	Correlations Between Clarity and Student Affect	
Study	**Design**	**Clarity Operationalized As**
Avtgis (2001)	Corr	Perception through TCSI Student motivation ($r = .67$) Affective learning ($r = .69$)
Chesebro (2003)	Exp	Clarity cluster ($r = .39$)
Chesebro and McCroskey (2001)	Corr	Perception through TCSI Affect for instructor ($r = .74$) Affect toward course ($r = .53$)
Comadena, Hunt, and Simonds (2007)	Exp	Structuring of presentation ($r = .38$)
Hines, Cruickshank, and Kennedy (1985)	Corr	Clarity cluster ($r = .46$)
Mottet et al. (2008)	Corr	Perception through TCSI In math and science courses ($r = .38$) In non–math and science courses ($r = .39$)
Sidelinger and McCroskey (1997)	Corr	Perceptions through TCSI Attitude toward content ($r = .60$) Enrolling in similar course ($r = .71$)
Titsworth (2001a)	Corr	High-inference semantic differential scale Affect for instructor ($r = .28$) Affect toward class ($r = .16$)
Zhang and Huang (2008)	Corr	Perception through TCSI ($r = .65$)
Zhang and Zhang (2005)	Corr	Perception through TCSI ($r = .44$)

Note: Corr, correlational design; Exp, experimental design. The *r* values show the relationship between clarity and student affect; in studies where multiple measures of affect were used, each *r* value is reported.

higher levels of student affect. Estimates of effect size indicate that the clarity-affect relationship is quite strong, with *r* values ranging from .38 to .74. Moreover, the size of the effects did not appear to differ depending on the type of affect (e.g., student motivation, affect toward the instructor, affect toward the course) assessed. Generally, effect sizes for the two experimental designs were lower than those effect sizes observed in correlational designs; yet all effect sizes could be described as strong. The only exceptions to this observation were the two effects reported by Titsworth (2001a); however, those effects resulted from correlated data where clarity was assessed using a high-inference, semantic differential scale rather than an established scale (i.e., the TCSI or the TCS).

A summary of 21 studies showing main effects of clarity on student cognitive learning is reported in Table 13.2. Contrary to the studies reviewed for affect, 82% of the cognitive learning studies used experimental designs. Findings from all the studies indicated that higher levels of clarity were associated with higher levels of student achievement. Negative correlations reported for several of the Smith and Land studies show that higher levels of vagueness, mazes, or uncertainty—all low-inference behaviors associated with poor clarity—are associated with lower levels of student cognitive learning. In addition to showing positive effects of clarity, most of the effect sizes could be characterized as moderate to strong, with some effect sizes as high as .70 or greater; only four of the effect sizes were lower than .20. Given the fact that nearly all these studies reported results of controlled experiments, the conclusion that clarity causes higher levels of student learning appears to be practically unquestionable.

Table 13.2	Correlations Between Clarity and Student Cognitive Learning	
Study	**Design**	**Clarity Operationalized As**
Chesebro (2003)	Exp	Clarity cluster ($r = .36$)
Chesebro and McCroskey (2001)	Corr	Perception through TCSI ($r = .52$)
Comadena et al. (2007)	Exp	Structuring of presentation ($r = .50$)
Denham and Land (1981)	Exp	Clarity cluster ($r = .75$)
Evans and Guymon (1978)	Exp	Clarity cluster ($r = .61$)
Hines et al. (1985)	Corr	Observed cluster of behaviors ($r = .63$)
Land and Denham (1979)	Exp	Clarity cluster ($r = .30$)
Land and Smith (1979)	Exp	Vagueness ($r = -.31$)
Land (1981b)	Exp	Clarity cluster ($r = .29$)
Land (1981a)	Exp	Clarity cluster ($r = .76$)
Land (1980)	Exp	Clarity cluster ($r = .28$)
Land (1979)	Exp	Clarity cluster ($r = .30$)
Smith and Land (1980)	Exp	Vagueness ($r = -.15$) Mazes ($r = -.19$)
Smith (1984)	Exp	Uncertainty ($r = -.14$) Lecture notes ($r = .21$)

(Continued)

Table 13.2	(Continued)	
Study	**Design**	**Clarity Operationalized As**
Smith (1985)	Exp	Uncertainty ($r = -.15$) Use of lecture notes ($r = .20$)

Spicer and Bassett (1976)	Exp	Organizational cues
		   Selected response test ($r = .25$)
		   Free recall test ($r = .30$)

Titsworth (2001b)	Exp	Organizational cues ($r = .30$)

Titsworth and Kiewra (2004)	Exp	Organizational cues
		   Detail test ($r = .50$)
		   Organization test ($r = .69$)

Titsworth (2004)	Exp	Organizational cues
		   Note details ($r = .35$)
		   Note organization ($r = .60$)

Zhang and Huang (2008)	Corr	Perception through TCSI ($r = .56$)
Zhang and Zhang (2005)	Corr	Perception through TCSI ($r = .33$)

Note: Corr, correlational design; Exp, experimental design. The *r* values show the relationship between clarity and students' cognitive learning affect; in studies where multiple measures of cognitive learning were present, each *r* value is reported.

THE SMITH AND LAND LANGUAGE STUDIES

In the period from 1979 to 1985, Land and Smith published more than 15 studies exploring specific linguistic dimensions of instructor clarity. Whereas the Ohio State studies attempted to operationalize clarity as a multidimensional, low-inference variable, Smith and Land isolated specific, low-inference aspects of clarity to serve as independent variables in a series of experiments. Smith and Land not only departed from the Ohio State group through the use of experiments; they also addressed the positive bias of the Ohio State studies by exploring what happens when teachers use imprecise language, confusing terms, and other unclear language choices.

Smith and Land's research program extensively explored five variables: (1) vagueness terms, (2) mazes, (3) utterances, (4) bluffing, and (5) uncertainty. *Vagueness terms* often are used by instructors who do not have sufficient understanding of the material for effective communication. Vagueness terms include unclear sets of words that mark a recovery point in a lecture (*bluffing*) or reveal an instructor's lack of assurance (*uncertainty*). *Mazes* include false starts and the use of redundant words, and *utterances* are vocalized pauses (e.g., "uh," "ah," "um") that detract from a teacher's level of verbal fluency. Smith and Land designed studies that took two approaches to manipulating these variables. One approach was to isolate individual variables (e.g., word mazes or vagueness terms) and treat them as separate factors in experiments. The "by variable" approach, of which there were seven studies, yielded impressive outcomes. Land and Smith (1979) observed an effect size of $r = .31$ in a study manipulating the use of vagueness terms. The other approach, which was used by Land in five studies, involved clustering variables together into "clear" and "unclear" conditions. For example, Land (1981b) combined vagueness terms and mazes and observed an effect size similar to the effect size obtained in the study that only examined vagueness terms ($r = .29$).

Smith and Land's program of research complemented the Ohio State studies in two important ways. First, their use of experimental designs allowed them to more directly test causal relationships between low-inference clarity variables and student achievement using videotaped lectures. Second, their program highlighted a set of low-inference variables, specifically the use of clear and unclear language, not prominently revealed in the Ohio State studies. However, their research was not without limitations. Variables identified by Smith and Land appear to conflate with each other. For example, vagueness terms, mazes, utterances, and uncertainty terms appear on face to be essentially the same variable. That is, the statement "This lesson might get you to understand a little more about some things we, ah, usually call number patterns" could be coded to contain all the imprecise variables in their program. Perhaps this observation is what led Land to cluster these variables in several of his studies.

INTERACTION EFFECTS OF CLARITY

Whereas previous sections described what are essentially "main effects" of clarity, scholars also have explored potential interaction effects. One such avenue involved potential interactions between instructor clarity and instructor immediacy. Researchers hypothesized two interaction patterns: the delivery distraction hypothesis and the additivity hypothesis. As explained by Titsworth (2001b), the delivery distraction hypothesis assumes that highly immediate delivery by the instructor could distract students from attending to and processing details. Conversely, the additivity hypothesis assumes that the positive main effects of immediacy and clarity will combine to create an ideal learning situation for students.

Compelling evidence points in favor of the additivity hypothesis. The additivity hypothesis received support in experiments conducted by Comadena et al. (2007) and Chesebro and McCroskey (1998b). In each study, patterns of mean scores show that students benefit from higher levels of immediacy and clarity. Although negligible interaction effects were observed in some of the studies, those effects point to an ordered pattern of mean scores where the high immediacy/high clarity condition was highest and the low immediacy/low clarity condition was lowest in terms of achievement. Although Titsworth (2004) found that high instructor immediacy led students to record fewer details in their notes, another study (Titsworth, 2001a) found that delayed retention was greatest when lectures contained both immediacy and clarity. Thus, while there may be a short-term distraction, in the long term, students benefit from immediate and clear instructors. Consequently, the conclusion that immediacy and clarity are both beneficial and largely work independently of one another seems warranted at this time.

In addition to exploring how clarity interacts with immediacy, Schonwetter, Struthers, and Perry (1995) explored how instructor clarity interacted with students' test anxiety. They manipulated lecture organization (high vs. low) and assessed whether students were high, moderate, or low in test anxiety. They found that while low and moderate test-anxious students benefited from organized lectures, high test-anxious students did not. The implication of this finding is that clarity may work differently for students who enter a class with different orientations toward learning, at least in terms of test anxiety.

Finally, several scholars have operated under the assumption that multiple low-inference clarity behaviors work in combination to improve achievement (e.g., Chesebro & McCroskey, 1998a). The assumption of these scholars is basically similar to the additivity hypothesis in that a linear positive relationship exists between the number of clarity behaviors enacted by an instructor and student achievement. Additional research is needed to determine whether there are conditions in which separate clarity behaviors might interact to differentially influence student learning.

In summary, experiments designed to test interactions have shown that instructor clarity and instructor immediacy do interact; however, the interaction effect is generally consistent with a main-effects model, where the two behaviors work together to produce an optimal learning condition for students. Isolated studies found that particular types of low-inference clarity behaviors may interact to influence students' achievement and that instructor clarity may have differential effects depending on students' test anxiety. Additional work replicating these latter two studies is clearly warranted.

TEACHER TRAINING AND DEVELOPMENT

Given the significant attention afforded to instructor clarity, few studies have explored how research findings can be translated into effective training programs. Of course, practical considerations intervene to some extent (e.g., experimental studies are difficult in disciplines such as education, where certification standards dictate uniform methods of training). Beyond bureaucracy, designing experiments that control for intervening variables while manipulating variables of interest in ongoing, naturalistic settings poses challenges for even the most ambitious researchers. That noted, three studies provide some evidence that teachers can be trained to be clear.

As mentioned previously, vagueness terms and mazes are related low-inference behaviors that result in unclear teaching. While the confluence of vagueness and mazes may pose some problems for researchers, the same problem should not confront professors hoping to train preservice teachers. Smith (1982) devised a training program testing whether secondary education student teachers could be trained to reduce the number of vagueness terms and mazes in a lecture. Results of Smith's study revealed no effect on word mazes; however, the group that received training significantly reduced their use of vagueness terms.

Stemming from the Ohio State program, Metcalf and Cruickshank (1991) created the Clarity Training Program (CTP) for preservice teachers. The training program consisted of four units comprising 17 specific skills that target clear teaching. For instance, Unit 3 focused on skills such as using examples, working examples, and explaining them; explaining unfamiliar words; showing similarities and differences between things; and explaining something and then pausing to allow students to think. A comparison of those skills with the low-inference items on the Ohio State teacher clarity scale highlighted obvious similarities. Analyses of outcome variables showed that preservice teachers who completed the CTP were clearer with their lessons; moreover, students of those same teachers scored higher on achievement tests. Despite the fact that intact groups were used in this design, Metcalf and Cruickshank's study provided meaningful evidence that rigorous clarity training can be integrated into existing teacher education programs and that such training can have short-term effects on student achievement. The same basic design was used in a subsequent study (Metcalf, 1992), which produced similar results.

A training/intervention study was reported by Gliessman (1987), who developed a training program for experienced teachers. Gliessman explored two specific behaviors: questioning and structuring. *Questioning* refers to the ways in which teachers sequence questions from lower-order to higher-order thinking skills (e.g., moving from a basic factual-level question such as "Who can tell me the different types of evidence?" to a higher-order question such as "In what situations would narratives be more effective than statistics as evidence?"); *structuring* refers to the ability of the teacher to clearly identify main and subordinate ideas in the lecture (e.g., a teacher might use transition statements to clearly move from one important point to another in a lecture). Although Gliessman's study lacked control because students were allowed to self-select into treatment groups, analysis of teaching demonstrations showed that multisequence questions increased from the beginning of the class to the end and that students receiving direct instruction on structuring improved their structuring skills.

CLARITY AND CULTURE

Undoubtedly, culture plays a vital role in the communication process, as cultural groups often share styles of language, symbols, and beliefs. Working from this assumption, Powell and Harville (1990) explored the relationship between instructor clarity, instructor immediacy, and instructional outcomes for students of white, Latino, and Asian American ethnic groups. Their results indicated that the positive effects of clarity remained relatively consistent across cultures, suggesting that culture may have little, if any, moderating effect on the clarity-learning relationship.

Extending instructor clarity research from U.S. classrooms to Chinese classrooms, Zhang and Zhang (2005) used a translated version of the TCSI and other pertinent scales to explore the association between instructor clarity and student classroom communication apprehension, state motivation, affective learning, and cognitive learning. Results revealed a significant positive correlation between instructor clarity and student affective learning ($r = .44$). These findings are consistent with conclusions generated from U.S. classrooms and suggest that, regardless of culture, clear teaching appears to positively influence student affect.

Citing a need to explore a possible mediated effect in the clarity-learning relationship, Zhang and Huang (2008) examined the impact of instructor clarity on student learning in U.S., Chinese, German, and Japanese classrooms. They argued that student state motivation functioned as a link between student affective and cognitive learning and subsequently hypothesized that student affective learning and state motivation mediate the effect of instructor clarity on student cognitive learning. Structural equation modeling revealed that when all variables (i.e., clarity, motivation, affective learning, and cognitive learning) were included in the model, the effect of instructor clarity on student cognitive learning was nonsignificant, which suggested full mediation for student affective learning and state motivation in the clarity-learning relationship.

Zhang and Huang's (2008) finding was somewhat inconsistent with prior research that suggests a partial mediation for student affective learning and state motivation in the immediacy-learning relationship (Zhang & Oetzel, 2006; Zhang, Oetzel, Gao, Wilcox, & Takai, 2007). They concluded that cultural effects might reduce the validity of instructional communication models across cultures. Zhang and Huang argued for cross-cultural validity testing to better determine the impact of teacher communication behavior on student learning.

THE NEGOTIATION OF CLARITY

Much of the instructor clarity research has been situated within the process-product paradigm, where instructor clarity is correlated with student outcomes. Put simply, this paradigm centers on the belief that clarity on the part of instructors leads to learning on the part of students. Civikly (1992) reviewed more than 50 instructor-clarity articles and argued for an expansion of the construct "to include (a) the clarity of the message or content, and (b) the role of the student as clarifier" (p. 138). She argued for a more constructivist view of clarity by including the learner in the teaching, clarity, and learning relationship, emphasizing that clarity highlights the central role of communication in the teaching and learning process.

Stemming from the relational perspective, a series of studies have highlighted the importance of student clarification tactics in the classroom. Darling (1989) studied college classrooms to understand how students signal comprehension problems. Following a series of weekly observations, she found that students commonly used three strategies to indicate their lack of comprehension: focused and directive (i.e., there is a problem, and the student proposes how to proceed), focused and nondirective (i.e., there is a problem, but the student is unclear about how to proceed), and personally qualified (i.e., there is a problem, and the student focuses on why he or she has the problem). Kendrick and Darling (1990) sought to explore the tactics students use to cope with potential misunderstandings in the classroom. After analyzing students' responses to open-ended survey questions, they determined that students' use of clarifying tactics varies often based on class size, the teaching method, and the type of problem experienced. Students tended to request elaboration from the teacher, express their confusion, or ask for examples.

Other scholars also have explored student question asking in the classroom as part of the clarity process. Pearson and West (1991) found that students tended to ask, on average, three questions of clarification and procedure in each hour of instruction. Students who typically asked questions were found to be independent and self-confident learners. In a later study, West and Pearson (1994) examined the types of questions students ask in classrooms and what instructors say before and after each type of student question. They analyzed classroom discourse in 30 classrooms across a university. An analysis of classroom audiotapes and transcriptions revealed six categories of student questions: classroom procedures, general inquiry (content), clarification, confirmation, general inquiry (teacher), and other. With respect to what instructors say, West and Pearson found that an instructor's question most often served as the antecedent to a student's question.

Recommendations for Future Research

Instructional clarity has natural, intuitive appeal for researchers, instructors, and students. From the perspective of researchers, clarity provides a key variable in the link between teaching and learning; for instructors, clarity is a tool, or process, that helps them guide students to deeper levels of learning; and for students, clarity is likely the difference between confident understanding and sheer confusion. For those reasons, it should be unsurprising that clarity has endured as a prominent variable in communication and education research. In light of research reviewed here, the following observations are offered.

OBSERVATION 1: CLARITY IS MULTIDIMENSIONAL

Once scholarship turned from the broad teacher-effects studies of the 1960s and 1970s, researchers interested in clarity adopted the assumption that multiple low- and intermediate-inference behaviors and dimensions constitute the larger construct of clarity. Most notably, the Ohio State studies demonstrated that numerous behaviors cause students to perceive their teachers as clear or unclear. Subsequent to the Ohio State studies, virtually all clarity research either followed in the tradition of assessing students' perceptions of multiple low-inference behaviors or isolated specific behaviors to manipulate in experiments.

Concluding that clarity is multidimensional was an important step. As noted earlier, high-inference, single-dimension constructs are difficult to study and even more difficult to teach; low-inference behaviors are more realistically assessed or manipulated and are relatively easy to incorporate into teacher training. The move to low-inference definitions did not come without challenges, however. The Ohio State studies showed that what could count as clarity was so broad it could be argued that all teaching behaviors generally relate to clarity in some way. The sheer breadth of what counts as clarity has made conceptual definitions of the construct difficult to generate. As Civikly (1992) noted, definitions of clarity are anything but clear.

In an attempt to synthesize the definition of clarity, Table 13.3 summarizes the intermediate-inference dimensions of clarity observed in the reviewed literature. As illustrated in the table, the process of being clear begins well before the instructor and students step into a classroom and continues through the entire instructional process. Based on the range of clarity behaviors, it is no longer fruitful to attempt to identify a single definition of clarity. Clarity is a process; as such, what constitutes clear teaching likely changes depending on the nature of a class and a group of students. Although it is possible to identify a broad range of behaviors that may contribute to clarity, it is not possible, or practical, to make definitive suggestions on behaviors that will always result in clear instruction from instructors and greater achievement for students. Prior research does suggest, however, that teachers who clearly communicate the relevance of course content to students' personal needs and career goals can influence their motivation to study (Frymier & Shulman, 1995).

Table 13.3	Components of Clarity Across the Research	
	Descriptor(s)	**Example**
Preinstructional clarity		
Advance organizers	Instructional objective; concrete and abstract; comparative and expository; conventional, linear, and matrix; question and descriptive	
Written organizational cues	Student notetaking handouts—outline format/matrix format	
Instructional clarity		
Verbal clarity	Vagueness terms	This lesson might get you to understand a little more about some things we, ah, usually call verbal clarity behaviors.
	Mazes	An idea, uh, concept, is a word or, ah, a phrase . . .
	Utterances	The sayings, uh, cues to help you move from one point to the next are called, umm, organizational cues, ok?
	Bluffing	Transition statements have reviews and previews, so to speak, obviously they will help you be clear.
	Uncertainty	Listen somewhat carefully and maybe take notes because you might be tested over the material.
	Pace of information flow	Use appropriate pausing to aid student comprehension/notetaking
Structural clarity	Verbal advance organizers	Today we will discuss two types of clarity—verbal clarity and structural clarity
	Transition statements	Now that we have discussed verbal clarity, we will discuss structural clarity.

(Continued)

Table 13.3	(Continued)	
	Descriptor(s)	**Example**
	Summaries	Today we discussed two types of clarity—verbal clarity and structural clarity
	Semantic cues	Here is an example of structural clarity . . .
	Written cues	Clear exam questions, clear syllabus
Process clarity		
Classroom understanding	Assignment expectations, relevance of material to students, teacher feedback, classroom policies Answers students' questions Student clarifies understanding	

OBSERVATION 2: FUTURE CLARITY STUDIES SHOULD EMPHASIZE PROCESS

Starting with Bruner (1960/1977) and continuing with Civikly (1992) and Simonds (1997), scholars have noted that clear teaching occurs when instructors and students negotiate meaning through communication. Bruner believed that this process begins when teachers select material and translate key principles of that material to knowledge structures appropriate to the developmental stage of the student. Civikly, Simonds, and other researchers expanded this notion to include processes where students and instructors engage in various clarifying behaviors such as asking questions, re-explaining, and using additional explanation to elaborate on meaning.

Explicit in these process-oriented perspectives is the notion that clarity is achieved through ongoing sequences of communication between instructors and students. Unfortunately, few studies exist to aid in understanding that process. Although a diversity of students has been represented in clarity studies (e.g., students ranging from elementary students to college students), little, if any, work (with the exception of Mottet et al., 2008), has attempted to identify how the process of clarity differs across situations involving students at different developmental levels. Obviously, what constitutes clear teaching for elementary school students likely would be inappropriate (and perhaps even confusing) for college students. Additional work exploring the developmental process of clarity would meaningfully expand an understanding of how this construct functions in the teaching and learning environment.

In addition to exploring how the process of clarity differs across diverse populations of students, additional work also should investigate clarity within and across disciplines. While some studies (e.g., Mottet et al., 2008; Smith & Land, 1980) have examined clarity within particular disciplines, key questions remain. For instance, does the process of clarifying differ when comparing STEM disciplines (science, technology, engineering, and math) with conceptual disciplines in the humanities and social sciences? How does clarity function in novel learning situations involving extensive group work or other experiential learning activities? Does this process differ in small classes by comparison with large classes? In essence, clarity research should attempt to recognize the diversity of learning situations facing students and begin to explore differences in the process of clarifying across those situations.

A particular learning context that deserves significant attention is in the burgeoning area of online pedagogy. Virtually all scholarship on clarity assumes a conventional face-to-face setting, where the instructor leads discussion in a traditional classroom. As such, much of what is known about clarity focuses on what the instructor says (e.g., the use of verbal examples, the use of verbal transitions). In online environments, lectures and other instructor-led presentations are de-emphasized in favor of written materials and multimedia presentations. Although some education research has explored clarifying text signals in expository text (see Lorch & van den Broek, 1997), no studies reviewed specifically explored these concepts in online environments. Future scholars should revisit some of the research designs reviewed and consider how those procedures could be adapted to explore clarity in online environments.

OBSERVATION 3: REMEMBER THE POSITIVE BIAS

The third observation returns to the criticism articulated by the Ohio State researchers that scholarship on clarity assumes that clarity is always related positively to achievement. Although the research reviewed certainly favors this assumption, the veracity of this assumption across varying types of students, disciplines, and learning environments should be tested. In communication studies, Eisenberg (2007) has highlighted situations in which ambiguity—the opposite of clarity—serves important organizational outcomes. Based on purely anecdotal evidence, this assumption also may be relevant in learning contexts.

Various scholars (Bruner, 1960/1977; Mayer, 1996b) note the importance of transfer in learning. That is, when students learn ideas, they must be able to transfer those ideas from examples and situations in the classroom to novel instances not explicitly addressed by instructors. If transfer happens, knowledge becomes useful for students across a wider variety of circumstances; if transfer does not happen, knowledge remains inert and largely unusable. Mayer's (1996a) work on problem solving suggested that teachers must scaffold instruction so that as students progress in knowledge, the teacher progressively removes prompts and cues on how to proceed so that students can learn how to transfer concepts from one problem to the next. Certainly, such instances require a certain degree of strategic ambiguity. Future research efforts should explore such learning situations to better understand the interrelationship between clarity and knowledge transfer on the part of students.

Conclusion

Starting with Rosenshine and Furst (1971) and continuing through recent studies on clarity, researchers have attempted to achieve a better understanding of how instructors can help students make sense of what they learn. For clarity to avoid being overly conflated with the more general class of good teaching behaviors, scholars should isolate specific low- and intermediate-inference clarity behaviors and dimensions to precisely indicate what aspects of clarity are relevant to the particular research questions being addressed. In so doing, scholarship on clarity can more meaningfully situate the construct within particular educational contexts and, by implication, begin to explore the processes involved in clarifying within those contexts.

References

Avtgis, T. A. (2001). Affective learning, teacher clarity, and student motivation as a function of attributional confidence. *Communication Research Reports, 18,* 345–353.

Brophy, J. (1988). Research on teacher effects: Uses and abuses. *Elementary School Journal, 89,* 3–21.

Bruner, J. S. (1977). *The process of education.* Cambridge, MA: Harvard University Press. (Original work published 1960)

Bush, A. J., Kennedy, J. J., & Cruickshank, D. R. (1977). An empirical investigation of teacher clarity. *Journal of Teacher Education, 28,* 53–58.

Chesebro, J. L. (2003). Effects of teacher clarity and nonverbal immediacy on student learning, receiver apprehension, and affect. *Communication Education, 52,* 135–147.

Chesebro, J. L., & McCroskey, J. C. (1998a). The development of the Teacher Clarity Short Inventory (TCSI) to measure clear teaching in the classroom. *Communication Research Reports, 15,* 262–266.

Chesebro, J. L., & McCroskey, J. C. (1998b). The relationship of teacher clarity and teacher immediacy with students' experiences of state receiver apprehension. *Communication Quarterly, 46,* 446–456.

Chesebro, J. L., & McCroskey, J. C. (2001). The relationship between teacher clarity and immediacy and student affect and cognitive learning. *Communication Education, 50,* 59–68.

Civikly, J. M. (1992). Clarity: Teachers and students making sense of instruction. *Communication Education, 41,* 138–152.

Comadena, M. E., Hunt, S. K., & Simonds, C. J. (2007). The effects of teacher clarity, nonverbal immediacy, and caring on student motivation, affective and cognitive learning. *Communication Research Reports, 24,* 241–248.

Darling, A. L. (1989). Signaling non-comprehension in the classroom: Toward a descriptive typology. *Communication Education, 38,* 34–40.

Denham, A., & Land, M. L. (1981). Research brief: Effect of teacher verbal fluency and clarity on student achievement. *Texas Tech Journal of Education, 8,* 227–229.

Eisenberg, E. (2007). *Strategic ambiguities: Essays on communication, organization, and identity.* Thousand Oaks, CA: Sage.

Evans, W. E., & Guymon, R. E. (1978, March). *Clarity of explanation: A powerful indicator of teacher effectiveness.* Paper presented at the meeting of the American Educational Research Association, Toronto, Ontario, Canada.

Faylor, N. R., Beebe, S. A., Houser, M. L., & Mottet, T. P. (2008). Perceived differences in instructional communication behaviors between effective and ineffective corporate trainers. *Human Communication, 11,* 149–160.

Frymier, A. B., & Shulman, G. M. (1995). "What's in it for me?" Increasing content relevance to enhance students' motivation. *Communication Education, 44,* 40–50.

Gliessman, D. H. (1987). Changing complex teaching skills. *Journal of Education for Teaching, 13,* 267–275.

Hines, C. V., Cruickshank, D. R., & Kennedy, J. J. (1985). Teacher clarity and its relationship to student achievement and satisfaction. *American Educational Research Journal, 22,* 87–99.

Kendrick, W. L., & Darling, A. L. (1990). Problems of understanding in classrooms: Students' use of clarifying tactics. *Communication Education, 39,* 15–29.

Kennedy, J. J., Cruickshank, D. R., Bush, A. J., & Myers, B. (1978). Additional investigations into the nature of teacher clarity. *Journal of Educational Research, 72,* 3–10.

Kibler, R. J., Cegala, D. J., Barker, L. L., & Miles, D. T. (1974). *Objectives for instruction and evaluation.* Boston: Allyn & Bacon.

Land, M. L. (1979). Low-inference variables of teacher clarity: Effects on student concept learning. *Journal of Experimental Psychology, 71,* 795–799.

Land, M. L. (1980). Teacher clarity and cognitive level of questions: Effects on learning. *Journal of Experimental Education, 49,* 48–51.

Land, M. L. (1981a). Actual and perceived teacher clarity: Relations to student achievement in science. *Journal of Research in Science Teaching, 18,* 139–143.

Land, M. L. (1981b). Combined effect of two teacher clarity variables on student achievement. *Journal of Experimental Education, 50,* 14–17.

Land, M. L., & Denham, A. (1979, February). *Effect of teacher clarity on student achievement*. Paper presented at the meeting of the Southwest Educational Research Association, Houston, TX.

Land, M. L., & Smith, L. R. (1979). Effect of a teacher clarity variable on student achievement. *Journal of Educational Research, 72*, 196–197.

Lorch, R. F., & van den Broek, P. (1997). Understanding reading comprehension: Current and future contributions of cognitive science. *Contemporary Educational Psychology, 22*, 213–246.

Mayer, R. E. (1977). The sequencing of instruction and the concept of assimilation-to-schema. *Instructional Science, 6*, 369–388.

Mayer, R. E. (1996a). Learners as information processers: Legacies and limitations of educational psychology's second metaphor. *Educational Psychologist, 31*, 151–161.

Mayer, R. E. (1996b). Learning strategies for making sense out of expository text: The SOI model for guiding three cognitive processes in knowledge construction. *Educational Psychology Review, 8*, 357–371.

Metcalf, K. K. (1992). The effects of a guided training experience on the instructional clarity of preservice teachers. *Teaching and Teacher Education, 8*, 275–286.

Metcalf, K. K., & Cruickshank, D. R. (1991). Can teachers be trained to make clear presentations? *Journal of Educational Research, 85*, 107–116.

Mottet, T. P., Garza, R., Beebe, S. A., Houser, M. L., Jurrells, S., & Furler, L. (2008). Instructional communication predictors of ninth-grade students' affective learning in math and science. *Communication Education, 57*, 333–355.

Pearson, J. C., & West, R. (1991). An initial investigation of the effects of gender on student questions in the classroom: Developing a descriptive base. *Communication Education, 41*, 167–180.

Powell, R. G., & Harville, B. (1990). The effects of teacher immediacy and clarity on instructional outcomes: An intercultural assessment. *Communication Education, 39*, 369–379.

Rosenshine, B. (1971). *Teaching behaviours and student achievement*. London: National Foundation for Educational Research.

Rosenshine, B. V., & Furst, N. F. (1971). Research on teacher performance criteria. In B. O. Smith (Ed.), *Research in teacher education* (pp. 37–72). Englewood Cliffs, NJ: Prentice Hall.

Schonwetter, D. J., Struthers, C. W., & Perry, R. P. (1995, April). *An empirical investigation of effective college teaching behaviors and student differences: Lecture organization and test anxiety*. Paper presented at the meeting of the American Educational Research Association, San Francisco, CA.

Sidelinger, R. J., & McCroskey, J. C. (1997). Communication correlates of teacher clarity in the college classroom. *Communication Research Reports, 14*, 1–10.

Simonds, C. J. (1997). Classroom understanding: An expanded notion of teacher clarity. *Communication Research Reports, 14*, 279–290.

Smith, L. R. (1982, March). *Training teachers to teach clearly: Theory into practice*. Paper presented at the meeting of the American Educational Research Association, New York.

Smith, L. R. (1984). Effect of teacher vagueness and use of lecture notes on student performance. *Journal of Educational Research, 78*, 69–74.

Smith, L. R. (1985). Teacher clarifying behaviors: Effects on student achievement and perceptions. *Journal of Experimental Education, 53,* 162–169.

Smith, L. R., & Land, M. L. (1980). Student perception of teacher clarity in mathematics. *Journal for Research in Mathematics Education, 11,* 137–147.

Spicer, C., & Bassett, R. E. (1976). The effect of organization on learning from an informative message. *Southern Speech Communication Journal, 41,* 290–299.

Titsworth, B. S. (2001a). The effects of teacher immediacy, use of organizational cues, and students' notetaking on cognitive learning. *Communication Education, 50,* 283–297.

Titsworth, B. S. (2001b). Immediate and delayed effects of interest cues and engagement cues on students' affective learning. *Communication Studies, 52,* 169–179.

Titsworth, B. S. (2004). Students' notetaking: The effects of teacher immediacy and clarity. *Communication Education, 53,* 305–320.

Titsworth, B. S., & Kiewra, K. A. (2004). Organizational lecture cues and student notetaking as facilitators of student learning. *Contemporary Educational Psychology, 29,* 447–461.

West, R., & Pearson, J. C. (1994). Antecedent and consequent conditions of student questioning: An analysis of classroom discourse across the university. *Communication Education, 43,* 299–311.

Zhang, Q., & Huang, B. (2008). How does teacher clarity affect student learning? A multi-cultural test for the mediated effect. *Texas Speech Communication Journal, 33,* 10–19.

Zhang, Q., & Oetzel, J. G. (2006). A cross-cultural test of immediacy-learning models in Chinese classrooms. *Communication Education, 55,* 313–330.

Zhang, Q., Oetzel, J. G., Gao, X., Wilcox, R. G., & Takai, J. (2007). A further test of immediacy-learning models: A cross-cultural investigation. *Journal of Intercultural Communication Research, 36,* 1–13.

Zhang, Q., & Zhang, J. (2005). Teacher clarity: Effects on classroom communication apprehension, student motivation, and learning in Chinese college classrooms. *Journal of Intercultural Communication Research, 34,* 255–266.

The Relational Side of Instructional Communication

14

An Examination of Instructors' Presentational Communication Traits

*Matthew M. Martin
and Scott A. Myers*

According to Scott and Nussbaum (1981), the factors that influence whether an individual is judged by others to be communicatively competent in interpersonal communication relationships are the same factors that also influence whether college students consider their instructors to be communicatively effective. In the classroom, these factors are encapsulated within a relational approach to teaching (DeVito, 1986; Frymier & Houser, 2000; Graham, West, & Schaller, 1992; Mottet & Beebe, 2006) and require an instructor to develop a host of relational teaching skills, which include, among others, the ability to listen, manage self-disclosure, become aware of verbal and nonverbal cues, and establish and maintain a supportive classroom climate (DeVito, 1986). Students respond favorably to instructors who are approachable, caring, and empathic (Chen, Lawler, & Venso, 2003; Smith, Medendorp, Ranck, Morrison, & Kopfman, 1994; Walsh & Maffei, 1994); they also report that an ideal instructor-student relationship is one in which there is open communication between instructors and students, a degree of mutual trust and honesty, and instructor willingness to listen to and counsel students (Garko, Kough, Pignata, Kimmel, & Eison, 1994). Together, these results suggest that effective teaching is interpersonally driven.

For many instructors, these relational teaching skills are manifested generally through their interpersonal communication traits and more specifically through their presentational communication traits. To examine the influence of instructor presentational traits in the classroom, this chapter is organized into three sections. In the first section, we examine the trait approach to the study of instructor communication. In the second section, we review the literature conducted to date on three instructor presentational communication traits: (1) instructor self-disclosure, (2) instructor communicator style, and (3) instructor sociocommunicative style. In the third section, we identify an agenda for future research.

The Trait Approach to the Study of Instructor Communication

One way to explain, understand, and predict how individuals communicate is to study their personality and communication traits (Daly, 1987; Daly & Bippus, 1998). Traits are considered to be the "distinguishable, relatively enduring way[s] in which one individual differs from others" (Guilford, 1959, p. 6) and are social constructs that reflect how individuals believe, think, and feel (Keyton & Frey, 2002). Although instructional communication researchers have examined the presence and influence of both instructor personality and communication traits in the classroom (e.g., McCroskey, Valencic, & Richmond, 2004; Teven, 2007), instructional communication researchers primarily are interested in the exploration of instructor communication traits. According to Infante, Rancer, and Womack (2003), a communication trait "is an abstraction which is constructed to account for enduring consistencies and differences in an individual's message-sending and message-receiving behaviors" (p. 77). Consonant with this definition is the expectation that an individual's communicative behaviors are relatively consistent across contexts and time as well as consistent within a context; yet "people differ in the degree to which they behave in accordance with their dispositions" (Daly, 1987, p. 23).

Communication trait researchers are interested in how, when, and why individuals' communication traits affect their interactions with other people (Daly, 1987). Infante et al. (2003) argued that from the trait perspective, individuals intentionally select situations and relational partners in accordance with their communication traits. Whether they exemplify the communicative behaviors associated with the trait, however, may depend on the individual, the situation, and the relational partners. It is possible that individuals engage in communicative behaviors that are indicative of several communication traits; they also may differ in their attribution of the primary trait that influences their use or choice of a particular communicative behavior (Buss & Craik, 1989). Hence, the evaluation of an individual's communication traits should occur over time rather than from one select interaction (Infante et al., 2003).

In the classroom, students observe their instructors over the length of the course (i.e., quarter, semester) and witness how their instructors communicate through their choice of teaching strategies (e.g., lecturing, facilitating class discussions), the numerous topics that they address (e.g., course content, student inquiries about course assignments, student problems and frustrations), and the contexts in which interaction occurs (e.g., before or after class, office visits, on campus); as such, students are able to make accurate observations about their instructors' communication traits. Additionally, if students believe that they know why their instructors are communicating or can assign an attribution to how their instructors are communicating (Kelsey, Kearney, Plax, Allen, & Ritter, 2004; McPherson & Young, 2004), they are better able to identify their instructors' communication trait behaviors (Read, Jones, & Miller, 1990). Based on the communication traits that students associate with a given instructor, then, students form expectations on how that particular instructor will communicate in any given situation in the classroom.

In providing a framework for classifying communication traits, Infante et al. (2003) identified four categories of communication traits: apprehension, which refers to the anxiety individuals possess when communicating with conversational partners (e.g., communication apprehension, unwillingness to communicate); aggression, which refers to how individuals use symbolic force with conversational partners (e.g., argumentativeness, verbal aggressiveness); adaptation, which refers to how individuals adjust their communication with their conversational partners (e.g., communication competence, interaction involvement, rhetorical sensitivity); and presentation, which refers to how individuals portray themselves with their conversational partners (e.g., predispositions toward verbal behavior, clothing consciousness). Although instructional communication researchers have demonstrated that instructors' communication traits from all four trait categories have an impact on students and the classroom environment (e.g., Knutson, 1979; Rancer & Avtgis, 2006; Waldeck, Kearney, & Plax, 2001), this chapter focuses specifically on how instructor presentational traits are intertwined with the relational approach to teaching.

The Study of Instructor Presentational Communication Traits

Although numerous presentational traits exist, the three traits of instructor self-disclosure, instructor communicator style, and instructor sociocommunicative style were selected for inclusion in this chapter for three reasons. First, although the origin and development of each trait can be traced to the interpersonal communication domain and have been researched extensively by interpersonal communication researchers, the study of each trait has migrated to the instructional communication context, where it has emerged as a prominent line of research (Cayanus, 2004; Nussbaum, 1992; Richmond, 2002; Sallinen-Kuparinen, 1992; Sorensen, 1989). Second, instructional communication researchers have established a link between each of these instructor presentational traits and teaching effectiveness, which refers both to students' positive evaluations of instructors and to students' reports of their affective, behavioral, and cognitive learning. Third, as Daly and Korinek (1980) aptly noted, "Talk is central to instruction" (p. 516). It is through classroom talk that instructors engage in self-disclosure, present a communicator style, and demonstrate the extent to which they are assertive and responsive (i.e., sociocommunicative style).

SELF-DISCLOSURE

Self-disclosure, which involves any information that a person divulges to another person (Cozby, 1973), emerges in the classroom as those statements made by instructors "that may or may not be related to subject content, but reveal information about the [instructor] that students are unlikely to learn from other sources" (Sorensen, 1989, p. 260). Not only does instructor self-disclosure occur voluntarily and involuntarily both in and out of the classroom (Fusani, 1994; Nussbaum & Scott, 1979), but it also varies in terms of its intent, amount, direction (i.e., positive or negative), honesty, and depth (Nussbaum & Scott; Wheeless & Grotz, 1976). Although not all instructional communication researchers have studied self-disclosure using these five dimensions, there is considerable support for the value of studying instructor self-disclosure and recognizing the multidimensionality of self-disclosure (Waldeck, 2008). (For a review of the development of this trait, see Derlega, Metts, Petronio, & Margulis, 1993.)

Viewed as an appropriate classroom behavior (Klinger-Vartabedian & O'Flaherty, 1989), instructors self-disclose a host of topics to their students. These topics include their families and friends; their educational and teaching experiences; their upbringing; their daily activities; and their opinions on current events, politics, and religion (Downs, Javidi, & Nussbaum, 1988; Javidi, Downs, & Nussbaum, 1988; Javidi & Long, 1989; McBride & Wahl, 2005; Nunziata, 2007; Nussbaum, Comadena, & Holladay, 1987). Sorensen (1989) found that good instructors (as rated by students) reveal positive information about themselves, whereas poor instructors do not. Instructor self-disclosure generally is used to clarify or extend course content, although it also serves as a vehicle through which instructors can promote class discussion, appear approachable, respond to student inquiries, create student affect, and enhance their credibility (Javidi et al., 1988; McBride & Wahl, 2005; Nunziata, 2007). Collectively, these findings demonstrate that instructors do, and should, control the information that they reveal to their students (Cayanus, 2004).

Instructors who self-disclose effectively are perceived more favorably by students. Javidi and Long (1989) found that experienced instructors connect their self-disclosures and narratives to course material more so than inexperienced instructors. Sorensen (1989) reported that good instructors are more intentional and honest in their classroom disclosures. Lannutti and Strauman (2006) noted that students gave their instructors higher teaching evaluations when they viewed their instructors' self-disclosures as honest, positive, and intentional, although the amount and depth of self-disclosure were not associated with instructor evaluations. Cayanus and Martin (2008) found that instructors whose self-disclosures are relevant and positive are considered by their students to engage in clarity. Mazer, Murphy, and Simonds (2009) reported that students consider instructors who are more self-disclosive (e.g., amount and intimacy) in their Facebook profile to possess more trustworthiness and to be more caring than instructors who are less disclosive in their profile.

Additionally, instructors' self-disclosures have an impact on students' attitudes and their classroom behaviors. Hill, Yun, and Lindsey (2008) conducted an experiment to test the impact of the relevance and the positiveness of instructor self-disclosure. Students in the positive self-disclosure conditions reported greater state motivation, instructor liking, and perceived instructor immediacy; there were no differences reported for the relevance self-disclosure conditions. Cayanus and Martin (2008) obtained positive relationships between instructors' amount, positiveness, and relevance of their self-disclosures with students' state motivation and interest (i.e., meaningfulness, competence, and impact). Students also report higher levels of state motivation and perceive the classroom climate to be favorable when shown a Facebook page of a high-disclosive instructor as compared with the Facebook page of a low-disclosive instructor (Mazer, Murphy, & Simonds, 2007).

When instructors' self-disclosures are overly positive, students are less likely to report that they communicate with their instructors for relational, excuse-making, participatory, and sycophancy reasons; when their self-disclosures are frequent and relevant, students are more likely to communicate with their instructors for functional and participatory reasons (Cayanus, Martin, & Goodboy, 2009). Cayanus, Martin, and Myers (2008) reported that when instructors' self-disclosures are overly positive, students are less likely to use the indirect, testing, and observing information-seeking strategies; when students consider their instructors' self-disclosure to be relevant, they are more likely to use the overt, third-party, and observing information-seeking strategies. Students also are more likely to participate during class (Goldstein & Benassi, 1994) and engage in out-of-class communication when their instructors self-disclose in the classroom (Cayanus & Martin, 2004).

Instructor self-disclosure also is related to students' learning. Nussbaum and Scott (1979) reported that positive relationships exist among instructors' overall communicator style, their competence of communicator style, and their honesty of self-disclosure with students' affective and behavioral learning; however, the relationships with cognitive learning were negative. They opined that if students like their instructors too much, the relationship becomes too social and cognitive learning suffers, though McCarthy and Schmeck (1982) noted that self-disclosure can influence positively student recall of course content. Cayanus and Martin (2008) found that amount and positiveness of instructor self-disclosure were the best predictors of student affect for the course, while amount, positiveness, and relevance were all significant predictors of student affect for the instructor. In a study of instructor self-disclosure on Facebook, Mazer et al. (2007) discovered that students reported greater affective learning for the more intimately disclosive instructor.

COMMUNICATOR STYLE

Communicator style, which refers to "the way one verbally and paraverbally interacts to signal how literal meaning should be taken, interpreted, filtered, or understood" (Norton, 1977, p. 527), is considered to be a pervasive form of self-presentation. Heavily influenced by theoretical work completed in the fields of interpersonal communication and psychology (Nussbaum, 1992), Norton (1983) proposed that communicator style focuses on the relational component of a message by centering on *how* an individual communicates any given message rather than *what* an individual communicates in the message. (For a review of the development of this trait, see Norton, 1983.)

Norton (1978, 1983) asserted that communicator style is composed of 10 dependent attributes (i.e., dominant, dramatic, contentious, animated, impression-leaving, relaxed, attentive, open, friendly, and precise) and one independent attribute (i.e., communicator image) that are manifested through an individual's use of verbal and paraverbal (i.e., nonverbal) communicative behaviors. *Dominant* communicators take charge of a situation by talking more loudly, longer, and more frequently than others. *Dramatic* communicators use picturesque language and stylistic devices (e.g., exaggerations, voice, rhythm, stories) to underscore content. *Contentious* communicators disagree with others and may get somewhat confrontational, hostile, quarrelsome, or belligerent. *Animated* communicators use eye contact, facial expressions, gestures, body movements, and posture to exaggerate content. *Impression-leaving* communicators have a memorable style that makes an impact on their relational partners. *Relaxed* communicators are poised and anxiety-free and remain calm and at ease when engaged in interactions with others. *Attentive* communicators express an interest in listening to others. They offer feedback, encouragement, and empathy. *Open* communicators are extroverted, unreserved, and straightforward. They do not have problems directly communicating their feelings, beliefs, thoughts, or emotions. *Friendly* communicators recognize others in a positive way and generally are considered to be kind and caring. *Precise* communicators try to be strictly accurate, using well-defined arguments and specific proof or evidence to clarify their positions. *Communicator image* refers to the assessment individuals make of their own communicative ability as compared with the communicative abilities of others.

From these 11 attributes, individuals select several attributes that constitute their communicator style and create a manner of communicating that is considered to be unique and personable yet habitual (Norton, 1983), though it should be noted that while each attribute is readily identifiable by a set of verbal and nonverbal behaviors, the same set of verbal and nonverbal behaviors (e.g., speaking loudly, gesturing wildly) can exemplify more than one attribute (e.g., dominant, animated). This style becomes associated with individuals, which then (a) guides their behaviors within and across communication contexts, (b) creates expectations for how they will communicate in a given context as well as expectations for how other individuals will respond to them, and (c) establishes boundaries for how messages should and should not be interpreted (Norton, 1983, 1986; Nussbaum, 1992).

In the classroom, instructors' communicator style is the way in which content is presented (Nussbaum, 1992) and influences heavily whether students consider their teaching to be effective (Norton, 1977, 1986; Scott & Nussbaum, 1981). Initial research conducted by Norton (1977) on the link between teaching effectiveness and instructor communicator style revealed that students consider effective teachers to be impression-leaving, attentive, friendly, not dominant, relaxed, and precise. Effective instructors are also considered dramatic (Norton & Nussbaum, 1980; Nussbaum, 1982) in that those instructors who are entertaining, tell stories, get students to laugh, and engage in double takes generally are viewed more positively than ineffective instructors (Norton & Nussbaum, 1980). Additionally, college students rate "better" instructors as being more dramatic, relaxed, open, impression-leaving, and friendly than "worse" instructors (Andersen, Norton, & Nussbaum, 1981; Schroeder & Leber, 1993); rate "above average" teachers as being more precise, more attentive, and less contentious than "below average teachers" (Bednar & Brandenburg, 1984); and report being satisfied with classroom communication when instructors are friendly, attentive, relaxed, and dramatic (Prisbell, 1994). Within organizations, "more effective" trainers are perceived to use the impression-leaving, open, dramatic, relaxed, and animated attributes at a higher rate than "less effective" trainers (Bednar & Heisler, 1985).

The link between communicator style attributes and teaching effectiveness may depend on two factors, which are instructors' impressions of their own style and student classification. Norton (1977), for instance, discovered that instructors rate their use of the attentive, relaxed, impression-leaving, and friendly attributes higher than their students do; they also consider themselves to be more effective than their students consider them to be. Comadena, Semlak, and Escott (1992) discovered that undergraduate students consider the impression-leaving, friendly, and attentive attributes to be indices of teaching effectiveness, whereas graduate students consider the impression-leaving, friendly, relaxed, attentive, lack-of-dominance, and precise attributes to be indices of teaching effectiveness.

Students also associate instructors' communicator style with their perceptions of their classroom learning. Across several studies, researchers have demonstrated that instructor communicator style is linked positively with students' perceived affective and behavioral learning (Andersen et al., 1981; Myers & Horvath, 1997; Nussbaum & Scott, 1979; Scott & Nussbaum, 1981), whereas instructor communicator style is linked either negatively with or not at all with students' cognitive learning (Andersen et al., 1981; Nussbaum & Scott, 1979). Nussbaum and Scott (1980) did establish, however, that the relationship between instructor communicator style and student learning is mediated by the degree of solidarity present in the instructor-student relationship. It is possible that other instructor communicative behaviors related to instructor communicator style (e.g., aggressive communication; Myers & Rocca, 2000) act as mediators in the instructor communicator style/student learning relationship (and should be considered in future research endeavors).

An instructor's communicator style also affects the extent to which students participate in the classroom. Myers and Rocca (2007) reported that student in-class participation (e.g., asking questions, expressing opinions) was related positively to the three profiles of instructor communicator style offered by Potter and Emanuel (1990): (1) the "human" instructor (i.e., the summed scores of the open, attentive, friendly, and relaxed attributes), (2) the "actor" instructor (i.e., the summed scores of the dramatic, animated, and impression-leaving attributes), and (3) the "authority" instructor (i.e., the summed scores of the dominant, contentious, and precise attributes), with the strongest relationship existing between in-class participation and the authority style. Myers, Mottet, and Martin (2000) found that the extent to which students are motivated to communicate with their instructors for relational, functional, participatory, excuse-making, and sycophantic reasons is predicted by the impression-leaving, animated, attentive, friendly, and contentious attributes.

SOCIOCOMMUNICATIVE STYLE

Sociocommunicative style is based on an individual's levels of assertiveness and responsiveness (Martin, 2008). The constructs of instructor sociocommunicative style (i.e., how instructors perceive themselves) and instructor sociocommunicative orientation (i.e., how students view instructors) build on earlier research conducted on psychological androgyny, social style, and instructor communication style (Bem, 1974; Kearney, 1984; Kearney & McCroskey, 1980; Lashbrook, 1974; Merrill & Reid, 1981). Based on their levels of both assertiveness and responsiveness, Merrill and Reid (1981) classified individuals into one of four categories of style: (1) expressive (i.e., an individual who is high in both assertiveness and responsiveness), (2) driver (i.e., an individual who is high in assertiveness and low in responsiveness), (3) amiable (i.e., an individual who is low in assertiveness and high in responsiveness), and (4) analytical (i.e., an individual who is low in both assertiveness and responsiveness). In subsequent instructional communication research, Richmond and McCroskey (1990) relabeled the four styles such that the expressive style became the competent style, the driver style became the aggressive style, the amiable style became the submissive style, and the analytical style became the noncompetent style. (For a review of the development of this trait, see Richmond & Martin, 1998.)

To understand sociocommunicative style, it is imperative to recognize the conceptual distinctions between assertiveness and responsiveness. Assertive communicators are strong in their interaction-management skills. Depending on their goals in a given situation, they are able to initiate, maintain, and terminate conversations; they are able to speak up for what is rightfully theirs; and they do not let others take advantage of them (Martin, 2008). Competitiveness, dominance, forcefulness, and independence are characteristics of an assertive individual (Richmond & McCroskey, 1990). Responsive communicators are other-oriented instead of self-centered. They are considerate of other individuals' feelings, consider these feelings when making decisions on how to communicate with these individuals, and are perceived as being caring, approachable, and concerned with the success of others (Martin, 2008). Helpfulness, compassion, friendliness, and sincerity are characteristics of a responsive individual (Richmond & McCroskey, 1990).

To date, researchers have examined instructor sociocommunicative style in one of two ways. The first way has centered on examining the two dimensions (i.e., assertiveness, responsiveness) of instructor sociocommunicative style in relation to students' perceptions of their instructor's communicative behaviors. Students who consider their instructors to be both assertive and responsive also consider them to be trustworthy (Wooten & McCroskey, 1996) and caring (Teven, 2001), clear in their teaching behaviors (Sidelinger & McCroskey, 1997), and less likely to engage in misbehaviors (i.e., incompetence, offensiveness, indolence), though the relationship observed between responsiveness and misbehaviors was stronger than the relationship observed between assertiveness and misbehaviors (Wanzer & McCroskey, 1998). Thomas, Richmond, and McCroskey (1994) found that although instructor assertiveness and responsiveness were not related to each other, students reported that nonverbally immediate instructors were high in both assertiveness and responsiveness. Similar results were obtained in a study that examined the relationships among athletes' perceptions of their coaches' assertiveness, responsiveness, and nonverbal immediacy (Rocca, Martin, & Toale, 1998).

Students' perceptions of their instructors' assertiveness and responsiveness also affect their learning and whether they communicate with their instructors. Teven (2005) found that both instructor assertiveness and responsiveness were correlated positively with students' reports of affect for the content and cognitive learning. Similar to the results obtained by Wanzer and McCroskey (1998), the relationships obtained between student learning and instructor responsiveness were stronger than the relationships obtained between student learning and instructor assertiveness. Allen, Long, O'Mara, and Judd (2008) reported that students who view their instructors as being both assertive and responsive report higher levels of affect for the course, the instructor, and the behaviors recommended in the course. They also noted that students high in communication apprehension were less likely to view their instructors as being assertive and responsive. In a study centered on out-of-class communication (OCC) between students and their instructors, Aylor and Oppliger (2003) discovered that while no significant relationships were obtained between instructor assertiveness and responsiveness and students' likelihood to engage in formal OCC (e.g., meeting in the instructor's office, e-mailing the instructor about questions about the course), students claimed to engage in informal OCC (e.g., talking before class starts, seeing an instructor on campus) with their instructors when they viewed their instructors as responsive. If they viewed their instructors as assertive, students reported not socializing with their instructors or discussing any personal problems with them.

The second way in which researchers have examined instructor sociocommunicative style has centered on the four categories (i.e., competent, aggressive, submissive, and noncompetent) of instructor sociocommunicative style in relation to students' perceptions of their instructor's communicative behaviors. Martin, Mottet, and Chesebro (1997) explored students' perceptions of instructor credibility (i.e., expertise, character, and caring) based on their instructors' perceived sociocommunicative style. Competent instructors were rated higher in perceived expertise than aggressive, submissive, and noncompetent instructors, while submissive and aggressive instructors were rated higher in expertise than noncompetent instructors. In terms of perceived character and caring, significant differences emerged among the four categories. For character, competent instructors were viewed the most favorably, followed by instructors who were considered to be submissive, noncompetent, and aggressive; for caring, competent instructors again were viewed the most favorably, followed by instructors who were considered to be submissive, aggressive, and noncompetent. Wanzer and Frymier (1999) reported that students found competent instructors to be higher in humor orientation than aggressive, submissive, and noncompetent instructors, though aggressive and submissive instructors were rated higher in humor orientation than noncompetent instructors. In a study involving instructor aggressive communication traits, students reported that competent instructors were considered to be more argumentative than submissive instructors, aggressive instructors were considered to be more argumentative than both noncompetent and submissive instructors, and noncompetent and aggressive instructors were considered to be more verbally aggressive than competent and submissive instructors (Myers, 1998).

Students' perceptions of their instructors' sociocommunicative style also affect their motivation for learning and for communicating with their instructors. Martin et al. (1997) found that students enrolled in courses with competent instructors reported the highest state motivation. Students enrolled in courses with aggressive and submissive instructors reported higher state motivation than students enrolled in courses with noncompetent instructors. Myers, Martin, and Mottet (2002) investigated students' sociocommunicative orientations, instructors' sociocommunicative styles, and students' motives for communicating with their instructors. They found that when students considered themselves to be competent and they viewed their instructors as competent, they were motivated to communicate with their instructors for relational and sycophancy reasons. Additionally, when students reported being assertive and viewed their instructors as responsive, they were likely to communicate for participatory reasons.

Generally, these collective results indicate that when instructors are assertive and responsive, students view their instructors more favorably and are more likely to play an active role in the classroom. However, in these research efforts, scholars largely have ignored the dimension of flexibility or versatility. Often mentioned as an essential component of the sociocommunicative construct (Martin & Rubin, 1995; Merrill & Reid, 1981; Richmond & Martin, 1998), flexible communicators are able to adapt their communication to meet the demands of the communicative encounter and, what is perhaps most important, to consider options and alternative ways of behaving in different situations (Martin, Anderson, & Thweatt, 1998). Examining this third dimension is warranted because not only should instructors be able to communicate assertively and responsively, but they also need to be able to adapt and adjust their behaviors (i.e., engage in flexibility or versatility) based on the students with whom they are communicating.

An Agenda for Future Research

As instructional communication researchers can attest, the study of instructor communication traits is a predominant area of research

(Staton-Spicer & Wulff, 1984; Waldeck et al., 2001). At the same time, instructional communication trait researchers who study instructor-student interaction need to heed attention to three issues. The first issue centers on the neglect of considering the situation in describing, explaining, and predicting student behavior. Infante (1987) stated that almost all communication trait researchers take an interactionist view, which posits that the situation interacts with individuals' predispositions and that this interaction then determines how they behave in the situation. He argued that "trait and situationist researchers should end their parochialism and integrate their models in order to move communication theory to a more unified and complete level" (p. 315). By focusing attention on the communicative situation or context, instructional communication researchers can discover *how* and *why* instructors' communication traits exert the greatest influence on their students' attitudes, behavior, and learning. As Daly (1987) noted, there are some contexts where the situation plays a greater role than individuals' traits in affecting how they behave in the situation. Seemingly, there are times when the situation in the classroom could supersede the influence of an instructor's communication traits.

A second issue is that most research examining communication traits in the instructional context has focused on students' reports of their instructors' communication traits; less research has centered on instructors' self-reports of their own communication traits or students' self-reports of their own communication traits (Waldeck et al., 2001). While some researchers have asked students to report on their own communication traits as well as their perceptions of their instructors' communication traits (e.g., Myers et al., 2002; Schrodt, 2003), few studies have asked instructors to report on their own communication traits while having students report on their own communication traits. One exception is the work completed by Valencic (2001), who asked 52 instructors to report on their extraversion, neuroticism, and psychoticism and 1,242 of their students to report on their instructors' perceived task attractiveness, nonverbal immediacy, credibility, assertiveness, and responsiveness, among other behaviors. Admittedly, this data collection and analysis effort is more extensive, but the benefit associated with such an effort is that researchers are able to collect responses from both the instructor and the student.

A third issue is the overreliance on student self-reports as the primary (and often sole) perspective of the instructor-student communication that occurs in the classroom. Although relying on student self-reports is an ideal method for an investigation (e.g., studying students' feelings of self-efficacy or asking students why they communicate with their instructors), relying only on self-reports simply is not sufficient. In 1980, Daly and Korinek proclaimed that "by almost any indicator, instructional communication scholars have been notorious in their avoidance of actually observing what is said and done in instruction" (p. 515). While this statement is not true of all researchers, too often the study of instructor communication traits has not examined the actual instructor communication that occurs in the college classroom.

Conclusion

In the classroom, the development of instructor-student interpersonal relationships can be "viewed as the means by which more effective, efficient, and satisfying teaching and learning may take place" (DeVito, 1986, p. 53). Instructors who pay attention to how they present themselves via their self-disclosure, communicator style, and sociocommunicative style may find that their students not only respond favorably to them but also report gains in their own learning outcomes. As such, taking a trait approach to instructor communication is one way in which the study of the relational approach to teaching can be enhanced.

References

Allen, J. L., Long, K. M., O'Mara, J., & Judd, B. B. (2008). Students' predispositions and orientations toward communication and perceptions of instructor reciprocity and learning. *Communication Education, 57,* 20–40.

Andersen, J. F., Norton, R. W., & Nussbaum, J. F. (1981). Three investigations exploring relationships between perceived teacher communication behaviors and student learning. *Communication Education, 30,* 377–392.

Aylor, B., & Oppliger, P. (2003). Out-of-class communication and student perceptions of instructor humor orientation and socio-communicative style. *Communication Education, 52,* 122–134.

Bednar, D. A., & Brandenburg, M. (1984). Relationships between communicator style and perceived teaching effectiveness in management classes. *Academy of Management Proceedings,* 111–116.

Bednar, D. A., & Heisler, W. J. (1985). Relationships between communicator style and instructional effectiveness in an industrial training setting. *Academy of Management Proceedings,* 114–118.

Bem, S. L. (1974). The measurement of psychological androgyny. *Journal of Consulting and Clinical Psychology, 42,* 155–162.

Buss, D. M., & Craik, K. H. (1989). On the cross-cultural examination of acts and dispositions. *European Journal of Personality, 3,* 19–30.

Cayanus, J. L. (2004). Using teacher self-disclosure as an instructional tool. *Communication Teacher, 18*(1), 6–9.

Cayanus, J. L., & Martin, M. M. (2004). An instructor self-disclosure scale. *Communication Research Reports, 21,* 252–263.

Cayanus, J. L., & Martin, M. M. (2008). Teacher self-disclosure: Amount, positiveness, and relevance. *Communication Quarterly, 56,* 325–341.

Cayanus, J. L., Martin, M. M., & Goodboy, A. K. (2009). Teacher self-disclosure and student motives to communicate. *Communication Research Reports, 26,* 105–113.

Cayanus, J. L., Martin, M. M., & Myers, S. A. (2008). The relationship between perceived instructor self-disclosure and college student information seeking. *Texas Speech Communication Journal, 33,* 20–27.

Chen, X. M., Lawler, E. M., & Venso, E. A. (2003). Improving teaching and learning: Students' perspectives. In C. M. Wehlburg (Ed.), *To improve the academy: Resources for faculty, instructional, and organizational development* (Vol. 21, pp. 238–254). Bolton, MA: Anker.

Comadena, M. E., Semlak, W. D., & Escott, M. D. (1992). Communicator style and teacher effectiveness: Adult learners versus traditional undergraduate students. *Communication Research Reports, 9,* 57–63.

Cozby, P. C. (1973). Self-disclosure: A literature review. *Psychological Bulletin, 79,* 73–91.

Daly, J. A. (1987). Personality and interpersonal communication: Issues and directions. In J. C. McCroskey & J. A. Daly (Eds.), *Personality and interpersonal communication* (pp. 13–41). Newbury Park, CA: Sage.

Daly, J. A., & Bippus, A. M. (1998). Personality and interpersonal communication: Issues and directions. In J. C. McCroskey, J. A. Daly, M. M. Martin, & M. J. Beatty (Eds.), *Communication and personality: Trait perspectives* (pp. 1–40). Cresskill, NJ: Hampton Press.

Daly, J. A., & Korinek, J. T. (1980). Instructional communication theory and research: An overview of classroom interaction. In D. Nimmo (Ed.), *Communication yearbook 4* (pp. 515–532). New Brunswick, NJ: Transaction Books.

Derlega, V., Metts, S., Petronio, S., & Margulis, S. T. (1993). *Self-disclosure.* London: Sage.

DeVito, J. A. (1986). Teaching as relational development. In J. M. Civikly (Ed.), *Communicating in college classrooms* (pp. 51–59). San Francisco: Jossey-Bass.

Downs, V. C., Javidi, M., & Nussbaum, J. F. (1988). An analysis of teachers' verbal communication within the college classroom: Use of humor, self-disclosure, and narratives. *Communication Education, 37,* 127–141.

Frymier, A. B., & Houser, M. L. (2000). The teacher-student relationship as an interpersonal relationship. *Communication Education, 49,* 207–219.

Fusani, D. S. (1994). "Extra class" communication: Frequency, immediacy, self-disclosure, and satisfaction in student-faculty interaction outside the classroom. *Journal of Applied Communication Research, 22,* 232–255.

Garko, M. G., Kough, C., Pignata, G., Kimmel, E. B., & Eison, J. (1994). Myths about student-faculty relationships: What do students really want? *Journal of Excellence in College Teaching, 5*(2), 51–65.

Goldstein, G. S., & Benassi, V. A. (1994). The relation between teacher self-disclosure and student classroom participation. *Teaching of Psychology, 21,* 212–216.

Graham, E. E., West, R., & Schaller, K. A. (1992). The association between the relational teaching approach and teacher job satisfaction. *Communication Reports, 5,* 11–22.

Guilford, J. P. (1959). *Personality.* New York: McGraw-Hill.

Hill, J. B., Yun, K. A., & Lindsey, L. (2008, November). *The interaction effect of teacher self-disclosure valence and relevance on student motivation, teacher liking, and teacher immediacy.* Paper presented at the annual meeting of the National Communication Association, San Diego, CA.

Infante, D. A. (1987). Enhancing the prediction of response to a communication situation from communication traits. *Communication Quarterly, 135,* 308–316.

Infante, D. A., Rancer, A. S., & Womack, D. F. (2003). *Building communication theory* (4th ed.). Prospect Heights, IL: Waveland Press.

Javidi, M., Downs, V. C., & Nussbaum, J. F. (1988). A comparative analysis of teachers' use of dramatic style behaviors at higher and secondary educational levels. *Communication Education, 37,* 278–288.

Javidi, M. N., & Long, L. W. (1989). Teachers' use of humor, self-disclosure, and narrative activity as a function of experience. *Communication Research Reports, 6,* 47–52.

Kearney, P. (1984). Perceptual discrepancies in teacher communication style. *Communication, 13,* 95–108.

Kearney, P., & McCroskey, J. C. (1980). Relationships among teacher communication style, trait and state communication apprehension and teacher effectiveness. In D. Nimmo (Ed.), *Communication yearbook 4* (pp. 533–551). New Brunswick, NJ: Transaction Books.

Kelsey, D. M., Kearney, P., Plax, T. P., Allen, T. H., & Ritter, K. J. (2004). College students' attributions of teacher misbehaviors. *Communication Education, 53,* 40–55.

Keyton, J., & Frey, L. R. (2002). The state of traits: Predispositions and group communication. In L. R. Frey (Ed.), *New directions in group communication* (pp. 99–120). Thousand Oaks, CA: Sage.

Klinger-Vartabedian, L., & O'Flaherty, K. M. (1989). Student perceptions of presenter self-disclosure in the college classroom based on perceived status differentials. *Contemporary Educational Psychology, 14,* 153–163.

Knutson, P. K. (1979). *Relationships among teacher communication style, trait and state communication apprehension, and teacher effectiveness.* Unpublished doctoral dissertation, West Virginia University, Morgantown.

Lannutti, P. J., & Strauman, E. C. (2006). Classroom communication: The influence of instructor self-disclosure on student evaluations. *Communication Quarterly, 54,* 89–99.

Lashbrook, W. B. (1974). *Toward the measurement and processing of the social style profile.* Eden Prairie, MN: Wilson.

Martin, M. M. (2008). Teacher socio-communicative style. In W. Donsbach (Ed.), *The international encyclopedia of communication* (Vol. 11, pp. 4994–4996). Malden, MA: Blackwell.

Martin, M. M., Anderson, C. M., & Thweatt, K. S. (1998). Individuals' perceptions of their communication behaviors: A validity study of the relationship between the Cognitive Flexibility Scale and the Communication Flexibility Scale with aggressive communication traits. *Journal of Social Behavior and Personality, 13,* 531–550.

Martin, M. M., Mottet, T. P., & Chesebro, J. L. (1997). Students' perceptions of instructors' socio-communicative style and the influence on instructor credibility and motivation. *Communication Research Reports, 14,* 431–440.

Martin, M. M., & Rubin, R. B. (1995). A new measure of cognitive flexibility. *Psychological Reports, 76,* 623–626.

Mazer, J. P., Murphy, R. E., & Simonds, C. J. (2007). I'll see you on "Facebook": The effects of computer-mediated teacher self-disclosure on student motivation, affective learning, and classroom climate. *Communication Education, 56,* 1–17.

Mazer, J. P., Murphy, R. E., & Simonds, C. J. (2009). The effects of teacher self-disclosure via "Facebook" on teacher credibility. *Learning, Media and Technology, 34,* 175–183.

McBride, M. C., & Wahl, S. T. (2005). "To say or not to say": Teachers' management of privacy boundaries in the classroom. *Texas Speech Communication Journal, 30,* 8–22.

McCarthy, P. R., & Schmeck, R. R. (1982). Effects of teacher self-disclosure on student learning and perceptions of teacher. *College Student Journal, 16,* 45–49.

McCroskey, J. C., Valencic, K. M., & Richmond, V. P. (2004). Toward a general model of instructional communication. *Communication Quarterly, 52,* 197–210.

McPherson, M. B., & Young, S. L. (2004). What students think when teachers get upset: Fundamental attribution error and student-generated reasons for teacher anger. *Communication Quarterly, 52,* 357–369.

Merrill, D. W., & Reid, R. H. (1981). *Personal styles and effective performance.* Radnor, PA: Chilton.

Mottet, T. P., & Beebe, S. A. (2006). Foundations of instructional communication. In T. P. Mottet, V. P. Richmond, & J. C. McCroskey (Eds.), *Handbook of instructional communication: Rhetorical and relational perspectives* (pp. 3–32). Boston: Allyn & Bacon.

Myers, S. A. (1998). Instructor socio-communicative style, argumentativeness, and verbal aggressiveness in the college classroom. *Communication Research Reports, 15,* 141–150.

Myers, S. A., & Horvath, C. W. (1997). A further examination of teacher communicator style and college student learning. *Journal of the Illinois Speech and Theatre Association, 18,* 37–48.

Myers, S. A., Martin, M. M., & Mottet, T. P. (2002). Students' motives for communicating with their instructors: Considering instructor socio-communicative style, student socio-communicative orientation, and student gender. *Communication Education, 51,* 121–133.

Myers, S. A., Mottet, T. P., & Martin, M. M. (2000). The relationship between student communication motives and perceived instructor communicator style. *Communication Research Reports, 17,* 161–170.

Myers, S. A., & Rocca, K. A. (2000). The relationship between perceived instructor communicator style, argumentativeness, and verbal aggressiveness. *Communication Research Reports, 17,* 1–12.

Myers, S. A., & Rocca, K. A. (2007). The relationship between college student class participation and perceived instructor communicator style. *Journal of the Speech and Theatre Association of Missouri, 37,* 114–127.

Norton, R. W. (1977). Teacher effectiveness as a function of communicator style. In B. D. Ruben (Ed.), *Communication yearbook 1* (pp. 525–542). New Brunswick, NJ: Transaction Books.

Norton, R. W. (1978). Foundation of a communicator style construct. *Human Communication Research, 4,* 99–112.

Norton, R. W. (1983). *Communicator style: Theory, applications, and measures.* Beverly Hills, CA: Sage.

Norton, R. W. (1986). Communicator style in teaching: Giving form to content. In J. Civikly (Ed.), *Communicating in college classrooms* (pp. 33–40). San Francisco: Jossey-Bass.

Norton, R., & Nussbaum, J. (1980). Dramatic behaviors of the effective teacher. In D. Nimmo (Ed.), *Communication yearbook 4* (pp. 565–579). New Brunswick, NJ: Transaction Books.

Nunziata, A. M. (2007, November). *College student perceptions of instructor communication privacy management.* Paper presented at the annual meeting of the National Communication Association, Chicago.

Nussbaum, J. F. (1982). The effective teacher: A communication nonrecursive path model. In M. Burgoon (Ed.), *Communication yearbook 5* (pp. 737–749). New Brunswick, NJ: Transaction Books.

Nussbaum, J. F. (1992). Communicator style and influence. In V. P. Richmond & J. C. McCroskey (Eds.), *Power in the classroom: Communication, control, and concern* (pp. 145–158). Hillsdale, NJ: Lawrence Erlbaum.

Nussbaum, J. F., Comadena, M., & Holladay, S. (1987). Classroom verbal behaviors of highly effective teachers. *Journal of Thought, 22,* 73–80.

Nussbaum, J. F., & Scott, M. D. (1979). Instructor communication behaviors and their relationship to classroom learning. In D. Nimmo (Ed.), *Communication yearbook 3* (pp. 561–583). New Brunswick, NJ: Transaction Books.

Nussbaum, J. F., & Scott, M. D. (1980). Student learning as a relational outcome of teacher-student interaction. In D. Nimmo (Ed.), *Communication yearbook 4* (pp. 553–564). New Brunswick, NJ: Transaction Books.

Potter, W. J., & Emanuel, R. (1990). Students' preferences for communication style and their relationship to achievement. *Communication Education, 39,* 234–249.

Prisbell, M. (1994). Students' perceptions of instructors' style of communication and satisfaction with communication in the classroom. *Perceptual and Motor Skills, 79,* 1398.

Rancer, A. S., & Avtgis, T. A. (2006). Argumentative and verbally aggressive communication in instructional contexts. In *Argumentative and aggressive communication: Theory, research, and application* (pp. 125–144). Thousand Oaks, CA: Sage.

Read, S. J., Jones, D. K., & Miller, L. C. (1990). Traits as goal-based categories: The importance of goals in the coherence of dispositional categories. *Journal of Personality and Social Psychology, 58,* 1048–1061.

Richmond, V. P. (2002). Socio-communicative style and orientation in instruction: Giving good communication and receiving good communication. In J. L. Chesebro & J. C. McCroskey (Eds.), *Communication for teachers* (pp. 104–115). Boston: Allyn & Bacon.

Richmond, V. P., & Martin, M. M. (1998). Socio-communicative style. In J. C. McCroskey, J. A. Daly, M. M. Martin, & M. J. Beatty (Eds.), *Communication and personality: Trait perspectives* (pp. 133–148). Cresskill, NJ: Hampton Press.

Richmond, V. P., & McCroskey, J. C. (1990). Reliability and separation of factors on the assertiveness-responsiveness measure. *Psychological Reports, 67,* 449–450.

Rocca, K. A., Martin, M. M., & Toale, M. C. (1998). Players' perceptions of their coaches' immediacy, assertiveness, and responsiveness. *Communication Research Reports, 15,* 445–450.

Sallinen-Kuparinen, A. (1992). Teacher communicator style. *Communication Education, 41,* 153–166.

Schrodt, P. (2003). Student perceptions of instructor verbal aggressiveness: The influence of student verbal aggressiveness and self-esteem. *Communication Research Reports, 20,* 240–250.

Schroeder, A. B., & Leber, R. L. (1993). Communicator style perceptions of "best" and "worst" teachers. *Forensic of Pi Kappa Delta, 78*(4), 11–16.

Scott, M. D., & Nussbaum, J. F. (1981). Student perceptions of instructor communication behaviors and their relationship to student evaluation. *Communication Education, 30,* 44–53.

Sidelinger, R. J., & McCroskey, J. C. (1997). Communication correlates of teacher clarity in the college classroom. *Communication Research Reports, 14,* 1–10.

Smith, S. W., Medendorp, C. L., Ranck, S., Morrison, K., & Kopfman, J. (1994). The prototypical features of the ideal professor from the female and male undergraduate perspective: The role of verbal and nonverbal communication. *Journal of Excellence in College Teaching, 5*(2), 5–22.

Sorensen, G. (1989). The relationships among teachers' self-disclosive statements, students' perceptions, and affective learning. *Communication Education, 38,* 259–276.

Staton-Spicer, A. Q., & Wulff, D. H. (1984). Research in communication and instruction: Categorization and synthesis. *Communication Education, 33,* 377–391.

Teven, J. J. (2001). The relationships among teacher characteristics and perceived caring. *Communication Education, 50,* 159–169.

Teven, J. J. (2005). Teacher socio-communicator style and tolerance for disagreement and their association with student learning in the college classroom. *Texas Speech Communication Journal, 30,* 23–35.

Teven, J. J. (2007). Teacher temperament: Correlates with teacher caring, burnout, and organizational outcomes. *Communication Education, 56,* 382–400.

Thomas, C. E., Richmond, V. P., & McCroskey, J. C. (1994). The association between immediacy and socio-communicative style. *Communication Research Reports, 11,* 107–115.

Valencic, K. (2001). *An investigation of teachers' temperament and students' perceptions of teachers' communication behavior and students attitudes' toward teachers.* Unpublished doctoral dissertation, West Virginia University, Morgantown.

Waldeck, J. H. (2008). Teacher self-disclosure. In W. Donsbach (Ed.), *The international encyclopedia of communication* (Vol. 11, pp. 4987–4989). Malden, MA: Blackwell.

Waldeck, J. H., Kearney, P., & Plax, T. G. (2001). The state of the art in instructional communication research. In W. R. Gudykunst (Ed.), *Communication yearbook 24* (pp. 207–230). Thousand Oaks, CA: Sage.

Walsh, D. J., & Maffei, M. J. (1994). Never in a class by themselves: An examination of behaviors affecting the student-professor relationship. *Journal of Excellence in College Teaching, 5*(2), 23–39.

Wanzer, M. B., & Frymier, A. B. (1999). The relationship between student perceptions of instructor humor and students' reports of learning. *Communication Education, 48,* 48–62.

Wanzer, M. B., & McCroskey, J. C. (1998). Teacher socio-communicative style as a correlate of student affect toward teacher and course material. *Communication Education, 47,* 43–52.

Wheeless, L. R., & Grotz, J. (1976). Conceptualization and measurement of reported self-disclosure. *Human Communication Research, 2,* 338–346.

Wooten, A. G., & McCroskey, J. C. (1996). Student trust of teacher as a function of socio-communicative style of teacher and socio-communicative orientation of student. *Communication Research Reports, 13,* 94–100.

Part III

Critical Communication Pedagogy

Critical Communication Pedagogy 15

Reframing the Field

John T. Warren and Deanna L. Fassett

In 2007, when we published *Critical Communication Pedagogy*, in which we worked to draw critical theory from the field of communication studies into the study of classroom interaction, our first inclination was to call the book *Toward a Critical Communication Pedagogy*. We soon realized that this sort of title presumed that we were advocating a new and uncharted way to do communication research about educational activity. This was not at all an accurate description of the field, either its research practice (conference and publication) or the way our colleagues teach in the classroom. Communication scholars have taken up the banner of critical theory (in all its many forms: Marxist, feminist, queer, postcolonial, etc.) with respect to research at the intersections of communication and instruction, but they have often found publishing such work difficult to do in the pages of our premier journal, *Communication Education*. Instead, critical scholarship often finds its home in education or cultural studies journals (e.g., Alexander, 2004; Cooks, 2007; Johnson, 2004; Nainby & Pea, 2003; Pineau, 1994; Warren, 2001b). Arguably, this is due to our discipline's protracted difficulties in engaging in cross-paradigmatic dialogue, especially as this plays out at the level of editorial politics and review board selection. Nevertheless, critical scholarship has appeared, albeit inconsistently, in the pages of *Communication Education* (e.g., see Cooks, 2003; Cooks & Sun, 2002; Fassett & Warren, 2004; Heinz, 2002; Hendrix, Jackson, & Warren, 2003; Howard, 2004; Johnson & Bhatt, 2002; Pelias, 2000; Perkins, 1994; Sprague, 1992, 1993, 1994; Warren, 2001a; Warren & Hytten, 2004; Wood & Fassett, 2003). However, in the end, the presence of scholarship at the intersections of communication, critical theory, and instruction has been, at best, uneven.

We dropped the "toward" in our title so that we could work with our readers to better recognize and articulate the role critical theory has played, for approximately 20 years now, in our quarters of the discipline. We further wanted to recognize scholars like Radhika Gajjala, Karen Lovaas, Bryant Alexander, and the others in this section of the *Handbook*, who have been doing critical communication pedagogy, though not always within this nomenclature, at our national and regional conferences for some time. Indeed, one of the first places we fell in love with the premise of critical pedagogy was, as graduate students, watching scholars in communication wrestle with issues of power, culture, justice, and desire in conference panels and sessions. It was at a conference where we first became inspired to write *Critical Communication Pedagogy*, a text that scholars across a variety of backgrounds and experiences could use to name and undergird their practice. These moments of naming and building alliances across desperate and resistant essays written by authors trying to work toward more socially just futures have been powerful. Inspired by these moments, our text has made possible continued, and perhaps more consistent, conversations. In both national and regional conferences, we have witnessed increasing numbers of panels dedicated to critical communication pedagogy, including new and seasoned communication scholars. We have seen work featured in multiple divisions at the national conference, including Basic Course, Critical/Cultural Studies, Ethnography, and Instructional Development. Yet publication outlets continue to be narrow; perhaps the most successful of these has been the *Basic Communication Course Annual* (*BCCA*) (e.g., Fassett & Warren, 2008; Fotsch, 2008; Pensoneau-Conway, 2009; Prividera, 2004; Treinen & Warren, 2001). As the rich work in this section of the *Handbook* suggests, the potential for contributions to the study of communication and education within a critical paradigm are both plentiful and exciting. Persistent publication in *BCCA* suggests the importance of linking critical, social-justice-oriented approaches to experiences and activities disciplinary readers recognize as relevant, such as our collective work in the foundations courses of our discipline.

In the end, the story these chapters (and the section as a whole) tell is one of potential and rich possibility. The work here is at once rigorous and insightful, diverse and complex. Whatever the history that has marginalized critical theory in our discipline, the work here reveals this research tradition as an established and continued presence in the study of communication and instruction.

The Chapters

The chapters in this section of the *Handbook* demonstrate two major characteristics of critical communication pedagogy. First, we include authors and topics that demonstrate the diversity of issues and content areas currently at issue in the field. We chose authors who are experts in their respective fields and who could offer not only a sense of the scholarly terrain but also a critical perspective on it. Second, we include writings that exemplify research engagement; that is, the authors explore their content areas through critical methods and writing styles. In this way, authors of each section in this handbook model the entailments of their particular paradigmatic perspectives; as communication education and instructional communication scholars embrace their own methods of empirical investigation, so too do the critical theorists in this section. In this way, the chapters are diverse not only in terms of content but also in terms of voice.

In Chapter 16, Leda Cooks offers her perspective on the philosophical and methodological foundations of critical communication pedagogy. Beginning with the tenets and critiques of critical pedagogy, Cooks provides a context for understanding the present terrain of critical work regarding communication and instruction. She locates Freire as a major figure who transcends the discipline of education and is often cited by colleagues in communication studies. From there, she clarifies the critical traditions that undergird the chapters in this section of the *Handbook*. That Cooks locates performance and performativity in critical foundations demonstrates the heuristic value performance studies has for critical communication pedagogy, an undeniably interdisciplinary effort.

In Chapter 17, Bryant Alexander takes up this exploration of performance, focusing on a significant line of investigation in critical communication pedagogy: performative pedagogy. Alexander's dedication to social justice pedagogy as both a classroom practice and a philosophical stance in research creates both context and history for performative pedagogy while also sharing a vision for future work, work that helps us see "the world anew." Alexander, in his chapter, serves as a model for how a scholar engaged in critical communication pedagogy research might speak into a rich foundational body of literature; his poetic voice demonstrates how bodies and minds might meet, and remain in productive tension, both in the world and on the page.

In Chapter 18, Bernadette Calafell explores identity scholarship in critical communication pedagogy. In a powerful narrative that juxtaposes her own lived experience as a student and professor with critical literature in communication, Calafell exemplifies how identity work in critical communication pedagogy illuminates and enriches understanding of one's own life; furthermore, her work models how reflexive investigation of one's own life may give shape to future research. Set at the intersections of gender, sexuality, race, and nation, Calafell crafts and illuminates a tensive relationship between herself and the academy.

In Chapter 19, in a rich and comprehensive review of critical race theory, especially as it plays out across both communication studies, in general, and critical communication pedagogy, in particular, Jennifer Simpson lends her own distinctive voice to ongoing dialogues about our discipline that address race and ethnicity. In her review, Simpson analyzes the intersections of critical communication pedagogy, critical race theory, and critical pedagogy, calling for careful consideration of how they inform and work together toward analyzing how individuals produce racial power and advocates that communication scholars work toward social justice via rigorous engagement in research. She ends her review by articulating a critical communication pedagogy that is substantively influenced by critical race theory.

In her chapter "Sexualities and Critical Communication Pedagogy" (Chapter 20), Karen Lovaas describes critical communication pedagogy along four levels of analysis, from public discourse to classroom practices. First, Lovaas discusses public discourse on sexuality and how that discourse produces knowledges about sexuality in ways that contribute to heteronormativity. Second, she explores how communication studies, as a discipline, has approached the study of sexuality, in general and with respect to instruction. Then, engaging in a still more local analysis, she considers institutional responses to sexuality, examining university structures and how various institutions generate proactive responses to issues of sexism and heterosexism. Finally, she moves to her own classroom practices, offering a reflexive account of her own pedagogical work as a heuristic for future research. In the end, she advocates a queer critical communication pedagogy, one that disrupts the status quo in our thinking and in our classrooms.

The section ends with Chapter 21, Radhika Gajjala, Natalia Rybas, and Yahui Zhang's dialogue on technology and critical feminist pedagogy, in which they advance a specific research project that carefully analyzes digitally mediated environments as sites of resistance and agency. Useful for multiple purposes, the chapter engages literatures in globalization, feminist pedagogy, and technology, locating each within and in relation to current research in critical communication pedagogy. As a research project, however, the essay charts new ground, asks new questions, and crafts a research agenda for those interested in how critical communication pedagogy might look within electronically mediated contexts. The essay also contributes to critical communication pedagogy by offering performative writing as a mode of analysis, producing a feminist pedagogy not only in content but also in form.

Together these chapters represent a significant contribution to the field of critical communication pedagogy. They offer a state of the field and, in their innovation, present a series of avenues along which we, as a community of scholars, might choose to grow and develop. While the various threads of critical theory (critical race theory, feminist theory, queer theory, performativity, etc.) are each unique in their own right, they are inextricably intertwined by their commitment to the various tenets of critical communication pedagogy. For instance, in *Critical Communication Pedagogy* (Fassett & Warren, 2007), we articulate and maintain 10 commitments that constitute a critical communication pedagogy. In general, these commitments include engaging and exploring fluid constructions of identity, culture as foundational, and both macro-critique and micro-analysis of power. Each of this section's chapters models and interrogates these paradigmatic commitments in heuristic ways.

Future Possibilities

Perhaps the most significant contribution of this *Handbook* is the way the chapters, in their aggregate, pose the question of the purposes to which we engage in research at the intersections of communication and instruction. Too often, disciplinarily, we fail to engage in substantive discussion of the purpose and value of our work, becoming mired instead in debates regarding what constitutes methodological rigor. Although rigor is significant, we are still learning, as a discipline, to embrace and engage a multiplicity of theoretical and methodological insights. Such sustained investigation will enable us to develop and sustain research that is purposeful and relevant to a variety of different constituents (within and beyond our discipline, inside and in community with the academy).

For example, the goal of work in communication education, as exemplified in this volume, is a collaborative effort to articulate and refine our educational practices within the site of communication classrooms. These discussions regarding service learning, "basic" course pedagogy, and preparing future faculty in communication are efforts at strengthening our own discipline-specific pedagogy, one that effectively meets the needs of our content and gives rise to the learning opportunities students need to succeed in communication study and practice. This differs in scope from instructional communication, which aims to isolate, predict, and alter communication phenomena across a broad array of teaching and learning contexts. In so doing, instructional communication scholars work toward the development of axiomatic theory, work that can be more universally applicable.

What critical communication pedagogy adds to these two foundational and enduring conversations is a productive reframing, a shift in focus that calls into question our purpose and function as researchers. For example, consider a time-honored communication education tradition: investigation of and in the introductory course. A critical paradigm challenges scholars engaged in this work to ask unsettling, reframing questions that move us from how best to teach the introductory public speaking course toward how we talk about our field and how our framing of this work can contribute to or detract from the pedagogy we advocate (and the values we espouse). For instance, if we continue to talk about our foundational communication courses as "basic," we risk students, colleagues (both in and beyond our discipline), and our communities believing that they are basic; that is, they will continue to be dismissed by our profession as burdensome and simplistic (Fassett & Warren, 2008). The way our field has talked about the introductory course and its pedagogy has, in many cases, become inextricably intertwined with how we think about the course, the students who take it, and the teachers who teach it and coordinate it. A critical communication pedagogy would remind the field of long-standing truths that we teach in our advanced classes: How we name something shapes and gives meaning to that thing. This "basic" idea is the foundational reason we demand that our students use gender-neutral language and reflect on their speech choices; language shapes our understanding in fundamental ways (Austin, 1975; Butler, 1997; Freire, 1970/2003; Morrison, 1994). This is an important reframing for our collective work to educate students about our discipline and its relevance to their lives.

Critical communication pedagogy also affords an important reframing of established lines of instructional communication research. For example, Sprague (1994) has raised a series of questions regarding power and compliance in the classroom that are worth our collective consideration. She notes that if we, as a discipline, cannot talk about what is at stake in definitions of "communication," "power," or "resistance," then we have lost sight of what it means to engage in research, in the substantive and rigorous analysis of shared concerns. Sprague's reframing of power asks us to reconsider our shared theoretical and methodological assumptions (from our use of particular metaphors to describe a phenomenon to what we believe counts as rigorous investigation); her concern regarding what it means for teachers to believe they can use power to force compliance (without a clear sense of the contextual, ethical, cultural, political, and ideological implications of such compliance) is a lasting contribution of critical theory to our work at the intersections of communication and instruction.

From our reading of the work produced by the authors of this section, we argue that as the body of critical communication pedagogy scholarship continues to grow, it has made and will continue to make five heuristic contributions to our discipline. These branches of prospective scholarship will help expand and complicate our understanding of communication as it relates to teaching and learning.

First, critical communication pedagogy invites attention to and careful consideration of work in both communication education and instructional communication. This is already evident as scholars work to question taken-for-granted norms in established research—for example, our own analysis of discourse about "at-risk" students (Fassett & Warren, 2004, 2005). Such work will continue to follow in the footsteps of Sprague's (1992, 1993, 1994) model.

Second, critical communication pedagogy will expand to address even more sites and issues than it currently does. The studies here only represent the depth and diversity lines of research in critical communication pedagogy; sites of investigation will likely grow and change. We anticipate attention to prison education, to how critical/transformative pedagogy can be enacted in institutional contexts where populations are under the watchful eye of authority. Attention will grow to include heretofore underexplored aspects of identity, such as economic class and ability. Furthermore, as work in this paradigm grows, we will see explorations of assessment, of how we can know efforts toward critical communication pedagogy are, indeed, successful in, for example, cultivating reflexivity; critical communication educators are also likely to examine and ask incisive questions regarding the nature and politics of and underexplored approaches to assessment.

Third, critical communication pedagogy will continue to address and complicate issues of theory and method as we study instructional sites. The critical paradigm (as Sprague, 1994, observes) radically reframes issues of theory and method from a predominant focus on social scientific approaches. Theoretical and methodological pluralism will bring additional complexity to communication analysis, especially as investigations draw into tension global or macro (i.e., social structures) and local or micro (i.e., individual actions) considerations.

Fourth, critical communication pedagogy renews our attention to the texts and technologies we use in our classrooms. While communication education, in many ways, already addresses this issue, the critical tradition invites investigation of how our pedagogical resources shape and define students, how we interact with students (virtually and physically), and the kinds of information we share with them. The critical paradigm challenges us to ask what kinds of knowledge about communication are worth knowing (and for whom, and who decides). That we have a profound disciplinary presence of introductory communication courses on campuses across the country is an incredible opportunity to raise awareness of important local, national, and global issues. For instance, public communication texts that center on environmentalism, corporate/capitalistic greed, or identity politics have the potential to change radically how we imagine our work in these courses.

Finally, critical communication pedagogy increases attention to issues of social justice as a fundamental and integral part of our work as researchers and teachers of communication. Too often, the rhetoric that surrounds being an academic invites us to rest comfortably in unquestioned assumptions, for example, that knowledge is valuable for its own sake or that education is inevitably competitive (or meaningfully meritocratic); however, the critical tradition calls such beliefs into question, asking instead how such knowledge works in the world and for whom such knowledge is produced. This point is not to say that all research should be "applied" or action oriented but that when we research the classroom, a site where power differentials are at play, we owe it to our students to do so in a manner that appreciates them in their full complexity and respects them as human subjects who have agency, cultural values, and beliefs that guide them.

In sum, the work represented here speaks as much to the future of our field as it does to the current state of it. By occupying the space between the present and the future, these essays become a space of possibility that brings us hope. In the end, research is a form of activism; in these instances, research is activism for a more humanizing and humane world. Thus, we close by chiming in with Bernadette Calafell, who, in Chapter 18, poetically pleads, "I hope for more. I *need* more. I want *you* to desire more." What inspires us most about the critical scholarship at the intersections of communication and pedagogy is what this activism can enable, how this activism can transform, and the possibilities that this activism can bring to bear. We want more, and here in these writings, we find hope for our ability to realize these possible futures.

References

Alexander, B. K. (2004). Racializing identity: Performance, pedagogy, and regret. *Cultural Studies <=> Critical Methodologies, 4,* 12–28.

Austin, J. L. (1975). *How to do things with words* (2nd ed.). Cambridge, MA: Harvard University Press.

Butler, J. (1997). *Excitable speech.* New York: Routledge.

Cooks, L. (2003). Pedagogy, performance and positionality: Teaching about whiteness in interracial communication. *Communication Education, 52,* 245–258.

Cooks, L. (2007). Accounting for my teacher's body: What can I teach what can we learn? *Feminist Media Studies, 7*(3), 299–312.

Cooks, L., & Sun, C. (2002). Constructing gender pedagogies: Desire and resistance in the "alternative" classroom. *Communication Education, 51,* 293–310.

Fassett, D. L., & Warren, J. T. (2004). "You get pushed back": The strategic rhetoric of educational success and failure in higher education. *Communication Education, 53,* 21–39.

Fassett, D. L., & Warren, J. T. (2005). The strategic rhetoric of an educational identity: Interviewing Jane. *Communication and Critical/Cultural Studies, 2,* 238–256.

Fassett, D. L., & Warren, J. T. (2007). *Critical communication pedagogy.* Thousand Oaks, CA: Sage.

Fassett, D. L., & Warren, J. T. (2008). Pedagogy of relevance: A critical communication pedagogy agenda for the "basic" course. *Basic Communication Course Annual, 20,* 1–34.

Fotsch, P. (2008). Race and resistance in the communication classroom. *Basic Communication Course Annual, 20,* 197–230.

Freire, P. (2003). *Pedagogy of the oppressed: 30th anniversary edition.* New York: Continuum. (Original work published in 1970)

Heinz, B. (2002). Enga(y)ging the discipline: Sexual minorities and communication studies. *Communication Education, 51*, 95–104.

Hendrix, K. G., Jackson, R. L., II, & Warren, J. R. (2003). Shifting academic landscapes: Exploring co-identities, identity negotiation, and critical progressive pedagogy. *Communication Education, 52*, 177–190.

Howard, L. A. (2004). Speaking theatre/doing pedagogy: Re-visiting theatre of the oppressed. *Communication Education, 53*, 217–233.

Johnson, J. R. (2004). Universal instructional design and critical (communication) pedagogy: Strategies for voice, inclusion, and social justice/change. *Equity and Excellence in Education, 37*, 145–153.

Johnson, J. R., & Bhatt, A. J. (2002). Gendered and racialized identities alliances in the classroom: Formations in/of resistive space. *Communication Education, 52*(3/4), 230–244.

Morrison, T. (1994). *The Nobel lecture in literature, 1993.* New York: Knopf.

Nainby, K. E., & Pea, J. B. (2003). Immobility in mobility: Narratives of social class, education and paralysis. *Educational Foundations, 17*, 19–36.

Pelias, R. J. (2000). The critical life. *Communication Education, 49*, 220–228.

Pensoneau-Conway, S. L. (2009). Desire and passion as foundations for teaching and learning: A pedagogy of the erotic. *Basic Communication Course Annual, 21*, 173–206.

Perkins, S. (1994). Toward a dramatic theory of instructional communication. *Communication Education, 43*, 222–235.

Pineau, E. L. (1994). Teaching is performance: Reconceptualizing a problematic metaphor. *American Educational Research Journal, 31*, 3–25.

Prividera, L. C. (2004). Assessing sensitivity: A critical analysis of gender in teaching basic communication courses. *Basic Communication Course Annual, 16*, 195–229.

Rodriguez, J. I., & Cai, D. (1994). When your epistemology gets in the way: A response to Sprague. *Communication Education, 43*, 263–272.

Sprague, J. (1992). Expanding the research agenda for instructional communication: Raising some unasked questions. *Communication Education, 41*, 1–25.

Sprague, J. (1993). Retrieving the research agenda for communication education: Asking the pedagogical questions that are "embarrassments to theory." *Communication Education, 42*, 106–122.

Sprague, J. (1994). Ontology, politics, and instructional communication research: Why we can't just "agree to disagree" about power. *Communication Education, 43*, 273–290.

Treinen, K. P., & Warren, J. T. (2001). Antiracist pedagogy in the basic course: Teaching cultural communication as if whiteness matters. *Basic Communication Course Annual, 13*, 46–76.

Warren, J. T. (2001a). Doing whiteness: On the performative dimensions of race in the classroom. *Communication Education, 50*, 91–108.

Warren, J. T. (2001b). Performing whiteness differently: Rethinking the abolitionist project. *Educational Theory, 51*, 451–466.

Warren, J. T., & Hytten, K. (2004). The faces of whiteness: Pitfalls and the critical democrat. *Communication Education, 53*, 321–340.

Wood, A. F., & Fassett, D. L. (2003). Remote control: Identity, power and technology in the communication classroom. *Communication Education, 52*, 286–296.

The (Critical) Pedagogy of Communication and the (Critical) Communication of Pedagogy

16

Leda Cooks

It is the end of a long and bumpy semester for all of us in my community-based learning course on race, ethnicity, and media literacy. For many years, students enrolled in some version of this course have studied the dynamics of race and power in society and in their lives and then worked with kids at a local "underperforming" and underresourced school on the topics of race, ethnicity, and nationality in their own lives and in the media. As these conversations take place and the learning becomes the teaching and vice versa, the performance of education as it typically occurs in the classroom is interrupted, the context changed, the roles mixed up, and the theories taken up and embodied across cultural contexts. At the end of the program, the children produce public service announcements on the topic, and we edit and show them in various venues: at their school, during "open house" for parents, at the university, and on the local cable access television channel. The class- and semester-long program is a lot of work for all involved: physical work, certainly, but mental and emotional work as well. It is the dimensions of that "labor" of learning—its production and evaluation as education—that lead me to question the ways we measure and define our teaching. Where do we locate pedagogy? How do we decide what and when something really important is known?

How does a teacher or "assessment administrator" break down the joy, anger, frustration, love, self-reflexivity, and transformation that my students expressed in video documentation of the process throughout the semester and in their taped (private) interviews and focus groups? As past students in the course still struggle with the meaning of the class and its impact on their lives, the puzzle grows larger when we include the middle school students, teachers, and administrators I have worked with over the years, as well as the parents and local community. All these relationships are pedagogical and all make the experience possible. But from the standpoint of instructional communication, what exactly makes this experience educative? Can we break it down into variables of immediacy? As one example, did my undergraduate students' frustration with the middle schoolers grow from their lack of experience with behavioral alteration techniques? (McCroskey, Richmond, Plax, & Kearney, 1985). Or perhaps there were other cultural expectations at work in their understanding of discipline and, moreover, of what constitutes knowledge of the media and their everyday lives.

And what about resistance? How do the segmentation and police enforcement of student bodies and of education, the standardization of knowledge through repeated everyday tests, and the elimination of creative curricula (and courses in music, health, art, physical education, etc.) contribute to middle school student resistance to schooling in general? How does one explain the confrontation of the students in my class with their own (racial, class, education) privileges not only in our university classroom but also in the context of their relationships with students from backgrounds far different from their own? Communication research in instructional contexts has produced techniques useful for preventing and managing resistance (Kearney & Plax, 1992; Kearney, Plax, Smith, & Sorensen, 1988; McCroskey et al., 1985), but how might educators learn from resistance about their own biases and values? How might they learn that resistance is occasionally educative, useful, and necessary for mental health and growth?

Starting with these questions, this chapter introduces the reader to an area of scholarship and teaching within the arena of communication, education, and cultural studies that combines ideas and concepts from critical pedagogy, cultural studies, and performance studies as well as interpretive and critical communication theory. Although subsumed in this volume within communication and instruction, what I heretofore refer to as critical communication pedagogy (CCP) is not specifically tied to teaching or to formal sites of instruction. Rather, it has as its goal a critique of the various manifestations of knowledge as sites of power and privilege, the uses of communication to secure or resist power, and the ability of communicative practices to invite change and allow spaces for agency and intervention in the hardened categories of education and schooling as a formal institutional practice. In other words, CCP offers a space for self-reflexivity[1] and critique in one's teaching and research, but always as a turning toward other places for action toward social justice. CCP is critical pedagogy *in*, *of*, and *for* communication. As such, it is positioned *in* and among discourses and performances, texts and bodies, processes (teaching/learning, knowing/doing) and products (education, evaluation, employment), and dialectics and dichotomies. Similarly, CCP is a critical pedagogy *of* communication; therefore, it is located in what it critiques, both as big "C" (disciplinary) and little "c" communication in educational contexts. Finally, CCP is a critical pedagogy *for* communication in that it moves beyond critique both in reflexivity and in advocacy for dialogic and democratic discursive forms.

In this chapter, I identify and briefly lay out the various influences on and concerns of CCP with the caveat that the area itself is yet (and always) in formation. Thus, my characterization of CCP is designed to introduce you to a set of concerns with an eye toward possibilities and to ask questions in the hope that the chapter might open up some conversations about the need for and future of such an area of study and practice. In particular, I identify a need for reflection on the structure not only of institutions of education (schools and the academy) and their implications for the formation of citizen/subjects/employees but also the structuring of epistemologies we use to make sense of those formations. In the following two sections, I discuss the primary ideas in critical pedagogy and communication theory that have influenced CCP through a cross-disciplinary body of scholarship whose main objectives can be found in the analysis and critique of power, identity, culture, and schooling toward social justice and social change.

Critical Pedagogy

The movement for progressive education in the United States can perhaps be traced back to the 1840s and Horace Mann's "radical" idea that education should be available to all (rather than only wealthy) children as a means to ensure a united citizenry. Yet it was not until the early 20th century and Dewey's (1938) writings on the ill fit between schooling and the experience of learning (or, for Dewey, experience *as* learning) that a larger critique of the educational system emerged.[2] Whereas the progressive movement failed to emphasize the inequities across race, class, and gender in the structures of schooling and society, the hidden curriculum movement in the 1960s and 1970s critiqued the discriminatory race and gender bias of school curricula (see Martin, 1997). Throughout these years, the radical school reform movement split into liberal and conservative traditions and attempted to come up with alternative means of educating students, with vastly different objectives and purposes (Livingstone, 1970).

A somewhat more united academic critique of schooling in the United States came in the 1980s on the heels of Paulo Freire's (1970) *Pedagogy of the Oppressed*. In this book, Freire argued that the traditional method of lecturing to students was inherently oppressive and inhumane, positioning the teacher as all-knowing and the student as a "blank slate." Freire named this tradition banking education: a method of teaching wherein a direct deposit of "knowledge" is inserted into a student's mind. He contrasted banking education with a *humanizing* method of *problem posing*. Problem posing asked students to indicate what issues and concerns they had and what they wanted to change in their community. Lessons were then constructed based on the knowledge students already held and what they wanted to know.

While Freire's concerns lay with empowering the oppressed as agents of their own learning and liberation, a more modernist and structural (Marxist) critique of schooling known as "critical pedagogy" emerged from scholars[3] in critical economics (Bowles & Gintis, 1976), education (Apple, 1996; Giroux, 1988; Kincheloe, 2008; Kozol, 1992; McLaren, 1998), linguistics (Chomsky, 2000), sociology (Aronowitz, 2000), cultural and postcolonial studies (Grossberg, 1994; Hall, 1997; hooks, 1994; Sandoval, 2000; Spivak, 1993; West, 1996), and literary studies (Gallop, 1995; Karamcheti, 1995; Zavarzadeh, 1992). Prominent in the critical/cultural analyses were themes of oppression and liberation, both accomplished through education, whether mind dulling, authoritarian, dictatorial, and one-way or creative, transformative, emancipatory, and dialogic. For the most part, these scholars focused on the ways schools socialized students into the maintenance of hegemonic structures of society, through creating and containing knowledge, and then dividing it up, assigning it value, and doling it out to those who could afford it financially and as a matter of social capital. Most of the early works were aimed at the macrostructures responsible for inequities in education and across society, and emphasis was placed on critique of these structures *as* pedagogy.

Thus, critical pedagogy had/has as its core a concern with social justice and the role of critique in changing the educational system toward democratic engagement in learning, radical critique of injustice, and openness toward other (diverse) ways of knowing than the dominant epistemologies favored in educational institutions. Critical pedagogy can be explicated through its concentration on the different dimensions of power, identity, and difference at work inside the classroom, as well as the social, cultural, national, and global networks (Castells et al., 1999; Giroux & Giroux, 2004) that give rise to commonsense knowledge of democracy, citizenship, race, gender, sexuality, civility, and merit (among many other ideas). As the critical and cultural scholars cited above turned their attention to the "problem" of education (primarily in the United States, the United Kingdom, and Australia), they analyzed the strategic places of education as well as the ways such places produced and schooled bodies in conjunction with other institutions to maintain hegemonic structures of race, class, gender, sexuality, religion, and ability, among other social categories of identity.

Citing this connection among structures, identities, and pedagogies, Giroux (1994) notes,

> [Critical] pedagogy . . . signals how questions of audience, voice, power, and evaluation actively work to construct particular relations between teachers and students, institutions and society, and classrooms and communities. . . . Pedagogy in the critical sense illuminates the relationship among knowledge, authority, and power. (p. 30)

Following from this relationship and the concerns articulated above, another key focus of critical pedagogy is on student resistance and the ways in which desire and creativity are managed, controlled, and disciplined into submission or, more often, apathy. Calling into question the emphasis on disciplining bodies, critical educators are interested in the myriad strategies students use to distance themselves from oppressive circumstances in the classroom. Rather than submitting themselves to mind-numbing drills for standardized tests or to curricula that not only ignore their culture but require that they live by (up to) the standards of the dominant group, some students find outlets for their creativity in mimicry, sarcasm, or composing alternative texts and performances for their peers. Other students simply "play dumb" (Shor, 1992), an activity that most teachers fail to recognize as resistance and even when recognizing it fail to question why such a strategy might be employed.

Critiquing Critical Pedagogy

The triumvirate of knowledge, authority, and power that has characterized much of critical pedagogy has also been the source of debate among its supporters and critics (and critic-supporters) (e.g., Delpit, 1996; Ellsworth, 1992; Lather, 1991; Keating, 2007). Some of the early writing in critical pedagogy held a fairly simplistic view of power as contained in teachers and other authority figures and their use of authority against students (e.g., Aronowitz & Giroux, 1986; McLaren, 1993). Teachers were the oppressors and students the oppressed; students could be liberated only through teachers giving up their power in favor of the democratic classroom. Postmodern, postcolonial, and feminist pedagogy scholars (and some critical race scholars writing in this area) felt that such bipolar arguments failed to acknowledge the dynamics of discursive power (Foucault, 1977, 1980), whether located in raced, gendered, sexualized, and so on, identities (Delpit, 1996; Ellsworth, 1992; hooks, 1994; Karamcheti, 1995; Luke, 1992;

Nieto, 1992) or fragmented and never completely embodied in the "essence" of teacher or student (Gore, 1992). Feminist critical pedagogues also introduced a more nuanced understanding of student (and teacher) resistance as part of desire, and as located in relationships (not positions) and contexts (Gallop, 1995; Kelly, 1997).

Still, perhaps the most popular critique of the fathers of critical pedagogy and their reliance on Marxist and critical theory was launched by those teachers and academics who felt that this body of work failed to address the everyday experiences and struggles of teachers who sympathized with their cause but could not *use* the theory. The call to apply critical pedagogy in the context of actual classroom interaction[4] was met with some occasional examples and anecdotes (e.g., Giroux & Giroux, 2004; hooks, 1994), but these were used to solidify the claims of theory, rather than as moments for exploration. Although there have been some notable exceptions in feminist studies and linguistics, most cultural studies scholars continue to address the classroom as a confluence of group identities and social structures and use critical pedagogical theory on a macrosocial level.

Apart from the territorial battles over which power relations are determined in the schools, the notion of empowering students and teachers has been viewed as problematic from a postmodern standpoint. Power emerged as a problem for theorists commenting on schooling and communication curriculum in postmodern society (e.g., Sprague, 1992, 1993), while power has remained a necessity for those who argue for social action research and emancipatory politics (e.g., Lather, 1991; McLaren, 1994; Zavarzadeh, 1992). Giroux and McLaren (1994) argued,

> Ideology needs to be understood as lived experience constructed as common sense, and hegemony as the process whereby students not only unwittingly consent to domination but sometimes find pleasurable the form and content through which such domination is manifested. Knowledge cannot be theorized in terms of rationality, nor can ignorance be relegated to the status of inadequate or inappropriate information or to distorted communication. Such a view denies that ideology is fundamentally related to the politics of pleasure, the typography of the body, and the production of desire. (p. 169)

The view of power expressed in this position is that of multiple sites of domination and resistance and of possible openings and spaces for emancipation through critiquing the discursive and situated practices that position both body and mind.

However, what does it mean to identify local contexts and moments of interaction in the context of the modernist goals of a liberatory pedagogy? First, locating practices and discussing them as critical pedagogy precludes a reflective look at the nature of teacher-as-educator. Gore (1992) argued that "no matter what one's political position, it is difficult to conceptualize educating others without also adhering to a certain conception of change or process" (p. 122). The democratic tradition of education in the United States assumes an antithetical relationship between authoritarian control/discipline and the autonomous individual capable of exercising freedom of choice. Liberal education presumes that participation equals education; critical pedagogy assumes that critical involvement on the part of teachers and students will lead to the undoing of hierarchical (and patriarchal) authority and create new spaces for learning. Neither approach has examined critically the power of pedagogy itself.

Deetz (1992) contends that "so called 'empowerment' and 'participation plans' may in fact most often occur in situations of hegemony" (p. 14). He further asserts that communication analyses can help demonstrate how these complex processes work. When students don't engage in the dialogue as asked, or when they participate too much, teachers (and classmates) tend to place them in categories of "good" or "bad" students. Sprague (1992) also comments on the need for research in education to place greater emphasis on communication as essential to the process of learning. Research that explores the constitutive processes through which critical involvement in education occurs, and through which power relations are constructed, makes communication central to critical pedagogical critique.

"Ideas" of Communication and Critique

The meanings of communication held by those who study and teach it play an important role in the ways an area of theory and practice is understood, and so, in what follows, I elaborate several ideas and metaphors for the process. In light of the important role they play in debates about the meaning of dialogue, the various understandings of the place and role of communication in critique should be discussed to better understand the perspectives advanced through CCP as well as debates among those who practice it over its goals and achievement thereof. Communication is most often defined as a transactional process through which meaning is made—the characterization of that meaning, as symbol, as message, or as power, as well as where and how and whose meaning is made evident play out in our notions of teaching, of learning, and of education and its assessment. Many metacommunication theoretical analyses (e.g., Baxter, 2006; Carey, 1989; Shepherd, St. John, & Striphas, 2006) have discussed the various metaphors of communication and their corresponding meanings and implications for theory, research, and practice. Although too numerous to discuss here, these metametaphorical analyses allow for a step back from our theorizing about communication for a bigger picture of what we have created and still might create.

Peters (1999) offers a historical look at the *idea* of communication and what it might represent in terms of Western philosophy, ontology, and epistemology. Drawing from the texts of Socrates and Jesus, Peters (1999) describes two general (Western) ideas about communication: as dialogue and as dissemination. Where dialogue (fashioned as Eros) denotes love and care for the uniqueness and particularity of the individual, dissemination cares not for the special case or the particular justness of a single cause. Jesus offered the same message to the multitudes (as represented in the Gnostic Gospels) in the hope, Peters argues, that those who have ears will hear. Given the impossibility of perfect communication (the matching of souls in dialogue), the more moral ideal of communication is as dissemination. Here, all are treated equally (if not always understood completely). Dialogue, however, can be both loving and brutish, demanding reciprocity when the gift of communication is given.

For critical communication theorists concerned with social justice, this distinction raises two important issues:

1. On whose shoulders do calls for dialogue and the articulation of voices that have been silenced place the burden of understanding? Ellsworth (1997) describes "understanding" content in the classroom context as sometimes a process of teachers demanding that their students "stand under" them, that is, engage in knowledge on the teacher's terms.

2. Is the hope for true dialogue too idealistic? However, if we turn to dissemination as the means to social justice, we can also see that the care for the multitudes most often translates into justice for those who are best represented: those who are members of the dominant culture.

For teachers and scholars engaged in critical work for social change, a careful look at the ways calls for dialogue can prefigure notions of individualism, and the importance of good (i.e., participatory) behavior, is called for, even as we must be aware of the danger of the voices lost in the crowd—those who fall into the cracks of "the system." Educational justice calls for an ethics of universal care and equal treatment; communication (or pedagogy) as dissemination is, after all, the purest form of democracy.

But democracy is also about dialogue, and to the extent that voice, participation, and representation are key to governance, it remains integral to ideas of citizenship. Here, too, the notion of a critical citizenry is directly linked to calls for dialogue in critical pedagogy (Freire, 1998; Giroux & Giroux, 2004; Lather, 1991; McLaren, 1993) and in CCP (Fassett & Warren, 2007). The tensions between dissemination and dialogue undergird the ethics of critical work in education and elsewhere and are sometimes debated in questions over what counts as critical work for social justice, the differentiation between critique and critical pedagogy, and on a broader level, what counts as good teaching.

Both of these seemingly antithetical ideas are held together in another important metaphor for communication: communication as gift. Shepherd (2006) observes that *munia*, or "gifts and services," is the root of the word *communication*. For Shepherd, communication is a gift of the *self*, freely given to one and all in an act of dissemination. At the same time, however, this gift giving is both an act of interdependence and a "sharing" of self. It is, after all, a dialogue. Gifts are about dialogue, too, in their implication of exchange. For Shepherd, and for seemingly most communication theorists, the self can give itself up to the other only if that other recognizes the "giver" as a self.

All communication, according to this view, is about (self/gift) exchange, and indeed we see traces of this metaphor in each of the subfields: interpersonal/relationship theories, intercultural theories, group communication theories, and so on. Exchanges of gifts are also transactions, with values placed on the appropriateness of the gift for the relationship. Here, the focus on the object—the gift, the message, and so on—exceeds and stands apart from the relationship itself. Its value is created by the market to be accumulated, saved, and counted. Just as dialogue can be seen to demand reciprocity, this form of gift giving implies and in fact needs a response to be recognized as a gift (for more on the circulation of gifts, see Bourdieu, 1997; Derrida, 1995, among others).

And so what does any of this have to do with pedagogy? If we extend the metaphor of the gift to pedagogy as gift (perhaps even more appropriate), we see that both dialogue and dissemination have an important place in ideas about what it means to engage in critical work for social justice. I will take this up in the final sections of the chapter, but for now, it is important to note that teaching as dissemination can imply the standardization of valid and reliable techniques as well as the Gnostic ethic of "scattering seeds" of education in a way that values all forms of knowledge equally. Of course, any teacher-researcher in education and communication may believe both, but it is the emphasis on one or the other that leads us to highly divergent views of power in the classroom.

In past decades, teachers and scholars in communication who focused on the role that power, identity, and embodiment played in their classrooms found little in the communication education and instructional communication literature that examined these dynamics. The power inherent in the socializing process of education, as well as its epistemological biases, was not reflected in the hypotheses tested and variables analyzed in the various communication research journals. Anytime a social phenomenon (relationship, group, organization) is broken down into constituent parts, they argued, it is much like focusing on the materials that make up the paints, canvas, and artist rather than on the painting itself.

These researcher-teachers came from a wide variety of areas of study within the communication discipline, but most, if not all, were critical scholars who questioned the dynamics of power in their classrooms and institutions (e.g., Cooks, 1993; Halualani, Chitgopekar, Morrison, & Dodge, 2004; Jackson & Heckman, 2002; Johnson & Bhatt, 2003; Pineau, 1994; Simpson, 2003; Warren, 2001). Moreover, they questioned the exercise of power in the process and product of research in educational contexts and, indeed, throughout the field, where one dominant cultural bias was made to stand for the experiences of an increasingly diverse country. In a discipline that prided itself on its relevance and importance in everyday lives, some scholars began asking, "Whose experiences? Whose lives?"

Others found, as Sprague (1992) put it, a vast gap between the research and actual teaching of instructional communication scholars. Sprague called for instructional communication scholars to teach their research and research their teaching, but with the pervasive bias toward scientific research, self-examination and theorizing about one's own practices (autoethnography) hardly seemed possible. Nonetheless, as the field shifted toward acceptance of alternative epistemologies and methodologies, Sprague's call to action began to be answered in the form of critical, performance, and autoethnographic writing (Alexander, 1999; Boyd, 1999; Pineau, 1994; Warren, 2001) about communication and education. Although I and others have called this area of research and teaching CCP, it has gone by a variety of names and will continue to do so. Those who write about CCP also may call themselves performance studies, cultural studies, intercultural, or interracial communication scholars. To them and for me, this affiliation, like many that I hold, is simply a connection of relationships and objectives held in common concern. For CCP, as with critical pedagogy, interdisciplinarity is central to answering questions that can only benefit from multiple perspectives.

Critical Communication Pedagogy

CCP is dedicated to the study of communication in instructional contexts to make changes in the ways we talk and think about teaching and learning: to alter the structures of schooling that train students in accordance with social class, race, gender, perceived ability, and sexuality; to open up the possibilities for different ways of knowing; and finally, to find different ways of communicating that knowledge beyond textbooks and lesson plans and into communities beyond the institution. CCP is about teaching and research as each informs the other and keeps praxis integral to deepening theory. The moral aspect, always present in critical work, demands a self-reflexivity in teaching and research; although CCP scholars (and indeed critical scholars in all fields) may differ over what it means to be a critical academic, as well as over what constitutes change toward social justice, most would recognize themselves and their work in this description.

CCP places communication as central to any understanding of what it is that we do when we teach and when we learn. That is, our expectations of what should take place in any instructional context are created in and through communication. Focusing on actual classroom interaction, CCP questions the exercise of power in the classroom in the service of student control (Fassett & Warren, 2004, 2007; Warren, 2003). Where variable analytic research programs have allowed, for example, a focus on power in the classroom (McCroskey & Richmond, 1992), teacher competence, teacher satisfaction, communication apprehension, or, on a more positive note, classroom immediacy strategies (Andersen, 1979; Frymier, 1994), CCP scholars are interested in what happens when teachers and students view the classroom as a richly layered context for possibility. If, as CCP insists, we construct our identities and, to some extent, our contexts through communication, programs of research such as the "Power in the Classroom" series, and its corresponding uses of behavior alteration techniques for classroom management, create the picture of a classroom where control and constraint are the primary needs of educators. Indeed, as any teacher will note, sometimes classrooms *are* out of control and teachers feel that they must fight daily just to complete their lesson plan. But the dominance of this metaphor and its ubiquitous rhetoric can leave teachers and students in the position of reacting in their entrenched roles of en/forcer of knowledge and recipient. Among teachers who have expressed powerlessness or who feel that they have lost control over the classroom and their students' education, there is also the implication that teachers desperately need power to do their job effectively.

So CCP asks, how is power constructed so that it might be gained or lost among populations that have traditionally been denied political and educational agency? That is, the poststructuralist move to decenter and disavow power assumes that one had power in the first place (Kendall & Wickham, 1999). For a (Latina, disabled, young) teacher to disavow her own power is to deny the subjectivity she never had; thus, despite the "apolitical" means, the consequences of education place the teacher in a precariously powerful position. For these reasons, the politics of location and the engagement of one's position in *context* are imperative to both the teaching and research of CCP.

In their book-length treatment of the topic, Fassett and Warren (2007) identify several commitments of CCP that rely on a constructionist and critical view of communication. Within these perspectives are the core concerns about identity and power discussed throughout this chapter. Regarding the commitment to a constitutive or social constructionist approach to communication, Fassett and Warren observe that for critical communication pedagogues, (1) identity is created through communication and thus is performed and performative in the actions that "make" a "star" pupil, a "C" student, and so on; (2) culture is created through socialization and therefore is central to pedagogy; (3) language and associated acts of naming our worlds create both presences and absences that are gaps in our pedagogy that we should analyze; (4) since all (and not just some) communication makes our reality, everyday practices are as important as more momentous events in the educational process; and (5) dialogue is "both metaphor and method for our relationships with others" (p. 54). As these commitments demonstrate, the focus of CCP is both on the process (the *doing*) of education and on what is made meaningful in and as a result of that process. Intimately connected to the imperative to study communication as meaningful, then, is the traditionally "critical" imperative of CCP scholars to identify power struggles in the name of social justice and change. To the above focus on communication as constitutive, Fassett and Warren (2007) add CCP's commitments to study and teaching about power: (1) power is dynamic and complex and is always more than just a tool or skill set for teachers to employ; (2) power (deployed as communication) creates structures and social systems; (3) given #2, CCP teachers and researchers hold a self-reflexive view of their own location and pedagogical praxis, as well as an abiding interest in and concern for the subjectivity and agency of others; and (4) we must analyze, describe, and critique the use of power in an effort to change power relations in educational contexts.

Fassett and Warren's (2007) commitments revolve around study of the *construction* of power and identity in the classroom and differentiate CCP from critical pedagogy. In CCP, both formal and mundane practices become the focus of study and attention: How do teachers and students make sense of what is largely unremarkable, as well as those moments in which something occurs to break the routine? In most writing on critical pedagogy (for exceptions, see Ellsworth, 1992; Keating, 2007), teacher and student roles and practices are commented on but remain largely abstract: The focus may be on cultural artifacts of education (e.g., movies, policies), or on the impact of educational socialization into race, class, gender, sexuality, ability, and other identity categories.

Beyond the concentration on power and identity in educational contexts, the body, embodiment, and performance hold a central place in CCP. Here, too, there are both similarities and differences to critical pedagogy. While certainly many critical pedagogical scholars have focused on the bodies of students (hooks, 1994; Giroux, 1988; McLaren, 1997), and occasionally of teachers (although, tellingly, this scholarship has come primarily from white female teachers and female teachers of color, e.g., Ellsworth, 1992; Gallop, 1995; hooks, 1994; Kelly, 1997), studies of the body as performance and as performative[5] are rare (for an exception, see Giroux & Shannon, 1997). In CCP, a primary object of focus has been the ways education and educating are embodied—as raced, sexed, gendered, aged, and so on. CCP scholars are interested in the forces that act on bodies to shape and give meaning to roles of student and teacher. Alexander's (1999) autoethnographic study of identity construction among African American students and professors demonstrated not only the importance of communication in creating and maintaining African American male identities but also that these identities were themselves complexly located in relations and contexts that could best be studied as *audienced* performance. Simpson's (2007) careful attention to her response to a student in a vulnerable moment for both of them allows for an analysis of the ways they both are situated, accountable, and responsible for the knowledge about racial identities they (together) produce. Similarly, Fassett and Morella (2008) focus on the creation and performance of (dis)ability as performative, that is, as an interruption in the roles of teacher and student, author and performer, knower and known that resituates not only the authors of the article but the roles of reader, teacher, student, and scholar. All these articles, and many others, bring together body, embodiment, and performance in the form of performance ethnography. While it is not my intention to narrow the range of methodologies in CCP scholarship, I turn now to a brief mention of performance ethnography as important to the development of CCP thus far.

Performance, Performativity, and Ethnography in Critical Communication Pedagogy

At the beginning of most of the classes I teach, I put out a spread. I have cooked, baked, and brought to my students soups and stews, casseroles, quiches, cookies, cakes, crepes—many a feast. As you might imagine, the students are initially surprised by this change in protocol. Once they get over the initial shock, they gather around the food in appreciation, laughter, and celebration. Once seated, we begin class. As I have done this over the past several years, I have received many comments from students. Most tell me that the food changes the atmosphere of the class; they relax and feel more comfortable discussing difficult and sometimes risky subjects.

For other students, the introduction of food into the classroom somehow reconfigures my authority in a negative way. I become too informal, frivolous about the topic, and somehow less erudite. I have read these sentiments in anonymous evaluations, but the fact remains that the food, my serving of it, and its foregrounded presence in the classroom has changed the relationship between bodies and knowledge. The place of the food—labored over and given freely—in this context of power upsets the spatial equation of mind, body, and knowledge. My celebration of food in this space of knowledge connects mind and body in a way that most of us try to avoid. On the other hand, a respected colleague allows no food or beverages in her 3-hour seminar, perhaps to preserve the integrity of the space. The sacred mind or the profane body: these oppositions play out in academic spaces and in academic bodies (Cooks, 2007) as performances and as performative of teaching and learning.

I mention performativity in the scene above as a site of rupture: an interruption in the everyday *performances* of the classroom that opens up the potential for making new and different meanings of the space (Madison, 2006). By focusing on the moment of difference, as opposed to, say, evaluation of the lesson or of student resistance to the content, I have opened up the possibility for different ways of knowing pedagogy and for understanding what different arrangements of spaces, bodies, and power might produce. As a research and teaching methodology, performance ethnography engages bodies and spaces and acts as powerful and purposeful—as accountable, although never fully knowable.

This sense of possibility inherent in the everyday and the links between meanings, practices, bodies, and (spatial) locations make performance ethnography an important part of CCP research. Indeed, as Denzin (2006) notes,

> Critical [communication] pedagogy, folded into and through performance (auto) ethnography attempts to disrupt and deconstruct these cultural and methodological practices performatively in the name of a more just, democratic and egalitarian society. Democracy-as-citizenship is radically performative, dialogic, transgressive, and pedagogical. (p. 333)

It is just this focus on moments and spaces, through embodiment, performance, and reflexivity, that positions CCP to answer the call for critical pedagogy to focus not only on pedagogy and power but on pedagogy *as* power—as creative, shifting, unfinished—and constituted through communication. Nevertheless, within this new area of CCP, there exist substantial differences over what constitutes critique and praxis in light of a commitment to social justice and social change. Where the majority of CCP has focused on critical "moments," that is, in the classroom or other interactions that occur within the educational context, their analysis has focused on the dynamics of the context and the ways in which the meanings made reflect outward on the roles, social and cultural structures, and institutions of education and identity (Fassett & Warren, 2004; Warren, 2003). Theory and practice are connected in these studies through self-reflexivity, performance, and critical theory. Whether implied or stated outright, social justice for these scholars occurs through reflection on theories, performances, and practices in educational settings. Critical theory's commitment to sites of struggle for the purposes of social change is answered through naming the struggle and through making visible to students and teachers, researchers and scholars, what has hitherto been hidden. For these CCP scholars, pedagogy/communication as dialogue is the moral imperative: the meeting of self with self in conversation.

For others working in this area, reflexivity and dialogue are not enough. While not forsaking dialogue, their interest is more in the pursuit of social justice through ruptures that create structural change (Conquergood,

1991; Simpson, 2003). Much as street and other forms of political theater have raised awareness outside the classroom that has led to change, these scholars are interested in educational and community justice. Some have combined CCP and community-based learning (Cooks & Scharrer, 2007; Cooks, Scharrer, & Paredes, 2004; Jovanovic, 2003). Others work with students to enact policy changes in media governance and elsewhere (Castañeda, 2008). For some CCP practitioners, critique allows for a detachment and distancing that must be bridged through the combination of self-awareness and collective action toward change.

Given such a range of commitments and contexts, CCP is not limited to performance and/or ethnographic methodologies. Rhetorical studies, critical discourse analysis, cultural studies analyses, and critical historical/genealogical studies are among the many methodological approaches to the ways in which education is made meaningful inside and outside the classroom. Where the emphasis is on relational dialectics over dichotomous categories of powerful/powerless, oppressed/oppressor, epistemology/ontology, or even creativity/constraint, methods that place the contextual—moments, tactics, language, interaction—in connection with structures and institutions are imperative.

Conclusion

We tend to ask, with the best of intentions: now that we know this, what are we going to do with it? The question might become, even as it seems to be right there, on the tips of tongues speechless with beauty and terror: now that we are unknown and deprived of knowingness, unlearned and learning, what are we going to do about it? (Pollock, 2006, p. 328)

Regardless of outside pressures for assessment, teachers constantly question if and how the educative process is working. The way those questions are posed, their framing as problems in need of solutions, as meanings embedded in relationships, or as complex flows of power, all influence the picture that we paint of education and of pedagogy (of teachers, students, and the knowledge that they together create). The end-of-semester questions that open this chapter are not answered definitively by CCP, but there is room for asking them.

Still, and despite our critical or radical inclinations, in the very assertion that we should not be perceived as Authorities, or as bearers of Truth, teachers are inscribed in the discourse of education. Part of "good" teaching is the sense that students have learned something—but that something must be packaged as content knowledge for purposes of evaluation and assessment. Good teaching, then, reinscribes the student-teacher relationship through the transference of bodies of knowledge to the willing student (body). Although critical pedagogy envisions the possibilities for articulations of power with, the teacher's role in this process is seldom problematized. If the teacher-student relationship is always already inscribed in the discourse of education, then the teacher can never completely divorce himself or herself from that power position. Hunter argues that "the importance of the teacher-student differentiation" in the "machinery of supervision" cannot be overemphasized (Luke & Gore, 1992, p. 124). Hunter comments that, much like the ethical self-shaping of the cultural elite, "authority is the inescapable product of the pedagogical imperatives and techniques and the purpose-built relations of supervision and correction deployed in the student-teacher couple" (p. 125). Thus, even when teachers do not assign grades, students act toward them in ways that re-create power relations.

Hall (1988) explains that ideology is effective; it frames the struggle over which meanings are naturalized as common sense. Thus, this analysis of the relationship between critical pedagogical thought and educational practices is grounded on the fact that epistemological choices embody power assumptions (Lannaman, 1991). I also recognize that simultaneously to use and to call into question a discourse, as Lather (1991) suggests is necessary, research must challenge dominant modes of learning and thinking while reflecting on its own use of those same interpretive lenses. To accomplish these purposes, future research in the area of CCP must necessarily be a conversation between critic and critique, a reflexive commentary on theory and practice, and, at times, a contradiction between research methods and the ideals of equality and democracy that are at the heart of critical pedagogical inquiry.

In *Reshaping the University: Responsibility, Indigenous Epistemes and the Logic of the Gift*, Rauna Kuokkanen (2007) argues that critical, cultural, and ethnic studies (Native Studies, Latin Studies, etc.) in higher education have recognized alternative cultures but not alternative epistemes.[6] For Kuokkanen, a shift toward indigenous epistemes would entail recognition of all meaning-making (communication) as relational, interdependent, and animated through human and nonhuman forms. For indigenous peoples, all life forms are connected through the logic of the gift. Kuokkanen refers to gifts and gift giving in this sense as the

> manifestation of reciprocity with the natural environment; it reflects the bond of dependency and respect for the natural world. . . . In this system one does not give primarily in order to receive but rather in order to ensure the balance of the world on which the well-being of the entire social order is contingent. (p. 33)

In this sense, Kuokkanen (2007) critiques CCP's metaphorical and foundational commitments to dialogue, dissemination, and gift as not enough. To really recognize and commit to the logic of the gift, for Kuokkanen, is to make a profound epistemological shift—to recognize as pedagogical one's *relational* embeddedness in the natural world. "Giving" here does not mean "giving up" something but rather volunteering an offering as acknowledgment of one's place in a larger web of connections. For CCP, such a shift means that learning about and acknowledging personal and cultural differences might be less important than examining, say, the higher esteem in which we hold reciprocity to other humans than reciprocity in nature, or epistemic assumptions at work in our conversations about ethics and culture. It also means acknowledging that we must include all the elements of our world in our dedication to "social" justice.

As critical scholars, what is our commitment, not only to diverse cultures, but to truly diverse epistemologies? Any movement that advocates a radical break from the way we think, a new understanding of scholarship and who we are, must also take into account the ways that we are sustained and re-created through current knowledge forms. In other words, it might be important to study not only the ways in which we know but also the ways we are intimately connected to and reason *through* what we know. If, as Dewey (1916) has observed, "the primary condition for growth is immaturity" (p. 41), and given that change exists as a condition of stability, new pedagogies must continue to interrogate the relationship between language, knowledge, and oppression.

Notes

1. Self-reflexivity is used here to differentiate between the act of self-reflection, or the examination of one's thoughts, and continuously examining *how* one is thinking and the implications of those thoughts (see Madison, 2006; Meyerhoff, 1982).

2. Notably, female scholars and scholars of color in the early 20th century do not figure into most historical accounts of critical pedagogy or critical literacy in the United States.

3. Please note that this is a very partial list. The critical pedagogy movement emerged at a moment when critical cultural studies was gaining momentum in the United States, and much of the scholarship crossed over into pedagogy.

4. Notably, Freire's student and coauthor, Ira Shor, produced two widely read books: *Critical Teaching in Everyday Life* (1987) and *Empowering Education: Critical Teaching for Social Change* (1992).

5. By performative, I am referring to the mundane actions of everyday life that, repeated over and over, become naturalized as roles (teacher, student, mother, son) and racial, sexual, gendered, and so on, identities. What is important is that performativity also refers to those moments of interruption that bring to light the sense making of common sense.

6. Kuokkanen (2007) describes *episteme* as a "fairly broad and flexible concept that covers aspects of epistemology, philosophy, cosmology, ontology, as well as various practices stemming from these, without being limited by them" (p. 56).

References

Alexander, B. (1999). Performing culture in the classroom: An instructional (auto) ethnography. *Text and Performance Quarterly, 19,* 307–331.

Andersen, J. F. (1979). Teacher immediacy as a predictor of teaching effectiveness. In D. Nimmo (Ed.), *Communication yearbook 3* (pp. 543–559). New Brunswick, NJ: Transaction Books.

Apple, M. W. (1996). *Cultural politics and education.* New York: Teachers College Press.

Aronowitz, S. (2000). *The knowledge factory: Dismantling the corporate university and creating true higher learning.* Boston: Beacon Press.

Aronowitz, S., & Giroux, H. (1986). *Education under siege: The conservative, liberal, and radical debate over schooling.* New York: Routledge.

Baxter, L. (2006). A dialogue. In G. J. Shepherd, J. St. John, & T. Striphas (Eds.), *Communication as . . . Perspectives on theory* (pp. 101–109). Thousand Oaks, CA: Sage.

Bourdieu, P. (1997). Selections from the logic of practice. In A. D. Schrift (Ed.), *The logic of the gift: Toward an ethic of generosity* (pp. 190–230). New York & London: Routledge.

Bowles, S., & Gintis, H. (1976). *Schooling in capitalist America: Educational reform and the contradictions of economic life.* New York: Basic Books.

Boyd, R. (1999). Compromising positions: Or, the unhappy transformations of a "transformative intellectual." *Communication Theory, 9,* 377–401.

Carey, J. W. (1989). *Communication as culture: Essays on media and society.* Winchester, MA: Unwin Hyman.

Castañeda, M. (2008). Transformative learning through community engagement. *Latino Studies, 6,* 319–326.

Castells, M., Flecha, R., Freire, P., Giroux, H. A., Macedo, D., & Willis, P. (1999). *Critical education in the new information age.* Lanham, MD: Rowman & Littlefield.

Chomsky, N. (2000). *Chomsky on miseducation* (Edited and introduced by D. Macedo). New York: Rowman & Littlefield.

Conquergood, D. (1991). Rethinking ethnography: Towards a critical cultural politics. *Communication Monographs, 38,* 179–194.

Cooks, L. (1993). *Critical pedagogy as communication education.* Unpublished dissertation, Ohio University, Athens.

Cooks, L. (2007). Accounting for my teacher's body: What can I teach what can we learn? *Feminist Media Studies, 7,* 299–312.

Cooks, L., & Scharrer, E. (2007). Communicating advocacy: Learning and change in the media literacy and violence prevention project. In L. Frey & K. Carragee (Eds.), *Communication activism: Media and performance activism* (Vol. 2, pp. 129–154). Cresskill, NJ: Hampton Press.

Cooks, L., Scharrer, E., & Paredes, M. (2004). Rethinking learning in service learning: Toward a communication model of learning in community and classroom. *Michigan Journal of Community Service Learning, 10*(2), 44–56.

Deetz, S. (1992). *Democracy in an age of corporate civilization: Developments in communication.* New York: State University of New York Press.

Delpit, L. (1996). *Other people's children: Cultural conflict in the classroom.* New York: New Press.

Denzin, N. (2006). Pedagogy, performance and autoethnography. *Text and Performance Quarterly, 26,* 333–338.

Derrida, J. (1995). *The gift of death* (D. Wills, Trans.). Chicago: University of Chicago Press.

Dewey, J. (1916). *Democracy and education.* New York: Free Press.

Dewey, J. (1938). *Experience and education.* New York: Simon & Schuster.

Ellsworth, E. (1992). Why doesn't this feel empowering? Working through the repressive myths of critical pedagogy. In C. Luke & J. Gore (Eds.), *Feminism and critical pedagogy* (pp. 90–119). New York: Routledge.

Ellsworth, E. (1997). *Teaching positions: Difference, pedagogy, and the power of address.* New York: Teacher's College Press.

Fassett, D. L., & Morella, D. L. (2008). Remaking (the) discipline: Marking the performative accomplishment of (dis)ability. *Text and Performance Quarterly, 28,* 139–156.

Fassett, D. L., & Warren, J. T. (2004). "You get pushed back": The strategic rhetoric of success and failure in higher education. *Communication Education, 53,* 21–39.

Fassett, D. L., & Warren, J. T. (2007). *Critical communication pedagogy.* Thousand Oaks, CA: Sage.

Foucault, M. (1977). *Discipline and punish: The birth of the prison.* London: Allen Lane.

Foucault, M. (1980). *Power/knowledge: Selected interviews and other writings: 1972–1977* (C. Gordon, Ed.; C. Gordon, L. Marshall, J. Mepham, & K. Soper, Trans.). New York: Pantheon Books.

Freire, P. (1970). *Pedagogy of the oppressed.* New York: Herder & Herder.

Freire, P. (1998). *Pedagogy of freedom: Ethics, democracy and civic courage.* Lanham, MD: Rowman & Littlefield.

Frymier, A. B. (1994). A model of immediacy in the classroom. *Communication Quarterly, 42,* 133–144.

Gallop, J. (Ed.). (1995). *Pedagogy: The question of impersonation.* Indianapolis: Indiana University Press.

Giroux, H. A. (1988). *Schooling and the struggle for everyday life.* Minneapolis: University of Minnesota Press.

Giroux, H. A. (1994). *Disturbing pleasures: Learning popular culture.* New York: Routledge.

Giroux, H. A., & Giroux, S. S. (2004). *Take back higher education: Race, youth, and the crisis of democracy in the post–civil rights era.* New York: Palgrave.

Giroux, H. A., & McLaren, P. (Eds.). (1994). *Between borders: Pedagogy and cultural studies.* London: Routledge.

Giroux, H. A., & Shannon, P. (1997). *Education and cultural studies: Toward a performative practice.* New York: Routledge.

Gore, J. (1992). What we can do for you! What can "we" do for "you"? Struggling over empowerment in critical and feminist pedagogy. In C. Luke & J. Gore (Eds.), *Feminism and critical pedagogy* (pp. 54–73). New York: Routledge.

Grossberg, L. (1994). Introduction: Bringin' it all back home: Pedagogy and cultural studies. In H. Giroux & P. McLaren (Eds.), *Between borders: Pedagogy and cultural studies* (pp. 1–25). London: Routledge.

Hall, S. (1988). *The hard road to renewal: Thatcherism and the crisis of the Left.* London: Verso.

Hall, S. (1997). The work of representation. In S. Hall (Ed.), *Representation: Cultural representations and signifying practices* (pp. 13–74). London: Sage.

Halualani, R. T., Chitgopekar, A., Morrison, J. H. T. A., & Dodge, P. S.-W. (2004). Diverse in name only? Intercultural interaction at a multicultural university. *Journal of Communication, 54*(2), 270–286.

hooks, b. (1994). *Teaching to transgress: Education as the practice of freedom.* New York: Routledge.

Jackson, R. J., & Heckman, S. M. (2002). Perceptions of white identity and white liability: An analysis of white student responses to a college campus racial hate crime. *Journal of Communication, 52*(2), 434–450.

Johnson, J., & Bhatt, A. (2003). Gendered and racialized identities and alliances in the classroom: Formations in/of resistive space. *Communication Education, 52,* 230–244.

Jovanovic, S. (2003). Communication as critical inquiry in service-learning. *Academic Exchange Quarterly, 7,* 81–85.

Karamcheti, I. (1995). Caliban in the classroom. In J. Gallop (Ed.), *Pedagogy: The question of impersonation* (pp. 138–146). Indianapolis: Indiana University Press.

Kearney, P., & Plax, T. (1992). Student resistance to control. In V. Richmond & J. C. McCroskey (Eds.), *Power in the classroom: Communication, control, and concern* (pp. 85–100). Hillsdale, NJ: Lawrence Erlbaum.

Kearney, P., Plax, T. G., Smith, V. R., & Sorensen, G. (1988). Effects of teacher immediacy and strategy type on college student resistance to on-task demands. *Communication Education, 37,* 54–67.

Keating, A. (2007). *Teaching transformation: Transcultural classroom dialogues.* New York: Palgrave Macmillan.

Kelly, U. (1997). *Schooling desire: Literacy, cultural politics and pedagogy.* New York: Routledge.

Kendall, G., & Wickham, G. (1999). *Using Foucault's methods.* London: Sage.

Kincheloe, J. (2008). *Critical pedagogy* (2nd ed.). New York: Peter Lang.

Kozol, J. (1992). *Savage inequalities: Children in America's schools.* New York: Harper Perennial.

Kuokkanen, R. (2007). *Reshaping the university: Responsibility, indigenous epistemes and the logic of the gift.* Vancouver, British Columbia, Canada: University of British Columbia Press.

Lannaman, J. W. (1991). Interpersonal communication research as ideological practice. *Communication Theory, 1,* 179–203.

Lather, P. (1991). *Getting smart: Feminist research and pedagogy with/in the postmodern.* New York: Routledge.

Livingstone, D. (1970). Radical school reform [Review article]. *Interchange, 1,* 107.

Luke, C. (1992). Feminist politics in radical pedagogy. In C. Luke & J. Gore (Eds.), *Feminism and critical pedagogy* (pp. 25–53). New York: Routledge.

Luke, C., & Gore, J. (Eds.). (1992). *Feminism and critical pedagogy.* New York: Routledge.

Madison, D. S. (2006). The dialogic performative in critical ethnography. *Text and Performance Quarterly, 26,* 320–324.

Martin, J. R. (1997). *Changing the educational landscape: Philosophy, women and curriculum.* New York: Routledge.

McCroskey, J. W., & Richmond, V. (1992). *Power in the classroom: Communication, control, and concern.* Hillsdale, NJ: Lawrence Erlbaum.

McCroskey, J., Richmond, V., Plax, T., & Kearney, P. (1985). Power in the classroom V: Behavior alteration techniques, communication training and learning. *Communication Education, 34*(3), 214–226.

McLaren, P. (1993). *Schooling as a ritual performance: Towards a political economy of educational symbols and gestures* (2nd ed.). London/New York: Routledge.

McLaren, P. (1994). Multiculturalism and postmodern critique: Toward a pedagogy of resistance and transformation. In H. Giroux & P. McLaren (Eds.), *Between borders: Pedagogy and the politics of cultural studies* (pp. 192–223). New York: Routledge.

McLaren, P. (1997). *Revolutionary multiculturalism: Pedagogies of dissent for the new millennium.* New York: Westview Press.

McLaren, P. (1998). *Life in schools: An introduction to critical pedagogy in the foundations of education* (3rd ed.). New York: Longman.

Myerhoff, B. (1982). Life history among the elderly: Performance, visibility and remembering. In J. Ruby (Ed.), *A crack in the mirror: Reflexive perspectives in anthropology* (pp. 261–286). Philadelphia: University of Pennsylvania Press.

Nieto, S. (1992). *Affirming diversity: The sociopolitical context of multicultural education.* New York: Longman.

Peters, J. D. (1999). *Speaking into the air: A history of the idea of communication.* Chicago: University of Chicago Press.

Pineau, E. L. (1994). Teaching is performance: Reconfiguring a problematic metaphor. *American Educational Research Journal, 31,* 3–25.

Pollock, D. (2006). Marking new directions on performance ethnography. *Text and Performance Quarterly, 26,* 325–329.

Sandoval, C. (2000). *Methodology of the oppressed.* Minneapolis: University of Minnesota Press.

Shepherd, G. (2006). Transcendence. In G. J. Shepherd, J. St. John, & T. Striphas (Eds.), *Communication as . . . Perspectives on theory* (pp. 22–30). Thousand Oaks, CA: Sage.

Shepherd, G. J., St. John, J., & Striphas, T. (Eds.). (2006). *Communication as . . . Perspectives on theory.* Thousand Oaks, CA: Sage.

Shor, I. (1987). *Critical teaching in everyday life.* Chicago: University of Chicago Press.

Shor, I. (1992). *Empowering education: Critical teaching for social change.* Chicago: University of Chicago Press.

Simpson, J. (2003). *I have been waiting: Race in U.S. higher education.* Toronto, Ontario, Canada: University of Toronto Press.

Simpson, J. (2007). "Can't we focus on the good stuff?" The pedagogical distance between comfort and critique. In L. Cooks & J. Simpson (Eds.), *Dis/placing race: Whiteness, pedagogy, performance* (pp. 247–269). Lanham, MD: Lexington Books.

Spivak, G. (1993). *Outside in the teaching machine.* London: Routledge.

Sprague, J. (1992). Expanding the research agenda for instructional communication: Raising some unasked questions. *Communication Education, 41,* 1–25.

Sprague, J. (1993). Retrieving the research agenda for communication education: Asking the pedagogical questions that are "embarrassments to theory." *Communication Education, 42,* 106–122.

Warren, J. T. (2001). Doing whiteness: On the performative dimensions of race in the classroom. *Communication Education, 50,* 91–108.

Warren, J. T. (2003). *Performing purity: Whiteness, pedagogy and the reconstitution of power.* New York: Peter Lang.

West, C. (1996). *The future of the race.* New York: Alfred A. Knopf.

Zavarzadeh, M. (1992). Theory as resistance. In M. Kecht (Ed.), *Pedagogy is politics: Literary theory and critical teaching* (pp. 25–47). Urbana: University of Illinois Press.

Critical/Performative/ Pedagogy **17**

Performing Possibility as a Rehearsal for Social Justice

Bryant Keith Alexander

So I asked students *to show* me what they learned from the assigned textbook reading . . .

and she did a frenetic dance, a choreography of emotion without a resolute ending.

I asked students *to critique* a particular theoretical perspective discussed in class . . .

and he engaged a hermeneutical poetics and wrote a poem without words: symbols, ellipses and an angry exclamation point (Alexander, 1999; Hurlock, 2002).

I asked students *to perform* their understanding of "the other" from the "other's" perspective . . .

and they performed ethnographically derived notes of homeless people, street vendors, day laborers and undocumented immigrants.

and white students performed scenes on racial inequality, while women of color performed aspects of Peggy McIntosh's (1997) "White Privilege and Male Privilege."

and "straight" students performed experiences of gays and lesbians through the ritual act of the marriage ceremony denied in the passing of California's Proposition 8.

I asked students *to engage* strategic action . . .

and they initiated a volunteer program at a local senior citizen's home connecting lonely college students and lonely seniors.

and they participated in immigration protests and gay marriage support rallies in downtown Los Angeles.

and they participated in a "Take Back the Night" march against sexual assault.

and they planned a "Day of Silence" commemorating the social silence on acts of violence against the lesbian, gay, bisexual, transgendered, transsexual, queer (LGBTTQ) community.

and they initiated a "Pens for Pals" program to collect school supplies for underprivileged children in their local communities and abroad.

and they initiated a mentoring program for young black men on campus as both recruitment and retention.

and they staged a sit-in at the Office of the University President to protest the raising of tuition, the conversion from quarters to semesters, and rising parking costs.

I asked students *to enact* the limits of potential and the horizons of possibility . . .

and in a plastic baggy she placed a tampon with menstrual blood next to a picture of her living child born a year earlier, and submitted it as a response—image as actualization and tampon as evidence of a liquid horizon—theorizing outward.

and he performed the experience of his brown Mexican American body trying to cross the border back into California with papers as passport and his body as a contested site—theorizing inward (Alexander, 1999, 2002a, 2002b, 2005).

I asked students to *place their bodies in the text, place their bodies on the line,* and *place their bodies betwixt and between* academic, cultural and political texts . . .

and they began, as I do, to flesh out the promises and possibilities of a critical performative pedagogy.

✶ ✶ ✶

Critical performative pedagogy promotes an active embodiment of doing as a key component of a pedagogical practice toward liberatory ends. Specifically, such practices are geared to having students and participants explore the possibilities of progressive cultural politics by constructing counternarratives to the master narratives of everyday and educational life (Bamberg & Andrews, 2004; Giroux, Lankshear, McLaren, & Peters, 1996), *engaging in active rehearsals of social justice* (Adams, 1997; Adams et al., 2000; Griffiths, 1998; Lea & Sims, 2008; O'Donnell, Pruyn, & Chavez, 2004; Richardson, 1996; Swartz, 2006), and promoting a dialogical performance that "struggles to bring self and other together so that they can question, debate, and challenge one another" on both the local and global levels (Conquergood, 1985, p. 9).

In this chapter, I seek to further outline key contributing logics to critical performative pedagogy as they are variously presented, explore a broadened construction of critical performative pedagogy that rightfully

extends outside the confines of traditional notions of engaging performance in the classroom, and explore the pitfalls and promises of critical
performative pedagogy toward developing a future agenda of its critical
import and application. The chapter necessarily works toward expanding
ways of thinking about critical performative pedagogy. Yet the basic
notion of a pedagogy that actively demands that students analyze social
issues through embodiment and engaged critical reflexivity on their own
positionality in relation to others, with the intent to transform social practice, is consistently present.

Contributing Convictions and Commitments

*Most people are mirrors reflecting the moods and emotions of the
times; few are windows, bringing light to bear on the dark corners
where troubles fester. The whole purpose of education is to turn
mirrors into windows.*

—Sydney J. Harris

In critical performative pedagogy, when students are given the opportunity to embody liberatory practices as a part of the pedagogical
endeavor, it makes real in them their potential to both see difference and
make a difference in the world. It is then that the reflective mirrors of theoretical postulating become refractive windows of possibility—altering
the wave of learning from just intellectual reverberations to seismically
dynamize the possibilities of education as an active tool for transformed
democratic practices reaching beyond the classroom. In the progressive
theories and techniques of his *Theatre of the Oppressed* variously trans-
posed, Augusto Boal (1979, 1995, 1998, 2002) uses the active gerund of
dynamizing as both description and dictate, to make the imagined possibility of transformation active and energetic, a forceful energy that
embodies and motivates change to do, not to make do. In his work, Boal
(1985) argues that "all theatre is necessarily political. Because all the activities of man are political and theatre is one of them" (p. ix); and so is performance and pedagogy as they interplay in the subject of our focus.

Critical/performative/pedagogy (CPP), like the contributing theoretical
antecedents of its construction—critical social and race theory (Darder &
Torres, 2004; Delgado, 1995; Ladson-Billings, 2000; Madison, 2005); performance, performance studies, and performativity (Conquergood, 1998, 2002;
Diamond, 1996; Hamera, 2005; Madison & Hamera, 2006; Pollock, 2006;
Reinelt & Roach, 1992; Schechner, 2006); and critical pedagogy (Freire, 1974,
1998, 2002; Giroux, 2001; Giroux & Shannon, 1997; Kincheloe, 2008;
McLaren, 1991, 1998, 1999; McLaren & Kincheloe, 2007; Shor, 1987; Wink,
2005)—engages an excavation of cultural knowing in the relationship

between the student, the classroom, and society in an alchemy of commitments at the nexus of this interdisciplinary project. In terms of critical theory, critical performative pedagogy engages in practices of unearthing "hidden forces and ambiguities that operate beneath appearances" in everyday cultural life and between borders of human experience as this relates to the differentiation of power among world citizens (Madison, 2005, p. 13). It also works toward "questioning uncomfortable liberal premises" that seem to undergird and guide the nature of human social relations pivoting on the materiality of raced and gendered bodies (Delgado, 1995, p. xiii).

As performance methodology, CPP actively engages "a deep kinesthetic attunement, developed through a rehearsal, that allows us to attend to experiential phenomena in an embodied, rather than purely intellectualized way" (Pineau, 1995, p. 46). As such, CPP engages the politics of performance (Cohen-Cruz, 2006; Conquergood, 1991, 2006; Dolan, 2006; Hamera & Conquergood, 2006; Kershaw, 1992), the relationship between performance and cultural politics (Diamond, 1996; Madison, 2005), and performance as acts of intervention (Román, 1998) in a deep "commitment to the three c's of performance studies: creativity, critique, [and] citizenship (civic struggles for social justice)" as an embodied pedagogical strategy (Conquergood, 2002, p. 152). In distinguishing performance and performativity, Della Pollock (2006) writes,

> Performance is the doing. The doing-of-the-thing-done [performativity is the thing done, the iteration of the expected] . . . the doing materializes the structural complexities shaping, pressing, and pulling at it. In so doing, performance is, for Diamond [1996], a kind of theorizing: it problematizes conditions of historical determination. (pp. 7–8)

In the more specific context of education, the link between performance and pedagogy in CPP is an embodied practice of critical pedagogy. Critical pedagogy, as a deep interrogative focus on pedagogical practice, "acknowledges school as a form of cultural politics . . . implicated in relations of power" and "argue[s] that teachers must understand the role that schooling plays in joining knowledge and power, in order to use that role for the development of critical and active citizens" (McLaren, 1998, p. 164). In whole, critical performative pedagogy works as critical praxis, "a thoughtful process of reflection and action" (Leistyna & Woodrum, 1996, p. 5) for progressive and resistant educators, those who *teach against the grain toward building a pedagogy of possibility* that is centered in the active body doing (Simon, 1992).

In her now germinal essays, performance studies scholar Elyse Lamm Pineau (1994, 1995, 1998, 2002), with whom I most readily attribute the nascent construction of critical performative pedagogy, married her "commitments to liberatory education with [her] conviction that performance offers an ideal lens for understanding and intervening in the cultural politics of education" (1998, p. 128). Pineau initially described critical performative pedagogy within a framework of "models of teaching and learning that are grounded in the sense-making capability and critical agency of our experiencing bodies" (p. 128), grounding this emergent construct in critical pedagogy.

In "Critical Performative Pedagogy: Fleshing Out the Politics of Liberatory Education," Pineau (2002) offers a set of undergirding themes that guide a focus on the active/performing body, making real the emancipatory prophecy of critical pedagogy. Drawing on the work of Peter McLaren (1999), she describes the *ideological body* at play in CPP—placing a dialectical emphasis on the sense-making body able to play, replay, and unplay behaviors. Drawing on the work of Dwight Conquergood (1991), she outlines *the ethnographic body*, "the cultural body situated in time, place, and history" (Conquergood, 1991, p. 187; Conquergood, 1986, 1992). And then she proposes a focus on *the performing body*, which extends the pedagogical value of students applying knowledge from the rudimentary form of performance as demonstration or showing to performance as a way of coming to know through sensory awareness and kinesthetic engagement, thus, learning by doing (Pineau, 1995).

Pineau's articulations of these fundamental foci of CPP lead to her outlined agenda for this still burgeoning pedagogical imperative:

- *Critical performative pedagogy* must acknowledge that inequities in power and privilege have a physical impact on our bodies and consequently must be struggled against bodily, through physical action and activism.

- *Critical performative pedagogy* must put bodies into action in the classroom because it believes that this is the surest way to help those bodies become active in the social sphere, thus using performance as a rehearsal of possibility.

- *Critical performative pedagogy* must develop research that accounts for how particular bodies present themselves in the classroom and provide detailed and evocative accounts of what one *sees* and *experiences* in the course of study.

- *Critical performative pedagogy* must take on the challenge of what it means to teach performatively across disciplines and at all levels of curriculum design and implementation. (Pineau, 2002, p. 53)

There are foundational variables in Pineau's agenda that clearly have become reality, resonating in a profusion of literature by key scholars engaging in projects that link critical theory, performance theory, and pedagogical discourse (see Alexander, 2005, 2006a; Denzin, 2006; Dimitriadis, 2006; Schutzman, 2006; Stucky, 2006; Valentine, 2006). In his groundbreaking work in the sociology of education, Henry Giroux (1998, 2001; Giroux & Shannon, 1997) called for a performative pedagogy, one that "opens up a narrative space that affirms the contextual and the specific while simultaneously recognizing the ways in which such spaces are shot through with issues of power" (Giroux, 1998, p. 145). Giroux (2001) fervently argues for an activation of the performative nature of the pedagogical, "that component that recognizes the partial breakdown, renegotiation, and reposition of boundaries as fundamental to understanding how pluralization is linked to the shifting nature of knowledge, identities, and the process of globalization" (p. 9). In such cases, performance is not exclusively the active body doing as much as a focus on the dynamic nature of culture and society reifying and defining itself based on social constructions of its own reality. Such recognitions in critical performative pedagogy capture these dynamic qualities and replay the processes of knowing and becoming as key components of a transformative pedagogy.

In his amalgamation of work that blurs the borders between a sociology of communication, social justice, and critical performance studies, Norman Denzin (2006) calls for a radical critical performance pedagogy, a pedagogy of hope. In short, Denzin's call advocates "a radical critical performance pedagogy that employs the strategies of a postcolonial, indigenous participatory theatre that uses historical restagings, masquerade, ventriloquism, and doubly inverted performances." He asks for "a radical critical performance pedagogy that uses performance and performance events as struggles and interventions; a form of revolutionary, catalytic political theatre, a project that provokes and enacts pedagogies of dissent for the new millennium" (pp. 325–335). What makes Denzin's call radical is the promotion of theater and performance as activism: a performative engagement that resists the reductive function of entertainment and escapism; a functional aesthetic that does the work of social change; a creative and artistic engagement that breaks the illusion of the fourth wall and penetrates the actuality of everyday life. Thus, critical performative pedagogy holds a reflective and refractive mirror up to society and then takes up arms in the processes of rebuilding social sensibilities of democracy.

The major contributions of Pineau, Giroux, and Denzin do not define the ends of critical performative pedagogy but in fact establish the directionality of the project. This project is grounded in the radical politics of using performance—creative, aesthetic, embodied, enacted presentations and representations of what is and what could be—as templates of critique and possibility but also as insurgent catalysts toward action, emancipation, and transformation.

Protocols, Procedures, and Possibilities

I hear and I forget; I see and I remember; I do and I understand.

—Confucius

I frame this section with this alliterative, triumphant quotation, knowing that these three categorical descriptives are not distinct. Each bleeds the borders of the other, for any radical method of doing, by nature of its shift from the center, knowingly invites critique and resists the fixities of proscription. Such definitional fixities would seek to both contain and limit the boundaries of its utility at the sacrifice of the vast creative, pedagogical, and political purposes of each who would dare to engage its undergirding principles. Like the shifting definitions of performance, critical performative pedagogy is a contested concept.

> Recognition of a given concept as essentially contested implies recognition of rival uses of it (such as oneself repudiates) as not only logically possible and humanly "likely," but as of permanent potential critical value to one's own use of interpretation of the concept in question. (Gallie, 1964, pp. 187–188, as cited in Strine, Long, & Hopkins, 1990, p. 183)

Certainly, a constructed political project such as critical performative pedagogy is already conflicted by the nature of the performance and theatrical biases that undergird the method (as well as the torrent of criticism that has historically trailed critical pedagogy like a recalcitrant lover desirous of its pleasures but resistant to its libidinal yearning that always demands more).

So in this section, I offer only skeletal templates, structural guides that further signal critical performative pedagogy at work. I offer snapshots of engagements that work toward achieving the varying agendas of critical performative pedagogy. In their burgeoning understanding of CPP as linked to the indebted influence of Boal's (1979) *Theatre of the Oppressed,* Harman and French (2004) offer what are key elements of critical performative pedagogy and particular features that offer challenge and thought. Here I outline and extend their critical contributions:

Critical performative pedagogy is collaborative (p. 110): Such practices are informed by the critical intentionality of the instructor, who develops creative engagements that ask students to test, by doing, the limits of theory and the delimited constructions of human social relation. The collaboration exists between the pedagogical intent of the instructor and the actualized participation of and between students and between the intense interplay of theory and application, of doing and the reflection on doing in a form of critical praxis. The collaboration exists in the interactive spirit of critique, exploration, and discovery within a particular sociopolitical and historical context that situates bodies in relation to each other; and it is a collaboration that works between the learning outcomes of a particular course, the broad goals of teachers as cultural workers, and participants as active citizens.

Critical performative pedagogy is self-questioning (p. 110): Like any critical and reflexive process, the instructor engaged in CPP must continually question her or his positioning, power, relations, and cultural capital—avoiding the trap of perpetuating the very power dynamic she or he is attempting to dismantle. Such a self-reflexive engagement then charges participants to splay open the nature of the particular power dynamics at work in any given situation that will be scrutinized and illuminated in performance. While insights are discovered in performance, CPP offers tools for critical explication of the theoretical knowledge that enriches the somatic experience, helping students articulate kinetic and kinesthetic senses engaged through/ within the performative experience.

Critical performative pedagogy is contextualized (p. 110): This is a project that resists a cookie-cutter model of application—for each social, cultural, and political context demands a tailored approach to investigation and problem solving. Such a thoughtful approach works to identify the cultural practices, traditions, and embodied experiences that signal the point of intervention and establish specific strategies/stratagems that re-create the conditions of particular experiences for the purposes of close scrutiny and illumination. And while CPP can be approached either as an individualized engagement (activity or exercise) linked to a particular learning outcome or as a paradigmatic frame that provides the framework for long-term educational practices and political campaigns as a way of teaching in/as social activism, it is equipment for living.

Critical performative pedagogy is action oriented (p. 110): This approach to teaching critically asks questions of local power relations and social justice issues so that teachers, students, and advocates can focus on specific strategies of resistance against social and cultural mores and local/state/global systems of oppression as well as those localized ways of seeing the self that stifle creative expression and the possibilities of self-actualization. At its core, CPP promotes change—in both the locations of deep attitude change and the ways in which such somatically informed cognitive shifts in knowing can inform necessary changes in bodily activities that are translated into acts of progressive and democratic citizenry.

Critical performative pedagogy is imaginative (p. 110): Play and imagination are pivotal in transformative education; each resists the traditional staid structures of educational practice that promote the Cartesian mind-body split (Freire, 1998; Greene, 2001; hooks, 1994). In particular, CPP both liberates and authorizes the body as a site of knowing and experiencing that is the nexus of all other forms of sense making—and particularly in the process of transforming play—from "make believe" to "making belief," illuminating the unrestricted processes of exploration, of trying on difference and exploring possible ways of being that are core to childhood practices of becoming, and making real the impulse of their desire (Alexander, 2002b).

Critical performative pedagogy is participatory and dialogic (p. 111): This is a pedagogy of engaged, structured doing in which instructors and planners try to project and anticipate the multiple variations of participatory experience as a hallmark of preparedness and caution for particular emergent outcomes. It is dialogic, not just in the sense of facilitators being engaged in the event as risk takers, but dialogic in Dwight Conquergood's (1985) sense of a dialogical performance that "struggles to bring self and other together so that they can question, debate, and challenge one another" (p. 9). In this sense, critical performative pedagogy is a system of interplay and critical sense making between people, cultures, and cosmologies; ways of seeing and knowing the world.

If these are broad descriptives of critical performative pedagogy, it is clear that a wide range of performance-based engagements could inform the interpretation of what might be included in such a project. For example, performance ethnography becomes critical performative pedagogy in a commitment that "takes as both its subject matter and method the experiencing body situated in time, place and history" (Conquergood, 1991, p. 187); it becomes a form of cultural exchange (Jones, 2002, 2006), a form of performative cross-cultural communication (Chesebro, 1998), and a theater form that establishes emancipatory potential in an ethnodrama that fuses a study of culture through performance (Mienczakowski, 1995, 2001; Park-Fuller, 2003). Performance ethnography is also a method of putting the critical sociological and sociopolitical imagination to work in understanding the politics and practices that shape human experience (Denzin, 2003). And hence the core variables in interpreting and evaluating effective performance ethnography might also apply to assessing critical performative pedagogy.

CONTENT

1. *Substantive Contribution* (Richardson, 2000, p. 254): Does the engagement contribute to the understanding of social life? Do the students/performers demonstrate a deeply grounded (if embedded) human-world understanding and perspective? How has this perspective been realized in the performance and the critical reflection on experience?

2. *Reflexivity* (Richardson, 2000, p. 254): How did the teacher/organizer come to conceptually form the pedagogical engagement? How was the information gathered? How has the author-performer's subjectivity been engaged as both a producer and product of this engagement? Is there adequate self-awareness and self-exposure for the participants to make judgments about their self-implication? Do author-performers hold themselves accountable to the standards of knowing and telling of the people and particularities they have engaged?

3. *Expresses a Reality* (Richardson, 2000, p. 254): Does this engagement present a fleshed out, embodied sense of a lived experience? Does it seem "true"—meaning a credible account of a cultural, social, individual, or communal sense of the "real"?

FORM

4. *Aesthetic Merit* (Richardson, 2000, p. 254): Does this piece succeed aesthetically? Does the use of creative analytical practice open up understanding and invite interpretive responses? Is the engagement artistically shaped, satisfying, complex, and interesting?

IMPACT

5. How does the critical performative engagement affect the performers/ students (emotionally, intellectually, and politically)? What new questions are generated in/through the performance? Does the performance move the performers/students/audience to try new ways of seeing and knowing the world, particular cultures, and particular research practices? Does the performance move the performers and audience to a particular action extending outside the borders of the immediate performative experience? (Alexander, 2005; Richardson, 2000, p. 254; Spry, 2001).

Pineau (2002) alludes to the practice of teachers requesting students to engage in auto-performances (i.e., performing personal narratives, autobiography, and autoethnography). While these practices can be reductively thought of as telling stories of the self, at their most rigorous application, these are instances in which students critically reflect on lived experiences situated in the context of family, race, gender, culture and society, and so on. They engage in a form of critical reflexivity with the intention not just of reflecting on experience, but of critically examining memory in the process of recall toward meaningful self-action in cultural and political landscapes (Alexander, 2006b, pp. xviii–xix; Madison, 2005, p. 177). In particular, autoethnography, with its orienting impulse to tell of experience in specific sociocultural and historical contexts, provides an intimate connection to critical performative pedagogy (Alexander, 2008; Ellis & Bochner, 2000; Spry, 2001).

The progressive theater work of Anna Deavere Smith (1993, 1994, 2003) takes, as its core impulse, a form of radical public performative pedagogy. By performing ethnographic interviews and re-creating public and private characters on stage, re-creating the cultural and political milieu of a happening, Smith's work is a form of performance ethnography that brings unlikely audiences and people into a conversation that seeks to illuminate racial and social politics for close public scrutiny. It is a form of *performance-conscious activism and activist-conscious performance* (Afary, 2009).

In her analysis of *The Laramie Project,* Jill Dolan (2005) writes that

> theatre can be a secular template of social and spiritual union not with a mystified, mythologized higher power, but with the more prosaic, earthbound, yearnings, ethical subjects who are citizens of the world community, who need places to connect with one another and with the fragile, necessary wish for a better future. (p. 137)

Such a utopian description of theater signals the potentials of a critical performative pedagogy that helps general and particularized audiences to meet and view restagings of problematic social and cultural experiences. Such stagings provide the opportunity for close examination with the opportunity to engage in a public discourse of possibility.

Three Brief Exemplars of Critical Performative Pedagogy

IN CLASS

Elyse Pineau (2002) offers the description of a student-generated engagement titled "Breasted Experience." The exercise occurred in a performance of gender course where undergraduate and graduate students explored everyday, as well as staged, performances of gender and sexual identity. Students had read Iris Marion Young's (1990) *Throwing Like a Girl;* in the book, Young argues that people experience their bodies in gender-specific ways and, further, that patriarchy eroticizes the female body by transforming it into an object of desire for men, while delimiting women's sense of their own physical capacity.

In the engagement, class members donned various sizes of "breasts" (bras filled with sacks of rice) while doing such everyday physical activities as running, lying down, hugging someone, and engaging in conversation. After each activity, students were asked to record their physical sensations as well as how those around them responded to the presence (enlargement) of their breasted bodies. Pineau notes that, predictably, male students were shocked to discover the sheer physical discomfort of running or lying on their stomachs. They reported changes in their posture, a reluctance to cross their arms for fear of accentuating breast size, and the unfamiliar intimacy of crushing their breasts against another man's chest when hugging. Pineau notes that one man offered an apology to all the women he had ever "complimented" by ogling their breasts. It should also be noted that several females discovered a new relationship to their body.

Pineau (2002) surmised that by performing their gender reflectively—critically—

> students began to come to terms with what breasts "mean" in a patriarchal society. . . . Whereas the Young text offered a way to think about gender bodies, the performance method taught students about how they "do" gender in immediate, concrete, and visceral ways. (p. 51)

Her very specific example also illuminates or describes a particular pedagogical methodology of having students embody and perform the meaningfulness of scholarly texts in general. A student's performance serves less as a singular response to an assignment and more as evidence of the student's active process of sense making. Students' performances mark the nascent beginnings of their own scholarly inquiry and production of scholarly work. In this way, students begin the process of developing arguments and responses to scholarly texts in the public setting of the classroom. In addition, they become more conscious of their own intellectual development and the critical link between theory, performance, and social awareness (see other examples in Alexander, 2002a, pp. 85–98).

PUBLIC, SOCIAL, AND POLITICAL CONTEXTS

The work of Augusto Boal (1979, 1995, 1998, 2002) undergirds an embodied participatory practice of rehearsing possibility, igniting a charge for civil engagement, and motivating social change. Below is a brief description of Boal's most compelling techniques. These techniques are applied and realized in a wide range of educational, social, cultural, and political contexts by educators and social activists around the world.

Image Theatre. Image theatre uses the human body as a sculpting medium to represent emotions, ideas, social dynamics, and relationships. Audience participants are encouraged to use existing bodies, volunteered for this purpose, to represent the most pressing of expressions, oppressions, and social forces as they are felt and experienced. Through body sculpting, participants are able to make the experience of oppression visible, then further manipulate the image to create alternative constructions to experience mobility, possibility, and emancipation.

Forum Theatre. Forum theatre engages improvisational rehearsal to create a scene of a specific oppression. Using the copresence of the protagonist (the person experiencing oppression) and the antagonist (the source of oppression or resistance), forum theatre stages scenes of everyday life, bodily interactions, and improvisationally created dialogue to reenact scenes of oppression. Participants play and re-create interactions as described by individuals or groups who are experiencing oppression in their daily lives. As participants replay the scene, often several times, audience members have the opportunity to intervene in the scene in the role of the protagonist—offering, rehearsing, and testing different strategies of empowering the voice against the resistance of the antagonist, who consistently tries to practice power. Discussion of participants' strategies follows the performance, focusing on the practical implementation of those possibilities in the actuality of similarly constructed scenes in everyday life.

The Rainbow of Desire. The rainbow of desire is a series of transformative techniques that further articulate and apply imaging techniques, as described in image theatre, as a psychodynamic exploration of group consciousness. These techniques allow participants to see how different desires, fears, and voices are contained and subdued at any one time, how they can be explored through embodied performance, and how participants can move toward navigating complex relationships. It is an embodied process of understanding self and others.

Legislative Theatre. Legislative theatre consists of applying "theatre of the oppressed" techniques, in the form of generated plays or scenes around hot-button social issues, to promote public involvement in political campaigns and in promoting democratic practices. During the structured performances directed by local organizers and performed in public spaces, audience members (people walking on the streets or those present for the engagement) are invited to participate in ways that further articulate the issues at play/in play. Legislative theatre can be used in public/community spaces to increase interest in local issues and developments and to empower targeted or disenfranchised populations to practice voice, particularly among individuals or target groups that may not engage through traditional methods such as public meetings. This method is particularly useful in assisting policymakers in understanding—through embodied visualizations and performances—the passions of the people as well as the potential and actual effects of particular political decisions that are made visible through performance.

CULTURAL AND COMMUNITY CONTEXTS

The Laramie Project, as performed by the Tectonic Theatre Project (Kaufman, 2002; Kaufman & the Members of the Tectonic Theatre Project, 2001) and described below by Jill Dolan (2005) in "The Laramie Project: Rehearsing for Example," offers a very specific example of how theater "can provide a place for radically democratic dissension and debate" (p. 137).

The Laramie Project used the idiom of performance to construct a public with which to examine the flaw in the social fabric illuminated by the murder of Matthew Shepard. On October 6, 1998, the twenty-one-year-old gay college student, out searching for a semblance of a queer life for himself in Laramie, Wyoming, was picked up in a bar by two local toughs who robbed Shepard, pistol-whipped him nearly to death, tied his wrists to a fence beside an isolated rural road, and abandoned him. Shepard was found the next day by a bicyclist, who called the local police. He was rushed to the hospital, where he died five days later, prompting demonstrations around the country and a national outcry against hate crimes. The Tectonic Theatre Project traveled to Laramie to create a performance based on the events; their motivating question, according to director Moisés Kaufman, was, "How is Laramie different from the rest of the country and how is it similar?" The play establishes a constellation of relationships, of kinship, and strangeness, of proximity and distance, as the Tectonic actors-cum-interviewers resided temporarily in Laramie, sifting through its people's public lives and secret feelings. (p. 113)

Dolan (2005) includes the explication of this project in her book, *Utopia in Performance: Finding Hope at the Theater*, in which she argues that "live performance provides a place where people come together, embodied and passionate, to share experiences of meaning making and imagination that can describe or capture fleeting intimations of a better world" (p. 2). In such cases, it is the power and magic of performance that makes possibility visible, or makes accessible and objectified the issues of living for close scrutiny. It is this element of the Laramie Project, similar to the work of Anna Deavere Smith, that brings such projects in alignment with the guiding principles of a critical performative pedagogy. While the bodies in action are relative, it is the occasion and intention of performative engagement that signal the potentials of awareness and knowledge that ignite action/activism.

In offering these brief exemplars, I have artificially created situational and contextual differences that seemingly distinguish the utility of the approaches in categories such as *the classroom, the public/social/political sphere,* and *cultural/community contexts.* These are only functional divisions of my labor, for these are not disparate locales, and the import of the human interactional intention of their purposes cannot be easily differentiated. Each site is infused with the politics of the other. These sites are *scenes of instruction* that reestablish what are teachable moments (Awkward, 1999). Each of these techniques and approaches to doing critical work are interchangeable in their applications and unified in their intentions. Each taps into the core of human experience, offers outlets to expression, and builds channels to possibility.

In *Critical Ethnography*, D. Soyini Madison (2005) outlines methods and ethics that undergird a performance-centered critical ethnography.

For my purposes, she offers three key questions in doing critical ethnography in/as/through what she refers to as a performance of possibilities:

> the possible suggests a movement culminating in creation and change. It is the active, creative work that weaves the life of the mind with being mindful of life, or merging the text with the world, of critically traversing the margin and the center, and opening more and different paths for enlivening relations and spaces. (p. 172)

Madison's construction of a performance of possibilities and the ensuing questions can also be applied to critical performative pedagogy. She directs the following interrogatives of method and intent:

> By what definable and material means will the Subjects themselves benefit from the performance?
>
> How can the performance contribute to a more enlightened and involved citizenship that will disturb systems and processes that limit freedoms and possibilities?
>
> In what ways will the performers probe questions of identity, representation, and fairness to enrich their own subjectivity, cultural politics, and art? (p. 172)

Madison engages in an explication of the questions in relation to *the subjects,* whose lives and words are being performed; *the audience,* who witness the performance; and *the performer,* who embodies and enacts the data. She concludes with a phrase that offers a synthesis of method and intent. She writes, "In a performance of possibilities, moral responsibility and artistic excellence culminate in an active intervention to break through unfair closures, remake the possibility for new openings, and bring the margins to a shared center" (p. 178). These are also the goals and objectives, as well as the methods and guides, for a critical performative pedagogy.

Pitfalls and Promises of Critical Performative Pedagogy

The classroom is a microcosm of society.

The preceding epigram is ubiquitous, almost commonplace to educational research. Yet, for me, its message has always been reductive. There is often a comfort offered in its iteration; but if the classroom is a microcosm of society, it means that the classroom presents the same challenges as society, and maybe with a highly concentrated dose of reality. Its consequences are not easily dissipated in the containment of the classroom, thus demanding added focus on intention and effect as key components of pedagogical engagement and the purpose of knowledge and experience to transform self in/and society. In their brief article "Critical Performative Pedagogy: A Feasible Praxis for Teacher Education," Harman and French (2004) outline what they frame as potential hurdles to critical performative pedagogy. And while some of their suggestions are situated within the specific context of teacher education, they offer two additional challenges that I would like to address directly. My intention is not a critique of their articulation but a collaborative venture in teasing at and subverting these oft-cited notions of limitations of critical performative pedagogy—reframing them as insurgent possibilities of this still burgeoning project. Harman and French offer these outlined hurdles to critical performative pedagogy:

> *Tapping Into Dangerous Zones:* Because the body is a site of charged political and sociocultural elements, working at this visceral level can lead to very emotional and potentially destructive outbursts. When facilitating CPP, we need to allow a lot of time for processing of emotions at the end of experiential workshops.

> *Reentry:* Having had such a powerful experience can make it difficult to return to one's everyday, possibly oppressive, life. There can be an expectation that such experiential work will lead to an immediate release from oppressive circumstances or that the change from this one experience will necessarily be a long-lasting one (pp. 110–111).

I suggest that each of these is critical to any form of transformative pedagogy and any engagement of liberatory practice. By its very nature, education taps into "dangerous zones"—cloistered spaces in the minds, hearts, and lived experiences of students, who are challenged to think and feel beyond the known. Such processes rightfully stir emotion and passion, consequently dismissing the aphorism of the classroom as a safe space. The questions are as follows: How can critical performative pedagogy tap into the dangerous zones of repressed emotions and suppressed hopes to build pedagogies of possibility? How can critical performative pedagogy help provide a channel for participants to direct those unleashed feelings in ways that are critical and reflexive? How can the emotional energy stirred up in critical performative pedagogy be channeled as productive outbursts of action, change, and transformation? How can the facilitators of a critical pedagogical engagement work to anticipate a range of possible responses and help participants also critically anticipate the emancipation that comes in expressing passion and articulating experience, in ways that are constructive and not parallel to the structures of their own oppression?

In terms of "reentry," while participants are engaged in a moment of possibilizing and a process of constructing belief, they are not disengaged from the realities of their everyday lives. In fact, all the practices, procedures, and protocols of critical performative pedagogy call participants into a more intense reflection of everyday life (and not an escape from everyday life). The impulse at the end of the engagements and workshops framed here as critical performative pedagogy is to invite participants to use aspects of the everyday—those components of living and human social engagement that weigh heavy on the body, and the dense particularity of their beings—as a source of empowerment, of growth, and of strategic engagement. These are the same bodies that exit the engagement enriched, energized, and informed with new strategies of/for living. Activities linked and framed as critical performative pedagogy are not magical fixes; such a caution appears in much of the work of Augusto Boal. These techniques, in fact, create an arena in which participants struggle to find workable solutions to everyday challenges. Knowing that such struggles in the moments of strategic play are symbolic of the work that is necessary to endure, transcend, and transform self, other, and society.

I want to offer you a brief glimpse into the conflicted complexities of a critical performative engagement in the form of a personal narrative, or what Giroux and Shannon (1997), citing Derrida, call a "performative interpretation," to address how critical performative pedagogy can not only unleash particular emotional states and traumatic memory but also provide a template for empowering acts of self-expression (p. 7). The mode of this example might also be described as *generative* or *generational* in the way in which the emergence of experience is spurred from triggering sources, speaking across borders of bodies, time, and space (Alexander, 2000; Pineau, 2000).

Earlier in this chapter, I offered an exemplar of critical performative pedagogy from Elyse Pineau (2002) based on Iris Marion Young's chapter, "Breasted Experience: The Look and the Feeling." And while I agreed with the narration of experience from the student-generated classroom engagement, each body experiences such activities differently. Maybe this is because of what Harman and French (2004) described as tapping into dangerous zones. I was a student in that class and, as a man who suffered(s) from a mild case of gynecomastia (enlargement of the breast in men), and who had experienced complications of that condition that same semester, being required to place bras filled with sacks of rice over my shoulders to simulate having breasts stirred up years of personal pain and grief. But, as someone who has also learned to *perform student well*, I participated. And, as a tamed act of resistance to the pedagogical intent of the engagement, I offered little commentary in the class discussion that followed.

I remember thinking that while the engagement may have been enlightening for many of the men in the class, my own lifelong body consciousness had sensitized me in ways that made the engagement less informing and more disturbing. I was not the predictable male student with a predictable response of shock in discovering the sheer physicality of having breasts. And, particularly as a gay man, who had never commodified the female body through ogling or indelicate comments, the lesson of respect and empathy/sympathy that seemingly undergirded the engagement was, to some degree, something I already knew, for I had similar (but certainly not the same) experiences. I felt more irritated by my required participation. And by the particular spectacle of embodiedness that I had to play out in this public arena, other than having to out my particularity, as a student, I felt that I had no choice but to participate. It wasn't until I was in another class, approaching another assignment that required me to engage performance as a strategic analytic, that I was able to truly reflect on issues and experiences stirred up in that previous engagement. I constructed a performance titled "A Breasted Experience" that explored the particularity of my experience of going to a local clinic for a mammogram, required by my doctor after I experienced pain in my "breasts" with the presence of small yet palpably felt lumps.

In the narrative, I recounted the lonely drive to the clinic and told meta-narratives about childhood encounters with boys who taunted me at a public swimming pool and the incongruent experience of seeing my little sister's joy of getting her first training bra. I took the audience into my experience and reflected on seeing commercials and ads encouraging women to get regular mammograms and how I never saw myself in those ads (and why should I?). I described the actual experience of having the mammogram, the discomfort and difficulty of the procedure, and the female technicians who told me how the experience would make me more empathetic to the routine experience of women having mammograms.

I first presented "A Breasted Experience" in a classroom situation with other students and the teacher, and then I reperformed it in two separate public performance venues. The engagement of the performance project and the actual performance not only allowed me a space to explore and explicate my own experience but also helped me liberate myself from the politics of body image that had long plagued me, from the ways in which our own cloistering of identity issues serves as a form of self-repression. The performance allowed me the opportunity to offer a subtle critique against those who would assume differentiated experiences of oppression between men and women, knowing of course that such experiences are not always equal but can inform each other.

The performance also allowed me, in the moment, and certainly now, nearly 15 years later at the time of this writing, to reflect on the critical impact of the initial classroom engagement. Not knowing the intimate details of every student's personal history, critical performative pedagogy certainly has the potential to tap into dangerous zones that teachers and facilitators have no way of understanding or anticipating. Pineau definitely alludes to this in her own essay. Critical performative pedagogy is a complicated matrix of intentions—teaching students how to think and learn through experiences, the possibilities of which may expand beyond the particularity of the experience, the intent of the experience, and how the student processes that experience. Critical performative pedagogy thus offers students equipment for living and critical mechanisms of sense making. And, whether in the exact moment of the pedagogical enterprise or in some later time of their own self-discovery, that knowledge, coupled with particular strategies of engagement, might lead to possibilities of personal liberation and public engagements of social value.

Critical Performative Pedagogy in/as/for Social Justice

In this chapter, I have attempted to offer you a broad understanding of critical performative pedagogy. I have offered you some of the undergirding principles as well as protocols, procedures, and practical applications and implications of a pedagogy that is bodily centered; a pedagogy of doing as a way of knowing; a pedagogy that seeks to inform and incite; a pedagogy that claims as its core mantra, *the active body doing, the active body knowing, the active body transforming*. But to what end? The title of this chapter suggests that the end is social justice.

What is social justice? There are shifting definitions of social justice that can be accessed through a wider range of resources and epistemological frameworks. But allow me a moment of being reductive by offering the following: Social justice is not a utopian reality of democracy and equality for all the citizens of the world fixed in time or place. Social justice is not an end, it is a practice; it is a doing. Social justice is a dynamic rehearsal that has no intention of a final performance. It is a rehearsal in everyday life toward a perfection of social interaction, a process of strategizing the multiple dimensions of being human—of being humane, of being in the company of others—that respects the multiple interpretations of that existential human possibility (Madison, 2006).

Social justice embodies not the possibility of difference but the reality of difference and then works to continually fashion cultures and laws within a global society of humanity where the rights of others are valued with equal justice. Social justice is not just about preventing human rights abuses, protecting other minority groups, though they (we) are most in need of such considered efforts. It is about establishing systems of humanity that negate instances of abuse as a result of unregulated power and the lack of empathic human understanding of specific embodied experience. Social justice is a political and social movement—a movement between bodies. It is a movement in doing and action toward knowing and a rehearsal for possibility. All campaigns for social justice seek to intervene in systems of oppression and establish structures of understanding and equality.

Earlier, I offered Pineau's (2002) agenda for a critical performative pedagogy, a list that is still valid and encouraged. While I have offered a broad frame for practices that can be constructed as *critical performative pedagogy*, the reference itself is most often linked with the educational context and what Pineau (1998) once engaged under the rubric of *performance across the curriculum*. Yet I argue that even within the sometimes cloistering context of an academic setting, and even within the confines of a book that focuses on the intersections of communication and instruction, critical performative pedagogy is built on foundations of social justice and must continue to empower students with strategies to critically articulate, translate, and apply such knowledge toward public and social transformation.

Critical performative pedagogy in educational contexts must reinforce the aims of social justice as its core tenets by asking key questions that link pedagogy and particular learning outcomes to strategies applied on a cultural level: How can we encourage students to translate embodied knowledge gained through performative engagement into social justice? How can we meaningfully link critical performative pedagogy with social activism in the communities surrounding where students live and learn? How can we link critical performative pedagogy with student internships, service learning, alternative spring breaks, and community-based projects in which students not only gain academic credit and professional experiences but also work in altruistic ways toward empowering needy communities and oppressed people? How can we teach students to make the links between critical performative pedagogy and engaged citizenship? How are students actually taught to translate the meaningfulness of experience in the context of a structured classroom engagement into the unfiltered practices of everyday life? If, in fact, all these factors of social justice are verifiable goals of a critical performative pedagogy, then they must be linked with strategies of application outside the moment of the engagement and outside the classroom—where the practices of an informed citizenry have their most palpable impact.

Critical performative pedagogy must not only continue strategic engagements of possibility in the classroom but also bring students into the public domain—the streets, the communities, and the doorsteps of local, state, and national leaders (Haedicke & Nellhaus, 2001). Critical performative pedagogy *is* local teachers' unions in California involving high school and college students in campaigns of protest at the state capitol against cuts in educational funding. In this practice, students are engaging in their own self-determination, making their voices heard in an embodied show of active political engagement. Like the work of José Cruz González, critical performative pedagogy *is magical realism* and *mature themes in performances for young audiences*, providing them with an age-appropriate but critical exploration of natural and social issues of the world (such as deforestation, global warming, death, the AIDS pandemic, etc.), without patronizing their intellect and the desperate necessity to know (Jennings, 2008).

According to Susan Mason (2008), in the work of González,

> magical realism may be described as a perspective of the oppressed whose lives are intricately bound to the natural world and may be understood in its terms . . . the children in his plays overcome violent and personal loss by remembering the lessons of their elders. (p. 23)

For me, critical performative pedagogy demands that its participants reconnect with kernel aspects of their being—elemental and indigenous forms of knowing that are excavated for reexamination and reactivation, to address current needs and the contingencies of living. In the work of González, as I am framing it as a critical performative pedagogy, there is teaching through performance; the play performed is a cultural script, a lesson plan that informs the social and cultural lives of young audiences. Such performative engagement with young audiences is an investment in our collective future, an investment in their critical citizenship.

Critical performative pedagogy *is* collaborative events between local artists, school age and college students using the arts to signify and critique atrocities committed against children (both local and abroad), the war on drugs, hate crimes, and the effects of violence: violence as "any relation, process, or condition by which an individual or group violates the physical, social, and/or psychological integrity of another person or group" (Bulhan, 1985, p. 53). Critical performative pedagogy *is* using Boalian techniques with athletes, fraternities, and sororities to explore the politics and consequences of staid and dangerous performances of gender as acts of intervention to rape, unreflective practices of power and class, and social and racial exclusion. Critical performative pedagogy *is* any strategic performative act that serves as a form of education, enlightenment, and transformation of problematic social and cultural practices, working toward re-creating the world anew.

If the classroom is truly a microcosm of society, then the instructional moment begins to establish a template for human social engagement. And if most people are mirrors reflecting the moods and emotions of the times, then the practices in critical performative pedagogy assist participants to become windows, bringing light to bear on the dark corners where troubles fester. And if it is true that embodied engagement leads to a more intense understanding, then the theoretical principles that inform critical performative pedagogy instill a deeper commitment to knowing the world anew, empowering students to continually rehearse for social justice; and critical performative pedagogy truly becomes a "pedagogy of difference" (Trifonas, 2003). As Debb Hurlock (2002) writes in reference to an interdisciplinary poetic pedagogy, which I now use for my own purpose, signaling the common focus on pedagogical invention and intervention, critical performative pedagogy "requires a faith in the process of experience and understanding, to believe that the process is as equally important as what will finally be found and offered back to the world for more conversation" (p. 17).

So I asked students to translate the meaningfulness of intellectual knowing to embodied doing, and embodied doing into intellectual power for emancipatory ends . . .

> and they began to critically analyze the ways in which the body acquires certain habits (enfleshment)—through race, culture, society, gender, and the overlaps of each.

> and they began to critically explore how a body can learn alternative behaviors (refleshment)—rehearsals for living, performing possibility as a rehearsal for social justice (McLaren, 1999; Pineau, 2002; Warren, 1999).

> and they began to see that the tools of learning can be used to emancipate both the mind and the body, for self and others.

> and they began to see possibility through performance, and performance as possibility.

> and they began to realize that the classroom can be a site of transgression, and pedagogy can be a tool for revolution (Ewing, 2005; hooks, 1994; McLaren, 2000).

References

Adams, M. (1997). *Teaching for diversity and social justice: A sourcebook.* New York: Routledge.

Adams, M., Blumenfeld, W., Castañeda, R., Hackman, H. W., Peters, M. L., & Zúñiga, X. (Eds.). (2000). *Readings for diversity and social justice: An anthology on racism, antisemitism, sexism, heterosexism, ableism, and classism.* New York: Routledge.

Afary, K. (2009). *Performance and activism: Grassroots discourse after the Los Angeles rebellion of 1992.* Lanham, MD: Lexington.

Alexander, B. K. (1999). Moving towards a critical poetic response. *Theatre Topics, 9,* 107–125.

Alexander, B. K. (2000). Skin flint (or the garbage man's kid): A generative autobiographical performance. *Text and Performance Quarterly, 20,* 97–114.

Alexander, B. K. (2002a). Intimate engagement: Student performances as scholarly endeavor. *Theatre Topics, 12,* 85–98.

Alexander, B. K. (2002b). Performing bodies: Student bodies (in the classroom). *Communication and Theater Association of Minnesota Journal, 27,* 57–74.

Alexander, B. K. (2005). Performance ethnography: The reenacting and inciting of culture. In N. K. Denzin & Y. S. Lincoln (Eds.), *The Sage handbook of qualitative research* (3rd ed., pp. 411–441). Thousand Oaks, CA: Sage.

Alexander, B. K. (2006a). Performance and pedagogy. In D. S. Madison & J. Hamera (Eds.), *The Sage handbook of performance studies* (pp. 253–260). Thousand Oaks, CA: Sage.

Alexander, B. K. (2006b). *Performing black masculinity: Race, culture and queer identity.* Lanham, MD: AltaMira Press.

Alexander, B. K. (2008). Autoethnography: Exploring modalities and subjectivities that shape social relations. In J. Paul, K. Kleinhammer-Tramill, & K. Fowler (Eds.), *Qualitative research methods in special education* (pp. 277–334). Denver, CO: Love.

Awkward, M. (1999). *Scenes of instruction: A memoir.* Durham, NC: Duke University Press.

Bamberg, M., & Andrews, M. (2004). *Considering counter-narratives: Narrating, resisting, making sense.* Philadelphia: John Benjamins.

Boal, A. (1979). *Theatre of the oppressed.* New York: Urizen Books.

Boal, A. (1985). *Theatre of the oppressed.* New York: Theatre Communications Group.

Boal, A. (1995). *The rainbow of desire: The Boal method of theatre and therapy.* London: Routledge.

Boal, A. (1998). *Legislative theatre* (A. Jackson, Trans.). London: Routledge.

Boal, A. (2002). *Games for actors and non-actors* (A. Jackson, Trans.). London: Routledge.

Bulhan, H. A. (1985). *Frantz Fanon and the psychology of oppression.* New York: Plenum Press.

Chesebro, J. W. (1998). Performance studies as paradox, culture, and manifesto: A future orientation. In S. J. Dailey (Ed.), *The future of performance studies: Visions and revisions* (pp. 310–319). Annandale, VA: National Communication Association.

Cohen-Cruz, J. (2006). The problem democracy is supposed to solve: The politics of community-based performance. In D. S. Madison & J. Hamera (Eds.), *The Sage handbook of performance studies* (pp. 427–445). Thousand Oaks, CA: Sage.

Conquergood, D. (1985). Performing as a moral act: Ethical dimensions of the ethnography of performance. *Literature in Performance, 5,* 1–13.

Conquergood, D. (1986). Performing cultures: Ethnography, epistemology, and ethics. In E. Slembek (Ed.), *Miteinander sprechen und handeln: Festschrift für Hellmut Geissner* (pp. 55–66). Frankfurt, Germany: Scriptor.

Conquergood, D. (1991). Rethinking ethnography. *Communication Monographs, 58,* 179–194.

Conquergood, D. (1992). Ethnography, rhetoric, and performance. *Quarterly Journal of Speech, 78,* 80–97.

Conquergood, D. (1998). Beyond text: Toward a performative cultural politics. In S. J. Dailey (Ed.), *The future of performance studies: Visions and revisions* (pp. 25–26). Annandale, VA: National Communication Association.

Conquergood, D. (2002). Performance studies: Interventions and radical research. *Drama Review, 46,* 145–156.

Conquergood, D. (2006). Rethinking ethnography. In D. S. Madison & J. Hamera (Eds.), *The Sage handbook of performance studies* (pp. 351–365). Thousand Oaks, CA: Sage.

Darder, A., & Torres, R. D. (2004). *After race: Racism after multiculturalism.* New York: New York University Press.

Delgado, R. (Ed.). (1995). *Critical race theory.* Philadelphia: Temple University Press.

Denzin, N. K. (2003). *Performance ethnography: Critical pedagogy and the politics of culture.* Thousand Oaks, CA: Sage.

Denzin, N. K. (2006). The politics and ethics of performance pedagogy: Toward a pedagogy of hope. In D. S. Madison & J. Hamera (Eds.), *The Sage handbook of performance studies* (pp. 325–338). Thousand Oaks, CA: Sage.

Diamond, E. (1996). *Performance and cultural politics.* New York: Routledge.

Dimitriadis, G. (2006). Pedagogy on the move: New intersections in (between) the educative and the performative. In D. S. Madison & J. Hamera (Eds.), *The Sage handbook of performance studies* (pp. 296–308). Thousand Oaks, CA: Sage.

Dolan, J. (2005). *Utopia in performance: Finding hope at the theater.* Ann Arbor: University of Michigan Press.

Dolan, J. (2006). The polemics and potentials of theatre studies and performance. In D. S. Madison & J. Hamera (Eds.), *The Sage handbook of performance studies* (pp. 508–529). Thousand Oaks, CA: Sage.

Ellis, C., & Bochner, A. P. (2000). Autoethnography, personal narrative, reflexivity: Researcher as subject. In N. K. Denzin & Y. S. Lincoln (Eds.), *The Sage handbook of qualitative research* (2nd ed., pp. 733–768). Thousand Oaks, CA: Sage.

Ewing, E. T. (Ed.). (2005). *Revolution and pedagogy: Interdisciplinary and transnational perspectives on educational foundations.* New York: Palgrave Macmillan.

Freire, P. (1974). *Education for critical consciousness* (M. B. Ramos, Trans.). New York: Continuum Press.

Freire, P. (1998). *Teachers as cultural workers: Letters to those who dare to teach* (D. Macedo, D. Koike, & A. Oliveira, Trans.). Boulder, CO: Westview Press.

Freire, P. (2002). *Pedagogy of the oppressed* (M. B. Ramos, Trans.). New York: Continuum Press.

Giroux, H. A. (1998). Critical pedagogy as performative practice: Memories of whiteness. In C. A. Torres & T. R. Mitchell (Eds.), *Sociology of education: Emerging perspectives* (pp. 143–153). Albany: State University of New York Press.

Giroux, H. A. (2001). Cultural studies as performative politics. *Cultural Studies <=> Critical Methodologies, 1,* 5–23.

Giroux, H. A., Lankshear, C., McLaren, P., & Peters, M. (1996). *Counternarratives: Cultural studies and critical pedagogies in postmodern spaces.* New York: Routledge.

Giroux, H. A., & Shannon, P. (1997). *Education and cultural studies: Toward a performative practice.* London: Routledge.

Greene, M. (2001). *Variations on a blue guitar: The Lincoln Center Institute lectures on aesthetic education.* New York: Teachers College Press.

Griffiths, M. (1998). *Educational research for social justice: Doing qualitative research in educational settings.* Buckingham, UK: Open University Press.

Haedicke, S. C., & Nellhaus, T. (Eds.). (2001). *Performing democracy: International perspectives on urban community-based performance.* Ann Arbor: University of Michigan Press.

Hamera, J. (Ed.). (2005). *Opening acts: Performance in/as communication and cultural studies.* Thousand Oaks, CA: Sage.

Hamera, J., & Conquergood, D. (2006). Performance and politics: Themes and arguments. In D. S. Madison & J. Hamera (Eds.), *The Sage handbook of performance studies* (pp. 419–425). Thousand Oaks, CA: Sage.

Harman, R., & French, K. (2004). Critical performative pedagogy: A feasible praxis for teacher education. In J. O'Donnell, M. Pruyn, & C. R. Chavez (Eds.), *Social justice in these times* (pp. 97–115). Greenwich, CT: Information Age.

hooks, b. (1994). *Teaching to transgress: Education as the practice of freedom.* New York: Routledge.

Hurlock, D. (2002). The possibility of an interdisciplinary poetic pedagogy: Reconceiving knowing and being. *History of Intellectual Culture, 2,* 1–17.

Jennings, C. (2008). *Nine plays by José Cruz-González: Magical realism and mature themes in theatre for young audiences.* Austin: University of Texas Press.

Jones, J. (2002). Performance ethnography: The role of embodiment in cultural authenticity. *Theatre Topics, 12,* 1–15.

Jones, J. (2006). Performance ethnography, performing ethnography, performance ethnography. In D. S. Madison & J. Hamera (Eds.), *The Sage handbook of performance studies* (pp. 339–345). Thousand Oaks, CA: Sage.

Kaufman, M. (Director). (2002). *The Laramie project* [Motion picture]. United States: Home Box Office.

Kaufman, M., & the Members of the Tectonic Theatre Project. (2001). *The Laramie Project.* New York: Vintage Books.

Kershaw, B. (1992). *The politics of performance: Radical theatre as cultural intervention.* New York: Routledge.

Kincheloe, J. L. (2008). *Critical pedagogy primer.* New York: Peter Lang.

Ladson-Billings, G. (2000). Racialized discourses and ethnic espitemologies. In N. K. Denzin & Y. S. Lincoln (Eds.), *The Sage handbook of qualitative research* (2nd ed., pp. 257–277). Thousand Oaks, CA: Sage.

Lea, V., & Sims, E. J. (2008). *Undoing whiteness in the classroom: Critical educultural teaching approaches for social justice activism.* New York: Peter Lang.

Leistyna, P., & Woodrum, A. (1996). Context and culture: What is critical pedagogy? In P. Leistyna, A. Woodrum, & A. Sherblom (Eds.), *Breaking free: The transformative power of critical pedagogy* (pp. 1–7). Cambridge, MA: Harvard Education Review.

Madison, D. S. (2005). *Critical ethnography: Methods, ethics, and performance.* Thousand Oaks, CA: Sage.

Madison, D. S. (2006). Staging fieldwork/performing human rights. In D. S. Madison & J. Hamera (Eds.), *The Sage handbook of performance studies* (pp. 397–418). Thousand Oaks, CA: Sage.

Madison, D. S., & Hamera, J. (Eds.). (2006). *The Sage handbook of performance studies.* Thousand Oaks, CA: Sage.

Mason, S. V. (2008). The playwriting of José Cruz-González. In C. Jennings (Ed.), *Nine plays by José Cruz González: Magical realism and mature themes in theatre for young audiences* (pp. 20–27). Austin: University of Texas Press.

McIntosh, P. (1997). White privilege and male privilege: A personal account of coming to see correspondences through work in women's studies. In R. Delgado & J. Stefancic (Eds.), *Critical white studies: Looking behind the mirror* (pp. 291–299). Philadelphia: Temple University Press.

McLaren, P. (1991). Schooling the postmodern body: Critical pedagogy and the politics of enfleshment. In H. Giroux (Ed.), *Postmodernism, feminism, and cultural politics: Redrawing educational boundaries* (pp. 144–173). New York: State University of New York Press.

McLaren, P. (1998). *Life in schools: An introduction to critical pedagogy in the foundations of education* (3rd ed.). New York: Longman.

McLaren, P. (1999). *Schooling as a ritual performance: Towards a political economy of educational symbols and gestures.* New York: Routledge.

McLaren, P. (2000). *Che Guevara, Paulo Freire, and the pedagogy of revolution.* New York: Rowman & Littlefield.

McLaren, P., & Kincheloe, J. L. (2007). *Critical pedagogy: Where are we now?* New York: Peter Lang.

Mienczakowski, J. (1995). The theatre of ethnography: The reconstruction of ethnography into theatre with emancipatory potential. *Qualitative Inquiry, 1*(3), 360–375.

Mienczakowski, J. (2001). Ethnodrama: Performed research: Limitations and potential. In P. Atkinson, A. Coffey, S. Delamont, J. Lofland, & L. Lofland (Eds.), *Handbook of ethnography* (pp. 468–476). London: Sage.

O'Donnell, J., Pruyn, M., & Chavez, C. R. (2004). *Social justice in these times.* Greenwich, CT: Information Age.

Park-Fuller, L. (2003). Audiencing the audience: Playback theatre, performative writing, and social activism. *Text and Performance Quarterly, 23,* 288–310.

Pineau, E. L. (1994). Teaching is performance: Reconstructing a problematic metaphor. *American Educational Research Journal, 31,* 3–25.

Pineau, E. L. (1995). Re-casting rehearsal: Making a case for production as research. *Journal of the Illinois Speech and Theatre Association, 46,* 43–52.

Pineau, E. L. (1998). Performance studies across the curriculum: Problems, possibilities and projections. In S. J. Dailey (Ed.), *The future of performance studies: Visions and revisions* (pp. 128–135). Annandale, VA: National Communication Association.

Pineau, E. L. (2000). "Nursing mother" and articulating absence. *Text and Performance Quarterly, 20,* 1–19.

Pineau, E. L. (2002). Critical performative pedagogy: Fleshing out the politics of liberatory education. In N. Stucky & C. Wimmer (Eds.), *Teaching performance studies* (pp. 41–54). Carbondale: Southern Illinois University Press.

Pollock, D. (2006). Performance trouble. In D. S. Madison & J. Hamera (Eds.), *The Sage handbook of performance studies* (pp. 1–8). Thousand Oaks, CA: Sage.

Reinelt, J., & Roach, J. R. (1992). *Critical theory and performance.* Ann Arbor: University of Michigan.

Richardson, L. (2000). Evaluating ethnography. *Qualitative Inquiry, 6,* 253–255.

Richardson, R. (1996). *Fortunes and fables.* London: Trentham Books.

Román, D. (1998). *Acts of intervention: Performance, gay culture, and AIDS.* Bloomington: Indiana University Press.

Schechner, R. (2006). *Performance studies: An introduction* (2nd ed.). New York: Routledge.

Schutzman, M. (2006). Ambulant pedagogy. In D. S. Madison & J. Hamera (Eds.), *The Sage handbook of performance studies* (pp. 278–295). Thousand Oaks, CA: Sage.

Shor, I. (1987). *Critical teaching and everyday life.* Chicago: University of Chicago Press.

Simon, R. I. (1992). *Teaching against the grain: Texts for a pedagogy of possibility.* New York: Bergin & Garvey.

Smith, A. D. (1993). *Fires in the mirror: Crown Heights, Brooklyn, and other identities.* Garden City, NY: Anchor.

Smith, A. D. (1994). *Twilight: Los Angeles, 1992.* Garden City, NY: Anchor.

Smith, A. D. (2003). *House arrest and piano.* Garden City, NY: Anchor.

Spry, T. (2001). Performing autoethnography: An embodied methodical praxis. *Qualitative Inquiry, 7,* 706–732.

Strine, M. S., Long, B. W., & Hopkins, M. F. (1990). Research in interpretation and performance studies: Trends, issues, priorities. In G. M. Phillips & J. T. Wood (Eds.), *Speech communication: Essays to commemorate the 75th anniversary of the Speech Communication Association* (pp. 181–204). Carbondale: Southern Illinois University Press.

Stucky, N. (2006). Fieldwork in the performance studies classroom: Learning objectives and the activist curriculum. In D. S. Madison & J. Hamera (Eds.), *The Sage handbook of performance studies* (pp. 261–277). Thousand Oaks, CA: Sage.

Swartz, O. (2006). *Social justice and communication scholarship.* Mahwah, NJ: Lawrence Erlbaum.

Trifonas, P. P. (Ed.). (2003). *Pedagogies of difference: Rethinking education for social change.* New York: Routledge.

Valentine, K. B. (2006). Unlocking the doors for incarcerated women through performance and creative writing. In D. S. Madison & J. Hamera (Eds.), *The Sage handbook of performance studies* (pp. 309–324). Thousand Oaks, CA: Sage.

Warren, J. T. (1999). The body politic: Performance, pedagogy, and the power of enfleshment. *Text and Performance Quarterly, 19,* 257–266.

Wink, J. (2005). *Critical pedagogy: Notes from the real world.* New York: Addison-Wesley Longman.

Young, I. M. (1990). *Throwing like a girl and other essays in feminist philosophy and social theory.* Bloomington: Indiana University Press.

When Will We All Matter? **18**

Exploring Race, Pedagogy, and Sustained Hope for the Academy

Bernadette Marie Calafell

I confess that my research interest in critical communication pedagogy studies was never planned. I had always assumed that my research trajectory would primarily be developing work in the areas of Latina/o performance and rhetorical studies. However, the lived experiences of an academic life led me to take a side road in my research, and since then I have often smiled fondly at my idealism and naïveté in truly believing that my presence as a woman of color in the classroom could go uninterrogated and in many ways ignored. In *Teaching to Transgress: Education as the Practice of Freedom*, hooks (1994) writes of a similar pain and the necessary turn to theory:

> I came to theory because I was hurting—the pain within me was so intense that I could not go on living. I came to theory desperate, wanting to comprehend—to grasp what was happening around and within me. Most importantly, I wanted to make the hurt go away. I saw in theory then a location for healing. (p. 59)

Reading these words for the first time several years ago, I felt them deeply resonating with me on multiple levels as a woman of color academic whose identities were political in every space in the academy whether or not I or others realized it. As Alexander writes of his experiences in the academy, "My very presence in academia signals a resistance to the combined expectations of my race and sex" (Alexander & Warren, 2002, p. 337). These words, as well as hooks's, further echoed the advice of a dear mentor who, when I shared an experience of unchecked racism in a class I was taking in my graduate program, urged me to "put it in your writing." This, he shared, was one of his strategies for surviving in an academic climate hostile to Others such as ourselves. Not a week goes by when I am not reminded of his words. Eleven years later, they continue to guide me as, in many ways, the work I have undertaken in critical communication pedagogy is driven not only by my need for sense making and answers but also by my desire for survival.

Furthermore, in turning to the body of work in critical communication pedagogy, I write to bear witness to experience. As Wright and Dinkha (2009) write,

> Women of color learn quickly that it is often not the quality of our education or even the content of our character that will be used by others to describe our life history. It is therefore essential to tell our own stories and document them in ways that may facilitate constructive change. (p. 103)

My desire to tell *our* stories and enable constructive change is what underlies this chapter. This desire in many ways resonates with a critical pedagogical perspective that comprises,

> at its best[,] . . . efforts to reflect and act upon the world in order to transform it, to make it a more just place for more people, to respond to our own collective pains and needs and desires. (Fassett & Warren, 2007, p. 26)

Complementing this view, Alexander (1999) writes, "Critical pedagogy is concerned with revealing, interrogating, and challenging those legitimated social forms and opening the space for additional voices" (p. 307). In articulating critical *communication* pedagogy, Fassett and Warren (2007) argue that culture is central, not additive. I follow their call in centering culture in my work and also by seeking to make explicit connections to our understandings of the relationship between the study of identity and critical communication pedagogy. I join an ongoing conversation about identities, positionalities, and power in the classroom and the academy at large by scholars such as Alexander (1999, 2004b, 2005), Alexander and Warren (2002), Allen, Orbe, and Olivas (1999), Carrillo Rowe and Malhotra (2006), Cooks (2003, 2007), Gust and Warren (2008), Johnson, Rich, and Cargile (2008), Warren (2003), Warren and Davis (2009), and Warren and Hytten (2004), who carefully unpack the interworkings of race, class, gender, and sexuality. These scholars remind us of the importance of understanding the materiality of ideology on the body. They work against reductionist critiques of identity and identity politics by demonstrating that "identities can be no less real for being socially and historically situated, and for being relational, dynamic, and at times ideological entrapments" (Alcoff & Mohanty, 2006, p. 6). These works importantly contour the complexities of the interworking of power, identities, and Otherness in the academy.

Specifically, in this chapter I operate from a critical communication pedagogy framework that is attentive to identity but is particularly seeking to give shape to the experiences of women of color. I do not assume that all women of color in the academy share the same experiences; however, like Hill Collins (2000), I understand the ways in which individual experiences are shaped by and feel the reverberations of histories and ideologies of racism, sexism, and heterosexism that create a unique relationship between the individual and collective. Furthermore, I privilege the perspectives of Others because it is not the common one we hear when we talk about critical pedagogy. More commonly, the experience of the white teacher entering the "multicultural" classroom is the focus.

Thus, in this chapter I ask, what would it mean to center the experiences of women of color faculty or Others in the classroom, particularly those who teach in the areas of race, class, sexuality, and gender? What would it mean to privilege the experiences of those who teach about the Other when the Other is the self (Henderson, cited in Johnson, 2003)? Alexander (2005) nuances this question as he writes, "When the in-class comments of students are suggestive of hatred and bigotry toward gays or other bodies that are 'queer' to them, my body and voice representatively stand in place to address those issues" (p. 251). Alexander (2005) elaborates,

> Teaching occurs at those intersections where sanctioned course content collides with lived experience—those moments when the "unspeakable" is spoken and the reverberation of the social exchange ricochets and resonates in the classroom. Those moments when the personal becomes political and the pedagogical imperative is to articulate understanding without silencing voice—that of both the student and of the teacher. (p. 253)

What would it mean if we explored more of the "impossibilities of (some) critical pedagogies" (Warren & Davis, 2009, p. 308)? Warren and Davis ask us to consider "the ways certain bodies enter the classroom . . . and the inability of current theory to provide space to understand and make space for all people" (p. 308). In this chapter, I delve into some of these impossibilities.

This critique of some critical pedagogies to account for the complexities of Other bodies and experiences in the classroom is further taken up by scholars such as Torres (2003), who challenges some uncritical uses of Freire (1970/2003) and the complexities that face women of color in the classroom who may embrace a Freirean perspective. Torres (2003) shares,

> As a product, and a proponent, of Freire's work, I have used his methods in both formal and informal settings. While they work wonderfully for many students—especially those who identify with oppressed groups—they are not as successful with those who either consciously or unconsciously identify with the oppressor. (p. 76)

Torres (2003) further elaborates,

As brilliant as they are, Freire's theories were developed in a completely different social, political, and historical context. . . . They did not necessarily consider how the process would work once the oppressed became the teachers, the subjects became the authors of their own experiences and the privileged became the students of the historical Other. The Freirean method calls for teaching in a way that validates the knowledge of the students and simultaneously decenters us as the only authority in the room. But as women of color, we enter the classroom already disempowered by existing gender and racial relationships, which may or may not be accompanied by class differences. (pp. 77–78)

Torres's (2003) critique is shared by Allen (2002), who complicates the oppressor and oppressed binary by turning to Patricia Hill Collins (2000) and her theorization of the matrix of domination, which is governed by four interrelated domains of power: the structural, disciplinary, hegemonic, and interpersonal. Hill Collins (2000) argues, "The structural domain organizes oppression, whereas the disciplinary domain manages it. The hegemonic domain justifies oppression, and the interpersonal domain influences everyday lived experience and the individual consciousness that ensues" (p. 276). Hill Collins (2000) asks us to consider identities from an intersectional perspective that takes into account the ways we occupy spaces of both empowerment and disempowerment simultaneously. These scholars challenge us to consider what a critical pedagogy might look like for faculty of color who teach courses in race, class, gender, and sexuality.

In locating my identities, I follow Hill Collins's (2000) lead in embracing an intersectional perspective toward identities. Thus, I am not just a woman of color, but I am also queer, able-bodied, and middle class. These various identities together afford me spaces of privilege and spaces in which I am disempowered and do not simply exist as additive labels. Furthermore, in embracing an intersectional perspective, I am attentive to Cohen (2005), who asks that we complicate our binary and homogeneous framing of various groups and identities through an intersectional perspective that recognizes the heterogeneity within groups and the potential for alliance building across groups. Cohen "envisions a politics in which one's relation to power, and not some homogenized identity, is privileged in determining one's political comrades" (p. 22). For example, Cohen (2005), who adds to the work of others who have challenged queer studies for its focus on whiteness and the West (Alexander, 2006, 2008; Calafell, 2007a; Carbado, 2005; Johnson, 2003; Keeling, 2005; Moreman, 2008; Muñoz, 1999; Nero, 2005; Ross, 2005; Zukic, 2008), writes,

While the politics of lesbian, gay, bisexual, and transgendered activists of color might recognize heteronormativity as a primary system of power structuring our lives, it understands that heteronormativity interacts with institutional racism, patriarchy, and class exploitation to define us in numerous ways as marginal and oppressed subjects. (p. 31)

She continues,

I emphasize here the marginalized position of some who embrace heterosexual identities not because I want to lead any great crusade to understand more fully the plight of "the heterosexual." Rather, I recognize the potential for shared resistance with such individuals. This potential is especially relevant not only for coalitional work but for a shared analysis, my vantage point, to "queer" people of color. (p. 36)

I take Cohen's (2005) view of intersectional politics to inform my understanding of identities and to underlie the possibilities of a critical communication pedagogy that seeks processes of alliance building and transformation (Alexander, 1999; Fassett & Warren, 2007).

In this chapter, I explore some moments of pedagogical (im)possibilities from an intersectional perspective drawing on both my experiences and literature on Other identities in the classroom. My use of the personal voice is informed by a performative writing perspective (Pelias, 2005; Pollock, 1998) that seeks to create an affective experience on the page. These narratives work against master narratives that position women of color as outsiders in the classroom and academia in general (Allen et al., 1999; Calafell, 2007b, 2009; Hughes, 2009; Owens Patton, 2004a, 2004b; Torres, 2003; Wright & Dinkha, 2009). It is a "performance of possibilities" that seeks to implicate you, the reader, into action (Madison, 1998). This is further consistent with the aims of a critical communication pedagogy that Fassett and Warren (2007) see as a

tactical form of research practice, in as much as something as sedimented and patterned as research practice can be tactical. It is a response, a recognition of patterns in discourse and thought. Critical communication pedagogy takes as a central principle a commitment to questioning taken-for-granted, sedimented ways of seeing and thinking. It forges alliances and builds new possibilities. (p. 100)

Thus, in turning to a performative and experiential voice, I seek to "forge alliances and build new possibilities" with you, the reader, in exploring moments of pedagogical impossibilities (Fassett & Warren, 2007). Addressing the theory and performance relationship, Madison (1999) writes,

The theory that gets in my head and sticks—the good parts or the parts relevant to what I must become and do in my life—performs. That *this* theory
performs me is an existential fact. That I choose to perform it is my craft.
I perform theory through time, through (un)conscious, nervousness,
and effort. This theory/performance coupling is not an easy assignment.
Performance thrills me, theory does not. I would surely lose myself without
performance, but I can not live well without theory. (p. 109)

Thus, like Madison (1999), I seek to straddle the theory-performance
coupling. This chapter is similar in form to handbook chapters written by
Calafell and Moreman (in press), Holman Jones (2005), and Adams and
Holman Jones (2008) in that it blends narrative with theory as illustra-
tive. This turn to experience is supported by a politics that privileges the
theory of the flesh (Moraga & Anzaldúa, 1983) to demonstrate and perform the complexities of lived experiences of raced, classed, and gendered
bodies. It is a politics that understands the importance of theorizing
through the body.

An Unconvincing Performance

Entering the ranks of teaching as a graduate student, I was both naive and
terrified. Naive because at that time, I believed in the idealism of the academy and all I thought it could offer me. I believed in the American Dream
and the promise of higher education. Being offered a teaching assistantship and a tuition waiver for a master's program, I thought I was set.
However, my idealism quickly waned as I became terrified because, after
about a week of teaching, I realized what I had gotten myself into. Vividly
I remember my orientation to teaching as my cohort and I were given
advice by more experienced (and somewhat jaded) graduate student
instructors about the ways in which we could establish and perform
authority and credibility in the classroom. These graduate student teachers were often handpicked by the faculty and administration for their
experience and reputation in the classroom. They were often the popular
graduate teachers in the department and, more often than not, they were
white, and, in many cases, they were heterosexual men. However, at this
time, I was not critically savvy enough to consider this. My memory does
not bring forth any faces of graduate student teachers of color speaking to
us or giving us "tips" about negotiating our presence in the classroom.
Furthermore, I cannot remember any mention of race, class, sexuality, or
gender in the equation, or if indeed it was mentioned, it was never dealt
with in any manner that took into account power. After my week's orientation to teaching, when I attempted to apply the strategies given by these
more experienced and department-endorsed graduate student teachers,

I failed. I was 23 years old, in many ways naive, thrown into a classroom in which I was clearly out of place in so many different ways.

My first semester was a nightmare not just because I actually *shook* in front of the class as I talked, trying to overcome my shyness, but because each class period posed a different set of challenges. For example, one day, it was the white male returning student who would continually ask my graduate student colleagues how old I was, as if he was being cheated out of an education and his money by having me as his instructor. The next day, it was the student who couldn't understand why I asked him to leave the class when he brought a gun for his visual aid for an informative speech into a building that clearly was marked with a sign that read "No firearms." All he cared about was whether or not he would lose points on his speech because I didn't allow him to use his visual aid. All this happened while the other women (please note: white) in my cohort didn't seem to have these difficulties. Sure, like many women in the classroom, they faced challenges to their authority, but their white middle-class performances of femininity and, in some ways, their socially correct beauty made their roads a little less rocky. Envious and blaming myself, I secretly hoped they would fail too.

More horror stories ensued and the inevitable "bad" teaching evaluations followed. Needless to say, my department was not happy with me, particularly the administrative structure that was led by two upper-middle-class white heterosexual women who terrified me both because of their over-the-top performances of white middle-class femininity and because I seriously doubted that they understood my perspective (nor did they want to). They failed to consider that the ethnicity of the instructor had a negative impact on credibility (Owens Patton, 1999) or that, "In general, women of color are more likely than white and/or male professors to experience situations where students question their expertise and teaching effectiveness" (Daufin, 1995, cited in Wright & Dinkha, 2009, p. 107). As Torres (2003) argues,

> We know that racism, sexism, classism, and homophobia reflect, create, and maintain a particular kind of hostility that is not in evidence when the instructor is white, straight, male, middle class, or some combination thereof. With a sense of entitlement that comes from deeply internalized dominance, such students eagerly display their assumed superiority, social authority, and their belief that they can afford to dismiss us. (p. 77)

The students and their intentions were never called into question, as I was constructed as a bad teacher. These women did not account for the ways women's bodies are read in the classroom (Cooks, 2007). None of this seemed to be compelling or recognized in my case because, in their minds, I was simply a problem. Looking back now from a critical frame, I understand that their abjection of me had less to do with me as an individual and more to do with my difference, more specifically my differences from them—everything that made me excessive—from my body to my class to my racial and ethnic affect (Calafell, 2007b, in press). At best, I'm sure my problems in the classroom were an irritation to them and, at worst, a reason to take away my teaching assistantship.

These women must have sensed the apprehension their presences caused me, because I was contacted by two faculty members I trusted and admired in the program to talk about my teaching. They shared that they had been consulted about my teaching, and they felt that it was better to be the ones to talk to me rather than the typical administrators. As we sat together in the office trying to figure out what was happening in the classroom, it was eventually suggested that perhaps I should stop talking about my ethnic identity. Subtly, I was told to pass (Alexander, 2004a) as white. As a light-skinned Chicana who was often misread, I had the "privilege" of not outing myself as a woman of color. It was suggested that I was overperforming my race. In some ways, I was performing my race incorrectly in this context and violating the administration's expectations (Alexander, 2004b; Calafell & Moreman, in press; Delgado, 2009; Inda, 2000; Moreman, 2008; Warren, 2003). I was left wondering if this would forever be my relationship to the classroom. Embarrassed and angry, I decided I would do whatever I needed to do to keep my assistantship.

This early experience in my teaching career has deeply shaped my orientation to the classroom and my general orientation to the academy. The suspicion I encountered from both the students and the administrators has manifested itself in multiple forms over the years. The tensions between insecurity and the recognition of racism, classism, and sexism in the classroom have driven my desire to become a better teacher and start to theorize pedagogy. Throughout the following text I write in the present tense because though the experiences I reflect on in this essay may have been in the past, the wounds of them live with me every day.

The Politics of Choice

Faculty and staff across campus are invited to include their names in the campus paper on one of two lists: one that lists you as being out on campus and the other that lists you as an LGBTQ ally. I hesitate, wondering where exactly to place myself. I understand Warren's words, as he writes,

> I do not tell many people that I am bi. It makes me uncomfortable. It makes me uncomfortable because I feel like I am assuming a risky identity which requires no risks—I get the privilege of "really" being married, of "really" being with a woman in public, of "really" appearing in every context, in every moment, as straight, as not-queer. (Warren & Zoffel, 2007, p. 236)

In my mind, my marriage to a man makes me a fraud. But I *am* queer and, to be quite honest, the marriage itself always was a bit subversive and in some ways queer (Calafell, 2008). It was a union that needed both financial and social "proof" to be justified as "real" to the Department of Homeland Security (Calafell, 2008). So, while I have certainly benefited from heterosexual privilege, I have also felt the tensions of nativism, paranoia, and hypernationalism after 9/11 in trying to "legalize" my Egyptian partner (Calafell, 2008). In the end, I choose the ally list despite the fact that I *feel* and *am* queer. I believe in queer politics and ideologies, *and* I *desire* both men and women. Like Warren, "I have a hard time naming [my] own location" (Gust & Warren, 2008, p. 117). Choosing the ally list instead of the out list is not easy. I don't want to be a fraud when I, as a married woman, benefit from heterosexual privilege. Also, quite frankly, for some of us queers of color, being out of the closet is not always a space of liberation (Ross, 2005). Ross argues that the binary of the closet and specifically being out of it signifies progress and modernity. This has implications for the ways queers of color are constructed, as power, history, and race are left unacknowledged. I consider both the subtle and explicit messages I received about sexuality while growing up. Sexuality in general was a taboo subject, and anything outside the purview of heterosexuality was not presented as an option for me as a Mexican American Catholic. From the questions about my age and my lack of a male partner, to the admonishing and badmouthing of a woman we knew who had just come out, to the suspicious looks at me and the first woman I had feelings for (who my family must have known was more than just a friend), I got the message very quickly. To them (at least the majority, not my mother), I would be flawed, a failure, should I not be a convincing heterosexual. All this history and its present reverberations continue to play in the back of my mind as I think about the lists. My colleague, a white bisexual woman, chooses to include her name on the out list, and I am listed as an ally. We are the only two from our department whose names appear on these lists.

The day the lists appear in the student newspaper, much panic among the communication student population ensues. The calls start to flood the department office: "Did I read this right? Is she a lesbian?" "I don't feel comfortable taking classes with her if she is a lesbian." These calls are not about my colleague whose name appears on the out list, they are about me. The students, while feeling like they have a handle on my racial performance and identity, are now confused and panicked about my sexuality, and the possibility that I have been a queer woman of color right under their noses scares them. Suddenly, I'm not so easy for them to make sense of and my presence is exponentially threatening. The administrative assistant assures me that she has "corrected" each and every caller. She has let them know that I am not a lesbian and I am married. My legal union to a man is all the "proof" they need. I guess they are more easily satisfied than Homeland Security. Outraged, I point out that my sexuality is none of the students' business, and she has no right to discuss it with them. She is reinforcing their fear of the Other and justifying their hatred. As Yep (2003) writes of heteronormativity,

> Through heteronormative discourses, abject and abominable bodies, souls, persons, and life forms are created, examined, and disciplined through current regimes of knowledge and power (Foucault, 1978/1990). Heteronormativity, as the invisible center and the presumed bedrock of society, is the quintessential force creating, sustaining, and perpetuating the erasure, marginalization, disempowerment, and oppressions of sexual others. (p. 18)

Heteronormativity and its violence are in full effect. The teacher's body is always sexualized (Gust & Warren, 2008) and, in this case, threatening.

Floored, angry, and disappointed with the students and the administrative assistant, I retreat to my office, close the door, and sit in silence and disbelief. Is my disbelief yet another marker of the heterosexual privilege I receive on a daily basis? In the end, I go to the Chair's office and ask that he send an e-mail to all the communication majors letting them know that homophobia will not be tolerated.

Almost 4 years later, I've left that school and find myself being honored at my new campus for my contributions to intellectual inquiry about queer life at the annual LGBTQIA Gala. I am pleased and humbled, mostly because I had no idea the award was coming and it was my graduate students who nominated me. I walk onstage to receive my award and stand silently as the woman giving me the award reads excerpts from my students' letters of nomination. In one of the letters, a student writes how wonderful it is to learn about critical sexuality studies and queer theory from a queer faculty member who is passionate and invested. I hear these words for the first time, and I smile at this moment of public outness that the student has given me. Does my queerness seem more authentic and comfortable to me because now I am single again without a man to mark me as heterosexual? What are the politics of this? I have not hidden my queerness here, but in many ways, I still feel like a fraud. Does it seem more authentic because I've told my mother that the next person I could be dating may be a woman? I don't know. But I smile, take my award, and return to my seat with my students.

"You Know She Hates White Men"

On more than one occasion, I have heard whisperings about a certain graduate student that refuses to take classes with me. It's very simple; he refuses to take classes from me because, according to him, I hate white men. He believes me to be so rigid that he *knows* we will clash. I have heard this more than once and from multiple sources. He has no problem sharing his belief with anyone. He believes that I hate white men even though whenever I see him on campus I smile and exchange pleasantries with him. This he believes because my courses center difference, and, as a white heterosexual male, he feels excluded and unduly implicated. My experience is not unique, and surely he is not the only one who feels this way. There are even a few white women who would probably join in his cause; he is just the most vocal. This experience of suspicion is one that has been shared by other faculty of color (Torres, 2003). I recall in one of my graduate programs hearing my fellow graduate students whisper about a prominent faculty member, that he hated white people. Was this because he was one of the leading scholars in critiquing white privilege and he was a person of color? In moments like this, our positionalities in these scenarios cannot be ignored (Cooks, 2003). The student who casts me as a racist is playing the "blame game" because I have forced him to see himself as a racialized subject, and he doesn't like it, so he's using diversionary tactics (Johnson et al., 2008). These dismissals seem like an easy way to try to discredit me because

> every critical remark I make from or about a subordinate location is viewed as an attack on them personally, as well as on their assumed objectivity and neutrality. I become political but they are not. Whatever I say from this position threatens their personal comfort, their endowment of privilege and power, and their commitment to the ideology of whiteness. (Torres, 2003, pp. 81–82)

This resistance takes so many forms, from inference (Owens Patton, 2004a) to acknowledgment, to diversion, to investment (Johnson et al., 2008), to colorblindness (Bonilla-Silva, 2003; Simpson, 2008), to a whole slew of other performances (Cooks, 2003; Nakayama & Krizek, 1995; Warren, 2003; Warren & Hytten, 2004) with which I'm sure many of us are familiar.

My supposed hatred of white men has surfaced at other times, in other places, and in other contexts (Calafell, 2007b). This hatred is not just imagined by the students; sometimes it comes from the administrators and colleagues too. At a previous institution, in a course on rhetoric and ethnicity, students were ready to revolt, waiting for any opportunity for me to slip up so they could pounce. My graduate student assistant, another woman of color, and I actually feared for our safety in that course. Finally, opportunity for the students to revolt was presented when I handed back some rather unexceptional papers. Unhappy with their grades, three students immediately headed straight to the Chair's office to complain. Soon after, I was called in to talk about what was happening in my classroom. My intention is not to focus on the students' actions but instead to consider the level of suspicion I was met with by my Chair; he performed and embraced whiteness, even though he was marked in his own way with Otherness (Carrillo Rowe & Malhotra, 2006). This man, who made no bones about the fact that he had wanted to hire me because I was a woman of color, began to interrogate me about what I did wrong. He had wanted to recruit people of color to the program but, like many others, had no desire to change the institutional climate or consider issues of retention (Owens Patton, 2004a). Confronted in this manner, I told him I did not need to teach at this university and could find a job somewhere else if this was how resistance to me would be met. As Torres (2003) argues, "Dealing with the sensitivities, hostilities, and defensiveness of privileged students cannot be my full-time concern. It robs marginalized and oppressed students of my attention and takes valuable time away from their engagement in the learning process" (p. 91). I would add that dealing with the sensitivities, hostilities, and defensiveness of administrators who have an investment in whiteness cannot be where I continually spend my energy.

Later my Chair would come to my office in a slightly less accusatory manner. I would come to find out that this was only after my white male colleague, who was his most trusted ally in the department, visited him (without my knowledge) and vouched for me and my efforts at breaking down racism in the classroom. This would come to be a pattern. I would be believed or understood only when this faculty member "translated" or vouched for me. Later, this same colleague became uncomfortable in this role when it mattered the most, and I, once again, became suspicious. In other places, this pattern has repeated itself, and I am left to wonder if this is a story that is familiar to other women of color in the academy.

Conclusions . . . Beginnings

I've offered these narratives as a way to flesh out some of the impossibilities of certain bodies in the academic setting. I've sought to shift the angle of vision to center the experiences of Others in the classroom. Alexander and Warren (2002) engage in a dialogic performance to present critical autopoetic narratives. In a similar manner, I invite you to engage in a dialogical performance (Conquergood, 1985) or intimate conversation with these narratives and this work. Perhaps they resonate with your own experiences; they are not so different, or maybe, they offer you an Other glimpse. Regardless of your positionality, I seek genuine conversation with you and these ideas. I hope for more. I *need* more. I want *you* to desire more. Anzaldúa (1990) writes, "Alliance work is the attempt to shift positions, change positions, reposition ourselves regarding our individual and collective identities" (p. 219). I ask you to shift positions and reposition yourself into an Other position. Previously, I have written about the politics of power of vulnerability and love (Calafell, 2007b). Can our work in critical communication pedagogy move from a place of rigidity and centeredness to a space of vulnerability, one that invites and expects connection and change through an affective experience with the Other? Conquergood (1985) argues that to engage in dialogic performance, we must be willing to be fully present and put our bodies on the line. This imperative as part of a larger performance paradigm requires vulnerability and demands social justice.

In this chapter, I not only implicate you, the reader, I also implicate an area of study to shift its angle of vision to an Other perspective because the performance scholar in me remains unsatisfied. Earlier, I asked what it would mean if we centered the experiences of women of color. Several years ago, at the National Communication Association convention, Patricia Hill Collins asked a similar question. In discussing her books *Black Feminist Thought* and *Black Sexual Politics*, Hill Collins noted that these works should be for everyone, not just black women. This point resonates for me as I wonder what critical communication pedagogy might look like if we start with the experiences of Others. What insights might we gather? Furthermore, while we are attentive to the ways power works, are we attentive to the *intersections* of identities and power? Can we find ways to intersectionally explore these experiences? Fassett and Warren (2007) demonstrate the importance of personal narrative in giving shape to a critical communication pedagogy. In this chapter, I have attempted to build on their work by giving shape to a critical communication pedagogy that is accountable to the intersections of identities and power through a narrative voice that invites reflection, connection, and vulnerability. Therefore, my aim in this chapter has been threefold. I have sought to center an Other experience as a form of intervention in critical communication pedagogy. I have attempted to perform intersectionality as a key imperative for our understandings and theorizings of identities in critical communication pedagogy. Finally, I have built on the work of scholars in critical communication pedagogy who have demonstrated the importance of the narrative voice. I further stake my claim in noting the importance of the narrative voice to give flesh to an intersectional perspective to identity. Narrative does not allow the nuances of intersectionality to be flattened by dry and meaningless numbers that quickly erase the humanness and complexity of people and their ordinary but extraordinary experiences. Continuing to bring a performance paradigm into critical communication pedagogy would open doors of invitation for Others to enter the dialogue and recenter theorizing away from the mind-body split, instead privileging Other ways of knowing that have come about because of histories of oppression (Conquergood, 1998). Thus, my call is for a social justice in critical communication pedagogy not only in terms of content but also in terms of form. I have begun this conversation as an invitation and only hope that you will join me.

References

Adams, T. E., & Holman Jones, S. (2008). Autoethnography is queer. In N. K. Denzin, Y. S. Lincoln, & L. T. Smith (Eds.), *Handbook of critical and indigenous methodologies* (pp. 373–390). Thousand Oaks, CA: Sage.

Alcoff, L. M., & Mohanty, S. A. (2006). Reconsidering identity politics: An introduction. In L. M. Alcoff, M. Hames-Garcia, S. P. Mohanty, & P. M. L. Moya (Eds.), *Identity politics reconsidered* (pp. 1–9). New York: Palgrave.

Alexander, B. K. (1999). Performing culture in the classroom: An instructional (auto)ethnography. *Text and Performance Quarterly, 19,* 307–331.

Alexander, B. K. (2004a). Passing, cultural performance, and individual agency: Performative reflections on Black masculine identity. *Cultural Studies <=> Critical Methodologies, 4,* 377–404.

Alexander, B. K. (2004b). Racializing identity: Performance, pedagogy, and regret. *Cultural Studies <=> Critical Methodologies, 4,* 12–27.

Alexander, B. K. (2005). Embracing the teachable moment: The Black gay body in the classroom as embodied text. In E. P. Johnson & M. A. Henderson (Eds.), *Black queer studies: A critical anthology* (pp. 249–265). Durham, NC: Duke University Press.

Alexander, B. K. (2006). *Performing Black masculinity: Race, culture, and queer identity.* Lanham, MD: AltaMira Press.

Alexander, B. K. (2008). Queer(y)ing the postcolonial through the West(ern). In N. K. Denzin, Y. S. Lincoln, & L. T. Smith (Eds.), *Handbook of critical and indigenous methodologies* (pp. 101–133). Thousand Oaks, CA: Sage.

Alexander, B. K., & Warren, J. T. (2002). The materiality of bodies: Critical reflections on pedagogy, politics and positionality. *Communication Quarterly, 50,* 328–343.

Allen, B. J., Orbe, M. P., & Olivas, M. R. (1999). The complexity of our tears: Dis/enchantment and (in)difference in the academy. *Communication Theory, 9,* 402–429.

Allen, R. L. (2002, April). *Pedagogy of the oppressor: What was Freire's theory for transforming the privileged and powerful?* Paper presented at the annual conference of the American Educational Research Association, New Orleans, LA.

Anzaldúa, G. (1990). Bridge, drawbridge, sandbar, or island: Lesbians-of-color hacienda alianzas. In L. Albrecht & R. M. Brewer (Eds.), *Bridges of power: Women's multicultural alliances* (pp. 216–231). Philadelphia: New Society.

Bonilla-Silva, E. (2003). *Racism without racists: Color-blind racism and the persistence of racial inequality in the United States.* Lanham, MD: Rowman & Littlefield.

Calafell, B. M. (2007a). *Latina/o communication studies: Theorizing performance.* New York: Peter Lang.

Calafell, B. M. (2007b). Mentoring and love: An open letter. *Cultural Studies <=> Critical Methodologies, 7,* 425–441.

Calafell, B. M. (2008). Performing the responsible sponsor: Everything you never wanted to know about immigration post-9/11. In A. Valdivia (Ed.), *Latina/o communication studies today* (pp. 69–89). New York: Peter Lang.

Calafell, B. M. (2009). "Your education wipes out your ethnicity": A "White" woman of color in the classroom: The turn to a personal voice. In D. Cleveland (Ed.), *When "minorities" are strongly encouraged to apply: Diversity and affirmative action in higher education* (pp. 93–101). New York: Peter Lang.

Calafell, B. M. (in press). Rhetorics of possibility: Challenging the textual bias of rhetoric through a critical race and feminist perspective. In E. Schell & K. Rawson (Eds.), *Rhetorica in motion*. Pittsburgh, PA: University of Pittsburgh Press.

Calafell, B. M., & Moreman, S. T. (in press). Iterative hesitancies and *Latinidad:* The reverberances of raciality. In R. T. Halualani & T. K. Nakayama (Eds.), *Handbook of critical intercultural communication*. Malden, MA: Blackwell.

Carbado, D. (2005). Privilege. In E. P. Johnson & M. A. Henderson (Eds.), *Black queer studies: A critical anthology* (pp. 190–212). Durham, NC: Duke University Press.

Carrillo Rowe, A., & Malhotra, S. (2006). (Un)hinging whiteness. In M. P. Orbe, B. J. Allen, & L. A. Flores (Eds.), *The same and different: Acknowledging the diversity within and between cultural groups* (International and Intercultural Communication Annual, Vol. 29, pp. 166–192). Washington, DC: National Communication Association.

Cohen, C. (2005). Punks, bulldaggers, and welfare queens: The radical potential of queer politics? In E. P. Johnson & M. A. Henderson (Eds.), *Black queer studies: A critical anthology* (pp. 21–51). Durham, NC: Duke University Press.

Conquergood, D. (1985). Performing as a moral act: Ethical dimensions of the ethnography of performance. *Literature in Performance, 5,* 1–13.

Conquergood, D. (1998). Beyond the text: Toward a performative cultural politics. In S. J. Dailey (Ed.), *The future of performance studies* (pp. 25–36). Annandale, VA: National Communication Association.

Cooks, L. (2003). Pedagogy, performance, and positionality: Teaching about Whiteness in interracial communication. *Communication Education, 52,* 245–257.

Cooks, L. (2007). Accounting for my teacher's body: What can I teach/what can we learn? *Feminist Media Studies, 7,* 299–312.

Delgado, F. P. (2009). Reflections on being/performing Latino identity in the academy. *Text and Performance Quarterly, 29,* 149–164.

Fassett, D. L., & Warren, J. T. (2007). *Critical communication pedagogy*. Thousand Oaks, CA: Sage.

Freire, P. (2003). *Pedagogy of the oppressed: 30th anniversary edition*. New York: Continuum. (Original work published 1970)

Gust, S. W., & Warren, J. T. (2008). Naming our sexual and sexualized bodies in the classroom and the important stuff that comes after the colon. *Qualitative Inquiry, 14,* 114–134.

Hill Collins, P. (2000). *Black feminist thought: Knowledge, consciousness, and the politics of empowerment* (Revised 10th anniversary, 2nd ed.). New York: Routledge.

Holman Jones, S. (2005). Autoethnography: Making the personal political. In N. K. Denzin & Y. S. Lincoln (Eds.), *The Sage handbook of qualitative research* (pp. 763–791). Thousand Oaks, CA: Sage.

hooks, b. (1994). *Teaching to transgress: Education as the practice of freedom.* New York: Routledge.

Hughes, R. L. (2009). Two degrees of separation and the good old professors network: Ivory tower tales. In D. Cleveland (Ed.), *When "minorities" are strongly encouraged to apply: Diversity and affirmative action in higher education* (pp. 135–145). New York: Peter Lang.

Inda, J. X. (2000). Performativity, materiality, and the racial body. *Latino Studies Journal, 11*(3), 74–99.

Johnson, E. P. (2003). *Appropriating Blackness: Performance and the politics of authenticity.* Durham, NC: Duke University Press.

Johnson, J. R., Rich, M., & Cargile, A. C. (2008). "Why are you shoving this stuff down our throats?" Preparing intercultural education to challenge performances of White racism. *Journal of International and Intercultural Communication, 1*, 113–135.

Keeling, K. (2005). "Joining the lesbians": Cinematic regimes of Black lesbian visibility. In E. P. Johnson & M. A. Henderson (Eds.), *Black queer studies: A critical anthology* (pp. 213–227). Durham, NC: Duke University Press.

Madison, D. S. (1998). Performance, personal narratives, and the politics of possibility. In S. J. Dailey (Ed.), *The future of performance studies* (pp. 276–286). Annandale, VA: National Communication Association.

Madison, D. S. (1999). Performing theory/embodied writing. *Text and Performance Quarterly, 19*, 107–124.

Moraga, C., & Anzaldúa, G. E. (Eds.). (1983). *This bridge called my back: Writings by radical women of color.* Brooklyn, NY: Kitchen Table.

Moreman, S. T. (2008). Hybrid performativity, south and north of the border: *Entre la teoría y la materialidad de hibridación.* In A. N. Valdivia (Ed.), *Latina/o communication studies today* (pp. 91–111). New York: Peter Lang.

Muñoz, J. E. (1999). *Disidentifications: Queers of color and the performance of politics.* Minneapolis: University of Minnesota Press.

Nakayama, T. K., & Krizek, R. L. (1995). Whiteness: A strategic rhetoric. *Quarterly Journal of Speech, 81*, 291–309.

Nero, C. I. (2005). Why are gay ghettos White? In E. P. Johnson & M. A. Henderson (Eds.), *Black queer studies: A critical anthology* (pp. 228–245). Durham, NC: Duke University Press.

Owens Patton, T. (1999). Ethnicity and gender: An examination of its impact on instructor credibility in the university classroom. *Howard Journal of Communications, 10*, 123–144.

Owens Patton, T. (2004a). In the guise of civility: The complicitous maintenance of inferential forms of sexism and racism in higher education. *Women's Studies in Communication, 27*, 61–87.

Owens Patton, T. (2004b). Reflections of a Black woman professor: Racism and sexism in academia. *Howard Journal of Communications, 15*, 185–200.

Pelias, R. (2005). Performative writing as scholarship: An apology, an argument, an anecdote. *Cultural Studies <=> Critical Methodologies, 5*, 415–424.

Pollock, D. (1998). Performative writing. In P. Phelan & J. Lane (Eds.), *The ends of performance* (pp. 73–103). New York: New York University Press.

Ross, M. B. (2005). Beyond the closet as raceless paradigm. In E. P. Johnson & M. A. Henderson (Eds.), *Black queer studies: A critical anthology* (pp. 161–181). Durham, NC: Duke University Press.

Simpson, J. L. (2008). The color-blind double bind: Whiteness and the (im)possibility of dialogue. *Communication Theory, 18,* 139–159.

Torres, E. E. (2003). *Chicana without apologies: The new Chicana cultural studies.* New York: Routledge.

Warren, J. T. (2003). *Performing purity: Whiteness, pedagogy, and the reconstitution of power.* New York: Peter Lang.

Warren, J. T., & Davis, A. M. (2009). On the impossibility of (some) critical pedagogies: Critical positionalities within a binary. *Cultural Studies <=> Critical Methodologies, 9,* 306–320.

Warren, J. T., & Hytten, K. (2004). The face of Whiteness: Pitfalls and the critical democrat. *Communication Education, 53,* 321–339.

Warren, J. T., & Zoffel, N. A. (2007). Living in the middle: Performances bi-men. In K. E. Lovaas & M. M. Jenkins (Eds.), *Sexualities & communication in everyday life: A reader* (pp. 233–242). Thousand Oaks, CA: Sage.

Wright, S., & Dinkha, J. (2009). Gendered reality, professional identity, and women of color in higher education. In D. Cleveland (Ed.), *When "minorities" are strongly encouraged to apply: Diversity and affirmative action in higher education* (pp. 103–118). New York: Peter Lang.

Yep, G. A. (2003). The violence of heteronormativity in communication studies: Notes on injury, healing, and queer world-making. *Journal of Homosexuality, 45,* 11–59.

Zukic, N. (2008). Webbing sexual/textual agency in autobiographic narratives of pleasure. *Text and Performance Quarterly, 28,* 396–414.

Critical Race Theory and Critical Communication Pedagogy

19

Jennifer S. Simpson

Over the past three to four decades, critical race theory has brought an urgency to the subject of race and to the problem of racism. In academic disciplines, it has repeatedly challenged the belief that race and racism are only marginally relevant to disciplinary content. From an instructional perspective, critical race theory indirectly asserts that racism is ordinary and widespread and thus that it has much to do with subject matter in a variety of courses. It assumes that when learning about, for example, the history of industrialization, the psychological development of children, the effects of unions on labor practices, the relevance of media to ideologies, or the links between identity and language, race is routinely bound up with human interaction. Critical race theory also distinguishes itself by stating directly that knowledge production and teaching that seek an end to racism are important and necessary.

Another body of work that prioritizes emancipation and antioppression is critical pedagogy. This body of thought focuses on the relationship of knowledge to power and sees all education as inherently political, or as having consequences related to how people live. Critical pedagogy seeks to make more transparent how ideologies and processes of social formation lead to injustice and stresses the importance of working at antioppressive practices in and outside the classroom. Many communication scholars who attend to issues of race, gender, sexuality, and class in their courses draw on critical pedagogy in their research and teaching. The work of these scholars has led to a loosely defined but identifiable body of work called critical communication pedagogy. Critical communication pedagogues offer rigorous attention to the ways in which communication is socially constructed, embrace the constitutive and embodied nature of all communication, and foreground the significance of human agency within particular contexts.

Critical race theory, critical pedagogy, and critical communication pedagogy have changed communication instruction. Even as large numbers of communication instructors may choose to ignore or only minimally acknowledge the theoretical, methodological, and pedagogical contributions of these three bodies of work, it is also the case that increasing numbers of textbooks, as well as disciplinary subfields, acknowledge their existence. All instructional paradigms center one set of questions and, in so doing, assign another set to a kind of pedagogical backstage. Critical race theory, critical pedagogy, and critical communication pedagogy insistently ask, "In what kind of world do we want to live?" "What is the role of communication in ensuring that that world is just and allows each of us to be fully human?" This chapter will address critical race theory and critical pedagogy, as well as their links to critical communication pedagogy and communication instruction. The final section will discuss contemporary tensions between critical communication pedagogy, critical race theory, and critical pedagogy.

Critical Race Theory, Critical Pedagogy, and Critical Communication Pedagogy: An Overview

Communication researchers and instructors have relied on critical race theory, critical pedagogy, and critical communication pedagogy to broadly affirm the socially constructed nature of reality and to attend more expressly to power. While there are distinct tensions among the three bodies of work, they demonstrate parallels related to a critique of acontextual analysis; the affirmation of reality as socially constructed; a belief in and emphasis on the complex relationship of agency and structure; attention to the significance of power; and claims about the primacy of material, lived, and embodied reality. These core theoretical starting points arguably challenge several often tacit but nevertheless consequential theoretical orientations in more traditional communication scholarship. These include the idea that individuals are the primary starting point for understanding communication; the minimization of the insistent interplay of individuals, ideologies, and institutions in all communication practices; and the tendency to approach communication practices as divorced from the material dynamics of power.

In addition to areas of overlap among the three bodies of thought, there are also significant points of tension among the three bodies of work. The existence and relevance of oppression (and discerning which type is primary); the necessity of racial minority experiences as a source of knowledge; a focus on antioppression and antiracism (versus, for instance, a heightened awareness of the existence of racism and/or oppression); and the distinctions between liberal multiculturalism and radical social transformation all represent areas of difference that have significant consequences for communication instruction. To understand these differences more clearly, and their relevance to communication instruction, it will be useful to more fully explore critical race theory, critical pedagogy, and critical communication pedagogy. I will draw out the primary theoretical components of critical pedagogy and critical communication pedagogy, especially as they relate to and engage critical race theory. An analysis of the intersections and gaps in all three can support rigorous and far-reaching attention to the future of communication instruction.

Critical Race Theory

Critical race theory, now evident in a range of disciplines, has its origins in legal scholarship. This body of work is "unified by two common interests. The first is to understand how a regime of white supremacy and its subordination of people of color have been created and maintained" in the United States. The second is not only to "understand the vexed bond between law and racial power but to *change* it" (Crenshaw, Gotanda, Peller, & Thomas, 1995, p. iii). In the 1960s and 1970s, there was a sense among many legal scholars that the gains won by the civil rights movement had stalled and were in some cases being "rolled back" (Delgado & Stefancic, 2001, p. 4). Critical race theory emerged in part as a response to these policy shifts. It seeks to understand the creation and maintenance of systems of racial oppression and to change the corresponding formations of power. It assumes that race and racial power are significant "within numerous vectors of social life" (Crenshaw et al., 1995, p. xxxii).

CRITICAL RACE THEORY: THEORETICAL COMPONENTS

There are six central components of critical race theory (Matsuda, Lawrence, Delgado, & Crenshaw, 1993). Critical race theory begins with the assumption that racism is ordinary to life in the United States. Rather than occasional or an exception, racism is "endemic in U.S. society, deeply ingrained legally, culturally, and even psychologically" (Tate, 1997, p. 234). Furthermore, for critical race theory scholars, racism exists not only at the level of individual prejudice, but "also in relation to the more subtle and hidden operations of power" at systemic and institutional levels (Gillborn,

2006, p. 21). For example, the established practice of denying African Americans and Latinos low-interest loans (ACORN Fair Housing, 2007), or the only recently legislatively addressed policy that has meted out far more severe punishment for possession of crack (used primarily by racial minorities) than cocaine (used primarily by whites) (Bebo, 1999; Johnson, Logan, & Davis, 2004), are two examples of how racism is embedded in institutions. Critical race theory scholars believe that racism represents the "common, everyday experience of most people of color" in the United States (Delgado & Stefancic, 2005, p. 6).

Along with asserting the ordinariness of racism, critical race theorists also "express skepticism toward dominant legal claims of neutrality, objectivity, colorblindness and meritocracy" (Matsuda et al., 1993, p. 6). Colorblindness is the belief that one's race does not have a significant effect on one's life experiences or opportunities. Meritocracy is the idea that success depends on individual effort and has little or nothing to do with institutional constraints. Both ideas can support the belief that we are largely "beyond" race, or that racism is over. In communication courses, textbooks often implicitly validate notions of colorblindness and meritocracy, allowing students and instructors, particularly those in the dominant group, to maintain the notion that racism is far removed from most communication interactions. For example, many communication textbooks include a specific chapter on cultural differences, implying that diversity itself is an exception, disconnected from the rest of the book's content. Furthermore, attention to race, gender, or class is often primarily offered at the individual level. For example, it is more likely for a communication instructor to consider stereotypes or individual prejudice than to acknowledge, for instance, the ways in which organizations rely on ideologies that privilege the dominant group in ways that legitimize institutional racism. In brief, critical race theory rejects ideas of objectivity and neutrality as overly simplistic.

A third tenet of critical race theory is the importance of historical analyses of the law and other institutions that shape how people live. Critical race theory assumes the necessity of context-based analysis and claims that all human interaction sits within a set of historical and present-day realities that are inescapably relevant. A recognition of context will lead to a parallel awareness of the prevalence of racism in social life, regardless of the setting (Matsuda et al., 1993, p. 6). In a class on health communication, in which course material includes attention to communication among providers and those seeking services, the instructor might encourage attention to how historical institutional racism differently effects cultural groups' relationships to publicly provided health care services. For instance, the Tuskegee experiments, in which the United States Public Health Service withheld information from and refused treatment to African American men who had syphilis in the interest of medical experimentation, might give the African American community reason to be suspicious of health care providers in general (Washington, 2006). This kind of historical and contextual analysis points to the ways in which social policies and practices often differently benefit various groups.

A fourth component of critical race theory is the necessity and significance of the experiential knowledge and analyses of racial minorities related to law and society. Centering the knowledge and lived realities of people of color serves to "act as a defence against the colour-blind and sanitized analyses generated via universalistic discourses" (Gillborn, 2006, p. 23). Relying on the knowledge of people of color as necessary rather than optional immediately challenges many common sense assumptions that the dominant white group may hold, about race as well as about other issues. Routine experiences undergone by all racial groups—receiving a speeding ticket, responding to a teacher's concern with one's child's behavior in school, interviewing for a job, seeking a place to live—might be rethought in light of contextual information and from the perspective of a racial minority. In the communication classroom, valuing the life experiences of racial minorities means that when a Latina student claims that an experience of racism occurred on her way to class, the instructor takes this claim seriously and encourages other students to do so as well.

Critical race theory is also committed to interdisciplinarity, rejecting the idea that the best way to understand the world in which we live is through tightly bound disciplinary categories, which should not overlap or be reciprocally informative. To fully understand the formation of laws that differently punish for possession of crack or of cocaine or the ways in which banks offer high-interest loans to one group and low-interest loans to another group, it is not sufficient to think only about legal or economic theories, respectively. Rather, to consider the latter example, it would be important to consider knowledge in a range of disciplines, including geography, history, law, sociology, business and economics, psychology, and communication. A final component of critical race theory is its insistence on the importance of "work[ing] toward the end of eliminating racial oppression as part of the broader goal of ending all forms of oppression" (Matsuda et al., 1993, p. 6). This point is crucial, particularly in academic settings where knowledge itself, rather than change, is often sufficient and desirable. In short, awareness is not enough for critical race theorists. Scholars who support critical race theory must pursue the end of racial and other forms of oppression.

CRITICAL RACE THEORY AND THEORETICAL ASSUMPTIONS: IMPLICATIONS FOR COMMUNICATION INSTRUCTION

These six characteristics have broad implications for communication instruction. They speak to core aspects of communication pedagogy, including where teaching and learning in communication classrooms begin, or pedagogical assumptions; what they include, or pedagogical content; and where they are going, or pedagogical outcomes. It is useful to consider these three components in connection with instruction in a specific course. Related to critical race theory and pedagogical assumptions in an interpersonal communication course, an instructor might begin with the beliefs that all identities are racialized, that interpersonal communication routinely involves expressions of race privilege and discrimination, that research about interpersonal communication has not sufficiently attended to race and is thus insufficient and/or misleading, and that interpersonal communication norms have a necessary relationship to racialized ideological norms and institutional rewards and restrictions for specific communication behaviors. In sum, rather than assuming that race is extraneous to interpersonal communication, or infrequently linked, this instructor might understand interpersonal communication to occur within racialized and other socially constructed identities.

In a critical race theory framework, pedagogical content in an interpersonal communication class might include the significance of racial stereotypes to interpersonal communication; the ways in which racism at ideological and institutional levels has shaped our interpersonal communication with those in similar and different racial groups; or how, in routine contexts where interpersonal communication occurs, individuals variously affirm, deny, and/or reject the knowledge and viewpoints of racial minorities. Finally, critical race theory urges that in an interpersonal communication class, pedagogical outcomes include at some level attention to ending racism in interpersonal communication, whether that be in particular contexts (family, school, workplace, etc.) or at the level of research and knowledge representation (e.g., in interpersonal communication textbooks).

It is also worth nothing that as critical race theory is a body of work aimed at making change and at transforming the way society works, its theoretical foundations set it apart from traditional forms of communication instruction. The purpose of theory for critical race scholars is not to control or predict, nor to assert a kind of universal, acontextual truth about how we live. Rather, critical race theory aims to illuminate "a set of interrelated beliefs about the significance of race/racism and how it operates in contemporary Western society" (Gillborn, 2006, p. 19). Critical race theory and many other critical theories assert that all theories have an agenda; begin with partial and subjective assumptions and values; and have specific consequences that matter to how people live. That is, all theories do something, act in the world in some way, and have specific effects. While many critical theorists pursue change and seek to resist and interrupt oppressive practices, other more traditional theories, including those in communication instruction, might work at maintaining social relations as they are, supporting, in large part, the way institutions currently operate. In a book that addresses a range of theories of communication instruction, it is important to note that many scholars in communication and other disciplines charge that critical theorists "have an agenda" or are simply asserting their "opinions" rather than offering rigorous attention to any subject matter. A critical theorist might ask in response, "How do more traditional understandings of communication, or those presented in textbooks, promote or affirm a certain way of thinking?" If a textbook repeatedly leaves race out, what is this author's agenda, especially related to race? Why is this agenda any more valid than one that claims that race is central to social interaction?

In brief, all theory and instruction speak to some aspect of how we live, advocating, whether openly or not, more of the same or a different approach. Most critical theorists are explicit about their scholarly agendas and often likewise receive the charge of being "biased" or "political." Many theories that do not label themselves critical and might assert their neutrality or unbiased nature also serve specific interests, routinely aimed at furthering "business as usual." As one scholar has pointed out,

> Most universities offer courses on managing some designated group . . . teachers learn how to discipline students . . . criminal justice students master skills of controlling deviant populations. Far fewer courses teach how to recognize and combat these strategies of control. Within this managerial climate, courses on union movements, Black political activism, global women's movements, and everyday subversive activities are few and far between. (Collins, 1998, p. xii)

In other words, all research and instruction has an agenda. Critical race theory raises a seemingly simple yet profound question for communication instruction: What do we want teaching and learning in communication classes to do?

CRITICAL RACE THEORY: METHODOLOGICAL COMPONENTS

In light of critical race theory's ends of antiracism and antioppression, three methodological tools are especially useful. Storytelling, counterstorytelling, and using narrative that builds on the experiences of people of color as a source of knowledge about social life comprise one tool. For critical race theory scholars, one primary barrier to ending racism is the set of beliefs and assumptions that tells people that racism is over, exceptional, and/or not a serious concern. A further issue is the invisibility of race discrimination and privilege, especially to those who are white. Storytelling and counterstorytelling might recount actual events in language that acknowledges the many layers of race; or might turn assumed wisdom on its head, offering accounts that simultaneously question reality and offer incisive analysis (see Bell, 1980, 2000; Delgado, 1995).

In addition to storytelling, another methodological tool for critical race theory is "interest convergence." This idea is generally linked to a 1980 article by Derrick Bell and proposes that gains for African Americans have come primarily and most extensively when whites have benefitted as well. For example, affirmative action, a program that most believe has significantly benefitted racial minorities, has in fact offered the most gains to white women (Ladson-Billings, 1998). Interest convergence is a tool for thinking about how race works, drawing attention to the analytical possibility of gains for racial minorities occurring primarily and often only when gains for whites also exist.

A third tool is that of critical white studies, which offers analyses of the privileges and constructions of what it is to be white. Critical white studies examines and critiques the learned behavior that often accompanies being white and that seeks to exclude or diminish racial minorities. For example, critical white studies seeks to understand ways in which whites in general learn to both ignore race and distance themselves from the consequences and origins of racism even as they routinely experience privileges because they are white. Critical race theory claims that there are racialized patterns to which whites subscribe. For example, the act of assuming a person of color is more likely than a white person to steal in a store selling clothes or music and the choice or policy that encourages an employee to follow a person of color around the store and not follow a white person are examples of whiteness. Critical race theory scholars believe that a thorough acknowledgment of how whiteness works, what it looks like, and what challenging it requires will be necessary to end racism.

CRITICAL RACE THEORY AND METHODOLOGICAL ASSUMPTIONS: IMPLICATIONS FOR COMMUNICATION INSTRUCTION

Related to communication instruction, these three methodological tools are highly relevant. First, centering storytelling and narrative, especially by racial minorities, would significantly shift the content and process of learning in many communication classrooms. Instructors might consider the perspectives of racial minorities related to a range of course material, especially when the theories, methods, and content that those in the discipline have represented have been those articulated by white scholars. Narratives from people of color, particularly related to their experiences in routine communication interactions—in the workplace, with law enforcement, in an interview, with other students or instructors—would serve to foreground a different set of priorities and realities than exist in most communication classrooms. Hearing from faculty or students of color quickly raises difficult questions regarding the politics of voice and representation (see Boler, 2004; Simpson, 2003, 2006, 2008). At a minimum, the use of storytelling in critical race theory asks communication instructors to grapple with the role of narratives from racial minorities in our classes.

Interest convergence encourages a realism and attention to actual benefits specific groups receive because of particular policies. This methodological approach challenges communication instructors to address the rhetorical or discursive levels of communication, or what we communicate with our words; the material levels of communication, or what we communicate with our actions; and how the two are intertwined. In short, it is wholly insufficient to attend to intent without a serious engagement with consequences. In this framework, comments that students or instructors often make such as "racism is mostly over," or that race and racism are "not really connected to most course content," would need to be examined for the assumptions on which they are based, and replaced by attention to the material realities of how people live. How do stereotypes and broader institutional practices affect communication interactions in interviews and hiring processes, for example? When we look at specific quality-of-life indicators, related to health care, education, and work, for example, how do specific racial groups fare? Interest convergence insists on careful attention to what policies mean for specific groups, an attention to the material effects of how people live that is often missing in communication classrooms.

Finally, critical white studies has made itself known as a body of work relevant to specific areas of communication scholarship (Cooks, 2003; Cooks & Simpson, 2007; Jackson, Warren, Pitts, & Wilson, 2007; Nakayama & Krizek, 1995; Warren, 2003). According to the authors of a chapter in a recent book on whiteness and pedagogy written by communication scholars, whiteness in communication classrooms includes seven themes:

(1) the (in)visibility of race; (2) the reality of conflict and denial of racism when students and teachers address race; (3) the prevalence of colorblindness; (4) the frustration that can come with learning about privilege; (5) the normalized racial boundaries that serve to powerfully maintain the status quo and which must be undone piece by piece; (6) the difficulty for particularly white students to know what it is to be racialized; and (7) the necessity of living and grappling with contradictions once whiteness is exposed. (Cooks & Simpson, 2007, p. 19)

In brief, communication scholars writing about whiteness have brought race into many communication classrooms, not only addressing how racial minority experiences bear on communication interactions, but also questioning the dominance of white norms and beliefs in most communication research, particularly that presented in textbooks. In summary, critical race theory, in its theoretical and methodological assertions, has both directly and indirectly had much to do with opening up communication instruction to a range of concerns, racial and otherwise. In many ways, it has shifted the subject, encouraging movement from an acontextual and individualistic understanding of communication to a complex view of communication interaction that engages the consequences of racism.

CRITIQUES OF CRITICAL RACE THEORY

Those who have found fault with critical race theory have primarily focused on the "suspect" nature of storytelling, a supposed lack of attention to class and capitalism, and questions regarding the usefulness of critical race theory in ending racism. Challenges linked to the appropriateness and validity of storytelling in legal and academic contexts are posed primarily by mainstream scholars, legal and otherwise, and criticize stories' lack of academic rigor and their "distortion of public discourse," due to their not always being "factually true" (Delgado & Stefancic, 2001, p. 91). In fact, these critiques often rest on a belief in objectivity and in acontextual truths that critical race theorists hold suspect. In this sense, the subversiveness of stories, their multidimensionality and adherence to lived reality, is what critical race theorists believe is useful in challenging knowledge that claims objectivity. From a critical race theory perspective, if knowledge is socially constructed, and if a belief in acontextual, universalistic notions of reality has fundamentally obscured the experiences of large numbers of people and especially racial minorities, storytelling becomes not only logical but necessary and desirable.

A second area of critique, primarily posed by critical pedagogues, asserts that critical race theory has not sufficiently attended to class. These scholars assert that critical race theory's emphasis on race results, in part, in a "fail[ure] to provide a systemic analysis of global capitalism and its effect on communities" (Parker & Stovall, 2004, p. 168). Indeed, two prominent critical race theorists, Richard Delgado and Jean Stefancic (2001), state simply, "Critical race theory has yet to develop a comprehensive theory of class" (p. 107). Although the question can be framed by pitting race against class (i.e., one or the other as most significant), many critical race theorists and critical pedagogues rely on the concept of intersectionality in their work, or the idea that class, race, gender, sexuality, and national origin have meaning not as isolated categories, but as categories that intersect. At the same time, some critical pedagogues (McLaren, 1998) insist on an anticapitalist analysis as primary to ending all forms of oppression.

Finally, many of those who work within critical race theory ask rigorous questions about its usefulness, particularly to communities of color.

What is [critical race theory's] practical worth? Why is it not down in the trenches, helping activists deal with problems of domestic violence, poor schools, and police brutality? . . . What is the purpose of critique unless one has something better to replace it with? (Delgado & Stefancic, 2001, p. 93)

There is a basic recognition among critical race theorists that the body of work they have produced has had significant and far-reaching consequences, related to how activists conceptualize race, the number of courses on critical race theory in law schools and in other disciplines, and judges' and attorneys' reliance on it (Delgado & Stefancic, 2001, p. 101).

Critical Pedagogy

Similar to critical race theory, critical pedagogy asks fundamental questions about the uses of power and the social construction of reality. As noted earlier, both critical race theory and critical pedagogy strongly critique acontextual, individualistic forms of knowledge production and instruction and advocate instead an attentiveness to the material realities of how people live, as well as radical change related to structures and practices that limit what it means to be human. Critical pedagogy draws extensively on the critical theoretical tradition of the Frankfurt School, which initially developed in the 1930s in Germany. This group of theorists shared a "belief that injustice and subjugation shaped the lived world. . . . Focusing their attention on the changing nature of capitalism, the early critical theorists analyzed the mutating forms of domination that accompanied this change" (Kincheloe, 2008, p. 46). In this section, I will discuss the main components of critical pedagogy and its tensions and critiques. As other chapters in this part of the book will focus at length on critical pedagogy, I will be brief and primarily attentive to the ways in which critical pedagogy intersects with critical race theory.

Critical pedagogy's insistent focus on the relationship of knowledge to power encourages attention to how power is used in racialized ways. Operating as a "rhetoric and a social movement" (Grande, 2004, p. 6), critical pedagogy identifies schools as "'sites of struggle' where the broader relations of power, domination, and authority are played out" (p. 6). Three theoretical components are central to critical pedagogy. These include (a) an analysis of knowledge and power, (b) an insistence on the importance of a democratic imagination in moving toward equity and justice, and (c) the belief that all learning represents opportunities for students to express agency and be a part of social change.

ANALYSIS OF KNOWLEDGE AND POWER

Attention to the relationship of knowledge and power represents the most far-reaching and consequential theoretical component of critical pedagogy (Giroux, 2007; Giroux & Searls Giroux, 2004; Kincheloe, 2008). This theoretical imperative insists on a relentless interrogation of how power works, and of the ways in which students' knowledge is tied up with dominant expressions of power. It asserts that learning begins when students critically reflect on what they have come to take for granted, and on the ways in which uses of power normalize oppressive conditions and practices (McLaren, 1998). For critical pedagogues, a thorough understanding of knowledge and power requires attention to ideologies, forms of oppression, the relationship of agency and structure, and capitalism. Students and instructors must consider ideologies: how they are shaped, particularly through the media; the ways in which they normalize repressive ways of thinking, feeling, and being; and how they might be challenged. In addition to considering ideologies, it is crucial to analyze forms of oppression and their effects on how people live related to the material, social, psychological, and spiritual aspects of life (Giroux, 2006; Kincheloe, 2008).

The relationship of agency and structure constitutes an additional area of concern related to knowledge and power, and focuses on how individuals make choices within a context-based and institutionally framed set of restrictions and possibilities (Grossberg, 1996). Finally, most critical pedagogues' attention to knowledge and power assumes that capitalism and its attendant consumerism and neoliberal policies in the United States and many other Western nations are antithetical to democracy and justice (McLaren, 2007). Related to this, a critique of capitalism and the ways in which it is exploitative is a necessary component for considering the relationship of knowledge and power.

A DEMOCRATIC IMAGINATION

For most critical pedagogues, the goal of a transgressive and emancipatory theory of knowledge is the realization of or substantive movement toward democratic practices and justice. This second theoretical component of critical pedagogy insists on the importance of "the responsibility of the present for a democratic future" (Giroux, 2007, p. 1). In this sense, schools become places where students can envision a more equitable society, in which people are "fully free to claim their moral and political agency" (Moyers, 2007). This also changes the content and ends of learning. Course material addressing weighty social issues and the possibilities of justice becomes part of disciplinary and curricular concerns. In communication classrooms, for example, learning is much more than functional, or the acquisition of certain skills and competencies. It also involves a combination of affective and ethical investments, a set of educative priorities that evoke a sense of caring for self and other, and of the possibilities of our own agency. For critical pedagogues working in communication classrooms, these commitments frame particular courses, such as interpersonal communication, small group communication, or intercultural communication. Likewise, in constructing a democratic imagination, there must be clear critiques of individualism, consumerism, and the discourse of privatization.

EDUCATION AND OPPORTUNITIES FOR AGENCY

Finally, critical pedagogy provides a thorough explication of the learning process itself. Critical pedagogues assert that for knowledge and power to be consistently questioned, and for democratic visions to be imagined and realized, all learning must stress responsibility, accountability, and agency. Students' experiences matter and are a source of knowledge and authority (Giroux, 2006). At the same time, students must learn to critically reflect on and challenge their own constructions of reality. As one author states, the "classroom becomes a dynamic place where transformations in social relations are concretely analyzed and the false dichotomy between the world outside and the inside world of the academy disappears" (hooks, 1994, p. 195).

Learning itself should be dialogical, places where the instructor has power and responsibility. In such classrooms, students learn to consider what they do and do not know and how their experiences limit and expand their knowledge (Boler, 2004). For critical pedagogues, a culture of critical questioning is central. Students learn to ask questions about how power is used and to what ends, and about what justice will require. Finally, as with critical race theory, critical pedagogy carefully attends to power, silence, and voice in the classroom. This can be in connection with the power of the teacher as well as with the power of individuals in the dominant race, gender, and socioeconomic groups to set norms and determine what counts as knowledge. Critical pedagogy insists on an attentiveness to how taken-for-granted practices of oppression and exploitation can play out in the classroom.

TENSIONS WITHIN CRITICAL PEDAGOGY

A central tension within various expressions of critical pedagogy is what can be identified as liberal versus radical forms of critical pedagogy. To a large degree, these tensions parallel the challenges critical race theory poses to liberal forms of multiculturalism. Liberal forms of critical pedagogy focus on what are called representational or cultural rather than material issues and present a multiculturalist logic rather than an anticap-italist logic (Grande, 2004). For critical pedagogy and critical race theory, ways of thinking that embrace liberalism and/or multiculturalism most often see racism and other forms of oppression as individual rather than systemic, and occasional rather than routine. In response to liberal forms of critical pedagogy, that for some critical pedagogues represent "pro-capitalist forms of schooling" (Grande, 2004, p. 23), critical pedagogues have articulated radical critical pedagogy, which rests on the importance of challenging capitalism, the necessity of historical-material analyses, and the requirement of "reimagin[ing] Marxist theory in the interests of the critical educational project" (p. 25). As will be noted later, this primary fault line between liberal and radical forms of critical pedagogy also arises in critical communication pedagogy.

More radical or progressive advocates of critical pedagogy and critical race theory assert that their liberal colleagues affirm difference in ways that underplay, deny, or ignore the existence of oppression. It is useful to consider this tension in relation to a class on intercultural communica-tion. Instructors teaching this class who opt for a more liberal or mul-ticultural understanding of intercultural communication and intercultural relationships might focus, as indeed most intercultural communication textbooks do, on high- and low-context cultures, on communication norms for specific racial groups, or on differences in masculine and feminine forms of communication. In contrast, commu-nication instructors who advocate more radical forms of critical race theory and critical pedagogy would be likely to frame all course content with, at a minimum, an acknowledgment of unequal power relation-ships among cultural groups. An instructor adopting a progressive stance in an intercultural communication course would not see commu-nication as a set of interactions that play out among equitably situated individuals in a generally fair world. Rather, he or she would seek to make more transparent the ways in which individuals, ideologies, and institutions are linked to forms of privilege and discrimination, and how the expressions of privilege and discrimination effect communication in nearly all social interactions.

CRITIQUES OF CRITICAL PEDAGOGY

Two primary critiques of critical pedagogy are particularly relevant, espe-cially in the context of critical race theory. First, some scholars fault criti-cal pedagogy for ignoring critical theories of race (Parker & Stovall, 2004; Wright, 2002). A related challenge is critical pedagogy's "theoretical underpinnings and practical utility for various racial groups" (Parker & Stovall, 2004, p. 172), leading one scholar to claim the existence of an "unremarked whiteness" in critical pedagogy (Wright, 2002, p. 6). A second broad area of critique of critical pedagogy is addressed in the book *Red Pedagogy* (Grande, 2004). It is worth noting that critical race theory and critical pedagogy have not drawn extensively or even moderately from the work of American Indians or other aboriginal peoples, even though that work has existed in academic contexts for at least two decades (Deloria, 1969, 1999; Maracle, 2005; Mihesuah, 1998; Mihesuah & Cavender Wilson, 2004). Grande's book *Red Pedagogy* (2004) represents a significant and timely call to account for a range of critical theorists. Grande acknowledges the potential of critical pedagogy to accomplish "a reconceptualization of the relationship between land (property) and democracy" (p. 50), a key objective for indigenous activists and scholars. She also asserts that it is critical

> to examine the degree to which critical pedagogies retain the deep structures of Western thought—that is, the belief in progress as change, in the universe as impersonal, in reason as the preferred mode of inquiry, and in human beings as separate from and superior to the rest of nature. (p. 3)

In particular, Grande's (2004) critique of the critical pedagogical norm of questioning everything is highly relevant to considering communication instruction. Grande asserts the importance of "belief and acquiescence" (p. 176) for American Indians, which challenges critical pedagogues to reconsider the nature and ends of questioning. Furthermore, Grande distinguishes between democratic ends, which in a liberal framework are associated with enfranchisement, and the aim of indigenization, which is sovereignty. Grande's work indirectly urges communication instructors also interested in emancipation and ending all forms of oppression to consider the qualities and content of liberation.

Critical race theory and critical pedagogy, particularly in their most radical and progressive forms, insist on both the existence of oppression and the need to end it. In this sense, they place specific and bold demands on communication instructors who share these objectives. Communication instruction becomes a way to engage existing knowledge and to change the ends to which knowledge is put. Critical race theory and critical pedagogy assert a kind of realistic and demanding hopefulness, one that "tak[es] on that knowledge" about racism, sexism, classism, and heterosexism, as well as the history and presence of discrimination and privilege, "and reach[es] for something different" (Cooks & Simpson, 2007, p. 14). How does critical communication pedagogy respond to this challenge? The final section of this chapter will address this question and conclude with specific assertions regarding the future of critical communication pedagogy in the context of critical race theory.

Critical Communication Pedagogy

Critical communication pedagogy includes growing attention in the past two decades to the ways in which power, often in the context of cultural group identities, bears on communication practices. At the time of this writing, I was not aware of a broad literature review identifying the primary components of, tensions within, and critiques of critical communication pedagogy. Indeed, while a search in "critical" and "communication" and "pedagogy" results in numerous resources, searching the term *critical communication pedagogy* produces very few results in academic databases. The comments in this section draw from communication scholarship that has parallels with critical work and that directly or indirectly engages questions of power. Critical communication pedagogy scholars work in fields such as whiteness studies (Cooks & Simpson, 2007), African American studies (Jackson, 2006), performance theory (Hamera, 2006), and gender and queer studies (Yep, Lovaas, & Elia, 2003). As the Web site for the journal *Communication and Critical/Cultural Studies* ("Aims and Scope," n.d.) asserts, these scholars understand communication "as a theory, practice, technology, and discipline of power . . . [and] promot[e] critical reflection on the requirements of a more democratic culture." In some cases, they also pursue knowledge and pedagogies that directly work at ending oppression. Critical work is identifiable and increasingly present in communication discourse. This is evidenced by, for example, National Communication Association divisions and caucuses and communication journals that focus on or include critical work.

At a very basic level, this group of scholars has changed course content. Departments offer new courses, such as interracial communication and performance ethnography. Existing courses, taught by instructors who take a critical approach, include different content and approaches than they did two or three decades ago. An intercultural communication class might address institutional racism. A course on organizational communication might attend to how sexism affects workplace practices. In many ways, for these scholars, the central organizing principle of communication has shifted from the individual to relationships (Simpson & Cooks, 2007). Students are more likely to encounter course content that considers communication and practices of privilege, discrimination, and oppression. Instructors challenge students to consider the questions, What is your experience? Where do you have privilege or not, and how does this affect communication, yours and others? What is the role of power? What is your relationship to communication when it supports discriminatory practices? Communication scholarship and instruction that support these questions have been crucial in opening up communication discourse. At the same time, it is worth noting that in most departments of communication, these kinds of content and questions are not the norm. Instructors who pursue this subject matter with our students are most often the numerical minority among our colleagues. For the most part, more mainstream communication instruction approaches continue to form most of students' learning experiences and outcomes.

A recent book by Fassett and Warren (2007) takes an autoethnographic approach to critical communication pedagogy, providing, as the book's cover states, "a synthesis of critical pedagogy and instructional communication, as both a field of study and a teaching philosophy." As there was at the time of writing this chapter very little scholarship that explicitly calls itself critical communication pedagogy, Fassett and Warren's book constitutes an important work in the context of this discussion. Chapter 2 of the book, which includes 10 commitments of critical communication pedagogy, is especially relevant. It is this chapter that most directly and conclusively states the theoretical underpinnings of what Fassett and Warren understand as critical communication pedagogy. In brief, these 10 commitments "draw together critical communication educators" and include the following assumptions or theoretical and methodological starting points (p. 39).

1. "Identity is constructed in communication" (p. 39).

2. Power is "fluid and complex" (p. 41).

3. Culture is not additive but central to critical communication pedagogy.

4. "Concrete, mundane communication practices [are] constitutive of larger social structural systems" (p. 43).

5. Critical communication educators "embrace social structural critique as it places concrete, mundane communication practices in meaningful context" (p. 45).

6. "Language is central to critical communication pedagogy" (p. 48).

7. "Reflexivity is an essential condition for critical communication pedagogy" (p. 50).

8. "Critical communication educators embrace pedagogy and research as praxis" (p. 50).

9. Critical communication pedagogy aims for a "nuanced understanding of human subjectivity and agency" (p. 52).

10. Dialogue is both "metaphor and method for our relationships with others" (p. 54).

Throughout these commitments, there is a clear theoretical and methodological adherence to the idea of communication as constitutive, relational, and embedded in sociostructural dynamics. Likewise, Fassett and Warren's (2007) examples throughout the book demonstrate the authors' ongoing concern for the pedagogical conditions in which students learn to challenge and question, particularly related to the uses of power, and to consider questions of communication and social life from a variety of angles. Fassett and Warren's articulation of critical communication pedagogy undoubtedly challenges traditional communication instruction. It insists on the presence of uncertainty, contradiction, and possibility.

The Work of Communication Instruction: Discussion and Implications

As stated earlier in this chapter, all communication instruction does something, has consequences, results in some ends and not others. As I mentioned earlier, drawing on Collins (1998), instructors might teach students how to control populations, or how to challenge methods of control. While the process of teaching and learning is never straightforward—students will take and leave a wide range of ideas and practices from the classroom—it is also never neutral. All learning will lead to certain ways of understanding the world and likewise to certain ways of being in the world. Communication students will learn to view cultural difference as a problem or a resource; to understand racism, sexism, and classism as rare or routine; to see themselves as persons who, for example, use their knowledge to contribute to the profits of a specific company or to further policy that supports a living wage. Critical race theory and critical pedagogy both begin with the assumption that oppression and injustice exist and are routine.

As a scholar, I also work with these assumptions. My own experience of learning—in and out of the classroom; from students, other instructors, and my own research—has taught me and continues to teach me that oppression exists; that it is routine; that it is fundamentally related to power and the construction of dominant and subordinate cultural groups; and that it makes itself known at all levels of our humanity, including mental, psychological, spiritual, and emotional levels. Another assumption with which I work is that a commonly understood definition of communication is the "shared process of making meaning" (e.g., see Craig, 1999). In response to the question, "What is it that communication instruction should do?," which I asked earlier in this chapter, one response is that communication's central contribution and responsibility to life in and outside the classroom is to make meaning in ways that lead to justice and the end of oppression. Communication instruction, then, becomes a way of imagining emancipation, of giving language to more just relationships, of identifying systemic oppression, and of articulating how we might be active in changing those forms of oppression. Communication becomes a way of making meaning that embraces hope, equity, and change, a way of constructing the world in which we want to live.

In considering the critical communication pedagogy articulated by Fassett and Warren (2007) and other communication scholars, as well as critical race theory and progressive forms of critical pedagogy, I see a significant distinction related to objectives. Critical race theory and progressive forms of critical pedagogy are clear about what it is they want to do: end racism and oppression. In contrast, if I rely on the 10 commitments of critical communication pedagogy articulated by Fassett and Warren, I am less certain of where Fassett and Warren want communication instruction to go and what they want it to do. Words such as meaning, reflexivity, and praxis, all in the 10 commitments, are important, as they indicate a clear departure from communication instruction that understands communication as independent from context, reflexivity as unimportant to knowledge, and praxis as a domain entirely separate from learning. At the same time, I wonder, meaningful for whom, and in what ways? Reflexivity that leads to what? Praxis that matters for whom, and how? In one sense, attention to reflexivity, meaning, and praxis might all be considered tools. As tools, they may be necessary to ending racism and oppression. Indeed, the work of critical race theorists and critical pedagogues indicates that they are necessary. As tools, however, they can be used to myriad ends, including those that maintain racism and oppressive practices.

Fassett and Warren's (2007) work centers on the importance of questioning for critical communication educators. They repeatedly return to the importance of students and instructors practicing reflexivity and asking questions—of themselves, each other, course content, social norms in and out of the classroom, department policy, and disciplinary content. For critical race theory and critical pedagogy, questions themselves are asked in relation to a particular set of norms and objectives. All questions situate, explicitly or not, those who ask and respond to a particular agenda, a particular way of seeing the world (e.g., see Simpson, 2003, pp. 144–145; Simpson, 2008). Fassett and Warren do not make the necessary objectives of questions, that to which they lead, explicit. In and of themselves, questions do not lead to the end of racism and oppression.

Critical race theory and critical pedagogy, in my mind, take two positions that set them apart from Fassett and Warren's (2007) critical communication pedagogy, as well as from many communication scholars' approach to critical communication pedagogy. First, critical race theorists and critical pedagogues insist on the routine existence of racism and oppression. They consistently and thoroughly make explicit the extensive harm racism, sexism, heterosexism, classism, and, for critical pedagogues, capitalism, do, especially to subordinate groups. In reading the work of critical race theorists and critical pedagogues, there is little doubt that existing structures and institutions, and the people who have power within them, drastically reduce the life choices and options for people who are women, racial minorities, queer, and/or working class or poor. Second, they have an explicit and liberatory agenda: that of ending all forms of oppression. This agenda is not left unstated or to chance. Its values and commitments are obvious. As McLaren (1998) asserts, those who critique liberal forms of critical pedagogy "have complained that critical pedagogy has been frequently domesticated in practice and reduced to student-directed learning approaches devoid of social critique and a revolutionary agenda" (p. 442). Put simply, in pursuing the aim of antioppression, critical pedagogy makes unequivocally clear the ways in which oppression exists. In reading this work, the existence and consequences of systems of oppression are obvious.

Researchers in critical race theory and critical pedagogy are committed to making the existence of any harm done by racism and other forms of oppression undeniable; and they insist on ending racism and oppression. These imperatives are, I would argue, what make both areas of thought "critical." It is worth considering the possibility that Fassett and Warren's (2007) commitments, and those of other critical communication pedagogues, might more closely align with what is called a constitutive approach to communication. At a minimum, the imperatives of critical race theory and critical pedagogy raise the issue of the substantive differences between a constitutive and a critical approach. Particularly in the context of (a) the use of communication instruction for functionalist or instrumentalist ends (i.e., a focus on skills that are often directly relevant to corporate interests); (b) the increasing calls for higher education to serve capitalist objectives (Giroux & Searls Giroux, 2004; Rhoads & Torres, 2006); and (c) the broad increase of individualism, consumerism, and privatization, there is a clear need for the commitments that critical race theory and critical pedagogy pursue. Furthermore, work that is not explicit about its ethical, affective, and political commitments will be consequential (i.e., all work has an agenda and has effects) and may be used to support oppressive ends.[1]

Critical communication pedagogy that draws from critical race theory and progressive forms of critical pedagogy will have two primary components. First, critical communication pedagogy will frame all scholarship in the concrete realities of how people live. This frame will center the ways in which communication acts to restrict or expand access to resources and the ability to make decisions about one's own life and the communities in which one lives. Such a frame will assess the significance of dominant and subordinate groups and will engage the ways in which privilege and discrimination, meted out among those groups, affect the conditions in which people live. Who has sufficient food and shelter, health care and work? How does communication work to maximize corporate profits at the expense of a living wage? To construct practices that locate the majority of toxic waste in communities primarily made up of people who are racial minorities and/or poor? What happens in the classroom when a student who is white wholly and without pause dismisses the experience of a racial minority sitting next to her? When a course on gender communication never comes around to discussing how heteronormative ideologies restrict options for all?

A second component of critical communication pedagogy is an understanding of communication that is committed to making a specific kind of meaning: one which centers and insists on equity and justice, in political, economic, and social terms. In this sense, communication itself in all forms and at all levels is a way of moving toward one set of practices and away from another; a way of imagining, creating, and maintaining a world in which justice is desired, possible, and (if only partially) realized. Furthermore, this attention to justice is concrete, plain, and insistent, with flesh and weight. It explicitly links the process of teaching and learning to practices that will change the world in which we live. Instructors urge students to ask questions, and insist on those students imagining the ends to which those questions are put: Now that you know about violence directed at queer youth, about the gentrification of neighborhoods and the corresponding decrease in affordable housing, about the continued profiling of blacks and Latinos, how will we respond? How can we communicate so that more just meanings prevail? The critical communication pedagogy at which I work seeks change that is realistic and hopeful; that is plain about the existence and consequences of oppression and bold about the need to face this oppression, without flinching. It dares to ask, as long as injustice exists, how can those of us working in a discipline that engages the process of making meaning turn our backs on questions of meaning that lead to justice: for whose benefit, for what gain, and at what cost to how people live?

Note

1. It is important to state clearly that adopting an antioppressive approach to education is not the equivalent of telling students how to think. Rather, it is about creating conditions in which a language for ending oppression and practicing justice is available and of value.

References

ACORN Fair Housing. (2007). *Foreclosure exposure: A study of racial and income disparities in home mortgage lending in 172 American cities.* Retrieved December 17, 2008, from www.acorn.org/fileadmin/HMDA/2007/HMDAreport2007.pdf

Aims and scope. (n.d.). *Communication and Critical/Cultural Studies.* Retrieved October 12, 2009, from www.gbhap.com/journals/titles/14791420.asp

Bebo, J. (1999). The war on drugs, crack cocaine, and the resulting sentencing disparities. *Discourse of Sociological Practice, 2*(1), 34–37.

Bell, D. A., Jr. (1980). Brown v. Board of Education and the interest convergence dilemma. *Harvard Law Review, 93*(3), 518–533.

Bell, D. A., Jr. (2000). After we're gone: Prudent speculations on America in a post-racial epoch. In R. Delgado & J. Stefancic (Eds.), *Critical race theory: The cutting edge* (2nd ed., pp. 2–8). Philadelphia: Temple University Press.

Boler, M. (2004). All speech is not free: The ethics of "affirmative action pedagogy." In M. Boler (Ed.), *Democratic dialogue in education: Troubling speech, disturbing silence* (pp. 3–13). New York: Peter Lang.

Collins, P. H. (1998). *Fighting words: Black women and the search for justice.* Minneapolis: University of Minnesota Press.

Cooks, L. M. (2003). Pedagogy, performance and positionality: Teaching about whiteness in interracial communication. *Communication Education, 52,* 245–257.

Cooks, L. M., & Simpson, J. S. (Eds.). (2007). *Whiteness, pedagogy, performance: Dis/placing race.* Lanham, MD: Lexington Books.

Craig, R. T. (1999). Communication theory as a field. *Communication Theory, 9*(2), 119–161.

Crenshaw, K., Gotanda, N., Peller, G., & Thomas, K. (1995). Introduction. In K. Crenshaw, N. Gotanda, G. Peller, & K. Thomas (Eds.), *Critical race theory: The key writings that formed the movement* (pp. xiii–xxxii). New York: New Press.

Delgado, R. (1995). *The Rodrigo chronicles: Conversations about America and race.* New York: New York University Press.

Delgado, R., & Stefancic, J. (2001). *Critical race theory: An introduction.* New York: New York University Press.

Delgado, R., & Stefancic, J. (2005, December). *The role of critical race theory in understanding race, crime, and justice issues.* Paper presented at the John Jay College of Criminal Justice, New York.

Deloria, V., Jr. (1969). *Custer died for your sins: An Indian manifesto.* New York: Macmillan.

Deloria, V., Jr. (1999). *Spirit and reason: The Vine Deloria, Jr., reader.* Golden, CO: Fulcrum.

Fassett, D., & Warren, J. (2007). *Critical communication pedagogy.* Thousand Oaks, CA: Sage.

Gillborn, D. (2006). Critical race theory and education: Racism and anti-racism in educational theory and praxis. *Discourse: Studies in the Cultural Politics of Education, 27*(1), 11–32.

Giroux, H. A. (2006). *The Giroux reader.* Boulder, CO: Paradigm.

Giroux, H. A. (2007). Introduction: Democracy, education, and the politics of critical pedagogy. In P. McLaren & J. L. Kincheloe (Eds.), *Critical pedagogy: Where are we now?* (pp. 1–5). New York: Peter Lang.

Giroux, H. A., & Searls Giroux, S. (2004). *Take back higher education: Race, youth, and the crisis of democracy in the post–civil rights era.* New York: Palgrave Macmillan.

Grande, S. (2004). *Red pedagogy: Native American social and political thought.* Lanham, MD: Rowman & Littlefield.

Grossberg, L. (1996). History, politics, and postmodernism: Stuart Hall and cultural studies. In D. Morely & K.-H. Chen (Eds.), *Stuart Hall: Critical dialogues in cultural studies* (pp. 151–173). London: Routledge.

Hamera, J. (2006). *Opening acts: Performance in/as communication and cultural studies*. Thousand Oaks, CA: Sage.

hooks, b. (1994). *Teaching to transgress: Education as the practice of freedom*. New York: Routledge.

Jackson, R. L. (2006). *Scripting the Black masculine body: Identity, discourse and racial politics in popular media*. Albany: State University of New York Press.

Jackson, R. L., Warren, J. R., Pitts, M. J., & Wilson, K. B. (2007). "It is not my responsibility to teach culture!" White graduate teaching assistants negotiating identity and pedagogy. In L. Cooks & J. S. Simpson (Eds.), *Whiteness, pedagogy, and performance: Dis/placing race* (pp. 67–86). Lanham, MD: Lexington Books.

Johnson, P. C., Logan, J. A., & Davis, A. J. (2004). *Inner lives: Voices of African American women in prison*. New York: New York University Press.

Kincheloe, J. L. (2008). *Critical pedagogy: Primer* (2nd ed.). New York: Peter Lang.

Ladson-Billings, G. (1998). Just what is critical race theory and what's it doing in a nice field like education? *International Journal of Qualitative Studies in Education, 11*(1), 7–24.

Maracle, L. (2005, June 23–26). *Some words on study as a process of discovery*. Paper presented at TransCanada: Literature, Institutions, Citizenship, Vancouver, British Columbia, Canada.

Matsuda, M. J., Lawrence, C. R., III, Delgado, R., & Crenshaw, K. W. (1993). Introduction. In M. J. Matsuda, C. R. Lawrence III, R. Delgado, & K. W. Crenshaw (Eds.), *Words that wound: Critical race theory, assaultive speech, and the First Amendment* (pp. 1–15). Boulder, CO: Westview Press.

McLaren, P. (1998). Revolutionary pedagogy in post-revolutionary times: Rethinking the political economy of critical education. *Educational Theory, 48*(4), 431–462.

McLaren, P. (2007). The future of the past: Reflections on the present state of empire and pedagogy. In P. McLaren & J. L. Kincheloe (Eds.), *Critical pedagogy: Where are we now* (pp. 289–314). New York: Peter Lang.

Mihesuah, D. A. (Ed.). (1998). *Natives and academics: Discussions on researching and writing about American Indians*. Lincoln: University of Nebraska Press.

Mihesuah, D. A., & Cavender Wilson, A. (2004). *Indigenizing the academy: Transforming scholarship and empowering communities*. Lincoln: University of Nebraska Press.

Moyers, B. (2007). *Discovering what democracy means*. Retrieved December 16, 2008, from www.commondreams.org/views07/0212-31.htm

Nakayama, T., & Krizek, R. (1995). Whiteness: A strategic rhetoric. *Quarterly Journal of Speech, 81*, 291–309.

Parker, L., & Stovall, D. O. (2004). Actions following words: Critical race theory connects to critical pedagogy. *Educational Philosophy and Theory, 36*(2), 167–182.

Rhoads, R. A., & Torres, C. A. (Eds.). (2006). *The university, state, and market: The political economy of globalization in the Americas*. Stanford, CA: Stanford University Press.

Simpson, J. S. (2003). *I have been waiting: Race and U.S. higher education*. Toronto, Ontario, Canada: University of Toronto Press.

Simpson, J. S. (2006). Reaching for justice: The pedagogical politics of agency, race, and change. *Review of Education, Pedagogy, and Cultural Studies, 28*(1), 67–94.

Simpson, J. S. (2008). "What do they think of us?" The pedagogical practices of cross-cultural communication, misrecognition, and hope. *Journal of International and Intercultural Communication, 1*(3), 181–201.

Simpson, J. S., & Cooks, L. M. (2007). Conclusion. In L. M. Cooks & J. S. Simpson (Eds.), *Whiteness, pedagogy, performance: Dis/placing race* (pp. 299–315). Lanham, MD: Lexington Books.

Tate, W. F. (1997). Critical race theory and education: History, theory, and implications. *Review of Research in Education, 22*, 195–247.

Warren, J. (2003). *Performing purity: Whiteness, pedagogy, and the reconstitution of power.* New York: Peter Lang.

Washington, H. A. (2006). *Medical apartheid: The dark history of medical experimentation on Black Americans from colonial times to the present.* New York: Doubleday.

Wright, H. K. (2002, April). *Homies don't play posties, homies don't play neos: Black critical ambivalence and the end(s) of critical pedagogy.* Paper presented at the annual meeting of the American Educational Research Association Conference (New Orleans).

Yep, G. A., Lovaas, K., & Elia, J. P. (2003). *Queer theory and communication: From disciplining queers to queering the discipline(s).* New York: Harrington Park Press.

Sexualities and Critical Communication Pedagogy

20

Karen E. Lovaas

> *In a sense, all new disciplines are bound to stutter, mumble, and cry as they grapple with and define their objects of study.*
>
> —Gunn and Rice (2009, p. 217)

When I was in fifth or sixth grade, I was walking back from school one afternoon a little way behind a girl who lived a few blocks away from me. I remember noticing, again, how beautiful those scooped areas behind the hinges of her knees were as she strode home ahead of me. I flashed on the idea that this must be the way that boys looked at girls' bodies. And I thought it must be something very unusual that I was able to see both as girls see and as boys do. I knew of no words to frame a recognition of the beauty of girls' bodies. I had no idea that there was anything other than cross-sex attraction. I had no idea what other kids at my elementary school were talking about when they used the phrase "fruit loop" to refer to the loop of fabric on the back of some tailored shirts, or what was meant when someone, usually a boy, said that if you wore green or yellow on a Thursday, you were a "fairy." It was clear that being so labeled was a form of ridicule. Though I made no direct connection between these comments and the "special skill" I discovered I had, I sensed, somehow, that it was something I should keep to myself. For a time, I believed that I would not live to adulthood; one of the factors for this was that in elementary school during the

Berlin and Cuban missile crises, we regularly participated in duck and cover bomb drills. Another was that I could not see any place or role for myself in the future. Seven or eight years later, when I learned the words homosexual, gay, and lesbian, I did not see myself in any of those terms, but I remember feeling both some relief that not everyone was readily and only destined to be matched with someone of the same sex and also some desire to know more about people who called themselves by those names. (By then, I had also been the student of a couple of extraordinary teachers—perhaps I could grow up to be a teacher?!) What I knew for sure, and had known since I was 5 or 6 years old, was that I did not want to have to fit myself into the only kinds of futures I saw in the gendered arrangements in my own family and those of my acquaintance.

✶ ✶ ✶

I speak briefly in this chapter about the existing scholarship and curriculum related to sexualities and communication. While I agree with Sloop (2006) about the difficulty of isolating research on sexuality from that on gender (the latter body of research is far more extensive, and there are numerous textbooks for gender and communication courses), it is my impression that, apart from the communication scholars whose research and interests specifically include sexualities, it remains all too easy to omit the subject or to settle for a nod at it by including sexual orientation in a list of social identity formations. I do not offer something definitive or conclusive about research or critical pedagogy related to sexualities and communication in this writing. We are not there and perhaps never will nor should be, given the glorious multiplicity and generativity of the subject: "Making love is not just becoming as one, or even two, but becoming as a hundred thousand" (Deleuze & Guattari, 1972/2004, p. 296). But I believe that we can and should do a better job of including sexualities in our work and continue to grapple, theorize, and say what we can.

In what follows, I consider sexualities and communication pedagogy along four levels: (1) public pedagogy (i.e., public discourse that informs a public; see Giroux, 2005), (2) the communication discipline, (3) the local level of institutional and curricular practices, and finally, (4) classroom practices. I view the field as spanning across each level, as they mutually inform each other. My compelling desire in this essay is to fuel the fires of our commitments to incorporating sexualities in our work, especially as teachers.

Public Pedagogy

As I was writing a portion of this chapter one afternoon, a local public radio station program was airing a discussion of whether former President Clinton's "Don't Ask, Don't Tell" policy, which "regulates" rather than bans the presence of gays, lesbians, and bisexuals in the military, should be rescinded. Nathaniel Frank, the author of a new book, Unfriendly Fire: How the Gay Ban Undermines the Military and Weakens America (2009), spoke with the program's host as well as responding to comments and questions from listeners calling into the show. Several of the callers expressed the precise sorts of prejudicial beliefs and fears that Frank argues account for the existence of a policy that has led to a sharp increase in discharges, hindered recruitment efforts, and hurt morale. Those in this group of callers were unable to imagine queer and straight recruits training and serving side by side without chaos ensuing and expressed certainty that recruits would not be able to trust and therefore work effectively with those whose sexuality differed from their own. How could these individuals, in this instance, all apparently heterosexual men, have come to believe that their personal safety was compromised by the presence of gay men, a conviction that they were willing to reveal to millions of public radio listeners?

✶ ✶ ✶

There is no easy way of knowing precisely how widespread such beliefs are today. Many of us interested in the subject of this chapter may assume that the military is a more heterosexist and sexist context than much of U.S. society. Whether or not that is an accurate assessment, we know that social institutions do not operate in vacuums; discourses promulgated in military, religious, family, organization, and media contexts, among others, frequently overlap, parallel, inform, and/or reinforce each other. Though we may not commonly speak of these institutions and discourses as such, all are sites of learning. The knowledge and prescriptions from these sources are elements of what Henry Giroux (2001) calls public pedagogies, which

> bridge the gap between private and public discourses, while simultaneously putting into play particular ideologies and values that resonate with broader public conversations regarding how society views itself and the world of power, events, and politics. (para. 8)

Readers of this *Handbook* likely have heard about differential suicide rates for queer and straight adolescents, almost certainly know about the killing of Matthew Shepard, have probably seen the evidence of the abysmal failure—and counterproductivity—of abstinence-only sex education (Hauser, 2008), and are undoubtedly aware of the struggles around the United States and other regions of the world for the right to marry one's same-sex partner. But how many of us are actively making the problems to which these few examples point a matter of personal concern? If we see them as emblematic of violent, misdirected, heterosexist public pedagogies, I wonder if we might be more inclined to view them as of professional concern as scholars and teachers.

Perhaps some of us may surmise that teachers are more likely to be open to and supportive of a wide range of students' expressions of social identities, both by virtue of their/our choice of a profession in which the majority of them/us work with young people and because in preparation to teach, one generally has succeeded in earning "advanced" academic degrees and/or certification. We may believe that the pedigreeing we have undergone has required us to divest ourselves of our biases, and it may be that it has indeed created opportunities for us to do some of this work.

Alas, more than half of the 96 respondents in a study of preservice elementary school teachers denounced male homosexuality (Maney & Cain, 1997). In an earlier study, more than three quarters of prospective teachers expressed negative attitudes toward gays and lesbians (Sears, 1992). Whether or not these findings are currently accurate, there is significant evidence that most students who identify as lesbian, gay, bisexual, transgender, or queer (LGBTQ) endure frequent harassment, both from fellow students and from the personnel of the school. The Gay, Lesbian, Straight Education Network (GLSEN) has conducted a study of the climate for LGBTQ students in U.S. schools every 2 years since 1999. The key findings of their latest report are as follows:

- Three fourths of students heard homophobic or sexist remarks often or frequently at school.

- Nine out of 10 students heard the word *gay* used in a negative way often or frequently at school.

- Remarks about students not acting "masculine" enough were more common than remarks about students not acting "feminine" enough.

- Nearly two thirds of students heard homophobic remarks from school personnel.

- Less than a fifth of students reported that school personnel frequently intervened when hearing homophobic remarks or negative remarks about gender expression (Kosciw, Diaz, & Greytak, 2008, p. 46).

The GLSEN survey does not include colleges and universities and does not specify the classes or other spaces within K–12 schools in which these comments are made (and communication classes, in the wake of "No Child Left Behind" policies, are exceedingly rare); thus, it is difficult to gauge how communication classrooms and teachers, specifically, fare in this regard. I am not aware of any indicators suggesting that our discipline is more immune than others.

Whatever the academic setting in which we labor, whatever the specific subject matter that we teach, study, and/or research, we have an obligation to do better for our students, our colleagues, our communities, and ourselves. This applies not only to treating each other with respect but also to making sure that our research and curricula include the subject of sexualities and communication.

Communication Studies

My academic training is primarily in communication and U.S. American Studies, and my work commonly stresses the discursive, interactional, and institutional. However, I do want to likewise acknowledge the unravelable interplay of inherited potentiality with discourses, institutions, and agency. I have been playing with Anne Fausto-Sterling's (2000) Russian nesting dolls as an apt metaphor for the interwoven strata of sexuality:

> *Academics can take the system apart for display or to study one of the dolls in more detail. But an individual doll is hollow. Only the complete assembly makes sense. Unlike its wooden counterpart, the human nesting doll changes shape with time. Change can happen in any of the layers, but since the entire assembly has to fit together, altering one of the component dolls requires the interlinked system—from the cellular to the institutional—to change. . . . Using Russian nesting dolls as a framework suggests that history, culture, relationships, psyche, organism, and cell are each appropriate locations from which to study the formation and meanings of sexuality and gender. (pp. 253–254)*

I might not choose the same number of layers or labels. I do not study sexuality and gender at the cellular level. None of this should suggest that I advocate that communication scholars join the search for a "cause" of sexual orientation, nor that I use classroom time debating the primacy of the factors typically referenced in such a debate. At the same time, and regardless of one's particular paradigmatic persuasion/s, the topic is in the classroom; students come from and bring in ideas from their science classes, their churches, their homes, and their media consumption. In relation to the last of those contexts, a search of general newspaper articles published in two recent years found that the primary analytical frame was that homosexuality either is caused by one's genes or is a matter of one's choice (Fausto-Sterling, 2007).

I recognize that I may be working against my own intentions by making it appear that to teach about sexualities and communication, one must be familiar/fluent with the literature of the biological sciences as well as with communication education, and perhaps critical pedagogy, sexuality studies, gender studies, philosophy, cultural studies, and . . . Were this the case, I would not consider myself, nor many others, adequately prepared to teach or do research in this area.

* * *

Communication scholarship related to sexualities is a relatively recent subject in a relatively young discipline; its approaches include the social scientific, interpretive, critical, and postmodern perspectives. The six threads of that scholarship over nearly three decades have been

> [(a)] the rhetoric of liberation politics (i.e., lesbian feminism, gay liberation, AIDS activism, and the conservative backlash); (b) innovations in language structure and use; (c) analyses of mainstream and alternative media representations; (d) identity formation and interpersonal relationships, including family, friends, and lovers; (e) classroom communication and queer pedagogy; and (f) critical and performative approaches to understanding identity politics in relation to power. (Lovaas & Jenkins, 2007, pp. 3–4)

(For critical reviews of communication scholarship on sexualities, see Heinz, 2002; Henderson, 2000; Sloop, 2006; Yep, 2003. Also see Nicholas, 2006, for a concise summary of key perspectives on LGBTQ identities in social science research and Gamson's, 2000, review of qualitative approaches to research on sexualities.)

There were three anthologies published in the 1980s and 1990s that made enormous contributions and introduced many in communication to gay and lesbian studies; two more have been published since 2000. The first of these five books was Jim Chesebro's (1981) *GaySpeak: Gay Male and Lesbian Communication*. In 1994, Jeffrey Ringer published *Queer Words, Queer Images: Communication and the Construction of Homosexuality* (Ringer, 1994b). Five years later came Larry Gross and James Woods's (1999) anthology, *The Columbia Reader on Lesbians & Gay Men in Media, Society, and Politics*; though its title referenced lesbians and gay men, some of the individual entries talked about bisexuals and a few mentioned queer theory.

Queer Theory and Communication (Yep, Lovaas, & Elia, 2003b) differs from much of the earlier work in communication in two key ways: (1) As opposed to the perspective that the homo/heterosexual binary is a significant matter for those who identify as homosexual, it adopts the universalizing view that the homo/heterosexual binary is an issue of tremendous importance in the lives of individuals across the spectrum of sexualities (Sedgwick, 1990). The universalizing view locates and exposes the incoherencies of terms such as "natural" sexuality, "woman," and "man" that stabilize heterosexuality (Jagose, 1996). (Yep, Lovaas, & Elia, 2003a, p. 4)

And (2) it treats sexualities as "multiple, unstable, and fluid social constructions intersecting with race, class, and gender, among others, as opposed to singular, stable, and essentialized social positionings" (Yep et al., 2003a, p. 4). Chapters in the book offer critical disciplinary and interdisciplinary analyses and reflections, including incisive critiques of the widespread heteronormativity in the discipline of communication (e.g., Nakayama & Corey, 2003; Owen, 2003; Yep, 2003). While many of the chapters focus on what their authors think queer studies has to offer, there is also considerable concern and ambivalence expressed regarding the shortcomings of queer theories (e.g., see Lee, 2003, and Martinez, 2003, on the omissions of race and the voices of women of color in queer theorizing). Of particular relevance to sexualities and pedagogy are articles examining the idealization of a particular type of heterosexual relationship in sexuality education and interpersonal communication (Elia, 2003), the heterosexist and sexist ideologies in much nonverbal communication scholarship and pedagogy (Lovaas, 2003), and reflections on the potential and challenges of queer theory and education (Halberstam, 2003; Kumashiro, 2003; Pinar, 2003).

It is worth noting that, of the 14 research articles and 12 reflection essays (as well as the Foreword and Introduction), none were reprints, most were original, and several were different versions of conference papers or adapted from dissertations. This reflected not only our desire, as editors and authors, to be current, but also our shared sense of discontent with the scholarship and pedagogy on sexualities in our disciplines, in particular, communication studies (Yep et al., 2003a). Fred Corey, Ralph Smith, and Tom Nakayama (2002) put together a bibliography of journal articles written by NCA and ICA members published between 1973 and 2002 that relate to LGBTQ issues. Of the 75 journal articles they list, eight articles appeared during the 17 years between 1973 and 1990, and 67 articles appeared in the 12 years between 1990 and 2002. Of the 67 articles between 1990 and 2002, three appeared in the journal *Communication Education*, all in 2002 (Cooks & Sun, 2002; Heinz, 2002; Russ, Simonds, & Hunt, 2002). I note that one other article in *Communication Education* that year, focusing on alliances across gender and race in the intercultural communication classroom, includes a discussion of challenging essentialist views of relationships among gender, sex, and sexual identities (Johnson & Bhatt, 2003). Since 2002, the only article in *Communication Education* to address sexuality in any way is a study of the impact of sex and physical setting on how students perceive high immediacy behavior by professors (Rester & Edwards, 2007). In contrast, *Text and Performance Quarterly* published three articles related to sexuality—though not sexuality pedagogy—in 2008 (Beasley, 2008; Dickinson, 2008; Zukic, 2008) and one thus far in 2009 (Buerkle, 2009).

Communication research that explores sexuality in the context of the classroom has, largely, explored how to create learning environments inclusive and supportive of LGBTQ voices. For example, in a conference paper, later published in Chesebro's (1981) *GaySpeak: Gay Male and Lesbian Communication*, Joe DeVito (1979) laid out what communication teachers can and should do to embrace students of all sexualities:

> Teachers and writers can approach the treatment of gay and lesbian students by focusing on promoting equal rights for all persons, by helping students to develop a positive self-concept about their identities, and by promoting mutual understanding and effective communication among students. Teachers should develop an intellectual and emotional recognition of gay and lesbian existence, history, and behavior; should avoid negative stereotypes of gays and lesbians; and should avoid the heterosexual presumption in teaching and writing, striving to eliminate discriminatory language usage and to prohibit abusive classroom criticism of the gay and lesbian cause. Teachers should also recognize the influence of affectional preference on communication with regard to such variables as self-disclosure, language usage, message encoding and decoding, contextual and subcultural differences, field of experience, and relational development and deterioration. (DeVito, 1979, p. 1)

The language of this abstract bespeaks its time and the author's perspective. A sampling of the literature related to pedagogy and sexuality since DeVito wrote does not lead me to believe that most communication teacher-scholars have taken most of those steps in a substantive manner. Twenty-one years later, Bettina Heinz (2002), in an article in *Communication Education*, contended that "communication educators, regardless of their own sexual orientation, still need be convinced of their educational responsibilities about g/l/b/t issues to all of their students" (p. 96). Heinz found that

> the everyday experience of gay, lesbian, bisexual and transgendered people is still largely excluded from the classroom discussions of U.S. high school and college students; that this exclusion is also evident in communication textbooks, syllabi, and curricula; and that unchallenged heterosexism and homophobia among U.S. high school and college students continue to pose interpersonal and social problems that might be partly resolved by communication pedagogy. (p. 95)

Heinz (2002) believes that communication scholars and teachers largely accept the importance of integrating gender and race matters in research and curriculum while continuing to explore specific approaches for doing so well. She notes that this is far less evident in relation to sexuality, particularly at its intersections with race, class, and ability/disability. While acknowledging increasing visibility in terms of greater numbers of conference presentations and publications in the communication discipline, concurrent with more characters who are lesbian, gay, or transgendered appearing in mainstream media, Heinz (2002), citing Dow (2001), reminds us that visibility does not equal progress in the political arena. Nor does it address the violence of lack of recognition in everyday interactions, including those in the classroom.

One method Heinz (2002) advocates for increasing the visibility of LGBTQ people and issues in the classroom is for LGBTQ faculty to openly identify themselves or "come out." This is a recurring topic in communication scholarship related to sexualities. Ringer (1994b) devoted one of the five sections into which his anthology, *Queer Words, Queer Images*, was divided to faculty disclosure of sexual identity: "Coming Out in the Classroom" (Jenkins, 1994; Opffer, 1994; Ringer, 1994a; Taylor, 1994). The subject continues to show up in journal articles and conference papers; for example, at a recent conference, Jacobs (2007) presented a paper describing his classroom practice of deliberately not revealing his sexual identity as a useful rhetorical strategy for interrupting heteronormative discourse.

While scholarship in this vein is often written from an interpretive perspective by an instructor who identifies as LGBTQ, there is also empirical work on the advisability of being "out" in the classroom (though many of these authors do not make reference to their own sexual identity). In their article "Coming Out in the Classroom . . . an Occupational Hazard? The Influence of Sexual Orientation on Teacher Credibility and Perceived Student Learning," Russ et al. (2002) report their finding that a guest instructor who referred to his male partner during a presentation to an introductory communication class was perceived in significantly more negative ways than the same speaker making reference to a female partner while giving the same presentation to another group of students. They recommend that, despite the many examples of prejudice found in their results, gay faculty should not hide their sexual orientation. I am a bit troubled by their suggestion for future work to "test if students actually learn less from gay instructors or if they simply perceive they learn less" (p. 323). More valuable, in my opinion, is their idea to investigate "how heterosexual teachers perceive and evaluate their gay, lesbian, bisexual and transgender students" (p. 323).

Work that addresses teaching in the communication classroom espouses a similar desire to illuminate and challenge heterosexism through communication about sexuality, though this end is made more difficult by pervasive beliefs and attitudes regarding sexuality. The stated goal of a recent article in *Communication Teacher* is "to increase empathy and tolerance for lesbians and gays, as well as those from diverse backgrounds, among students in a basic communication course" (Rivers, 2000, p. 8). As a step toward achieving this goal, the author proposes a classroom activity in which students analyze and respond to a cartoon strip in which one friend comes out as gay to a straight friend. Instructions to a faculty member using this activity include this recommendation: "Try to separate yourself from the subject matter; if you're offended by homosexuality, try to put it aside and empathize with these people and their pain" (p. 9). If such a vital facet of the lives of the LGBTQ students with whom a teacher likely works in every college classroom—their sexuality—is so unacceptable, perhaps those teachers should ask themselves whether they are well suited to the profession of teaching. To the author's credit, she also relays her practice of "continual inclusion of gays and lesbians during discussions of romantic relationships," a practice revealing that, among her students, "many are deeply uncomfortable with, perhaps even openly hostile to, any suggestion of homosexuality" (p. 9).

In another effort in this vein, Pawlowski (2006) discusses how to include the "delicate" and "sensitive" subject of sexual communication in the family communication course and provides an activity in which, following reading about the topics of intimacy and self-disclosure, students are asked "to reflect upon what they have learned regarding their experiences with being taught about sex" and to respond in writing to some related questions. The term *sex* is repeatedly used in the questions regarding what, when, how, and from whom one learned about sexuality. Students then meet in triads to discuss what they have written. Next, each group of students is given a scenario and asked to consider how they would handle it. There are four different scenarios, the last of which is described as "optional," a choice influenced by whether the class goes on to participate in another activity, which involves reading an article (Saltzburg, 2004) regarding the experience of parents of adolescents who disclose that they are "gay or lesbian" (p. 109). (The Saltzburg, 2004, article problematically assumes that parents are heterosexual and that such disclosures are inherently difficult for parents.) Should the instructor choose not to use "the follow-up article and activity, then this scenario will encourage students to cover sexual orientation and familial communication" (Pawlowski, 2006, p. 102). I flinched a little as I read this, recalling that I have caught myself talking about the need to "cover" a particular area of subject matter, as if my approach to teaching primarily involved being sure to provide at least some information on each of a series of topics.

While not focused on the subject of integrating sexuality in communication courses, Johnson and Bhatt (2003) include the subject of how they discussed sexual orientation in the midst of a lecture on gender during an intercultural communication class; much of that presentation was dedicated to differentiating between sex, gender, and sexual orientation. Like Cooks and Sun (2002), the authors identify with critical pedagogy. They approach the classroom as a potential space in which teachers and students can and should resist dominant discourses that shape our knowledge of social identities and differences. An example of how they sought to facilitate this work in relation to sex, gender, and sexuality during this particular class period is Johnson's use of her own body as a text for the students to interpret, looking for markers of sex and gender. Johnson extended this exploration of her gender performances by introducing other behaviors and attributes for them to consider; in the midst of the discussion, Johnson disclosed that she identifies as a lesbian. Bhatt also invited students to comment on "what they knew about" her gender and sexual identities. Johnson and Bhatt (2003) do not suggest that collaborations or alliances across differences are simple, readily accomplished matters. Rather, they describe their own work together as being

> born out of a commitment to critical dialogue and experiencing significant pain and conflict. . . . [W]e have consciously engaged around the ways whiteness, heterosexuality, colonialism, sexism, and class differences have structured our relationship. It is precisely in engaging those issues actively, that we have come to a place of alliance professionally and politically. (p. 242)

Future research at the intersections of communication and instruction must interrogate, from the outset, its own heteronormativity, as well as the overlaps and assumptions that surround both popular and academic discussions of sex, gender, and sexuality. We are beginning to see exciting, intersectional work in this vein (e.g., B. K. Alexander, 2005; Bell, 2007; Calafell, Chapter 18, this volume; Gust & Warren, 2008; Johnson, 2007; Tuder, 2007; Warren & Zoffel, 2007), though we may have to look beyond *Communication Education* to find it.

In terms of communication textbooks related to sexuality, since the Chesebro (1981) and Ringer (1994b) anthologies, there have been two anthologies related to media and sexual identities (Carstarphen & Zavoina, 1999; Gross & Woods, 1999) and the single-authored textbook by Larry Gross (2001), *Up From Invisibility: Lesbians, Gay Men, and the Media in America*. There are many other textbooks and anthologies in sexuality studies, sociology, literature, cultural studies, anthropology, psychology, geography, and other disciplines disciplinary and interdisciplinary that include sections related to cultural studies and sexuality. However, in our field specifically, I am only aware of two: The aforementioned anthology, *Queer Theory and Communication* (Yep et al., 2003b), and the more recent one *Sexualities and Communication in Everyday Life: A Reader* that Lee Jenkins and I edited (Lovaas & Jenkins, 2007).

Before Lee and I decided to put together a textbook on sexualities and communication, we had each spent considerable time assembling spiral-bound course readers because we could not find a sufficiently current textbook that was appropriate for our upper-division undergraduate students (both the Chesebro, 1981, and Ringer, 1994b, anthologies were used in earlier versions of the course). We wanted a book that would under-gird our main pedagogical aims and speak to the primary challenges we had faced in the classroom; at the same time, we anticipated that it might be of interest to others who were teaching in this area and seek-ing a textbook, looking for supplementary materials for related courses such as gender and communication, or considering developing a course on sexualities and communication. We include readings that help estab-lish a conceptual foundation for studying sexuality while introducing students to a few individuals from several disciplines whose ideas have been influential in shaping contemporary sexuality studies. We believe that it is crucial to augment and enhance the communication field by more fully incorporating the study of sexuality in its intersections with gender, race and ethnicity, nationality, age, and ability. We were excited, for example, to include the pioneering article by E. Patrick Johnson (2007), first published in 2001, in which he argues that queer theory has not adequately attended to race and class and offers *quare studies*, which attends to "the racialized bodies, experiences, and knowledges, of trans-gendered people, lesbians, gays, and bisexuals of color" (p. 77) and insists that we "must make theory work for its constituency" (p. 297). The potential we saw for an article to push how we think about the sub-ject of sexualities and communication was key in our decision to include it. For example, two readings that have consistently generated vigorous discussions in our classes at San Francisco State University (SFSU) frame the topics of weddings (Bell, 2007) and same-sex mar-riages (Yep, Lovaas, & Elia, 2007) in unfamiliar, provocative, and, we think, productive ways. Future work at the intersections of communi-cation and instruction will, necessarily, entail the creation of antholo-gies, readers, and textbooks that substantively address current issues at the intersections of sexuality and other aspects of human identity. This scholarship will emerge from and speak directly to our work in the communication classroom.

INSTITUTIONAL AND CURRICULAR PRACTICES

Though I had taken undergraduate courses in subjects such as women in U.S. history, it was Sally Gearhart's graduate class in patriarchal rhetoric at SFSU in the late 1970s that first set me on fire in reading and thinking and talking about the politics of sex, gender, and sexuality, and how they are related to other areas of life, such as culture, race, age, and spirituality. I read and was inspired by Adrienne Rich and Audre Lorde, among others (Lorde, 1984; Lorde & Rich, 1984; Rich, 1980). Sally also helped me—first, by her own classroom alchemy and second, by encouraging me to read Paulo Freire's Pedagogy of the Oppressed (1970)—to better imagine myself as a teacher.

I feel fortunate to now be a faculty member in Communication Studies at SFSU, which has often been at the forefront of progressive pedagogy. In 1972, for example, Nancy McDermid, assisted by Sally Gearhart, Lee Jenkins, and Cathy Decker, created an undergraduate course titled "The Rhetoric of Sexual Liberation," which Sally Gearhart (2003) describes as "overtly feminist and the first such course to be offered nationally in our discipline" (p. xxiii). The course morphed into "Sex Roles and Communication" and, later, "Gender and Communication." In 1989, Lee Jenkins developed "Sexual Identity and Communication," which has been offered approximately once a year ever since. Our department also offers graduate seminars in both areas every year or two. Starting in Spring 2010, we will have an undergraduate course in masculinities and communication, developed by Gust Yep, for a total of six courses related to gender and/or sexuality.

The majority of colleges and universities offer courses in culture and communication; gender and communication classes are also increasingly common. However, as of this writing, there appear to be very few regularly scheduled college courses on sexuality and communication in the United States. Some departments offer classes that examine media representations of gender and sexuality; many more include race, class, and gender, but generally do not specify sexuality, age, ability, religion, and so on. A number of programs occasionally offer special topics courses that either focus on or include sexuality. For example, Southern Illinois University, which recently instituted a graduate area of study in gender, sexuality, and communication, has offered a special topics seminar in postcolonial queer theory. University of Wisconsin at Milwaukee has an issues in communication seminar in communication and sexuality. At the undergraduate level, the University of South Florida has a special topics course in communication, spirituality, and sexuality. Apart from SFSU, I am aware of only two communication programs that regularly offer undergraduate courses that concern sexuality, both grouping it with gender. Regis University has a class offered every other year titled "Gender, Sexuality, and Communication," and Columbus State University teaches "Communication, Gender, and Sexuality."

Though not the result of a comprehensive search, the impression I am left with after my online searching for evidence of communication courses about sexuality is that there are few such courses in comparison with courses related to gender and culture, that the courses that exist are often taught intermittently, and that the number of such courses is slowly increasing. Online catalog descriptions of communication courses related to gender, culture, media, and interpersonal, relational, and family communication are more apt to make reference to sexuality or sexual orientation than 10, or even 5, years ago. During my recent term as introductory course director,

I looked at all the hybrid and survey textbooks currently available for use in the fundamentals of oral communication course and noted that, while gender is more often integrated in these books, it is still atypical to see more than an example or two related to sexualities.

Why is it uncommon to see communication courses related to sexualities? Why does the subject appear to receive limited attention in many courses? Among the possible explanations that come to mind are the following: We may feel a variety of kinds of discomfort with the subject matter, including viewing it as too politically charged. We may believe that sexuality is a special case, too private or intimate to discuss in the classroom context. We may have questions about the appropriateness of sexualities as a legitimate subject for the communication discipline; we may deem that other departments, such as human sexuality or biology, are already sufficiently addressing the subject of sexuality and doing a better job of it than we would. We may worry that the content will entail explicit discussion of sexual practices. We may have never taken a related undergraduate course or graduate seminar, or read the germane communication studies literature; we may feel intimidated by some of the frequently cited theories and theorists associated with sexuality studies, such as queer theory, poststructuralism, Foucault, and Butler. Those of us who identify as heterosexual may assume that, as heterosexuals, we are not qualified to teach this subject; we may also be anxious that teaching a sexualities and communication course will cause others to question our sexual identity. Those of us who identify as LGBTQ may be concerned about becoming too closely linked with the subject, thinking that others assume that we are naturally best suited to teach in this area. We may recognize in these ideas the whispers and commands of the public pedagogies of heteronormative sexuality; though I teach both "Sexual Identities and Communication" and "Gender and Communication," though I have coedited books and published articles and encyclopedia entries related to the subject, I still hear them.

Given the length of my combined experiences at SFSU as a graduate student, lecturer, and full-time faculty member, I focus in the remainder of this section and in the next on this particular local context for sexuality and communication pedagogy, in the hope that it may be of some value, particularly for those who are taking or anticipate taking steps toward a more sexually diverse and inclusive pedagogy.

However, it is important to note that, though I live and work in the San Francisco Bay Area, a place widely perceived as virtually an oasis of sexual positivity and freedom, queer bashing and heteronormativity are alive and well here (as is homonormativity). The local organization CUAV (Community United Against Violence) reported that "hate crimes against LGBTs in San Francisco increased by seven percent in 2007, according to an analysis conducted by national anti-violence groups" (Gilligan, 2007, para. 1). Furthermore, the Web site for the Department of Sexuality Studies at SFSU (2009) proclaims, "San Francisco is one of the birthplaces of sexual liberation in the U.S. that has also fostered sexuality studies in the academy. San Francisco State University has nurtured and developed sexuality as a field of study" (para. 1); yet a colleague, who attended an online sexual harassment training that was required of all California State University supervisors in late 2007, shared with me that in the module dealing with how to avoid sexual harassment, one of the slides advised that "the most effective and prudent way to avoid being the subject of a harassment complaint is to never discuss or refer to sex, sexuality-related topics, or any of the protected categories while on the job." I do not know how the university system came to purchase this particular program, but I am curious as to whether those who made the selection were aware that it would be impossible to do one's job effectively in any department offering courses related to sexuality "or any of the other protected categories." Imagine making no reference, whenever you are "on the job," to race, sex, sexuality, age, ability, or religion, even curiously, at a university whose mission statement begins with the aim "to create and maintain an environment for learning that promotes respect for and appreciation of scholarship, freedom, human diversity, and the cultural mosaic of the City of San Francisco and the Bay Area" (SFSU, 2009). Wherever we live and work, we are not separate from the webs of heterosexist and sexist ideologies, never far from warnings that sexuality is a minefield.

In this richly multivalent milieu, I have been teaching "Sexual Identity and Communication," the course's current title, since 1999. SFSU's bachelor of arts in communication studies has eight breadth areas, one of which is communication diversity, which includes courses in gender, culture, sexuality, and dialogues across differences. The objectives on my latest syllabus for the course are as follows:

1. To understand how sexualities are constructed, expressed, and negotiated through communication in a variety of social contexts;

2. To recognize the influence of sociohistorical context and power relations on the communication of sexualities, including analyzing the impacts of heterosexism, sexism, and other interrelated forms of oppression;

3. To evaluate the ethical implications of theories, research, and practices regarding sexualities and communication; and

4. To apply knowledge of sexualities and communication to enhance our capacities for self-reflection, respect for self and others, dialogic communication, and critical social engagement.

These objectives echo themes in the learning objectives for all the courses in the communication diversity area, while adding more specific and explicit reference to sociohistorical context, power relations, and praxis. Though it may not be sufficiently apparent in this list of objectives, we examine dominant and counterdiscourses on sexualities, especially contemporary ones, and have opportunities both to reflect on how our own assumptions, beliefs, and practices may support, resist, and/or interrupt them, and to imagine other possibilities.

While located in the Communication Studies Department, the sexualities course also fulfills a general education requirement; before this was the case, I understand that a smaller percentage of students in the class identified as heterosexual, and a larger percentage specifically sought out the course because of an interest in the subject, not primarily to fulfill a university requirement. The broader student base means greater diversity of student backgrounds and interests; it also means that we have more students who come into the classroom with little notion of what a class with this title will address. The last time I taught the class, for example, several students told me that they were surprised by the course content, having expected more of a "speech course." There are students who have not discussed sexuality in any prior classroom setting, and who have had limited interactions—at least as far as they are aware—with those whose sexual identifications differ from their own. I have had students who identify as heterosexual tell me that they have deliberately avoided being in the company of people who are not straight. Several years ago, a student in my class confided to me that where he came from, homosexuals were buried in the sand up to their necks and stoned to death. I do not know how many of those who drop the class do so because of the course content; in a time when enrollment is up and, due to budget cuts, the number of classes offered is down, there is a strong incentive to complete the course.

Happily, all the students in the above examples remained in the class and most let me know that they were glad they had done so. As with other courses deemed "controversial," it is very possible to speak to what is considered controversy without either defensiveness or the delivery of a curriculum designed to make everyone feel "safe" at all times.

CLASSROOM PRACTICES

Once a week for much of the semester, a group of students facilitate our discussion of a reading. They are asked to read the material well, develop "juicy" questions to stimulate substantial conversation, and bring in artifacts that relate to topics within the reading that are of particular interest to them. As a group, they meet briefly to compare notes, prioritize, and order the sequence of questions. I had an intensifying headache accompanied by nausea the afternoon we were discussing Lisa Diamond's (2002) article, "'Having a Girlfriend Without Knowing It': Intimate Friendships Among Adolescent Sexual-Minority Women," and contemplated ending class early. But at times during the class conversation that day, my fervent responses to students' comments allowed the pain to recede to the edges of my awareness. I told them how tired I am of the old When Harry Met Sally conversation, the conventional wisdom that one's relationships must be either "platonic" or "romantic," that it concerns me when we view sexuality— especially some people's sexuality—as uncontrollable, so that once they felt attracted to someone they could always only see the person through a lens of sexual interest. I shared my memory of the time I sat in a hot tub across from a longtime friend from my reading group and realized, for the first time, how gorgeous and sensual and sexy she was. I asked them if they were sure and, if so, how, that one was always either in a friendship or a sexual relationship and never the twain shall or should meet. I said that I hoped that they some- times enjoy the experience of desire that is not openly—or perhaps in the smallest, most subtle little ways—acknowledged by both parties, or all 3 or 4 or 10. Never spoken aloud, the choice to imagine the possibilities, to simulta- neously sample and exercise restraint, was a delicious treat. I admitted that I often had this experience, sometimes in the college classroom.

✶ ✶ ✶

According to my old American Heritage dictionary, the definition of *anec- dote* includes "hitherto undivulged particulars of history or biography" (Morris, 1980). This anecdote, then, like the one with which this chapter launched, appears in print for the first time in this volume. Knowing this, I feel both discomforted and comforted.

Comfort comes from the Late Latin *confortare,* "to strengthen." Everyday references to strength carry a very positive connotation much of the time. I will hazard that a common desire of teachers is that, in the course of their work together in a class, students are in some ways strengthened. It could sound, conversely, like an exercise in abuse to hope to weaken something about one's students. But I know that some of the most valued learning with my most treasured teachers has involved an undermining of solid notions that I have held. About why things are the way they are. About historical events. About similarities and differences among and between individuals and peoples. It is discomforting, some- times frightening, when a cozy old "given" is questioned. In my experience as a teacher, courses in the "diversity" curriculum, and particularly those related to sexuality and gender, involve a remarkable amount of this dis- comfort. A question I/we repeat often during the course of a semester is how do I/we know what I/we know?

A favorite activity early in my sexualities class is the emissary from a distant star. I usually work with a teaching assistant (TA) in this class, and in this exercise, the TA and I play the role of emissaries (miraculously, English speaking) from beings elsewhere in the cosmos, who have been watching Earth's human upright, bipedal occupants in particular and who are curious about the reasons for many related phenomena they have observed. Students working in small groups are charged with the task of planning how to explain the sex/gender/sexuality matrices of humans to the emissaries. Each group then begins to present their explanation to the emissaries, who respond with question after question. While able to understand English grammar and simple vocabulary, the emissaries do not know words such as *male*, *female*, or *reproduction*, the labels for parts of human anatomy, and so on. Scores of words are written on the board as students explicate bodies and gender norms and forms of desire. Ignorant as well of the whys and many hows, the emissaries have been able to observe a great deal of human action. The device of the emissaries requires students to explain what has not needed explaining, "facts" and webs of meaning that they have not attempted to explain before. What are sex, gender, and sexuality? How does one distinguish a male from a female? Does this distinction hold for everyone? Does everyone make this distinction? How do we account for similarities and differences in humans? What differences do differences make?

Besides engaging all of us in thinking about how we know what we know, recognizing some of the limits of our knowing, and noticing that things we take as set, as fact, as always, as universal, may be arbitrary arrangements and conventions, the activity helps establish that question posing and discussion facilitation will be central parts of the role of the teacher. It is both discomforting and comforting as we stretch our description and analysis muscles and laugh a lot. After debriefing this activity, we create our class ground rules or working agreements, brainstorming ways of being together in the context of a university classroom with its panoply of rules and norms, some more pliant than others.

From this chapter's location in the critical communication pedagogy section of the *SAGE Handbook of Communication and Instruction* and what I have said thus far in citing influential personal events, teachers, colleagues, theorists, and course objectives, does the chapter advocate a critical, feminist, queer pedagogy, then?

Conclusion

I became a critic of the institution of gender in childhood and was thrilled when feminism provided me with a vocabulary with which to better analyze and communicate my nascent critique of the gender regimes in which I lived. At points, the first versions of feminism I encountered were both helpful tools and obstructions, as I so wanted "sisterhood," an overarching web of connections among all women and feminist men, as schema and activist community. It was more years of formal and informal schooling and unschooling, an unfinished and unfinishable process, before I recognized how gender oppression interrelated with systems of oppression based on race, class, sexuality, and ability, for example.

> In a sense, all new disciplines are bound to stutter, mumble, and cry as they grapple with and define their objects of study. (Gunn & Rice, 2009, p. 217)

Even as I stutter, mumble, cry, and grapple, I love teaching a course on sexualities and communication and no longer allow myself the out of "there's really not much good research in the field of communication yet on this subject in relation to sexualities" as a reason not to do the necessary work to include sexualities in any course I teach. Though I enjoy working with a reader I coedited for the sexualities and communication course, I am never entirely satisfied with the materials or my pedagogy. Upcoming versions of the book and course can and must do better on the interlocking dynamics of sexualization, globalization, and transnationalism; of sexualization and racialization and class; and of abilities, religion, and spirituality. More is needed on bisexualities, transsexualities, heterosexualities, and homonormativity.

The editors suggested that I provide a vision for the field for the next 10 years. I have a sense of some of my own tentative next steps, but from where I currently sit in relation to sexualities and critical communication pedagogy, most of all, I want to see more of it! I do not want to attempt to define myself or the field by a single appellation or a string of them. I remember feminism as home and how some of the ways I embraced it blinded me from seeing what womanist and Third World and postcolonial feminisms exposed. Queer was another homecoming. I had never felt at home with heterosexual, lesbian, or bisexual, and queer better matched my range of desire, politics, and suspicion of sexual labels. But others called my attention to how/where queer theory was eliding race (e.g., Alexander, 2003; Johnson, 2007), obscuring the importance of material conditions and institutional practices (e.g., Hennessey, 2000; Kirsch, 2006; Morton, 1996), and ignoring trans lives (Namaste, 2000). I am drawn to and grateful for the work of scholars whose work is clearly informed by life experience and demonstrates that they are informed by and are critical of queer studies (e.g., Halberstam, 2005; Johnson & Henderson, 2005). Anytime I get too comfortable with identifying with a group label, I want to remind myself of this:

> But the problem is, precisely, to decide if it is actually suitable to place myself within a "we" in order to assert the principles one recognizes and the values one accepts; or if it is not, rather, necessary to make the future formation of a "we" possible, by elaborating the question. Because it seems to me that the "we" must not be previous to the question; it can only be the result—and necessarily the temporary result—of the questions as it is posed in the new terms in which one formulates it. (Foucault, 1984, para. 11)

After Freire's *Pedagogy of the Oppressed* (1970), bell hooks's *Teaching to Transgress* (1994) was the next book to stir and inspire me as a teacher. Rising to the top of my must read bookshelf right now is M. Jacqui Alexander's (2005) anthology, *Pedagogies of Crossing: Meditations on Feminism, Sexual Politics, Memory, and the Sacred*. There are articles I find persuasive espousing trans pedagogy (Olson, 2002) and bisexual pedagogy (Nathanson, 2009). I am excited by and picking up what I can from my colleagues at SFSU, for example, Amy Kilgard's development of interventionist performance pedagogy. How many critical pedagogies do we need? What is to be gained from a queering of critical communication pedagogy?

I am working from, with, and toward a sexualities and communication pedagogy that is critical in the Freirean sense of involving an ongoing process of moving between acting and reflecting, and recalling that "the emancipatory project is not a one shot deal achieved solely in a classroom context" (Lovaas, Baroudi, & Collins, 2002, p. 181). I think our sexualities and communication pedagogy can take from queer theory the impulse to question all identity categories, without dismissing them, and keeping in mind "that the postmodern push to theorize identity discursively must be balanced with theories of corporeality and materiality" (Johnson, 2002, p. 118); I want it to interrogate the normative: hetero-, homo-, white, Eurocentric, patriarchal, ableist, and otherwise. I think it is productive for us, at least for a while, to continue to think, as teachers and scholars, in terms of sexing, gendering, and sexualizing processes, and to continue to add plurals in more of the places where we have only seen singulars, such as heterosexualities.

My university students today are generally much better informed than I was at their age, let alone than when I was in elementary school. In a recently assigned paper, two students used terms I had never heard of in discussing sexual identities: cissexual and sapiosexual. Perhaps you are already familiar with these terms; if not, I am going to let you use them as an opportunity to think about what they might mean and what else has yet to be named. For me, it was a reminder that we continue to be creative in giving voice to our desires, whatever opposition we may face from forces at public, local, and classroom levels that would tame them.

> My concern is what can be done by means of education to enable people to transcend their private terrors and act together to give freedom a concrete existence in their lives. (Greene, 1975, p. 4)

References

Alexander, B. K. (2003). Queering queer theory again (or queer theory as drag performance). In G. A. Yep, K. E. Lovaas, & J. P. Elia (Eds.), *Queer theory and communication: From disciplining queers to queering the discipline(s)* (pp. 349–352). Binghamton, NY: Harrington Park Press.

Alexander, B. K. (2005). Embracing the teachable moment: The black gay body in the classroom as embodied text. In E. P. Johnson & M. G. Henderson (Eds.), *Black queer studies: A critical anthology* (pp. 249–265). Durham, NC: Duke University Press.

Alexander, M. J. (2005). *Pedagogies of crossing: Meditations on feminism, sexual politics, memory, and the sacred.* Durham, NC: Duke University Press.

Beasley, M. M. (2008). "Tribute to the ancestors": Ritual performance and same-gender-loving men of African descent. *Text and Performance Quarterly, 28*(4), 433–457.

Bell, E. (2007). Performing "I do": Weddings, pornography and sex. In K. E. Lovaas & M. M. Jenkins (Eds.), *Sexualities and communication in everyday life: A reader* (pp. 145–164). Thousand Oaks, CA: Sage.

Buerkle, C. W. (2009). Metrosexuality can stuff it: Beef consumption as (hetero-masculine) fortification. *Text and Performance Quarterly, 29*(1), 77–93.

Carstarphen, M. G., & Zavoina, S. C. (1999). Sexual rhetoric: Media perspectives on sexuality, gender, and identity. Santa Barbara, CA: Greenwood Press.

Chesebro, J. W. (Ed.). (1981). *Gayspeak: Gay male and lesbian communication.* New York: Pilgrim Press.

Cooks, L., & Sun, C. (2002). Constructing gender pedagogies: Desire and resistance in the "alternative" classroom. *Communication Education, 51*(3), 293–310.

Corey, F. C., Smith, R. R., & Nakayama, T. K. (2002). GLBTQ bibliography by NCA/ICA members. Retrieved September 28, 2009, from www.ncaglbtq.org/glbtcommbiblio.html

Deleuze, G., & Guattari, F. (2004). *Anti-Oedipus* (R. Hurley, M. Seem, & H. R. Lane, Trans.). London and New York: Continuum Press. (Original work published 1972)

Department of Sexuality Studies, San Francisco State University. (2009). *Department history.* Retrieved September 28, 2009, from http://hmsx.sfsu.edu/about%20us/history.htm

DeVito, J. (1979, November 1). *Educational responsibilities to the gay and lesbian student.* (ERIC Document Reproduction Service No. ED184167)

Diamond, L. M. (2002). "Having a girlfriend without knowing it": Intimate friendships among adolescent sexual-minority women. *Journal of Lesbian Studies, 6*(1), 5–16.

Dickinson, P. (2008). Love is a battlefield: The performance and politics of same-sex marriage in North America. *Text and Performance Quarterly, 28,* 277–297.

Elia, J. P. (2003). Queering relationships: Toward a paradigmatic shift. In G. A. Yep, K. E. Lovaas, & J. P. Elia (Eds.), *Queer theory and communication: From disciplining queers to queering the discipline(s)* (pp. 61–86). Binghamton, NY: Harrington Park Press.

Fausto-Sterling, A. (2000). *Sexing the body: Gender politics and the construction of sexuality.* New York: Basic Books.

Fausto-Sterling, A. (2007). Frameworks of desire. *Daedalus, 136*(2), 47–57.

Foucault, M. (1984). *Polemics, politics and problematizations.* Retrieved September 28, 2009, from http://foucault.info/foucault/interview.html

Frank, N. (2009). *Unfriendly fire: How the gay ban undermines the military and weakens America.* New York: St. Martin's Press.

Freire, P. (1970). *Pedagogy of the oppressed.* New York: Seabury Press.

Gamson, J. (2000). Sexualities, queer theory, and qualitative research. In N. K. Denzin & Y. S. Lincoln (Eds.), *Handbook of qualitative research* (pp. 347–365). Thousand Oaks, CA: Sage.

Gearhart, S. M. (2003). Foreword: My trip to queer. In G. A. Yep, K. E. Lovaas, & J. P. Elia (Eds.), *Queer theory and communication: From disciplining queers to queering the discipline(s)* (pp. xxi–xxx). Binghamton, NY: Harrington Park Press.

Gilligan, H. T. (2007). *Hate crimes against LGBTs increased in 2007.* Retrieved September 28, 2009, from www.cuav.org/article/5

Giroux, H. A. (2001). *Private satisfactions and public disorders: "Fight Club," patriarchy, and the politics of masculine violence.* Retrieved July 22, 2009, from www.henryagiroux.com/online_articles/fight_club.htm

Giroux, H. A. (2005). *Cultural studies in dark times: Public pedagogy and the challenge of neoliberalism.* Retrieved July 22, 2009, from www.henryagiroux.com/online_articles/DarkTimes.htm

Greene, M. (1975). *Education, freedom, and possibility.* Inaugural Lecture as William F. Russell Professor, Teachers College, Columbia University.

Gross, L. (2001). *Up from invisibility: Lesbians, gay men, and the media in America.* New York: Columbia University Press.

Gross, L., & Woods, J. D. (Eds.). (1999). *The Columbia reader on lesbians & gay men in media, society, and politics.* New York: Columbia University Press.

Gunn, J., & Rice, J. E. (2009). About face/stuttering discipline. *Communication and Critical/Cultural Studies, 6*(2), 215–219.

Gust, S. W., & Warren, J. T. (2008). Naming our sexual and sexualized bodies in the classroom: And the important stuff that comes after the colon. *Qualitative Inquiry, 14*(1), 114–134.

Halberstam, J. (2003). Reflections on queer studies and queer pedagogy. In G. A. Yep, K. E. Lovaas, & J. P. Elia (Eds.), *Queer theory and communication: From disciplining queers to queering the disciplines* (pp. 361–364). Binghamton, NY: Harrington Park Press.

Halberstam, J. (2005). *In a queer time and place: Transgender bodies, subcultural lives.* New York: New York University Press.

Hauser, D. (2008). *Five years of abstinence-only-until-marriage education: Assessing the impact.* Retrieved July 22, 2009, from www.advocatesforyouth.org/index.php?option=com_content&task=view&id=623&Itemid=177

Heinz, B. (2002). Enga(y)ging the discipline: Sexual minorities and communication studies. *Communication Education, 51*(1), 95–104.

Henderson, L. (2000). Queer communication studies. In W. B. Gudykunst (Ed.), *Communication yearbook 24* (pp. 465–484). Thousand Oaks, CA: Sage.

Hennessy, R. (2000). *Profit and pleasure: Sexual identities in late capitalism.* New York: Routledge.

hooks, b. (1994). *Teaching to transgress: Education as the practice of freedom.* New York: Routledge.

Jacobs, A. T. (2007). *"I'm here! Am I queer?" Analyzing the discourse of being openly closeted.* Paper presented at the annual meeting of the NCA 93rd Annual Convention, Chicago, IL [Online]. Retrieved September 28, 2009, from www.allacademic.com/meta/p188633_index.html

Jenkins, M. (1994). Ways of coming out in the classroom. In R. J. Ringer (Ed.), *Queer words, queer images: Communication and the construction of homosexuality* (pp. 332–334). New York: New York University Press.

Johnson, E. P. (2001). "Quare" studies, or (almost) everything I know about queer studies I learned from my grandmother. *Text and Performance Quarterly, 21,* 1–25.

Johnson, E. P. (2002). Performing blackness down under: The café of the gate of salvation. *Text and Performance Quarterly, 22*(2), 99–119.

Johnson, E. P. (2007). "Quare" studies, or (almost) everything I know about queer studies I learned from my grandmother. In K. E. Lovaas & M. M. Jenkins (Eds.), *Sexualities & communication in everyday life: A reader* (pp. 69–84, 297–299). Thousand Oaks, CA: Sage.

Johnson, E. P., & Henderson, M. G. (2005). *Black queer studies: A critical anthology.* Durham, NC: Duke University Press.

Johnson, J. R., & Bhatt, A. J. (2003). Gendered and racialized identities alliances in the classroom: Formations in/of resistive space. *Communication Education, 52*(3/4), 230–244.

Kirsch, M. (2006). Queer theory, late capitalism, and internalized homophobia. In K. E. Lovaas, J. P. Elia, & G. A. Yep (Eds.), *LGBT studies and queer theory: New conflicts, collaborations, and contested terrain* (pp. 19–45). Binghamton, NY: Harrington Park Press.

Kosciw, J. G., Diaz, E. M., & Greytak, E. A. (2008). *2007 National School Climate Survey: The experiences of lesbian, gay, bisexual and transgender youth in our nation's schools.* New York: GLSEN.

Kumashiro, K. K. (2003). Queer ideals in education. In G. A. Yep, K. E. Lovaas, & J. P. Elia (Eds.), *Queer theory and communication: From disciplining queers to queering the discipline(s)* (pp. 365–368). Binghamton, NY: Harrington Park Press.

Lee, W. (2003). *Kuaering* queer theory: My autocritography and a race-conscious, womanist, transnational turn. In G. A. Yep, K. E. Lovaas, & J. P. Elia (Eds.), *Queer theory and communication: From disciplining queers to queering the discipline(s)* (pp. 147–170). Binghamton, NY: Harrington Park Press.

Lorde, A. (1984). *Sister outsider: Essays and speeches.* Trumansburg, NY: Crossing Press.

Lorde, A., & Rich, A. (1984). An interview: Audre Lorde and Adrienne Rich. In A. Lorde (Ed.), *Sister outsider: Essays and speeches* (pp. 81–109). Trumansburg, NY: Crossing Press.

Lovaas, K. E. (2003). Speaking to silence: Toward queering nonverbal communication. In G. A. Yep, K. E. Lovaas, & J. P. Elia (Eds.), *Queer theory and communication: From disciplining queers to queering the discipline(s)* (pp. 87–107). Binghamton, NY: Harrington Park Press.

Lovaas, K. E., Baroudi, L., & Collins, S. M. (2002). *Trans*cending heteronormativity in the classroom: Using queer and critical pedagogies to alleviate trans-anxieties. *Journal of Lesbian Studies, 6*(3/4), 177–190.

Lovaas, K. E., & Jenkins, M. M. (2007). Introduction: Setting the stage. In K. E. Lovaas & M. M. Jenkins (Eds.), *Sexualities and communication in everyday life: A reader* (pp. 1–17). Thousand Oaks, CA: Sage.

Maney, D. W., & Cain, R. (1997). Preservice elementary teachers' attitudes toward gay and lesbian parenting. *Journal of School Health, 67*(6), 236–241.

Martinez, J. M. (2003). Racisms, heterosexisms and identities: A semiotic phenomenology of self-understanding. In G. A. Yep, K. E. Lovaas, & J. P. Elia (Eds.), *Queer theory and communication: From disciplining queers to queering the discipline(s)* (pp. 109–128). Binghamton, NY: Harrington Park Press.

Morris, W. (Ed.). (1980). *The American Heritage dictionary of the English language.* Boston: Houghton Mifflin.

Morton, D. (Ed.). (1996). *The material queer: A LesBiGay cultural studies reader.* Boulder, CO: Westview Press.

Nakayama, T. K., & Corey, F. C. (2003). Nextext. In G. A. Yep, K. E. Lovaas, & J. P. Elia (Eds.), *Queer theory and communication: From disciplining queers to queering the discipline(s)* (pp. 319–334). Binghamton, NY: Harrington Park Press.

Namaste, V. K. (2000). *Invisible lives: The erasure of transsexual and transgendered people.* Chicago: University of Chicago Press.

Nathanson, J. (2009). Bisexual pedagogy: Bringing bisexuality into the classroom. *Journal of Bisexuality, 9*(1), 71–86.

Nicholas, C. L. (2006). Disciplinary-interdisciplinary GLBTQ (identity) studies and Hecht's layering perspective. *Communication Quarterly, 54*(2), 305–330.

Olson, T. (2002). TA/TG: The pedagogy of the cross-dressed. *Bad Subjects, 59.* Retrieved November 19, 2008, from http://bad.eserver.org/issues/2002/59/olson.html

Opffer, E. (1994). Coming out to students: Notes from the college classroom. In R. J. Ringer (Ed.), *Queer words, queer images: Communication and the construction of homosexuality* (pp. 296–321). New York: New York University Press.

Owen, A. S. (2003). Disciplining "Sextext": Queers, fears, and communication studies. In G. A. Yep, K. E. Lovaas, & J. P. Elia (Eds.), *Queer theory and communication: From disciplining queers to queering the discipline(s)* (pp. 297–317). Binghamton, NY: Harrington Park Press.

Pawlowski, D. R. (2006). Sexual communication in the family: Handling a delicate topic in the family communication course. *Communication Teacher, 20*(4), 100–104.

Pinar, W. F. (2003). Queer theory in education. In G. A. Yep, K. E. Lovaas, & J. P. Elia (Eds.), *Queer theory and communication: From disciplining queers to queering the discipline(s)* (pp. 357–360). Binghamton, NY: Harrington Park Press.

Rester, C., & Edwards, R. (2007). Effects of sex and setting on students' interpretation of teachers' excessive use of immediacy. *Communication Education, 56*(1), 34–53.

Rich, A. (1980). Compulsory heterosexuality and lesbian existence. *Signs: Journal of Women in Culture and Society, 5,* 631–660.

Ringer, R. J. (1994a). Coming out in the classroom: Faculty disclosures of sexuality. In R. J. Ringer (Ed.), *Queer words, queer images: Communication and the construction of homosexuality* (pp. 322–331). New York: New York University Press.

Ringer, R. J. (Ed.). (1994b). *Queer words, queer images: Communication and the construction of homosexuality.* New York: New York University Press.

Rivers, M. J. (2000). For better or worse? Let's make it better. *Communication Teacher, 14*(4), 8–10.

Russ, T. L., Simonds, C. J., & Hunt, S. K. (2002). Coming out in the classroom . . . an occupational hazard? The influence of sexual orientation on teacher credibility and perceived student learning. *Communication Education, 51*(3), 311–324.

Saltzburg, S. (2004). Learning that an adolescent child is gay or lesbian: The parent experience. *Social Work, 49*(1), 109–118.

San Francisco State University. (2009). *University mission.* Retrieved September 28, 2009, from www.sfsu.edu/~puboff/mission.html

Sears, J. (1992). Educators, homosexuality, and homosexual students: Are personal feelings related to professional beliefs? *Journal of Homosexuality, 22*(3/4), 29–80.

Sloop, J. M. (2006). Critical studies in gender/sexuality and media. In B. J. Dow & J. T. Wood (Eds.), *The SAGE handbook of gender and communication* (pp. 319–333). Thousand Oaks, CA: Sage.

Taylor, J. (1994). Performing the (lesbian) self: Teacher as text. In R. J. Ringer (Ed.), *Queer words, queer images: Communication and the construction of homosexuality* (pp. 289–295). New York: New York University Press.

Tuder, J. (2007). "Holly Kowalski": Sex across the curriculum. In K. E. Lovaas & M. M. Jenkins (Eds.), *Sexualities and communication in everyday life: A reader* (pp. 243–245). Thousand Oaks, CA: Sage.

Warren, J. T., & Zoffel, N. A. (2007). Living in the middle: Performances bi-men. In K. E. Lovaas & M. M. Jenkins (Eds.), *Sexualities and communication in everyday life: A reader* (pp. 233–242). Thousand Oaks, CA: Sage.

Yep, G. A. (2003). The violence of heteronormativity in communication studies: Notes on injury, healing, and queer world making. In G. A. Yep, K. E. Lovaas, & J. P. Elia (Eds.), *Queer theory and communication: From disciplining queers to queering the discipline(s)* (pp. 11–59). Binghamton, NY: Harrington Park Press.

Yep, G. A., Lovaas, K. E., & Elia, J. P. (2003a). Introduction: Queering communication: Starting the conversation. In G. A. Yep, K. E. Lovaas, & J. P. Elia (Eds.), *Queer theory and communication: From disciplining queers to queering the discipline(s)* (pp. 1–10). Binghamton, NY: Harrington Park Press.

Yep, G. A., Lovaas, K. E., & Elia, J. P. (Eds.). (2003b). *Queer theory and communication: From disciplining queers to queering the discipline(s).* Binghamton, NY: Harrington Park Press.

Yep, G. A., Lovaas, K. E., & Elia, J. P. (2007). A critical appraisal of assimilationist and radical ideologies underlying same-sex marriage in LGBT communities in the United States. In K. E. Lovaas & M. M. Jenkins (Eds.), *Sexualities & communication in everyday life: A reader* (pp. 165–177). Thousand Oaks, CA: Sage.

Zukic, N. (2008). Webbing sexual/textual agency in autobiographical narratives of pleasure. *Text and Performance Quarterly, 28*(4), 396–414.

Producing Digitally Mediated Environments as Sites for Critical Feminist Pedagogy

21

Radhika Gajjala, Natalia Rybas, and Yahui Zhang

The meaning of race and the challenges of racism change for each generation, . . . and the new challenges we face demand a new language for understanding how the symbolic power of race as a pedagogical force as well as a structural and materialist practice redefine the relationship between the self and the other, the private and the public. It is this latter challenge in particular that needs to be addressed more fully if racism is not to be reduced to an utterly privatized discourse that erases any trace of racial injustice by denying the very notion of the social and the operations of power through which racial politics are organized and legitimated.

—Giroux (2003, pp. 191–192)

Calling out a more complex, nuanced understanding of identity as emergent from communication commits us to more complex and nuanced understandings of power, privilege, culture, and responsibility.

—Fassett and Warren (2007, pp. 41–42)

The two quotes above assert the importance of critical pedagogy in shifting generational and political climates and the centrality of communication in identity formation. To challenge any form of oppression, we have to start with trying to understand how it manifests contextually and in concrete and mundane communication practices. While teaching generations of "digital natives," it is a must that we engage Web 2.0 pedagogically and strategically. In relation to current structures of globalization and migrant labor, race is a nuanced category intersecting with class, gender, geography, caste, and histories of colonialism and corporate globalization in complex ways. At various contexts where technologies ("old" and "new") encounter human beings together with local, global, economic, and social processes, we see race and class produced against specific contextual backdrops.

How might we proceed to convey an understanding of the complexity of race through our research and pedagogy? The analysis is based on efforts to interrogate issues of identity in cyberspace through classroom assignments. This work is a part of a larger project that examines issues of race in cyberspace and provides a variety of possible pedagogic interventions and practices to engage the problem of racialization within cyberspace. Giroux (2003) suggests,

> In its current manifestation, racism survives through the guise of neoliberalism, a kind of repartee that imagines human agency as simply a matter of individualized choices, the only obstacle to effective citizenship and agency being the lack of principled self-help and moral responsibility. (p. 191)

Taking his suggestion into account and foregrounding the understanding that concrete, mundane communication practices are "constitutive of larger social structural systems" (Fassett & Warren, 2007, p. 43), we find it imperative that we examine the different venues and habits within which everyday praxis authorizes various forms of discrimination. Race, class, caste, gender, geography, and specific located histories of colonization *intersect* with specific place-based configurations of access to various literacies associated with the communities of production. These communities shape constructs of identity and ignorance, which, in their turn, reproduce existing sociocultural patterns of inclusion and exclusion. The sociocultural patterns overlap with geographically, culturally, historically, and nationally produced place-based configurations of race and engender contradictory manifestations of racism and acts of silencing online. Thus, we strive to show *how* these manifest in specific instances, especially in controlled environments of classrooms.

The methodology for teaching and researching in class projects is based on critical feminist pedagogies, critical communication pedagogy (Fassett & Warren, 2007), and what we term *epistemologies (and pedagogies) of doing* (Gajjala, Rybas, & Altman, 2007). It can be problematic to pinpoint a feminist pedagogy, given its many strands of theoretical underpinnings. However, some basic principles exemplify feminist pedagogy: egalitarian relationship in the classroom, students valued as individuals, and personal experience as a learning resource (Welch, 1994, p. 156). While finding feminist pedagogy useful for our classroom praxis in valuing our students and validating students' experiences, critical communication pedagogy's attention to the constitutive nature of communication (Fassett & Warren, 2007, p. 3) renders it possible and imperative for us to focus on the everyday communication practices of our students in Web 2.0 environments. To make Web 2.0 environments "transformative, generative spaces of dialogue" (p. 43), the epistemologies of doing (Gajjala et al., 2007) emphasize hands-on application with simultaneous engagement in theory building. By emphasizing an epistemology of doing, therefore, we merely attempt to recover what it means to engage the process of learning and understanding. Of course, in these situations, our dilemma often is to maintain a "strategic certitude" in delivering assignments while balancing it with "strategic ambiguity." Thus, we draw examples from teaching and learning contexts to illustrate the production of identities. Some of these contexts include classroom settings, digital videos, MOO (multiuser dimension object-oriented) environments, Web sites and video podcasts produced in class assignments, Second Life and social networking explorations in and outside of "classroom" activities with advisees and collaborators, student journaling, and discussions around these productions and explorations. This research sheds light on multiple pedagogical and learning techniques as well as multiple contingent practices in cybercultures at online/offline intersections. It also focuses on the process of how selves are produced in interpersonal interactions in digitally mediated environments.

In sync with the multiple locationality of the research, this chapter is formed through engagement of diverse relational positions. To begin with, we are all of international origin, with multilingual and multisociocultural backgrounds. Existing notions of race, gender, class, and sexuality in the United States affect us differently. Therefore, conceptualizing issues of racialization at various local/global and online/offline intersections leads us to an understanding of geographic, economic, and linguistic intersections embedded within U.S.-centric articulations of race, gender, and sexuality. Also, we are dynamically engaged in complex relations with each other. During the collaboration, one of the authors (RG) was the instructor in a majority of the classes to which we refer, and the other two (NR and YZ) were graduate students, who were enrolled in some of Radhika's classes and assisted with some other classes. Radhika served as an adviser for Natalia and Yahui during graduate programs. Under the guidance of Radhika, Natalia has completed her dissertation on identities in cyberspace, and Yahui has finished her dissertation on Chinese women bloggers from a postcolonial feminist perspective. Currently, we all continue teaching communication as university professors: In our pedagogical practice and research engagement, we face the critical issues of racialization in concrete instances of interactions in classrooms.

Interwoven with the research process is a continuing concern and anxiety over the process of teaching, as we engage students in activities that they are used to seeing as playful and social and not directly related to academic coursework. As several feminists (e.g., Klein, 1987) have noted, while a male body is automatically granted authority in a situation where technology is used, a female teacher negotiates complex issues—even today—when teaching hands-on technology to students. In addition, inviting students into critical dialogues and asking them to experiment so that they understand technology-mediated environments critically creates further problems for the feminist teacher. Therefore, in articulating pedagogical tactics and learner-advisee perspectives, the authors reflect on these techniques. Even though, structurally, the power is invested in the tenured professor, the lines between learner and teacher and adviser and advisee are blurred sometimes in actual practice. To reflect these complex relationships, voice in this essay manifests in different forms. Sometimes we write as if in one voice; thus, the literature review and analysis of some particular examples does not distinguish between our three voices. However, in sections that require an articulation of pedagogic philosophy and reflection as either teacher or student and/or observer of the pedagogic practices, we use first person narrative. At such times, the subsection has the name of the first person writer. In between, we insert autoethnographic and performative writing segments drawn from interaction within the online environments that serve to illustrate the affective and processual nature of our research and teaching in such spaces.

Pedagogical Influences

We would like to borrow the simile of "weaving a tapestry" as used by bell hooks (1994, p. 52) to explicate the pedagogical influences that shape who we are as teachers, students, and researchers. It is not very productive to focus on only one pedagogical perspective when, in fact, many critical pedagogies inform and enrich one anther. Let us first begin with critical feminist pedagogy.

Critical feminist pedagogy pays attention to the intersections of gender and race, class and sexuality, and history and geography. The feminist classroom definitely approaches the content of the course through the lens of gender, but the attention to gender alone does not bring out true feminist educational impact. Critical feminist pedagogues of color (Collins, 1990; hooks, 1994; Lorde, 1984; Moraga & Anzaldúa, 1983; Smith, 1983) have contributed to a more comprehensive understanding of feminist pedagogy by bringing in the issue of the interlocking systems of oppression resulting not only from gender but also from race, class, and sexuality. They have also articulated the importance of understanding multiple locations of both oppression and privilege in knowledge production. In addition, they explicitly engage with the political aspects of education. As bell hooks notes in *Teaching to Transgress: Education as the Practice of Freedom,* "no education is politically neutral" (p. 37). At the same time, critical feminist pedagogy is concerned with historicizing knowledge and disrupting colonial discourse (Spivak, 1993). Critical feminist pedagogy calls for sensitivity to gender, race, class, sexuality, disability, multiculturalism, postcolonial criticism, and globalization (Wicker, Miller, & Dube, 2005).

Feminist pedagogy is characterized by four vital aspects: participatory learning, validation of personal experience, encouragement of social understanding and activism, and development of critical thinking and open-mindedness (Hoffmann & Stake, 2001, p. 80). Frances Maher and Mary Kay Tetreault (1994) describe a feminist classroom as encompassing "the entire process of creating knowledge, involving the innumerable ways in which students, teachers, and academic disciplines interact and redefine each other in the classroom, the educational institution, and the larger society" (p. 57). For critical feminist pedagogues, the collaborative, experiential, egalitarian, interactive, empowering, relational, affective, and not least, rational classroom environment is meant to cultivate more sensitivities to the theoretical concerns of critical feminist pedagogy.

To create a participatory learning environment, students are encouraged to contribute their experiences and perspectives. At the same time, teachers engage themselves in the process for self-actualization (hooks, 1994). Instead of being the expert imparting knowledge, the feminist pedagogue becomes a facilitator and learner at the same time. Both the students and teachers are understood as embodied, lived, and situated beings who must take active responsibility for "transgressing" racial, sexual, class, and geographical boundaries. Such an environment elicits growth of both the teachers and the students. Weiler (1995) elaborates that such a classroom is an arena for students to investigate multiple realities and engage in discussion with peers and faculty (p. 103).

Valuing the personal as a source of legitimate and valid knowledge, critical feminist pedagogues encourage students to understand personal experience as political, historical, and socially constructed. More important, the goal is to help students develop a critical framework that will enable and empower them to link personal experience with institutional structures of subordination (hooks, 1994; Klein, 1987).

The cultivation of a critical framework and a process of self-actualization is not only for the empowerment of individuals. Critical feminist pedagogy emphasizes the importance of translating these feminist principles into the transformation of social lives and social justice. Feminism is committed to social change, and feminist practice is integral to a feminist pedagogy. Miller (2005) reflects on feminist pedagogy as a liberative praxis. She contends, "Feminist pedagogy is concerned with the ideology of teaching and the methods. It introduces into the classroom a plethora of possibilities that resist easy answers and disallow the maintenance of homogeneous neatness" (p. 36). Struggles in the community and issues controversial and urgent in the society can all become opportunities for the praxis of critical feminist pedagogy.

Critical feminist pedagogy also takes great effort to foster in students the courage to take a critical stance toward authority and to be open-minded to diverse perspectives and experiences. The feminist classroom seeks to promote in students "connected knowing." Students are encouraged to put the voices of "experts" in dialogue with their own and others' voices and experiences (Belenky, Clinchy, Goldberger, & Tarule, 1986). Open-mindedness also entails, for both students and professors, coming to terms with ambiguity, contradiction, and the uncertainty that distinguishes a deep self-criticality and reflexivity from a mere rhetorical one (Ellsworth, 1989, p. 312). It also means engaging with diverse others "dialectically and dialogically" (Klein, 1987, p. 191).

This elaboration of what critical feminist pedagogy entails does not foreclose its connection with critical communication pedagogy as espoused by Fassett and Warren (2007). In fact, there are several important connections between the two bodies of scholarship that warrant some elaboration. Both critical feminist pedagogy and critical communication pedagogy have been inspired by the liberatory pedagogy of Paulo Freire (1971, 1985), who eloquently explores themes of oppression and liberation in his works. Kathleen Weiler (1991) and bell hooks (1994) cite Paulo Freire as the educational theorist whose work comes closest to feminist pedagogy. Perhaps the best evidence to support this inference is Freire's central view that "besides being an act of knowing, education is also a political act. That is why no pedagogy is neutral" (Freire & Shor, 1987, p. 13; see also Freire, 1985).

Similarly, the thought-provoking critique and lived experiences with critical pedagogy both as students and educators by Fassett and Warren (2007) lead them to the conclusion that

> critical pedagogy, at its best, is inherently Freirean: efforts to reflect and act upon the world in order to transform it, to make it a more just place for more people, to respond to our own collective pains and needs and desires. (p. 26)

This conscious awareness of one's agency to engage with and to influence one's social worlds in an always political environment is what defines both feminist pedagogy and critical communication pedagogy. In addition, the attention to the fluid nature of power draws these two areas of research even closer.

The reflexive consideration of the relationship between knowledge and power leads to feminist theorists' realization that power differentials exist between teacher and students (Ellsworth, 1989). As Elizabeth Ellsworth succinctly puts it, all voices are "partial, multiple and contradictory" (p. 312), and all of us occupy a variety of "socially constructed positions of privilege . . . [or] subordination" (p. 313), including the teacher.

Likewise, one of the key commitments of critical communication pedagogy understands "power as fluid and complex" (Fassett & Warren, 2007, p. 41). As such, all of us participate in structures of power to some degree, and we have to be sensitive to our exercise of power and to the consequences of our actions. Fassett and Warren direct us to "a focus on concrete, mundane communication practices as constitutive of larger social structural systems" (p. 43). Furthermore, they encourage critical communication educators to "embrace social, structural critique as it places concrete, mundane communication practices in a meaningful context" (p. 45). In other words, communication matters, regardless of context.

The connections between these two pedagogical perspectives are also evidenced in their commitment to social justice, teaching as a liberatory praxis, and engagement in dialogue within a learning community. However, a new level of insight that is very salient in critical communication pedagogy is the centrality of communication. As Fassett and Warren (2007) clearly state, "A central goal of this book is to articulate a language of critique that accounts for how communication creates and makes possible our ability to see and respond" to social inequalities (p. 7). As they caution us, "If we do not engage communication as constitutive, if we continue to see communication as a mirror (however cloudy) for reality, we fail to see the mechanisms of production in the classroom" (p. 45). This discriminating attention to communication in our concrete and mundane everyday communication practices, whether online or offline, makes it possible for us to see "the mechanisms of production" and, thus, to create possible spaces for change.

To make Web 2.0 environments "transformative, generative spaces of dialogue with students" (Fassett & Warren, 2007, p. 43), the epistemologies of doing (Gajjala et al., 2007) comprise one more piece of the triad that addresses the issues of producing, consuming, and using technology. "Doing" is conceptualized as hands-on application with simultaneous engagement in theory building. In an ideal situation, this is what we do every day in our classrooms; in actuality, we know that the methods we use for teaching often end up being top-down transmissions of skill sets and/or scholarly literature. The circular and uneven nature in which learning happens through doing is often not privileged even in the ways we grade. In *epistemologies of doing*, we work to "race the interface" while *doing* technologies as they are located in specific contexts and moments.

To gain nuanced understandings of power, we engage technology in relation to the interlocking issues of race, class, caste, gender, geography, and specific located histories of colonization in the discursive context of computer-mediated communication. As both instructors and students, we carry with us a critical communication feminist praxis to open up different ways for examining issues of race, gender, class, and geography in cyberspace and to provide a variety of possible pedagogic interventions and practices to engage the problem of racialization within cyberspace that is clearly situated in unequal power relations manifested within current "global" economies.

Yahui's Reflections on Critical Feminist Pedagogy

"Building Cyberfeminist Webs" exposed me to feminist pedagogy for the first time. I took the class during the summer of 2003 because how to build a Web site was something I was interested in learning, coming from a first year, master's program background. I was eager for the professor to show us the technical steps of *how* but discovered very soon that she was more interested in stirring feelings and thoughts, challenging us to do projects that touched our personal lives.

This was something very new to me, because for many years of my schooling, from elementary to secondary to college to graduate school, I was used to taking notes regarding what my teachers said and then trying to understand and memorize what was imparted to me. I never even thought that my personal experience would matter and count in the pursuit of knowledge. I always felt small and trivial in front of the big names, the gatekeepers who define what knowledge is, such as my teachers and professors. When I was first asked to seek deep in my heart about what I was really passionate about in doing a project, I felt the voice and image of my mother speaking to me not only on her behalf but also on behalf of many nameless Chinese women who toiled day and night for their families, who went through all kinds of political campaigns in China, who endured hardships and extreme poverty, but who survived and triumphed with love and passion. In the end, I produced a digital video project narrating the frustrations, hardships, and hope of my mother's life as a Chinese woman.

Our class took a seminar format. There were reading assignments and a lot of class discussions about how we could extend the concepts and theories in the readings to our projects. By the end of the 6-week summer class, there were a wide variety of projects for presentations. One of the classmates was a miracle baby. She did a digital video using the photos her parents took for her over the years to show us how she transformed from a baby in an incubator who had a slight chance of survival to the graduation ceremony where, accompanied by her loving parents, she received her bachelor's degree. There were two classmates who did a Web site. One of them focused on the insidious impact media had on the body image of American teens, while the other centered on the philosophical foundations of feminism using a Web site as a medium. Two other projects left me with a lasting impression. One was done by a faculty member from the Women's Studies program. She felt strongly that obesity was very much exaggerated. In her project, she did interviews with health professionals to clear the myth about this so-called national problem, especially in relation to women. Her research had a nice combination of literature, theory, and interviews so that body issues became the focus of her study. Women's bodies had been and still are continually reshaped according to prevailing ideology through fashion, exercise programs, foot binding, and so on.

The other project I want to share was on the mundane daily life of a lesbian couple. Before taking this class, I never had any chance of getting to know lesbian or gay people in my personal life. I knew vaguely that they existed and they were "different" from me. Coming from a culture where heterosexual marriage is almost a universal practice, sitting in a classroom with a self-declared lesbian was itself a big eye-opener for me. During the seminars, she shared with us her daily life with her partner, her relationship with her stepchildren, her family business in the training of horses for kids, and how she had to juggle all these with her academic identities as a graduate student and a grant writer. I began to look at life through her eyes and realized that sexual oppression was a part of the daily routine that this classmate and her partner had to face. I understood that heterosexism exists in a repressive manner, and it affects the lives of my classmate and many people like her. This was the first time that I began to confront my own unconscious heterosexism. Her final project was a beautiful digital narrative of her mundane life and how it strengthened her and her partner to endure together.

I am in my 30s and have been in the academic world for almost all my life. I have taken numerous classes with different teachers and professors. However, if you asked me to share with you some unforgettable moments of my long schooling, I am afraid I cannot remember much. The countless classes I have taken over the years seem to blur together. But this "Building Cyberfeminist Webs" class stays with me, and I can recall so many details of the process I went through for my project and remember what my classmates did. This is perhaps the most amazing and powerful evidence of what a feminist pedagogy can do to a student. It stirs thoughts and transforms the ways I look at things and people and myself in relation to them.

Radhika's Reflections on Critical Feminist Pedagogy

Yet it was these students, students such as Yahui—now my collaborator on various projects to do with critical feminist pedagogy and technology—who were some of my most severe critics in class. In 2003, for instance, a former doctoral advisee proceeded to "rewrite" my syllabus in order to interpret it within her own grid of certainty. Eventually, by the end of the semester, she began to realize that the strategic ambiguity with which I had delivered the class material and defined projects and their content was what had allowed her to take control of her own knowledge production in the class while dialoguing clearly with issues raised in the readings and discussions. What she learned was that while she was free to define her own project, she would not be allowed to define it outside of classroom concerns. Her assignments would need to take into account the multivocality possible in the classroom. Therefore, she did not have permission to be an isolated "individual" working on her own concerns in relation to the class topics but had to build theory relationally and contextually. As Yahui points out in her narrative here, different students in class were forced to confront their situatedness while designing and producing their projects.

Both Natalia and Yahui have begun to understand how multivocality and relationality, as well as individual voice and context, connect in these classrooms through strategies of ambiguity and certitude at the interface where they are not explicitly told what to do and how to reproduce the status quo but are asked to discover what the status quo asks of them and where their points of departure and points of entry into this status quo are. So now they (re)write (with) me as my mirrors—telling me and showing me my own practice of teaching and research—alerting me to vagueness in my articulations, pointing to ways in which I could better narrate what I do in class.

Discussions of Race and the Internet in Class

To illustrate how discussions around race in cyberspace in an average undergraduate (and sometimes even graduate) class tend to take place—even now, after more than a decade of the Internet having become a part of our everyday discourse and use—we use the example of discussions from one particular class taught by Radhika in 2004. The content in this class called attention to how issues of race, class, gender, and sexuality within digitally mediated environments are all interconnected and layered. The contingent and processual nature of identity and meaning making online and their inextricability from mundane practices of living, doing, and communication were examined/illustrated through activities in online environments such as a MOO and Blackboard and through an online collaboration with students from another university involving the creation of a Web site.

Both critical feminist pedagogy and critical communication pedagogy emphasize that teachers are facilitators in the process of knowledge production, and students in this process play an active part. Online discussion boards in course management software such as Blackboard can be used for facilitation in this manner, even though the technical interface of such courseware is actually not conducive to effective dialogue. The design of discussion boards and the process of asynchronous communication based in the design of the course and the assignment can work for, or against, critical feminist pedagogy, depending on how they are used (student comments from graduate courses also attest to this in various ways). The key to using these fora effectively is in developing strategies for facilitating critical engagement. The readings and activities are delivered in a different time frame and format, and they are received, read, and discussed differently than reaction papers and discussions in a face-to-face classroom setting. This is what was used to allow for reflection and dialogue in these discussion assignments, rather than using the discussion board as a "portal" where the teacher transmits information and the students deliver the "correct" content. Thus, the process of how the discussion board was used is important. The irony, of course, is that to facilitate the dialogue necessary for critical thinking and feminist pedagogical approaches to classroom activities, it was necessary to structure the assignments with very careful planning and understanding of the online fora concerned. The exchanges that happened in this venue provided one of multiple modes of interaction in that class and helped set the stage in preparing students to think in terms of social change in action. The role of professors in an active discussion space is to watch the directions of the discussions and jump in with some comments or questions to spark more ideas. Some of the recurring themes on the discussion section of the Blackboard were about how race does matter in the online setting; how our online and offline lives influence each other; how the Internet can be a double-edged sword; how stereotypes are perpetuated rather than eliminated in the online space; and how the otherness of other people and places are exploited, thus creating a form of cybercolonization.

At the beginning of the semester, one of the students posted a message saying that "race is irrelevant online unless you make it relevant." The reason behind this assumption was that, in a textual format, the absence of physical features renders race unnecessary. This post generated a lot of discussion. One of the responses read, "I don't believe that race is something you can make matter or not as you let it or wish. Race is NOT an ON/OFF switch." This response expresses the idea that race is not something one can put on or take off at will. It is part of who that person is. Race is deeper than skin color.

The same student who argued that race is not a switch went on to discuss identity performance in online and offline contexts:

Tell me that you are Korean and try to pass for being Korean . . . probably I won't believe that you are. Why? I'm sure that you will fail to answer some questions that I may ask you regarding experiences of being raised in a Korean family. Then, are you still Asian/Korean because you only claim that you are even though I don't believe that you are?

A careful reading of this posting reveals the underlying tone that race is much more complicated than the surface value of physical features and body colors. It involves one's upbringing, education, and social environments.

Of course, other students took part in the discussion, expressing their ideas that race cannot be taken as an appendage or accessory. In addition, the discussion surfaced that designers who create an interface without taking race into consideration (for instance, not giving "race" as an option for self-identification on online fora) are usually blamed for the reproduction of racial prejudices online. However, in reality, designers work for their clients, who have the final say regarding the visuals and the content of the online spaces they design. The discussions on race were multifaceted, but many agreed that race does matter in online spaces.

The interplay of online and offline lives is another commonly discussed topic among the students. There were students who expressed their concerns about not being able to trust anyone online because of the possibility of people lying, and there were other students who thought that the Internet provided the freedom for people to do whatever they liked. However, in the same discussion forum, postings such as the following tell another story.

> First of all, I understand what you mean, but I find it dangerous to conceptualize the internet as a world distinctively different from "real world." It is because in the end it is human beings who live their daily life in "real world" who participate in those online social interactions. So, to some degree, we bring our experience into those online social contexts. . . . I would rather say that it is much more fruitful to conceptualize the internet as a social world that is interwoven with "real world." Secondly, I wouldn't call it "freedom." Early scholars of identity in cyberspace have been criticized for conceptualizing cyberspace as a "free" place where people can explore their identities by crossing over genders, races, etc. [However, we cannot.] It is because essentially our identity is "negotiated" rather than something that we "freely" choose.

Students began to see and articulate connections between offline/online and virtual/real, concepts that are nuanced and based in everyday discourse and practices. They are not mutually exclusive binaries, nor are "real" and "offline" always synonymous, because the practices and effects of online engagement as part of our everyday life are as real and everyday as when we are interacting offline. Thus, students began to realize how online social reality is produced through online/offline practices.

Students' discussion also identified that the Internet can be a double-edged sword. One of the groups examined the issues of race, masculinity, and relationships, and their reading assignment was Roy's (2003) "From Khush List to Gay Bombay." Roy argues that "the very convenience of the Internet can lull people into a comfortable sense of 'keyboard activism'" (p. 189). One of the group members responded to the reading this way:

> The net is most effective as a way of providing access to information; . . . for those who most need the net because their physical environment is not safe, it can be more of a crutch and could dissuade them from forming groups in their immediate area.

However, one group also shared the following reflections on these issues.

> The primary concern with regards to this openness online that is generated through relative anonymity is that while online communities can be beneficial to providing emotional and informational resources to those lacking them in their immediate physical environment, in order to truly develop, these individuals must translate these identities to the offline world.

Online activism and offline actions should go hand in hand for any constructive change in the "real world." This is indeed a very important and insightful realization that the students reached through engaged discussions.

If the interplay between the online and the offline worlds exists, it is small wonder that the students found in their discussions that stereotypes were perpetuated rather than eliminated in the online space. Relevant here are their discussions on two articles: Nakamura's (2000) "Where Do You Want to Go Today?'" and González's (2000) "The Appended Subject: Race and Identity as Digital Assemblage." One of the postings stated,

> The appendages that González talks about and the avatars that Nakamura addresses in relation to the Internet both relate to stereotypes that stem from social constructs in the real world. . . . The perpetuation of stereotypes on the Internet is ironic since the World Wide Web is supposed to be a catalyst for merging differences. However, the Internet, like the digital body, goes against the original intent of being "utopic and inclusive" (González, p. 33) and instead accentuates differences.

The discussion participants also noticed

> that even within these fantastic realms, such as the planetary realm of the future, the avatars are limited to past stereotypes in that "aliens are either black men or blue space creatures; heroes are white men with blond hair; killers wear African headdresses; and cult images include nude women of color" (González, p. 33). These communities unconsciously reinforce these stereotypical characteristics.

These reflections were not confined to how stereotypes were enacted in the online spaces. They went a step further by analyzing how other cultures and people are depicted and cyber colonization comes into existence.

It is clear that the forming of these dissected avatars can be seen as a type of colonization whereby the conquerors categorize these different characteristics and then occupy them as they wish. This aside, it is simply interesting to see that the construction of these avatars, no matter how dissected they are, still retain the qualities of stereotypes of before.

Another student group also mentioned that the Internet cannot be a solution to social problems and pointed to the discrepancies existing between the West and the East.

We see that the cyber-exploitation of the Other as the Western perspective of these different cultures rather than the assertion of these cultures independently. It is to the point where the Internet depiction of these Other places becomes a form of cyber-colonization.

More important, as one student pointed out,

But more than just hegemony over the Other, I think that the corporations are creating hegemony over even Western consumers. By perpetuating the current perceptions of the Other, corporations are able to make their customers believe that technology actually can bridge the gap between cultures.

While these were not the only major themes arising from the Blackboard discussions over the course of the semester, the purpose of presenting these themes is to show one particular effort to "race the interface" through the problematization of the notion of a raceless Internet in class discussion. Digitally mediated environments such as Blackboard can contribute to the core components of critical feminist pedagogy by creating participatory learning environments, valuing personal experience, encouraging social understanding and activism, and fostering critical thinking and open-mindedness—but only when the content and process strongly guide the discussion into such critical thinking. Thus, rather than claiming that critical feminist pedagogy needs to "empower" student participation, we experience feminist pedagogy as grounded in particular values and ideologies as well as processes that reframe the way power manifests in the classroom. The shift is not that the student gains power; rather, the shift is that a feminist and critical understanding of the topics becomes privileged, challenging students to express and articulate issues from this other frame of reference.

We frame the remainder of the chapter with this illustration to ground the notion of a pedagogy of doing within a specific epistemological framework that, although it questions and critiques the mainstream forms of knowledge building, equally is based in the exercise of power in the classroom. To us, there is no illusion that feminist and critical pedagogy are about dispelling student-teacher hierarchies. The "empowerment" that occurs in such situations is the empowerment of discourses traditionally marginalized in mainstream academic discourse and process. What this sort of critical feminist pedagogy does is to make possible particular alternative discourses to emerge through the careful framing of content and activities in the course. In technology-mediated courses, this can be done through the positioning and use of technology in comparatively unexpected ways.

Natalia's Reflection on Class With Radhika

Since Spring 2002, when I took a class with Radhika, I have firmly realized that I cannot learn something unless I do it, read it, talk it, discuss it, critique it, apply it, and write it. To preface, I draw my sense of pedagogical engagement from teaching foreign languages as a foreign language speaker living in a country where people speak neither my native nor my acquired tongues. Building the interconnected layers of awareness is complex: connecting words with grammar, texts with speaking, singing, and drawing; structuring and making mistakes, listening and dialoging, walking and dancing with students; writing and teaching to write, reading and teaching to read. All forms of being in the language produce an unimaginable boost in foreign language mastering. Doing research with (computer, Internet) technology in my doctoral program, I continue the Radhik-al multisited approach to studying things by doing them. Here is one episode of such process.

After a very busy day, I was finishing my work. In a moment of relaxation, I signed into my e-mail box. There was a message of invitation to join Twitter from Radhika. It was not the first invitation from her; we often work and play in various social environments online as we explore cyberspace and the technoculture from inside. I assumed that this was "yet another social network system" (Heer & Boyd, 2005). Curiously, I clicked on the provided link and went to the sign-up page. At this time, very little info was needed to open an the account: "real" name, password, e-mail, and image. Questioning the "real" in the real name line, I chose Nat Ryb (I later changed it to Kiki Mora), which comes from a combination of online and offline fantasy-based interactions. For the image, I uploaded one of the formatted pictures I keep on the desktop of my computer. After registration, I moved to the next screen; a very simple, blue color background interface, with the question on the very top of the screen, "What are you doing now?" and a box to write answers. This innocent yet intricate query made me pause. What did it mean, "What am I doing?" This question invited a reflexive monologue:

Who is asking? Who is watching? Who is reading? Who cares what I am doing? Why should I respond? Where am I? What am I doing when I am supposed to be working? What is *work* anyway? After a moment of musings, I decided to enter the dialogue, typing my answer to the tricky question: "I'm opening an account on twitter.com." While I was typing and exploring the interface, I noticed that my friend is Cyber Divalive. Then my note appeared right above her invitation. These lines intertwined in a dialogic exchange of messages. The question remained at the top, demanding more answers. I posted a couple more responses as the question continued to haunt me: "What am I doing?"

Living in this episode is one of many instances when I participate in building, applying, and reproducing theory while living in specific contexts. As I go through the experience of signing up and using Web software, I reproduce the social conventions embedded in the computer program. I respond when the computer asks me, I provide a name when I am asked, I post a picture when I am asked. I also reproduce technical conventions constituting the software: I move my fingers and push the keys to type my answers (rather than saying them by employing my vocal cords), I upload a picture to represent myself (rather than drawing it), I click on the link in the e-mail and teleport to another Web site. I know how to operate the interface even if the program is new to me. However, I do not register my cell phone on Twitter to avoid skyrocketing bills, I do not instant message to avoid distractions, I do not add random friends to avoid meaningless conversations. I perform some aspects of social and technical literacy ethnomethodologically—actualizing rules while interpreting social reality and inventing life "in a permanent tinkering" (Coulon, 1995, p. 17). I formulate abstractions about the specific program based on my past experiences and, more important, based on imagined experiences of possible consequences of inactions. Writing and thinking about these practices adds a layer of explicit reflecting. Thus, I theorize technology by isolating the logic of experience from the experience in the moment of doing and then reproducing and re-creating in writing. The piece I am composing now builds up as I word my understanding by wording the experience. I engage technology, theoretically, and practically through multiple facets and develop a puzzle-like layered awareness of the context.

Radhika's Reflection on Teaching With/in Technology

Kiki Mora (Natalia) introduced the notion of what she humorously calls the "Radhik-al" approach. But this is a collaborative approach—strongly contingent on how she interacts with my pedagogy, my advising. In understanding the way I ask her to throw herself into various online/offline environments, she connects to her own research process, further developing methodologies for studying and teaching these environments, making connections between Garfinklean ethnomethodology, Foucauldian analyses, traditional ethnographies, critical ethnography, and cyberethnography. She provides me a mirror. She teaches me to see and articulate how I teach and research (as do several other advisees and students in my classes). My pedagogy and research practice as a feminist have their roots in how I engage technology in my personal life, every day.

When did this become my profession; when did this become my life? I cannot unblur these. When I write up my syllabi, I make the effort anew each time.

✶ ✶ ✶

This morning as I chugged away on the exercise machines, first running on the treadmill and then the elliptical runner—with my iPod trinket playing in my ears, my mind seeking out words of wisdom, some sign perhaps from all the songs I've heard many times before over and over again. Hoping for the random shuffling of the songs to talk to me—knowing I have embedded my father's voice and his poem for my mother in the midst of a medley of old and new Bollywood songs, South Indian and North Indian classical music, Western Classical music, a bit of remix and Desi rap as well as some other mixed music from the 1980s and 1990s . . . Every morning it's pretty much the same—I seek to get a sign from all these technologies I use. Perhaps this is the root of my fascination with technologies—they are my modern-day spirits. Like Samantha in *Bewitched* and Jeannie in *I Dream of Jeannie*, I will twitch my nose or blink my eyes and my family and friends will teleport toward me, converse with me, laugh with me and give me words of wisdom or sarcasm to live and laugh by . . .

So I entered Second Life again and clicked something and found myself on a boat with a guy who was cursing about lag . . .

"Hello," he said.

"Hello," I said.

"Where am I," I said.

"lol," he said. . . .

Dorothy is not in Kansas anymore, I thought.

Darn those English metaphors again.

But I am writing in English . . . my audience won't get my linguistic twists and metaphors from another language and context—and if I tried to explain, they would be no fun anymore . . .

Yes, that is why I disappear into technospaces. That is why I am so aware of technologies—for you, my audience, here and now are the technologies shaping me and speaking to me and giving me a "sign" that I must interpret as either validation or rejection or neither through my own lenses of understanding and affect . . .

You sit around me . . . and I think, what are my secrets today?

I click on your profile button—but it tells me nothing I want to know.

I set my profile button—to tell you nothing you need not know.

But we must establish some bonds of trust if we are to write together like this . . .

✶ ✶ ✶

When did this become my profession; when did this become my life?

Engaging Privilege and Social Boundaries Online and Offline

In this section, we describe one particular example of how offline/online intersections were mobilized in a clear attempt to make students understand the importance of race, class, and geography when learning about the consumption and production of digital media. In one of the activities in a course on computer-mediated cultures offered in Spring 2005, undergraduate students worked in groups researching identities of Mexican American teens at online/offline intersections through user interviews, textual analyses, and linking/living online in their social networks. The Mexican American teens were from low-income neighborhoods of northwestern Ohio and had (limited) access to computers and the Internet in a community center after school. This group of teenagers were involved in a social networking environment online as an alternative to e-mail or instant messaging, to share content on friends' profiles and occasionally have fun. The assignment directed the university students to examine how the social network systems of MySpace.com and Facebook.com play into the production of raced and classed subjectivities in online/offline environments. To accomplish this objective, students in the undergraduate class also needed to understand how the two social network systems worked by creating profiles on them (if they did not already have one) and by exploring the process of living and interacting in these spaces. The project design allowed multiple contingencies to interact: student researchers' location, larger technosocial phenomena of MySpace, preconceptions about Mexican Americans, and social panics about MySpace.

These contingencies emerged as soon as the project participants made decisions about methodological approaches. Because many of the university students had Facebook accounts, they seemed quite familiar with online networks. However, a few of the students expressed discomfort at the possibility of starting MySpace accounts and ethnographically examining them in relation to the Mexican American users. These students chose to concentrate on the textual analysis of the MySpace profiles without engaging in profile production and online interaction. It appeared that MySpace and Facebook carried class markers drawing a divide between the two groups: The university students preferred Facebook, while their subjects—students in the community center—chose MySpace. Such zoning of Internet social network activities highlights the subtle character of social clustering whereby users avoid crossing the boundaries of digital neighborhoods. Boyd (2006) argues that on social network sites "people define their community egocentrically" (para. Egocentric Networks), as the lists of friends in a network constitute the context for both members and the audiences and signal the expected social boundaries. Entering a certain context in social networks online happens through affiliation with other individuals who construct sets of interests and communication practices. In the spring of 2006, Facebook accepted for registration only .edu e-mail addresses; this meant that only university students could open Facebook accounts. However, MySpace welcomed all users. Thus, signing up for a new MySpace account implied, on the one hand, entering an unrestricted zone with a potentially unlimited population and, on the other hand, becoming affiliated with the dwellers of that zone. Those who chose the safety of textual analysis preferred to maintain the social boundaries between the university students and the Mexican American teenagers from a low-income community.

The prevalence of stereotypes was the most evident to the student researchers involved in the textual analysis of the MySpace profiles. The undergraduate students observed that these Internet accounts contribute to the negative stereotypes of the Mexican American community. The researchers considered the objective of the community center in the opposite direction—that is, in eliminating the stereotypes. One of the students suggested on the discussion board that the children created a certain kind of identity to fit the community and avoid considering the role of stereotypes. Another student continued with the idea that the teenagers do not understand that they perpetuate the existing notions of themselves but try to fit into a group of their peers. These observations contribute to maintaining similar social boundaries between the researchers and their "subjects." The inferences about the profile content contribute to the othering of the profile creators. Warren's (2003) work on performativity of whiteness suggests that such dissecting of nonwhite stereotypes positions privileged individuals as free of such collective generalizations. The analysis made by student researchers assigns responsibility for stereotyping to the hands of the stereotyped and distances the observers from the process of racing-classing-gendering.

In addition to textual analyses, the undergraduate students engaged in online interactions with the Mexican American teens. The student researchers were producing cyberselves in social networking sites by linking to community members as friends and using multiple interactive features available on MySpace. Those students who chose not to participate in online interactions expressed their anxieties and discomfort about the unhealthy social atmosphere of the sites where the teens preferred to hang out. However, those who were on Facebook and also interacted on MySpace made more careful and nuanced observations, pointing to the complexity of identities performed and linked. This suggests to us that those student researchers who were self-reflexive and also understood how to navigate the technical interface within a specific networking site were able to come to a more nuanced understanding of the users and their uses. These researchers tended to raise more contextually relevant and complex questions in class. Simultaneously, the lack of familiarity about how social networking systems work or avoiding involvement in specific technologies gave rise to some misreadings or partial interpretations.

The visits to the community center, in-depth interviews with Mexican American teenagers and staff members, and textual analysis of the teens' MySpace accounts were followed by similar analyses of white-appearing profiles on MySpace. A student explains how she filters her perception of the identities she observed on MySpace:

> To make a confession . . . When I did a textual analysis for the white teens, I came across photographs of teens that appeared to be like me (looks, that is). However, once I opened up their page, they had rap music playing and all sorts of strange photos I wouldn't dare have on a page if I made one. So in a way two stereotypes were made by me. First, I assumed the girls' photos I looked at were pretty much like me, but when I read past the picture, I made other judgments about their character that may or may not be true. (KT)

The expectations about groups of people inform the reading of online identity or the information one puts forth in the profile. Such a group-based, essentially stereotypical, approach to understanding people struck another student as odd. She says,

> I originally thought all of the "white" teens shared at least some things in common, but as I read their profiles, I found that there are so many subcultures within the "white" cultures that that assumption is a false one. In fact, there are many African American or Latino people who have more things in common with white teens than other whites. (LM)

She sees individuals connected at the affective and imaginary level as she observes the users of MySpace weave the "taste fabric" that constitutes shared identity and culture (Liu, Maes, & Davenport, 2006, p. 43). Common interests and common friends help envision the members and draw connections between their beliefs and values. The ethnographic engagement with the MySpace profiles produces the imagined community (Anderson, 1991; Gajjala, 2004) and redraws/reconstructs the group affiliations, as in the case of KT and LM. They make an inferential leap based on their embodied involvement in the online and offline praxis of identity building. Even though LM's observations are overly optimistic, they may still require some significant critical analysis from this student and her peers. Such critique may take the direction toward exploring the difference "not in the body but rather made through the bodily acts" (Warren, 2003, p. 29). It implies that social meanings of difference—in terms of race, gender, geography, and other markers—reside in the bodily movements, including rhetoric. So what are the "bodily acts" that the white female interacting on MySpace draws from? Through a close look at LM's response, we see her constitute everyday whiteness performatively in reference to other members of the social network of Facebook. LM makes her analysis of MySpace—where diverse socioeconomic groups connect—from a whitened perspective. In particular, she seems to erase the differences existing along racial and class lines, and based on her hidden privilege within this hierarchy, ends up reading and articulating sameness (p. 56) in interests and profile design. The similarity comes from the common dwelling of the users on MySpace; this sharing of space, according to her, allows MySpace to bridge the divide and create a peaceful coexistence while other differences cease to matter. Pointing at the performative nature of race implies that being white or black does not come with just or only the skin color, depending considerably on one's biological heritage. As Wiegman (2003) states, it is not the same to have a certain skin and identify with white privilege.

> The myriad minute decisions that constitute the practices of the world are at every point informed by judgments about people's capacities and worth, judgments based on what they look like, where they come from, how they speak, even what they eat, that is, racial judgments. (Dyer, 2000, p. 539)

The meaning of these trivial, yet serious, differences is socially negotiated in performative acts that support relativity of race: It exists only in relation to other identities, only as a contrast. Thus, LM pays attention to "Latino and African Americans with very high education levels on MySpace and some whites with low education levels" as if these people fall out of the norm for social networking. Yancy (2004) writes, "Whiteness superiority thrives vis-à-vis black inferiority. Whiteness is parasitic upon blackness" (p. 7). This implies that whiteness must have a counterpart to project its power; and if the other seems exotic, the situation looks especially comfortable. If "an equal number of white people [are] reporting that they like rap music as African Americans," as LM observes, she overlooks the historical heritage and the cultural status of rap music.

Conclusion: Pedagogies of Doing (Radhika)

What I term *pedagogies of doing* are based on several layers of interrelated course activities and projects that are organized under specific categories and pursue specific objectives. We usually start with application within specific technological interfaces with an objective to reproduce the status quo. This way, students engage in the everyday practices of technology; they learn about digitally mediated "genres" as they are doing the activity. For instance, when I ask students to work through distance technologies to form groups with members of a class from another university in order to produce YouTube videos, I am asking them actually to reproduce existing practices of online social networking for virtual work. There is nothing counter status quo in this assignment. It is the newness of the activity in the context of an academic course that makes it seem as if this is not so. It is also the readings and content of the classroom discussions that allow for an assumption that somehow this application and practice is not mainstream. My strategic ambiguity in this instance encourages the students to struggle and think through the encounters and processes as they code and decode what it means to complete this sort of assignment. The strategic certainty I have provided is that the video must be of a certain length, must be collaborative in nature, and is definitely due at a certain time. It is not in this application and practice itself, therefore, that I engage in feminist and/or critical communication pedagogic intervention. Later, when I require that they articulate the process in journals and in reflective papers engaging critical readings and theoretical frameworks introduced in class, they begin to reflect on the issues through feminist and critical lenses. This then allows for the examination and critique of status quo through reproduction of status quo with a twist, for example, through the requirement that the YouTube videos be focused on themes related to race, gender, sexuality, geography, and class in such a way to appear non–status quo. This activity leads to the examination of existing theories and literature—both critical feminist and "mainstream"—while responding to the readings through lenses provided by the practices. The examination of existing theories is followed by the activity of applying the theories considered through the production of content for the YouTube videos. This application of theories takes the form of reproducing the frameworks introduced in readings through the practices at online/offline intersections and, further, feeds into extending and building theory. The students begin to understand how the academic content introduced in class is relevant to the application together with how the very application can feed into the critique and extension of the theoretical frames brought up by class. Thus, the students leave the class with a great deal to process and think about yet with a clear understanding that the context and nuanced nature of online/offline existence cannot be reduced to simplistic generalizations. They become conscious of the need to work with broad conceptual categories while entering the space in order to gain a more complex understanding.

The pedagogy of doing responds to the objective to teach social and cultural situatedness as well as to help the students understand the contextual and contingent nature of how technology design and use are rendered sensible. I realized that the only way to do this is to "plunge" the students into activities that engage them in offline/online contexts around doing technology. Drawing from feminist critiques of knowledge building (see Alcoff & Potter, 1993), where the difference between propositional knowledge and processual understanding is laid out, the methodology I call "epistemologies of doing" is based on critiques of epistemologies that devalue understanding and knowledge of contextual skills and expertise through the process of learning *how to* in favor of knowledge-making processes that privilege propositional knowledge. Dalmiya and Alcoff (1993) describe an epistemological hierarchy between propositional and practical forms of knowledge that is implicit in modern ways of knowing. In describing how all knowledge in modern epistemology becomes propositional (i.e., information transmitted through impersonal propositions), they cite the example of how the expertise of midwives was invalidated as ignorant "old wives' tales." Such epistemic invalidation of old wives' tales has been caused in part by the fact that modern epistemology has forgotten the lesson from Aristotle that knowledge can come in two forms: propositional and practical (p. 220). These issues are related to layered coexisting and contradictory sociocultural and economic systems of production and meaning-making processes as well as subtle and not-so-subtle shifts within the globalizing economy and postcolonial hierarchies, even as individuals and local communities retain different degrees of agency within structural constraints.

References

Alcoff, L. M., & Potter, E. (Eds.). (1993). *Feminist epistemologies.* New York: Routledge.

Anderson, B. (1991). *Imagined communities: Reflections on the origin and spread of nationalism.* London: Verso.

Belenky, M. F., Clinchy, B. M., Goldberger, N. R., & Tarule, J. M. (1986). *Women's ways of knowing: The development of self, voice and mind.* New York: Basic Books.

Boyd, D. (2006). Friends, friendsters, and top 8: Writing community into being on social network sites. *First Monday, 11.* Retrieved January 12, 2007, from www.firstmonday.org/issues/issue11_12/boyd

Collins, P. H. (1990). *Black feminist thought: Knowledge, consciousness and the politics of empowerment.* Boston: Unwin Hyman.

Coulon, A. (1995). *Ethnomethodology* (J. Coulon & J. Katz, Trans.). Thousand Oaks, CA: Sage.

Dalmiya, V., & Alcoff, L. (1993). Are "old wife tales" justified? In L. Alcoff & E. Potter (Eds.), *Feminist epistemologies* (pp. 217–244). New York: Routledge.

Dyer, R. (2000). The matter of whiteness. In L. Back & J. Solomos (Eds.), *Theories of race and racism: A reader* (pp. 539–548). New York: Routledge.

Ellsworth, E. (1989). Why doesn't this feel empowering? Working through the repressive myths of critical pedagogy. *Harvard Educational Review, 59,* 297–324.

Fassett, D., & Warren, J. T. (2007). *Critical communication pedagogy.* Thousand Oaks, CA: Sage.

Freire, P. (1971). *Pedagogy of the oppressed.* New York: Herder & Herder.

Freire, P. (1985). *The politics of education.* Basingstoke, UK: Macmillan.

Freire, P., & Shor, I. (1987). *A pedagogy for liberation.* Basingstoke, UK: Macmillan.

Gajjala, R. (2004). *Cyber selves: Feminist ethnographies of South Asian women.* Walnut Creek, CA: AltaMira Press.

Gajjala, R., Rybas, N., & Altman, M. (2007). Epistemologies of doing: E-merging selves online. *Feminist Media Studies, 7,* 209–213.

Giroux, H. (2003). Spectacles of race and pedagogies of denial: Anti-black racist pedagogy under the reign of neoliberalism. *Communication Education, 53,* 191–211.

González, J. (2000). The appended subject: Race and identity as digital assemblage. In B. Kolko, L. Nakamura, & G. Rodman (Eds.), *Race in cyberspace* (pp. 27–50). New York: Routledge.

Heer, J., & Boyd, D. (2005). Vizster: Visualizing online social networks. *IEEE symposium on information visualization.* Retrieved January 15, 2007, from http://jheer.org/publications/2005-Vizster-InfoVis.pdf

Hoffmann, F. L., & Stake, J. E. (2001). Feminist pedagogy in theory and practice: An empirical investigation. *NWSA Journal, 10,* 79–97.

hooks, b. (1994). *Teaching to transgress: Education as the practice of freedom.* New York: Routledge.

Klein, R. (1987). The dynamics of the women's studies classroom: A review essay of the teaching practice of women's studies in higher education. *Women's Studies International Forum, 10,* 187–206.

Liu, H., Maes, P., & Davenport, G. (2006). Unraveling the taste fabric of social networks. *International Journal on Semantic Web and Information Systems, 2,* 42–71. Retrieved December 15, 2006, from http://mf.media.mit.edu/pubs/journal/TasteFabric.pdf

Lorde, A. (1984). *Sister outsider: Essays and speeches.* New York: Crossing Press.

Maher, F., & Tetreault, M. K. (1994). *The feminist classroom: An inside look at how professors and students are transforming higher education for a more diverse society.* New York: Basic Books.

Miller, A. S. (2005). Feminist pedagogies: Implications of a liberative praxis. In K. O. Wicker, A. S. Miller, & M. W. Dube (Eds.), *Feminist New Testament studies: Global and future perspectives* (pp. 17–40). New York: Palgrave Macmillan.

Moraga, C., & Anzaldúa, G. (1983). *This bridge called my back: Writings by radical women of color.* New York: Kitchen Table: Women of Color Press.

Nakamura, L. (2000). "Where do you want to go today?" Cybernetic tourism, the Internet, and transnationality. In B. E. Kolko, L. Nakamura, & G. B. Rodman (Eds.), *Race in cyberspace* (pp. 15–26). New York: Routledge.

Roy, S. (2003). From Khush list to gay Bombay: Virtual webs of real people. In C. Berry, F. Martin, & A. Yue (Eds.), *Mobile culture: New media in queer Asia* (pp. 180–197). London: Duke University Press.

Smith, B. (1983). *Home girls: A black feminist anthology.* New York: Kitchen Table: Women of Color Press.

Spivak, G. C. (1993). *Outside in the teaching machine.* London: Routledge.

Warren, J. T. (2003). *Performing purity: Whiteness, pedagogy, and the reconstitution of power.* New York: Peter Lang.

Weiler, K. (1991). Freire and a feminist pedagogy of difference. *Harvard Educational Review, 61,* 449–474.

Weiler, K. (1995). Revisioning feminist pedagogy. *NWSA Journal, 7,* 100–106.

Welch, P. (1994). Is a feminist pedagogy possible? In S. Davies, C. Lubelska, & J. Quinn (Eds.), *Changing the subject: Women in higher education* (pp. 149–162). London: Taylor & Francis.

Wicker, K. O., Miller, A. S., & Dube, M. W. (Eds.). (2005). *Feminist New Testament studies: Global and future perspectives.* New York: Palgrave Macmillan.

Wiegman, R. (2003). "My name is Forrest, Forrest Gump": Whiteness studies and the paradox of particularity. In E. Shohat & R. Stam (Eds.), *Multiculturalism, postcoloniality, and transnational media* (pp. 227–255). New Brunswick, NJ: Rutgers University Press.

Yancy, G. (Ed.). (2004). *What white looks like: African-American philosophers on the whiteness question.* New York: Routledge.

Author Index

Subject Index

453

About the Contributors

Bryant Keith Alexander is a professor of performance, pedagogy, and culture in the Department of Communication Studies at California State University Los Angeles. He is the author of *Performing Black Masculinity: Race, Culture and Queer Identity* and a coeditor with education scholars Gary Anderson and Bernardo Gallegos of *Performance Theories in Education: Pedagogy, Identity and Reform*. His essays appear in a wide variety of scholarly journals and book volumes, including *Communication, Race, and Family*; *Philosophies of Research and Criticism in Education and the Social Sciences*; *Qualitative Research Methods in Special Education*; *Opening Acts: Performance in/as Communication and Cultural Criticism* (Sage); *Queer Theory and Communication: From Disciplining Queers to Queering the Discipline(s)*; *Men and Masculinities: Critical Concepts in Sociology*; *The Sage Handbook of Performance Studies*; *The Sage Handbook of Qualitative Research* (3rd edition); *The Sage Handbook of Critical and Indigenous Methodologies*; *Contesting Empire/Globalizing Dissent: Cultural Studies After 9/11*; *Black Queer Studies: A Critical Anthology*; and *Communicating Ethnic and Cultural Identity*. He received his PhD from Southern Illinois University in 1998.

Melanie Booth-Butterfield is the Peggy Rardin McConnell Chair of Speech Communication and Professor of Communication Studies at West Virginia University. Her research focuses on humor, emotion and interpersonal/relational interactions, and health communication, emphasizing how various communication patterns and traits affect message reception, decoding, and behavior. Her research has been published in *Communication Monographs, Human Communication Research, Communication Education, Journal of Applied Communication, Communication Quarterly, Southern Journal of Communication, Western Journal of Communication, Communication Reports*, and *Communication Research Reports*. She is the editor of *Communication Education*, past president of the Eastern Communication Association, and author of *Interpersonal Essentials*. She received her PhD from the University of Missouri in 1985.

Bernadette Marie Calafell is an associate professor and Associate Chair in the Department of Human Communication at the University of Denver. Her research converges around issues of performance, rhetoric, and intersectionality, particularly within Chicana/o and Latina/o communities. Her publications include articles in the *Journal of International and Intercultural Communication, Critical Studies in Media Communication, Text and Performance Quarterly, The Communication Review, Cultural Studies <=> Critical Methodologies*, and *Communication, Culture, and Critique*. She is also author of the book *Latina/o Communication Studies: Theorizing Performance*. She received her PhD from the University of North Carolina.

Rebecca M. Chory is an associate professor in the Department of Communication Studies at West Virginia University. Her research primarily focuses on media entertainment, verbal aggression, and antisocial communication and behaviors (e.g., injustice, aggression, deception) in organizational and instructional contexts. Her research has been published in various journals, including *Communication Education, Communication Monographs, Journal of Broadcasting & Electronic Media, Journalism and Mass Communication Quarterly, Western Journal of Communication, Communication Quarterly*, and *Communication Studies*. In 2009, Dr. Chory was a Fulbright Scholar in Budapest, Hungary. She received her PhD from Michigan State University.

Leda Cooks is a faculty member in the Department of Communication at the University of Massachusetts, Amherst. Her teaching and research explore the intersections among race, culture, identity, and community with an emphasis on pedagogy, performance, and social justice. She received her PhD from Ohio University in 1993.

Deanna P. Dannels is an associate professor of communication and director of Graduate Teaching Assistant Development in the Department of Communication, and the associate director of the Campus Writing and Speaking Program at North Carolina State University. Her current research explores theoretical and curricular protocols for designing, implementing, and assessing oral communication within the disciplines. She has published widely in areas of composition, teaching and learning, design and engineering education, business and technical communication, oral communication genres, and professional identity construction. Her primary theoretical writing focuses on the distinct nature of oral genre learning—specifically, her contributions include the "communication in the disciplines" and "relational genre knowledge" frameworks for oral communication across the curriculum. She received her PhD from the University of Utah in 1999.

Ann L. Darling is an associate professor and Chair of the Department of Communication at the University of Utah. Her work focuses on questions related to communication and instruction. She has written numerous articles addressing issues of teacher socialization, graduate teaching assistant socialization, and graduate teaching assistant training. Her most recent work explores communication, instruction, and social justice, particularly in the context of applied communication research. Her work has appeared in journals such as *Communication Education, International Journal of Qualitative Research in Education, Teaching and Teacher Education, Journal of Thought,* and the most recent *Handbook of Applied Communication Research.* She received her PhD from the University of Washington in 1987.

Deanna L. Fassett is an associate professor of communication studies at San José State University. In addition to teaching graduate and undergraduate coursework in communication education and instructional communication, she serves as her department's graduate teaching associate supervisor. Her research interests include power, privilege, identity, and culture as they shape and are shaped by classroom communication and communication about the classroom. She has published *Critical Communication Pedagogy,* coauthored with John T. Warren, as well as articles in journals such as *Communication Education, Basic Communication Course Annual, Text and Performance Quarterly,* and *Communication and Critical/Cultural Studies.* She is currently writing an introductory course text with John T. Warren, titled *Communicating Culture: An Introduction to Communication as Social Action,* as well as the guide, *Coordinating the Communication Course: Continuity, Professional Development and Advocacy.* She received her PhD from Southern Illinois University in 2000.

Radhika Gajjala is a professor of communication and cultural studies and director of women's studies at Bowling Green State University, Ohio. Her book *Cyberselves: Feminist Ethnographies of South Asian Women* was published in 2004. She has coedited *South Asian Technospaces* and *Webbing Cyberfeminist Practice* and is currently working on a single-authored book, *Technocultural Agency: Production of Identity at the Interface.* She received her PhD from the University of Pittsburgh in 1998.

Alan K. Goodboy is an assistant professor in the Department of Communication Studies at Bloomsburg University. He specializes in instructional and interpersonal communication with an emphasis in quantitative research methodologies. His original research has been published in various journals, including *Communication Education, Communication Quarterly, Communication Research Reports, Human Communication, Journal of Instructional Psychology, North American Journal of Psychology, Psychological Reports,* and *Western Journal of Communication.* He received his PhD from West Virginia University.

Katherine Grace Hendrix is an associate professor in the Communication Department at the University of Memphis. She is an instructional communication scholar with an interest in the pedagogical contributions of and credibility challenges faced by professors and graduate teaching assistants (GTAs) of color—including international GTAs who speak English as a second language. Employing critical and feminist standpoint theories, she also examines the epistemological and axiological assumptions of research communities that function to sanction scholarship reflecting particular ideologies while excluding others. Her research has been published in journals and edited books, including *Communication Education*, the *Howard Journal of Communications*, the *Journal of Black Studies*, *New Directions for Teaching and Learning*, and *Qualitative Inquiry*. She received her PhD from the University of Washington in 1994.

Patricia Kearney is a professor of communication studies and recipient of the Distinguished Scholar Award at California State University, Long Beach. Her research and teaching, both theoretical and applied, focus on communication in the instructional process. A former editor of *Communication Education*, Kearney has written a variety of textbooks and industrial training packages, and she has published more than 100 research articles, chapters, and commissioned research reports and instructional modules. She is listed among the 100 most published scholars and among the top 15 published female scholars in her discipline. She received her EdD from West Virginia University.

Karen E. Lovaas is Associate Professor and Graduate Studies Coordinator in the Department of Communication Studies, and Co-Director of the Global Peace, Human Rights, and Justice Studies Program at San Francisco State University. Her teaching and research are in the areas of sexuality, gender, culture, the prison industrial complex, and critical pedagogy. She is currently developing a new course in the rhetoric of ecology. She coedited the anthology, *Sexualities & Communication in Everyday Life* (Sage, 2007), with department colleague Lee Jenkins. *LGBT Studies and Queer Theory: New Conflicts, Collaborations, and Contested Terrain* (2006) was coedited with SFSU colleagues John Elia and Gust Yep. *Queer Theory and Communication: From Disciplining Queers to Queering the Discipline(s)*, also coedited with Gust Yep and John Elia, came out in 2003. She has also published several articles and encyclopedia entries related to sexualities, gender, and communication. She is a regular presenter at the National Communication Association and Western States Communication Association annual conferences. She received her PhD in American Studies from the University of Hawai'i.

Jason M. Martin is a doctoral student in the Department of Communication at the University of Kentucky. He serves as an editorial assistant for *Communication Teacher*, research assistant for the Director of Undergraduate Studies in Communication at the University of Kentucky, and chair of the University of Kentucky Communication Mentoring Program. He has collaborated on various projects addressing an array of communication related topics and has presented his work at national and regional conferences. His teaching experience includes public speaking, persuasion, interpersonal communication, and intercultural communication courses. He received his master's degree from the Ohio State University at Columbus in 2003.

Matthew M. Martin is a professor in the Department of Communication Studies at West Virginia University, where he also serves as the department chair. He teaches courses in instructional communication, communication theory, and interpersonal communication. His research interests center primarily on communication traits and interpersonal relationships in the instructional context. He coedited the book *Communication and Personality: Trait Perspectives* (1998). He currently serves on numerous journal editorial boards, including *Communication Education, Communication Monographs, Communication Quarterly*, and the *Journal of Intercultural Communication*. He received his PhD from Kent State University in 1992.

Joseph P. Mazer is an assistant professor in the Department of Communication Studies at Clemson University. His research interests focus on instructional communication, interpersonal communication, and new communication technologies. His research encompasses a range of issues, including emotion in teaching and learning, student academic support, teacher use of slang, and virtual social networks such as Facebook. His research articles have appeared in *Communication Education, Communication Research, Communication Research Reports, Qualitative Research Reports in Communication, Communication Research Measures II: A Sourcebook, Learning, Media and Technology*, and *The Journal of General Education*. He received his PhD from Ohio University in 2010.

Matt McGarrity is a lecturer in the Communication Department and the director of the Public Speaking Center at the University of Washington. His research focuses on public speaking pedagogy. This includes analyses of specific rhetorical concepts in public speaking textbooks, works that present models for effective teaching, and analyses of the framing of public speaking education by teachers, textbook authors, and policymakers. He has won a number of teaching awards including the National Speakers Association's Robert Henry Outstanding Professor Award. He received his PhD degree from Indiana University at Bloomington in 2005.

Scott A. Myers is a professor in the Department of Communication Studies at West Virginia University. He teaches courses in instructional communication, small-group communication, and interpersonal communication. His research interests center primarily on the student-instructor relationship in the college classroom, with his research appearing in *Communication Education, Communication Research Reports*, and *Communication Quarterly*. He is a former editor of *Communication Teacher* and a former executive director of the Central States Communication Association (CSCA), and he currently serves as the Second Vice President of CSCA. He received his PhD from Kent State University in 1995.

Keith Nainby is an assistant professor of communication studies at California State University, Stanislaus. His research interests are at the intersections of communication pedagogy, philosophy of communication, and performance studies; these vectors of inquiry especially support his work with aspiring educators (at both the K–12 and the college levels) in the diverse landscape of California public schooling. His most recent publication is "Effacement and Metaphor: Searching for the Body in Educational Discourse," in *Liminalities: A Journal of Performance Studies*. He is currently pursuing two separate studies of social class discourse: one on a program for first-generation university students and another on social class in film. He received his PhD from Southern Illinois University in 2003.

Timothy G. Plax is a professor of communication studies and director of the Hauth Center for Communication Skills at California State University, Long Beach (CSULB). He has served on the faculties of the University of New Mexico and West Virginia University. His research and teaching focus on social influence and interpersonal and organizational communication, but he is best known for his research in instructional communication. His experiences include 6 years as a member of the executive staff at the Rockwell International Corporation and 25 years as a consultant in corporate and instructional arenas. He has published more than 150 manuscripts, including several textbooks, chapters, research articles, and commissioned research reports. He is listed among the 25 most published scholars in his discipline. He received his PhD from the University of Southern California.

Natalia Rybas is an assistant professor of communication at Indiana University East. Her teaching and research interests revolve around issues of identity and relationships in the context of computer-mediated communication. Her publications have appeared in *Qualitative Inquiry*, *Feminist Media Studies*, and edited collections.

Paul Schrodt is the Philip J. and Cheryl C. Burguières Professor and an associate professor in the Department of Communication Studies at Texas Christian University. His research in instructional and family communication has appeared in *Human Communication Research*, *Communication Monographs*, *Communication Education*, the *Journal of Social and Personal Relationships*, and *Personal Relationships*, among other outlets. He is a former recipient of the Franklin Knower Article Award from the Interpersonal Communication Division and the Sandra Petronio Dissertation Excellence Award from the Family Communication Division of the National Communication Association, as well as the Outstanding New Instructor Award from the Central States Communication Association. He received his PhD from the University of Nebraska–Lincoln in 2003.

Deanna D. Sellnow is Gifford Blyton Endowed Professor and Director of Undergraduate Studies in Communication at the University of Kentucky.

She has published and presented her scholarship in international, national, regional, and state venues. Her work focuses on problem-based learning, service learning, experiential education, learning style theory, teacher training, assessment, technology-enhanced learning, and gender issues in the classroom. She has conducted workshops for professional groups and university faculty across the country. Her work with learning styles is also currently being used to help shape messages to instruct various publics during crisis events. She received her PhD degree from the University of North Dakota at Grand Forks in 1991.

Timothy L. Sellnow is a professor of communication and Associate Dean for Graduate Programs in the College of Communications and Information Studies at the University of Kentucky. His research focuses on all forms of communication in risk and crisis situations. His work in instructional communication focuses predominantly on service learning and on the instructional dynamics of risk and crisis messages. His work appears in journals such as *Communication Education, Communication Teacher, Communication Yearbook,* and the *Journal of Applied Communication and Research.* He is coauthor of the 2009 book *Effective Risk Communication: A Message-Centered Approach.* He has also engaged in funded research for agencies such as the Centers for Disease Control and Prevention and the Department of Homeland Security. He received his PhD from Wayne State University, Detroit, in 1987.

Jennifer S. Simpson is an interdisciplinary scholar with a focus in communication and an associate professor in the Faculty of Arts at the University of Waterloo (Waterloo, Canada). In collaboration with Leda Cooks, she is the coeditor of *Whiteness, Pedagogy, Performance: Dis/placing Race* (2007). She is also the author of *I Have Been Waiting: Race and U.S. Higher Education* (2003). She has published articles in *The Review of Education, Pedagogy, and Cultural Studies; Journal of International and Intercultural Communication; Journal of Intercultural Communication Research;* and *Journal of Contemporary Ethnography.* She does research in the areas of race, whiteness, critical pedagogy, intercultural communication, and democracy and justice. The courses she teaches include intercultural communication, public communication, persuasion, gender and communication, and communication and social justice. She is currently working on a book that addresses higher education and democratic practices, particularly as related to undergraduate education. She received her PhD from Northwestern University.

Scott Titsworth is an associate professor and Associate Director for Graduate Studies in the School of Communication Studies at Ohio University. His research examines how classroom communication affects learning and emotional experiences in the classroom. His research articles have appeared in *Communication Education, Journal of Applied Communication Research, Journal of Communication, Communication Studies, Basic*

Communication Course Annual, Contemporary Educational Psychology, and *Argument and Advocacy*. He is an author of four communication textbooks related to the introductory communication course and quantitative methods. He received his PhD from the University of Nebraska–Lincoln in 1999.

Paul D. Turman is the Associate Vice President for Academic Affairs for the South Dakota Board of Regents. He was previously a tenured associate professor at the University of Northern Iowa. He continues to conduct research in areas of instructional and group communication, publishing work in *Communication Education, Small Group Research, Journal of Applied Communication Research, Communication Studies, Communication Quarterly*, and the *Western Journal of Communication*. He has been recognized for outstanding teaching at the institutional, state, and regional level. He received his PhD from the University of Nebraska–Lincoln in 2000.

Jennifer H. Waldeck is an assistant professor of communication studies at Chapman University, Orange, California. Her research interests are in organizational, business, and instructional communication, with emphases on mentoring, training and development, effective assimilation of corporate employees, and the role of advanced communication technologies at work and in higher education. Her research has appeared in *Communication Monographs, Communication Education, Journal of Applied Communication Research*, and *Communication Yearbook* and in several edited volumes. Her experience includes 3 years as Director of Curriculum Development for a consulting firm that provided services to global organizations such as Ford Motor Company, Cendant, Coldwell Banker, and Toyota. She has received her PhD from the University of California, Santa Barbara.

Melissa Bekelja Wanzer is a professor in the Communication Studies Department at Canisius College. Her research interests focus on instructional communication, interpersonal communication, and health communication. Her research has appeared in *Communication Education, Communication Research Reports, Communication Teacher, Health Communication*, and *The Journal of Health Communication*. She is currently a consulting editor for *Communication Education*. She also serves on the editorial board for *Communication Quarterly, Communication Research Reports, Qualitative Research Reports*, and *The Journal of Intercultural Research*. Her recent scholarship includes a coauthored interpersonal communication textbook, *Interpersonal Communication: Building Rewarding Relationships*. She received her EdD from West Virginia University in 1998.

Jami L. Warren is a doctoral student in communication at the University of Kentucky, Lexington, where she also completed her bachelor's and master's degrees. Her work focuses primarily on instructional communication and, more specifically, on service learning and student learning outcomes.

John T. Warren is an associate professor of communication pedagogy in the Department of Speech Communication at Southern Illinois University, Carbondale. His research and teaching interests examine the intersections of identity/difference and performance in the classroom. His books include *Critical Communication Pedagogy* (2007, coauthored with Deanna L. Fassett, Sage), *Casting Gender: Women and Performance in Intercultural Contexts* (2005, coedited with Laura Lengel), and *Performing Purity: Whiteness, Pedagogy, and the Reconstitution of Power* (2003). He has been published in journals such as *Communication Education, Text and Performance Quarterly, Educational Theory,* and *Communication and Critical/Cultural Studies.* He is currently writing an introductory course text with Deanna L. Fassett, titled *Communicating Culture: An Introduction to Communication as Social Action* (Sage). He received his PhD from Southern Illinois University in 2001.

Paul L. Witt is an associate professor in the Department of Communication Studies at Texas Christian University (TCU). His research in teacher immediacy has appeared in *Communication Monographs, Communication Education, Communication Quarterly,* and *Communication Reports,* among others. He and his coauthors earned the John E. Hunter Award from the International Communication Association for their meta-analysis of immediacy and learning research. He was selected as the outstanding professor from the TCU College of Communication and earned several awards for excellence in the teaching and mentoring of students. He received his PhD from the University of North Texas in 2000.

Yahui Zhang is an assistant professor of communication and media studies at Wayland Baptist University in Texas. Her research interest has been driven, motivated, and constituted by her fascination with how mundane communication both reflects and reshapes the intricate structures in which we participate. She is committed to pedagogy as praxis so that teaching and learning becomes a process for constantly engaging in meanings and their bearings. She received her doctoral degree in communication studies from Bowling Green State University in Ohio.

Supporting researchers for more than 40 years

Research methods have always been at the core of SAGE's publishing program. Founder Sara Miller McCune published SAGE's first methods book, *Public Policy Evaluation*, in 1970. Soon after, she launched the *Quantitative Applications in the Social Sciences* series—affectionately known as the "little green books."

Always at the forefront of developing and supporting new approaches in methods, SAGE published early groundbreaking texts and journals in the fields of qualitative methods and evaluation.

Today, more than 40 years and two million little green books later, SAGE continues to push the boundaries with a growing list of more than 1,200 research methods books, journals, and reference works across the social, behavioral, and health sciences. Its imprints—Pine Forge Press, home of innovative textbooks in sociology, and Corwin, publisher of PreK–12 resources for teachers and administrators—broaden SAGE's range of offerings in methods. SAGE further extended its impact in 2008 when it acquired CQ Press and its best-selling and highly respected political science research methods list.

From qualitative, quantitative, and mixed methods to evaluation, SAGE is the essential resource for academics and practitioners looking for the latest methods by leading scholars.

For more information, visit **www.sagepub.com**.